THE ECONOMICS OF NATIONAL SECURITY

Lee D. Olvey

James R. Golden

Robert C. Kelly

AVERY PUBLISHING GROUP INC.

Wayne, New Jersey

For Kathleen, Elaine and Helen

Copyright © 1984 by Avery Publishing Group, Inc.

In-house editor: Joanne Abrams

Library of Congress Cataloging in Publication Data

Golden, James Reed.
    The economics of national security.

    Includes bibliographical references and index.
    1. United States—Military policy—Economic aspects.
2. United States—National security—Economic aspects.
I. Kelly, Robert C., 1946-   . II. Olvey, Lee D.
(Lee Donne) III. Title.
HC110.D4G64 1984   338.4'76234'0973   83-15734
ISBN 0-89529-117-7
ISBN 0-89529-237-8 (pbk.)

Printed in the United States of America

10 9 8 7 6 5 4 3 2 1

CONTENTS

PREFACE

Twenty years have now passed since *The Economics of Defense in the Nuclear Age* was written by Charles J. Hitch and Roland N. McKean. That text treats defense as an economic problem and argues that the limited resources available for defense could be used more wisely if economic analysis were applied in the management process. The arguments concerning program budgeting that are presented in that text became the basis for the reorganization of the decision making processes in the Department of Defense. Emphasis was placed on explicit linkages of expenditures to national security objectives, and quantitative estimates of the costs and benefits of alternative programs.

The Economics of National Security attempts to build on the foundation laid by Hitch and McKean, but places more emphasis on mobilization, the impact of supply factors on macroeconomic objectives, and the dramatic expansion of economic interdependence. In these latter areas, this text is in the tradition of a series of studies of mobilization, resource limitations, and national security issues, completed in the Department of Social Sciences at the U.S. Military Academy in the 1950's under the direction of the late General George A. Lincoln.

Our objective in writing this book is to show how economic theory may be used to analyze and illuminate a wide variety of issues related to national security. We begin each section with a brief review of the relevant economic theory and then move on to applications of that theory to current issues. Wherever possible, specific examples, illustrations, or case studies are used to reinforce the theoretical point that is being made.

In some cases, readers with a limited background in economics may wish to scan some of the more advanced discussions of economic theory. Similarly, those with a solid background in economic theory may wish to scan or omit the introductory chapter in each section. We have attempted to make the pertinent economic theory as accessible to as wide an audience as possible, and in doing so we have accepted the risk of including material that readers may find either too simple or too sophisticated. We hope we have found the proper balance between accessibility and sophistication.

The text is organized into seven major parts, each of which deals with a different aspect of economic theory. Part I provides an overview of different perspectives on defense spending and highlights the ways in which economic analysis fits into each perspective. Part II presents a model of how defense spending affects the economy and how budgetary decisions are made in the context of overall economic objectives. Part III explores the concept of cost-benefit analysis and its practical relevance in defense decision making. Part IV reviews the principles of market behavior and discusses the impact of defense decisions on the labor and capital markets, and the effect of defense research on technological change. Part V uses input-output analysis to trace the critical interactions of the defense sector with the rest of the economy. Part VI develops the international aspects of the economics of national security, beginning with trade theory, continuing with various issues of economic interdependence, and ending with the national security implications of East-West trade. Finally, Part VII provides an overview of issues in comparative economic systems and defense spending, with a discussion of different economic systems in general, the Soviet command economy in particular, arms race issues, and problems related to the developing nations.

This text grew out of the authors' interests in various aspects of national security policy, and their frustration with teaching the ideas without the benefit of a comprehensive current book. A survey of numerous courses on the economics of national security indicated that other teachers were suffering from the same constraint and were forced to fall back on a series of readings on the relevant topics. In many cases the best readings were quite dated, and in each case the instructor was forced to try to impose a sense of order on a series of disjointed topics. This book attempts to pull most of the most important ideas together, using a format that is oriented on the perspective provided by economic theory.

Lee Olvey's experience in teaching cost-benefit analysis, his work on economic development in Brazil, and his studies of international relations gave us insights into national security policy, the impact of cost-effectiveness analysis on defense decision making, and issues in comparative military spending. James Golden's work as a Senior Staff Economist with the Council of Economic Advisers provided much of the background for our analysis of the integration of defense issues in the budgetary process, and the major problems involved with economic interdependence and East-West trade. Robert Kelly's manpower studies for the Office of Management and Budget, and his doctoral research on defense and economic development provided the foundation for our analysis of defense supply issues and issues concerning the developing nations. The entire text, however, is a joint effort, and each of us benefitted from the insights and comments of the other authors.

We have received assistance from many of our colleagues in the Department of Social Sciences at West Point in the preparation of this text. In particular we would like to thank Stephen Strom for his comments in editing the text, and Mrs. Margaret Murphy and Mrs. Verda Lare for their superb typing support. The authors claim full responsibility for any remaining errors or omissions. The views expressed in the text are those of the authors, and do not purport to reflect the views of any government agency.

Lee D. Olvey, Professor
James R. Golden, Professor
Department of Social Sciences
United States Military Academy

Robert C. Kelly, Director of Corporate Development
Continental Resources Company

INTRODUCTION

Economic theory has a great deal to contribute to the enlightened analysis of national security issues. Indeed, that is precisely the point of this book. We must hasten to add that other disciplinary perspectives are also very useful in understanding national security issues, and in many cases economic factors will be subordinated to other concerns. However, the economic framework of highlighting the resource implications of various decisions that affect national security does provide useful insights even when economic factors do not dominate policy judgments.

Figure 1 provides a highly simplified view of the levels of analysis involved in developing a foreign policy strategy, and in developing a defense budget that reflects that strategy. The figure shows an outer ring that represents the international and domestic environment within which national security decisions are made. The second ring depicts the institutions and actors who gather information, form perceptions about the environment, and participate in the process of developing a strategy and budget. Finally, the interior of the diagram

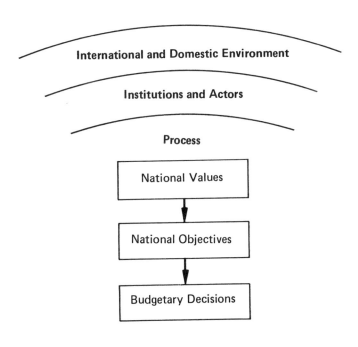

Figure 1 Defense Environment, Institutions and Process

emphasizes the process by which resources are allocated among competing social objectives. The process shown suggests that national values are translated into specific national objectives, and ultimately into budgetary decisions, although we will discover that decisions on budgets and objectives also have impact on national values.

Various theories of policy formulations stress different aspects of the environment, the actors and institutions, and the decision-making process. Clearly, each element is important in policy formulation, and the remainder of this book will attempt to show how an economic perspective can contribute to each level of analysis.

The first part of the book is devoted to a careful examination of the alternative perspectives of the facts that influence the development of a defense budget. This discussion emphasizes two different views of the budgetary process — the foreign policy planning approach and the domestic policy planning approach — and then considers the importance of various institutions and actors in determining the ultimate budgetary decisions. This section concludes with an integrated model that shows how each of these perspectives is interrelated with the others.

The remaining six parts of the book demonstrate how economic theory is applied throughout the process of establishing national security objectives and allocating resources to meet those objectives. Indeed, economics is the study of allocating scarce resources among competing uses. In order to highlight different dimensions of economic theory, this broad area is subdivided into macroeconomics, microeconomics, international economics, and comparative economic systems. The following provides a brief introduction to these areas and explains how each deals with a different aspect of national security economics.

The Macroeconomics of National Security

Macroeconomics emphasizes the performance of the entire national economy and the impact of different spending and production patterns on total output and price levels. The level of defense spending has a major impact on the macroeconomic performance of the U.S. economy. In fiscal year 1980, the defense budget of the U.S. was estimated to total 135.5 billion dollars, or about 650 dollars for every person in the country.[1] This amount of money could have been used to purchase 2.71 million $50,000 houses, or 19.3 million $7,000 automobiles. Just as the level of defense spending has a significant impact on national output and prices, competing macroeconomic priorities place limitations on the economically feasible and politically acceptable levels of defense outlays.

The second part of this book deals with the macroeconomic issues surrounding national security problems. The defense budget makes up a significant share of the total amount spent by the Federal Government on goods and services in any one year, and the level and changes in the defense budget can result in substantial changes in aggregate output, inflation, and the rate of unemployment. The macroeconomics section also examines the development of the budget through the budget cycle, and the "burden" of the defense budget from an aggregate perspective.

Resource Allocation in the Defense Sector

Microeconomics stresses the efficient allocation of resources to meet the objectives of individual actors — primarily firms and consumers, but more generally any economic decision maker. The study of microeconomics naturally leads into an analysis of the economic environment of the decision maker, and of the structure of the market within which the individual buys or sells resources and products.

The level and composition of defense spending clearly depends on a wide range of decisions made by individuals involved in defense budgeting and procurement. Microeconomic theory highlights the process that should be used to insure the efficient allocation of scarce defense resources. This objective may be stated either as obtaining the largest possible contribution to national security for a given defense outlay or, conversely, as determining the combination of resources that will produce a desired level of security at the least possible cost.

The third part of the book deals with the major issues of resource allocation in the defense sector. In both the foreign policy area and the domestic policy area, the selection of a program to meet an objective may be analyzed using the microeconomic tools of Cost Benefit or Cost Effectiveness analysis. Part III shows how optimizing techniques can be used to choose among alternative methods of attaining a specified objective.

Microeconomic Issues

Judgments on cost and relative effectiveness depend in turn on an understanding of actual markets in which defense inputs — personnel, weapon systems, and energy — are purchased. Once again, microeconomic theory has a good deal to say about the operation of different markets and can shed considerable light on defense procurement problems. The pattern of defense outlays over different industries, labor groups, and regions also has a significant impact on a number of important markets, and microeconomic theory can help to evaluate the implications of defense outlays for those individual markets.

In the fourth part of the book we explore the structure of various defense related markets and demonstrate how microeconomic theory can be used to develop and implement policy decisions. For example, an analysis of the military labor market is an essential ingredient in making policy decisions on pay and allowances for military manpower. Without some understanding of the nature of the supply of labor to the military services, the Department of Defense would not be able to meet the predetermined policy of maintaining a given sized force in terms of manpower, or to determine future labor costs for the budget process. This section reviews the structure of various economic markets, and then develops some of the special problems related to defense mobilization and technological change.

Interindustry Relations and the Defense Sector

A special branch of microeconomics provides a bridge to macroeconomic issues by emphasizing "interindustry analysis." This approach stresses the flows of goods in process from one industry to another and the ways in which changes in the output of one industry affect the rest of the economy. The fifth section of the book applies the economics of interindustry analysis to national security problems. Interindustry analysis is important in tracing the effects of changes in the amount of defense spending (or any other component of final aggregate demand) on the specific industries that produce the goods required for the defense sector. In the foreign policy planning area, interindustry analysis is important in devising military strategies, and this section indicates how an examination of an adversary's industrial structure may yield important targeting information for both conventional and nuclear forces. The section also shows how interindustry analysis may be used to forecast the price and employment effects of various changes in defense programs.

The International Aspects
of the Economics of National Security

International economics treats the allocation of resources and the specialization of production processes across nations, and develops the impact of different trade and financial flows on individual nations. Patterns of international specialization and trade have clear impacts on national security. International trade theory stresses the trade-off between the efficiency that results from specialization and the vulnerability that follows from dependence. At a broader level, international trade and the resulting financial transactions constitute a major area of international intercourse, and national security interests are affected whenever national values, such as acceptable living standards, are at stake in the international arena. Trade with potential adversaries poses a special national security problem in which the possible gains from trade must be weighed against contributions to military capacity. In each of these areas international economic theory provides important insights regarding the consequences of different trade patterns and the national security implications of international economic transactions.

In the sixth section of the book we review the broad theory of international trade and specialization, and discuss the implications of various international financial transactions. The section goes on to examine the importance of shifting economic realities and resource dependencies for our alliance structure, and concludes with an analysis of the implications of East-West trade in general, and high-technology exports in particular.

Comparative Economic Issues

The study of comparative economic systems focuses on the ways in which different economies are organized to solve the fundamental economic questions of what should be produced, how it should be produced, and who should receive the output. Each of these perspectives is extremely useful in understanding important dimensions of public policy processes in general and national security decision making in particular.

For example, the overall economic performance of our major potential adversary, the Soviet Union, and its ability to sustain different levels of defense expenditure and high quality weapons production are obviously central to any evaluation of the security of the United States. Similarly, the possible impact of different levels of defense spending in the United States on levels of expenditure in the Soviet Union must be considered in deciding whether or not additional outlays might add to or reduce national security. The theory of economic systems can also be useful in understanding the economic choices faced by developing nations and the impact of different levels and patterns of defense spending on their economic growth. In particular, economic theory can be very useful in assessing the appropriate role and expected impact of foreign military arms sales.

The seventh section of the book deals with these comparative economic issues. The section begins with a theoretical discussion of the differences between the major economic systems, and proceeds with an evaluation of the Soviet command economy. Particular stress is placed on the Soviet economic base for military expenditures. The section concludes with a study of developing economies with emphasis on expanding competition for scarce resources, and the consequences of various military assistance and arms sales programs.

Summary

In terms of the simplified model depicted in Figure 1, the first five sections of the book emphasize processes and institutions involved in the development of defense policy, and the last two sections stress the importance of the international environment, and the perceptions of that environment, in the policy-making process. In each section we stress the interrelationships of the environment, the actors and institutions, and the process.

The discussions that follow are designed to present a menu of important applications of economic analysis in the defense area, and to whet your appetite for further reading on these important policy issues. In the first section we turn our attention to a more detailed examination of defense decision-making perspectives.

NOTES

1 *Department of Defense Annual Report Fiscal Year 1980* (Washington, D.C.: Government Printing Office, 1979), p. C–10.

Part I

Perspectives on Defense Spending

An idealist believes the short run doesn't count. A cynic believes the long run doesn't matter. A realist that what is done or left undone in the short run determines the long run.

Sydney J. Harris

You took the good things for granted. Now you must earn them again. For every right that you cherish, you have a duty which you must fulfill. For every good that you wish to preserve, you will have to sacrifice your comfort and your ease. There is nothing for nothing any longer.

Walter Lippmann

Chapter 1
Economics and National Security

THE GENERAL NATURE OF THE ECONOMIC PROBLEM

Every society is faced with the problem of allocating and distributing scarce resources. The general nature of the economic problem can best be understood by utilizing the concept of a production possibility frontier. Every society is endowed with a limited supply of productive resources which include land, labor, capital, and entrepreneurial talent. Given the existing state of technology, these resources can be combined to produce alternative combinations of goods and services. The production possibility frontier describes the output alternatives of an economic system by showing the combinations of commodities that can be produced when society is employing its resources in the most efficient manner.

A typical production possibility frontier is shown in Figure 1.1. The axes of the graph show the output of the two hypothetical goods produced in the economy, Q_1 and Q_2. Given the resource endowment of society and the state of technology, the economic system can produce any combination of these two commodities on, or below, the production possibility frontier. If the economic system is efficient, then the output combination produced will be somewhere on the frontier, such as at point A or point B. Any point below the frontier, such as point C, indicates that the economy is operating inefficiently in that by using a better technology or by utilizing all of society's resources, more of at least one commodity could be produced without a reduction in the output level of any other commodity. At point C, for example, if the best technology were being employed, or if more of the resources available within the economy were utilized, the output of Q_1 could be increased from Q_1^C to Q_1^A without changing the output of Q_2.

On the other hand, output combinations that lie above the production possibility frontier, such as point D, are not currently attainable. In order to attain such a combination of outputs, the society in question would have to either increase the amount of productive factors (through capital accumulation or population growth, for example) or develop improved technologies (through such actions as investment in research and development programs).

A major problem that all societies face is that decisions to change the economic *status quo* involve opportunity costs. The opportunity cost of deciding to move from point A to point B in order to increase production of Q_2 is a reduction in the potential output of Q_1 from Q_1^A to Q_1^B. The concept of opportunity cost results from the downward slope of the production possibility frontier, which implies that in order to produce more of any commodity there must be an increase in the amount of resources utilized in the production of that commodity. Thus, to move from point A to point B, resources must be taken from the production of Q_1 and put into the production of Q_2. This implies a reduction in Q_1 in order to produce more of Q_2.

The concavity of the production possibility frontier implies that as resources are used more intensively in the production of one commodity, factors are employed in proportions that result in diminishing marginal returns to the additional unit of each factor employed. Thus if society desires to push the production of Q_2 to very high levels, relative to its capacity to produce Q_2, factors of production may have to be employed in proportions that are less efficient than those utilized at lower levels of production.

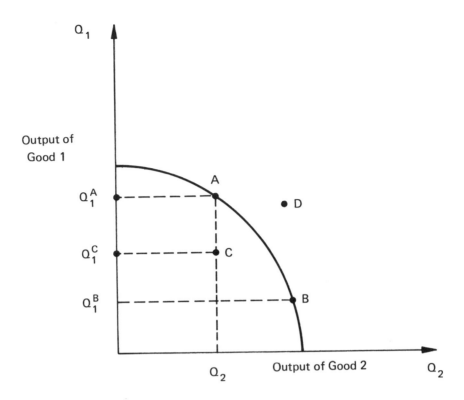

Figure 1.1 Production Possibility Frontier

Thus the production possibility frontier depicts the possibilities of an economic system, or what can be produced. The general economic problem for any society, however, is not only the technical question of what can be produced, but also involves the normative questions of what should be produced and who should receive the benefits of the output. To answer these questions society must possess some criteria, either explicit or implicit, for both choosing from among alternative feasible output combinations and for distributing the output. To do this, most economic systems employ some combination of two methods of economic organization: the command system and the market system.

In the command economic system, the questions of what should be produced and how output should be distributed are answered by having those in political power specify both output levels and the distribution of the product. Such a process would require the political leaders to evaluate the social benefits of feasible alternatives and to select that output combination that yields, according to their value system, the greatest social benefit.

The alternative to the command system is the market system, in which the general interaction of buyers and sellers in markets, reflected in the price system, leads to the selection of an output combination. Here, rather than the political leadership specifying output levels, buyers and sellers are free to follow their own self-interest and to trade so as to maximize their own well-being. In such a system, if markets are competitive, a set of relative prices is established for all goods — Q_1 and Q_2 in this case — that leaves consumers maximizing their welfare, and entrepreneurs maximizing their profit, given the distribution of initial factor endowments and individual tastes in the society.

In the United States, the predominant form of economic organization is the market system. Thus, most discussions of economics generally deal with the economic theory of goods produced and consumed in various types of market structures. Indeed much of the substantive material involved in a study of the economics of national security involves nothing more than the application of basic economic concepts to the national security problem. The production possibility frontier, for example, can be redrawn, as in Figure 1.2, to indicate the trade-offs possible between the production of defense goods and civilian goods. This concept can then be used to indicate the nature of the opportunity costs of defense spending.

However, there are a number of ways in which the economics of national security differ from more conventional economic treatments, in theory as well as in content. We will emphasize those differences which, although not generally new, are not frequently dwelt upon in conventional economic discussions. The following section discusses the special nature of national security economics, and some of the major differences between conventional economic treatments and those in this book.

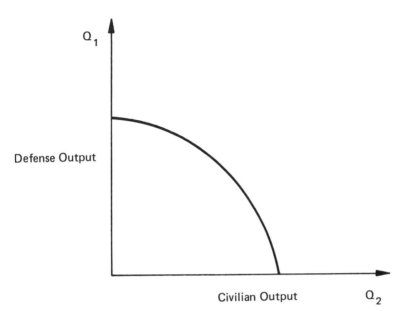

Figure 1.2 Defense and Civilian Goods Production Possibility Frontier

THE SPECIAL NATURE OF NATIONAL SECURITY ECONOMICS

As noted in the preceding section, many issues in national security economics can be dealt with by applying basic economic concepts to the problem being considered. One example of such a problem is that of supplying labor to the armed forces. If the issue to be examined is the impact of changes in wages on the supply of military labor, then the conventional theory of the labor supply curve can be applied to the specific issue of military recruiting.[1]

On the other hand, there are some special features of the national security economic problem that warrant more emphasis than is given in a basic economic theory text. A number of these features are discussed in the following paragraphs. Although the list is not all inclusive, it does point up some of the major theoretical differences between conventional treatments of economics and the material relevant to the study of defense economics.

Public Good Nature of National Defense

National defense is a classic case of a public good. A public good is a commodity or service that, if it is produced for a single member of the economy is provided for all.[2] Because it is impossible to prevent those who do not desire to pay for national defense from receiving its benefits, the market system will not lead to the optimal production of national defense even if it is in society's interest to have the service provided. In this case, the good must be provided by the government and paid for through the general revenue system, or it will not be provided at all. In such cases, the price of the service provided is not determined in a market, thus precluding the calculation of the economic benefits of such a product except on a subjective basis.

The Large Share of Output Spent on Defense

Defense spending absorbs a substantial share of American national output. Table 1.1 gives total gross national product, expenditures on national defense, and the percentage of output spent on defense for selected years between 1955 and 1980. As the data indicate, the share of output spent on defense declined over the period shown. Nevertheless the amount of expenditure remained a significant percentage of total output. Thus, changes in the levels of defense spending have a major impact on all sectors of the economy in terms of the level of employment and the rate of inflation, not only directly as indicated above, but also indirectly through the multiplier as indicated in the macroeconomics section.

Table 1.1
The Fraction of U.S. Output Spent on Defense: 1955–1980

Year	Output ($ Billion)	Defense ($ Billion)	Defense as a Percent of Output (%)
1955	399.3	38.4	9.6
1960	486.5	45.6	9.4
1965	688.1	60.3	8.8
1970	982.4	73.5	7.5
1975	1528.8	83.9	5.5
1980	2626.1	135.9	5.2

Source: Economic Report of the President, 1978, p. 257; 1982, pp. 233, 317.

Special Market Structures

While much of the emphasis in conventional economics is on the competitive model, many of the market structures dealt with in the defense area are noncompetitive. Many of the expenditures being made in the defense sector involve the Defense Department (DoD) exclusively ordering products from an industry in which there are very few suppliers. Thus in many cases the market for defense goods represents a combination of monopsony (single buyer) and monopoly (single seller) or oligopoly (few sellers). In the case where DoD is the only buyer and the selling firm is the only supplier, the economic market structure is a bilateral monopoly rather than a competitive market.

International Externalities in Consumption of Defense

Expenditures on national defense are generally intended to assist a nation in achieving its national security objectives. The national security objectives of the nation are, however, generally affected by the consumption of national defense by other nations. Thus many of the costs and benefits of national security are based on the interdependence of decisions made outside of the U.S. market for defense goods. An external economy in consumption results when an *ally* increases its expenditure on defense,[3] while an external diseconomy results when an *adversary* increases its expenditure on defense.[4] Changes in the level of spending by both our allies and adversaries, therefore, may result in changes in the level of spending by the United States. The reactions of the United States to such changes in spending by our allies and adversaries is similar to the strategies employed in oligopolistic market structures.

Peak Load Requirements

The demand for many goods and services is fairly uniformly distributed over time. Thus the capacity that is employed in producing most goods is fully or at least evenly utilized at all times. National defense, on the other hand, has a demand time profile that can be compared to that of an electric utility company in a large metropolitan area.[5] The utility generally operates at peak capacity at certain times during each day, while the defense sector only operates at peak capacity during a war. This special aspect of defense goods makes the economic decisions surrounding their use akin to the peak-load pricing problem in economics. In this case the relevant questions are: how much capacity should be built, how much should be spent on defense during peak load, and how much capacity should be stockpiled in non-peak times?

THE ROLE OF ECONOMICS
IN NATIONAL SECURITY DECISION MAKING

A distinction is frequently made between the *positive* use of economics to address issues of efficiency and the *normative* use of economics to consider issues involving more explicit value judgments, such as the distribution of income. The positive use of economics implies that there is a clear objective and that the problem is to find the most efficient way to use the limited available resources in order to reach that objective. Normative economics goes beyond such issues of technical efficiency, and explores the issues of which of the feasible sets of outputs *should* be produced, and the related issue of how the output should be distributed to different individuals. Normative economics therefore involves the fundamental issue of what the society's objectives should be.

It is unlikely that any economic model will enable a decision maker to mechanically determine how society should utilize its resources in terms of either the division of resources between defense and non-defense goods, or even among different types of goods within the defense budget. The factors involved in such allocational and distributional questions, especially when public goods are involved, are generally determined in the political arena, and involve decision makers employing subjective value judgments on the marginal usefulness of a particular good or service relative to the social costs of procuring it.

Because no economic model can be constructed to replace the preference system of the decision maker, it is unlikely that economc theory can answer the general question of "How much is enough?"[6] The use of economics in a positive fashion can, however, indicate the consequences of a value system to the decision maker. By developing economic alternatives through such constructs as the production possibility frontier and other general behavioral and technical relationships among economic variables, the full range of options can be developed, and the impact of a particular value system can be more clearly defined. Thus it is in the development of the alternatives and opportunity costs that economics can have its greatest impact on the national security decision-making process.

CONCLUSION

The discipline of economists is generally concerned with allocating and distributing scarce resources among competing uses. Expenditures on national security utilize a substantial portion of the national product, and the efficient allocation of resources, both within the defense sector and between defense and non-defense goods, can significantly affect social welfare.

While conventional economic theory can be applied to many problems in the national security area, the peculiar characteristics of the defense sector warrant special emphasis. Thus the public good nature of defense goods, the large share of output which the defense sector commands, the special market structures, the externalities in consumption, and the peak load demand for defense output make economic analysis in the national security area substantially different from the more traditional analysis of a perfectly competitive industry.

Lastly, while normative or welfare economics can yield little in terms of decision-making rules concerning allocation and distribution questions, the positive approaches to the subject can generally crystalize the alternatives and reveal the consequences of pursuing a particular national security policy.

NOTES

1 See, for example, the treatment of the supply of Volunteers to the military in Richard Lipsey and Peter O. Steiner, *Economics* (New York: Harper and Row, 1974), pp. 110-115.
2 See Robert Haveman, *Economics of the Public Sector,* 2nd ed. (New York: Wiley, 1976), pp. 25-26 for a definition and discussion of the nature of public goods.
3 See Chapter 21. See also Mancur Olsen and Richard Zeckhauser, "An Economic Theory of Alliances," *Review of Economics and Statistics,* Vol. 48 (August, 1966), pp. 266-279, for an example of the effect of external economies resulting from defense spending by allies.
4 See Chapter 25. See also Martin McGuire, "A Quantitative Study of the Strategic Arms Race in the Missile Age," *Review of Economics and Statistics,* Vol. 59 (August, 1977), pp. 328-339, for a discussion of the impact of external diseconomies resulting when adversaries change their consumption of national defense.
5 See Peter O. Steiner, "Peak Loads and Efficient Pricing," *Quarterly Journal of Economics,* Vol. 71 (November, 1957), pp. 585-610, for a discussion of the peak load pricing problem as it relates to the electric utility industry.
6 Alain Enthoven and K. Wayne Smith, *How Much is Enough, Shaping the Defense Program 1961–1969* (New York: Harper and Row, 1971).

SELECTED REFERENCES

Alain Enthoven and K. Wayne Smith, *How Much is Enough, Shaping the Defense Program 1961–1969* (New York: Harper and Row, 1971).

Robert Haveman, *The Economics of the Public Sector,* 2d ed. (Santa Barbara California: John Wiley and Sons, Inc., 1976).

Charles J. Hitch and Roland N. McKean, *The Economics of Defense in the Nuclear Age,* Ninth Printing (New York: Atheneum, 1975).

Chapter 2
Foreign Policy Planning and Defense Spending

INTRODUCTION

In his treatise on war, the great Prussian military strategist Clausewitz noted that war is but an extension of the nation's international political pursuits.[1] This concept is important because it highlights the fact that one of the important determinants of the amount that any nation spends on its military program is that nation's foreign policy.

This chapter examines the relationship between foreign policy objectives and the defense budget. While it is clear that domestic policy and institutional forces also affect the amount of resources that are spent on defense, here we attempt to isolate the direct links between a nation's foreign policy objectives and the force requirements, with the ultimate goal of developing the budgetary links between various objectives and the defense budget.

The analysis in this chapter essentially provides one method by which a defense budget and force structure can be conceptually developed. Two analytical sequences are possible. In the first sequence, an analysis of national values and the consequent foreign policy objectives is developed, leading to a strategy and resultant force structure designed to meet those specified objectives. The cost of such a force structure yields the defense budget. In the second sequence, a given budgetary ceiling leads to a variety of force structure alternatives. The alternative that is then chosen is the one that best meets the specified set of national security objectives. In either sequence, if the final result is unacceptable, revision of the initial assumption and further analysis are required.

In the following discussion we label the first sequence, which flows from national values and foreign policy objectives down to a defense budget, the "foreign policy approach." In the next chapter we address the second sequence, which emphasizes budgetary constraints, under the label of the "domestic policy approach." Obviously, each approach emphasizes only one aspect of an integrated process. However, by focusing first on the foreign policy process we will be able to emphasize the impact of national values on the determination of the defense budget.

To develop this model of defense budgeting, we shall initially examine the process of refining national values and reducing them to more narrowly defined national interests or objectives. Following the theoretical development of foreign policy objectives, we will briefly survey the post-World War II foreign policy history of the United States and attempt to isolate some of the national values and interests that evolved from the post-war power relationships.

The theoretical analysis then continues with an examination of the relationship between national interests or objectives, and the strategy employed to attain those objectives. This leads, in turn, to a generalized discussion of the specific defense programs that support the strategy. Finally, the programs that are developed to support the strategy result in the specification of identifiable economic resources devoted to defense use. The defense budget in the United States is specified in resource (i.e. manpower, capital, etc.) or input terms, and the budgetary process may be viewed as the translation of output programs (i.e. strategic forces, conventional forces, etc.) into input requirements. The ultimate defense budget is thus the cost of such inputs.

The rationale for using this perspective as a model of defense planning is that the development of the defense budget within the defense establishment is primarily concerned with these aspects of the planning process. Thus the foreign policy planning approach can be viewed as the process utilized by a specific set of actors within the government, including the Defense Department, the National Security Council, and the State Department, in arriving at a defense budget. Other major actors in and out of the government concentrate on other perspectives which are dealt with in succeeding chapters.

Foreign Policy and National Security Objectives

The foreign policy of the United States (or any other nation for that matter) can be viewed as being developed to promote what are generally described as national values within the context of the relationship of the United States to other major actors in the international arena.[2] These national values are defined by Trager and Simonie as, " . . . the most fundamental principles on which the social, political, and physical existence of the state are based."[3]

National values are, of course, difficult to define precisely and to rank order. They are difficult to define because a nation state is composed of many individuals and institutions, all of which generally possess divergent views on national values. They are difficult to rank order because, particularly in a democratic political system, rank ordering of values is generally fraught with inconsistencies and usually impossible without some type of dominant decision maker.[4]

These difficulties aside, it is generally conceded that one of the most basic and important values of a nation state is its survival.[5] This value dominates most others in that if a nation does not exist, no other national values have meaning.

Other national values that may be high on the pecking order include the promotion of a particular political philosophy, such as democracy; and the promotion of a particular economic philosophy, such as capitalism. Each of these national values will also affect the conduct of foreign policy.

According to the foreign policy planning model, the defense budget is linked to a set of national values and an evaluation of the international environment in which those values are at risk. The values that are defined by decision makers may not necessarily all relate to the conduct of foreign policy; but in the context of developing such a value system the attainment or promotion of the national values may require interactions with other nation-states, and thus necessitate a foreign policy consistent with the attainment of the values.

National values, however, are broad general concepts and must be narrowed in order to develop a usable framework. As noted by Trager and Simonie:[6]

> They [national values] are thus unsuitable as guidelines for the day to day conduct of national security policy. More concrete intermediate objectives which we shall call "interests" are necessary as connecting links between basic values and national security operations.

Thus it would be extremely difficult, as an analyst, to formulate a consistent foreign policy or national security policy by simply working from the value of national survival or the promotion of democracy. We must first narrow the values into a set of more concrete, more precisely defined interests or objectives. Within the framework proposed by Trager and Simonie we shall refer to the operational refinement of a value as an objective, in this case a foreign policy objective.[7]

Admittedly the line between values and objectives is a fine one. The idea behind the formulation of objectives, however, is to refine the general concept of a value so that in an operational sense, the analyst or policy maker can develop the implementing strategy. Thus, objectives give a specific operational definition to national values and enable the decision maker to make the leap from national values to the actual instruments designed to accomplish the task of attaining those values. So while survival might be a national value, an operational definition of survival, or foreign policy objective, might be nuclear deterrence.

A strategy is generally defined as a specific method or plan devised to attain objectives. Within the context of this analysis, the use of force or defense resources to attain our foreign policy objectives can be further defined as military strategy.[8]

Military strategies, therefore, involve a plan to meet an objective by the use of military resources, and therefore necessarily involve the examination of various specific force alternatives. The task of moving from the military strategy to the specific defense programs designed to accomplish that strategy in the United States is generally accomplished using the Planning, Programming and Budgeting System (PPBS). Before elaborating further on the conceptual framework used to develop the defense budget from the foreign policy perspective, however, it may be helpful to review our conceptualization of the formulation of the defense budget from the foreign policy perspective down through the development of the military strategy. This is done in Figure 2.1.

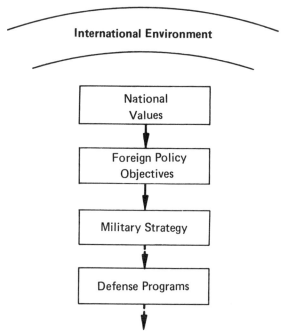

Figure 2.1 Planning and Military Strategy

Although Figure 2.1 shows the next link in the process of developing the defense budget, it will be helpful at this point to digress to a brief historical review of the foreign policy environment of the United States from the end of World War II through the 1970s. This review highlights some of the concepts developed thus far and provides some empirical basis for dealing with the issues to follow.

HISTORICAL OVERVIEW OF THE NATIONAL SECURITY ENVIRONMENT

World War II to the 1980s

The national security environment in the several decades since the end of World War II can be characterized in terms of the relationships between the major international actors during several subperiods of this era, as well as by the military strategy that evolved in response to these relationships. The historical subperiods relevant to this overview include The Cold War (1947–1965), the Vietnam Era (1965–1973), and the Era of Detente and Multipolar Competition (1973–   ). The military strategies that evolved over the post-World War II period, as described by Rainey, include the strategies of containment, massive retaliation, flexible response, and nuclear sufficiency.[9]

The Cold War resulted from conflicting national values and the immense military power possessed by the United States and the Soviet Union following World War II. The perception of Soviet aggressive intentions in Europe and Asia, combined with a philosophical opposition to the Soviet political system, led the former war-time allies into an era of intense competition characterized by belligerent rhetoric, near-military confrontations in Berlin in 1948 and Cuba in 1962, as well as actual participation by one of the two superpowers in two limited military conflicts: the Korean War in 1950–1952 and the Soviet-Hungarian intervention in 1956. During The Cold War Era, which we shall define as the period from 1947 to 1965, the strategy adopted by the United States evolved from the strategy of containment, to massive retaliation, and finally to a strategy of flexible response.

The strategy of containment evolved during the Truman administration and was enunciated by George Kennan in 1947.[10] The strategy generally involved the use of U.S. military power to counter Soviet expansionist tendencies in Europe and Asia. While it is beyond the scope of this brief review to critique each strategy, the problem with implementing the strategy of containment was the lack of U.S. and allied conventional capability (i.e. non-nuclear) to deal with Soviet conventional threats. The result of this situation was that U.S. nuclear forces were relied upon as the means to deter the Soviet use of military force in conjunction with expansionist political policies.

The strategy of containment evolved into the strategy of massive retaliation with the emergence of the People's Republic of China, and the increasing interests of the United States in preventing Chinese expansionism in Asia, following the Korean War. This strategy relied upon the nuclear superiority of the United States over the Soviet Union to forestall any Soviet or Chinese expansionism.[11] The strategy of massive retaliation, however, suffered from two severe drawbacks. The first was that, due to the continued lack of conventional capability, the options of the United States in response to a crisis became limited to either doing nothing or initiating a potential nuclear holocaust. Additionally, as the nuclear superiority of the United States declined, the potential costs to the United States of exercising the nuclear option, in the event of a Soviet retaliation, became significantly greater. This was perceived as weakening the credibility that the nuclear option would be used, thereby reducing its effectiveness as a deterrent.

The third major strategy of the Cold War evolved logically from an analysis of the flaws in the doctrine of massive retaliation. This strategy, called flexible response, was based upon the policy of graduated responses to Soviet or Chinese initiatives. Thus, to counter Soviet use of conventional forces in pursuit of foreign policy objectives, the United States would respond with conventional forces, rather than with the all-or-nothing nuclear option.

The evolution of American strategy following the adoption of flexible response is clouded by the conflict in Vietnam. During the Vietnam Era, the United States was made aware of the limitations of conventional power and the problems inherent in a strategy of flexibility when that strategy implied the waging of a protracted, limited war. The Vietnam Era also represented a watershed in terms of change in the international political environment from a primarily bi- or tri-polar world to a world of more diffused interests and political relationships. The intentions of the Soviet Union and the Chinese were not the only factors critical to the formulation of American policy during the Vietnam and post-Vietnam period. The aspirations of the developing world and traditional allies increasingly became focal points for the formulation of foreign policy objectives. The growing economic and political interdependence of the world made a simple bi-polar model of American foreign policy-making obsolete.

In response to the changing international environment and the growing strength of the Soviet Union, American strategic doctrine evolved into one of "nuclear sufficiency."[12] The attempt by the United States and the Soviet Union to attain nuclear superiority gave way to an era of "detente" and attempts by the superpowers to limit the escalation of both nuclear and conventional weapons. The Strategic Arms Limitation Talks (SALT) and the Mutual and Balanced Force Reduction (MBFR) negotiations in the 1970's signaled an attempt by the two major superpowers to accommodate each other's power in an era of political competition marked by a reduction in tensions over the earlier years of The Cold War.

With the beginning of the 1970s, the international environment was characterized by the ascendancy of the "oil states" and the increasing economic interdependence of both the Western and Eastern worlds. The foreign policy objectives of the United States necessarily became enmeshed in considerations of economic relationships, both between friends and allies. The simple bi-polar strategic doctrine became obsolete as the foreign policy objectives of the United States necessarily were refocused on multiple rather than single power relationships. The Era of Detente and Multipolar Competition resulted in a need to rethink American strategic doctrine, not only along the lines of Soviet-American or Chinese-American relationships, but along lines directed at American interests regarding the oil states and other economic powers. The era of strategies that could easily be summarized by single slogans had ended. Future American strategies would necessarily involve several conceptual ideas directed at major actors within the multipolar world arena, as well as along broad "functional" areas of interest.

DEFENSE PROGRAMS, STRATEGY, AND FOREIGN POLICY OBJECTIVES

The development of a defense budget requires that a strategy resulting from a set of foreign policy objectives be supported by a specific set of force structure programs. The rational process by which the United States presently accomplishes this task was initially developed during the period when Robert McNamara was the Secretary of Defense (from 1961 to 1968), and is entitled the Planning Programming and Budgeting System (PPBS). While the specifics of PPBS are discussed at length in Chapter 8, it will be helpful at this point to discuss the formulation of the defense budget in general terms by indicating some basic American foreign policy objectives, discussing the nature of American strategy, and outlining the broad American force structure in terms of defense programs.

The basic public document that outlines the result of the PPBS process is the *Annual Report of the Secretary of Defense*. Each year, by law, the Secretary of Defense is directed to submit to Congress a written annual report on " . . . the foreign policy and military force structure of the United States for the next fiscal year, how such force structures relate to each other, and the justification for each."[13] A general review of the *Annual Report of the Secretary of Defense, Fiscal Year 1980* indicates the following foreign policy objectives, strategy, and force structure to meet that strategy for fiscal year 1980.

Foreign Policy Objectives

As noted in the preceding review of the international environment, foreign policy objectives of the United States in the last quarter-century of the twentieth century will be focused on multiple centers of power, both military and economic. This concept is clearly indicated in the Fiscal Year 1980 Annual Report, which notes:

> . . . the overriding objective of our foreign policy is to maintain U.S. interests under conditions of international peace and stability. At present our basic interests remain intact. Perhaps the greatest immediate threat to them comes from economic and monetary forces. It would be a mistake, however, to underestimate the military problems created by the military buildup of the Soviet Union.[14]

The specific objectives or interests are further clarified when the Report notes:

> To survive, to prosper, to preserve our traditions we need political as well as military allies, trading partners, access to raw materials and supplies of energy; we need freedom of the seas and international airspace as well as space, and a pluralistic environment conducive to national and individual freedom.[15]

Thus the distillation of national values inherent in these statements indicates a set of objectives aimed at American survival in an interdependent world in the 1980s and 1990s.

Strategy

The strategy employed to meet objectives in 1980 and beyond stresses the concept of flexibility inherent in the flexible response doctrine of the sixties and seventies. This flexibility includes not only that involved in the choice between nuclear and conventional forces, but also flexibility within the nuclear option — the ability to choose between strategic nuclear (i.e. use of ICBMs, SLBMs) and theater nuclear (i.e. use of tactical nuclear weapons) options.

The overall nature of the strategy is summarized in the following statement from the FY 1980 Annual Report of the Secretary of Defense:

> It has become a truism of modern defense policy that we must maintain military capabilities at three basic levels: strategic nuclear, theater nuclear, and non-nuclear. The degree of dependence we should place on each is much less obvious. This administration like its four predecessors, has decided that it will keep the barrier to nuclear warfare — primarily in the form of our non-nuclear capabilities — at a high level.[16]

This general statement of strategy must of course be refined to develop a specific force structure to support the strategy.

Defense Programs

The development of a specific type of force to support the strategy is accomplished by means of what are termed defense "programs." This terminology, adopted from the McNamara era, reflects the output side of the defense effort — what capabilities are purchased, rather than what resources are used. The purpose of such a concept is to enable policy makers to better evaluate the defense budget by arranging the inputs, insofar as feasible, into programs having an identifiable, common output.

The specific programs designed to support the strategy outlined above generally include strategic forces, theater nuclear forces, general purpose forces, and other capabilities. The following paragraphs review each of these programs in terms of their role in meeting the general set of objectives outlined above.

Strategic forces include those elements of our military force designed to deliver strategic nuclear weapons. The basis of this force is the concept of the triad — a mixture of land-based missiles, submarine-based missiles, and manned bombers. The strategic nuclear forces are generally designed to meet the objective of international peace and stability by deterring the Soviet Union and any other potential adversary from threatening such stability by a nuclear attack on the United States or on American allies. The specific requirement for such a force as stated in the Fiscal Year 1980 Annual Report is as follows:

> . . . [the requirement is] met if our retaliatory forces can satisfy the following conditions: survive in adequate numbers and types after a well-executed surprise attack on them by the Soviets; penetrate Soviet defenses and destroy a comprehensive set of targets in the U.S.S.R. . . . ; if necessary, inflict high levels of damage on Soviet society . . . ; and retain a reserve capability in the wake of a controlled exchange.[17]

Theater nuclear forces are also designed to meet the objective of stability, with a response less than a strategic nuclear exchange. The use of theater nuclear forces is primarily oriented toward Western Europe where:

> . . . these forces must be capable of carrying out serious military tasks within NATO's strategy of flexible response if deterrence fails, with the aim of controlling escalation.[18]

General purpose forces are designed to attain the overall objective of stability as well as many of the specific objectives outlined above. General purpose forces include most of what are termed conventional forces, less the mobility elements designed to move the forces over great distances. The primary objective of general purpose forces is to promote stability by countering the:

. . . heavy concentration of Soviet Forces in Eastern Europe and the Western military districts of the USSR. These forces represent a direct and growing threat to the security of Western Europe, on both the central front and flanks.[19]

Other foreign policy objectives may provide a rationale for use of general purpose forces. As noted in the Annual Report:

To stress Europe is not to rule out a major contingency elsewhere. Nor is it to preclude a smaller attack by the Soviet or other forces in such sensitive areas as the Middle East and the Persian Gulf, or the Korean peninsula. For planning purposes, however, it seems appropriate to pose the size of our general purpose combat forces on the assumption of having to halt more or less simultaneously one major attack . . . and one lesser attack elsewhere.[20]

This "one-and-a-half war strategy" is designed to meet the objective of stability with emphasis on central Europe, while at the same time leaving enough conventional capability to meet the other objectives such as the security of trading partners, access to raw materials, and the availability of access to energy sources.

The remaining defense programs include such elements as intelligence and communications, airlift and sealift, guard and reserve forces, research and development, training, and other programs. These elements are designed to complement the employment and mission of the strategic, theater nuclear and general purpose forces.

In summary, the foreign policy planning model suggests that the set of foreign policy objectives derived from our national values results in a strategy and set of programs to implement that strategy. From an output point of view, the defense programs listed above are designed to enable the nation to attain its foreign policy objectives. The PPBS system makes the translation from objectives to programs and finally to the budget by an analysis of the most effective combination of forces that will result in attainment of the objectives. The "most effective" combination of forces is generally determined by use of the techniques of cost-effectiveness and cost benefit analysis, discussed in Chapters 10-12.

DEFENSE PROGRAMS AND DEFENSE SPENDING

The impact of the foreign policy approach to defense spending on the defense budget is determined by first accounting for the costs of each of the programs that result from this approach. The evolution of program costs over the period from fiscal year 1964 to fiscal year 1980 is shown in Table 2.1. The usefulness of reviewing such figures is that it gives an indication of the trends in fiscal emphasis concerning the various programs within the defense budget.

The figures in Table 2.1 represent the cost of purchasing the outputs of the defense sector used to implement American military strategy. The trends shown should not be interpreted as changes in the physical volume of the defense effort in each area, but simply as the current dollar value of purchasing the specific force component shown on each line. Over the time period indicated, changes in the price level, changes in technology, and changes in relative prices must be taken into account before we can determine whether capabilities have been affected and, if so, what areas have been affected. To see this, we note in Table 2.2 some major indicators of physical components in each program for selected years between fiscal year 1964 and fiscal year 1980. As these figures indicate, the trends in current dollars do not necessarily bear any relation to the trends in physical components within each program area. While the current dollar costs for strategic forces, for example, between fiscal year 1968 and fiscal year 1980 increased by 52 percent, the number of landbased missiles remained constant and the number of strategic bomber squadrons, manner fighter intercepter squadrons, and air defense firing batteries all decreased.

Physical aggregates are also fraught with problems in terms of comparing capabilities. Is an Army division of 1968 equivalent to a 1980 Army division? Or has the change in capital, both human and physical, as well as our technological advancement increased the capability of an American division to conduct ground combat?

The important point to note here is that trends in program budgets do not necessarily indicate changes in capability, but rather reflect the cost of various programs.

Besides being useful in terms of analyzing trends in each area of the defense budget, the general concept of program cost can be used in a rough sense to indicate the trade-offs within major program areas. These comparisons of various budget levels are helpful in indicating the opportunity cost of attaining various objectives, as well as answering questions concerning the mix of forces necessary to attain a given set of objectives.

Defense program budgets, therefore, indicate the cost of the force structure designed to implement a given strategy. Historically, however, the defense budget as submitted to Congress identifies defense spending not from the output side, but from the cost of purchasing defense inputs. The method of converting the program budget to a budget amenable for submission to Congress is accomplished by simply listing all resources used to produce the program outputs specified in Table 2.1 according to the general budget title line items shown in Table 2.3.

The line items shown in Table 2.3 are mostly self-explanatory. Each line item refers to the purchase of an input used in the current production of defense services. One major exception to this description is the line item entitled "retired pay" which actually represents deferred compensation paid to those who have served on active or reserve duty in the past and are now eligible for retirement benefits.

The input breakdown of the defense budget is helpful in identifying trends in the aggregate costs of specific inputs to the military sector such as manpower, capital, and operations and maintenance funding. Trends in current dollar outlays in these areas should be interpreted cautiously, however, for many of the same reasons cited in the above analysis concerning the program budgets.

The aggregate defense budget sent to Congress reflects the sum total of each general line item shown in Table 2.3 for each fiscal year. Once a final budget is negotiated and passed by both houses of Congress and is signed by the President, it becomes law and funds are then expended to provide defense services (see Chapters 7 and 8 for a detailed examination of the budgetary process).

Table 2.1

Total Obligational Authority by Program

(In Millions of Dollars — Current)

FY 1964 – 1980

Summary by Program	1964	1968	1972	1976	1980
Strategic Forces	8,387	7,128	7,156	7,225	10,834
General Purpose Forces	16,417	30,537	25,560	32,972	49,974
Intelligence and Communications	4,380	5,542	5,458	6,674	9,116
Airlift and Sealift	1,040	1,747	1,114	1,262	1,907
Guard & Reserve Forces	1,768	2,177	3,258	5,380	7,113
Research & Development	4,834	4,270	5,749	8,655	11,758
Central Supply & Maintenance	4,638	8,385	8,663	9,740	13,770
Training, Medical, Other General Personnel Activities	6,921	12,151	15,198	21,539	27,887
Administration & Associated Activities	1,079	1,239	1,693	2,180	2,557
Support of Other Nations	81	1,789	2,652	244	583
Total	49,547	74,965	76,502	95,881	135,500

Source: Annual Report of the Secretary of Defense FY 1980, *p. A–1*.

Table 2.2
Department of Defense
Summary of Selected Active Military Forces: 1964 – 1980

	Actual Jun 30 1964	Actual Jun 30 1968	Actual Sep 30 1978	Estimated Sep 30 1980
Strategic Forces:				
Intercontinental Ballistic Missiles:				
Minuteman	600	1,000	1,000	1,000
Titan II	108	54	54	54
Polaris-Poseidon Missiles	336	656	656	656
Strategic Bomber Squadrons	78	40	25	25
Manned Fighter Interceptor Squadrons	40	26	6	6
Army Air Defense Firing Batteries	107	81	0	0
General Purpose Forces:				
Land Forces:				
Army Divisions	16⅓	19⅔	16	16
Marine Corps Divisions	3	4	3	3
Tactical Air Forces:				
Air Force Wings	21	30	26	26
Navy Attack Wings	15	15	12	12
Marine Corps Wings	3	3	3	3
Naval Forces:				
Attack & Antisubmarine Carriers	24	23	13	13
Nuclear Attack Submarines	19	33	70	75
Other Warships	363	385	166	181
Amphibious Warships	133	157	64	63

Source: Annual Report of the Secretary of Defense FY 1980, *p. C-1.*

Table 2.3

**Department of Defense Total Obligational Authority
by Input Categories: FY 1964 – 1980**

(In Millions of Dollars)

Summary by Budget Title	FY 1964	FY 1968	FY 1972	FY 1976	FY 1980
Military Personnel	12,983	19,961	23,147	25,430	30,328
Retired Pay	1,211	2,093	3,889	7,326	11,466
Operation & Maintenance	11,693	20,950	21,242	28,848	11,466
Procurement	15,028	22,528	18,526	21,213	35,425
Research, Development Test, & Evaluation	7,053	7,263	7,584	9,520	13,606
Special Foreign Currency Program	——	——	12	3	7
Military Construction	977	1,557	1,262	2,148	2,167
Family Housing & Homeowners Assistance Program	602	612	839	1,259	1,608
Revolving & Management Funds	——	——	——	135	——
Total	49,547	74,965	76,502	95,881	135,500

Source: Annual Report of the Secretary of Defense FY 1980, *p. A–1.*

CONCLUSION

This chapter has reviewed the formulation of the defense budget from a foreign policy perspective. The entire process is summarized in Figure 2.2, which gives the set of concepts inherent in formulating a defense budget from a national perspective based on foreign policy considerations.

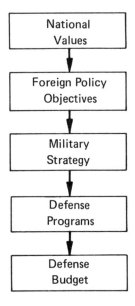

Figure 2.2   Foreign Policy Planning and the Defense Budget

The arrows shown in the figure represent the planning path described in this chapter, i.e., a formulation that begins with a development of national values and ends with a defense budget. The model can also conceptually be utilized to work from a given defense budget back to a set of objectives that are attainable with the given budget. This does not imply that we would somehow derive our national values or our foreign policy objectives from a given defense budget. Working this process in reverse, however, would certainly be useful in indicating the consequences to decision makers of fixing the defense budget at a given level.

The approach outlined here is admittedly a great simplification of a terribly complex process. The process as described above also leaves open-ended the issue of what impact the size of the defense budget has on the attainment of those national objectives which are not primarily related to the foreign policy process. In addition, it fails to take into account the effect of relevant actors on the outcome of the process. The following chapters deal with these issues by looking at the formulation of the defense budget from alternative perspectives. In particular, Chapter 3 deals with domestic political and economic policy and the formulation of the defense budget, while Chapter 4 deals with the institutional actors in the defense decision-making process and their impact on the defense budget.

NOTES

1 An article of selected extracts of Karl von Clausewitz, *On War*, can be found in Frank N. Trager and Philip S. Kronenberg, eds., *National Security and American Society* (Lawrence, Kansas: University Press of Kansas, 1973), pp. 75–89.

2 The concepts of national values, interests, and objectives can be found in numerous texts and articles on the theory of foreign policy and national security policy. Examples include Gene E. Rainey, *Patterns of American Foreign Policy* (Boston, Massachusetts: Allyn and Boem, Inc., 1975); John Spanier and Eric M. Uslander, *How American Foreign Policy is Made* (New York: Praeger, 1974); and Frank N. Trager and Frank L. Simonie, "An Introduction to the Study of National Security," in Frank N. Trager and Phillip S. Kronenberg, eds., *National Security and American Society* (Lawrence, Kansas: University Press of Kansas, 1973), pp. 35–48.

3 Trager and Simonie, *op. cit.*, p. 38.

4 See Kenneth Arrow, *Social Choice and Individual Values* (New York: John Wiley and Sons, 1951).

5 Trager and Simonie, *op. cit.*, p. 38.

6 *Ibid.*, p. 43.

7 As noted by William J. Taylor, Jr., in "Interdependence, Specialization, and National Security," *Air University Review* (July–August 1979), Vol. XXX, No. 5, pp. 17–26, the distinction between foreign policy and national security policy is becoming imperceptible. We shall consequently use foreign policy and national security policy interchangeably in the following discussion.

8 Rainey, *op. cit.*, p. 234.

9 Rainey, *op. cit.*, p. 235-237. See Amos A. Jordan, William J. Taylor, and Associates, *American National Security*, Chapter V, Johns Hopkins Press, 1981, for detailed review of the evolution of American strategic doctrine from post-World War II.

10 Rainey, *op. cit.*, p. 235.

11 *Ibid.*

12 *Ibid.*, p. 236.

13 *Annual Report of the Secretary of Defense FY 1980* (Washington, D.C.: U.S. Government Printing Office, 1979), p. 30.

14 *Ibid.*, p. 59.

15 *Ibid.*, p. 8.

16 *Ibid.*, p. 12.

17 *Ibid.*, p. 13.

18 *Ibid.*

19 *Ibid.*

20 *Ibid.*

SELECTED REFERENCES

Amos A. Jordan, William J. Taylor and Associates, *American National Security* (Baltimore: Johns Hopkins Press, 1981).

Gene E. Rainey, *Patterns of American Foreign Policy* (Boston: Allyn and Boem, Inc., 1975).

Frank N. Trager and Phillip S. Kronenberg, eds., *National Security and American Society* (Lawrence, Kansas: University Press of Kansas, 1973).

Chapter 3
Domestic Policy Planning and Defense Spending

INTRODUCTION

In the preceding chapter, defense budget decisions were described as a rational process that focuses primarily on the foreign policy aspects of the defense problem. While the level of defense spending certainly depends on foreign policy objectives, viewing the budgetary process solely from the foreign policy perspective ignores the constraints that domestic issues place on defense decision-makers.

The national values that were the basis of foreign policy objectives may also lead to the formulation of objectives that focus on domestic concerns and have little bearing on foreign policy. Promotion of the free enterprise system and a vigorous economy as a national value, for example, may result in numerous objectives that have little direct effect on foreign policy, but have significant consequences on the defense budget. In this analysis, such objectives are regarded as domestic policy objectives.

This distinction does not mean that certain national values that result in domestic policy objectives may not lead also to foreign policy objectives. The promotion of a vigorous economy, for example, certainly results in a number of foreign policy objectives, such as access to raw materials and freedom of the seas. The same value may also imply objectives, such as the development of a national highway system, that have little direct bearing on the conduct of foreign policy or military strategy but which utilize resources that might also be utilized in the defense sector, i.e., have a cost in terms of defense opportunities. It is this *opportunity cost* of attaining various objectives that links the two sets of issues and that is the focus of this chapter.

The following section develops a method of formulating a defense spending target within the context of domestic policy planning. The second section of the chapter deals with the formulation of various domestic policy objectives from national values, specifically focusing on those objectives that (1) compete with defense programs for funds or (2) place overall limits on the availability of funds to the public sector. The third section of the chapter develops a model that relates both types of domestic policy objectives to the aggregate amount spent on defense, while the final section summarizes the domestic policy planning process.

Once again, it should be noted that the development of an aggregate defense budget using the domestic policy planning approach is only one perspective of the defense budgetary process. As noted in the previous chapter, foreign policy considerations play a key role in the formulation of the defense budget. The purpose of describing the domestic policy aspects of defense budgeting is to isolate a perspective that many major actors and institutions have of the defense budgeting process. These institutions and actors include the President, nondefense government agencies, the Office of Management and Budget, the Council of Economic Advisers, and nondefense related committees of Congress, as well as many nondefense related private interest groups.

DOMESTIC POLICY OBJECTIVES

The initial phases of formulating a defense budget from the domestic policy planning perspective are similar to those developed in the foreign policy planning approach described in Chapter 2. The starting point is the set of national values that represent, as noted earlier, the broad philosophical or ideological orientation of the nation. These values must be refined into more specific interests or objectives in order to institute the planning procedure. A broad national value such as the promotion of the free enterprise system is ill-suited for policy planning and must be refined into a specific set of objectives before a strategy and its resulting programs can be formulated.

In the context of the domestic policy planning approach, the refinement of objectives is subject to several qualifications that are important in making the approach useful from a budgeting perspective. First it should be noted that some objectives that result from a refinement of national values do not entail the expenditure of resources but, instead, reflect a change in the tone of national policy. Thus, an objective such as a presidency that is open in terms of more press conferences or a change in congressional budgetary procedures, may not involve resource costs. These types of objectives we shall define as *noneconomic*. Other objectives, such as the improvement of environmental standards by imposition of tighter controls on the private sector, impose economic costs that are not reflected in the budget. For the most part, the impact of such measures is ignored in the formal budgetary process, although clearly there are cases in which explicit treatment is required, particularly in the area of energy policy.

The remaining set of objectives resulting from the crystallization of national values are defined as economic objectives, in that they entail the expenditure of resources to attain the objective. These objectives can furthermore be subdivided into those objectives that limit aggregate public expenditures, and those objectives that compete for specific amounts of available public funds.

Economic objectives which limit aggregate public expenditure include the broad set of macroeconomic objectives which affect the total allocation of resources between the public and private sectors. Economic objectives which compete with the defense sector for available public resources include the objectives inherent in the missions of nondefense agencies within the Federal government. The following section develops the relationships among these various concepts.

DOMESTIC POLICY OBJECTIVES AND THE DEFENSE BUDGET

The discussion of the domestic policy planning approach can be summarized in Figure 3.1 which describes the refinement of national values into various categories of domestic policy objectives. As in the illustration of the foreign policy planning approach, Figure 3.1 omits nonbudgetary related items from the model of the planning process.

Macroeconomic Objectives

There are a number of key laws and documents where the refinement of national values into specific macroeconomic objectives is accomplished. As noted in the *Economic Report of the President* for 1979:

> The Employment Act of 1946 has been the basic guide for the President and Congress in the development of economic policies. The Employment Act charged the government with responsibility to promote maximum employment, production, and purchasing power through the use of policy tools at its disposal. Since 1946 the instruments of fiscal and monetary policies have been used in ways that contributed to economic prosperity.[1]

Thus the guidance for overall economic policy generally stems from the Employment Act. In 1978, however, Congress further delineated the macroeconomic objectives of the nation in the Full Employment and Growth Act of 1978, otherwise known as the Humphrey-Hawkins Act. The nature of the act is indicated in the 1979 *Economic Report of the President*:

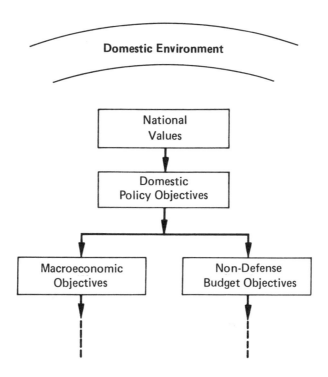

Figure 3.1   National Values and Domestic Policy Objectives

　　　The new law strengthens the Employment Act in three essential respects. It explicitly identifies national economic priorities and objectives; it directs the President to establish, and the Congress to consider, goals based on those priorities and objectives; and it creates new procedures and requirements for the President, the Congress, and the Federal Reserve to improve the coordination and development of economic policies.[2]

The initial objectives of the Humphrey-Hawkins bill were specified in terms of 1983 targets for unemployment and inflation. The unemployment target was specified as 4 percent for workers over 16 and a rate of inflation in consumer prices of 3 percent.[3]

Another key macroeconomic objective implicit in the Humphrey-Hawkins Act and important from a budgetary perspective is the rate of economic growth. As noted in the *Economic Report of the President for 1979*:

　　　Lower unemployment and inflation rates are basic objectives, but they are not the only economic aims of the Administration or the new act. As noted earlier, the Humphrey-Hawkins Act places a high priority on encouraging the growth of investment and capital formation, reducing the share of Federal Spending in the nation's output, and balancing the budget.[4]

Thus another macroeconomic objective is higher growth through increased investment. One of the ways of increasing private investment is to reduce public consumption and revenues, therefore increasing the amount of income which the private sector has available to both invest and consume. This entails a secular trend of smaller shares of government spending and therefore places some restraint on the overall availability of resources to the public sector.

Macroeconomic Objectives and Macroeconomic Variables

As noted above the primary macroeconomic objectives which concern policy makers involved in the budgetary process are the rate of inflation and the rate of unemployment. While a detailed discussion of the relationship between such objectives and the budget is given in Chapter 6, it will be helpful at this point to sketch the relationship between these objectives and the size of the Federal budget.

The choice of a set of macroeconomic targets for inflation and unemployment presents policymakers with a dilemma usually depicted by means of a Phillips Curve. The Phillips Curve, as discussed in detail in Chapter 6, reflects the combinations of inflation rates and unemployment rates attainable given the capacity of the economic system and the values of inflation and unemployment from past periods. A typical Phillips Curve is shown in Figure 3.2. As indicated, the Phillips Curve implies that inflation rates and unemployment rates are inversely related. The policy maker selecting a set of macroeconomic targets, therefore, attempts to select the inflation rate and unemployment rate which in some sense leaves society best off. The dilemma inherent in the policy choice is that improving either target usually makes the other target worse off. Thus moving from point A to point B in Figure 3.2 reduces the unemployment rate but results in a higher rate of inflation.

Once a policy target for inflation and unemployment is selected, the job of the macroeconomic policy maker is to insure that the level of aggregate income, or the gross national product, is consistent with the policy goals. There are a variety of policy instruments which can be employed to affect the level of income. These instruments generally come under the heading of monetary and fiscal policy. While the detailed effects of changes in monetary and fiscal policy are described in Chapter 6, we shall be content at this point to note that the level of aggregate income is increased by increases in the supply of money, decreases in the level of taxation, and increases in the level of government spending. Given the supply of money and the level of taxation, therefore, the level of income rises with an increase in total purchases of goods and services by the government, and falls with a decrease of such purchases.

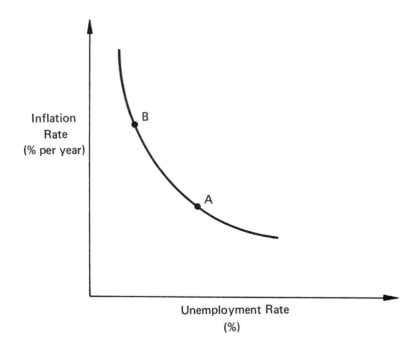

Figure 3.2   The Phillips Curve

In developing the overall Federal budget, the President through his Council of Economic Advisers and the Office of Management and Budget attempts to balance the objectives of the defense and nondefense sectors with the objectives of macroeconomic policy.[5] This will imply that fiscal and monetary policy should be expansionary in periods where the emphasis of the administration is on decreasing the rate of unemployment rather than dealing with the rate of inflation. In periods where inflation appears to be the primary concern, then monetary and fiscal policy would move towards restraint. The cyclical swings in the economy between periods of high inflation and high unemployment thus affects the decision on whether the growth of government expenditures, as a part of the fiscal package, will incrementally accelerate or decelerate.

In the *Economic Report of the President for 1982*, the Reagan administration outlined a new set of priorities with respect to the federal budget:

> This administration has a different set of spending priorities than those reflected in the budgets of the recent past. This difference is expressed in the following guidelines used in developing the Administration's plan for restraining the growth of Federal spending.
> - Strengthen the national defense.
> - Maintain the integrity of social insurance programs while reforming entitlement programs to ensure that they serve those in greatest need.
> - Reduce subsidies to middle- and upper-income groups.
> - Apply sound economic criteria to programs where subsidies are justified.
> - Recover costs that can clearly be allocated to users of services provided by Federal programs.
> - Reduce the Federal role in allocating credit by restraining on- and off-budget credit activities.[6]

Thus, the overall size of the federal budget is, in an incremental fashion, affected by the perceptions of the President and his economic advisers of trends in the key macroeconomic variables and a general philosophy concerning the appropriate roles of government.

Another macroeconomic objective noted above, which deserves some mention from a budgetary perspective, is the rate of economic growth. Economic growth as previously noted depends to a certain degree on the rate of investment undertaken by the private sector. One way of increasing investment is to increase the disposable income of members of the economic system by reducing the amount of taxes used to finance public consumption, an approach now referred to as "supply side" economics and adopted by the Reagan administration. This cannot be done, however, without decreasing the level of government expenditures. If taxes are reduced without a concomitant decrease in government spending, then the government is forced to borrow to make up the deficit. This borrowing increases the demand for funds in money markets and competes with private investors for the limited amount of financial resources. As a result, private investment is "crowded out" in the bidding process and is reduced below that level which would occur in the absence of the government expenditure reduction.

Thus in a period of full employment the percentage of total output which is utilized in consumption by the public sector has opportunity costs in terms of economic growth. A target of increasing economic growth, therefore, implies a fiscal policy of restraint which will place some limits on overall Federal expenditures.

Nondefense National Objectives

The second major aspect of the domestic policy planning approach to defense spending is the determination of the nondefense Federal budget. The size of these expenditures relative to the size of the defense budget is shown in Table 3.1, which gives total Federal outlays for FY 1981 and FY 1983. It should be noted at this point that some aspects of nondefense objectives will relate to the attainment of foreign policy objectives.

Budget outlays such as international affairs and general science, space, and technology expenditures certainly have spillover effects into the defense sector. But for purposes of simplification a specified portion of the Federal budget can be assumed to be related to primarily domestic policy issues. Given this assumption, the determination of the nondefense portion of the Federal budget can be accomplished in a method similar to that used in determination of the defense portion of the budget. A "domestic" strategy is developed to support domestic objectives in each of the functional budget areas. Programs are developed to support the strategy, and the costing of those programs in terms of inputs leads to a conventional budget request in each functional budget area.

While specific domestic policy objectives are detailed in the budget requests of Federal agencies that have responsibility for domestic policy, it is instructive to observe the overall emphasis at the presidential level on various domestic policy budget areas. In addition to these cyclical variations, trends in Federal spending are also affected by philosophical views on the appropriate role of government. *The Economic Report of the President for 1982* suggests the importance of this philosophical perspective in the Reagan administration:

> Because of these philosophical beliefs and economic judgments, the Administration has initiated a major transformation of the role of the Federal Government in the U.S. economy. The Administration's economic recovery program will change both the size and the nature of government involvement, reversing the trend of recent decades when the Federal budget usually grew faster than the rest of the economy as the Federal Government took upon itself responsibilities that had previously been left to the private sector or to State and local governments.[7]

The result of agency requests balanced with presidential emphasis is a set of budget requests for the domestic portion of the Federal budget.

Table 3.1
Federal Budget Outlays: 1981–1983
(Billions of Dollars)

	FY 1981 (Actual)	FY 1983 (Estimate)
National Defense	159.8	225.1
International Affairs	11.1	12.0
General Science, Space, Technology	6.4	7.6
Energy	10.3	4.2
Natural Resources and Environment	13.5	9.9
Agriculture	5.6	4.5
Commerce and Housing Credit	3.9	1.6
Transportation	23.4	19.6
Community and Regional Development	9.4	7.3
Education	31.4	21.6
Health	66.0	78.1
Income Security	225.1	261.7
Veterans Benefits	23.0	24.4
Administration and Justice	4.7	4.6
General Government	4.6	5.0
Fiscal Assistance	6.9	6.7
Interest	82.5	112.5
Offsetting Receipts	−30.3	−44.7
Total	657.2	757.6

Source: Economic Report of the President, 1982, p. 317.

Domestic Policy and the Defense Budget

The implications of the preceding discussion for the defense budget can now be developed. The domestic policy objectives of the government lead to two broad sets of budgetary effects. Macroeconomic objectives and the resulting macroeconomic strategy, implemented by means of fiscal and monetary policy, determine the overall share of the national product which is allocated towards public consumption. The resources which are available for public consumption for domestic policy needs are simultaneously determined by the budgetary activities of nondefense Federal agencies. From a domestic policy planning perspective the defense budget can then be viewed as the residual between the overall allocation of resources for public consumption and the domestic portion of the budget. This approach is illustrated in Figure 3.3 which outlines the domestic policy constraints on the defense budget.

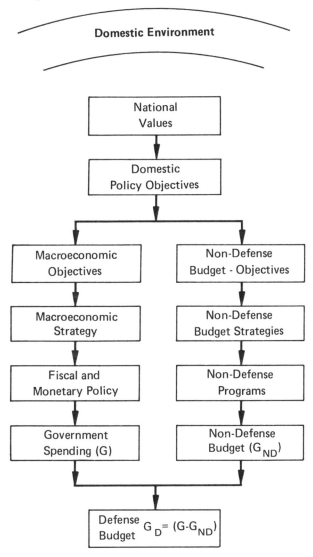

Figure 3.3 The Domestic Policy Perspective on the Defense Budget

CONCLUSION

The domestic policy planning approach to defense spending is useful in analyzing the domestic policy constraints on the defense budget. This perspective on defense budgeting also appears to have been the method actually used to allocate rsources to the defense sector under the Truman and Eisenhower administrations. In their analysis of defense budgeting, *How Much is Enough*, Alain Enhoven and K. Wayne Smith note:

> Starting with the Truman administration and continuing under Eisenhower, the President, relatively early in the budget cycle, provided guidance to the Secretary of Defense on the size of the defense budget which he thought was economically and politically feasible for the next fiscal year. The problem was that this figure was usually arrived at by simply estimating the government's total revenues then deducting fixed payments (such as interest on the national debt and payments to veterans), the estimated costs of domestic programs, and expenditures on foreign aid. Whatever "remained" was then allocated to the military.[8]

The budgeting process is obviously not as mechanistic as portrayed in this or any budgetary model. The defense budget, the domestic budget, and the overall level of public expenditure are determined simultaneously in an interactive process which attempts to balance all national objectives within the given institutional framework associated with the budget process. Those concerned with domestic policy, however, would most likely tend to view the defense budget along lines similar to those developed in this chapter.

As in the foreign policy planning perspective on defense budgets, the direction of the lines of implied sequence can go in either direction. This chapter on the domestic policy planning perspective has been developed assuming that the initial step in the process is the determination of national values. In some cases, such as a war or other national military emergency, the defense budget may be the driving factor and the residuals could be macroeconomic objectives or domestic policy objectives. In either case, the model emphasizes the effect of domestic policy considerations on defense budget decision-making and the linkages between the various domestic policy objectives and the size of the defense budget.

In both the foreign policy planning and the domestic policy planning approaches to defense budgeting, the role of the specific actors in the budget process has been understated. The following chapter reviews the actors and institutions in the budgeting process and stresses their influence on its outcome.

NOTES

1 *The Economic Report of the President, 1979*, p. 106.
2 *Ibid.*, p. 107.
3 *Ibid.*, p. 108.
4 *Ibid.*
5 The role of the President is discussed in detail in Chapter 4.
6 *The Economic Report of the President, 1982*, pp. 78-79.
7 *Ibid.*, p. 84.
8 Alain C. Enthoven and K. Wayne Smith, *How Much is Enough?* (New York: Harper and Row, 1971), p. 13.

SELECTED REFERENCES

James T. Lynn and Charles L. Schultze, *The Federal Budget: What are the Nation's Priorities* (Washington, D.C.: American Enterprise Institute for Public Policy Research, 1976).

Joseph A. Pechman, ed., *Setting National Priorities: The 1980 Budget* (Washington, D.C.: The Brookings Institution, 1979).

N. Singer, *Public Microeconomics: An Introduction to Government Finance,* 2nd ed. (Boston: Little, Brown & Co., 1976).

Chapter 4
The Institutional Perspective on Defense Spending

INTRODUCTION

The preceding chapters have outlined two related approaches, both of which assume that the relevant policymakers involved in the formulation of the defense budget arrive at defense spending totals based on a "rational" application of the methodologies outlined in Chapters 2 and 3.

While these approaches do indicate methods that can be and are used in the American defense budgetary process, the discussion thus far has ignored the various institutional interests — as well as the institutions themselves — that play a significant role in formulating decsions on defense spending. In order to understand fully the defense budgetary process, it is necessary to explore the ways in which the various institutions and decision makers within the budgetary process reconcile the differences between the defense spending totals arrived at by the previously discussed competing methodologies.

The institutional approach to defense budget formulation requires an understanding of the general decision-making framework involved in the budget process. In this regard, two key points should be noted that outline important aspects of the institutional perspective. The first is that the budget document is proposed by the executive branch and disposed of, through the legislative process, by Congress. Thus, the key decision maker in the budgetary process is the president, although Congress certainly plays an important role in affecting the final disposition of presidential initiatives.

The second key point to be noted is that the president is affected in his budgetary decision-making by a number of other institutions. The general institutions that affect presidential decisions concerning the defense budget in the United States include the following: presidential advisers (the White House staff, National Security Council, Office of Management and Budget, and the Council of Economic Advisers), the Defense Department, other cabinet-level agencies (the State Department, Central Intelligence Agency, and all other departments competing for limited funds), Congress, special interest groups, and the media. Each of these institutions exerts some pressure on the president when he is making budgetary decisions, and the relative magnitude of each of these pressures determines the general direction of budgetary policy. As noted by Morton Halperin in his analysis of national security decision making:

> the President . . . in dealing with a particular problem will have little weight of past experience and little firsthand knowledge. Issues tend to come to him and his closest associates in an abstract or generalized form, and pressure will be brought from many sides. The White House tends to relate each theory to its sponsors and to appeal to the allegiance of as many groups as possible.[1]

Thus, to understand the outcome of the budget process, it is necessary to understand the institutions that exert pressure, their institutional interests, and their relative importance in terms of influence.

The institutional perspective on defense spending examines these factors and their impact on the defense budget. The approach is summarized in Figure 4.1, which diagrams the president as the center of the budget decision-making process and the various institutions that exert pressure on the president as agents of influence

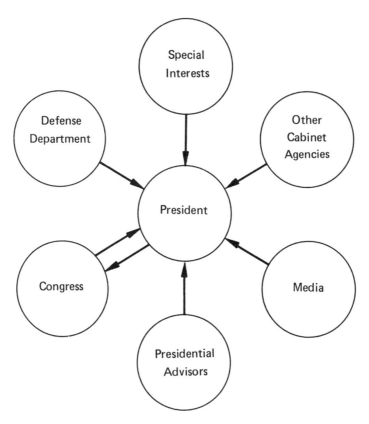

Figure 4.1 Institutional Pressures in Presidential Defense Budget Decisions

surrounding the president. The arrows represent the flow of input to decision-makers in the budgetary process. Thus, single arrows emanate from each agent of influence; only the president and Congress, which is a decision maker through the legislative process, are both agents of influence and decision-makers. The president sends the proposed budget to Congress for a legislative decision, and the Congress sends the budget back to the president for signature into law.

Figure 4.1 is clearly a simplification of a complex web of interactions. It emphasizes the early stages in the formulation of the president's budget submission to Congress. After submission of the president's proposed budget, the institutions direct their efforts at Congress. As we will discover in Chapters 7 and 8, however, Congress considers the budget for one fiscal year while the president is already developing the budget for the following fiscal year. Thus a more realistic view of the process would show a continuous flow of inputs from each institution to both the president and the Congress.

The following sections in this chapter briefly discuss each of the major institutions outlined in the general model described above. The descriptions indicate the nature of each institution, their relative closeness to the president in terms of access, and their magnitude of influence in general budgetary decision making.

THE PRESIDENT

The single most important participant in the defense budgetary process from the institutional perspective is the president. The importance of presidential influence on defense budget policy results from the three critical roles that the president plays in American government: the chief executive of the federal bureaucracy, the American head of state, and the leader of his political party. Each of these roles results in the president's exerting considerable influence on the final outcome of the defense budget process.

In his role as chief executive of the federal government and the federal bureaucracy, the president is charged by law with presenting the federal budget to Congress each year. Since the defense budget is a major subcomponent of the federal budget, and the president is the final approving authority of the budget, the influence of the president on defense budget submission is direct and obvious.

It should be noted, however, that there may be a substantial difference between a presidential budget submission and the ultimately approved budget. The actual approving authority of the budget is Congress, and Congress may add or subtract from a presidential budget submission. In his study of the budgetary process, Aaron Wildavsky presents some statistics that indicate the relationship of the actual presidential budget submission and the final appropriation voted by Congress. In a study of 444 appropriation histories of 37 bureaus dealing with domestic policies over the period from 1947 to 1959, Wildavsky's data show that in only 62 (or 14 percent) of the appropriations' histories were there no differences between the presidential budget request and the amount appropriated by Congress. In the remaining 382 appropriation histories — 86 percent of total histories — the amount appropriated by Congress differed from the president's request.[2] Thus, the president plays a significant role in determining the defense budget by submitting an initial negotiating position in his proposed budget, and by serving as the approving authority of the federal budget. The fact that the president approves a budget submission, however, does not necessariy imply that the president sets the defense budget. On the contrary, as Wildavsky's data show, more often than not the budget submission of the president is substantially altered by Congress.

The second factor that results in substantial presidential influence on the defense budgetary process is the president's role as head of state. As such, the president is the key decision-maker and chief spokesman for the United States on matters of foreign policy. The importance of the president in this area is indicated by Morton Halperin in his analysis of bureaucracy and foreign policy in the United States:

> The President stands at the center of the foreign policy process in the United States. His role and influence over decisions are qualitatively different from those of any other participant. In any foreign policy decision, the President will almost always be the principal figure determining the general direction of actions. Thus it was President Johnson who made the final decision that the United States should deploy an ABM system.
>
> Furthermore the President serves as the surrogate for the national interest. Many senior participants look to the President as to a blueprint for clues to the national security. His perception and judgment of what is in the national interest are dominant in the system.[3]

The implications of the presidential role as head of state are critical to the formulation of the defense budget from the foreign policy perspective. The president essentially shapes and enunciates the national interests and national security objectives of the United States through his role in the foreign policy process. Thus the overall nature of the force structure and defense program are keyed to the presidential conceptualization of the national values and the national interest.

The third presidential role that results in significant effects on the defense budget is that of leader of his political party. The leadership of the political party implies that presidential decisions on the defense budget will not only be shaped by foreign policy considerations, but also by domestic politics. The implication of both of these factors is that the President in his role as the leader of a major political party must weigh the political costs and benefits of various budget alternatives and choose the set of alternatives that most advances the national interest and at the same time allows the president and his party to maintain political power.

PRESIDENTIAL ADVISERS

The closest institutional group to the president, in terms of access as well as physical proximity, is the set of presidential advisers that constitute the Executive Office of the president. This group include four major subcomponents that are relevant to defense budget decision-making: the White House staff, the Office of Management and Budget, the National Security Council, and the Council of Economic Advisers.

The White House Staff

The White House staff includes a set of usually five to ten assistants to the president who constitute the president's direct staff. These advisers generally include a chief of staff, a domestic policy adviser as a minimum, a national security adviser, a press secretary, and an appointments secretary. Each of these individuals filters much of the information that flows up to and down from the president. Their appointments are based on a close personal relationship with the president, as well as their expertise in policy administration. The influence of these staff members on the defense budget is substantial as they assist the president in weighing the political costs and benefits of controversial issues within the defense budget request.

The Office of Management and Budget

The Office of Management and Budget (OMB) also plays a critical role in managing the budget process. The purpose of OMB is to translate initial presidential guidance on the budget to the major federal government agencies into a final budget request which the president submits to Congress. In this capacity, OMB acts as the president's budget watchdog and attempts to reconcile differences within the executive branch between presidential budget guidance and the budget requests of the various federal agencies.

In managing the budget process, OMB conducts several reviews of each agency budget prior to final presidential review and approval. During these reviews, the OMB staff and the staffs of the various agencies attempt to work out compromises to preclude major squabbles from reaching the heads of agencies, the director of OMB, and the president.[4]

Another function of OMB is to conduct an independent analysis of federal programs and to develop budget issues out of this analysis. The budget issues tend to focus the attention of each federal agency on the specific area within their respective budgets that OMB feels deserve management review.

The influence of OMB on the defense budget is substantial. Except for major issues which demand presidential attention, OMB essentially is delegated approval authority from the president for routine increments in or decrements from the federal budget. Thus while the president exercises final approving authority on budget submissions, OMB in fact resolves most issues concerning the budget prior to final presidential review.

The National Security Council

The National Security Council (NSC) was created by the National Security Act of 1947, and includes the president, vice-president, secretaries of state and defense, the director of Central Intelligence, and the chairman of the Joint Chiefs of Staff.[5] The purpose of the NSC is to coordinate national security policy, although the particular method by which the NSC is utilized depends on presidential style.

The NSC has a permanent staff which analyzes various national security issues and briefs the members of the Council when the NSC is called into session by the president. The president's national security adviser is generally appointed to serve as the Executive Secretary of the Council and to record the Presidential Decision Memoranda that result from presidential decisions within the NSC framework.[6]

The NSC's recognized purpose is both to deal with national security crises and to review overall American security strategy. Within the budget framework developed in the foreign policy planning approach, the NSC strategy review assists the president in shaping his view of national values and specific national security objectives.[7] In this sense, the NSC plays a significant role in affecting the outcome of the defense budgetary process by refining national values and shaping the budget guidance that the president hands down to the Defense Department.

The Council of Economic Advisers

The Council of Economic Advisers (CEA) was established by the Employment Act of 1946. The purpose of the Council is described in the following paragraph from the 1978 *Economic Report of the President:*

> . . . The Council of Economic Advisers analyzes economic problems and interprets trends and changes in the economy in order to help the President develop and evaluate the national economic policies. The Council prepares regular reports on current economic conditions in the United States and abroad and prepares forecasts of future economic developments. The Council also performs an advisory role within the Executive Office of the President and participates in interagency groups that analyze economic problems and develop programs to address them.[8]

The role of the Council is therefore critical to the development of domestic policy.objectives, and instrumental in affecting the defense budget from the domestic policy perspective. The major input that the CEA has in the process is the development of macroeconomic objectives and the overall ceiling on total federal spending. Through its economic forecasts and models, the CEA in effect helps determine the president's views on the division of national output between the public and private sectors.

THE DEFENSE DEPARTMENT

The Department of Defense (DOD) obviously plays a critical role in the defense budget process. DOD has responsibility for translating United States national military strategy into defense programs. The secretary of defense is the cabinet officer with the primary responsibility for developing the defense portion of the federal budget and advising the president on matters of military policy.

The organization of the Department of Defense is shown in Figure 4.2. The DOD organization can be initially subdivided into three major subcomponents, which include the Joint Chiefs of Staff, the military departments, and the office of the secretary of defense. The latter subcomponent includes the primarily civilian portion of the staff headed by the under- and assistant secretaries of defense.

The Joint Chiefs of Staff

The Joint Chiefs of Staff are the principal military advisers to the secretary of defense, but also have the unique ability within the department to offer independent advice to the president and the National Security Council. The Joint Chiefs of Staff became operational in 1947 as a result of the fear of many military advisers that placing the military services totally under the authority of a presidentially and politically appointed secretary of defense would prevent independent military opinions from filtering through to the president.

The Joint Chiefs include the senior ranking military officer of each service as well as the chairman, who is appointed by the president. Thus the Joint Chiefs include the Chairman of the Joint Chiefs, the Chief of Staff of the Army, the Chief of Naval Operations, and the Chief of Staff of the Air Force. Because the Marine Corps is a component of the Navy, the Commandant of the Marine Corps is not an official member of the Joint Chiefs, although he does attend the meetings of the Joint Chiefs regularly and sits coequally with the other members of the Joint Chiefs in matters relating directly to the Marine Corps.

The Joint Chiefs of Staff have three primary functions that affect their role in the budgetary process. First, as the primary military advisers to the president, the Joint Chiefs help shape presidential views on foreign policy objectives and military strategy. Secondly, as the principal integrated military planning staff in the Department of Defense, the Joint Chiefs are responsible for evaluating military requirements in a coordinated fashion and presenting the secretary of defense with coordinated guidance for the development of the

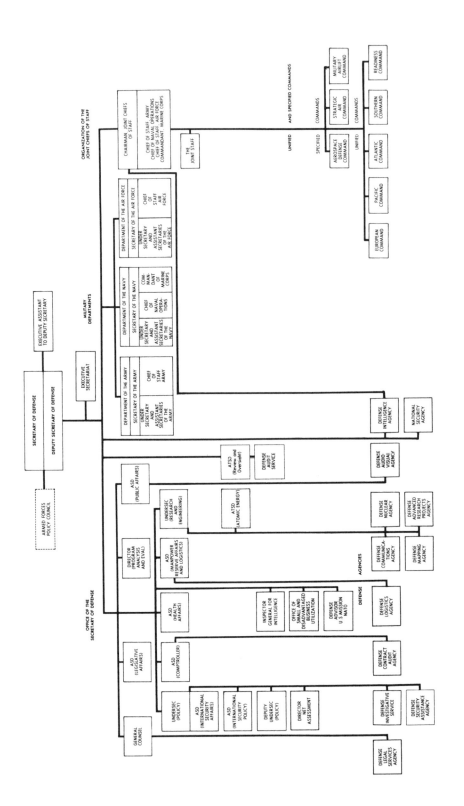

Figure 4.2 Organization of the Department of Defense

Source: The United States Government Manual 1982/83, p. 801.

defense budget. Lastly, as direct members of the chain of command with authority over specified commands, the Joint Chiefs receive input from the units in the field on the actual effectiveness of programs and policies, and use these inputs in reassessing the effectiveness of programs and military strategy in the budget process.

The Military Departments

While the chain of command in the United States military structure flows from the president through the secretary of defense and the Joint Chiefs of Staff to the unified and specified commands, the operation and efficiency of each of the services is the responsibility of that particular military department, each of which is headed by a civilian secretary. The military departments include the Department of the Army, the Department of the Navy, and the Department of the Air Force. As previously mentioned, the Marine Corps is a subcomponent of the Department of the Navy.

Perhaps the single most important aspect of these subcomponents of the organizational structure of DOD from the budgetary perspective is that each service submits a separate budget, and the total defense budget is integrated at the DOD level. The basic development of defense programs to support the military strategy is done by each service.

The fact that each service submits a separate budget leads to some organizational conflicts regarding the roles and missions of each service. While it may seem obvious that the Army is responsbile primarily for ground combat, the Navy for sea combat, and the Air Force for air combat, there are numerous areas of overlap which create friction between the services and should be understood in order to keep budget controversies in perspective. As Halperin notes:

> The three classic disputes which divided the military services in the 1940s and continue to divide them now are: (1) the struggle between the Navy and Air Force over naval aviation; (2) that between the Army and Air Force over combat support; and (3) that between the Army and Marines over Marine participation in ground combat operations.[9]

The struggle between the services not only exists in the area of roles and missions but also in the area of relative budgetary power. Each of the services desires to be the key service in overall influence, and that influence depends to a large degree on budget shares. In this regard, Halperin notes:

> As a precaution, each of the services tends to resist proposals which though promising more funds, may lead to a less than proportionate increase in its budget as compared with other parts of the defense establishment. The Services individually prefer the certainty of a particular share of the budget to an unknown situation in which budgets may increase, but shares may change. For example, in 1957, the Gaither Committee appointed by President Eisenhower recommended substantial increases in the budgets of all three services. . . . However, none of the services supported these proposals, in part because none was certain how the expanded budget would be divided.[10]

Thus, the military departments influence budgetary policy not only by their explicit budgetary functions, but also by their organizational interests and their relationships with the other services.

The Office of the Secretary of Defense

The Office of the Secretary of Defense is the direct staff of the secretary of defense, and serves to develop coordinated policy in terms of military strategy and the defense budget. Within the OSD staff, two suborganizations that play key roles in formulating the defense budget are the Office of the Undersecretary of Defense for Policy and the Office of the Assistant Secretary of Defense for Program Analysis and Evaluation.

The Undersecretary of Defense for Policy is the staff officer within DOD who is primarily responsible for the integration of plans and policies of all DOD organizations with overall national security objectives.[11] Thus the DOD position on national security objectives and the coordination of service programs to meet those objectives is developed by the policy staff.

The Office of the Assistant Secretary of Defense for Program Analysis and Evaluation (PAE) formulates coordinated programs and budgets to support the national military strategy. The PAE staff, therefore, has the role of analyzing the various programs submitted to the secretary of defense by the services, and insuring that the service budget submissions support the national strategy while at the same time meeting overall budgetary guidance from the executive branch to the secretary of defense.

OTHER CABINET LEVEL DEPARTMENTS AND AGENCIES

While all other federal departments and agencies compete with DOD for funds within the federal budget, at least two other cabinet level departments have direct inputs into the defense budgetary process in terms of their roles in the national security policy process. These two agencies are the Department of State and the Central Intelligence Agency.

The Department of State

The secretary of state is the Cabinet officer responsible for overall supervision of American foreign policy. The Department of State has the mission of promoting the long-range security and well-being of the United States in terms of American relations with other nations. The State Department analyzes, plans, and executes those aspects of American foreign policy that generally involve nonmilitary activities. The department plays a key role in advising the president on foreign policy and on the refinement of national values into national security objectives.

Within the State Department, the Bureau of Politico-Military Affairs is specifically responsible for advising the secretary of state on those issues under his purview that affect national security. The Bureau works closely with the Defense Department in coordinating the military and nonmilitary aspects of American foreign policy.[12]

The Central Intelligence Agency

The Central Intelligence Agency (CIA) was established under the supervision of the National Security Council by the National Security Act of 1947.[13] Although the CIA is technically in the Executive Office of the president and operates under the direction of the National Security Council, the size and functions of the CIA make it of sufficient importance to view the agency along the same lines as the Department of State.

The Central Intelligence Agency is responsible for collecting, producing, and disseminating foreign intelligence. The agency is also responsible for conducting special activities approved by the president which may also include covert operations outside the United States. By controlling the information relevant to the national security policy process, the CIA plays an important role in shaping opinion within the government on national security objectives. The ability to conduct covert paramilitary operations tends to overlap with the mission of the military services, resulting in some organization friction. The small number and scope of such operations, however, make this a minor problem.

The director of the Central Intelligence Agency is also the head of the intelligence community. This community includes the intelligence branches of each service (army, navy, air force), the National Security Agency (NSA), the Defense Intelligence Agency (DIA), and the Bureau of Intelligence and Research within the Department of State. Each of the above organizations plays a role similar to the CIA within their respective organizations, thus providing a variety of views from differing agencies within the executive branch on the assessment of the threat and appropriate policy responses.

The director of the Central Intelligence Agency coordinates the preparation of intelligence community-wide efforts such as the National Intelligence Survey (NIS), which presents a comprehensive intelligence survey of each nation,[14] and the National Intelligence Estimate (NIE), which represents the intelligence community's best forecast of the military capability and course of action of any given nation-state.[15] These sources help shape presidential opinion on the nature of our relations with other states, thereby influencing the nature of the national security objectives which set the tone of defense policy.

The critical role of the intelligence community in shaping defense policy is illustrated by the impact of the intelligence analysis on the Cuban Missile Crisis in 1962. In his analysis of the crisis, Gene Rainey notes that Robert Kennedy, while examining the photographs of the Russian missile sites in Cuba, found that neither he nor the president could distinguish differences between the missile site and a football field. Yet as Rainey indicates:

> In October 1962, President Kennedy accepted the belief of his intelligence community that the photo he was examining was of a missile site and not a football field. On the basis of this information, he chose a series of policy options that brought the world close to nuclear conflict.[16]

While the above incident relates to a short-run crisis in national security policy, similar types of analysis and information are used by all participants in the budgetary process.

CONGRESS

As previously noted, Congress is a key decision-maker in the defense budget process. Congress receives the presidential budget submission and passes funding legislation. While the details of the budget process are discussed in detail in Chapter 7, it will be helpful here to briefly overview the Congressional role and to discuss the organizational interests that shape the defense budget.

The president's proposed defense budget is sent to both houses of Congress, which separately vote on defense spending legislation. Prior to each house reviewing the budget, however, the Budget Committees of Congress, in accordance with the Budget Control Act of 1974, set an overall budget guideline based on macroeconomic considerations.[17] Each functional area, including defense, is given a guideline figure in order to meet the recommended total spending figure. Thus, in this way Congress plays a key role from the domestic policy perspective in limiting overall spending in accordance with domestic policy objectives.

After the overall budget limit has been set by the budget committees, the individual appropriation committees and subcommittess in each house of Congress examine the budget in detail and pass legislation for each separate appropriation category. The key committees in this regard for the defense budget are the House and Senate Appropriations and Armed Services Committees and the Senate Foreign Relations Committee. The Appropriations and Armed Services Committees are tasked with the specific examination and reporting of most defense appropriation bills, while the Foreign Relations Committee examines overall American foreign policy objectives in light of Congressional interests.

After the examination of each appropriations bill, Congress may, and often does, amend the bill, adding or subtracting incremental amounts from each piece of legislation before submitting the bill to the full Congress for a vote. Differences between the two houses are resolved in conference committees. After each house votes on the amended bills, the bill is submitted to the president who can sign, veto, or permit the bill to become law without signature.

Several organizational features of Congress and the budget process limit the ability of Congress to make more than minor additions or deletions in the president's budget. First, the nature of the budget process is such that Congress is presented with a finished budget by the president. Congress — without much of the information available to the executive branch — must then publically debate, in the individual committees, the merits of each particular bill. As Wildavsky notes:

> . . . the (President) announces himself (with respect to the budget) with trumpet blasts from on high while the latter (Congress) sounds more like the Tower of Babel than the Heavenly Chorus. The President's budget is made in private, the Congressional budget in public. Congressmen see how their budget is made; knowing what went into it. They are, like sausage makers, leery of what will come out of it. Unaware of what has been going on in the Executive Office of the President, they respect its products more because they know the ingredients less. Thus have Congressmen come to prefer other people's errors to their own.[18]

Traditionally Congress has been leery of deviating from the announced presidential budget due to the superior information available to the executive branch and to fear of publically making errors. Prior to recent changes in budgetary procedures, the fragmented nature of Congress made it an unwieldy organization unable to produce a unified budget.[19] Thus the role of the Congress generally has been to make incremental changes to presidential initiatives. Although Congress can and does vote down individual items within each appropriations category, the thrust of the budget is presidentially determined.

SPECIAL INTEREST GROUPS

Special interest groups are organizations composed of individuals with similar views on a particular issue that attempt to influence policymakers to make decisions that will be advantageous to their group. While there are a large number of groups that attempt to influence policy decisions and budget decisions in particular, the groups can be subdivided into two areas for ease of discussion. These two areas include those groups that are motivated by the financial effects of policy decisions, and those groups that are motivated by the ideological effects of policy decisions.[20]

Groups that are concerned primarily with financial effects certainly include business lobbies, but also can include nonbusiness groups concerned with the impact of defense spending on the overall level of spending, or with the economic effects of defense decisions in a particular region. Business lobbies have a substantial interest in influencing presidential decisions, not only on the total amount spent on defense, but more importantly, from the lobbyist's perspective, on the particular share of defense spending that is made in an area that can affect the lobbyist's firm. In fiscal year 1983, DOD was programmed to spend $114 billion for research, development and acquisition of weapons systems.[21] These contracts play a key role in the profitableness of many firms and result in intense efforts on the part of lobbyists at all levels to affect decisions in the budget process.

Other nonbusiness special interest groups include citizens' groups concerned with such issues as the size of the tax burden or defense spending in a particulr state or urban area. These groups tend to have less of a continuing influence than business lobbies in that they generally form to deal with a specific issue arising at a particular time, such as a proposed base closing. During the period of that particular issue, these groups, usually through direct pressure on the president or their own representatives in Congress, can exert considerable influence on budgetary policy.

Groups motivated by ideological considerations are generally concerned more with the shaping of national security objectives than with direct influence on the budget process. Examples of such groups include the Israeli and Arab lobbies in the United States which attempt to influence American policy in the Middle East. These special interest groups can generate domestic political pressure by appealing to ethnic groups living within the United States to influence policy. They also benefit from the leverage that their client state can exert, such as the oil weapon of pro-Arab special interest groups.

THE MEDIA AND PUBLIC OPINION

The final major institution that plays a role in defense budget decision-making from the institutional point of view is the "media," which shapes public opinion on defense budget issues. The "media" is a catch-all phrase used to describe mechanisms by which information is distributed. The term "mass media" implies the use of such mechanisms to distribute information to a large audience. The mass media in the United States include the press, television, radio, and film.

The mass media can affect budgetary policy in various ways, depending on the type of information that is disseminated. In general, the types of information produced by the mass media can be divided into three categories: (1) reporting of current events, (2) investigative reporting of particular issues, and (3) editorializing.

Reporting of current events provides the public and, to some degree, policymakers with current intelligence on fast-breaking domestic and foreign policy developments. This type of information generally has little direct effect on overall budgetary policy unless it is processed in terms of a specific study relevant to specific issues in the budgetary process.

Investigative reporting entails an extensive examination of a particular issue. Once again, although the report may be on a particular issue relevant to budgetary decision-making, the direct influence of a press report usually depends on a follow-up study or analysis of the issue in question.

Editorializing is a means whereby the press management can give independent analysis and opinions on public policy issues. While such commentary is helpful in the debate on policy issues, it usually has a less direct effect on the budgetary process.

From the perspective of the executive branch, which has direct access to the detailed information required to formulate the defense budget, the press plays some role but not as great a role as it does in the Congressional area. In an analysis of the effect of the media on public policy, James Reston, a prominent *New York Times* foreign policy analyst, notes:

> Congressmen are different. Unlike officials of the executive branch, they live most of the time in the open. They think the good opinion of the press is important to their reelection, which dominates much of their thinking; consequently they see reporters and some of them even read us.[22]

The link between the importance of the press to budgetary policy and the Congress is noted by Reston when he points out that:

> Its [the press's] influence is exercised primarily through the Congress, which confuses press opinion with public opinion. . . .[23]

Thus Congressmen, in voting on spending legislation, may use press reports on the proposed legislation as indicators of public opinion, and vote in a way that the representative feels most closely reflects the interests of his or her constituency. Press reports also shape public opinion of Congressional constituents and may lead to constituent pressure. On many issues, representatives may vote in accord with a content analysis of constituent mail and telephone inputs. Much of the information on which constituents base their opinions comes from the media.

CONCLUSION

The president, approving the defense budget, tends to temper "rational" approaches to the budget process with the pressure exerted by the various institutions and groups described in the preceding sections. Indeed, the use of the "rational" approaches to defense decision-making requires inputs from the various institutions under consideration. The actual outcome of the defense budget process from the institutional perspective therefore depends on the various views held by each institution and group, and the pressure which that group can exert on the president and, to a lesser extent, on Congress. Those groups that are able to gain influence over and access to the president have far more of an effect on the defense budget than would be indicated in the foreign policy planning or domestic policy planning models. Of course, in the actual budgetary process each of these factors is important, and in the following chapter we develop a more integrated model of defense spending.

NOTES

1 Morton Halperin, *Bureaucratic Politics and Foreign Policy* (Washington, D.C.: Brookings, 1973), p. 24.
2 Aaron Wildavsky, *The Politics of the Budgeting Process,* 2nd ed. (Boston: Little Brown, 1974), p. 41.
3 Halperin, *op. cit.*, p. 17.
4 The details of the budgeting process are treated in greater detail in Chapter 7.
5 *United States Government Manual 1978/79* (Washington: U.S. Government Printing Office, 1978), p. 98.
6 Gerald Rainey, *Patterns of American Foreign Policy* (Boston: Allyn and Bacon, Inc., 1975), p. 157.
7 Such a review is usually written up in a document called a Presidential Review Memorandum (PRM).
8 *The Economic Report of the President, 1978* (Washington: U.S. Government Printing Office, 1978), p. 244.
9 Halperin, *op. cit.*, pp. 40–41.
10. *Ibid.*, p. 58.
11. *United States Government Manual 1978/79, op. cit.*, p. 175.
12. *Ibid.*, p. 412.
13. *Ibid.*, p. 98.
14. Rainey, *op. cit.*, p. 168.
15. *Ibid.*, p. 170.
16. *Ibid.*, p. 165.
17 See Robert H. Haveman, *The Economics of the Public Sector,* 2nd ed. (New York: John Wiley & Sons, 1976), pp. 97–99, for details of the 1974 Act.
18 Wildavsky, *op. cit.*, p. 210.
19 Rainey, *op. cit.*, p. 211.
20 *Ibid.*, p. 115.
21 *Annual Report of the Secretary of Defense FY 1982*, p. III-127.
22 James Reston, "The Difference of the Press," in Frank N. Trager and Philip S. Kronenberg, eds., *National Security and American Society* (Lawrence, Kansas: University Press of Kansas, 1973), p. 238.
23 *Ibid.*, p. 233.

SELECTED REFERENCES

Les Aspin, "The Defense Budget and Foreign Policy: The Role of Congress," *Daedalus*, Vol. 104 (Summer, 1975), pp. 154–174.
Morton Halperin, *Bureaucratic Politics and Foreign Policy* (Washington, D.C.: Brookings Institution, 1973).
Aaron Wildavsky, *The Politics of the Budgeting Process,* 2nd ed. (Boston: Little Brown, 1974).

Chapter 5
An Integrated Model
of Defense Spending

INTRODUCTION

In the preceding chapters we developed three separate ways of viewing the process by which the defense budget is determined: the foreign policy perspective, the domestic policy perspective, and the institutional perspective. The first two perspectives emphasize the link between national values and the defense budget. The third perspective isolates the institutions and actors that affect the amount of resources that the United States devotes to defense.

In this chapter we integrate the three approaches, indicate the ways in which each approach is related to the others, and explain the method by which differences in the amounts determined in each approach are reconciled. In the final section of the chapter, the various components of the integrated model are related to the major functional areas of economics, thus indicating the ways in which economics can be used in examining the defense budget decision-making process.

The purpose of integrating the three viewpoints on the determinants of defense spending is to avoid the misconception that defense budgets are made in a vacuum, where each particular approach is independent of the other. While it may be true that during any one period of time the institutions and actors that play roles in the defense budget process may tend to emphasize one approach over another, it is generally the case that all approaches simultaneously affect the outcome of the process, and each plays a role in shaping the amount spent in defense.

The above points are well summarized, from the viewpoint of the Department of Defense, in the *Annual Report of the Secretary of Defense for FY 1980:*

> Although the fact is not widely appreciated, the defense budget is shaped by the way in which it is prepared. At one extreme the budget total can be reached by building from the ground up. This approach requires a detailed specification of needs, and an aggregation of those needs into a posture that we would then attempt to acquire at the least cost, but without regard to what the total might be in relation to federal revenues. At the other extreme, some percentage of the federal budget can simply be allocated to defense, and we could then attempt to create the most effective possible posture out of those resources.
>
> For a variety of reasons, we must resort to some combination of these approaches. . . .[1]

Thus, a true picture of the defense budgetary procedure emerges after we analyze the interactions of the various perspectives.

THE RATIONAL APPROACH AND BUREAUCRATIC POLITICS

The foreign policy planning and domestic policy planning approaches to the formulation of the defense budget have been denoted as "rational" approaches to the problem of defense spending. By a "rational" approach we generally mean that the policy model employed fits the decision-making paradigm described by Graham Allison as the Rational Actor Model of decision-making. The characteristics of such a model are defined by Allison in his classic analysis on public policy decision-making theory, *The Essence of Decision.*[2] In describing a series of models of the decision-making process in foreign policy and international politics that characterize the Rational Actor Model, Allison notes:

> Each assumes that the actor is a national government. Each assumes that the action is chosen as a calculated solution to a strategic problem. For each, explanation consists of showing what goal the government was pursuing when it acted and how the action was a reasonable choice, given the nation's objective. This cluster of assumptions characterizes the Rational Action Model.[3]

Spanier and Uslander in their study on the making of foreign policy delineate the particular steps used in policy analysis using the rational actor model:

> The rational actor model assumes that the decision makers will (1) select the objectives and values that a given policy is supposed to achieve and maximize, (2) consider the various alternative means of achieving these purposes, (3) calculate the likely consequence of each alternative course, and (4) choose the course most likely to attain the objectives originally selected. The government is often viewed as a unitary actor when the rational actor model is used. . . .[4]

Thus it may appear that both the foreign policy and domestic policy planning models fit the description of a Rational Actor approach to defense budgetary decision-making. The problem with such a rational approach to defense budget policy, however, is that the decisions are not made by a single actor, but by many of the actors and institutions described in Chapter 4. Additionally, the rational actor models described in Chapters 2 and 3 can lead to two different amounts for the defense budget, depending on whether the focus is on foreign or on domestic policy.

The alternative approach to the Rational Actor Model is that of Bureaucratic Politics. The nature of this model is given by Allison in the following passage from *The Essence of Decision*:

> . . . the Government (or Bureaucratic Politics Model) sees no unitary actor but rather many actors as players who focus not on a single strategic issue but on many diverse intranational problems as well; players who act in terms of no consistent set of strategic objectives but rather according to various conceptions of national, organizational and personal goals; players who make government decisions not by a single national choice but by the pulling and hauling that is politics.[5]

Clearly the institutional perspective on defense spending highlights those actors — or players, as Allison describes them — who influence the defense budget from a bureaucratic politics viewpoint.

As noted in the excerpt from the *Annual Report of the Secretary of Defense,* a combination of the foreign policy and domestic policy planning models is used in shaping the defense budget. The bureaucratic politics model, however, is useful in describing how the two rational approaches to defense budgetary policy are reconciled.

AN INTEGRATED MODEL OF DEFENSE BUDGET FORMULATION

The various approaches and paradigms previously discussed can now be integrated into a singly analytical and descriptive model of defense budget decision making. The integrated model, presented in Figure 5.1, stresses the importance of the international and domestic environments, the actors who interpret those environments and make decisions within a number of interrelated institutions, and the process within which national values, objectives, programs, and budgets are determined.

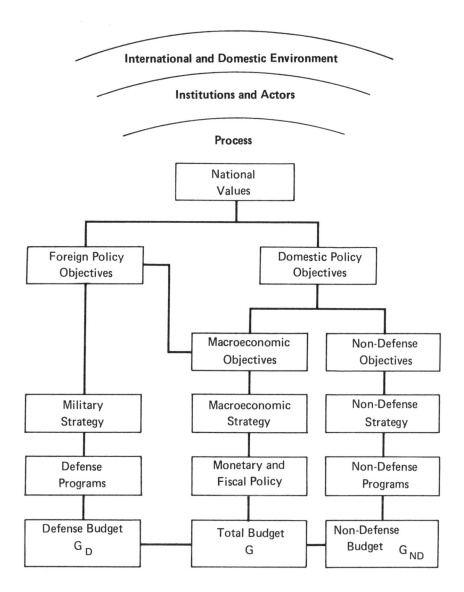

Figure 5.1 An Integrated Model of Defense Budget Determination

A key point to note in the integrated model is that no arrows have been drawn to indicate either a sequence of events or relative priorities. Just as changes in the international and domestic environments can produce changes over time in institutions, actors, and process, so changes in process and institutions can change perceptions of the domestic and international environment. Moreover, each of the steps shown in the process of matching national values with budget allocations is jointly determined. This means that decisions do not flow neatly from national values downward, but rather resource constraints ultimately affect objectives and, in some cases, even national values.

In the chapters on foreign policy planning and domestic policy planning the models were developed using national values and objectives as starting points. This view of the process has often been described as the "requirements approach" in which output requirements are first defined and a supporting budget is developed to meet those requirements. In the integrated model, however, it is clear that national objectives are constrained by the availability of resources. Thus there are no such things as "requirements" which must be met. Rather the nation has a wide range of values, and it must decide how its limited resources should be allocated to attain the highest degree of conformity to those values.

Suppose that the nation's decision makers have two national values: national survival and an acceptable standard of living. The national value of survival is translated into the objective of deterring a strategic nuclear or major conventional attack on the United States, an objective which is pursued through a military strategy of flexible response including the forward deployment of forces in Europe, a strategic reserve in the United States, and a strategic nuclear capability at least as great as that of the Soviet Union. The national value of an acceptable standard of living is translated into the objective of a minimum level of real per capita income; and an economic strategy emphasizing free competitive markets, and macroeconomic monetary and fiscal policies designed to maintain a vital private sector. Suppose that military planners conclude that the strategy requires ten million men and women in uniform, or roughly ten percent of the U.S. labor force. Will this "requirement" actually drive budget and force structure decisions?

As indicated in Figure 5.1, changing the defense budget will require a change in the total budget, a change in nondefense spending, or both. In some periods, a shift in national values or a change in perceptions about the international environment may produce substantial adjustments in the resources allocated to defense. The sustained increase in Soviet military spending in the late 1970s and the Soviet invasion of Afghanistan in late 1979 may have triggered a fundamental reassessment of defense programs in the United States. In other periods resources available to defense may be fixed by competing macroeconomic or nondefense objectives. Thus it would certainly be inappropriate to assert that "requirements" determine defense spending, but it would also be inappropriate to conclude that the level of spending is unrelated to perceived military requirements.

Indeed, the budgetary process is designed to bring requirements and spending into balance. In the case of defense programs, the differential between requirements derived from the current strategy and resources allocated in the current budget is typically labeled as the "level of risk." When divergence in requirements and resources is great—that is, when the risk level is high—serious distortions can arise in the planning process. For example, force structure and strategy may be tied to objectives, but manning levels and readiness may be tied to available resources. The result can be an allocation of resources that fails to produce the highest attainable level of security. Perceived military requirements always exceed available resources, and therefore this allocation problem will always exist. One of the purposes of the budgetary process is to highlight such problems so that decision makers will understand the consequences of inconsistencies in the planning process.

Another way of showing the limitations of the "requirements" approach is to observe that there are only two "degrees of freedom" in formulating the overall federal budget when various levels of defense spending, nondefense spending, and the total budget are considered. By this we mean that with an arbitrarily given set of foreign policy objectives and domestic policy objectives, the resulting figures for the total budget (derived from macroeconomic objectives), the nondefense budget (derived from nondefense budget objectives), and the defense budget (from foreign policy planning objectives) may not be consistent. Thus, if two of the three general sets of objectives are met, the third will in all likelihood not be met.[6] At this point the mechanism that resolves the conflict is assumed to involve the bureaucratic politics that the various actors and institutions conduct to make their rational perspective prevail. A reconciliation of the differences of the various approaches requires, therefore, that the actors in the process modify initial budget proposals to make the overall results of the process consistent. The adjustments which can be made include changes in either programs, strategies, or objectives. If programs and strategies have been efficiently designed, however, it may be impossible to reconcile the subcomponents and the total spending figure without changing the sets of objectives or even perhaps national values.

An important consequence of this particular approach to the formulation of the defense budget and the total federal budget, therefore, is the fact that our national values and objectives may not necessarily remain unchanged in the budgeting process. The process itself may in fact alter our objectives and values.

For example, a war, which necessitates high levels of defense spending, may require that macroeconomic objectives such as low rates of inflation, or nondefense budget objectives, such as a high level of social welfare spending, be curtailed. A high priority on fighting inflation, on the other hand, may require reduced spending on defense, and force a reduction in commitments abroad. The important point to emphasize is that changes in the defense budget in one direction or another entail opportunity costs in terms of meeting foreign and domestic policy objectives. The rational actor component of the defense spending model indicates the linkages that force the trade-off between various objectives, while the bureaucratic politics aspects of the process determine the objectives that win or lose in key budget contests.

INTEGRATING INTERNATIONAL AND DOMESTIC FACTORS IN THE MODEL

The integrated model presented in Figure 5.1 has been simplified in order to emphasize different perspectives of the planning process. The model suggests that foreign and domestic policy objectives are defined somewhat independently, based on national values and assessments of the international and domestic environments. In fact many institutions in the U.S. government are divided precisely along such international and domestic lines, and the model is not entirely unrealistic. There are, however, many important linkages between foreign and domestic policy objectives.

In Figure 5.1, a line has been drawn from both foreign policy objectives and domestic policy objectives to the box labeled "macroeconomic objectives." This particular linkage is emphasized because of the large and growing importance of international economic factors to both domestic economic policies and the broader spectrum of foreign policy objectives. These international economic factors will be emphasized in the sixth section of this book. However, some of the central linkages may be introduced here.

If U.S. citizens are buying more foreign goods and investing more overseas than the offsetting expenditures by foreign citizens in the United States, foreign citizens will accumulate claims for dollars. This increased availability of dollars on world markets will tend to lower the value of the dollar in terms of other currencies. As a result, when U.S. citizens want to buy foreign products, the price of those products in terms of dollars will be higher. One of the consequences of a balance of payments deficit may therefore be a higher rate of inflation, fueled in part by higher import prices.

The U.S. might attempt to solve the balance of payments problem by simply restricting foreign imports, either through import quotas or through tariffs. As an alternative, the U.S. could seek to attract dollars back to the United States by raising the interest rates that foreign investors can obtain. Unfortunately, restricting imports is inefficient because in the long run it means that consumers would be limited to goods produced in the U.S., and this would eliminate the benefits of international specialization. The alternative of driving up interest rates in the U.S. has the disadvantage of lowering output and growth, because funds for domestic investment would consequently be more expensive to U.S. firms.

Just as each response to the balance of payments problem might have damaging consequences for the domestic economy, each response would also risk alienating members of the military alliance developed to meet foreign policy objectives. Not only would increased tariff barriers risk retaliatory restrictions from other nations, they would also run the risk of poisoning potential cooperation on a wide range of common military interests. Similarly, efforts to raise domestic interest rates to attract foreign funds may be opposed by foreign governments seeking to solve their own balance of payments problems. Because the dollar is a widely held reserve currency—a currency used to settle international payments—many important prices, such as the price of crude oil, are denominated in dollars. Efforts by the United States to raise the value of the dollar may therefore have a direct impact on the price of oil in Western Europe.

Such interrelationships will be addressed in far more detail in later chapters. These examples, however, should indicate the dangers inherent in treating foreign and domestic policy objectives in isolation. Indeed, the failure to develop an institutional framework that places greater emphasis on such interrelationships may have been one of the major policy problems of the last decade.

ECONOMIC THEORY AND THE INTEGRATED MODEL

Economic theory may be used to highlight important factors at each point in the integrated model developed in Figure 5.1. Beginning at the top of the figure, economic theory can be used in analyzing important aspects of the international and domestic environments. Although the behavior of actors and institutions lies more in the realm of sociology and political science, economics allows us to gain a deeper appreciation of the markets in which defense production occurs, and the analytical techniques used by many of the key actors and institutions.

International economics highlights the trade-offs implicit in international specialization and trade. Comparative economic analysis stresses the common problems faced by all economic systems, and assists in an assessment of the potential strengths and weaknesses of both allies and potential adversaries. Microeconomic theory addresses decision rules for allocating resources which affect specific programs, choosing among alternatives, resources, and reviewing specific program expenditures. Macroeconomic theory is an essential tool in analyzing the domestic policy portion of the budgetary process.

In each of the following sections of the book, we begin with an analysis of these fields of economic theory and proceed to a discussion of their application within the context of the integrated model of defense planning and budgeting. Macroeconomic factors have a crucial role in the model, because they concern both foreign and domestic policy objectives. In addition, macroeconomic issues have a dominant role in determining the total level of federal outlays. In the following section we begin our detailed exploration of the integrated model with an analysis of macroeconomic objectives, macroeconomic strategy, and monetary and fiscal policy.

NOTES

1 *Annual Report of the Secretary of Defense FY 1980* (Washington: U.S. Government Printing Office, 1979), p. 27.
2 Graham Allison, *The Essence of Decision: Explaining the Cuban Missile Crisis* (Boston: Little Brown and Company, 1971).
3 *Ibid.*, p. 13.
4 John Spanier and Eric M. Uslander, *How American Foreign Policy is Made* (New York: Praeger, 1974), p. 103.
5 Graham Allison, *The Essence of Decision, op. cit.,* p. 144.
6 A consistent budget requires that G (total government spending) = G_{ND} (nondefense spending) + G_D (defense spending). If all three variables are determined independently as indicated in the separate perspectives, then the probability is small that the three values will, *ex ante*, be consistent with the budget identity.

SELECTED REFERENCES

Graham Allison, *The Essence of Decision: Explaining the Cuban Missile Crisis* (Boston: Little Brown and Company, 1971).
Jack Kemp and Les Aspin, *How Much Defense Spending is Enough?* (Washington, D.C.: American Enterprises Institute, 1976).
John Spanier and Eric M. Uslander, *How American Foreign Policy is Made* (New York: Praeger, 1974).

Part II

The Macroeconomics of National Security

A billion here, a billion there. Before you know it, it starts to add up to real money.

Everett Dirkson

Government expands to absorb revenue—and then some.

Tom Wicker

When George Washington threw that dollar across the Rappahanock River, he didn't realize he was establishing a precedent for government spending.

Harold Coffin

Chapter 6
National Income Determination and Government Spending

INTRODUCTION

In Part I of this book we emphasized the link between the level of defense spending and the overall fiscal policy adopted by the federal government in the attempt to meet its economic policy objectives. Defense spending is a major component of federal government purchases of goods and services, and it is one of the few components of government purchases that can be controlled or substantially altered in the annual budget. Other types of expenditures are often tied to longer term legislation, and spending levels are more or less determined for the duration of the legislation. Defense purchases, particularly procurement of weapon systems, can be accelerated or restricted depending on the objectives of fiscal policy. Thus, defense spending is more closely linked with annual shifts in economic policy than are other government programs.

This chapter examines the framework within which economists evaluate the level of government purchases, and hence defense expenditures, which is most consistent with the nation's economic objectives. There are two major schools of thought on the way in which *fiscal policy* decisions on government spending and taxation and *monetary policy* decisions on the supply of money and interest rates affect the economy. Keynesian economists, advocates of the ideas first proposed by John Maynard Keynes, stress the importance of fiscal policy. Monetarist economists, led by Nobel Prize laureate Milton Friedman, stress the importance of monetary policy. The position of Keynesian economists is that the federal government has an obligation to use fiscal and monetary policies to prevent undesirable fluctuations in the level of economic activity. Thus when the economy slows down, the federal government should stimulate the economy by cutting taxes and expanding the level of government spending. When the economy is overheated and the price level is rising rapidly, the government should restrict spending and increase taxes. Monetarist economists place more emphasis on the importance of variations in the supply of money on the level of economic activity, and generally believe that counter-cyclical fiscal and monetary policies actually exacerbate our economic problems. They favor a steady expansion in the supply of money, broadly defined, and a smaller economic role for government in general, and the federal government in particular.

Thus Keynesian economists would see a countercyclical role for defense spending, increasing outlays in recession and cutting spending in an expansion. Monetarists, on the other hand, would see such fluctuations as counterproductive and probably destabilizing.

The relative weight given to these different views in policy decisions at the national level has varied from administration to administration. The Nixon and Ford administrations tended to place more emphasis on the monetarist approach, reflecting the views of three conservative chairmen of the Council of Economic Advisers: Paul McCracken, Herbert Stein, and Alan Greenspan. The Carter administration adopted a somewhat more active fiscal role for the federal government, reflecting the approach of Council chairman Charles Schultze. But the distinctions have been less important than the similarities. The monetarist position that fluctuations in the supply of money have a major impact on the level of economic activity is now generally accepted. This acceptance, however, has done little to alter the basic view that fiscal policy should be used to control economic cycles. The real debates are over the extent of government intervention, and over the importance of different economic objectives.

The Keynesian approach is embodied in the economic models used by policymakers in setting fiscal policy, and that approach will be used here. We will begin with a very simple Keynesian model that shows how the level of national income is determined, and explains the impact of government purchases on national income. We will then proceed to a more complex view of how aggregate demand and aggregate supply interact to determine the real output of the economy and the price level, and discuss how the "supply-side" thrust of the Reagan administration fits into the general model. Throughout this chapter we will emphasize domestic economic policies, but we will present a framework within which our subsequent examination of international economics may be considered.

NATIONAL ECONOMIC OBJECTIVES

Economic indicators are indirect and incomplete measures, at best, of the nation's standard of living. The Gross National Product measures the nation's annual output of those goods and services that are delivered to the ultimate user, but only goods and services that pass through the marketplace are counted. Changing price levels and changing product quality make it very difficult to distinguish between *"real"* increases in output and *apparent* increases that are only the result of inflation. Nevertheless, the economic indicators that are available are widely used by policymakers in describing the nation's economic objectives, and they do provide some insight into the shifting patterns of economic activity.

A variety of public documents outline our economic policy objectives. The president's annual assessment is presented in his *Economic Report* to Congress, which is released each year in January. These reports consistently emphasize six major policy objectives, stating that we must:

1. Maintain high levels of *"real"* per capita national income where *real* income is measured in constant, not inflated, dollars.
2. Maintain a rate of growth in real incomes that, as a minimum, provides for the employment of new workers entering the work force and provides some expansion in real per capita national income.
3. Minimize involuntary idleness as reflected in the unemployment rate.
4. Minimize the disruptive effects of inflation by restricting the rate of price increases and preventing wide variations in annual rates of inflation.
5. Provide for an equitable distribution of national output.
6. Maintain a favorable U.S. balance of payments position and a strong dollar, in an open and growing world economy.

Other objectives might be added, but these are clearly the six that are most frequently cited in public documents. The objectives, unfortunately, are rarely consistent with each other. Restricting inflation may mean increases in unemployment. Lowering unemployment may mean higher levels of inflation and a weaker dollar. A more "equitable" distribution of income may reduce the incentives for investment and lower economic growth. The choices among competing objectives are often difficult and painful.

The economic purist would argue that the choice of objectives and the setting of priorities is a function of the political process, and that economists merely advise on the most efficient means of reaching the designated objectives. In practice, of course, the economists in government play an important role in establishing economic priorities, and their economic and political philosophies influence their recommendations. The apparent inconsistencies in the recommendations of the country's leading economists stem as much from differences in normative, or value, judgments as they do from differences in positive, or objective, analysis. The views of monetarist economists have a great deal to do with their assessment of the impact of big government on economic freedom and their concern for the impact of inflation on financial markets, and the views of Keynesian economists are certainly related to the priority they tend to place on the distribution of national output and the importance of high levels of employment.

Our economic policy consists of a set of priorities for our multiple objectives, and a plan for reaching those objectives by using the various policy "variables" such as the level of government purchases, the tax structure, the supply of money in the economy, and so on. Policies that affect taxes and government purchases are called "fiscal" policies, and those that affect the supply of money, the availability of credit, and interest rates are called "monetary" policies. Fiscal policy is controlled by the executive branch and the Congress, while monetary policy is set by the independent Federal Reserve Board with little direct executive or Congressional control.

Fiscal policy is determined as part of a continuous cycle of evaluating the performance of the economy, setting economic priorities, preparing the president's bugetary proposals to Congress, and passing legislation to fix the level of federal government receipts and expenditures. This process will be reviewed in some detail in Chapter 7, but it is important to note that this cycle is geared to produce an annual budget.

In the context of this short period of time, policymakers are apt to place the greatest emphasis on the period remaining until the next election. Although there has been considerable discussion of the advantages of longer term planning, and some such planning has been mandated by the Humphrey-Hawkins Act (1978), short term considerations still dominate the budgetary process. This has led some critics to argue that the nation does not in fact have any "economic policy," but simply moves through a sequence of predictable cycles from one crisis to the next. Herbert Stein, President Nixon's chairman of the Council of Economic Advisers, makes the point in his explanation of how our "economic policy" normally evolves:

> There will be an attempt to pump the economy up to ambitiously high levels of employment and low levels of unemployment. This will lead to a "surprising" amount of inflation. The government will respond to this by an incomes policy, or even by controls. However, these measures will yield at most temporary restraint. They will break down in a wave of inflation, whereupon we will turn for awhile to the "old-time religion" of tight fiscal and monetary policy. But this conversion will last only until the inflation rate subsides a bit, and the cycle will then start over. This course of action does not constitute a policy, any more than the turning of the sunflowers towards the sun constitutes a policy. That is, it is not a pattern of behavior that was deliberately chosen and intended. However, it is not only predictable; it is also more and more predicted.[1]

Of course, whether or not the government controls policy or is the victim of previous policy errors is at the heart of the controversy between noninterventionist monetarists and the interventionist Keynesians. In any case, governments have long intervened in attempts to meet their policy objectives, and there is little evidence that they are about to abandon the practice. While there is continuing discussion of the importance of long term planning, there is little evidence that the short term exigencies of the budgetary cycle are about to give way to longer run issues. Keynes' observation that "In the long run we are all dead," has political as well as economic implications.[2]

STATISTICAL MEASURES OF ECONOMIC OBJECTIVES

The income received each year by American citizens in the form of payments for their contributions to the production process is perhaps our principal measure of economic welfare. The *National Income* measures the payments received each year by those providing the factors of production (land, labor, capital, and entrepreneurial skill) to firms that produce the desired goods and services. By summing these payments for labor (wages and salaries), capital (interest), land (rent), and entrepreneurial skill (profit) over a given year and adding transfer payments, we obtain the total National Income generated by the economy. Since the firms are simply places at which output is produced, the value of all of the goods and services sold by the firms must be equal to the payments made to the owners of the factors of production used to make the output. In other words, National Income is equal to *Aggregate Spending*. This relationship is shown in Figure 6.1, which shows that all of the receipts of the firms are passed on to people who, in their role as purchasers of goods and services, are conventionally called "consumers."

With some slight modifications National Income, or Aggregate Spending, is equal to the widely used measures of national producton known as the *Gross National Product* and the *Net National Product*. Aggregate Spending includes the indirect business taxes (sales taxes) incorporated in the prices of products as well as the expenditures made to replace capital used up in the production process (depreciation). When we subtract indirect business taxes from aggregate spending the residual is the Gross National Product, and when we subtract depreciation from the GNP we have the Net National Product.

The Gross National Product thus represents the total value of all "final" goods and services produced in the nation in a given year, evaluated at market prices. Intermediate goods are not counted, as they merely reflect exchanges that are made in the process of production. Goods and services only enter the GNP when they are sold to the ultimate user. For example, it would be double (or triple) counting to include the coal and iron ore used to produce steel, the steel used to produce the automobile, and the automobile in computing national output. The GNP includes only the value of the automobile.[3]

The Circular Flow of Income

The GNP can be measured by either adding up all of the components of aggregate spending, or adding up the payments made to the owners of the factors of production. Using the aggregate spending approach we may divide the GNP into homogeneous clusters of goods and services based either on the industry producing the product; the characteristics of the product, such as durability; or by the purchaser. One typical approach is to divide the GNP into purchases made by consumers (*consumption*), purchases made by firms buying capital goods (*investment*), purchases made by foreign citizens (*exports*), and purchases made by all levels of government (*government purchases of goods and services*). Because our calculations should only include purchases of products produced in the United States, imports must be subtracted out of our statistics to obtain the GNP. Thus the GNP (Y) is equal to consumption (C), plus investment (I), plus government purchases (G), plus exports minus imports (X–M), or:

$$Y = C + I + G + (X-M)$$

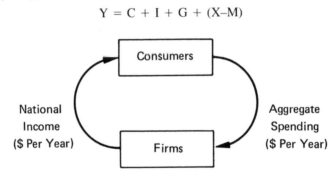

Figure 6.1 National Income Equals Aggregate Spending

Note:
This figure assumes that there are no government or foreign sectors. Figure 6.2 includes those sectors.

There is nothing sacred about this particular formulation, and we could divide the GNP into as many subcategories of expenditure as we desire. Consumption includes purchases of services, durable goods, and nondurable goods. Investment includes purchases of plants and equipment by producers, residential investment by individuals, and changes in the inventories maintained by producers. Government purchases include the procurement of goods and services by all levels of government, but do not include "transfer payments," such as Social Security, which simply redistribute income and do not directly add to output. Similarly, net exports could be broken down by product category, or destination, or both. The four sector approach used above is typically used to teach introductory Keynesian economics, but economists wishing to investigate economic activity in greater detail typically divide the GNP into smaller, more homogeneous categories.

Figure 6.2 outlines the flow of income using the four categories of aggregate spending discussed above. The figure shows that all of the income received by firms is passed on to the individuals who contribute the factors of production. In their role as consumers these individuals purchase some of the output directly (consumption). Some of the consumers' income goes to the government in the form of taxes (the government also makes some transfer payments to individuals, so the flow to the government is called "net taxes"). Some of the consumers' income is used to purchase financial securities (stocks, bonds, savings accounts) through financial intermediaries (banks, stock brokers, insurance companies); this income, which is set aside in an attempt to increase future income, is called *saving*. Firms borrow funds through the financial intermediaries to supplement their retained earnings so that they may invest (i.e., purchase additional capital plant and equipment or increase their inventories). Finally, the "rest of the world" purchases exports from U.S. firms. Foreign imports also flow into the United States, so the arrow actually depicts "net exports."

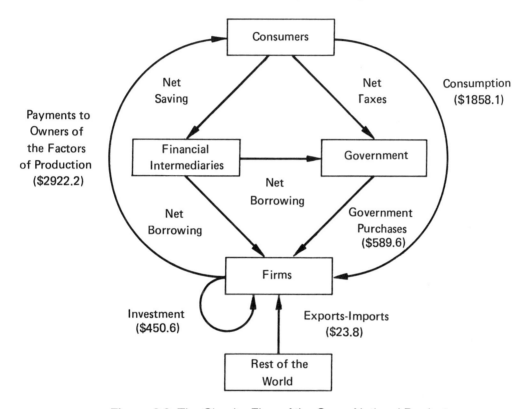

Figure 6.2 The Circular Flow of the Gross National Product

Note:
All figures shown in parentheses are flows that occurred in 1981 in billions of dollars. Total payments to the owners of the factors of production were $2922.2 billion. This equals the sum of aggregate spending on consumption, investment, government spending, and net exports.

Note that each arrow represents a flow of dollars; goods and services flow in the opposite direction. The figures in parentheses show how the 1981 GNP of $2922.2 billion was divided among the four elements of aggregate spending.

Figure 6.2 also illustrates the important principle that changes in aggregate spending produce changes in the level of income received by consumers. As we will see later in this chapter, the Keynesian approach to predicting changes in the gross national product emphasizes the impact of shifts in aggregate spending on consumer income.

Table 6.1 shows how the GNP and its components have varied over a thirty-year period. The GNP, consumption, and government purchases increase year after year. The levels of investment and net exports are less predictable. Investment actually fell in 1974 and 1975, and net exports were negative in 1972, 1977, 1978, and 1979. Because net exports are a small percentage of the total U.S. GNP, variations in the rate of growth of GNP are most closely related to variations in the level of investment.

Table 6.1
Selected Components of the National Income Accounts and Price Indices: 1950 – 1981

Year	Y[1]	C[2]	I[3]	X–M[4]	G[5]	P[6]	Q[7]	CPI[8]	PPI[9]
1950	286.2	192.0	53.8	1.9	38.5	53.6	533.5	72.1	79.0
1955	399.3	253.7	64.8	2.2	75.0	61.0	654.8	80.2	85.5
1960	506.0	324.9	76.4	4.4	100.3	68.7	736.8	88.7	93.7
1965	688.1	430.2	112.0	7.6	138.4	74.3	925.9	94.5	95.7
1970	982.4	618.8	140.8	3.9	218.9	91.4	1075.3	116.3	110.3
1971	1063.4	668.2	160.0	1.6	233.7	96.0	1107.5	121.3	113.7
1972	1171.1	733.0	188.3	–3.3	253.1	100.0	1171.1	125.3	117.2
1973	1306.6	809.9	220.0	7.1	269.5	105.8	1235.0	133.1	127.9
1974	1412.9	889.6	214.6	6.0	302.7	116.0	1217.8	147.7	147.5
1975	1528.8	979.1	190.9	20.4	338.4	127.2	1202.3	161.2	163.4
1976	1702.2	1089.9	243.0	8.0	361.3	133.7	1273.0	170.5	170.3
1977	1899.5	1212.0	303.3	–9.9	396.2	141.7	1340.5	181.5	180.6
1978	2127.6	1350.8	351.5	–10.3	435.6	152.1	1399.2	195.4	194.6
1979	2368.5	1509.8	386.2	–3.5	476.0	165.5	1431.1	217.4	215.9
1980	2626.1	1672.8	395.3	23.3	534.7	177.4	1480.7	246.8	247.0
1981[10]	2922.2	1858.1	450.6	23.8	589.6	193.6	1509.6	272.4	269.8

1 Gross National Production (billions of dollars).
2 Personal Consumption Expenditures (billions of dollars).
3 Gross Private Domestic Investment (billions of dollars).
4 Net Exports of Goods and Services (billions of dollars).
5 Government Purchases of Goods and Services (billions of dollars).
6 Implicit Price Deflator for the Gross National Product (1972 = 100).
7 Gross National Product in 1972 dollars (billions of 1972 dollars).
8 Consumer Price Index (1967 = 100).
9 Producer Price Index for Finished Goods (1967 = 100).
10 Preliminary Estimates.

Source: Economic Report of the President, 1980, 1982.

The Price Index

Unfortunately, the steady increase in the GNP depicted in Table 6.1 is deceiving. The GNP is computed using the prices that exist in each year, and therefore changes in the GNP reflect changes in price levels as well as changes in real output. The procedure we use to correct for changes in the price level involves the totalling up of the monetary value of goods and services using the relative prices that existed in some "*base year*." Suppose that we selected 1972 as our base year. We would then be interested in what the GNP would have been in each year if prices had not changed since 1972, and we would call our estimates "real GNP in 1972 dollars." Since prices rose from 1972 to 1979, we know that our 1979 GNP of $2368.5 would be lower if output were valued at 1972 prices, but how much lower would it be?

In order to convert current, or nominal, GNP into real GNP evaluated in the "*constant*" dollars of some base year, we need an index that tells us how much prices have risen since the base year. For example, suppose that prices rose by 65.5% between 1972 and 1979. The price level in 1979 would then be 165.5% of the 1972 level. In constructing a *price index* we assign a value of 100.0 to the base year, and in every other year the index shows the percentage change since the base year. In our illustration the value of the price index in 1979 would be 165.5.

We may now construct a simple ratio. The GNP in constant dollars of some base year (Q) is to the current dollar GNP (Y) as the value of the price index in the base year (Pb)is to the value of the price index in the current year (Pt).

$$\frac{\text{GNP in Constant \$}}{\text{GNP in Current \$}} = \frac{\text{Value of Price Index in Base Year}}{\text{Value of Price Index in Current Year}} \tag{6.2}$$

or

$$\frac{Q}{Y} = \frac{Pb}{Pt}$$

This may easily be solved for real GNP (Q) as:

$$Q = \frac{Y \cdot P_b}{P_t} \quad \text{or} \quad Q = \frac{Y}{P_t / P_b} \tag{6.3}$$

Since the value of the price index in the base year is 100.0, this reduces to:

$$Q = \frac{Y}{P_t / 100.0} \tag{6.4}$$

To continue our illustration, to find the real value of the output of 1979 expressed in constant dollars of 1972 we would divide the current dollar GNP (Y = $2368.5 billion) by the ratio of the price index in 1979 P_t = 165.5 to 100.0, and solve for Q.

$$Q = \frac{\$2368.5 \text{ billion}}{165.5 / 100.0} = \$1431.1 \text{ billion}$$

In other words, if the output of 1979 had been produced in 1972, it would have been valued at $1431.1 billion.

Growth and Inflation

As our national economic policy objectives indicated, we are concerned with the level of real output (Q), the rate of growth in real output, and the rate of increase in the price level (i.e., inflation).

Table 6.1 shows the pattern of prices and real output over a thirty-year period. Note that real GNP (Q) is obtained by dividing current dollar GNP (Y) by the ratio of the price index (P) to 100.0. The *rate of growth* in real GNP may be computed as:

$$\text{Real Growth} = \frac{Q_t - Q_{t-1}}{Q_{t-1}} \tag{6.5}$$

where the subscript t indicates the year and t–1 indicates the prior year. Similarly the *rate of inflation* may be computed as:

$$\text{Inflation} = \frac{P_t - P_{t-1}}{P_{t-1}} \tag{6.6}$$

Thus from 1978 to 1979 the rate of growth in real GNP was 2.28% per year (1431.1–1399.2)/1399.2, and the rate of inflation using the GNP price index was 8.81% per year (165.5–152.1)/152.1.

Note that the pattern of change in real GNP (Q) in Table 6.1 is more erratic than the steady increase in nominal GNP (Y). In fact the real GNP actually declined in 1974 and 1975 while the nominal GNP, buoyed by rising prices, kept right on climbing. Most economists define a decline in the real GNP that persists over two consecutive quarters as a "recession." The word recession has such negative connotations, however, that politicians dislike hearing their economic advisers using such a term in public. In 1978, President Carter's chief inflation fighter, Alfred Kahn, predicted that unless the rising rate of inflation were brought under control the country was headed for a recession. Apparently he was chastised for using the term "recession," and in a subsequent news conference he vowed that he would never use that word again, but he reiterated that unless inflation were brought under control the nation was headed for a "big banana."

The Price Index and Inflation

The rate of inflation computed for any given year clearly depends on the price index selected for the computation. Thus far we have discussed the index used to "deflate" the current dollar GNP to estimate real output in the constant dollars of some base year. This index is called the *GNP deflator* and measures changes in the prices paid for all final goods produced in the country in a given year. Individual consumers, however, are not concerned with the prices paid for capital goods, exports, or government purchases. In order to measure changes in the prices paid by consumers, a *Consumer Price Index* (CPI) has been developed which uses only the prices consumers pay for food, housing, transportation, clothing, and so forth, weighted by the relative importance of these expenditures in the typical consumer's budget. This index is keyed to the price levels in urban areas and the expenditure patterns of urban "blue-collar" workers.

Numerous wage contracts are linked to the CPI. Whenever the CPI goes up by 1%, about 9 million people covered by cost-of-living adjustment clauses receive an extra 5¢ to 10¢ per hour. In addition, Social Security benefits going to 35 million people and federal pensions going to an additional 1.5 million retirees are also tied to changes in the CPI.

Besides the GNP deflator and the CPI, there are a number of producer price indexes that measure the prices paid by producers for goods in various stages of processing. The values of the Producer Price Index (PPI) for finished goods, the CPI, and the GNP deflator for a thirty-year period are presented in Table 6.1. Note that the rate of inflation in 1978 was 7.66% per year using the CPI [(195.4–181.5) / 181.5], 7.75% using the PPI for finished goods [(194.6–180.6) / 180.6], and 7.34% using the GNP deflator. In periods of rapid change in the rate of inflation, the three indices do not move together quite so closely. In 1979 the CPI was increasing at an annual rate of 11.3%, while the GNP deflator was rising at an annual rate of 8.8%. Thus our estimate of the rate of inflation may vary considerably with the price index selected.[4]

We should emphasize that these statistics are based on sampling techniques, and that errors are to be expected. For example, the CPI is based on prices observed in selected stores in a sample of urban areas. Changes in these stores and areas may or may not accurately reflect changes in other locations. Our estimates of the unemployment rate are also based on survey data collected by the Bureau of Labor Statistics in the Department of Labor. We define the unemployment rate as the ratio of the number of people over 16 years of age who are actively searching for work, to the total work force. The work force is defined as those searching for work plus those who are employed. The relevant numbers are estimated through a phone survey in which individuals are questioned on their employment status and recent attempts that they have made to find work. Note that the unemployment rate depends on the number of people who are looking for work, and this number may vary with expectation that work can be found. Thus the unemployment rate does not measure the number of people who are so disenchanted that they have given up the search for work, it does not measure "underemployment," and it does not tell us how many of those who are working are working all the hours they desire.

This brief review of economic statistics has highlighted the problems involved in measuring our progress toward the national economic objectives of high levels of real GNP, high growth in real GNP, price stability, and low levels of unemployment. We have observed that there is a continuing flow of income in the economy which is determined by the levels of aggregate spending. Changes in aggregate spending may be the result of an increase in real output, or simply of higher price levels. Variations in the level of aggregate spending are primarily related to fluctuations in the level of investment. The Keynesian approach to macroeconomics calls on the federal government to intervene in the economy to control variations in the level of aggregate spending by offsetting the impact of shifts in the level of investment, and in the next section we outline the simple Keynesian model of income determination.

A FOUR-SECTOR KEYNESIAN MODEL OF INCOME DETERMINATION

A Keynesian model of the economy is developed by dividing aggregate spending into as many components as desired, and then providing a behavioral equation to estimate the level of each component. A typical Keynesian model used in actual forecasting might have twenty or more equations for an equal number of components of aggregate spending. The principles involved in the larger Keynesian models, however, may be illustrated with the model discussed earlier in which aggregate spending is divided into four major components: consumption (C), investment (I), government purchases (G), and net exports (X–M). After we have estimated the value of each component, we may simply add them all up to estimate the GNP using the following accounting identity:

$$Y = C + I + G + (X–M) \qquad (6.6)$$

The complexity of the Keynesian model depends on the number of components of GNP that we attempt to estimate, but it also depends on the number of variables that are determined by the model (the endogenous variables) and the number that are determined outside the model (the exogenous variables). The simplest Keynesian model treats I, G, and X–M as exogenous variables that are provided by some source outside the model. The only endogenous variables then would be the level of consumption (C) and the level of the GNP (Y).

Keynes postulated that the primary determinant of the level of consumption was the level of income received by consumers, and he felt that this "consumption function" was linear. The form of this simple consumption function would be:

$$C = a + bY \qquad (6.7)$$

where a and b are constants. This consumption function is plotted on Figure 6.3 which shows that "a" is the intercept of the linear function and "b" is the slope. Keynes called the slope, b, the *marginal propensity to consume* (mpc) since it represented how much of an additional dollar of income would be spent on consumption (note on Figure 6.2 that the rest of the additional dollar of income would go to savings or taxes).

If we substitute this linear consumption function into our aggregate spending equals GNP identity we obtain:

$$Y = a + bY + I + G + (X–M) \qquad (6.8)$$

If we know the values of I, G, and (X–M), we may solve this equation for Y as follows:

$$Y – bY = a + I + G + (X–M);$$

or collecting Y terms

$$Y (1 – b) = a + I + G + (X–M);$$

or dividing by 1 – b

$$Y = (\frac{1}{1-b}) \; [a + I + G + (X–M)] \qquad (6.9)$$

The term $(1/1 – b)$ is called the "*multiplier*." If there is a change in the value of I, G, or (X–M), the level of the GNP will shift by the change in that exogenous variable times the "multiplier."

Let's try out some of these ideas using the data in Table 6.1. First, go back to our simple consumption function:

$$C = a + bY \qquad (6.7)$$

Because this is an equation of a straight line, if we knew two points on the line we could solve for the slope, b, and the intercept, a. In Table 6.1 we observe that in 1977 the values of C and Y respectively were $1210.0 and $1899.5 billion, and in 1978 the values of C and Y were $1350.8 and $2127.6 billion. The values for 1977 and 1978 thus provide two points on the consumption function. The simplest way to solve for the slope, b (the marginal propensity to consume), is to observe that the slope will be the change in C divided by the change in Y, or:

$$b = \frac{\Delta C}{\Delta Y} \qquad (6.10)$$

In this case:

$$b = \frac{(1350.8 - 1210.0)}{(2127.6 - 1899.5)} = \frac{140.8}{228.1} = .617$$

This suggests that for every additional dollar of GNP produced, about 62¢ goes to satisfy the demands of consumers. Substituting the value of the slope back into the consumption function we may solve for the intercept, a, using the data for either 1977 or 1978. In this case we arbitrarily use the data for 1978:

$$C = a + bY$$
$$a = C - bY$$
$$a = 1350.8 - .617\ (2127.6)$$
$$a = 1350.8 - 1312.7 = 38.1$$

The multiplier would be $1/(1-b)$ or 2.611. If we multiply 2.611 times the sum of $a + I + G + (X-M)$ using the values in Table 6.1, we obtain a GNP for 1978 of 2127.7 billion dollars. Of course the accuracy of these computations is in no way a test of the Keynesian *theory*, because we used only the data for one year to solve for the parameters of the consumption function. In other words these computations have only demonstrated an accounting identity. The assertion of Keynesian theory is that the marginal propensity to consume, and hence the multiplier, will be relatively constant over time. In testing this theory we would estimate the marginal propensity to consume using values of consumption and income that were observed over a period of time, and test to see how well the linear consumption function "fit" the observed data.

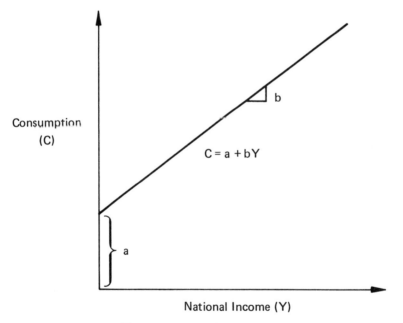

Figure 6.3 The Consumption Function

The idea of the multiplier applies to Keynesian models that are far more complex than the simple model presented here. The system of equations in the model may be solved to show how the GNP varies with the change in any policy variable available to the government (government spending, tax rates, or the supply of money). If the multiplier for government spending were stable at a value of 2.611, we could use the multiplier to predict the change in GNP that would result from a change in government spending. Suppose that business expectations about the future drop, or the availability of credit drops, or interest rates rise. Firms are apt to cut back on their investment plans, and aggregate investment will fall. How much would the GNP drop if the level of investment falls by $100 billion? Using the multiplier we would expect a decline of $261.1 billion. Swings in the level of investment would have a multiplied impact on the GNP. The "multiplier" is greater than one because a change in investment would reduce aggregate spending, consumer income would fall, consumption would drop, aggregate spending would then fall further, and consumption would decline even more. Keynes observed that business cycles resulted from the erratic performance of investment, but he also noted that the multiplier effect also applied to changes in government purchases. In order to offset the decline in the GNP of $261.1 billion we "only" have to increase government purchases by $100 billion. In this case the multiplier increases the GNP since the increase in G raises aggregate spending, which increases consumer income, which increases consumption, which increases aggregate spending, which adds to consumer income, which produces even more increases in consumption.

The Full-Employment Budget

The preceding section suggested that the level of GNP can be varied by selecting the appropriate level of government spending. In our simple model we can select precisely that level of government purchases that will eventually shift GNP to the desired level, because we know the value of the multiplier and we know precisely how much we wish to change the GNP. In practice, however, we only have estimates of the multiplier, we are not sure precisely how long it will take the GNP to shift to the desired level, and we also know that while we are waiting, a number of other factors (the level of investment, for example) may also change. We may well adopt a fiscal policy that stimulates the economy beyond an output that can be produced with an acceptable level of inflation.

The size of the budget deficit is not a very good guide to the level of stimulation being provided by our fiscal policy. Large deficits may develop either because we have added to aggregate spending by driving up government purchases and cutting taxes, or because the economy is growing slowly and tax receipts are low compared to the continuing level of government purchases. In the former case the large deficit would reflect a great deal of fiscal stimulus, but in the latter case the deficit is simply the result of the poor performance of the economy.

Because there are dangers of overstimulating the economy by trying to find the precise level of government purchases that will bring us to our current output target, and because the balance in the current budget is often a poor guide to the amount of fiscal stimulus being provided, many economists advocate "*balancing the budget at full employment output*." Full-employment output, "*potential GNP*," is the level of GNP at which we have achieved the highest rate of employment of the labor force consistent with an acceptable level of inflation. In general, as output and employment increase, wages will rise, and there will be pressure on prices to rise as well. These pressures may build up in many sectors of the economy long before the economy as a whole is at capacity output. The definition of "full-employment output" then is essentially a political judgment on the acceptable trade-off between inflation and unemployment. When the idea of full employment or "potential" output was introduced in the early 1960s, the acceptable rate of inflation was about 3% per year, and the level of unemployment typically associated with this rate of inflation was about 4% of the labor force. In the 1980s an acceptable rate of inflation may be closer to 6% per year, and the corresponding rate of unemployment may be about 5.5% of the labor force. The potential GNP then is the GNP consistent with the target rate of unemployment, and the difference between the actual and potential GNP is a measure of how close we are to our desired level of GNP. In 1978 the potential GNP was estimated at $1,423 billion 1972 dollars, which was about 1.7% above the actual GNP of $1399.2 billion 1972 dollars.[5]

The idea of balancing the budget at full employment suggests that the government should attempt to set government purchases of goods and services at a level equal to what tax receipts would be if the economy were at full employment. Figure 6.4 illustrates this concept. Note that the tax structure and the pattern of government spending have been set so that when the economy is operating at potential GNP (Y_p) government purchases equal tax receipts. This combination of tax structure and government purchases would then be pursued *regardless* of the level of actual GNP. If the actual GNP were below potential (Y_1), the budget would be in deficit providing some fiscal stimulus to the economy. If the actual GNP were above potential (Y_2), tax receipts would be greater than government purchases and the actual budget would be in surplus. If the actual GNP equalled the potential GNP, the actual budget would be in balance, providing no fiscal stimulus for further expansion or contraction.

Of course, if we wish to push the economy toward its potential output at a faster rate, we can raise the level of government purchases even further. Note that the result would be a budget deficit even if the economy were at full employment. This full employment budget deficit would be a far more accurate measure of the fiscal stimulus being provided than the actual budget deficit.

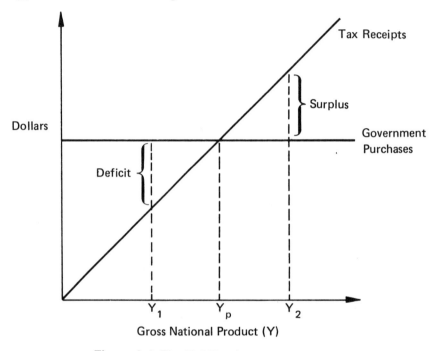

Figure 6.4 The Full Employment Budget

A GENERAL KEYNESIAN MODEL OF INCOME DETERMINATION

Our ability to apply countercyclical Keynesian economics to control the level of the GNP depends on the stability of the behavioral equations in the model and on the government's ability to modify its spending or taxing patterns in time to achieve the desired level of output. The simple model that treats investment, government purchases, and net exports as exogenous and assumes that consumption is related only to the level of the GNP is obviously far too simplistic for actual policy decisions. We may develop a more generalized model, however, which is quite a bit more realistic, and comes closer to capturing actual behavioral patterns.[6]

The simple Keynesian model discussed changes in current dollar or nominal GNP. We must now be more precise because we would like to sort out how much of the change in nominal GNP is the result of changes in real output, and how much is the result of changes in the price level. To explore this we will need to expand our discussion to include aggregate supply as well as aggregate demand. The aggregate spending approach only tells us what the demand for output will be. We now ask whether or not that output can be produced and how the supply of output will vary with the price level. To proceed with our analysis we will first develop a more generalized model of aggregate demand and then proceed to aggregate supply. From this point on, our output and aggregate spending variables will be expressed in constant dollars of some base year unless otherwise indicated.

Aggregate Demand

The level of consumption is clearly related to the level of income (Q) received by consumers. But we also assume that consumers with more accumulated assets, that is greater wealth (W), consume more in a given period of time. Many durable goods (automobiles, appliances) are purchased by borrowing funds on credit and then paying back the loan over time. Thus credit availability (CA) measured by the down-payment required, the ease with which funds may be obtained, the size of monthly payments and the duration of the loan, all affect consumption. Consumers are also aware of possible future changes in their income, and we expect current consumption to be a function of expected future income (Q*) as well as current income. The structure of the tax laws (t) including the level and composition of taxes (income, property, sales) also affects consumption. The impact of the price level (P) on consumption is not quite as clear. At first glance one might argue that high prices depress consumption, but here we are concerned with the level of all prices rather than relative prices. A higher price level raises both prices and income level, and can leave the amount of consumption unchanged. A high price level, however, can have two effects that lower consumption. First, a higher price level lowers the value of any assets that are denominated in dollars (bonds, savings accounts) and reduces wealth. Second, the higher price level lowers the real money supply, raising interest rates and lowering credit availability. For these reasons we assume that a higher price level lowers the level of consumption. Using a plus sign over a variable to indicate a positive association with the level of consumption, and a minus sign to indicate a negative association, our consumption function can be written as:

$$C = f(\overset{+}{Q}, \overset{+}{W}, \overset{+}{CA}, \overset{+}{Q^*}, \overset{-}{t}, \overset{-}{P}) \tag{6.11}$$

The level of investment was exogenous in our simple introductory model, but we expect the level of investment to vary with the price of capital goods (P_c), the return stream of earnings (R*) expected to result from the addition of new capital, and the rate of interest (r) representing the cost to the firm of obtaining funds with which to purchase the capital goods. Using the same plus and minus sign notation this investment function is written as:

$$I = f(\overset{-}{P_c}, \overset{+}{R^*}, \overset{-}{r}) \tag{6.12}$$

Leaving government purchases and net exports as exogenous variables, we may substitute these behavioral equations into our aggregate spending equals GNP identity as follows:

$$Q = C + I + G + (X–M) \tag{6.13}$$

$$Q = C\ (\overset{+}{Q}, \overset{+}{W}, \overset{+}{CA}, \overset{+}{Q^*}, \overset{-}{t}, \overset{-}{P}) + I\ (\overset{-}{P_c}, \overset{+}{R^*}, \overset{-}{r}) + G + (X–M)$$

or putting this in the most general form:

$$Q = f\ (\overset{+}{W}, \overset{+}{CA}, \overset{+}{Q^*}, \overset{-}{t}, \overset{-}{P}, \overset{-}{P_c}, \overset{+}{R^*}, \overset{-}{r}, \overset{+}{G}, \overset{+}{X}, \overset{-}{M}) \tag{6.14}$$

If we could measure each of these variables and estimate the model, we could solve for the multiplier impact that each variable would have on the GNP. We could plot the GNP against any of these variables to highlight a particular relationship. In Figure 6.5 we plot the GNP versus the price level, showing that the real GNP should fall as the price level increases. A change in any of the other variables affecting aggregate spending would cause this aggregate demand curve to shift. An increase in a variable with a plus sign would cause the aggregate demand curve to shift to the right, and an increase in a variable with a minus sign would cause the aggregate demand curve to shift to the left. For example, an increase in government purchases or a cut in taxes would cause the aggregate demand curve to shift to the right to AD′ in Figure 6.5.

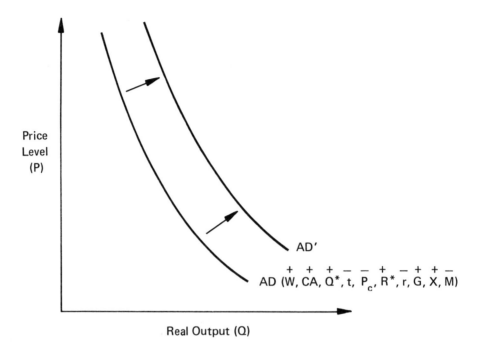

Figure 6.5 The Aggregate Demand Curve

Aggregate Supply

We know that an increase in government purchases will shift the aggregate demand curve to the right, but how will this shift be divided between an increase in real output and an increase in the price level? To answer this question we need to know how the aggregate supply of real output varies with the price level. The quantity of output that firms are willing to provide will be a function of the prices they receive for their products (P); the prices they must pay for inputs such as wages and raw materials (P_{in}); the stock of capital plant and equipment (K); the technology available for producing output from the available inputs (Z); the restrictiveness of government health, safety, environmental, and economic regulation (R_{eg}); and the tax laws (T) affecting the supply of labor, the availability of credit, and after tax profits. Higher prices are needed to call forth more output because most firms face diminishing returns to their fixed factors of production making it increasingly more costly to produce additional units of output. Using our plus and minus sign convention we may write the aggregate supply function as:

$$Q = f \ (\overset{+}{P}, \ \overset{-}{P}_{in}, \ \overset{+}{K}, \ \overset{+}{Z}, \ \overset{-}{R}_{eg}, \ \overset{-}{T}) \tag{6.15}$$

We can plot the supply of output versus any of these variables. Figure 6.6 shows aggregate output plotted against the price level. Note that the aggregate curve becomes very steep when output is pushed beyond the level of potential or full employment output (Q_p), because firms begin to use their least efficient capital as they press to produce their maximum output and because the firms are forced to hire less efficient labor as the unemployment rate drops. An increase in any of the other variables in the aggregate supply function will cause the aggregate supply curve to shift to the right (plus sign) or left (minus sign), and a decrease will cause a shift in the opposite direction. For example, if workers expecting higher prices demand a pay increase to protect themselves against inflation, the result will be an increase in the price of inputs (labor in this case) and a shift of the aggregate supply curve to the left (to AS' in Figure 6.6).

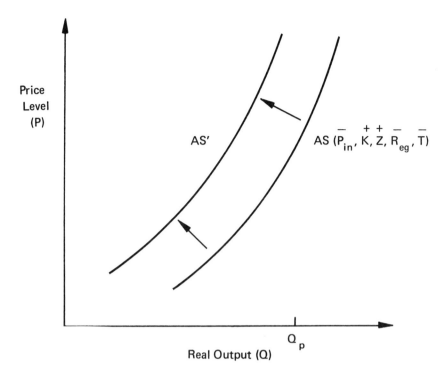

Figure 6.6 The Aggregate Supply Curve

We may now put the aggregate supply and demand curves together and determine the equilibrium price and output levels. Figure 6.7 shows that equilibrium will be produced at that price (P_e) and output (Q_e) that equate aggregate supply and aggregate demand. At that point the output that firms desire to produce will just equal the output that consumers, firms, government, and foreign citizens desire to purchase. Note that a change in any of the other variables affecting aggregate supply or aggregate demand will cause a change in the equilibrium price and output by shifting the relevant curve. For example, an increase in government purchases will cause the aggregate demand curve to shift to the right (to AD′ in Figure 6.7), causing an increase in both output and prices.

STAGFLATION: AN APPLICATION

In the early 1960s President Kennedy ran on a platform of "getting the country moving again," and he proposed a tax cut along Keynesian lines to stimulate aggregate demand. The tax cut, actually passed in 1964 after Kennedy's death, preceded the increased expenditures of the Johnson administration for the war in Vietnam and the "*Great Society*" programs aimed primarily at rapid urban development. President Johnson refused to sacrifice his domestic programs and was slow to recommend increased taxes to finance the war. The result was a sharp shift of the nation's aggregate demand curve to the right as shown in Figure 6.7. The economy approached full employment of its resources, the level of output expanded, but prices also began to rise.

The increased rate of inflation brought the expectation of continuing price increases, and workers attempted to protect themselves by bargaining for wage hikes keyed to the rate of inflation. These wage increases pushed up the cost of inputs, shifted the aggregate supply curve to the left, and added to inflationary pressures.

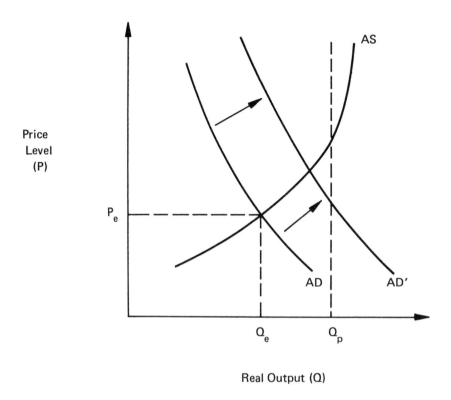

Figure 6.7 Aggregate Demand and Aggregate Supply

Unfortunately, the 1970s brought a number of other pressures that tended to shift the aggregate supply curve to the left. First, the sale of 25 percent of our grain crops to the Soviet Union in 1972 produced sharp increases in the price of feedgrain inputs to meat production in particular and food products in general. Next the OPEC embargo and associated crude oil price increases in 1973 sharply increased the price of energy inputs to the production process. Then the rate of growth in output per worker (productivity) fell in the United States, caused in part by a slackening in the rate of capital investment. The decline in productivity increased the labor costs per unit of output produced. Fourth, there was a sharp increase in legislation aimed at improving environmental quality, health, and safety. While resultant regulations reflected a concern with important public issues, they also placed increasing costs on producers. The impact was not only on current operating costs, but also on the expectations of future regulations and thus on the rate of capital formation. Each of these problems on the supply side tended to shift the aggregate supply curve to the left.

Figure 6.8 shows the impact of a leftward shift in aggregate supply following a shift to the right in aggregate demand. In this case the government began by expanding government purchases, shifting the aggregate demand curve from AD_1 to AD_2. Note that the final shift from B to C produces a sharp rise in the price level but a decline in the level of output. Thus we are faced with the dilemma of simultaneous increases in unemployment and prices, a dilemma economists label "stagflation." Keynesian manipulation of aggregate demand may be ineffective in handling stagflation since the real culprit is the shifting aggregate supply curve. Presumably at some point the rising level of unemployment will dampen the inflationary pressures in the economy and lower the expectation of future inflation, but this process may take a considerable amount of time. Note that efforts by the government to combat unemployment by stimulating aggregate demand may not only be ineffective, they may actually worsen the unemployment problem by accelerating the shift in the aggregate supply curve.

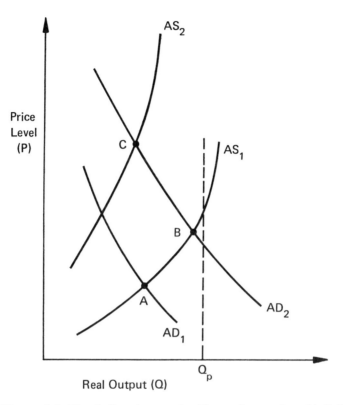

Figure 6.8 Stagflation: Increasing Unemployment and Inflation

Note:
Strictly speaking this figure shows that the price level will increase, but it does not show what the rate of increase will be. Whether or not the rate of inflation will be higher or lower depends on the rate at which the curves shift and how rapidly the prices converge on the new equilibrium level.

THE PHILLIPS CURVE: AN ILLUSION

The *Phillips Curve* purports to show the trade-off between the level of unemployment and the rate of inflation. If the aggregate supply curve is constant, then an increase in aggregate demand will expand output, lower unemployment, and raise prices. Thus we might plot this trade-off as shown in Figure 6.9. At low levels of aggregate demand unemployment will be high and the rate of inflation will be low. As demand expands unemployment will fall and prices will rise.

But this trade-off is based on the assumption that the higher rate of inflation will leave conditions in the labor market unchanged, that is, the wage demands of workers will be unaffected. If workers attempt to protect themselves against the inflation with higher wages, the aggregate supply curve will shift to the left. At a given level of unemployment inflation will now be higher, and the Phillips Curve will shift to the right (from PC_1 to PC_2 in Figure 6.9). Thus attempts to use monetary and fiscal policies to move along the inflation–unemployment trade-off of the current Phillips Curve may simply result in a shift in the curve, and a less acceptable trade-off between unemployment and inflation.

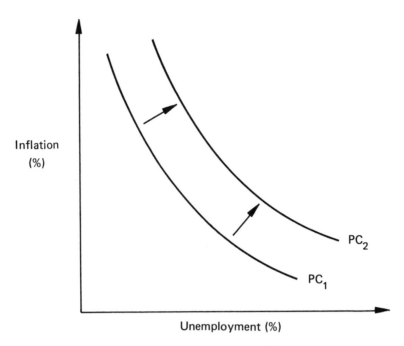

Figure 6.9 The Phillips Curve

Note:
Anything which causes the aggregate supply curve to shift to the left will produce an equilibrium at which a higher price level is associated with a given level of output and hence a given level of unemployment. A shift of the aggregate supply curve to the left is associated with a shift of the Phillips Curve to the right. The Phillips Curve will only be stable if the aggregate supply curve does not shift.

Over the decade of the 1970s a number of factors combined to shift the Phillips Curve to the right. In addition to those factors affecting the aggregate supply curve noted previously, the larger participation of teenagers and women in the work force and the increases in unemployment compensation have tended to increase the average level of unemployment in the economy. Teenagers and women have historically entered and left the work force at a higher turnover rate than the rest of the work force, and improved unemployment compensation has lengthened the period of job search and reduced the motivation to accept just any job opportunity. The shift of the Phillips Curve to the right is the mirror image of the factors on the supply side that have shifted the aggregate supply curve to the left.

The result is that policymakers now face a far more complex set of trade-offs than were confronted in the 1960s. Policies that might reduce inflationary expectations such as wage-price controls or tight monetary and fiscal policies have undesirable side effects. Wage-price controls distort the pattern of relative prices in the economy, and may simply defer the accumulating inflationary pressures until the controls are removed. Tight monetary and fiscal policies slow current growth and add to unemployment. Thus most public officials consistently refer to the possibilities of a "soft landing," that is a gradual lessening of aggregate demand to reduce inflation without an increase in the level of unemployment.

SUPPLY SIDE VERSUS DEMAND SIDE ECONOMICS

The Reagan administration has emphasized attempts to increase economic growth and simultaneously reduce inflation by stressing efforts to stimulate aggregate supply. Much of its economic program incorporates the supply factors outlined above in seeking more emphasis on cost-effectiveness in regulatory programs and lowering business taxes to stimulate investment. The new idea in President Reagan's "supply side" economics, however, is that a cut in marginal individual tax rates can both increase incentives for greater productivity and generate additional savings. Those additional savings would then provide a greater pool of funds for investment, lower interest rates, and stimulate an increase in aggregate supply. The catch is that the traditional analysis outlined above suggests that the tax cut would also stimulate more consumption and increase aggregate demand. The test for the "supply side" tax cut passed in 1981 providing for annual cuts over a three-year period of five, ten and ten percent in 1982, 1983 and 1984 respectively, therefore rests on the relative shifts in aggregate demand and aggregate supply. If supply were to increase more rapidly, the result would be higher real growth and lower inflation. On the other hand, if demand increased more rapidly the result would be higher inflation and a lower increase in real output. In practice, however, circumstances did not permit a pure test of this supply-side tax theory, because the Federal Reserve Board, with the administration's support, simultaneously pursued a classic monetarist strategy of low rates of growth in the money supply to counter inflation. The combination of low money growth and large budget deficits combined to drive up interest rates, reduce investment and increase unemployment. The fiscal stimulus of the tax cut was more than offset by rising interest rates, aggregate demand fell, and unemployment increased. As a result inflation was reduced not by the desired supply-side impact, but by a traditional lowering of aggregate demand.

CONCLUSION

Keynesian economics suggests that the government should play an active role in manipulating aggregate demand in order to achieve our economic policy objectives. In simplest terms the Keynesian prescription is to offset fluctuations in aggregate demand caused by shifts in the level of investment, by shifting the level of government purchases and the tax structure. Keynesian models attempt to develop multipliers that show what impact the change in some policy variable will have on the level of national output. These multipliers are used in the budgetary process to select the desired level of government expenditures. Because defense expenditures are a major component of government purchases of goods and services, these decisions on economic policy can have a significant impact on the defense sector.

In order to deal with the complex problems of stagflation, however, a more complete economic model is needed. Many of our problems in the 1970s were more concerned with shifts in the level of aggregate supply than with the aggregate demand stressed by Keynesian analysis. In making their budgetary decisions, policymakers must also consider the impact the budget will have on inflationary expectations and the rate of capital formation. While these considerations have increased concern for supply conditions, the federal government has only indirect impacts on many supply factors. Thus the fiscal policy decisions reflected in the budgetary process continue to be the centerpiece of our economic policy. In the next chapter we will examine the institutional setting in which these budgetary decisions are made and the process by which economic analysis is integrated in the analysis.

NOTES

1 Herbert Stein, "Waiting for Phase II," *The AEI Economist* (October, 1978), p. 2.
2 John Maynard Keynes, as quoted by Robert L. Heilbronner, *The Worldly Philosophers, 4th ed.* (New York: Simon and Schuster, 1972), p. 279.
3 The Gross National Product may be further defined as the sum of the output of each final good or service produced in year t, q_{it}, multiplied by the price of each good or service in that year, p_{it}. Thus the Gross National Product (Y) may be expressed as:

$$Y_t = \sum_{i=1}^{n} q_{it} p_{it}$$

4 "Which Price Indicator Do You Believe?" *Business Week* (May 14, 1979), p. 120.
5 *The Economic Report of the President 1979* (Washington, D.C.: Government Printing Office, 1979), p. 75
6 The following discussion follows the development of the aggregate demand model in James R. Golden and Robert H. Baldwin, *Economics and Public Policy: Principles, Problems and Applications (Wayne, New Jersey: Avery Press, 1979), Chapters 14–21.*

SELECTED REFERENCES

William J. Baumol and Alan S. Blinder, *Economics: Principles and Policy* (New York: Harcourt Brace Jovanovich, Inc., 1979)

William H. Branson and James M. Litvack, *Macroeconomics* (New York: Harper and Row, 1976).

James R. Golden and Robert H. Baldwin, *Economics and Public Policy: Principles, Problems and Applications*, 3rd ed. (Wayne, New Jersey: Avery Press, 1981).

Chapter 7
The Federal Budget

INTRODUCTION

The national budget is the most direct statement of our national priorities. Although the budget is often seen as a dry collection of statistics, it is an important political, as well as economic, document which outlines those projects that we care about enough to support with scarce government funds, and those projects that do not warrant such support. The budget explains how much of our national output is to be diverted to government programs through taxes, how much of government expenditures will go to the purchase of goods and services, and how much of the government's tax receipts will be transferred to selected citizens in the form of "transfer payments."

Table 7.1 outlines the sources of revenue going to the federal government from 1970 to 1981 and the uses to which those funds were put. The federal government budgets its expenditures based on a fiscal year that begins on October 1 of each year, but Table 7.1 translates these figures to a normal calendar basis as they would appear in the national income accounts. In each of the years presented, the annual budget was in deficit, a deficit that was financed by increasing the national debt in the form of government bonds.

It is difficult for most of us to grasp the size and impact of the federal budget. The budgets of the late 1970s were labeled as "*austere*" because of their attempts to limit government spending, and hence aggregate spending, to counter inflationary pressures. Yet the budget for 1980 represented over $2,400 for every individual in the United States. Viewed in other terms, over 20 percent of the national output flows through the *federal* government. In a 1976 article in *Newsweek*, Milton Friedman wrote, " . . . Each of us works, as it were, from Jan. 1 to the end of March for the Federal government, then to late May for his state and local government, and only then for himself."[1] Clearly, the federal budget has a dramatic influence on all of our lives and a major impact on the distribution of our national output.

Personal income taxes remain the largest single source of income for the federal government, although social security taxes rose rapidly during the 1970s from about 25 percent of total receipts in 1970 to almost 33 percent in 1980. The personal income tax has a *progressive* rate structure so that the marginal tax paid on an additional dollar of income increases as income increases, although in practice the use of tax shelters keeps the tax less progressive than the rates themselves suggest. We might note that as inflation increases nominal (current dollar) income, the average tax rate automatically increases. Social security payments are made by individuals and their employees, and tend to be regressive since they constitute a smaller percentage of income as income increases. The greater reliance on social security payments as a source of revenue has made our tax system more regressive with a heavier burden being placed on low-income families.

On the expenditure side only 33 percent of federal outlays in 1980 were projected to go to the purchase of goods and services. The largest single source of expenditure in the federal budget is transfer payments such as social security, unemployment insurance, and federal pensions. In 1980 such expenditures were about 42 percent of the federal budget. The largest share of actual purchases of goods and services (desks, payrolls, tanks) goes to the defense sector.

These carefully unbalanced totals (note the annual deficits which must be financed with an increase in government debt) of receipts and expenditures are the result of a process of evaluating national priorities, gauging impacts on the economy, bargaining, and debating that extends over the two-year budget cycle. The first budget proposals come from the executive branch when the president delivers his budget address in January. The president's budget proposal is the result of an annual process of analysis and bargaining orchestrated by the Office of Management and Budget in the Executive Office of the President. But the president's proposal is simply the clarion call for continuing debate in the Congress. The process of Congressional review was overhauled in the 1970's and now includes an analytical capability in the Congressional Budget Office and a Budget Committee in each house, in addition to the traditional finance, appropriations, and legislative committees.

In this chapter we will first examine how the president's closest economic advisers use economic analysis to provide a framework for the budget debate. Next we will examine the budgetary processes within the executive and legislative branches, before summarizing some of the most important characteristics of the entire budgetary process. Finally we will consider "reforms" of the budgetary process in the executive branch—program budgeting and zero-based budgeting—that have been proposed in the name of increased efficiency. In the following chapter we will explain how the Department of Defense fits into the overall budgeting process.

Table 7.1
Federal Transactions in the National Income Accounts: 1970 – 1981
(Billions of Current Dollars)

Description	Actual									Estimate		
	1970	1971	1972	1973	1974	1975	1976	1977	1978	1979	1980	1981
Receipts												
Personal Taxes	93.6	87.5	100.3	107.3	122.6	127.1	136.9	165.9	186.3	223.5	245.1	279.7
Corporate Profit Taxes	33.0	32.0	34.2	41.0	43.7	42.1	51.9	58.8	67.2	78.4	76.5	77.1
Indirect Business Tax	19.2	20.0	19.9	20.7	21.4	22.2	24.2	24.5	27.2	29.4	38.5	53.0
Social Insurance	49.2	52.9	59.1	71.5	84.2	92.1	100.9	116.1	133.1	152.4	170.5	199.9
Total Receipts	194.9	192.5	213.5	240.5	271.8	283.5	313.9	365.3	413.8	483.7	530.6	607.7
Expenditures												
Purchases of Goods and Services	97.0	94.8	100.9	101.7	104.6	118.0	126.2	140.7	151.1	162.4	185.6	202.9
(Defense)	75.3	72.1	72.5	73.3	74.1	80.3	85.5	92.3	98.1	105.9	118.7	132.1
(Nondefense)	21.7	22.7	28.4	28.4	30.5	37.6	40.7	48.4	53.0	56.5	66.9	70.8
Transfer Payments	57.0	70.1	78.9	89.7	104.7	134.3	156.5	169.6	181.8	201.7	235.1	267.6
Grants to State and Local Governments	22.6	26.8	32.6	40.4	41.6	48.4	57.5	66.2	74.6	79.3	84.3	90.7
New Interest on Debt	13.6	14.2	14.1	15.9	19.8	21.9	25.2	28.4	33.7	40.4	49.2	52.2
Subsidies Less Surplus of Government Enterprises	5.4	6.8	6.4	9.1	8.0	5.7	6.1	7.0	9.4	9.8	10.0	12.9
Total Expenditures	195.6	212.7	232.9	256.2	278.8	328.7	371.5	412.0	450.6	493.6	564.2	626.3
Surplus (+) or Deficit (−)	−.6	−20.2	−19.5	−15.7	−7.0	−45.3	−57.6	−46.7	−36.8	−9.9	−33.6	−18.6

Source: Special Analyses Budget of the United States Government, Fiscal Year 1981, p. 72.

THE PRESIDENT'S ECONOMIC ADVISERS

The history of economic advising is spotty at best, but many trace the process back to Joseph and the Pharoah in Egypt. You may recall that Joseph's success came from his ability to translate the Pharoah's dreams, and it has been suggested that many of his successors have relied on the same approach. Unfortunately many of those dreams have turned out to be nightmares.

Council of Economic Advisers and the Joint Economic Committee

A more recent history might begin with the Employment Act of 1946, which established the three-member *Council of Economic Advisers* in the Executive Office of the President and the *Joint Economic Committee* in Congress. The act committed the government to maintaining high levels of employment and established agencies staffed with professional economists placed in positions to have significant impact on economic policy. The Joint Economic Committee has no legislative responsibilities, but its hearings have provided an important forum for economic issues, and it has attracted a long line of influential chairmen: Robert Taft, Paul Douglas, William Fulbright, John Sparkman, Charles Percy, Jacob Javits, Edward Kennedy, Hubert Humphrey, Wright Patman, Wilbur Mills, Henry Reuss, and Richard Bolling, to name a few.

The impact of the Council of Economic Advisers, with a staff of only 50 and an annual budget under $2 million, has been enormous and is the result of close relationships that have evolved between a series of council chairmen and the president. The chairman of the CEA has a number of important advantages in the advisory process. First the chairman is charged with acting in the general interest, and his level of responsibility and span of economic interests, both domestic and international, parallel the president's. The chairman is unencumbered by the administrative responsibilities of heading a major agency and the political constituencies that go with such responsibilities. Second, many issues are handled through interagency task forces. Because these studies typically require the participation of agencies with conflicting interests, a referee is needed, and the council chairman is a logical referee in cases of economic policy. Although many people would define a committee as a group of people who individually don't know what to do, and collectively decide that nothing can be done, much of the important work of government is done within such committee structures. Third, many issues are now framed in program analysis formats, which lend themselves to the professional expertise of the council chairman. Finally, the chairman is charged with the preparation of the president's annual *Economic Report*, and the formal presentation of ideas in the report is an important part of generating economic policy.[2]

The Council of Economic Advisers has two members in addition to the chairman, and traditionally one member focuses on macroeconomic and international issues while the other concentrates more on microeconomic issues related to particular industries. The council is supported by a staff of some ten to twelve senior staff economists, normally drawn from the ranks of associate professors of economics who serve for one or two years, and a handful of junior staff economists. Thus the staff is extremely small, but it benefits from a limited institutional commitment and can serve an important role in performing relatively "neutral" analyses of policy issues.

The influence of the chairman of the Council of Economic Advisers is, in the final analysis, a function of his ability to influence the decisions of the president and therefore depends on the personal relationships between the two. In the early 1970s chairmen Herbert Stein and Alan Greenspan had very close personal relationships with Presidents Nixon and Ford, respectively. Chairman Charles Schultze's relationship with President Carter was somewhat more formal, but Schultze wielded considerable influence as the result of his recognized expertise in a wide range of government issues. Schultze had been the director of the Bureau of the Budget under President Johnson, before it was reorganized as the Office of Management and Budget under President Nixon in 1970.

Office of Management and Budget

The *Office of Management and Budget*, with a staff of about 650, is charged with the preparation of the president's annual budget proposals. The office is organized around budget categories such as National Security and International Affairs; Human and Community Affairs; Economics and Government; and Natural Resources, Energy, and Science. Budget examiners for each agency in the federal government review agency budget proposals and identify important issues for detailed analysis. The director of the Office of Management and Budget is in a key position in implementing the distribution of resources desired by the president. President Reagan's OMB director, David Stockman, played a particularly influential role in spearheading the drive for the supply-side tax cut of 1981.

Secretary of the Treasury

The third major economic adviser is the secretary of the treasury, who administers a department with more than one hundred thousand people (including the Internal Revenue Service) in addition to assuming the traditional role of personal adviser to the president on economic issues. The input of the secretary of the treasury, the chairman of the Council of Economic Advisers, and the director of the Office of Management and Budget on fiscal policy is so important that these individuals are often called the economic "*troika*."

In purest terms, the chairman of the CEA is concerned with forecasting the performance of the economy and determining the appropriate level of fiscal stimulus. The director of OMB insures that the level of government expenditures remains at the desired level, and the secretary of the treasury is concerned with developing tax policy, collecting taxes, and financing any deficit. In practice, each of the agency staffs has some expertise in all of these areas, and policy is formulated through a committee process aimed at achieving consensus or highlightling key issues that require a presidential decision.

Policy Coordination

During the Nixon administration the process of coordinating economic policy was centralized under strong secretaries of the treasury. George Schultz was given the title of "*economic czar*" by the press because of his dual roles of treasury secretary and personal adviser to the president. Schultz's successor, John Connally, continued in the role of principal coordinator of economic policy. Under this system there was considerable emphasis on the generation of a consensus policy, and there was little public debate on issues that might reflect differences of opinion within the administration. President Nixon added a *Council on International Economic Policy* (CIEP) to the Executive Office of the President in an attempt to improve the coordination of international economic policy, but CIEP did little to change the actual decision-making process. Nixon also created a Defense Programs Review Committee to review the consistency of defense programs with our other economic and domestic objectives, but as we will see at the end of this chapter this committee met infrequently and had little impact on the defense budget.

Under the Ford administration, emphasis was placed on insuring that differing viewpoints reached the president. An *Economic Policy Board* chaired by the secretary of the treasury was created to provide a formal forum for considering different viewpoints and forwarding recommendations to the president. The EPB had a staff in the White House directed by William Seidman, a close friend of the president, to provide summaries of the positions taken by different agencies. The EPB included most cabinet members with economic interests and the president's national security adviser, Henry Kissinger, as well as the director of OMB, the secretary of the treasury, and the chairman of the CEA.

The Carter administration reorganized the EPB slightly and named it the *Economic Policy Group*. The substitution of the word "group" for "board" in the title accurately suggests a less formal coordinating body. The EPG placed less emphasis on presenting a consensus position to the president, and the entire framework permitted much more public debate of key issues by the principals in the administration. Where President

Ford preferred an *oral* briefing of an Economic Policy Board *consensus*, President Carter preferred a decision process in which *written* analyses of *many* alternatives reached him. This system gave the appearance of decentralization in permitting the public expression of a variety of administration views, but it actually centralized a great deal of influence in the hands of the president since so many decisions were only made after different positions reached the "oval office." President Reagan restored a more informal policy process with more emphasis on oral briefings.

Managing Fiscal Policy

Within this overall framework of policy coordination the three agencies of the "*troika*" continue to have the greatest impact on the evolution of fiscal policy. In the last chapter we saw that fiscal policy can be used to stimulate the economy if unemployment is seen as the major problem, or to reduce aggregate demand if the problem is inflation. The dichotomy between inflation and unemployment, of course, fails to do justice to the challenge to economic policy during recent years in which the economy has been beset by unacceptable rates of both inflation and unemployment—the so-called problem of *stagflation*.

In a period of stagflation, the administration attempts to walk a difficult tightrope in an attempt to lower unemployment without adding to inflationary pressures. Such subtlety in policy is extremely difficult to manage in a bureaucracy characterized by thousands of decentralized decision centers. Instead, there is a strong tendency to "*manage by campaign*" so that the president can influence the way in which the entire bureaucracy will lean on a variety of issues. The Kennedy slogan of "getting the country moving again," the Johnson emphasis on the "Great Society," the Ford effort to "Whip Inflation Now (WIN)," and the Carter emphasis on inflation as the number one priority sent clear signals to the bureaucracy. For example, when President Carter shifted the emphasis from lowering unemployment in the first year of his administration to fighting inflation in the second, the thrust in a variety of programs changed. Regulations aimed at improving environmental quality, health, and safety came under much closer scrutiny because of the impact strict regulations would have on inflation. Few specific presidential decisions were required to reverse policy, since the weight of anti-inflationary arguments automatically increased throughout the bureaucracy. Management by campaign can be difficult to reverse if the wrong opponent is selected. The WIN campaign slowly died of its own weight as the country slipped into recession in 1974 and 1975, and unemployment became the new priority.

Yet despite the tendency to manage by campaign, there is a great deal of effort to fine-tune the economy based on recent projections of economic performance. For example, the Council of Economic Advisers constantly monitors the projections of a variety of large macroeconomic models of the economy. In the late 1970s the Data Resource Institute's model could be quickly accessed with "on-line" computer terminals at the Council, and the model's multipliers could be used to estimate the impact that different economic policies would have on the future performance of the economy. There are several large (several hundred equation) computer models of the economy which are widely used in the government and in private research centers to predict the performance of the economy. The Brookings Institution, the Wharton School of Business at the University of Pennsylvania, and the University of Michigan, in addition to the Data Resource Institute, maintain some of the more widely used models. In addition, there are numerous smaller models, although they are generally less useful in policy formation, because they contain so few policy variables. They are widely used, however, to predict changes in the overall level of national output. For example, the St. Louis Federal Reserve Bank maintains an eight equation model of the economy that emphasizes the importance of changes in the stock of money on the level of output and prices.

The projections of the macroeconomic computer models are supplemented with a great deal of qualitative evaluation of specific sectors of the economy in order to produce the best possible estimates of future economic performance. These estimates are continuously revised throughout the year in a series of meetings of the members of the "troika." The final estimates of the year, produced in November and December, become the basis of the president's budget submissions to Congress and the annual Economic Report of the President.

The annual budget prepared by OMB and the Economic Report produced by CEA are carefully coordinated to insure that the fiscal policy reflected by the budget is justified by the economic analysis in the Economic Report. These two documents are the clearest statements of economic policy produced by the administration each year, and they should be read together to gain an understanding of the priorities being established and the administration's arguments for those priorities. While the economic analysis is carefully presented to support precisely the level of fiscal stimulus provided in the budget, the actual budget is the result of an unending struggle for funds that continues in the executive branch until the last minute before the budget goes to press, and then shifts to the Congress until funds for the actual budget are finally appropriated. In the next section we turn to the budgetary process in the executive branch and the coordination of that process by the Office of Management and Budget.

THE EXECUTIVE BUDGET

The budget prepared by the Office of Management and Budget for submission by the president to Congress each January is a legislative proposal. Prior to 1921 there was no unified federal budget and agencies negotiated directly with Congress for funds. In 1921 the Bureau of the Budget was created to give the president greater influence on the budget and hence on the evolution of national priorities which it reflects. In 1970 the Bureau of the Budget was reorganized as the Office of Management and Budget, emphasizing the role of the agency as one of the president's major means of managing the burgeoning federal bureaucracy.

The budget includes both revenues and expenditures, but these two halves of the budget are separated both in the process of analysis in the executive branch and in subsequent review in the Congress. Revenues are the result of tax laws which are subject to infrequent change, and therefore revenues for the next fiscal year can be forecast based on the structure of those laws. Although many expenditures are also fixed by law, and are therefore "*uncontrollable*" without changes in legislation, a portion of the expenditures may be altered each year. The budget process is therefore dominated by analysis of the appropriate level of total government expenditures and the composition of those expenditures.

The budgetary process in the executive branch may be outlined quite quickly. The process begins in the spring before the budget is submitted. At this point the director of OMB, the secretary of the treasury, and the chairman of the Council of Economic Advisers (the "troika") recommend initial overall budget guidelines to to the president. Simultaneously, budget examiners in OMB begin evaluation of programs in their areas of responsibility, identify budget issues, and submit their own ideas for budget revision. In the summer before budget submittal, the president announces his preliminary fiscal policy appraisal and sets general budget guidelines for OMB. In the fall the OMB examiners review the budget proposals of each agency and the director of OMB then submits his budget recommendations to the president. The phase of the process taking place in the summer and early fall is highlighted by continuing negotiation between the staff of OMB and the budgetary staffs at the agencies. As fall approaches the budget review process escalates to a level at which agency heads and their staffs deal with associate directors in OMB.

Negotiations over the composition of the budget continue into November, even as the "troika's" economic forecasts are being revised and the president is evaluating his fiscal policy. In December the final decisions on economic policy are developed and the final changes in agency budgets are made so as to bring the level of government expenditures in line with the revised fiscal policy. On the 15th day after Congress convenes in January, the president submits his budget proposal.

In our forthcoming discussions of program budgeting and zero-based budgeting we will have more to say about the details of the budgeting process in the executive branch, but before doing so we will trace the carefully prepared executive budget through the Congress. As a result of the reforms to the Congressional budgetary process of the 1970s, we will find that there are strong parallels between the executive and Congressional procedures.

THE CONGRESSIONAL BUDGET

In the early 1970s President Nixon *impounded*, or refused to spend, funds that had been appropriated for specific projects by Congress, on the grounds that the approved levels of spending would be inflationary. The success of his impoundments was the result, in part, of a widespread recognition that the budgetary procedures used in Congress did not place sufficient emphasis on the economic impact of the entire budget. At that time, the President's budget submission was sent directly to the legislative committees in the House of Representatives to "authorize" the expenditure of funds for specific programs up to a given ceiling, and then to the appropriation committees in the House to designate a precise level of approved spending. The same process was then repeated in the Senate, differences were resolved in joint committees, the pieces were put back together to form the total budget, and the entire package was returned to the president for his signature. Revenues were considered in a completely separate process through the House Ways and Means Committee and the Senate Finance Committee. As a result of this extreme specialization of function, the fiscal stimulus provided by the approved budget was not a major concern of or constraint on the ultimate budget.

Selective impoundment of funds by the president is obviously a powerful tool in modifying government priorities. The precedents for such impoundment go back to President Jefferson, and in a 1921 memorandum the first director of the Bureau of the Budget argued that Congressional appropriations are ceilings, not directives. The Employment Act of 1946 provided a basis for using impoundment as an anti-inflationary tool. The issue of impoundment came to a head in a clash over the Federal Water Pollution Control Act Amendments of 1972. Congress appropriated $24.7 billion to clean up the nation's waterways by 1985. The amendments were passed on October 4, 1972, and vetoed by the president on October 17 on the grounds that the expenditures would be inflationary. On October 18 Congress overrode the veto by a vote of 247–23 in the House, and 52–12 in the Senate. On November 20 the director of the Environmental Protection Agency, William Ruckelshaus, announced that only $2 billion of the $5 billion appropriated for fiscal year 1973, and $3 billion of the $6 billion for fiscal year 1971 would actually be available to the states.

President Nixon's impoundment of funds led the Congress to establish a Joint Study Committee on Budget Control in 1972 in order to determine what steps should be taken to expand Congressional control of the budgetary process. The ultimate result of that study was the Budget Control Act of 1974 which established a new committee structure, revised the budget timetable, and provided for ceilings on overall spending, revenue, and deficits through a process of joint budget resolutions.

The new organization established a Budget Committee in each house and a Congressional Budget Office. The Budget Committees were designed to guide each house in its consideration of the appropriate level of fiscal stimulus that should be provided by the budget based on an analysis of current and projected economic conditions. In addition to the staff of each Budget Committee, the new organization provided for a Congressional Budget Office to provide economic analyses in support of the budgetary process. The CBO has a staff of about 200 of which some two-thirds are professional economists or budget specialists. The CBO monitors the forecasts of the major computer models of the economy, reviews the projections made by the executive branch, and provides its own estimates of future economic performance. As a result, the CBO plays much the same role in Congressional review of the budget as the Council of Economic Advisers plays in the formulation of the executive budget, and since the CBO staff is much larger it also provides many specific budget analyses similar to those provided by the Office of Management and Budget in the executive branch.

The Congressional Budget Office, however, does not serve the same function as OMB in coordinating the budgetary process. This function of imposing fiscal responsibility on the consideration of the detailed components of the budget is executed by the Budget Committees in each house. Under the revised Congressional timetable (presented in Table 7.2), by April 15 each year the Budget Committees analyze the initial reports of the other committees and the Congressional Budget Office, and report the first concurrent resolution proposing a level of government expenditures, receipts, and deficits consistent with overall economic objectives. The first concurrent resolution on the budget is approved by about the 15th of May at the same

---

Table 7.2

Congressional Budget Process Timetable

1. November 10	President submits current services budget.
2. 15th day after Congress meets	President submits his budget.
3. March 15	Committees and joint committees submit reports to Budget Committees
4. April 1	Congressional Budget Office submits report to Budget Committees.
5. April 15	Budget Committees report first concurrent resolution on the budget to their respective Houses.
6. May 15	Committees report bills and resolutions authorizing new budget authority.
	Congress completes action on first concurrent resolution on the budget.
7. 7th day after Labor Day	Congress completes action on bills and resolutions providing new budget authority and new spending authority.
8. September 15	Congress completes action on second required concurrent resolution on the budget.
9. September 25	Congress completes action on reconciliation bill or resolution, or both, implementing second required concurrent resolution.
10. October 1	Fiscal year begins.

---

time that the legislative committees are reporting out the new "budget authority," or ceilings, for each program. This separation of authorization from appropriation remains a key aspect of the process. The process of deciding on specific levels of *spending authority* takes place in the appropriations committees, or, more specifically, in the subcommittees of these committees which consider specific areas of spending. About one week after Labor Day Congress completes action, authorizing the funding of approved programs and appropriating specific spending authority to those programs. By the middle of September the Congress acts on the second concurrent budget resolution, which may revise the fiscal targets based on changing analysis of economic conditions. By the end of September the Congress completes action, reconciling approved levels of spending and receipts with the fiscal limits set by the second concurrent resolution. On October 1 the new fiscal year begins, and assuming the appropriations bills are signed by the president, spending begins at the new authorized levels. The process of implementing the budget and controlling the level of expenditures then reverts to the executive branch in general, and the Department of Treasury in particular.

This iterative process of setting tentative budget ceilings, reviewing specific appropriations, revising the ceilings based on shifting economic conditions, and then reconciling spending authority with the revised constraints, has made the entire budgetary process in Congress far more responsbile. The budget as a whole may be defended as consistent with overall economic policy as well as relative government priorities. The Budget Committee evaluation is central to this process, and its guidance on overall ceilings as well as ceilings for specific functional areas in the budget (e.g., national defense, international affairs, agriculture, health, income security) has had a major impact on the budgetary process. The evidence to date shows that the budget timetable has been maintained and that the concurrent budget resolutions have acted as an effective constraint on the total level of spending.

AN OVERVIEW OF THE BUDGETARY PROCESS

Any budgeting process is concerned with identifying objectives, planning programs to meet those objectives, and allocating funds to those programs on an annual basis. The federal budgeting process emphasizes incremental additions to current spending levels, continuous interaction between the legislative and executive branches, the distribution of spending rather than the efficiency of specific programs, and the near term consequences of budgeting decisions. In addition, the process develops a momentum of its own, and it may take a new president years actually to gain control of the executive budget submissions.

Incrementalism

Despite continuing attempts to use formal analytical techniques to decide on the composition of the budget, the budget process remains essentially "incremental." One reason for this is the time constraint on key budget analysts and decision makers. It is simply not possible to review every category of government expenditures in detail each year. Another reason for incrementalism is that any government program immediately builds a supporting constituency composed of the beneficiaries. Thus government programs are easy to initiate and expand, but very difficult to reduce or eliminate. In addition, as Peter F. Drucker observed in his analysis of the bureaucracy and the budget, incremental budgeting is reinforced by a psychology that sees an expanding agency budget as a measure of success. Drucker noted that, "The importance of a budget-based institution is measured essentially by the size of its budget and the size of its staff. To achieve results with a smaller budget or a smaller staff is, therefore, not 'performance.' It might actually endanger the institution."[3] The dominance of the role of incrementalism in the budget may be judged by the fervor with which alternate approaches to budgeting are continuously presented as revolutionary concepts. This was true of program budgeting in the 1960s and zero-based budgeting in the 1970s. In each case there is little evidence of a dramatic departure from traditional incrementalism in the budgeting process.

Of course the quantitative evidence of incrementalism, which is based on a quick scan of the annual budget totals for virtually any agency, can be deceiving. Analysis of the budget does produce changes in the composition of spending on specific programs, and on rare occasions a program may actually be eliminated. But the bulk of this analysis is on the budgetary increment reflected in the addition of new programs or the expansion of existing programs. Thus to argue that the budgetary process is incremental does not necessarily imply that it is not analytical.

While the executive branch often analyzes program outputs in making its budgetary decisions, the budget is presented to Congress in terms of *"line items"* (manpower, maintenance, procurement) in the form of inputs rather than outputs. This approach tends to reinforce an incremental analysis of the budget and to focus attention on personnel increases and major new capital expenditures.

As part of the new budget timetable, the president provides Congress each November with an estimate of the cost of simply continuing current programs, adjusted for inflation, into the next fiscal year. This *"Current Services Budget"* provides a baseline against which proposals for new expenditures may be compared. This approach, which was popularized by the studies of the Brookings Institute in the early 1970s, emphasizes the increment to the budget and focuses analysis on changes in existing programs and the room for new initiatives in the budget. A large portion of the budget is *"uncontrollable"* in the next fiscal year, since expenditures are mandated by existing legislation. The current services budget for fiscal year 1980 was estimated at $544.1 billion, compared with the administration's ultimate budget proposal for fiscal year 1980 of $531.6 billion.[4] Clearly the administration's proposals left little room for new initiatives.

A Process of Continuous Interaction

The neat progression of the budgetary timetable from initial formulation of proposals in the executive branch to ultimate appropriations by Congress may tend to distort many of the important dynamic interactions of the process. For example, as the Office of Management and Budget is reviewing agency proposals for fiscal year 1984, the Congress will be evaluating authorizations and appropriations for fiscal year 1983. The individuals involved with the executive budget proposals must monitor and testify in both processes.

The executive branch will be fine-tuning its proposals for fiscal year 1984 before it knows the fate of its proposals for fiscal year 1983. The appropriation process does not end with the beginning of the new fiscal year. Supplemental appropriations may be requested by the executive branch to fund expenses that were not anticipated at the time of the initial budget submission. In many ways the budget process is less a sequential progression from executive branch proposals to Congressional appropriations, than a continuing process of interaction among the key participants.

As a result, there is a tendency for the participants to see the budgetary process from an historic perspective. In this sense certain portions of the budget may be emphasized in a given year, since the participants know that a major review of some other program dominated an earlier budget cycle. The participants are apt to emphasize items that have been changed significantly since the last review, rather than beginning the analysis from scratch each year. Similarly, the executive budget is apt to be influenced by the expected fate of proposals in Congressional review. Historically the executive budget has been expanded during the budget process in Congress, and administration officials may well cut programs below desired levels in their proposals knowing that they will be expanded in Congress.[5]

The budgetary process is also highly personal. The administration officials who provide input to the executive budget also testify before Congress on the executive proposals. Such testimony is coordinated by the Office of Management and Budget, and the official statements of members of the executive branch are expected to be consistent with the executive's proposal. In practice, testimony before the legislative and appropriations committees begins with the official position, but personal views are then interjected in response to questioning. For example, in an exchange recounted by Aaron Wildavsky, the Senate Appropriations Subcommittee was conducting hearings on the Navy's Polaris submarine budget. Senator Ellender asked Admiral Burke how the House subcommittee came to the conclusion that the Navy wanted nine submarines, when the budget proposal called for only two. When asked if the admiral had suggested that nine was the appropriate number, Burke replied, "No, sir; however, let me amplify that. This number was brought out under specific questioning by the Defense Subcommittee of the House. We had recommended to the secretary of defense that there be nine."[6] The personal relationships established between administration officials and key congressmen can have an important impact on ultimate budgetary decisions.

As a continuous process of interaction between key executive officials and the Congress, the budgetary process is intensely political. As Frederick Mosher noted in a "Letter to Editor-in-Chief" of the *Public Administration Review*, " . . . the budget process is a 'due process' of administration wherein the facts, the analyses, the interests, the politics and the prejudices of people enter."[7] Economists traditionally differentiate between decisions that affect the efficiency with which outputs are produced from the available inputs (positive economics) and decisions concerning how the outputs of the economy are to be distributed (normative economics). Although efficiency considerations can have an impact on some budgetary decisions in which we are comparing two similar outputs which are designed to reach the same social objectives, most budgetary decisions concern the allocation of funds over programs with very different objectives. The ways in which the budget decisions are made, therefore, have important normative implications. Centralization of the budgetary process might make it simpler to manage, but it would also alter the pattern of checks and balances that determine the distribution of outputs consistent with our democratic values.

The Attempts at Long-Term Planning

Despite continuing attempts to refocus the budget on long-term national priorities, the current process continues to be dominated by concern for the next fiscal year. The political exigencies of reelection tend to reinforce this short-run concern, as does our limited ability to forecast the performance of the economy more than one or possibly two years in the future. Although budget projections for the next five fiscal years are now included in all budget documents, this is really an extension of the "current services" budget approach. That is, the budget projections portray the costs of continuing current programs and the future costs of new initiatives in the budget, but the budgeting process does not address the long-range consequences of current decisions in any meaningful way.

For example, the *Humphrey-Hawkins Full Employment and Balanced Growth Act of 1978* is an attempt to force an expansion of the planning process to incorporate long-term goals. The act requires long-term goals for unemployment, national output, productivity, and inflation, and a series of reports on how these goals are to be met. In practice, the forecasts for the future performance of the economy simply assume that the economic goals will be met, but there is no adjustment in programs to see that the goals (which are currently quite unrealistic as specified in the act) are actually met. Indeed the Humphrey-Hawkins Act may actually have made our long-term planning far less useful in considering the current budget, since the act mandates such unrealistic planning assumptions.[8]

Finally, the budgetary process has a strong momentum of its own. When a new president is elected in November, the executive budget for the next fiscal year has already been largely formulated. The new chief executive has only a few weeks in January to prepare modifications in the budget proposal before the annual budget address to Congress. The first budget prepared by his administration is not proposed until the following January, and much of that proposal is dictated by prior legislation, which established existing programs. Thus a new president only gains real control of the budgetary process near the end of his first, and perhaps last, term.

In summary, the budgetary process is an intensely political activity which is characterized by continuous interaction between the executive and legislative branches. The personal relationships of the key actors in the process are extremely important in providing a flow of information between the two branches. The momentum of the budget is staggering, and the emphasis of the budgetary process is on increments over prior levels of expenditure.

But perhaps the most obvious fact about the budget process over the last two decades is that it is continuously being "reformed." We have seen that the Congressional reforms of the 1970s have had an important impact on the ability of Congress to keep fiscal policy in line with changing economic objectives. Next we will examine the impact of two other "reforms" of budgeting in the executive branch: program budgeting and zero-based budgeting.

Program Budgeting

On August 25, 1965, President Johnson issued an executive order requiring the heads of all executive agencies to introduce "*program budgeting*." Although there is no one simple definition of program budgeting, the vast literature on the subject stresses four major characteristics:

1. Decisions on expenditures should be based on output categories, such as health care, or programs, rather than the "*line item*" inputs, such as pay or maintenance, of conventional budgeting.
2. The planning process supporting the actual budget submission should seek out alternative ways of meeting designated objectives by comparing the costs and the benefits of each alternative.
3. The full life-cycle cost of accomplishing the objective should be considered, rather than only those expenses incurred in the first few fiscal years.
4. The relationship of each program with specific objectives should be highlighted so that the budget may be allocated to those programs that make the greatest contribution to the stated objectives.

Program budgeting came to the government as a revolutionary idea produced at the RAND Corporation, and implemented by then Secretary of Defense Robert McNamara's comptroller, Charles J. Hitch. Many analysts have argued that the approach was not all that revolutionary, that it simply emphasized particular steps in the budgetary process, and that the literature on the subject goes back much further than the early RAND studies.[9] But the important point is that as the concept was applied in the Department of Defense, program budgeting marked a sharp departure from normal practice. As Wildavsky observed in 1974, program budgeting is the antithesis of conventional practice. "Interestingly enough, the distinguishing characteristics of the program procedure are precisely the reverse of those of the traditional practice. Federal budgeting today is incremental rather than comprehensive, calculated in bits and pieces rather than as a whole, and veils policy implications rather than emphasizing them."[10]

The idea of the "*program*" is at the heart of this approach. The program is a package of related end-products that contribute to a specific mission of the agency. In the Department of Defense beginning in 1961 the major output programs were designated as: strategic forces; general purpose forces; intelligence and communciations; airlift and sealift; guard and reserve forces; research and development; central supply and maintenance; training, medical, and other general personnel activity; administration and associated activities; and support of other nations. The program cut across conventional service (Army, Navy, and Air Force) lines, and emphasized horizontal similarities in function rather than vertical integration into the operations of specific services.

The major impact of program budgeting in the Department of Defense was a centralization of the decision-making process in the Office of the Secretary of Defense. This centralization occurred because the program structure emphasizes functions that transcend traditional service boundaries, and because the process emphasizes quantitative estimates of the effectiveness and costs of different weapon systems. The analysts assembled under the assistant secretary for systems analysis in the Department of Defense provided the critical quantitative evaluation favored by Secretary McNamara.

The system as applied in DoD was known as the *Planning, Programming and Budgeting System* (PPBS). The system was and is most effective in dealing with weapon systems with comparable outputs. It has been less effective in dealing with force structure questions where the outputs cannot be easily quantified (for example, General Purpose Forces). In addition, Wildavsky stresses three major problems with program budgeting compared to the conventional approach: the process decreases agreement among the participants, increases the burden of calculation on the partcipants, and the inevitable centralization of decision-making changes the outputs of the budgeting process.[11] These problems are more pronounced when the responsibility for related activities cuts across agency lines.

Despite President Johnson's directive and some initial flirtations with program budgeting in the Departments of Agriculture and State, the initiative to spread program budgeting throughout the government slowly died and was not revived by the Nixon administration. Its demise *outside* the Department of Defense may be traced to a resistance to any reorganization of governmental function along program lines, the difficulties of defining useful programs, and the lukewarm support of the revised approach in the then Bureau of the Budget. Programs, like beauty, are in the eye of the bcholder. There is nothing sacred about a particular combination of functions. The program approach, therefore, clarifies certain relationships, but it obscures others. As Mosher observes, in the case of many programs that cut across the responsibilities of different agencies, the first decision-maker with responsbility for the entire program may well be the president. "While some reorganizations in this direction would undoubtedly be helpful, the objectives of different organizations will inevitably cross over into others, however they are defined; all have multiple purposes. All have, and inevitably will have, their own committees and subcommittees in Congress, including the appropriations subcommittees. How then to develop rational program budgets?"[12] For a while the Bureau of the Budget issued vague guidelines on the implementation of program budgeting, but conventional budgets continued to be issued as well, and eventually the facade of program budgeting was dropped.

Program budgeting remains at the Department of Defense, but it has been only an internal management technique. The annual budget submissions were never changed from the conventional line item (personnel, procurement, maintenance) format, and Congress never adopted the program budget as a way of analyzing defense expenditures. Program budgeting in the rest of the federal government ended, "not with a bang, but a whimper." The fad shifted from incremental additions to programs to "zero-based" review of the entire budget each year.

ZERO-BASED BUDGETING

Zero-based budgeting came to Washington from the Texas Instrument Corporation via the State of Georgia. Peter A. Pyhrr used a process for evaluating the 1970 budget for the staff and research divisions of

Texas Instruments and reported the results in the Harvard Business Review. Jimmy Carter, then Governor of Georgia, read the article and asked Pyhrr to assist him in implementing zero-based budgeting for the State of Georgia in fiscal year 1973. In 1977 President Carter brought this approach to the federal government.

A short extract from Pyhrr's 1973 book outlines the approach.

> The process requires each manager to justify his entire budget request in detail, and puts the burden of proof on him to justify why he should spend any money. Each manager must prepare a "decision package" for each activity or operation, and this package includes an analysis of cost, purpose, alternative courses of action, measures of performance, consequences of not performing the activity, and benefits. Managers . . . must identify a minimum level of spending—often about 75% of their current operating level—and then identify in separate decision packages the costs and benefits of additional levels of spending for that activity. This analysis forces every manager to consider and evaluate a level of spending lower than his current operating level; gives management the alternative of eliminating an activity or choosing from several levels of effort; and allows tremendous trade-offs and shifts in expenditure levels among organizational units.[13]

The concept is simple enough. Managers start at the lowest "cost centers" for each activity in the organization, isolate the costs associated with various levels of operation, and outline why each activity exists and how much it costs. The *decision package*, which goes to the next highest manager in the organization, evaluates the implications of different levels of operation and establishes spending priorities. As this is done at higher and higher management levels, priorities are revised, the different activities are reviewed, and funds are finally allocated in the revised budget.

Such a review can break down conventional barriers to the exchange of such information in an organization, and may permit substantial reallocations of funds. In 1977 Southern California Edison reported that it was saving $300,000 per year as the result of a new maintenance approach suggested in its zero-based review, and Westinghouse Electric Corporation's turbine division may have saved $4.2 million in overhead costs in 1976 from a zero-based budget review. But such reviews are time-consuming and involve a huge amount of paperwork. A Navy experiment in zero-basing its $10-billion dollar operations and maintenance budget produced justification documents some 2,000 pages long, compared with its normal submissions to Congress of 150 pages.[14]

In the spring of 1977 President Carter directed all federal agencies and departments to zero-base their fiscal year 1979 budget requests. A bulletin from the Office of Management and Budget to the heads of executive departments and establishments outlined the required steps of:

1. Identifying objectives and key performance indicators;
2. Identifying decision units or "cost centers";
3. Preparing decision packages including minimum levels of expenditure, current levels, and other appropriate increments;
4. Ranking decision packages;
5. Reviewing the rankings of subordinate managers.

The bulletin identified the expected benefits to the government as: focusing the process on a comprehensive analysis of objectives; improving coordination of program and activity planning, evaluation, and budgeting; identifying trade-offs between programs; and providing managers at all levels with better information on budget priorities.[15]

At this point it is not clear whether or not zero-based budgeting will have an important impact on the budgeting process in the executive branch, but the odds are definitely against it. Zero-based budgeting faces the same kind of bureaucratic resistance and inertia that program budgeting encountered. The problems of defining programs, now "activity centers," remain under the new approach. The sheer workload of an annual review of every federal program will be staggering, and whatever format is used in the executive branch, the budget must still be defended in Congress using the conventional line-item approach.

The reports on the impact of zero-based budgeting in Georgia are not encouraging. According to Georgia's legislative budget officer, Pete Hackney, "Zero-based budgeting exists in name only." He should know, because he is the official who receives the executive branch analyses and then disregards them; the legislature continues to use the line item approach.[16]

The returns on zero-based budgeting are certainly not yet in. A variety of states and hundreds of companies are experimenting with it and many are reporting successes, at least from a one-time zero-based review. In addition, the zero-based approach at the federal level had the strong support of President Carter and the Office of Management and Budget during his administration. Yet it would be surprising if the incrementalism of conventional budgeting, with all of its bureaucratic and organizational support, could be overcome by a new packaging of the analysis performed in the executive branch.

Some experts on the zero-based approach are not optimistic. According to Robert N. Anthony, "Compared with the procedures that are already in use in the federal government, it has nothing of substance to offer. The new parts are not good, and the good parts are not new."[17] Anthony, a professor of management at Harvard Business School, is particularly concerned with the insufficient time for such a review and the simultaneous consideration of both planning and budgeting decisions. But as Anthony notes, there is also a distinct possibility that zero-based budgeting can be used as a campaign slogan to press for more effective review of current programs, to emphasize outputs rather than inputs, and to emphasize measurable results.

CONCLUSION

The campaigns for program budgeting and zero-based budgeting were attempts to focus attention on particular aspects of the budgeting process. Their emphasis on outputs, alternatives, and efficiency places them in contrast to the conventional budgetary process with its emphasis on inputs, increments, and distribution. Efficiency seems inevitably to argue for centralization, but the democratic notion of balancing outputs over competing interests may be more consistent with a decentralized process. We may therefore anticipate continuing claims for greater emphasis on efficiency to be countered with arguments for greater concern for distribution. In "pure" economics, concerns for efficiency and distribution may be separated, but when it comes to the operation of actual organizations the two issues may not be independent.

The momentum of prior budgetary decisions is overwhelming. There is little concern in the budgetary process for adjustments in that momentum that will only be achieved in the future, despite the continuing argument for reform in that direction. Budget decisions are closely tied to the *short term* performance of the economy. In the executive branch, the Office of Management and Budget provides the link between fiscal policy planning by the "troika" and the actual budget proposals. In the Congress, the Congressional Budget Office monitors economic conditions and provides analysis of the appropriate level of fiscal stimulus. The Budget Committees in each house use this input and their own analysis in coordinating joint resolutions that link the Congressional budgeting process to fiscal objectives. Thus the entire budgetary process is dominated by the momentum of prior spending, modified by adjustments to bring overall fiscal policy into line with short-term economic objectives.

In the next chapter we will discuss the role of the Department of Defense in the budgeting process. Because defense expenditures account for a large portion of government goods and services, and because the pace of those expenditures may be altered in the near term, the defense budget is closely tied to the level of fiscal stimulus required by our economic objectives.

NOTES

1 Milton Friedman, "Ford's Budget," *Newsweek* (February 9, 1976), p. 64.

2 Some of these ideas on economic advising were drawn from a paper presented by Paul W. McCracken, President Nixon's first Council chairman, at the Princeton University Conference on "Advising the President," Princeton, New Jersey, October 31, 1975.

3 Peter F. Drucker, *Management: Tasks, Responsibilities, Practices* (New York: Harper and Row, 1974), p. 142.

4 *Special Analyses Budget of the United States Government, Fiscal Year 1980* (Washington, D.C.: Government Printing Office, 1979), p. 14.

5 See, for example, Norman Jones, "Playing Charades with the Budget," *Business Week* (January 26, 1976), p. 29.

6 Aaron Wildavsky, *The Politics of the Budgetary Process*, 2nd ed. (Boston: Little Brown and Co., 1974), p. 89.

7 Frederick C. Mosher, "Letter to Editor-in-Chief," *Public Administration Review* (March, 1967), p. 68.

8 See, for example, Herbert Stein, "Statement Presented to the Committee on the Budget of the House of Representatives" (February 7, 1979), reprinted in the *American Enterprise Institute Economist* (February, 1979).

9 See, for example, Frederick C. Mosher, *op. cit.,* pp. 67–70.

10 Aaron Wildavsky, *op. cit.,* p. 135.

11 *Ibid.,* pp. 189–194.

12 Frederick C. Mosher, *op. cit.,* p. 68.

13 Peter A. Pyhrr, *Zero-Base Budgeting* (New York: John Wiley & Sons, 1973), pp. xi–xii.

14 "What It Means to Build a Budget from Zero," *Business Week* (April 18, 1977), p. 160.

15 "Zero-Base Budgeting," Bulletin No. 77–9, Office of Management and Budget (April 19, 1977).

16 "What It Means to Build a Budget from Zero," *op. cit.,* p. 162.

17 Robert W. Anthony, "Zero-Base Budgeting is a Fraud," *The Wall Street Journal* (April 27, 1977), p. 22.

SELECTED REFERENCES

Peter F. Drucker, *Management: Tasks, Responsibilities, Practices* (New York: Harper and Row, 1974).

Peter A. Pyhrr, *Zero-Base Budgeting* (New York: John Wiley & Sons, 1973).

Charles L. Schultze, *The Politics and Economics of Public Spending* (Washington, D.C.: Brookings Institution, 1968).

Chapter 8
The Defense Budget and the Impact of Defense Spending

INTRODUCTION

The ultimate economic constraint on the level of outlays for national security is the nation's productive capacity, or potential Gross National Product. This level of output assumes that all of the nation's resources are used to capacity in the production process. In practice this level of output is rarely reached. Usually, some of the nation's capital and labor go unemployed or underemployed, and the actual GNP is less than the potential.

If we were concerned with the limitations on mobilization for an extended, major conflict, the nation's potential to produce would be the relevant contraint. In addition, we would be concerned with the sectoral composition of the potential output and our ability to shift resources from private to defense production. Projections of the availability of critical supplies required for defense production would then be taken as constraints on our mobilization capacity. Many of the early texts on the economics of national security were primarily concerned with the problems of mobilization, and therefore focused on the availability of critical supplies.[1]

While the problems of mobilization remain significant, the most pressing issues concern the deterrent impact of our forces in being and their ability to contain attacks short of strategic nuclear exchanges. This emphasis on forces-in-being shifts our attention from the capacity of the nation under full mobilization, to its capacity to support the required level of forces on a sustained basis. The achieved GNP is therefore a better measure than potential GNP of the nation's capacity for sustained defense.

There are, however, many other important claims on the nation's annual output, including consumer goods, private capital formation, and other government programs. Thus there is, in addition, a political constraint as to the share of GNP that can be made available to defense purposes. The intensity of this political constraint at any given time is clearly a response to the seriousness of the threat to national security, as perceived by national leaders and the society as a whole; in general the greater the perceived threat, the larger the share of GNP that can be made available for defense. Obviously, the basic subsistence needs of society always must be satisfied. It is important to remember, however, that even during the World War II years from 1940 to 1945, U.S. consumption levels continued to increase in real terms. The massive war effort was financed more out of expanded production than by a reduced standard of living. The fact that consumption is rarely cut to permit expanded military expenditure has led some writers to question the relevance of GNP as a measure of total economic capacity for defense. (See Chapter 25 for discussion of comparative defense spending.)

The annual federal budget defines the actual limitations on defense outlays in any given year. In this chapter we will examine how the Department of Defense fits into the general scheme of the federal budget, and how the defense budget is allocated to different programs. We will pay particular attention to the continuing impact of the Planning, Programming, and Budgeting System (PPBS) introduced in the early 1960s.

The level of spending for national security is one of the most controversial political issues of our day. Proposed defense spending for fiscal year 1983 was roughly $258 billion, a huge amount by any standard.[2] The changing level of defense spending, however, is not accurately depicted by changes in current dollar outlays, because spending is influenced by inflation as well as real purchases, and the capacity of the economy to support defense outlays is also constantly shifting. Later in the chapter we will propose measures to assist in evaluating the relative size of defense outlays.

Finally we will turn to the economic impacts of the defense sector on the rest of the economy. This issue concerns not only the current "opportunity costs" or alternatives that must be foregone to support defense spending, but also the impact of defense spending on the future productive capacity of the economy and its distribution. While arguments about the "military–industrial complex" are often more emotional than enlightening, we will consider some of the major impacts of the size and distribution of defense outlays and propose a format for debating the issues.

DEFENSE BUDGETING

The budgetary process as a whole should address the objectives of defense spending, how different levels of spending allocated in the most efficient way to competing defense programs affect progress toward those objectives, the value to society of the alternative uses of funds in the public and private sectors, and the appropriate balance between defense spending and other priorities. Defense "requirements" cannot be determined solely from an analysis of the capabilities of potential enemies and the force levels which would be needed to meet any contingency. The most we can hope for is an analysis of the risk that will remain after a given level of spending has been allocated to defense. Thus each of the budgeting questions is related to all of the others. We must know our objectives in order to evaluate the contribution of different levels of spending to national security, and to evaluate the contribution of each level of spending we must know the most efficient way of allocating funds over different defense programs. To compare the return on defense spending with the return on other government programs or with increased spending in the private sector, we must have a comprehensive view of all government programs. Knowing the opportunity costs of defense spending will help us to determine how much risk should be accepted in reaching our national security objectives.

The Traditional Budgeting Process

The information needed to determine the appropriate level of defense expenditures should be organized to show how increments in spending will move the nation closer to its security objectives. The traditional approach to budgeting, however, which was outlined in Chapter 7, tends to submerge the linkage of outlays to objectives. The traditional process centers the budget debate on line item entries such as personnel and procurement, rather than the expected outputs of agency programs. In the Congressional budget process outlays are first authorized for different purposes in the legislative committees (the House and Senate Armed Services Committees) and then the authority to obligate funds for specific line items is set by the Appropriations Committees (and particularly the specialized subcommittees).

Note that the final approval to commit funds, or "obligational authority," extends over several fiscal years. For example, funds for fiscal year 1982 were obligated by Congressional actions going back to 1976. About one-third of annual defense expenditures are based on the authorizations of earlier fiscal years, and two-thirds are based on authorizations passed in the same fiscal year.[3] Thus in any given year defense outlays are different from the "obligational authority" appropriated by Congress in that year.

If we examine the defense budget from the traditional perspective of line items, we will quickly discover that line item entries tell us very little about defense programs. Figure 8.1 describes the levels of defense obligational authority for 1980, 1981, and 1982 by appropriation category. Note that each of the appropriation categories represents an *input* of personnel, equipment, research, or maintenance, rather than an *out-*

put of some defense program. The link between objectives and outlays in the traditional budgeting process is obviously a bit hazy, and this formulation of the budget suggests why the budget review centers on increments to specific input categories.

Table 8.1
Department of Defense Budget by Appropriation Category: 1980–1982
(Billions of Current Dollars)

Appropriation Title	Current Dollars Total Obligational Authority		
	FY 1980	FY 1981	FY 1982
Military Personnel	31.1	36.7	43.0
Retired Pay	11.9	13.7	15.0
Operation and Maintenance	46.6	55.2	63.0
Procurement	35.3	47.8	65.4
Research, Development, Training & Evaluation	13.5	16.6	20.0
Military Construction	2.3	3.4	5.1
Family Housing	1.6	2.0	2.3
Revolving Management Funds	——	.5	.5
TOTAL	142.2	176.1	214.2

Note: Totals may not add due to rounding.

Source: Caspar W. Weinberger, *Department of Defense Annual Report, 1983,* January 31, 1982, p. A-1.

The Planning, Programming, and Budgeting System

In the early 1960s Secretary of Defense McNamara introduced a Planning, Programming and Budgeting System (PPBS), which was designed to emphasize the link between planning and budgeting by examining the budget in terms of output related programs (see Chapter 7 for discussion of PPBS). Under PPBS, increments to programs were considered in the planning phase, and these increments were then translated into line item entries for the traditional budget submission. With minor changes the PPBS approach introduced by McNamara is still in use today.

Table 8.2 outlines the defense budget for fiscal years 1981 to 1983 in terms of ten output oriented programs. Note that under this formulation less than 10 percent of the budget is allocated to strategic forces (ICBM's, Trident submarines, intercontinental bombers), and about 40 percent goes to general purpose forces (fighter wings, naval forces, Army and Marine divisions). The program categories give us a clearer idea of how defense funds are allocated by function, and provide a clearer link to our defense objectives.

Each program is divided into subprograms (e.g., Army forces—divisions, brigades, combat support forces—under General Purpose Forces) and subprograms are further divided into program elements (e.g., Army battalions). The Department of Defense's Five Year Defense Progam (FYDP) spells out the projected levels of forces and weapons systems in each program element over the next five fiscal years and the associated levels of required expenditure. The annual planning and programming debate within the Department of Defense centers on how programs relate to current defense objectives and how defense funds should be allocated over the different programs. These decisions, made in the context of the FYDP become the basis for the annual budget negotiated between the Department of Defense and the Office of Management and Budget, and ultimately for the executive branch's submissions to Congress. As noted earlier, however, the actual submission to Congress and the subsequent debate in Congress is still based on the line item format.

Our current budgetary process is designed to handle incremental changes in the balance among competing programs. Initial fiscal guidance comes to DoD from the Office of Management and Budget, based on the initial analysis of our fiscal policy objectives and prior levels of defense spending. This fiscal guidance is used along with the policy and strategy guidance of the Secretary of Defense to constrain force structure planning conducted by the Joint Chiefs of Staff, and the programming of outlays by the services. An iterative exchange of proposals by the services and the Secretary of Defense leads to an updating of the Five Year Defense Program. The next fiscal year of the FYDP becomes the basis for the budgeting debate with the Office of Management and Budget. The president's ultimate budget requests for national security are derived from a balancing of the arguments provided by DoD, the review of the proposals by OMB, the overall budget constraints indicated by shifting economic conditions, and an assessment of the appropriate balance between defense and other programs.

In Congress, the defense budget faces the review of the Budget Committees in the initial competition for funds with other programs in the first concurrent resolution on the budget, and then goes through an authorization process in the Armed Services Committees and the appropriation process in the subcommittees of the Appropriations Committees. Finally the defense budget must survive the final reconciliation of the overall budget with the fiscal objectives contained in the second concurrent resolution.

Table 8.2
Department of Defense Budget by Major Program: 1981–1983
(Billions of Current Dollars)

Military Program	Current Dollars Total Obligational Authority		
	FY 1981	FY 1982	FY 1983
Strategic Forces	12.7	16.2	23.1
General Purpose Funds	68.3	88.0	106.5
Intelligence and Communications	11.2	14.0	18.0
Airlift and Sealift	2.9	4.0	4.4
Guard and Reserve Forces	9.9	11.6	14.3
Research and Development	14.2	16.9	20.1
Central Supply and Maintenance	17.6	19.2	22.2
Training, Medical and Other Personnel Activities	35.0	39.8	44.2
Administration and Associated Activities	3.4	3.6	4.3
Support of Other Nations	.9	1.0	.9
TOTAL	176.1	214.2	258.0

Source: Caspar W. Weinberger, *Department of Defense Annual Report, 1983,* January 31, 1982, p. B-7.

The Evolution of PPBS Since Secretary McNamara

In the 1960s, PPBS was a "revolution" since it tended to focus so much power in the hands of the Secretary of Defense. Programs cut across traditional service lines, and the analysis of programs emphasized quantified estimates of the costs and effectiveness of different program elements. The analysts who came from RAND with Charles Hitch, McNamara's comptroller, had a clear advantage over the services, at least initially, in performing this type of analysis.

The record of PPBS under McNamara was mixed. Perhaps the greatest successes were in the area of strategic weapons, where the outputs could be measured in comparable quantitative terms (payload, accuracy, reliability). It was less successful in the area of general purpose forces, where the outputs were less quantifiable and forces had multiple purposes. As issues concerning general purpose forces grew with the expansion of the war in Vietnam, PPBS had less impact in reallocating defense funds. The linkage of planning and programming in the initial PPBS was marred by the separation of the force structure planning of the Joint Chiefs of Staff from the actual programming decisions. The Joint Strategic Operations Plan (JSOP) of force structure requirements was completed without considering fiscal constraints, and thus it had little impact on programming decisions. Time constraints were also a major problem, and budget submissions frequently preceded completion of the Five Year Defense Program. Moreover, the presentation and debate of the budget in Congress continued in the form of traditional line items, and many members of Congress resisted the apparent centralization of authority in the hands of the Secretary of Defense.[4]

But the PPBS approach has endured at the Department of Defense, despite its failures in other areas of the federal government. A major advantage of the Department of Defense is that virtually all defense-related programs fall within its jurisdiction, and therefore meaningful programs may be created that relate DoD outputs to the DoD budget. PPBS has evolved since Secretary McNamara to permit a greater service role in the evaluation of program alternatives, and thus much of the friction of the early years has been reduced. The Joint Chiefs of Staff now first establish defense requirements without considering budget limitations and then consider fiscal constraints in recommending actual force structures and acceptable levels of risk. As a result, planning and programming are more thoroughly integrated. PPBS remains because, as its initial proponents claimed, it helps to make the planning process more realistic. As Charles Hitch observed in "Decision-Making in Large Organizations":

> The function of the program is to cost out the plans to keep them feasible and realistic, to make planners face up to the hard choices. The function of systems analysis is to get dollars into the calculations at an earlier stage—into the planning process, into the evaluation of alternative ways of achieving a military objective. You can't choose the optimal way or even a good way without knowing about the alternatives—what the alternatives achieve and what they cost.[5]

A Critique of PPBS

Although PPBS ultimately gets high scores on the planning side, its impact on budgeting is perhaps more questionable. In the budgeting process the internal defense decision meets the world of politics and program budgeting appears to have had little impact on the format or substance of the political debate. Wildavsky asserts that, " . . . PPBS did not change budgetary decisions in DoD to any significant degree. Programming has not had the anticipated effect on budgeting. Rather, the yearly appropriations have placed limitations on programs."[6] Murdock is more sanguine about the impact of PPBS but he notes that the impact of the analysis in such a system is still limited by the "political interests of participants and the personal proclivities of the central decision-maker."[7]

The real issue is whether or not the introduction of PPBS has raised the quality of debate on defense issues in determining how much defense spending is enough. Since the 1960s the locus of influence over the defense budget has shifted. In a period of expanding defense expenditures in the early 1960s Secretary McNamara had the full support of Presidents Kennedy and Johnson; the National Security Council apparatus relied upon so heavily by President Eisenhower was largely disregarded if not dismantled; and the Bureau of the Budget had a minor role in reviewing defense spending. The issues were debated by Secretary McNamara, supported by PPBS analysis, and by Congress, whose staff was limited and whose budget review process was decentralized and often ineffective. Since then there have been major changes in each of these areas.

Although the Secretary of Defense is still one of the most powerful administration officials, there is now considerably more external review of defense spending proposals within the administration than existed in the 1960s. The role of the Office of Management and Budget and of the National Security Council staff in reviewing defense proposals has expanded sharply. At the same time the quality of Congressional review of defense programs has been improved with the addition of the staffs of the Budget Committees in each house and the Congressional Budget Office (see discussion in Chapter 7). The revised budgetary process in Congress emphasizes the trade-offs among competing programs, and places these issues before the Congress as a whole, rather than merely placing it before specialized committees. The net result of these shifts is that the defense budget receives more intense scrutiny outside the Department of Defense.

PPBS has facilitated external review of defense proposals because it organizes information on spending by output programs and it shows how those programs relate to specific defense objectives. On the other hand PPBS has not shifted the focus of debate away from incremental adjustments to current programs.

This process remains incremental, but it has become more and more comprehensive in considering the trade-offs betwen defense and other government programs. The entire process also provides the Department of Defense with earlier projections of budget constraints, from the initial fiscal guidance from OMB through the indications provided by the first concurrent resolution in Congress. Earlier fiscal guidance should continue to improve the planning and budgeting process in DoD.

It remains to be seen whether or not the zero-based budgeting approach initiated by President Carter will survive under President Reagan or have much impact on the incremental approach to budgeting. As we noted in the last chapter, the pressures for incremental budgeting in our bureaucracy are enormous. But to the extent that zero-based budgeting searches for alternatives and emphasizes the impact of different levels of expenditure, it should reinforce the importance of the program budgeting approach in the Department of Defense.

In the final analysis, the critical question of how much defense spending is enough can never be answered with certainty. The central questions involve the level of risk we are willing to accept and the estimate of the opportunity costs of defense outlays. In our judgment, the Planning, Programming and Budgeting approach used by DoD provides the necessary framework for analyzing the budgetary implications of different defense programs and providing the decision makers in the budgetary process with the appropriate information on which to base their decisions on these important issues.

THE SIZE OF THE DEFENSE BUDGET

The defense budget is an extremely important assessment of our political priorities. Lawrence Korb in *The Price of Preparedness* stresses five major impacts of the defense budget:

1. Of fifteen major federal government functions, national security accounts for the second highest level of expenditures, surpassed only by income security costs.
2. The defense budget contains a large portion, over fifty percent, of the "controllable" or discretionary funds in the federal budget. Thus changes in government spending required by shifts in fiscal policy are generally absorbed in the defense budget.
3. The force structure that may be purchased with the budget reflects and constrains our national security policy.
4. Budget decisions have long term consequences. As we noted earlier, roughly one-third of the funds appropriated in any fiscal year will actually be spent in future years. The weapons systems procured in any year will affect the force structure for years to come.
5. The size and composition of our defense expenditures are taken as signals to our allies of our commitment and intentions, just as we use the budgets of our allies in interpreting the extent of their capability and commitment.[8]

We might add that the defense budget also has a significant impact on the regional and industrial composition of national output, and important consequences for our balance of payments.

As we have seen, the defense budget is subjected to thorough scrutiny in the executive branch and in Congress. Korb adds that the review also extends to numerous research institutes (e.g., the American Enterprise Institute, the Brookings Institution, the Center for Defense Information, and the National Urban Coalition), and the defense budget is a major topic in presidential campaigns and an early target for presidential action.

> In the post-World War II period, each new administration has moved quickly to reshape the defense budget drawn up by the outgoing administration. In 1953, President Eisenhower slashed $4.9 billion, or 12%, off of President Truman's proposed $40.7 billion defense budget for FY 1954. Eight years later, President Kennedy added $5.2 billion, or 12.2 percent, to President Eisenhower's proposed $42.9 billion FY 1962 budget. In 1969, President Nixon cut $1.5 billion, or 1.8 percent, from President Johnson's proposed FY 1970 budget of $83.2 billion. Within one month of taking office, President Carter reduced the Ford administration's FY 1978 budget by $2.8 billion, or 2.3 percent.[9]

Changes in the level of defense spending have important political, strategic, and economic implications, but changes in absolute levels of spending are a poor guide to the real size and impact of defense outlays. We have already considered two ways of looking at the defense budget: in terms of appropriation title, and in terms of major military programs. A glance at Table 8.2 suggests that spending on every military program increased from FY 1981 to FY 1983; the total budget expanded by almost fourteen percent in just two years from 1978 to 1980, and is projected to rise by some 47 percent from 1981 to 1983 under the Reagan buildup. During this period, however, prices increased, the size of the federal budget changed, the productive capacity of the nation increased, and military expenditures by the Soviet Union expanded. Thus our view of the changing defense budget will be influenced by the standard we use for our comparison. In this section we will use five criteria for evaluating defense outlays: the defense budget expressed in the constant dollars of some base year; defense expenditures as a share of the federal budget; defense expenditures as a percentage of federal purchases of goods and services; the defense budget as a percentage of the nation's gross national product; and defense employment as a percentage of government employment and the civilian work force.

Real Defense Expenditures

As we discussed in Chapter 6, inflation will increase the dollar value of goods and services even if the level of real output is constant. In order to net out the impact of inflation, we divide expenditures in current dollars by a price index that shows how much prices have changed compared to some base year. If we convert the total obligational authority shown in Tables 8.1 and 8.2 to constant dollars of 1980, we find that Total Obligational Authority (TOA) was $131.8 billon in fiscal year 1978, $133.2 billion in 1979, and $135.5 billion in 1980.[10] Note that our estimate of fiscal year 1978 and fiscal year 1979 authority increases when we express it in terms of the inflated 1980 dollar, but of course fiscal year 1980 expenditures are unchanged. As a result of shifting our dollar figures to the constant standard of the base year—1980 in this case—the apparent increase in defense spending is sharply reduced. The "real" increase from fiscal year 1978 to fiscal year 1980 is less than three percent compared with our initial estimate of fourteen percent based on the current dollar figures.

Of course our estimate of "real" defense expenditures depends on our choice of a price index, or deflator, to transform the current dollar figures. The appropriate price index weighs changes in the prices of items in the defense budget by their relative importance in defense expenditures. Such indexes are produced by the Office of Management and Budget and the Department of Defense, and in general their movement parallels that of the GNP deflator discussed in Chapter 6.

Figures 8.1 and 8.2 display the pattern of defense obligational authority and outlays from 1964 to 1980. The data for 1964 are generally taken as an indication of defense expenditures prior to the Vietnam War. Note that when the defense budget is expressed in current dollar terms, the defense budget appears to increase from year to year except for the small reductions in the early 1970s resulting from the force reductions after the Vietnam War. When we examine the constant dollar pattern, however, the picture is quite different. Expressed in real terms, the defense budget remained below the 1964 level from 1972 to 1980. Note that changes in Total Obligational Authority (TOA) "lead" changes in total outlays, a relationship that can be seen most clearly in the Vietnam buildup of the late 1960s.

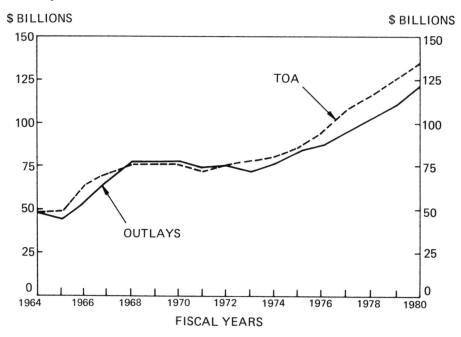

Figure 8.1 Department of Defense Budget Trends (Billions of Current $)

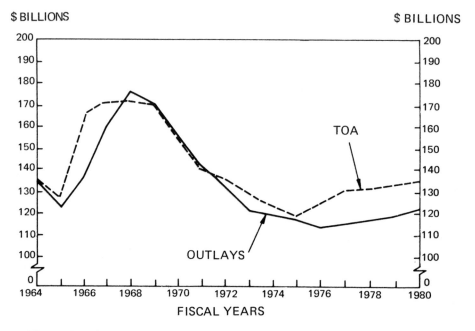

Figure 8.2 Department of Defense Budget Trends (Billions of Constant FY 1980 $)

Source: Harold Brown, op. cit., p. 318.

These "real" trends in budget expenditures expressed in constant dollars reflect real changes in force structure. In 1964 there were about 2.7 million active duty military personnel, by 1968 the number had risen to 3.5 million, by 1972 it was back down to 2.3 million, and in 1979 it stood at 2.1 million.[11] Of course some elements of the force structure expanded in this period (Polaris–Poseidon missiles went from 336 in 1964, to 656 in 1979; and nuclear attack submarines went from 19 to 72), but other elements declined (strategic bomber squadrons went from 78 to 25, and manned fighter interceptor squadrons went from 40 to 6).[12] These adjustments reflect shifts in the relative effectiveness of different components. However, the constant dollar budget figures tell us that the market value of the personnel and equipment purchased by the 1964 budget was, on balance, greater than the market value of the personnel and equipment purchased with the budgets of the late 1970s.

Defense Share of the Federal Budget, Federal Purchases, and the GNP

Another way of examining the defense budget is to trace the portion of the federal budget allocated to national security. In the period from 1948 to 1950, defense purchases came to 30.8 percent of federal expenditures, from 1958 to 1960 they were 51.1 per cent, from 1968 to 1970/41.0 percent, and from 1978 to 1980 they were down to 21.6 percent. The major cause of this downward trend in defense outlays as a portion of the budget was a dramatic rise in transfer payments. In the period from 1968 to 1970, transfer payments (domestic, foreign, and grants-in-aid to state and local governments) came to 38 percent of federal expenditures, but by 1978 to 1980 they stood at 56.4 percent. Even if we count only federal purchases of goods and services we detect a decline, although a much less precipitous decline in the share of defense spending. In 1970 defense accounted for 78 percent of such purchases, in 1975 for 68 percent, and for 65 percent in 1980. Although the federal budget has been expanding over this period, its growth has been only slightly higher than the growth in the national economy. The federal budget was 14.6 percent of GNP in 1948 to 1950, 18.8 percent in 1958 to 1960, 20.5 percent in 1968 to 1970, and 21.8 percent in 1978 to 1980.[13]

The result of the decline in the defense share of federal expenditures and the stability of federal outlays as a share of GNP, suggests that defense expenditures as a portion of the total economic production of the nation have been declining. This indeed was the case in the 1970s. Table 8.3 traces Department of Defense budgets as a share of federal budget outlays, the Gross National Product, the labor force, and net public spending (including state and local government). Compared with the pre-Vietnam budget for fiscal year 1964, the budgets for the end of the 1970s reflect a sharp decline in defense spending by each of these criteria.

Our conclusion must be that the stability of federal expenditures as a portion of the GNP, despite the rapid increase in domestic spending, has come at the expense of a declining share of the budget for defense. Thus we are faced with three alternative prospects for the 1980s. Either the defense budget must continue to decline as a portion of federal outlays; or the rate of increase in domestic programs must be reduced; or the share of the federal budget in the GNP, and hence the share of taxes, must be increased. There is of course no law, legislative or social, that limits the share of federal budget outlays to something around 20 percent of the GNP, and the share tends to increase each year based on the progressive structure of our tax laws, but the current social mood seems to favor reductions in government programs rather than expansion.

The Reagan administration's preferences have been clear, and the extended pattern of declines in defense budgets in both real terms and as a percentage of federal outlays has been reversed in current budget projections. The build-up outlined in Table 8.2 suggests a dramatic expansion in obligational authority between 1981 and 1983. Whether or not those projections can be sustained in conjunction with the supply-side tax cuts and large projected budget deficits remains to be seen.

Table 8.3
Department of Defense Budget Financial Summary: 1964–1980

Department of Defense as Percentage of	FY 1964	FY 1968	FY 1977	FY 1978	FY 1979	FY 1980
Federal Budget (Outlays)	41.8%	43.3%	23.8%	22.8%	22.7%	23.1%
Gross National Product	8.0%	9.3%	5.2%	5.0%	4.9%	4.9%
Labor Force	8.3%	9.9%	4.9%	4.9%	4.9%	4.9%
Net Public Spending	27.9%	29.5%	15.6%	15.1%	14.8%	14.9%

Source: Harold Brown, op. cit., p. 322.

THE MACROECONOMIC IMPACTS OF DEFENSE SPENDING

The Reagan administration has announced its intention to expand defense expenditures in an attempt to make up for dramatic increases in defense spending by the Soviet Union during the 1970s. Unless these spending increases are offset by reductions in other areas of government spending, those outlays for defense can be expected to add to inflationary pressures in the economy. In this section we examine the expected consequences of increased defense expenditure, consider the possibility of using wage-price controls to moderate inflationary pressures, and then discuss the macroeconomic impact of the opposite case of reductions in defense expenditure. We will discover that while in theory compensatory fiscal policies may be used to offset the consequences of either increases or decreases in defense outlays, in practice it is far more difficult to moderate the impact of increases in defense spending.

Increased Defense Expenditure

As we have seen, defense spending accounts for about five percent of our gross national product and about one-quarter of annual federal expenditures. If the economy is operating at far less than full employment, the opportunity cost of increased defense expenditures may be only a modest increase in inflationary pressure. This would be shown as a shift in the aggregate demand curve to the right as indicated in Figure 8.3 from AD_1 to AD_2. But the closer we come to full employment (Q_F), the stronger the inflationary pressure will be, as shown by the shift from AD_2 to AD_3. If the increase in defense spending is not compensated for by an increase in taxes or a decline in other areas of government spending, the inflation will be an implicit tax, shifting resources away from the private sector to the public sector. If the federal government financed the increased defense outlays with an increase in taxes, the transfer of resources from the private to the public sector would be more explicit, but the pressure on prices would be reduced because the tax increase would shift the aggregate demand curve back to the left. If the government adjusted to the increased level of defense outlays by cutting other public programs, the shift in aggregate demand to the right would also be reduced or eliminated, there would be no shift of resources from the private to the public sector, and the only economic impact would come from the redistribution of expenditures.

Depending on which of these approaches is selected, the opportunity cost of increased defense outlays will be higher inflation, reduced spending in the private sector, or reduced spending on other government programs. In periods of high employment the opportunity costs may be quite low, but in a period when the economy is approaching full employment or when there is already substantial inflationary pressure, the opportunity costs could be quite severe.

In theory the inflationary pressures could be offset by tax increases or cuts in government programs which would shift the aggregate demand curve back to the left. From a practical point of view, however, it is difficult to increase taxes or reduce other government programs to make room for increases in defense outlays. In the late 1960s, President Johnson was slow to propose a tax increase to fund the Vietnam War, and he was also reluctant to cut his "Great Society" domestic programs. The result was a sharp increase in inflationary pressures.

Although we have the fiscal tools to manage the economic impact of shifts in defense spending, the record of the late 1960s suggests that we may occasionally lack the political will. It would be a gross exaggeration to lay the inflationary problems of the 1970s, which stemmed primarily from problems of aggregate supply, at the feet of defense spending. But the lesson is clear that defense spending does have opportunity costs, and attempts to hide those costs by refusing to adjust taxes or other elements of government spending can have disastrous economic consequences.

Price Controls

The fiscal remedies to control inflation—increased taxes or reduced government spending—are politically painful. The monetary solution—slower growth in the supply of money and increased interest rates—is no more popular. As a result refuge is often sought in some form of wage and price controls, programs which are often labeled *incomes policies* because they deal directly with controlling private income.

The major impact of price controls is to produce an excess of demand over supply. Normally prices would adjust to bring demand and supply into balance, but when prices are prevented from performing this role, shortages inevitably develop. Because the demand for goods exceeds the supply, some way must be found to allocate the existing supply without letting prices rise. This might be done with rationing stamps, as in World War II, through a regional allocation scheme, by having people wait on queues for available supplies, or through illegal black markets. Thus price controls are typically accompanied by some sort of allocation scheme. The price controls of the early 1970s were imposed in an attempt to control the inflationary pressure resulting from the fiscal policies of the late 1960s. The controls produced major shortages, particularly in processed foods and lumber, and were abandoned when the pressure for price increases in some markets became too great. The result was a surge of inflation in 1973 and 1974, prompting a tightening of monetary and fiscal policies which contributed to the recession of 1974 to 1975.

The record of temporary price controls in the American economy has been a dismal failure. Government tinkering in the market system seems to promote shortages and misallocation of resources without relieving inflationary pressures. The long lines at gasoline stations in the late 1970s resulted as much from government controls on gasoline prices as from reductions in the supply of crude oil, and the shortages produced by the controls probably increased the pressure for gasoline prices to rise. The regional allocation scheme used to shift available gasoline supplies exacerbated the problem by preventing market pressures from reallocating supplies to the areas of greatest need. Advocates of controls suggest a permanent system so that inflationary pressures would not simply be shifted to a future period when controls were ended. Such a scheme, however, would also mean a permanent system of allocating supplies, since the pricing system would no longer balance supply and demand. Having government agencies set prices and allocate supplies may be feasible, but it would be a major departure from our market system and it would mean a sharp reduction in economic freedom.

Decreased Defense Expenditures

Although the impetus of the 1980s is apparently toward expanded defense outlays with the accompanying threat of inflationary pressure, the opposite problem of sharp cuts in defense expenditures with the accompanying threat of expanded unemployment must also be considered. Critics of large defense programs frequently suggest that reduced military expenditures would free valuable resources for social programs, and there is always pressure to reduce defense outlays when international tensions ease. Similarly at the end of any actual conflict sharp drops in defense spending must be anticipated. How can the economy adjust to sharp cuts in defense outlays?

A reduction in defense outlays could free resources for other competing purposes if the economy is operating near full employment. On the other hand, if the reduction in defense outlays were not compensated for with an increase in other government programs or a tax cut to shift resources to the private sector, the result of the cut in defense spending could be a decline in real output and an increase in unemployment. This would be shown as a shift from AD_3 to AD_1 on Figure 8.3. In addition to the decline in aggregate demand, the economy would be forced to adjust to a shift in the industrial and regional distribution of outlays caused by the reduction in defense expenditures.

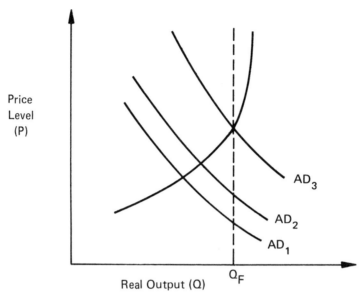

Figure 8.3 The Impact of a Shift in Aggregate Demand on the Price Level as the Economy Approaches Full Employment

Concerns for the ability of the economy to adjust to reduced levels of defense expenditures have taken center stage during periods of conflict. During World War II, and the Korean and Vietnam Wars, there was substantial concern with the problems of demobilization on the one hand, and the question of how to allocate the "peace dividend" on the other. Actually, the concern with the impact of reduced spending in the 1960s grew even before the Vietnam War began. The high levels of defense spending in the early 1960s, spurred by an attempt to eliminate an apparently nonexistent missile gap, and by a shift in spending to provide a more "flexible response" to a variety of conventional force contingencies, had produced a substantial increase in defense capabilities, and a period of declining defense expenditures was foreseen. Indeed, in 1963 President Kennedy established the Committee on the Economic Impact of Defense and Disarmament, chaired by Gardner Ackley of the Council of Economic Advisers, to examine the likely impacts of cuts in defense spending.

The Ackley Committee noted that the demobilization from World War II, when defense outlays accounted for more than 35 percent of the GNP, was extremely rapid, and despite the release of over 9 million men from the armed services there was no significant increase in unemployment. The adjustment to the end of the Korean War, which involved a smaller decline in defense spending, did see unemployment rise to 5.6 percent of the labor force in 1954; but tax reductions and backlogs in the demand for durable goods brought the unemployment rate down to 4.4 percent in 1955.[16]

The Committee, however, went on to note that shifts in the composition of defense spending might make future adjustments to cuts in defense spending more difficult.

However, we must recognize that some of the "conversion" problems that we are likely to face in the immediate future—whether arising from over-all reductions or simply from shifts in composition—may be more difficult to solve than were "conversion" problems in the past. The character of many goods procured by the military has become increasingly different from that of nonmilitary goods. Further, there appears to have been some tendency for defense production to become more concentrated geographically and to develop and use more highly specialized resources—human, capital, and natural. In earlier defense cut-backs, the problem was largely one of reconversion—a return to production of previously produced goods. . . . Today, many firms in the defense industries have never produced for nonmilitary markets to any significant degree.[17]

We will return to this issue of the composition of defense production in a moment, but first we must pause to emphasize the Committee's central conclusion: The problem of managing shifts in defense spending at the macroeconomic level is no different from managing other shifts in aggregate demand. As long as the correct compensatory fiscal policies are taken, there need be no major disruption in the economy as the result of shifts in defense outlays. "Even general and complete disarmament would pose no insuperable problems; indeed it would mainly afford opportunities for a better life for our citizens."[18]

In the case of reduced defense expenditures the appropriate fiscal policies—tax cuts and increases in government expenditures in other areas—and monetary policies—expansion in the supply of money and re-duced interest rates—are politically popular. Thus in practice it has been much simpler to adjust mac-roeconomic policy to offset defense cuts than it has been to moderate the impact of increased defense outlays.

THE DISTRIBUTION OF DEFENSE SPENDING AND THE MILITARY–INDUSTRIAL COMPLEX

The Ackley Committee noted that the ability of the economy to adapt to shifts in defense spending was be-coming more restricted in the mid-1960s as a result of the increasing specialization of defense production. Charles Hitch also noted this shift in the nature of defense spending in 1968 as he highlighted four major changes that made the impact of the defense sector on business different from earlier impacts: the high level of defense spending, the sustained high level of spending, the growth of defense industries, and the push to ex-tend weapon capabilities beyond the limits of current technology.[19] In short, the sustained level of specialized expenditures was producing a new industry that produced primarily for defense and that was being pushed into new, economically risky, investments in new technology. Hitch also underscored the Ackley Committee's earlier concern for the impacts of defense spending on the composition of the nation's output, the regional dis-tribution of production, the characteristics of manpower in defense industries, and the distribution of research and development.

Industry Impacts

In 1966, Wassily Leontief and his associates, using the input-output techniques for which Leontief sub-sequently won the Nobel Prize in economics, investigated the industrial impact of changes in defense outlays (see detailed discussion of this technique in Chapters 18 and 19). Assuming a 20 percent cut in defense spend-ing and an equal, offsetting increase in nondefense spending, Leontief found that five industries would suffer losses in production greater than the gains in any industry. The losses in those five industries were projected as follows: aircraft (–16%), ordnance (–15%), research and development (–13%), electronics equipment (–5%), and nonferrous metals (–2%). Although Leontief's projections showed that the gains to the entire economy would exceed the losses, the losses tended to be concentrated in a small number of industries.[20] One implica-tion is that the gains from defense cuts would be widely distributed but would have a small impact on each in-dustry, producing few vocal advocates, but the losing industries would have a major concern and would be or-ganized and vocal in supporting current defense programs. Although the study suggests that gains in nonde-fense production would exceed defense production losses, the net impact on employment is not clear.

Regional Impacts

Although the statistics on the distribution of defense outlays are incomplete, defense procurement is con-centrated in the aircraft, communication, shipbuilding and ordnance, instruments, electronic components, and machinery sectors.[21] These industries in turn tend to be concentrated by geographic region, although subcontracting tends to diffuse the regional patterns. In estimating the regional impact of defense outlays we need to know not only the size of such expenditures, but also their percentage impact on the local economy. If we use wages and salaries paid by defense-related industries and defense agencies as a proportion of personal income as our standard, defense spending has the greatest impact in Alaska and Hawaii, followed by Virginia, California, Maryland, Utah, and Washington. Outlays are also large in New York, Texas, and New Jersey, but the greater diversification of the economy in those areas lessens the relative impact of defense outlays.[22]

Defense outlays are further concentrated by community. For example, the Los Angeles and San Diego sections of California, Seattle, Boston, Wichita in Kansas, Hunstville in Alabama, and Cape Kennedy in Florida are very dependent on defense expenditures.[23] In an extraordinary projection of the regional implications of changes in defense outlays John H. Cumberland showed major impacts on the unemployment rates in such Standard Metropolitan Statistical Areas (SMSAs) as: Brockton, Massachusetts; Duluth, Minnesota; Fayetteville, North Carolina; Johnstown, Pennsylvania; Lawton, Oklahoma; Monterey, California; San Diego, California; and Waterloo, Iowa.[24]

The Military–Industrial Complex

Such regional and industrial concentrations of defense-related expenditures might be expected to produce substantial political pressure on the level and distribution of defense outlays. The theory of the *military–industrial complex* suggests that military decision makers, corporations which produce primarily for the defense sector, and political representatives of regions in which defense spending is concentrated exert pressure for levels of defense expenditure in excess of legitimate national needs. Moreover, the theory continues, the pressure which is exerted tends to be focused on particular weapon systems and excessive spending for those systems reduces the effectiveness of defense outlays. Thus the theory attacks both the level and composition of defense expenditure.

President Eisenhower expressed his concern for the possible evolution of the military–industrial complex in his famous farewell address:

> Now this conjunction of an immense military establishment and a large arms industry is new in the American experience. The total influence—economic, political, even spiritual—is felt in every city, every state house, every office of the Federal Government. We recognize the imperative need for this development. Yet we must not fail to comprehend its grave implications. Our toil, resources, and livelihood are all involved; so is the very structure of our society.
>
> In the councils of Government, we must guard against the acquisition of unwarranted influence, whether sought or unsought, by the military–industrial complex. The potential for the disastrous rise of misplaced power exists and will persist.
>
> We must never let the weight of this combination endanger our liberties or democratic processes. We should take nothing for granted. Only an alert and knowledgeable citizenry can compel the proper meshing of the huge industrial and military machinery of defense with our peaceful methods and goals, so that security and liberty may prosper together.[25]

Translating the hypothesis of a military–industrial complex into an operational theory is extremely difficult because so many factors enter every decision on military spending. The crude theory suggests that an interlocking network of defense-related groups acting in their own economic and political self-interest have a major impact on defense outlays. There are, however, alternate explanations of shifts in defense outlays, such as shifts in Soviet capabilities. Some private interests will inevitably be served by defense procurement programs, but it does not follow that the policy was determined to satisfy those private interests. On balance, an assessment of the influence of the "military–industrial complex," however defined, rests on assumptions about the nature of potential threats to national security.[26] As Stephen Rosen notes, "If one believes that the external threat is in fact being exaggerated, the theory of the military–industrial complex is both more plausible and more useful as a concept."[27] In its extreme form as a unicausal explanation of military spending, the theory of the military–industrial complex is woefully inadequate, but taken as one of many factors affecting the pattern of defense outlays, the theory may be helpful.

Testing the theory, however, is no easy task. Proponents of the theory typically cite expenditure patterns in aircraft procurement, and they argue that contracts are awarded to keep current production lines in operation rather than on the basis of competitive bidding. Annual purchases by NASA and DoD are a major proportion of the total sales of General Dynamics (the F-111), North American Rockwell (the space shuttle, the B–1 bomber), Boeing (Minuteman missiles), Lockheed (the C–141 and C–5A transport aircraft, and the Poseidon), McDonnell-Douglas (the F–4 fighter, the ABM, the F–15 fighter), and Grumman (subcontracts for the F–111 fighter, the F–14 fighter). While these firms are highly dependent on the Department of Defense, DoD is also dependent on the production capability of these highly specialized firms. DoD also has an interest in extending the production runs of these companies through foreign arms sales in order to spread the enormous research and development costs over more aircraft, thereby lowering average procurement costs. James Kurth claims that the awards of aircraft contracts from 1960 to 1971 can be explained by the desire to maintain production in each major contracting firm, according to what he calls the "bail-out imperative."[28] The $250 million loan guarantee by the federal government for Lockheed in 1972 is further evidence of the perceived need to keep production lines open. But is this evidence of the military–industrial complex at work, or is it evidence of sensible management by DoD to insure future production potential? Unfortunately, efforts by the aircraft industry to diversify and reduce dependence on DoD contracts have been largely unsuccessful, and the interdependence of DoD aand the industry remains a fact of life in defense procurement.[29]

As a group, the top military contractors are somewhat more diversified than the aircraft industry. Major industrial corporations receive the majority of defense contracts, and the magnitude of their other sales reduces their dependence on DoD. Of the one hundred largest industrial corporations in 1968, only sixteen reported military contracts totalling more than 25 percent of total sales.[30] Of course, these firms may still find that the marginal sales to DoD have an important impact on annual profits, but since they are less specialized, their concern is perhaps more for the level of government outlays in general than for defense spending in particular.

Labor Impacts

The distribution of defense outlays has produced a concentration of spending in a few specialized defense industries, some mutual interdependence of the Department of Defense with those industries, and a somewhat concentrated regional expenditure pattern. It has also tended to shift a large proportion of the highly specialized scientific and engineering communities into the defense sector, and has had important impacts on the distribution of national spending on research and development. In the positive sense, outlays have stimulated greater education and training in the sciences and have produced spillover benefits in the form of technological breakthroughs which have been transferred to the private sector. On the other hand, it is also clear that these "spillovers" could have been produced at less cost if the outlays had been made directly on civilian research, and that the shift of research and development to defense has imposed an opportunity cost on research in other areas.

The labor force in defense-related employment tends to be somewhat more skilled than the private labor force, and represents a very large proportion of total employment for aeronautical engineers, airplane mechanics, physicists, and electrical engineers.[31] About half of all federal government expenditures for research and development are funded by the Department of Defense, and when atomic energy and space research is added, the programs account for more than half of the research in industrial laboratories, and the majority of the research performed by universities and other nonprofit institutions.[32]

Thus, shifts in defense expenditures can have important impacts on the industrial and regional composition of national output, on the structure of the work force, and on the composition of the nation's research and development efforts. While the overall performance of the economy can be managed by shifting fiscal policy to accommodate increases or cuts in defense outlays, the impacts of such changes on a number of firms, communities, and occupational groups can be significant.

CONCLUSION

The defense budget has enormous implications for the national economy. It is our clearest political statement of the opportunity costs we are willing to impose on the nation in order to reduce perceived threats to our national security. The budget also outlines how defense funds will be allocated to achieve our national security objectives. The budgetary process has been dramatically improved by the implementation of program budgeting within the Department of Defense, and by improved review of defense programs within the Office of Management and Budget and in the Congressional appropriations process. As a result, defense outlays receive careful scrutiny to insure that they are in line with our overall national objectives, including our objectives for the national economy. This review process, however, remains essentially incremental, and fundamental shifts in defense policy take years to work their way through the budgetary process. The shift to zero-based budgeting may have some impact on this incremental approach, but the obstacles are overwhelming.

By any criterion, the defense budget claims a huge share of our national resources. In the 1970s, however, real defense spending remained relatively constant while other government programs expanded and the capacity of the national economy to produce increased. Defense spending actually fell as a proportion of the federal budget and as a share of the GNP. Under the Reagan administration these trends have been reversed.

Defense expenditures impose opportunity costs on the rest of the economy. At the macroeconomic level, the costs are either increased inflation, lower consumption and investment in the private sector, or reductions in competing government programs. The impacts of changes in defense outlays can be offset by applyng stabilizing fiscal policies. Such policies as increasing other government programs or cutting taxes to compensate for reductions in defense spending are politically popular, and easy to implement. On the other hand, restrictive fiscal policies to offset increases in defense outlays such as increasing taxes or cutting other programs are much less popular and far more difficult to implement. Price controls are no panacea for fiscal irresponsibility, and merely delay inflationary pressures while creating shortages that become more and more difficult to manage.

At the industry level, defense outlays tend to be concentrated in technical sectors (such as the aircraft industry), which require a specialized labor force and major research and development programs in the areas of science and engineering. The impacts of changes in defense spending therefore tend to be concentrated by industry, occupation, and region. Macroeconomic policies to offset shifts in defense outlays may have to be supplemented with regional policies to offset the impacts of sharp increases or cuts in defense outlays.

The theory of the military–industrial complex suggests that the level and composition of defense outlays may be strongly influenced by the self-interest of groups involved in defense production. The theory is difficult to test because of the multiple causes of shifts in defense outlays. The current Congressional budgetary process involves the entire Congress rather than a few specialized subcommittees, and fiscal constraints imposed by the entire budgetary process restrict defense outlays. Thus, while the defense industries are clearly represented in the budgetary process, there appear to be adequate restraints on the "acquisition of unwarranted influence . . . by the military–industrial complex" at the macroeconomic level. At the level of individual contracts, the requirement to maintain future defense production capacity will continue to impose interdependence on the Department of Defense and the defense industries in the more technical areas of military procurement.

NOTES

1 One of the earliest of these resource oriented analyses was *Economics of National Security* (New York: Prentice Hall, 1954) by the late George A. Lincoln, Head of the Social Sciences Department at West Point while the authors were students and instructors at the Military Academy. This text is due in large part to his example and influence.
2 Caspar W. Weinberger, *Department of Defense Annual Report, Fiscal Year 1983* (Washington, D.C.: U.S. Government Printing Office, 1982).

3 Lawrence J. Korb, "The Price of Preparedness: The FY 1978–1982 Defense Program," *AEI Defense Review*, No. 3 (June, 1977), p. 5.

4 See, for example, *Planning–Programming–Budgeting: Initial Memorandum,* Government Operations Subcommittee on National Security and International Operations (the "Jackson Subcommittee"), U.S. Senate, 90th Congress, 1st Session, 1967.

5 Charles J. Hitch, "Decision-Making in Large Organizations," in Louis C. Gawthrop, ed., *The Administrative Process and Democratic Theory* (New York: Houghton Mifflin Company, 1970), p. 22.

6 Aaron Wildavsky, *op. cit.,* p. 199.

7 Clark A. Murdock, *Defense Policy Formation* (Albany: State University of New York Press, 1974), p. 164.

8 Lawrence Korb, *op. cit.,* p. 2.

9 *Ibid.,* p. 3.

10 Harold Brown, *Department of Defense Annual Report, 1980, op. cit.,* p. 317.

11 *Ibid.,* p. B–4.

12 *Ibid.,* p. C–1.

13 *Special Analyses Budget of the United States Government, Fiscal Year 1980, op. cit.*

14 Harold Brown, *op. cit.,* pp. 32–34.

15 See for example Barry M. Blechman, "The Defense Budget," in Joseph A. Pechman, ed., *The 1978 Budget: Setting National Priorities* (Washington, D.C.: The Brookings Institution, 1977), pp. 81–141.

16 *Report of the Committee on the Economic Impact of Defense and Disarmament* (Washington, D.C.: Government Printing Office, July, 1965), pp. 9–10.

17 *Ibid.,* pp. 10–11.

18 *Ibid.,* p. 1.

19 Charles J. Hitch, "The Defense Sector: Its Impact on American Business," in *The Defense Sector and the American Economy* (New York: New York University Press, 1968), p. 19.

20 Wassily Leontief, et. al., "The Economic Impact—Industrial and Regional—of an Arms Cut," in *Input–Output Economics,* Wassily Leontief, ed. (New York: Oxford University Press, 1966), pp. 194–197.

21 R. Oliver, "The Employment Effect of Defense Expenditures," *Monthly Labor Review* (September, 1967), pp. 10–11.

22 Report of the Committee on the Economic Impact of Defense and Disarmament, *op. cit.,* pp. 6–7.

23 *Ibid.,* p. 7.

24 John H. Cumberland, "Dimensions of the Impact of Reduced Military Expenditures on Industries, Regions, and Communities," in Bernard Udis, ed., *The Economic Consequences of Reduced Military Spending* (Lexington, Mass.: Lexington Books, 1973), pp. 114–128.

25 Dwight D. Eisenhower, "Liberty is at Stake," Farewell Address delivered to the nation, Washington, D.C., January 17, 1961, in *The Defense Sector and the American Economy, op. cit.,* p. 97.

26 See, for example, Jerome Slater and Terry Nardin, "The Concept of a Military–Industrial Complex," in Steven Rosen, ed., *Testing the Theory of the Military Industrial Complex* (Lexington, Mass.: Lexington Books, 1973), pp. 27–60.

27 Steven Rosen, "Testing the Theory of the Military Industrial Complex," in Steven Rosen, ed., *op. cit.,* p. 5.

28 James R. Kurth, "Aerospace Production Lines and American Defense Spending," in Steven Rosen, ed., *op. cit.,* pp. 135–156. Kurth's analysis is discussed in more detail in Chapter 15.

29 Murray L. Weidenbaum, "Industrial Adjustments to Military Expenditure Shifts and Cutbacks," in Bernard Udis, ed., *op. cit.,* pp. 33–38.

30 Stanley Lieberson, "An Empirical Study of Military–Industrial Linkages," in Steven Rosen, ed., *op. cit.,* p. 66.

31 Bernard Udis and Murray L. Weidenbaum, "The Many Dimensions of the Military Effort," in Bernard Udis, ed., *op. cit.,* pp. 33–38.

32 *Ibid.,* pp. 42–43, and *The Report of the Committee on the Economic Impact of Defense and Disarmament, op. cit.,* p. 8.

SELECTED REFERENCES

Lawrence Korb, "The Budget Process in the Department of Defense, 1947–77: The Strengths and Weaknesses of Three Systems," *Public Administration Review* (July–August, 1977), pp. 334–346.

Lawrence Korb, "The FY 1981–1985 Defense Program: Issues and Trends," *AEI Foreign Policy and Defense Review*, Vol. 2, No. 2, 1980.

Steven Rosen, ed., *Testing the Theory of the Military Industrial Complex* (Lexington, Mass.: Lexington Books, 1973).

Bernard Udis, ed., *The Economic Consequences of Reduced Military Spending* (Lexington, Mass.: Lexington Books, 1973).

Chapter 9
The Theory of Defense Production

INTRODUCTION

Thus far in this section we have discussed the economic implications of different levels of defense expenditures and the budgetary process within which decisions on defense outlays are considered. The budgetary process links national security objectives with defense programs and the required inputs of manpower, equipment, and supplies to implement those programs. From an economic perspective, this process may be summarized in the framework of a "production function" that describes how different levels of output are related to different levels and combinations of inputs. From the viewpoint of economic efficiency we seek to find the least cost method of reaching a given level of defense output, or to find the highest level of output that can be obtained for a given budgetary outlay. Because expenditures are tied to inputs, and inputs are linked to outputs through the production function, this approach suggests that the appropriate allocation of defense resources should be related to the prices of the various inputs and to the contribution of each input to the desired output. In other words, changes in the prices of inputs or changes in the contribution of each input to defense output should lead to a reallocation of defense spending.

In this chapter we present the economic theory of the production function, and discuss the solution to the problem of finding the least cost combination of inputs to achieve any level of defense output. We then apply this approach to the defense problem in general and to the defense manpower problem in particular. Although we will encounter numerous problems with defining defense outputs, and hence in estimating the specific form of the defense production function, we will find that the approach still yields important insights into the efficient allocation of defense resources.

THE PRODUCTION FUNCTION

The *production function* describes the maximum level of output that can be obtained from any combination of inputs using the most efficient conversion or production process available. Outputs of final goods and services (haircuts, automobiles, tanks) are the result of the combination of inputs (labor, capital, supplies) used in the production process. In mathematical notation we might write this relationship as:

$$Q = f(I_1, I_2, \ldots I_n) \tag{9.1}$$

where Q is the output produced and I_1 through I_n are the inputs used. In this form the units of input and output would be expressed in real terms, such as the number of tanks produced in a year, manyears of labor, tons of steel, kilowatts of energy, and so forth.

To simplify the description of the production process it is convenient to group the inputs into more homogeneous categories such as labor, capital, and supplies. In this form the production function would be written as:

$$Q = f(L_1 \ldots L_n; K_1 \ldots K_n; S_1 \ldots S_n) \tag{9.2}$$

assuming that there are "n" categories of labor, capital, and supplies. For example, L_1 might be electronics engineers, L_2 could be secretaries, and so forth.

To further simplify the production function we could aggregate, or combine, the inputs in each group to form an index of the level of total labor, capital, and supplies used in the production process. Our production function would then read:

$$Q = f(L,K,S) \qquad (9.3)$$

Whenever we aggregate, we lose some information. For example, by defining the input of labor as the total number of manyears, we lose information on the skill levels of different workers in our work force. Similarly, when we add up the services provided by the stock of machinery used in the production process, we must now add up the contributions of different types of equipment, and the same is true in estimating the input of supplies. We use the dollar values, in some cases estimates, of the capital and supplies used in order to aggregate different types of capital and supply inputs. Thus when we begin to aggregate, we shift from measuring inputs and outputs in real physical terms to measuring them in terms of dollar values. If our output consisted of several products, we would measure total output in terms of the dollar value of all the outputs produced in a given period.

Estimating the contribution of the stock of capital to the production process is difficult, because a given piece of equipment will continue to contribute to production over many years. What we would really like to know is how much it would cost to rent the machine for one production period, but if the machinery is purchased and there is no rental market from which to draw our data, the cost of the capital used in the production process must be "imputed" or indirectly estimated. Normally we assume that the contribution of each piece of equipment during a production period is proportional to its purchase price, but this assumption must be modified when different pieces of equipment deteriorate or depreciate at different rates.

In order to facilitate a graphical description of the production process, we will assume that the level of output produced is a function only of the inputs of capital and labor as follows:

$$Q = f(K,L). \qquad (9.4)$$

If we assume that in the short run the stock of capital is fixed at a level K_2, we may plot the relationship between output and labor as shown in Figure 9.1. This curve demonstrates that total output increases as the number of manyears of labor increases, but that the rate at which output increases ($\Delta Q/\Delta L$ or the slope of the curve) declines as more and more labor is used. In other words the "*marginal product*," or the amount of output produced by an additional worker, tends to decline as more and more workers are hired. This widely observed phenomenon is termed "diminishing returns" to an input, and it occurs because one of the inputs, capital in this case, has been held constant. As a result we are applying more and more units of labor to a fixed amount of machinery, and eventually this constraint lowers the incremental output that an additional worker can produce. If we increase the stock of capital from K_2 to K_1, the entire production function will shift upward (we now produce more output from a given input of labor) but we will still observe that the marginal product of labor will fall as more and more units of labor are used.

ISOQUANT AND ISOCOST ANALYSIS

Figure 9.1 suggests that any level of output could be produced from a variety of combinations of capital and labor. For example, output Q_1 could be produced from L_1 units of labor and K_1 units of capital, or with L_2 units of labor (more labor) and K_2 units of capital (less capital). If we were to plot all of the combinations of capital and labor that could be used to produce output Q_1, we would trace out an *isoquant* or a curve of constant output as shown in Figure 9.2.

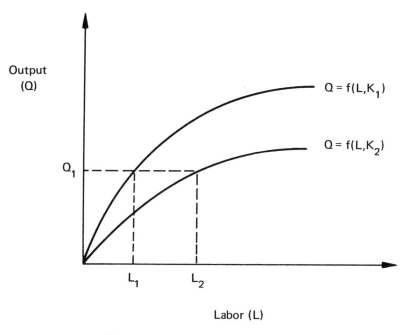

Figure 9.1 The Production Function

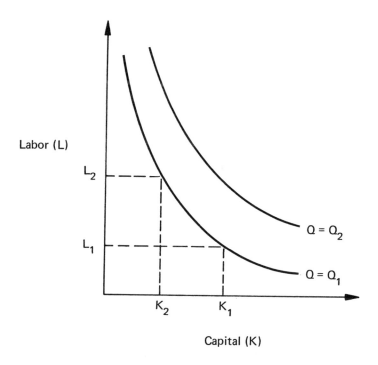

Figure 9.2 Isoquants

The isoquant for a level of output higher than Q_1 would be to the right of the Q_1 isoquant. In order to produce more output from a given stock of capital, more labor must be added; in order to produce more output from a given amount of labor, more capital must be added. In Figure 9.2, Q_2 must be a higher level of output than Q_1. The isoquants thus map out different output levels in the same way that contour lines map out different altitudes on a contour map.

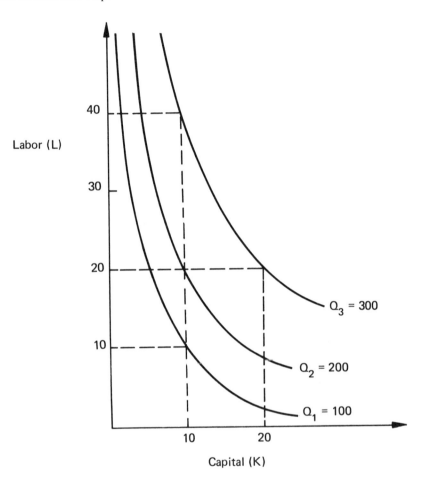

Figure 9.3 Returns to Scale and Returns to Labor

Note:

Returns to Scale are Increasing

K	L	Q
10	10	100
20	20	300

Returns to Labor are Diminishing

K	L	Q		$\Delta Q/L$
10	10	100	⟩	10
10	20	200	⟩	
10	40	300		5

Returns to Scale and Marginal Products

Isoquants may be used to illustrate the idea of *"returns to scale."* We have seen that if we hold one input constant and increase the other, the "returns" or increases in output attributable to the variable input will become smaller and smaller. In other words, the marginal product of the variable input will decline as more and more of the variable input is used. However, if all of the inputs are changed by the same proportion, the change in the level of output is the result of a change in the scale of operation. If we increase all of the inputs by some proportion and find that output increases by the same proportion, the "returns to scale" are constant; if output goes up by a larger proportion, returns to scale are increasing; and if output goes up by a smaller amount, returns to scale are decreasing.

Consider Figure 9.3. Note that as we move from 10 units of labor and capital to 20 units of each, the output shifts from 100 to 300. In this case the returns to scale are increasing, because when the inputs of labor and capital are doubled the level of output triples. This is the result of *"economies of scale"* that may be obtained as the level of production increases, perhaps because of improved organization or the benefits of increasing specialization. We can also see on Figure 9.3 that when capital is fixed at 10 units there are diminishing returns to labor becaue larger and larger increments of labor are required to expand output by the same amount as we go from isoquant to isoquant. When labor goes from 10 to 20, output goes from 100 to 200, so the marginal product of labor is 10 ($\Delta Q/\Delta L = 200-100 / 20-10$); but when labor goes from 20 to 40, output goes from 200 to 300, and the marginal produce of labor drops to 5 (300–200 / 40–20).

Marginal Rate of Factor Substitution

The shape of the isoquants suggests that as we use less capital, more and more labor must be substituted to maintain the same level of output. The rate at which one input must be substituted for another in order to maintain the same level of output is called the *"marginal rate of factor substitution."* In this case the marginal rate at which labor must be substituted for capital is equal to the negative of the ratio of the marginal product of capital (MPK) to the marginal product of labor (MPL).[1] As we move to the left along the Q_1 isoquant, the stock of capital drops and the marginal product of capital rises; and at the same time the amount of labor increases and the marginal product of labor drops. In order to maintain the same level of output, more and more labor must be substituted for each unit of capital. Similarly, as we move to the right along the Q_1 isoquant, the marginal product of capital falls and the marginal product of labor rises. Thus less and less labor needs to be substituted for each unit of capital in order to maintain the same level of output.

Minimizing the Cost of Producing a Given Level of Output

Suppose that we have decided to produce output Q_1, and we are trying to determine what combination of inputs will produce output Q_1 at the least cost. If P_k were the price of capital and P_L were the price of labor, the cost, C, of any combination of inputs would be:

$$C = P_k K + P_L L. \tag{9.5}$$

One way of proceeding would be to calculate the cost associated with each combination of capital and labor that could be used to produce Q_1. Assume that we do this and we find that the least cost combination of capital and labor that can be used to produce output Q_1 is C_1 dollars using inputs K_1 and L_1 as shown in Figure 9.4. Of course we could use C_1 dollars to buy more units of capital and fewer units of labor, or more units of labor and fewer units of capital. If we sketch out all of the combinations of capital and labor that could be purchased with C_1 dollars, we would trace an isocost line representing a constant level of expenditures. The isocost line for an outlay of C_1 dollars is also shown in Figure 9.4. The slope of the isocost line is the negative of the ratio of the price of capital to the price of labor, since this represents the number of units of labor that may be purchased for each unit of capital that is given up.[2] Note that no combination of inputs that can be purchased with C_1 dollars can produce more than Q_1 units of output.

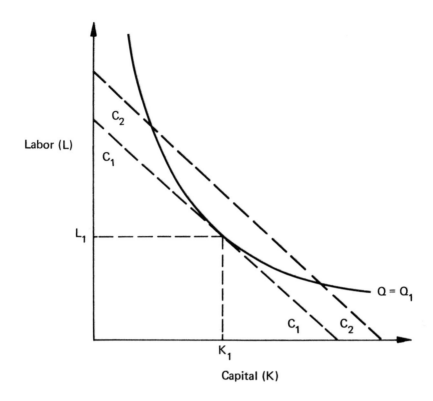

Figure 9.4 Isoquant and Isocost Lines

We could, of course, produce Q_1 units of output at a higher cost. Consider an isocost line corresponding to a higher level of expenditure, C_2, as shown in Figure 9.4. This isocost line crosses the Q_1 isoquant in two places, but if we chose to produce output Q_1 with the inputs indicated by those intersections, the cost would obviously be higher than if we used the preferred combination of L_1 and K_1.

We are now ready for an important conclusion. The least cost at which a given output may be produced is given by the isocost line that is just tangent to the isoquant for that output. Alternately, the highest output that can be produced from a given outlay is given by the isoquant that is just tangent to the isocost line for that outlay. We can see that this is true graphically, but the full significance of these conclusions can be developed by examining the point of tangency more carefully. At this point, the marginal rate of factor substitution (the slope of the isoquant) must be just equal to the price ratio (the slope of the isocost line), or:

$$-\frac{MPK}{MPL} = -\frac{P_K}{P_L} \tag{9.6}$$

This condition suggests that the rate at which one input can be substituted for another in the production process is equal to the rate at which one input may be substituted for another in the marketplace. If the relative productivity of capital is higher than its relative price, we should be using more capital in the production process.

Another way of viewing this efficiency condition is to rearrange the marginal condition to read:

$$\frac{MPK}{P_K} = \frac{MPL}{P_L} \tag{9.7}$$

In this form, the condition is to equate the marginal product per dollar spent on capital and labor. Suppose that the marginal product of labor divided by the price of labor were greater than the marginal product of capital divided by the price of capital, as shown at point A on Figure 9.5 (note the slope of the isoquant is less than the slope of the isocost line). This would suggest that an additional dollar spent on labor would increase output by more than a reduction of a dollar spent on capital would cut production. For the same total cost we can increase output by shifting to an input combination with more labor and less capital (for example point C). Similarly we could produce the same output with less cost by substituting more labor for less capital (for example, a shift to point B).

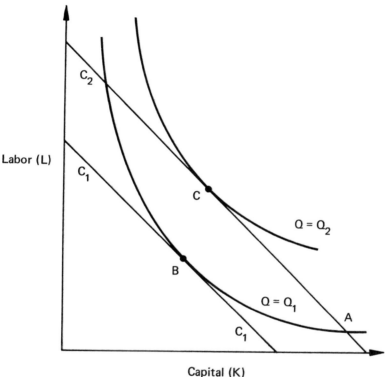

Figure 9.5 Adjustment from an Inefficient to an Efficient Input Mix

Note:

At point A: $\dfrac{mpL}{P_L} > \dfrac{mpK}{P_K}$

At points B and C: $\dfrac{mpL}{P_L} = \dfrac{mpK}{P_K}$

Our central conclusion for the efficient allocation of resources is that a mix of inputs should be selected that insures that the marginal contribution to output of the last dollar spent on each input is equal. If some inputs produce more of a contribution to output per dollar spent, the use of that input should be expanded and the use of other inputs should be reduced. This conclusion holds whether we see the problem as minimizing the cost of some fixed level of output, or as maximizing the output consistent with some fixed level of expenditure.

APPLICATIONS TO DEFENSE PRODUCTION

Our national security goals are essentially unlimited, but the resources available to meet those goals are constrained by our production capacity and our willingness to accept the opportunity costs imposed by defense spending on other social priorities and private investment and consumption. Resource constraints imposed by the budgetary process require that our general national security goals be translated into feasible objectives. National security objectives are therefore not absolute, but rather they are formed in a continuing process of defining goals, evaluating available options for meeting those goals, selecting the most efficient options, and trading off different defense objectives against competing claims on our national resources.

For example, one of our national security goals since the end of World War II has been to deter attacks by the Soviet Union on Western Europe and defeat such attacks if they should occur. We might translate this general goal into a series of defense objectives, beginning with the most expensive.

Objective 1: Maintain sufficient conventional and nuclear forces to halt any conventional Soviet attack at the eastern border of West Germany with conventional weapons, and defeat such an attack with nuclear weapons if the Soviet Union initiates their use.

Objective 2: Maintain sufficient conventional and nuclear forces to halt any conventional Soviet attack at the Rhine with conventional weapons, or with nuclear weapons if the Soviet Union should initiate their use.

Objective 3: Maintain sufficient conventional forces to contain a Soviet advance long enough to permit negotiation prior to the use of nuclear weapons, and sufficient nuclear forces to defeat the Soviet attack if the initial containment and negotiation are unsuccessful.

Clearly these objectives are only illustrative, and many other objectives could be posited. The point is that each objective is related to our broader national security goal, and the question we must ask concerns how much we are willing to spend in order to meet the goal.

In this case, our primary goal would be to deter attack, and this would of course depend on a large number of factors beyond decisions on the force structure of the United States. Deterrence would also depend on the Soviet Union's interpretation of our national commitment, on the commitment of our allies, on the confidence the Soviets had in their allies, on the capabilities of Soviet forces, and so forth. In addition we would have to consider the likely Soviet response to each increment in our capability to defend in Europe. If the Soviet response were simply to expand their capability, more defense spending might not move us any closer to our national security goal. Higher levels of preparedness in the United States might transmit the wrong signals to the Soviet Union. Forces deployed forward in sufficient strength to achieve Objective 1 might also have the capability and posture of offensive action.

This brief discussion suggests that it may be very hard to find a direct linkage between defense inputs and our national security goals along the lines suggested by a production function. Such a linkage becomes more reasonable when we begin to discuss objectives, and even more reasonable when we evaluate the specific missions assigned to the forces charged with meeting the objectives.

Following the conceptual approach developed by Richard Cooper in *Military Manpower and the All-Volunteer Force*, we may think of our national security output (Q) as a function of the specific missions our forces can accomplish $(M_1 \ldots M_n)$.[3] This national defense production function would then be expressed in mathematical notation as:

$$Q = f(M_1 \ldots M_n) \tag{9.8}$$

Each specific mission in turn would be a function of the capital and labor inputs allocated to it, or:

$$M_i = f(K_i, L_i) \tag{9.9}$$

where the subscript "i" refers to the "ith" mission. If each mission were independent—that is, if the capital and labor allocated to one mission had no impact on the accomplishment of other missions—we could achieve an efficient allocation of defense resources by finding the most efficient mix of capital and labor for each mission taken separately. For example, resources allocated to general purpose forces could not easily be reallocated to increase strategic nuclear forces.

As Cooper notes, this formulation of the defense production function has important implications. Unless we identify resource needs by mission, we cannot solve the aggregate defense management problems of linking inputs to outputs. However, because the aggregate levels of capital and labor used by the Department of

Defense are simply the sums of the capital and labor allocated to each mission, aggregate DoD output can be related to aggregate DoD input if the mix of missions remains constant. If defense objectives and hence the mix of missions remain stable over time, we may use the aggregate production function as an analytic tool for evaluating the allocation of resources in the Department of Defense.

In other words if capital and labor are allocated to *independent* missions, and if the mix of missions is roughly constant over time, we are justified in aggregating the production functions for each mission into an aggregate defense production function of the form:

$$Q = f(K, L) \tag{9.4}$$

where K is an index of all capital used by the Department of Defense, and L refers to the aggregate manpower level. Suppose that there are two defense missions (M_1 and M_2) that we will call conventional defense in Europe (M_1) and strategic deterrence (M_2). We define the output of the conventional defense mission as the number of days of defense until a Soviet force of stated size reaches the Rhine, and the output of the strategic mission as the number of kilotons that can be delivered on specified targets after a Soviet first strike of stated size. We find the most efficient combination of capital and labor for mission one (K_1 and L_1) and for mission two (K_2 and L_2). Our aggregate production function suggests that defense output Q could be expressed as:

$$Q = f(K_1 + K_2, L_1 + L_2). \tag{9.10}$$

But what would be the units on Q? How can we add numbers of days of defense and kilotons delivered on target?

The answer of course is that we cannot. This is one of the arguments for management at the mission level. We might note that when we are adding up the contribution of defense programs to the gross national product in the national income accounts, we dodge the whole issue of measuring output and assume that the output is simply equal to the sum of the inputs. This rule is applied throughout the public sector. Productivity in the public sector is arbitrarily defined to be one; output is equal to input. No matter how efficient government becomes in providing some service or output, it receives no credit when it is time to add up our national output. Of course, inefficiency is hidden under the same umbrella.

We cannot even aggregate different outputs in the conventional way of adding them up by applying market prices, because there are no markets for defense outputs. Thus we have no recourse to a market solution of our aggregation problems.

But before you discard the aggregate defense production function on the grounds that we cannot measure aggregate defense output, recall the conclusion of our isocost and isoquant analysis. Defense resources will be efficiently allocated as long as the marginal product per dollar spent on each input is equal. It may be extremely difficult to estimate changes in marginal products for each input, although we may have some qualitative arguments along these lines (for example, a rapid improvement in anti-tank weapons would suggest an increased marginal product for mechanized infantry and a decline for armor). We do, however, have data on shifts in relative costs. If the marginal productivity of different inputs remains relatively constant, shifts in input prices should lead to shifts in the defense force structure in order to maintain an efficient allocation of resources.

Consider Figure 9.6. Based on the original relative prices of capital and labor reflected in cost line C_1, the most efficient combination of capital and labor for achieving output level Q_1 is given at point A. Now if the relative price of capital dropped, the slope of the cost line would decline (recall that the slope is $-P_K/P_L$) as shown by C_2, and the most efficient combination of inputs to produce output Q_1 would be at point B. In other words, the decline in the relative cost of capital should produce a shift in the allocation of inputs to the use of less labor and more capital. Note that this conclusion holds regardless of the units in which output is measured. Thus, if the productivity of different inputs remains constant, shifts in relative prices should be matched by shifts in the input mix, and hence in force structure.

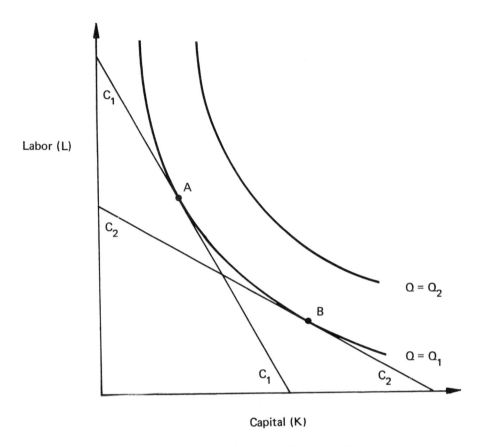

Figure 9.6 Defense Outlays and Changing Prices

DEFENSE CAPITAL AND LABOR RATIOS: AN APPLICATION

Richard Cooper applied the theory of defense production in an evaluation of the adjustment of capital and labor to shifting input prices from 1956 to 1977.[4] His estimates of the Department of Defense labor input were derived by simply summing all uniformed, direct-hire, indirect hire, and contract personnel not engaged in training activity. Although some adjustments for different skill levels could be applied, Cooper found that they made little difference in his estimates. He relied on Charles Robert Roll's technique for estimating the replacement cost of all the equipment (planes, typewriters, tanks) in the defense inventories in order to obtain constant dollar estimates of the size of the aggregate capital stock.[5]

Cooper found that the DoD capital stock varied much less over the period from 1956 to 1977 than the labor input. The fiscal year DoD capital stock was estimated to be about $268 billion in 1976. The annual depreciation, based on replacement cost, of that stock was estimated at about $25 billion in that year. Just to maintain the existing capital stock in 1976 would have cost $25 billion, but the actual procurement was only $16.5 billion. In other words, the dollar value of the capital in defense inventories actually fell in 1976. But the major point is that enormous outlays are required to make even modest percentage increases in the size of the capital stock.[6]

On the other hand, the supply of labor can be altered quite rapidly through reserve mobilization or a draft. Thus while the defense capital stock rose slowly through the 1960s and fell slowly through the 1970s, the labor supply rose rapidly during the Vietnam War years of the late 1960s and fell even more precipitously with the demobilization of the early 1970s.

During this same period, the shift to an all-volunteer force and general wage increases associated with sharp general inflation produced a rapid increase in personnel costs. The cost of capital, measured by the Bureau of Labor Statistics' index of the cost of machinery and equipment in the private sector, also rose substantially, but at a rate considerably below the increase in labor costs. As a result, the relative price of capital fell through the 1970s.

Economic theory suggests that in the face of a falling relative price of capital, force structure should be adjusted to increase the input of capital and reduce the input of labor. Cooper found that the capital to labor ratio remained virtually constant from 1957 to 1971, rose 10 percent from 1971 to 1974, and then actually fell from 1975 to 1977 to about the same ratio as that in 1964. Over this period, the cost of capital dropped about 40 percent compared to the cost of labor, but the ratio of capital to labor used in the Department of Defense rose only about one percent. In addition, the shifts in the ratio that did occur were the result of cuts in personnel, rather than increases in the capital stock. As noted above, the capital stock continued to fall throughout the 1970s.

Cooper's central conclusion is that, "It would thus seem that the defense establishment has not taken full advantage of substitution opportunities. Given the dramatic rise in the cost of labor relative to the cost of capital, it appears that substantially more substitution could yield major efficiency gains, as reflected in either reduced defense budgets or increased military capability, or both.[7]

While such analyses of potential adjustment to shifting input costs can be very enlightening, we should emphasize the assumptions behind the analysis. First, we assumed that the mix of missions remained relatively constant. Second, the analysis thus far is essentially static, because it assumes that the new input price ratios will remain constant during the current planning period, and it assumes that there will be no changes in the relative productivity of the input factors. Third, we have not yet directly addressed the time dimension involved in planning for current capability and future mobilization. In the next section we expand our analysis to include some of these dynamic considerations.

DYNAMIC CONSIDERATIONS IN EVALUATING DEFENSE OUTPUT

Decisions on defense expenditures involve judgments not only on the proper allocation of current resources, but also on the most efficient allocation of resources over time. Our ability to accomplish a given mission at some future point in time depends on the inputs of capital and labor available at that time. We can revise our mission production function to show this dynamic relationship and state it as:

$$M_{1t} = f(K_{1t}, L_{1t}) \qquad (9.11)$$

where the subscript 1 indicates the first mission and the subscript t indicates the year in which the mission must be accomplished. Our aggregate production function would then be expressed as:

$$Q_t = f(M_{1t}, M_{2t}, \ldots M_{nt}) \qquad (9.12)$$

where there are n missions. Our ability to meet our national security objectives will, however, be affected by our perceived ability to accomplish the required missions in the future as well as in the present, and the production function should be modified to include future missions as follows:

$$Q_t = f(M_{it}, \ldots, M_{im}; \ldots; M_{nt}, \ldots, M_{nm}) \qquad (9.13)$$

where there are n missions and our current defense output is influenced by future capabilities extending out to year m.

The efficient allocation of resources now requires that we consider the future stream of capital and labor allocated to each mission over time. Thus we must modify our earlier analysis to include trade-offs between current and future capabilities, the rate at which different input factors may be adjusted to meet future requirements, our time preference for current versus future levels of output, and anticipated future changes in the prices and the productivity of different inputs.

Suppose, for example, that mission number one is a conventional defense of Western Europe. The mission requires some forces to deter a surprise attack by Soviet forces from their current positions and to provide an effective defense in the case of attack until reserves are mobilized. Thus we must consider current Soviet capabilities, capabilities that will exist at different time intervals after Soviet mobilization, current allied capabilities, and allied capabilities that will exist at different time periods after allied mobilization. The appropriate current defense posture depends on our estimates of the rate and nature of the forces that could be mobilized on each side, and the locations in which they could be deployed.

A *"short war"* scenario might assume that any war would be fought essentially with forces-in-being that were already deployed in Western Europe. According to this scenario, reinforcement from the United States would be seriously limited by contested control of the sea and air lanes. The war in Europe would be a "short war" with devastating losses on each side in the early days of fighting. The result would either be a rapid conventional victory by allied forces, or a subsequent escalation to tactical or even strategic nuclear weapons. This scenario suggests that defense resources should be committed to forces deployed in Europe with a high "tooth to tail," or combat to support force, ratio. Few funds would be allocated to strategic mobility since reinforcement would be unlikely. Similarly, funds would be allocated primarily to active rather than reserve forces.

A *"long war"* scenario might assume that there would be sufficient early warning of any Soviet attack to provide substantial time for allied mobilization. According to this scenario, naval and air forces might be able to maintain sufficient superiority to preserve open air and sea lanes. The war in Europe would be a "long" war with no decisive battles in the early days of fighting. The result might be an extended conventional conflict, perhaps with tactical nuclear exchanges, but without escalation to strategic nuclear exchanges. This scenario suggests that defense resources should be committed to some forces deployed forward in Europe, to some active forces designated for rapid reinforcement, to a reserve system capable of reinforcing the active forces, to a higher ratio of support to combat forces, and to sufficient strategic mobility capabilities to reinforce the forward deployed forces.

These two scenarios are obviously caricatures drawn to highlight differences in force structure, but they illustrate the idea that defense output must be viewed as a stream of future capabilities. The output profiles shown in Figure 9.7 illustrate the differences between our "short" and "long" war scenarios. Note that designing our forces for either scenario runs some risks and involves some opportunity costs. Under the short war scenario, our emphasis on current forces reduces our mobilization capability, and under the long war scenario, our emphasis on mobilization capability reduces the effectiveness of our current forces. In practice, some mix of capabilities is selected based on shifting estimates of the likelihood of each scenario.

A long war strategy would probably argue for a higher ratio of current capital to labor on the grounds that capital is harder to expand than manpower is during a mobilization, and that capital forward deployed and prepared to be issued to the reinforcing troops would greatly simplify the reinforcement problems. The short war strategy might argue for a higher ratio of manpower to capital, on the grounds that sufficient manpower could not be mobilized in time to use the excess capital effectively. In economic terms, the short war strategy tends to raise the marginal productivity of labor compared to the marginal productivity of capital. This argument, however, can be overstated, and many military leaders have argued for a larger manpower ratio to provide the leadership core required to handle mobilization.

In summary, each mission has a dynamic profile that requires the defense decision maker to trade off current and future capabilities. Different scenarios lead to different estimates of the relative productivity of capital and labor in accomplishing the mission. In addition, the timing of capital procurement must be very sensitive to the pace of technological advance. By delaying major procurements and sustaining the life of current capital through increased maintenance, there may be a possibility of procuring an improved system. Given the long life of military capital, current procurement decisions affect the force structure for the next decade and often longer. As we shall see when we discuss arms races in general, procurement decisions must also be linked to changes in the capabilities of potential enemies and the prospect of future innovations that would reduce the capability of our own systems.

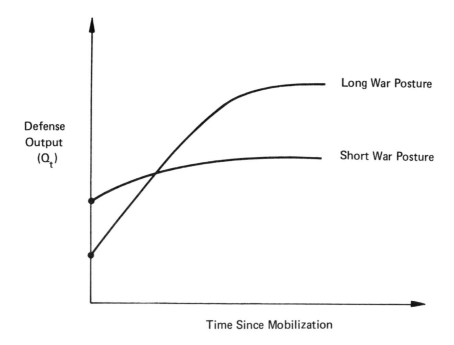

Figure 9.7 Long and Short War Output Profiles

Finally, changes in the expected future prices of different defense inputs must also be considered in evaluating the most efficient allocation of defense resources. As we have seen, the cost of defense manpower rose relative to the cost of defense capital during the 1970s, suggesting a shift toward greater expenditures on capital. In a dynamic sense, however, adjusting the mix of inputs to the shifting relative prices of the last decade would make little sense if we anticipated a shift in relative prices in the other direction in the next decade. There are several indications that the relative increase in military pay will continue over the next decade despite the cuts in real military pay of the late 1970s resulting from antiinflationary policies. First, there are major problems in filling reserve and national guard units at current pay levels. Second, we know that the population pool of potential recruits will fall sharply in the 1980s. There is some prospect of continued substitution of women for men in some defense jobs, but the extent of possible substitutions in combat assignments is still the subject of debate. On balance it is difficult to foresee how the volunteer force, as currently structured, can survive the next decade wihout substantial pay adjustments. We will return to this argument in our subsequent discussions of defense manpower, but for the present the point to emphasize is that the efficient allocation of defense resources requires consideration of possible shifts in relative input prices.

CONCLUSION

The theory of defense production links output and input decisions. At the aggregate level, the theory suggests that shifts in the relative prices of inputs or the relative productivity of different inputs should lead to a reallocation of defense resources in order to provide the desired output most efficiently. Applying these ideas in practice requires an evaluation of expected changes in missions, input productivity, and input costs, because future as well as current capabilities must be considered. The central idea that the efficient allocation of resources requires evaluation of input costs, however, applies even in a more dynamic evaluation of defense production.

Isocost and isoquant analysis provides a useful framework for summarizing decisions on defense production. From the point of view of our aggregate economic policy, the defense budget is constrained at a given isocost line, and the problem for defense planners is to find the allocation of resources that produces the highest output consistent with that cost constraint. From the point of view of national security strategists, the process may be seen as evaluating the "required" level of defense output (selecting the desire isoquant) and then minimizing the cost of reaching that level of output. In a more general sense, however, defense decisions should be made by considering the least cost at which different levels of defense output may be produced, and then trading off different levels of defense capability against competing national objectives. Whichever of these perspectives one uses, the conclusion for resource management remains the same. Resources should be allocated over different inputs to insure that the return from the last dollar spent on each input is the same.

In the following chapters we will turn to a detailed examination of the markets for defense inputs in order to evaluate how the prices of those inputs are determined, and how defense management decisions are affected by the markets in which the inputs must be procured.

NOTES

1 This may be shown using calculus. The production function is:

$$Q = f(K, L)$$

Taking the total derivative we have:

$$dQ = \frac{\delta Q}{\delta K} dK + \frac{\delta Q}{\delta L} dL$$

Along an isoquant dQ equals zero. Therefore the slope, dL/dK, is derived as:

$$\frac{\delta Q}{\delta K} dK = -\frac{\delta Q}{\delta L} dL \quad \text{and} \quad \frac{dL}{dK} = -\frac{\delta Q/\delta K}{\delta Q/\delta L}$$

$\delta Q/\delta K$ is the marginal product of capital (MPK) and $\delta Q/\delta L$ is the marginal product of labor (MPL). The marginal rate of factor substitution is therefore the negative of the ratio of the marginal products of the inputs, or $-MPK/MPL$.

2 This may be shown using algebra. the isocost equation is:

$$C_1 = P_K K + P_L L.$$

Solving for L we have:

$$L = C_1 / P_L - (P_K / P_L) K,$$

where $-P_K / P_L$ is the slope.

3 Richard Cooper, *Military Manpower and the All-Volunteer Force* (Santa Monica, California: Rand, 1977), pp. 273–274.

4 *Ibid.*, pp. 278–190.

5 Charles Robert Roll, Jr., *Capital and Labor Shares in the Department of Defense* (Santa Monica, California: Rand, 1978).

6 Cooper, *op. cit.*, p. 281.

7 *Ibid.*, p. 288. The optional mix of capital and labor is discussed in more detail in Chapters 15 and 16.

SELECTED REFERENCES

Richard Cooper, *Military Manpower and the All-Volunteer Force* (Santa Monica, California: Rand, 1977).
Edwin Mansfield, *Microeconomics: Theory and Applications* (New York: W. W. Norton & Co., Inc., 1970).

Part III

Resource Allocation in the Defense Sector

Management by objectives works if you know the objectives. Ninety percent of the time you don't.

Peter Drucker

What we gain in power is lost in time. For every grain of wit there is a grain of folly. For everything you have missed you have gained something else, and for everything you gain, you lose something.

Ralph Waldo Emerson

Chapter 10
Basic Concepts of Efficiency in Resource Allocation

INTRODUCTION

In this and the two following chapters we will be concerned with the concept of efficiency in defense resource allocation and with the two analytical methods for achieving such efficiency: namely, Cost Benefit Analysis and Cost Effectiveness Analysis. Possibly the most typical choice in defense economics involves whether or not to approve a specific project, e.g., procurement of a new weapons system. The techniques apply and our interest extends to a much wider variety of problems, however, ranging across issues as diverse as military compensation, tactical doctrine, and alliance policies, and embracing literally any policy issue in which scarce resources are involved and in which some element of choice is present. In some cases the economic considerations are predominant; in others economic considerations take a back seat to political factors. In some cases economic analysis provides a powerful tool for identifying the preferable course of action; in others the complexities are such that the analysis is less productive. In most cases, however, a careful economic analysis is both appropriate and useful. The trick is neither to overstate nor understate its role.

Cost Benefit Analysis applies in those cases in which the proposed project or policy is expected to confer benefits that can be measured or at least approximated in dollar terms. For example, the construction of a dam or other water resource improvement project can be analyzed with this technique. The crucial aspect for Cost Benefit Analysis is that the benefits and costs are commensurate in that they are capable of being measured in common terms—in this case, in dollars. For most defense spending, the output cannot be measured or evaluated in dollar terms. A weapons system such as a tank or fighter plane, for example, can be analyzed in terms of combat effectiveness in various contexts against various types of opposing forces, and in comparison to various alternative systems. It is not feasible, however, to evaluate combat effectiveness in dollar terms. This lack of commensurability between cost and benefit creates special problems and requires somewhat more restrictive techniques of analysis. Such techniques come under the heading of Cost Effectiveness Analysis, in which costs are measured in dollars and effectiveness is measured in some other units.

In all cases, however, the basic idea to remember is that defense problems are economic problems. The expenditure of scarce resources for defense purposes must be subjected to the same type of economic scrutiny as should any other use of public funds. Defense spending consumes scarce resources, diverting them from use in the satisfaction of other economic wants. The resulting cost of defense spending is reduced opportunity for consumption, either in the private sector or the nondefense public sector. This opportunity cost must be taken into account in determining the amount of resources to allocate to defense. Furthermore, those scarce resources must be used in the most effective manner possible. In choosing between two competing designs for a tank, plane, or ship, for example, the model that exhibits the best performance characteristics is not necessarily the best choice. Enhanced effectiveness normally means higher cost, and the analyst and ultimately the policymaker have an obligation to evaluate what that cost is, and to judge whether the enhanced effectiveness justifies the higher cost.

The relevance, indeed the indispensability, of cost considerations in defense resource allocation is patently obvious. Yet a sytematic effort to perform cost analysis is a relatively recent phenomenon that has met considerable resistance. After surveying the methods of Cost Benefit Analysis and Cost Effectiveness Analysis, we will examine briefly the history of the application of these techniques, including a look at why such ordinary economic notions have been able to generate such heated controversy.

Our objective, then, is to explore how economic analysis can be used to achieve efficient resource allocation in the public sector of the economy, specifically with respect to defense spending. We cannot talk sensibly about efficiency in the public sector, however, without a clear and common understanding of what we mean by efficiency in the private sector. We need a frame of reference, and for this purpose certain concepts and understandings are indispensable. The remainder of this chapter is devoted to that purpose. Our discussion will be limited to a survey of the most important concepts.

MARKET PRICES AND OPPORTUNITY COSTS

The central purpose of economic activity—at least, as that purpose is understood in a democratic pluralist society—is the satisfaction of individual economic wants. Given the fact that resources are limited, the test of the efficiency of resource allocation must be based on the degree to which the goods and services produced actually satisfy the economic wants of the individuals in the society.

This is an extraordinarily difficult task. The most formidable difficulty lies in the nature of the objective: satisfying human wants that are complex, that vary widely among individuals, and that by their very nature are private to each individual and not subject to external measurement. The task is also made difficult by the sheer immensity of the problem. Affecting millions of participants, the task requires coordinated daily choices regarding the composition of output, its distribution to users, and the inputs and methods of production to be employed.

Fortunately, in a mixed-market economy the preponderance of the allocation is handled by the market mechanism. The quantity of resources to be allocated to each activity is determined on a decentralized basis, through the interaction of supply and demand. The market prices established in this process serve as a signalling device that, subject to certain qualifications, insures that each resource is allocated to its most efficient use. The system of market prices is the key to efficient resource allocation in the private sector and, as we shall see, these prices also provide an indispensable framework for analyzing efficiency of allocation in the public sector.

The aspect of market prices that renders them invaluable as a basis for resource allocation is that they reflect *opportunity cost*. As mentioned earlier, by opportunity cost we mean the cost of using resources measured in terms of the value of the alternative output that those resources might produce, were they not diverted to whatever project or purpose is being analyzed. Of course, in making this comparison we are interested in looking at the *best* alternative, since the objective of our concern is the best possible use of our resources.

The way in which the market mechanism succeeds in pricing resources in a manner that reflects their opportunity cost can be shown by reference to an ordinary supply demand analysis, illustrated in Figure 10.1.

We initially assume that the market for the resource in question is "competitive," meaning that both the suppliers (or sellers) and the demanders (or buyers) are sufficient in number so that no single individual is able by his own actions to influence the market price significantly. We also assume the absence of collusion, so that no group of individuals acting in concert is able to gain market power and influence the price.

In labelling the diagram "Market for any Resource or Product," we make the point that the analysis that follows is generally applicable. The resource in question might be a *primary resource* or "factor of production," such as labor, land, or capital. It might be any of the millions of *intermediate products* representing resources still in the process of transformation and not yet ready for final consumption. Such intermediate products constitute the bulk of the inputs to industrial production and include raw materials and semi-finished items such as steel, lumber, glass, plastic, textiles, etc. Intermediate products also include completed items purchased by business firms and utilized for other production rather than consumption. Finally, our diagram applies to *final products*, or finished goods and services purchased by consumers to satisfy their economic wants.

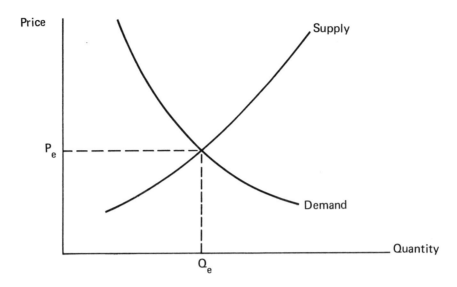

Figure 10.1 Market for any Resource or Product

The demand and supply curves shown in the diagram graphically depict the behavior of the buyers and sellers in the market for the resource or product. More specifically, the demand curve illustrates variations in the quantity of the resource or product that will be demanded, these variations being a decreasing function of the market price. Similarly, the supply curve illustrates variations in the quantity supplied, but as an increasing function of the market price.

The market demand curve is an aggregate relationship, depicting the value to potential buyers of the resource or product in terms of dollars, based on the potential buyers' willingness to pay. In the case of a final product, this willingness stems from the ability of the product to satisfy economic wants. In the case of primary resources or intermediate products, the willingness to pay is motivated by the productivity of the item in the next stage of the production process. In either case the buyers, limited by their own budgetary constraints and motivated by their desire to maximize their individual satisfaction of economic wants, can be expected to search for the cheapest or most economically effective ways of satisfying their needs.

The supply curve is essentially a cost of production relationship. The motivating force for individual suppliers is the production and sale of the item for profit, profit being the difference between sales revenue and production cost. Accordingly, suppliers seek to minimize their production costs, and the standard analysis of supplier behavior under competitive conditions demonstrates that the market supply curve is equivalent to the marginal cost of production.[1]

It is through the interaction of these patterns of supply and demand behavior that the market price is determined. The equilibrium price, given by the intersection of the supply and demand curves, represents that price at which the quantity supplied is equal to the quantity demanded, and the market is consequently cleared. In conjunction with establishing an equilibrium price, the market also decides the allocation issue: namely, the quantity of the resource or product that will be produced.

To understand the manner in which competitive market prices reflect opportunity costs, we need to look for a moment at how the market mechanism might function in a specific case. For this purpose, consider Figure 10.2 and suppose it represents supply and demand for a certain type of cotton cloth.

As the diagram shows, the current equilibrium price, as set by the market, is $50 per bolt; and the quantity exchanged at this price is some 20,000 bolts per week. What is the significance of the $50 per bolt price of cotton cloth?

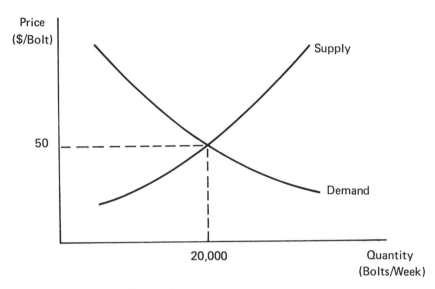

Figure 10.2 Supply and Demand for Cotton Cloth

From the standpoint of the demand curve, we note first that $50 does *not* represent the value of cotton cloth in terms of the price individual users generally would be willing to pay. For amounts greater than the equilibrium quantity of 20,000 bolts per week, the value of the cloth to users is considerably in excess of $50 per bolt. For amounts greater than the equilibrium amount, the cloth has some value, although the value is always less than $50. The nature of the market mechanism is such that, barring the presence of various imperfections, which we will assume for the moment to be absent, the equilibrium price of $50 will be paid and received on *all* cotton cloth exchanged in the market. This means that all the users will receive all the cloth they purchase for a price of $50 a bolt, which is generally less than what they would be willing to pay, except for the *marginal use*. By marginal use we mean the last and least valuable use, or that use which would be discontinued if for some reason the price rose to $51 and the quantity demanded declined accordingly. Another way of stating this characteristic of a market price is to note that all those uses which have a value in excess of $50 per bolt of cloth are satisfied, while those values less than $50 remain unsatisfied. It should be noted that these uses may be highly diversified, ranging across many types of clothing, industrial, and other uses. In each case, of course, substitute items are available, and the buyer's demand for cotton cloth reflects an implicit comparison and evaluation of those substitute items, taking into account relative prices, product performance, individual taste, etc. Thus the $50 price reflects the marginal value of cotton cloth in each of its many uses. The same analysis may be made at any price, and the demand curve may be interpreted as a marginal valuation curve, each point representing the marginal value of coton cloth at that particular output level.[2]

By requiring all purchasers of cotton cloth to pay a price of $50, the market has taken an important step towards allocative efficiency. The 20,000 bolts produced go to the most valuable uses. If, by contrast, some portion of the 20,000 bolts were diverted to purposes in which their use was valued at less than $50 per bolt, that diversion could be characterized as a misallocation.

The $50 price is also of fundamental importance from the standpoint of supply, representing as it does the marginal cost of production. Just as cotton cloth has a market price, so also do all those factors or inputs used in making it, such as, cotton yarn, labor, weaving machinery, energy, processing chemicals, and so on. In each case the established price reflects a similar balance between the marginal cost of production of that item and its marginal value in each of its various uses. When we consider the total system of market prices, ascribing to each price this property of reflecting both marginal value in use and marginal cost of production, we can understand what is meant by saying that competitive prices reflect opportunity costs.

Consider, for example, the consequence of increasing the production level of cotton cloth by one bolt. We known that an additional $50 of resources are required to produce the cotton, divided in some fashion among the various inputs involved. We assume that the primary productive factors of land, labor, and capital are fixed. Hence, the ultimate impact of the additional cotton will be reduced levels of output of *other* goods or services. We also assume that the price set on each resource used to make additional cotton reflects that resource's marginal value in alternatives uses. It follows that the ultimate consequence is a reduciton in output of other final goods in the same amount as the increase in cotton, namely $50. In other words, the opportunity cost of an additional $50 worth of cotton cloth is $50 less of something else.

The significance of this remarkable property of competitive market prices is profound. It means that, subject to the qualifications that we will discuss presently, the market system achieves efficiency in resource allocation, in the sense that the "value" of total output is maximized. This maximum value of output is based on a system of relative prices that reflect the marginal value to consumers of the various items in the output mix, as revealed by their willingness to pay for the items. We can use these market prices to evaluate specific public projects, measuring benefits and costs in terms of their market value. If benefits exceed costs, then the project represents an efficient use of resources—at least in the sense that it leads to an increase in the value of total output. It is on the basis of this concept of efficiency and this use of market prices that cost benefit analysis is conducted.

There are, however, serious qualifications to the above formulation. The major qualification concerns a shortcoming in our concept of efficiency in resource allocation. We must also qualify the argument because, for a number of reasons, in practice market prices at best only approximate the competitive model, and in many instances diverge sharply from it. The following sections consider each of these problems in turn.

EFFICIENCY AND EQUITY IN RESOURCE ALLOCATION

The fundamental objective of efficiency in resource allocation is to maximize the economic well-being, or welfare, of members of society. Unfortunately, we are unable to measure individual economic welfare directly. That being the case, and assuming economic welfare to be a function of goods and services available for consumption, the conventional approach to the problem is to seek to maximize the "value" of the goods and services that our limited resources produce. Using market prices as weights, the value of total output can be measured in money terms. Employing this approach, the scheme of resource allocation leading to the greatest dollar value of output may be said to be the most "efficient." In the competitive market, the allocation of resources tends to be efficient in this particular sense.

The main problem with this formulation is that a dollar's worth of additional output is treated identically, without regard to the way in which the additional output is distributed. An additional dollar's worth of goods and services for the most affluent member of society receives the same credit as an additional dollar for the least affluent member. What this means, to state the difficulty in a more persuasive way, is that by our definition, any reallocation of resources that leads to an increased value of output has to be deemed more "efficient" no matter what the distributional impact. This would even apply, for example, to a reallocation that reduced the income of some, provided that others enjoyed an improvement sufficient in magnitude to cause a net increase overall.

Obviously this will not do. Efficiency alone, in the sense we have defined it, is not a sufficient basis for evaluating resource allocation—in general or in specific instances. The distribution of outputs to different individuals also matters, and the question of whether "more is better" depends in an essential way on "who gets it." In other words, we must be concerned with both efficiency and *equity* of distribution in evaluating different patterns of resource allocation.

Given the impossibility of measuring economic welfare in a way that would permit interpersonal comparisons, economists have tended to avoid the problem of equity. In the absence of any scientific, objective basis for evaluating the equity of alternative allocation schemes, it has been felt that such issues were best left to resolution through the political process. Economists, of course, do have views and make judgments on distribution or equity issues. The point is that in doing so they are understood to be engaging in a different type of activity—one that is inherently subjective. There is no generally acceptable criterion for evaluating equity, and in the final analysis each individual is entitled to his own criterion. Given this lack of ground rules, economists have preferred to segregate the two issues, devoting the bulk of their attention to the efficiency problem, but seeking to analyze the efficiency issue so as to avoid prejudging the questions of equity or slipping in hidden assumptions or biases with respect to such issues.

This leads in effect to a two-stage process. Efficiency is analyzed first, insofar as can be accomplished without prejudging the issue of equity. Equity judgments are then made individually or through the political process, hopefully incorporating efficiency considerations and resulting in better policy decisions.

Given their propensity to avoid value judgements in constructing economic theory, economists have, on occasion, been criticized for avoiding the difficult issues and focusing too much of their energy on less important matters. In their defense, however, a great deal can be said for treating value judgments as explicitly and openly as possible. In practice this means taking care to avoid the imbedding of particular ideological preferences in the theory. In any event, that is the approach we will follow in this text.

PARETO OPTIMALITY AND PARETO IMPROVEMENTS

The central concept in defining efficiency in resource allocation so as to abstract from the problem of income distribution is the notion of *Pareto Optimality.*. Resource allocation in a given system is said to be Pareto Optimal if in every possible reallocation of resources that would result in the improvement of one or more individuals' economic welfare, at least one other individual would experience a reduction in economic welfare. The closely related concept of a *Pareto Improvement* is defined as a reallocation in which at least one individual gains in economic welfare, while no one is harmed. Thus Pareto Optimality may be defined in terms of an allocation scheme in which no Pareto Improvement is possible. Once Pareto Optimality has been achieved, all possible sources of improvement in the efficiency of resource allocation have been exhausted, save, of course, those which reward some by reducing the welfare of others.

Efficiency in Exchange: Distribution of the Output

Recall from Chapter 9 that we may represent levels of output produced from different combinations of inputs with a series of production contour lines, or lines of constant output, known as "isoquants." Similarly in the case of an individual we may map out "indifference curves" which trace combinations of goods, say X and Y, that provide the individual with constant levels of satisfaction or economic welfare.

For example, Figure 10.3 depicts a welfare map for Jones. Each contour line, or "indifference curve," represents a constant level of satisfaction. According to the curves shown, if Jones loses some of Good X he must be compensated with more of Good Y in order to remain at the same level of satisfaction. Contours further to the right represent higher levels of satisfaction, because at any level of Good Y, Jones has more of Good X as well. Thus, J_3 represents a higher level of satisfaction than J_2.

The meaning of Pareto Optimality may be illustrated using an Edgeworth Box diagram, which compares the levels of satisfaction attained by two individuals based on different distributions of fixed amounts of Goods X and Y.

The solid contoured lines, J_1 to J_7, portray the indifference curves of Jones, depicting his ranking of alternative allocations. It is assumed that Jones values both goods, and generally prefers more of either, so that his contours or indifference curves depict higher levels of economic welfare as we move up and to the right from J_1 to J_7.[3] Similarly, the dashed lines reveal Smith's preference function with Smith's welfare increasing as we move to the left and down from S_1 to S_7.

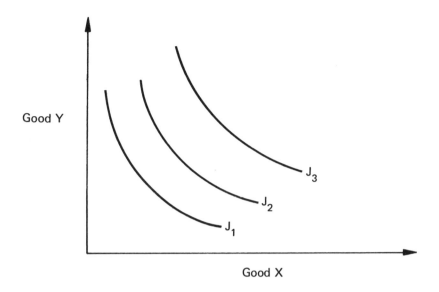

Figure 10.3 Individual Welfare Map

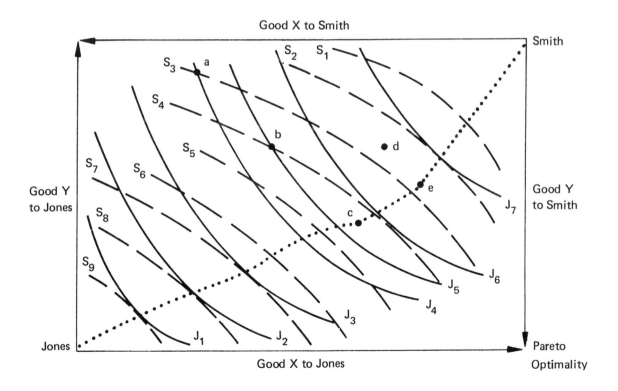

Figure 10.4 An Edgeworth Box Diagram Illustrating Efficiency in Exchange

For both individuals, the indifference curves depicted are "ordinal." This means that a point on a higher contour represents a preferred allocation, or a higher level of economic welfare. We can attach no significance, however, to the distance between any two contours—we cannot make an inference as to "how much" one point is preferred over another. By the same token, we can make no inference as to the comparative level of welfare of the two individuals. These assumptions impose serious limitations on our ability to define an efficient allocation scheme. The assumptions are necessary, however, given the limits of our ability to measure or compare the underlying preference functions.

Particular importance attaches to the slope of an indifference curve, which is known as the *marginal rate of substitution* (MRS). The MRS, at a given point, represents the rate at which the individual is willing to exchange one good for the other, moving along his present contour and experiencing no increase or decrease in economic welfare. The dotted line, known as the *contract curve*, depicts the locus of points of tangency between the indifference curves of Jones and Smith, i.e., all the possible allocation schemes for which the $MRS_{Jones} = MRS_{Smith}$. *All points lying on the contract curve satisfy the conditions for Pareto Optimality with respect to the simple problem of exchange we have defined.*[4] By examining any point on the contract curve, the reader may readily verify that a movement in any direction inevitably harms one of the two individuals, i.e., it moves him to a lower indifference curve. A movement along the contract curve, in other words, improves the welfare of one while lowering the welfare of the other. A movement from a point on the contract curve to a point not on this curve may even harm both, although not necessarily.

As discussed previously, we have no scientific basis for comparing the welfare of Jones and Smith. Hence, in evaluating various allocation schemes, we are limited to comparisons that do not require us to trade off one man's gain against another man's loss. The contract curve is important because it takes us as far as we can go towards achieving efficient allocation without getting involved in such equity trade-offs. From any point on the contract curve, there is no reallocation that benefits both parties. Conversely, from any point *not* on the contract curve, it is always feasible to make reallocations that *do* benefit *both* parties. In the diagram, for example, a reallocation from Point a to Points b or c would have that effect. Such a movement would constitute a Pareto Improvement. To reiterate, once we achieve a Pareto Optimal allocation such as Point c on the contract curve, no reallocation benefitting both parties is possible. This means we have exhausted the possibilities for improving economic welfare via more efficient allocation. It might of course be judged that some other allocation is more desirable, such as e on the contract curve, or even d, which lies off the contract curve. Such a judgment, however, would have to be based on arguments of equity. Questions are involved in this case that economic science cannot answer.

Efficiency in Production: The Choice of Factor Inputs

The above discussion has developed the concepts of Pareto Optimality and Pareto Improvement in terms of the problem of efficiency in exchange—that is, we took the amounts of goods available as given and focused solely on their distribution. By analogous reasoning, the concept may be extended back into the production process, addressing the questions of (1) the amounts of each good to be produced, and (2) the choice of technology and input combinations to be employed in production processes. Each of these two important dimensions of efficiency in resource allocation may also be illustrated with a single diagram.

In Figure 10.5 the Edgeworth Box is used to show what is meant by Pareto Optimality with respect to choice of inputs. The case illustrated is again a simple two-factor, two-good case. We assume that the factors K (capital) and L (labor), represented respectively by the horizontal and vertical dimensions of the Edgeworth Box, are available in fixed amounts.

These two factors are employed in the production of two products, A and B, and may be combined in varying proportions, producing levels of output according to functions depicted by solid line production contours, or "isoquants," for A and dashed line isoquants for B. As in the previous example, any point inside the box represents a feasible allocation scheme. At Point a, for example, K_A units of capital are allocated to the produc-

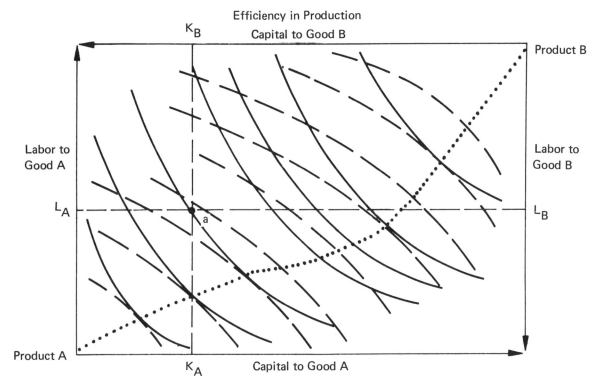

Figure 10.5 An Edgeworth Box Illustrating Efficiency in Production

tion of A, and the remaining K_B units to B. Each isoquant represents a given level of output, which increases as we move to the right and up in the case of A, and increases as we move to the left and down in the case of B. The slope of the production contour at any point is known as the *marginal rate of factor substitution* (MRFS), and gives the (marginal) rate at which one factor may be substituted for the other, holding output constant. The reader should note that the rate is depicted as varying, with the trade-off worsening as we move to a higher intensity of use of either factor. This assumption regarding the nature of the production function, discussed in Chapter 9 and known as the generalized law of diminishing returns, is crucial to this analysis.[5]

Our objective in this allocation problem is to employ the given amounts of capital and labor so as to maximize output of Goods A and B. A Pareto Optimal solution, perfectly analogous to the exchange problem previously analyzed, is that the allocation be accomplished in such a manner that no additional output of either good is possible, except at the cost of reducing the output level for the other good. It may easily be shown that the necessary condition for achieving Pareto Optimality is that the factors be allocated so that their marginal rate of factor substitution in the production of both products is identical, i.e., $MRFS_A = MRFS_B$.[6] This condition is satisfied at any point on the dotted line, which is the locus of points of tangency between the two production functions and is analogous to the contract curve discussed above.

The meaning of Pareto Optimality in this sense is best illustrated using the conventional idea of a production possibility frontier introduced in Chapter 1 and reproduced here in Figure 10.6. Points inside or on the frontier represent feasible output levels of the two goods, given fixed amounts of factor inputs. In other words, points inside or on the curve correspond to points inside the Edgeworth Box in Figure 10.5. All points on the frontier represent efficient production schemes, corresponding to a point on the dotted line in Figure 10.5. Any point inside the frontier is inefficient, since more of *both* goods could be produced. Satisfacton of the Pareto Optimality condition in allocation of the factors guarantees that the output levels are pushed out to a point on the production possibility frontier.

Choice of Outputs

We have seen that Pareto Optimality involves efficiency in exchange (Figure 10.4) and efficiency in production (Figure 10.5). The third dimension of Pareto Optimality concerns the choice of an output pattern, i.e., the selection of a particular point on the production possibility frontier. In order to explain this aspect of efficiency we need to return to the concept of opportunity cost, in which the cost to society of an increase in the output of any good is measured in terms of the corresponding reduction in output of some other good. In our two-good case, the opportunity cost of more of A is less of B. This opportunity cost of A is given by the slope of the production possibility frontier in Figure 10.6, and we will refer to it as the *marginal rate of transformation* (MRT). At Point a, for example, where the slope is one, one additional unit of A can be had at the cost of one unit of B. As we expand A's output, however, given the shape of the production possibility curve, the MRT changes so that the opportunity cost increases. At Point b the cost of an additional unit of A is two units of B.

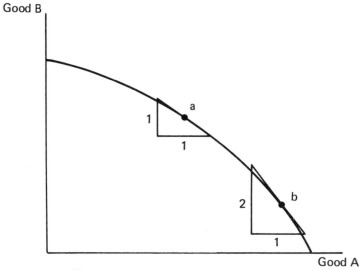

Figure 10.6 Production Possibility Frontier

Which pattern of output is best? Clearly the answer depends on how society values Good A with respect to Good B. Since we must assume that individual preferences vary, and since in any event we cannot measure or compare directly the individual valuations, choosing the output pattern to best satisfy society's preferences sounds like a formidable task. Once more, the concept of Pareto Optimality suggests an approach.

As we have previously specified, the condition of efficiency in exchange in our two-good, two-person economy requires that the marginal rate of substitution between the two goods be equal for both consumers. We now impose an additional condition, that *this marginal rate of substitution—whatever it is—must also be equal to the marginal rate of transformation*. Thus an output pattern must be selected such that the slope of the production possibiltiy frontier at that point is equal to the marginal rate of substitution. The rate at which society is *able* to transform one good into the other must equal the rate at which consumers are *willing* to exchange the one good for the other.

The logic of this condition is easily understood by considering any output pattern for which the condition is *not* satisfied. Suppose, for example, referring again to Figure 10.6, that the society is producing the output of Point a, with the opportunity cost of Good A equal to one unit of Good B. In other words, society is able to transform one unit of Good B into one unit of Good A. Suppose further that at these levels of output, consumers are generally willing to give up two units of B in exchange for an additional unit of A. What this means is that an additional unit of A would be worth more than its opportunity cost. Clearly it would make for greater efficiency in resource use, therefore, if less of B and more of A were produced. The value of the output to consumers would be greater. As long as there is a divergence between the opportunity cost and the value of marginal output of one good relative to the other good, it will always be possible to enhance the value of output by reallocation.

Given the assumed shapes of production and preference contours, such reallocation will tend to bring about the necessary equality between MRS and MRT. As more of A is produced, its opportuntiy cost rises. At the same time, its increasing availability makes it of less value to consumers, relative to B.

The Pareto Efficiency Conditions

The preceding discussion was couched in terms of two-good, two-person economics to facilitate graphical illustrations of what Pareto Optimality means. The argument, however, is easily extended to any number of goods and persons, and the conditions as stated then apply to any pair of goods and any pair of consumers. The three conditions we have developed correspond to the three allocation problems of How, What, and For Whom. In summary we restate them.

1. *Efficiency in Production: Choice of Factor Inputs (the "How" problem).* In any two production processes utilizing two production factors in common, the marginal rate of factor substitution must be the same.
2. *Choice of Outputs (the "What" problem).* The marginal rate of transformation between any two products must be equal to the marginal rate of substitution.
3. *Efficiency in Exchange: Distribution of the Output (the "For Whom" problem).* Final output must be distributed so that the marginal rate of substitution between any two products is the same for all consumers of both products.[7]

Given satisfaction of these three conditions, Pareto Optimality is achieved. This means that no reallocation with respect to factors, outputs, or distribution of the outputs can improve any individual's economic welfare without reducing the welfare of at least one other. No Pareto Improvements are possible.

It would be difficult to exaggerate the importance of these conditions, since they constitute the basic conceptual framework for all efforts to promote efficient use of resources in a general, economy-wide sense. As such, they are indispensable to an understanding of Cost Benefit Analysis.

PARETO OPTIMALITY AND THE MARKET SYSTEM

The relevance of the Pareto Conditions to economic policymaking depends, of course, on the feasibility of implementing them. The marginal trade-offs and rates of substitution referred to above are fine theoreticallly, but unless they can be measured in an operational way they would be of limited value for policy purposes. It should come as no surprise to the reader that we rely on the market pricing system to measure these trade-offs. What this all boils down to, therefore, is the question of whether market price ratios do indeed measure, or at least approximate, the underlying economic realities—namely, the MRS's and MRT's as defined above.

The Market and Efficiency in Exchange

The answer to this question is yes, albeit a highly qualified yes. Earlier in the chapter, in the discussion of supply and demand in competitive markets, the assertion was made that an equilibrium market price does indeed reflect both the marginal value in use (from the buyer's point of view) and the opportunity cost (from the seller's point of view). We can state essentially the same results in a form that is easier to relate to the Pareto Optimality conditions by using *price ratios*. For any buyer (e.g., Jones or Smith) of any two goods (e.g., A and B), it can be shown that the rational individual will arrange his purchases within his budgetary constraint so that

$$\frac{P_A}{P_B} = MRS_{Jones} = MRS_{Smith}, \tag{10.1}$$

where P_A and P_B represent the competitive market prices of A and B respectively. Why it is rational to behave in this way is easily seen in Figure 10.7, which depicts a preference function and a budget line for Jones. The budget line indicates the combinations of Goods A and B that may be purchased with the consumer's income. Although any point on the budget line is feasible, Point a, where the budget line is tangent to a preference contour, brings Jones to the highest contour within his budgetary capability. The slope of the budget line is the negative of the price ratio P_A/P_B, and it represents the rate at which Jones can substitute the two goods. That is to say he must give up P_A/P_B units of B to obtain an additional unit of A. In attempting to maximize his satisfaction, Jones will adjust his purchases of A and B to the point at which his marginal rate of substitution is equal to the price ratio.[8]

The power of the market system comes into play with the fact that *every* consumer, each adjusting to the given market price ratio, winds up with the same MRS. Our condition for efficiency in exchange is thereby satisfied.

The Market and the Choice of Outputs

For sellers of goods A and B, assuming as we do that profit maximization is the driving motive, the rational behavior involves supplying the good up to point at which the marginal cost of producing it is equal to the market price.[9] Stating this result in terms of the price ratio of the two goods, we have

$$\frac{MC_A}{MC_B} = \frac{P_A}{P_B}, \tag{10.2}$$

where MC_A and MC_B represent the respective marginal costs of Good A and Good B. It may be shown that the left hand ratio is the marginal rate of transformation, which the reader will recall is the slope of the production possibility frontier. This is easily understood in terms of the opportunity cost concept. If A is cotton cloth and costs \$50 to produce (at the margin), and B is nylon cloth and costs \$100 (again at the margin), then the resources released by producing one less unit of nylon would permit production of two additional units of cotton. By combining equations 10.1 and 10.2 we obtain

$$MRT = \frac{P_A}{P_B} = MRS_{Jones} = MRS_{Smith}, \tag{10.3}$$

thereby satisfying our condition for efficiency in choice of outputs.

The Market and Efficiency in Production

Finally, the condition for efficiency in production is guaranteed by our assumption that profit maximization is the motivating force in the behavior of suppliers. A corollary to maximizing profit is to select inputs for any level of output so as to minimize production costs. This means that in each production process, inputs will be combined so that the marginal rate of factor substitution between any two factors is equal to the market price ratio.[10] Considering capital and labor as two factors and denoting their marginal rates of substitution in production of A and B respectively as $MRFS_A$ and $MRFS_B$, we have

$$\frac{P_K}{P_L} = MRFS_A = MRFS_B \tag{10.3}$$

Once again, individual decision makers, in this case producers acting individually but on the basis of a common set of market prices, are led to behavior that insures satisfaction of the Pareto Optimality conditions.

The Market and Pareto Optimality

The above discussion presented in outline forms the argument that allocation based on competitive market prices will be efficient, at least in the sense of Pareto Optimality. This is a significant result. It is the principal basis for defense of the market-based solution to problems of economic allocation. It is also significant with respect to cost benefit and cost effectiveness analysis. The point here is that competitive market prices do indeed reflect the opportunity costs and the marginal values of individual factors and products. Consequently, they do in general constitute reliable guides to policymakers in evaluating the cost of diverting such goods and factors to alternative purposes—be they defense, the nondefense public sector, or other uses.

PARETO IMPROVEMENTS AND POTENTIAL PARETO IMPROVEMENTS

A Cost Benefit analysis is a comparison of two allocation schemes—the current scheme, and the one which would replace it upon implementation of the project being analyzed. Neither of these schemes is likely to be optimal. Hence, rather than defining conditions for optima, the practical tasks of economic analysis boil down to judgments as to whether a proposed change leads to an improvement in economic welfare.

One criterion for making a favorable judgment is that the change constitutes a Pareto Improvement. We defined a Pareto Improvement as a change resulting from some specific reallocation of resources, such that one or more individuals experience an improvement in economic welfare and no one suffers a reduction. The market allocation process may be characterized as a continual search for Pareto Improvements, i.e., transactions from which both parties gain. If the market functions smoothly, relatively free of certain distorting influences to be discussed below, it will approach Pareto Optimality. That is to say it will do a good job of identifying and taking advantage of Pareto Improvements.

Unfortunately, this concept is of limited use in evaluating allocation issues that stem from governmental intervention in the market process. Such intervention typically differs from a market transaction in that something more than a voluntary, mutually rewarding exchange between two parties is involved. Typically there is some element of coercion, exercised through governmental tax or regulatory authority, and typically there are some "losers." Even though benefits exceed costs in aggregate terms, the benefits and costs are so distributed that for some individuals the costs exceed the benefits.

Given our inability to make interpersonal comparisons of economic welfare—at least on a scientific basis—governmental actions of this nature fall outside the purview of economic analysis. No matter how large the net benefits, if a single individual suffers a net reduction in welfare, then it can well be argued that, strictly speaking, economics has nothing to say. To leave matters here would condemn economists to silence on most important economic issues. As discussed above, the conventional way of skirting this thorny problem is to attempt to abstract from the *distributional* aspects of benefits and costs. In order to clarify what this means one further concept from the jargon of welfare economics is required, the concept of a *Potential Pareto Improvement*.

We define a Potential Pareto Improvement as change that would make all affected parties net gainers provided there is an appropriate redistribution of the benefits and costs, for example, through money transfers. In others words, a Potential Pareto Improvement is a reallocation that may be converted into a Pareto Improvement through redistribution. If we think in terms of a government project that entails costs and benefits measurable in monetary terms, and if we assume the redistribution will take the form of monetary compensation, it would appear that any project for which benefits exceed costs would qualify as a Potential Pareto Improvement. Indeed, Cost Benefit analysis may be characterized as a search for Potential Pareto Improvements.[11]

It turns out that deciding whether a given project does or does not constitute a Potential Pareto Improvement is a process fraught with conceptual and practical problems. These problems are discussed in the following chapters. Without going into detail at this point, suffice it to say that we aspire to make a determination as to whether the gainers place sufficient value on the benefits to enable them to compensate the losers, leaving some net benefit. This of course does *not* suffice as a basis for undertaking the project, if in fact the compensation is not actually paid. What it does provide is a partial evaluation of costs and benefits in dollar terms, implicitly assigning the same weight to a dollar of benefit or a dollar of cost, without regard to who receives the benefit and bears the cost. The distribution of these benefits and costs must be judged separately.

Qualifications Due to Market Imperfections

We wish to use actual market prices to indicate relative marginal values and relative marginal costs, and we have presented some arguments in support of doing that when the prices in question are determined in competitive markets. In practice, real world prices diverge from those of the competitive model because few real world markets are perfectly competitive. In the following paragraphs we will discuss briefly the principal causes of these *market imperfections*, or departures from the competitive model, and their impact on the accuracy of actual prices as guides to resource allocation.

Limited Information

Market imperfections stem from many sources. Probably the most pervasive problem is simply the lack of complete information on the part of buyers and sellers regarding the opportunities the market affords. Our previous account assumed success of the market in establishing a common price on each product, for all buyers and sellers. This would only be achievable in a static world of perfect knowledge; zero transactions costs; and simple, homogeneous products whose quality and designs were unobscured by brand names and exaggerated advertising claims. In the real world the search for the best deal costs time and money, and is frustrated by the complexity of the products involved and constantly changing conditions. The resulting prices afford a much less precise definition of opportunity cost than those suggested by the concept of the equilibrium price in the competitive model.

Despite these inaccuracies the market pricing system remains the best available guide to opportunity cost, and we have no substitute for it. We do have an interest in improving the performance of the market system, however, especially with regard to identifying and rectifying any situations that lead to a systematic bias in prices.

Monopoly

The most serious source of a systematic bias occurs when either buyers or sellers are able, individually or in groups, to influence the market price to better serve their own interest. The classic case is that of *monopoly*, when there is a single supplier to the entire market for some good for which close substitutes are not available.[12]

Monopoly power may result from exclusive control of a particular resource or from exclusive production rights protected by patent or government license. Perhaps a more troublesome source of monopoly power is the presence of economies of scale that make it economically impractical for more than one firm to supply the market. This problem arises when there are extremely high fixed costs, such as those that occur in public utilities inovlving heavy investment in a distribution system, e.g., for water, electricity, or telecommunications. The high fixed cost can also take the form of outlays for research and development, or result from an economic scale of production that is so large that a single firm satisfies the entire market demand.

The problem with monopoly is that the seller sees his opportunities for earning revenue in terms of the downward sloping market demand curve, rather than in terms of a fixed market price that is beyond his control. In this different circumstance, profit maximization systematically leads to an allocation involving a higher price and a lower level of output for the monopoly good than would occur in a competitive situation.

The discrepancy is illustrated in Figure 10.7, which depicts the monopolists' marginal cost curve MC, the market demand curve D, and the associated marginal revenue curve MR. The marginal cost curve represents the opportunity cost of producing one more unit of output based on the price of the inputs required to produce that last unit. The *marginal revenue* curve represents the additional revenue the monopolist will receive from selling one more unit, and is the key to profit maximization for the monopolist. To maximize profit, he should expand output only to that point at which his marginal revenue is at least as great as his marginal cost.[13] In the diagram this leads to a monopoly output Q_m, which he will be able to sell at the monopoly price P_m given by the demand curve. Note that the monopoly price P_m is substantially greater than the marginal cost of production at that output level. This allocation scheme may be contrasted with the "efficient" output and price designated by Q_c and P_c respectively, at which price and marginal cost are equal. The price of the monopoly good does not reflect its opportunity cost, and because of this distortion, less of the good than the optimal amount will be consumed.

As a result of this discrepancy, and because monopolists are thereby generally able to charge a price that is excessive in terms of a "fair" return on the resources they control, societies normally seek to impose some form of government control on the pricing mechanism, whether by outright government ownership or by price regulation. Whereas this explanation fairly adequately conveys the manner in which monopoly creates problems for the market mechanism, it must be emphasized that the regulatory process in practice is far more complex than this simple diagnosis might suggest. We have relied on nothing more than the general shape of the de-

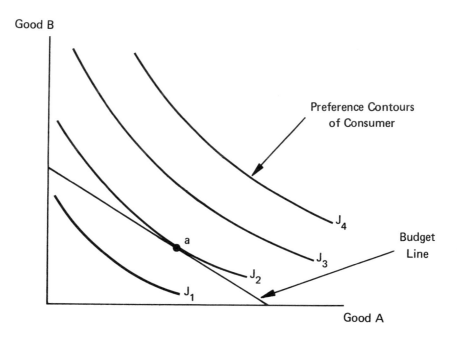

Figure 10.7 Rational Consumer Choice

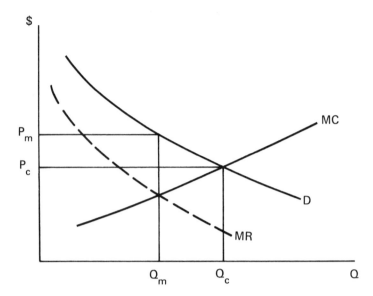

Figure 10.8 Monopoly Output and Price

mand curve and the Marginal Cost curve to demonstrate the presence of a discrepancy. The magnitude of the discrepancy, however, is obviously dependent on the specific shape of both cost and demand curves, and the information required to correct this discrepancy through regulation involves a detailed knowledge of actual costs—something that in practice is difficult and costly to obtain.

Oligopoly

A more common market structure is that of *oligopoly*—a situation in which a few large suppliers dominate the market, i.e., account for the bulk of total sales. A widely used measure of the extent of oligopoly is the so-called "four firm concentration ratio," which is the percentage of total sales accounted for by the four largest firms in a particular sector. The concentration ratio is above 50 percent for most U.S. manufacturing sectors, and in many cases it is in the 80–90 percent range. This particular measure of concentration is, of course, arbitrary, but it does give some indication of the extent to which market power is present.

In contrast to the monopoly case, there would be no simple model for predicting the allocation pattern under oligopoly even if we had perfect knowledge of the underlying demand and production cost conditions. The basic difficulty is an element of unpredictability caused by the presence of more than one seller, which results in a sharing of the total market and hence of the profits to be earned. Collectively, the oligopolists have an interest in maximizing the total profits obtainable, but individually each also has an interest in increasing his share of that total. If the sellers agree on the sharing, they can all benefit by holding prices at the monopoly price level, thereby maximizing the total profit pie. Even if governments outlaw explicit collusion in price setting, monopoly profits may be obtained through tacit cooperation in which prices move together or one firm assumes the role of price leader and others follow suit. In such a case, the oligopolistic market structure behaves much like a pure monopoly.

In practice, cartels and other oligopolistic market sharing schemes tend to break down because of the ever-present opportunity and temptation for one or more members to increase their share by reducing the price. Even though prices themselves may exhibit very stable behavior, suggesting the absence of overt competition, the same result can be achieved through competition that takes other forms, primarily with respect to product design. About the best that can be said regarding the way in which these forces balance out is that the result lies somewhere between the theoretical extremes of the monopoly price and the competitive price. Presumably, the larger the number of firms or the lower the concentration ratio—the closer the result to the competitive ideal. Empirical estimates of the extent of the problem are handicapped by lack of adequate data. The studies that have been made suggest that the problem is not that great, but any conclusions are at best tentative.[14]

Some critics charge that these departures from the competitive model have become so widespread and create such serious distortions in the pricing system that it no longer is in society's interest to permit prices to be set by the market. The counter argument states that while our pricing system is certainly less than perfect, the relative prices it sets do in fact provide a reasonable correspondence to the underlying economic realities and, more importantly, they are vastly superior in this regard to any available alternative. Price setting by bureaucratic fiat, for example, could not begin to respond to the continuous shifting of costs and demand conditions with the flexibility that our admittedly imperfect pricing system is able to provide.

THE PROBLEM OF EXTERNALITIES

A second qualification to the reliability of market prices as indicators of opportunity costs comes under the heading of *externalities*. In developing the relationship between Pareto Optimality and the market system of allocation, it was suggested that the price set in a market transaction reflects marginal cost to the seller and marginal value for the buyer. There is a possibility, however, that the production of the good involves costs other than those borne by the producer or seller. From a practical point of view, the most important cases in recent times involve pollution. A manufacturing process that discharges pollutants into the air or a river or lake imposes costs on other uses of the air or the water. Since a property right to the air or to water systems is normally not established, their use is external to the market mechanism. Hence, in the absence of remedy in the form of governmental regulation or other supplemental allocation means, such external effects are omitted from the market price.

Externalities may be positive or negative, and they may occur on either the production or consumption side of the market. A firm may provide specialized training to workers who then leave and go on to work elsewhere with greater productivity as a result of their training. The externality in this case is on the production side, but it is a benefit rather than a cost. Examples of externalities in consumption are also easy to find. General education, for example, is generally thought to confer social benefits above and beyond those enjoyed by the individual receiving the education, the argument being that a more highly educated populace is conducive to greater social welfare.

In any event, the problem created by the presence of externalities is that the impact, be it a cost or a benefit, is not reflected in the market price. Hence, in the presence of externalities, market prices will not reflect true opportunity costs and the allocation schemes resulting from decisions based on those prices will not be Pareto Optimal. Continuing industrial and population growth, combined with greater public awareness of the resulting problems, have led in recent years to more intensive efforts to repair this failing of the market system. As in the case of monopoly, although the nature of the problem is conceptually straightforward, effective policy is hampered by the cost and unavailability of data, and by the problems inherent in any bureaucratic alternative to the market mechanism. A major difficulty in most cases is that the external effects fall outside the participants in the market transaction, and some redistributional impact results from any regulatory scheme. In other words, policy may be shaped more by political reality than by economic reason.

CONCLUSION

Where do these problems leave us with respect to the reliability of market prices as a basis for resource allocation? More specifically, how do these failings in our pricing system affect the use of market prices to measure costs and benefits, aa we will be using them in the following chapter?

First of all, when we use specific prices to measure benefits or costs, we intend those prices to reflect opportunity costs. Hence we should use competitive prices, corrected for distortions created by market imperfections or externalities or any other market failure we may know of. If some such difficulty is present to a significant degree, corrections should be made if feasible. This is easier said than done, and in most cases lack of adequate, reliable data renders such corrections infeasible. Cases do arise, however, in which we can improve cost and benefit estimates by taking these problems into account. Much of cost benefit analysis is applied to situations in which, for one reason or another, the market system is unable to handle the allocation function. Not surprisingly, the problems we have raised are frequently present.

There is a more subtle way in which the above qualifications call the efficacy of the pricing system into question. This is the so-called problem of "Second Best."[15] We have asserted that directing resources to their most valuable uses, as measured by competitive market prices, leads to efficiency in resource allocation. This is the "Best" allocation. If the actual prices of the goods in question are distorted in some measurable fashion, we have further asserted that resources should be directed to their most valuable uses in terms of corrected prices. Suppose, however, that market failure and imperfections are known to occur throughout the system, so that resources in general are being allocated on the basis of prices that fail to reflect opportunity costs. The question then naturally arises as to whether the efficiency conditions we have described remain valid in any specific instance, unless they hold true throughout the economy. In other words, given that some of the marginal conditions are not met, is the "Second Best" solution to meet as many of them as possible? The theoretical answer to this question is a clear and unequivocal no.[16]

We can respond to this disturbing conclusion in several ways. First, we can, of course, give up on any attempt to evaluate economic policy. Secondly, we can ignore the problem by "assuming" the Pareto Conditions to be satisfied. Finally, we can seek to identify the necessary data so that the impact of distortions that relate to the problem under study can be taken into account and second-best optima developed. The third alternative obviously is the preferred one, although practice to date leans more heavily on the second.

NOTES

1 Profit is defined as $\pi = P \cdot Q - C(Q)$, where P and Q represent price and quantity respectively and C(Q) denotes total cost as a function of the output level Q. The first order condition for profit maximization is given by

$$\frac{d\pi}{dQ} = P - \frac{dC}{dQ} = 0.$$

Thus price must equal

$$\frac{dC}{dQ},$$

which is "marginal cost"—the rate of change of cost as a function of output.

2 Technically speaking, the ordinary demand curve overstates the marginal value of the product if it is a "normal" good, and understates the value in the case of an "inferior good." For the relationship to be exact, a "compensated" demand curve is required as discussed in Chapter 11.

3 The indifference contours are shown as nonintersecting, downward sloping, and convex to the origin. For a discussion of the rationale behind these assumptions, see Donald Watson and Mary A. Holman, *Price Theory and its Uses,* 4th ed. (Boston: Houghton Mifflin Co., 1972).

4 An algebraic statement of this requirement may be derived as follows, using the technique of Lagrangian multipliers. Formulate the Lagrangian expression

$$L = U_J(X_J, Y_J) + \lambda [U_S(\bar{X} - X_J, \bar{Y} - Y_J) - U_S^\circ]$$

where U_J and U_S are the respective utility levels of Jones and Smith, $\bar{X}$ and $\bar{Y}$ are the total amounts of the two goods to be distributed to Jones and Smith, and λ is a Lagrangian multiplier. It may be shown that maximization of L is equivalent to maximizing Jones' utility, subject to the condition that Smith's utility is fixed arbitrarily at U_S°. First order conditions for a maximum require that the partial derivatives vanish, thus

$$\frac{\partial L}{\partial X_J} = \frac{\partial U_J}{\partial X_J} - \lambda \frac{\partial U_S}{\partial X_S} = 0$$

$$\frac{\partial L}{\partial Y_J} = \frac{\partial U_J}{\partial Y_J} - \lambda \frac{\partial U_S}{\partial Y_S} = 0$$

$$\frac{\partial L}{\partial \lambda} = U_S - U_S^\circ = 0$$

The first two equations may be reduced to the form:

$$\frac{\partial U_J / \partial X_J}{\partial U_J / \partial Y_J} = \frac{\partial U_S / \partial X_S}{\partial U_S / \partial Y_S}$$

which is equivalent to $MRS_J = MRS_S$. See Henderson and Quandt, Chapter 7.

5 A function with this property is said to be quasi-concave. Although plausible for most cases, circumstances may arise in which this assumption is not justified, in which case the First Order Conditions are unreliable. For discussion of the associated problems see Henderson and Quandt.

6 The proof in this case is perfectly analogous to that described in Note 4, except that production functions are used in lieu of utility functions.

7 It is important to realize that the marginal equalities are only required in the case of consumers who actually consume both products. If the marginal conditions imply a *negative consumption level that is infeasible, the optimum involves a "Corner Solution," with zero consumption of one good and without the marginal conditions being satisfied.*

8 First Order conditions for maximizing utility subject to a budgetary constraint are obtained by setting the partial derivatives of the appropriate Lagrangian expression equal to zero.

$$L = U(A,B) - \lambda[P_A \cdot A + P_B \cdot B - M^\circ]$$

$$\frac{\partial L}{\partial A} = \frac{\partial U}{\partial A} - \lambda P_A = 0$$

$$\frac{\partial L}{\partial \beta} = \frac{\partial U}{\partial \beta} - \lambda P_B = 0$$

$$\frac{\partial L}{\partial \lambda} = P_A \cdot A + P_B \cdot B - M^\circ = 0$$

The first two equations yield

$$\frac{\partial U / \partial A}{\partial U / \partial B} = \frac{P_A}{P_B} \quad \text{or} \quad MRS = \frac{P_A}{P_B}$$

9 See Note 1.

10. Algebraically, the producer wishes to minimize the cost of producing any specified level of output. Thus,

$$L = P_K \cdot K + P_L \cdot L - \lambda[Q_A(K,L) - Q_A^\circ]$$

$$\frac{\partial L}{\partial K} = P_K - \lambda \frac{\partial Q_A}{\partial K} = 0$$

$$\frac{\partial L}{\partial L} = P_L - \lambda \frac{\partial Q_A}{\partial L} = 0$$

$$\frac{\partial L}{\partial \lambda} = Q_A - Q_A^\circ = 0$$

Dividing the first two equations yields the condition

$$\frac{P_K}{P_L} = MRFS_A$$

11 See E. J. Mishan, *Cost-Benefit Analysis*, New and Expanded Edition (New York: Praeger Publishers, 1976), Chapter 59.
12 See Chapter 13 for an expanded discussion of market structures.
13 For the monopolist, market price is not treated as fixed but rather as being a function of his level of sales. If we define profit π as total revenue R less total cost C, the first order condition for profit maximization is given by

$$\frac{d\pi}{dQ} = \frac{dR}{dQ} - \frac{dC}{dQ} = O,$$

which means that marginal revenue must equal marginal cost. If the demand curve is downward sloping, the marginal revenue curve will always lie *beneath* the demand curve.
14 Efforts to estimate the magnitude of monopoly distortions in the U.S. pricing system are highly controversial. For a classic paper on this subject see Arnold Harberger, "Monopoly and Resource Allocation," *American Economic Review*, 1954.
15 See R. Lipsey and K. Lancaster, "The General Theory of Second Best," *Review of Economic Studies*, 1956–7.
16 *Ibid.*

SELECTED REFERENCES

Robert H. Haveman and Kenyon A. Knopf, *The Market System*, 3rd ed., (New York: John Wiley & Sons, 1978).
James M. Henderson and Richard E. Quandt, *Microeconomic Theory: A Mathematical Approach,* 2nd ed. (New York: McGraw-Hill Book Co., 1971).
Donald S. Watson and Mary A. Holman, *Price Theory and its Uses*, 4th ed. (Boston: Houghton Mifflin Company, 1972).

Chapter 11
Cost Benefit Analysis

INTRODUCTION

Cost Benefit analysis is the evaluation of the economic dimension of public policy issues. Such analysis typically has been applied to public works involving large capital investments, e.g., a bridge, dam, highway system, or canal. In recent decades, however, the scope of Cost Benefit analysis has been extended to a much broader array of public actions, including evaluation of legal or administrative regulation of economic behavior such as pollution controls, safety regulations, zoning laws, or health laws. Any policy issue that involves the use or production of economic goods or services is in principle amenable to such analysis. The issue may involve *whether* to undertake the given action, *when* to undertake it, or *which* of several mutually exclusive actions is best.

The distinctive aspect of Cost Benefit analysis is that it is undertaken in behalf of society as a whole. It is the *public* interest that is to be served, as opposed to that of any particular group or region. Furthermore, we require a generally acceptable definition of public interest, not some private notion of the individual analyst as to what is best. The ultimate objective is the increased economic welfare of the members of society. Given our ability to measure that welfare in a comparative way, this aspiration to scientific objectivity poses serious problems. In brief, there is no straightforward answer to the question, "What does society seek to maximize?" Thus we need some fairly elaborate conceptual machinery for the task at hand. As discussed in Chapter 10, we employ the concepts of efficient resource allocation, based on Pareto Optimality, as one test of the "efficiency" aspect of the project. Final judgment is based on that *plus* an additional, separate evaluation of the distributional or "equity" aspects of the project.

In performing the first step—the efficiency test, which is the heart of Cost Benefit analysis—we rely on competitive market prices or approximations thereof in order to estimate benefits and costs. These prices are assumed to reflect opportunity costs, and the analysis boils down to a comparison of the value society places on the benefits of the project to the value of benefits lost due to the diversion of resources from other uses. If the benefits exceed the costs, the project constitutes a "better" use of the resources involved, at least in terms of allocative efficiency. Both benefits and costs are measured in money terms. A dollar of benefit and (minus) a dollar of cost are equally weighted, no matter how they are distributed. This latter feature of the approach is the reason a separate evaluation of distributional aspects is mandatory.

Given the intimate relationship between Cost Benefit and ordinary analysis of allocative efficiency, the reader may question the need for treating Cost Benefit as a separate subject. On a theoretical level, there is no difference. Cost Benefit represents nothing more than an effort to apply the conventional economic notions of allocative efficiency to specific policy issues. Even though no theoretical novelty is involved, however, the practical problems of doing this are formidable. We have stressed, for example, the key role of competitive market prices. The theoretician develops his efficiency criteria in terms of such prices. Yet the practitioner has to deal with situations in which such prices are either seriously flawed or nonexistent. This is not surprising. If markets were established for the goods or services in question, and were functioning so as to generate prices that accurately and comprehensively reflect opportunity costs, there would be little need for government intervention in the first place. The literature of Cost Benefit analysis, accordingly, is largely concerned with finding practicable methods for working around problems of inadequate data. We cannot present these methods in any detail in this chapter. We can, however, survey the basic principles employed, and highlight some of the typical problems encountered. Additional reading is suggested at the end of the chapter.

MEASURING BENEFITS—INDIVISIBILITIES AND CONSUMER'S SURPLUS

The basic situation we wish to address is the case in which a proposed act of public policy (a "project") is to be evaluated in terms of its economic consequences. The positive consequences we refer to as benefits; the negative ones as costs. To be a bit more specific, we will consider a case in which the major impact of the project is to increase the quantity available for public consumption of some good (or service), which we denote by X. We will assume for the moment that the information we have as to the value of X takes the form of an *ordinary demand curve*, such as that depicted in Figure 11.1. Figure 11.1 provides an estimate of the amount of X that would be purchased at any given price P.[1] Let the current quantity and market price of Good X be denoted by X_o and P_o respectively, and let it be assumed that the project we are evaluating will provide an increase in X to the level of X_1 as shown in the diagram. The increase is thus $X_1 - X_o$, or ΔX. Our first task is to put a monetary value on this increase, thus providing a valid measure of the benefit of the project.

We will approach this problem in terms of three situations: (1) the price of X does not change significantly as a result of the project; (2) the price does change, but the quantity ΔX may be adjusted in a continuous manner; (3) the price changes, and the quantity change is not continuously adjustable. For example, the only alternative in case 3 is to remain at X_o or, by adopting the project, to go all the way to X_1. No interim amounts are feasible. Before considering each of these cases, recall that we are, for the moment, treating all benefit dollars as equal, irrespective of their distribution. We also assume that conditions of Pareto Optimality hold elsewhere in the economy.

Case 1: Constant Price

In Case 1, the price remains constant despite the change in the quantity of X. This situation could occur if the amount ΔX is small relative to that of X_o. It could also occur if there exists a close substitute for X. The reader should imagine a horizontal demand curve, rather than the one depicted. In this simplest of all cases, we have a straightforward measure of the benefit in monetary terms. We merely evaluate each additional unit of X in terms of the constant price P. The result is the product $P \cdot \Delta X$, which measures the revenue that could be ob-

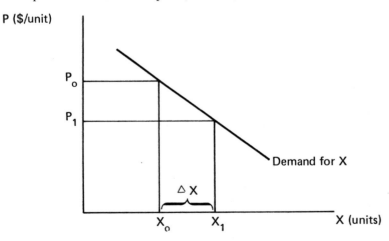

Figure 11.1 An Ordinary Demand Curve

tained from the sale of ΔX under ordinary market conditions. The reader is cautioned to remember the strengths and limitations of this measure. The strength is that it measures dollar benefit in terms of the willingness of users to pay in dollars for the additional X. The weakness is of course that, implicitly, each dollar receives equal weight, no matter what the economic status of the individual who pays it. Hence our measure remains subject to a strong caveat as to the distribution of the benefits.

Case 2: Price Change with Continuous Adjustment of Quantity

Case 2 raises the complexity of the problem somewhat, since the price P does vary from P_0 to P_1 in response to the increase in X. In this case, however, we are able to vary the amount by which X increases. Hence this case permits application of basic marginal analysis. Rather than evaluating the *total* benefits (and costs) of the project, we may evaluate the *marginal* benefit (and cost) at varying levels of X. As long as the marginal benefit of additional X exceeds the marginal cost, further expansion is called for. Once a point is reached where marginal cost equals or exceeds marginal benefit, expansion should be halted. The nice feature of the ordinary demand curve depicted in Figure 11.1 is that it provides the measure of marginal benefit at each level of X. The price P_1, for example, represents the value of X to the marginal user at output level X_1, measured of course in terms of willingness of the user to pay dollars for the good. Hence there is a sense in which we can interpret the ordinary demand curve as a marginal valuation curve. If X is variable and can be chosen so as to balance this marginal value with the marginal cost of producing X, the market price provides the measure of marginal benefit that our analysis requires.

Case 3: Price Change and Indivisibilities in Output

Although each of the two previous cases may occur, they serve primarily to illuminate the problems that arise in the more common situation represented by Case 3, in which the price of X changes, and we are constrained to a discrete increase, e.g., from X_0 to X_1 in Figure 11.1. To facilitate the explanation, we provide a numerical example in Figure 11.2, that illustrates an increase in X of 400 units in association with a fall in market price from \$10 to \$6. What are these 400 units of X "worth"?

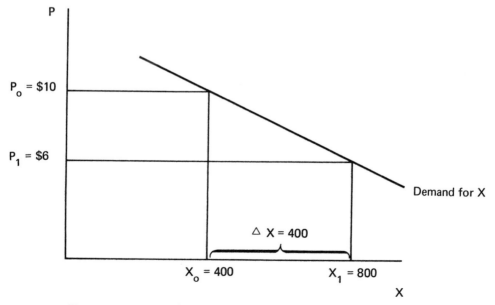

Figure 11.2 Price Changes Due to Increase in Good X

The first point to be noted is that the change in market value or revenue, R, associated with the increase does *not* provide an adequate estimate. By that measure we would have

$$\Delta R = P_1 X_1 - P_0 X_0 = 6(800) - 10(400) = \$800 \tag{11.1}$$

According to this calculation, the entire increment of 400 additional units is worth only $800—an average of $2 apiece. Yet the demand curve suggests a unit value ranging between $6 and $10! The problem is that in order to sell 800 units, we would have to reduce the price to $6 on *every* unit, including the original 400 *and* 400 additional. The value to users does not go down with this price decrease, but of course, the revenue collected does. Clearly we need something in addition to the revenue in order to evaluate the benefit.

One approach that has a great deal of intuitive appeal involves the summing of the value of each of the 400 additional units on a unit-by-unit basis, noting that the first additional unit could be sold for $10 and that each unit thereafter for 1¢ less with $6.00 for the last additional unit. (Over the total 400 unit increase, price drops $10–$6 = $4.) Thus we would have the change in benefit, ΔB, associated with the increase in X from 400 to 800 given by

$$\Delta B = \$10.00 + 9.99 + 9.98 + \ldots + 6.00 = \$3200 . \tag{11.2}$$

Summed in this way, the benefit amounts to the area beneath the demand curve between X_0 and X_1, a trapezoid whose area is given by

$$\Delta B = \tfrac{1}{2}(P_0 + P_1)(X_1 - X_0) = \tfrac{1}{2}(16)(400) = \$3200 \tag{11.3}$$

For any straight line demand curve, this amounts to using the "average" price over the relevant range. More generally, the area beneath the demand curve is given by

$$\Delta B = {}_{X_0}\!\int^{X_0 + \Delta X} P(X)dX \tag{11.4}$$

where ΔB is the additional benefit, X_0 is the initial level, ΔX is the increase in X, and $P(X)$ is the inverse demand curve, or price as a function of quantity. This is, in fact, the measure most commonly used. Despite its obvious intuitive appeal there are some problems associated with this particular measure, and although we do advocate its use as normally the best available, it is important to recognize these shortcomings.

What we really desire to have is a dollar estimate, ΔB, of the value of ΔX, such that ΔB represents the amount of dollars we could take *from* the users in return for providing them the increase ΔX, leaving their level of economic welfare unchanged. Our estimate of ΔB as $3200 is obviously much greater than the additional $800 they would pay if the increase in X were marketed in the normal way, as shown by Equation 11.1. The

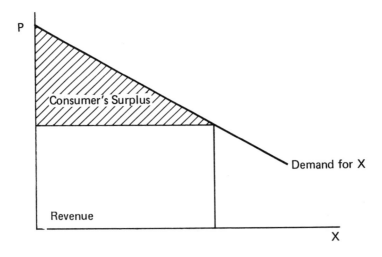

Figure 11.3 Consumer's Surplus

difference between the two sums constitutes a residual that goes to consumers in the form of a surplus of the value of their consumption above and beyond the amount they actually have to pay. It is known, not surprisingly, as *consumer's surplus* (CS) and may be approximated by the triangular area beneath the demand curve and above the price line, as shown in Figure 11.3.[2]

The total area beneath the demand curve, therefore, consists of the sum of two parts: consumer's surplus plus revenue.

$$B = R + CS \tag{11.5}$$

Frequently our interest is directed towards the change in consumer's surplus (ΔCS) associated with a change in X.

In that case, the change in consumer's surplus consists of the area between the two price lines, the demand curve, and the vertical axis as shown in Figure 11.4, which continues with our numerical example. The reader will note that ΔCS is, in this case, equal to

$$(10 - 6) \cdot (400 + 800) \cdot \tfrac{1}{2} = \$2400.$$

Thus:

$$\Delta B_{(\$3200)} = \Delta R_{(800)} + \Delta CS_{(2400)} \tag{11.6}$$

We can see that the change in benefit, as we defined it, is equal to the change in revenue *plus* the change in consumer's surplus. Whereas a private decision maker might evaluate the ΔX in this case as worth only $800, from the public point of view we would also count the change in consumer's surplus, placing a total value of $3200 on the increase. The data were selected to make the point that consumer's surplus can be important. Of course, it does not always or even usually play that large a role. Whenever the price—or marginal dollar value—of the good in question does change, however, we must somehow take that change into account, and the above treatment represents the conventional way of doing so in a Cost Benefit analysis.

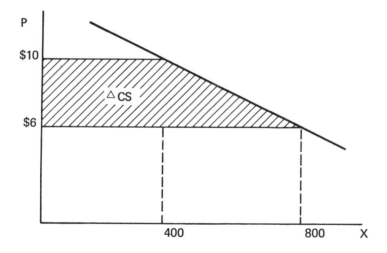

Figure 11.4 Change in Consumer's Surplus

Objections to the Use of Consumer's Surplus

Objections to the concept of consumer's surplus take two forms: (1) the estimate provided by the area beneath an ordinary demand curve is biased; (2) the aggregation of dollar amounts across different consumers is a "cardinalist" approach to consumer satisfaction, giving each dollar equal weight.

The reason for the first objection is easily understood by recalling the basic premises of an ordinary demand curve. It represents the amount, X, of the good that will be purchased, assuming *each* unit carries some *common* price P, and all other prices and income are held constant. Thus our demand curve indicates that, at a common price of $6, 800 units of X will be purchased. In interpreting the area beneath the demand curve as the amount consumers would pay for, say, an additional 400 units, we have tacitly violated those premises. Instead of charging $6 for each of the additional units sold, we have charged a price ranging from $10 down to $6. We have robbed the consumer of the surplus, in effect reducing his purchasing power below the amount *originally* assumed in estimating the demand curve. If we do in fact extract this higher payment, sometimes referred to as the amount a "perfectly discriminating monopolist" could charge, we would find our consumers somewhat less enthusiastic about purchasing additional units of X. Hence, to obtain an accurate measure of the monetary value of ΔX on a lump sum basis, we need a more sophisticated demand curve, known as a "compensated" or "constant utility" demand curve. If the good in question is a "normal" good, namely one of which less will be purchased given a reduction in income, the compensated demand curve will lie beneath the ordinary demand curve, as depicted in Figure 11.5.[3]

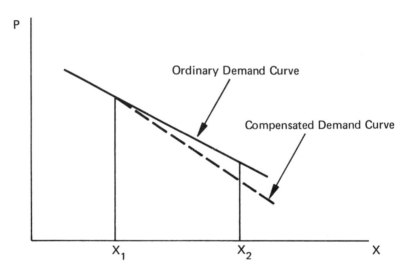

Figure 11.5 Compensated Demand Curve

The problem is that, as a practical matter, compensated demand curves are not available for empirical work, and we are either left with the measure we have suggested or left with no measure at all. Two partially redeeming points can be made. In some cases, it may be argued that the difference between our approximation and the true value is relatively unimportant. The discrepancy is related to the so-called "income-effect," namely the effect on demand of a change in income, resulting in this case from our removal of consumer's surplus. If the good plays a small role in the typical consumer's budget, this effect will be small. Secondly, it should be borne in mind that even ordinary demand curves cannot be estimated with precision. They are best interpreted as fairly rough approximations, even in the best of circumstances, and the bias resulting from the income effect may be small relative to the the likely errors in the demand curve itself. Hence although the theoretical objection is perfectly well founded, in real world applications it may be a relatively minor problem—at least in comparison to other problems.

The second objection is not so much an objection to consumer's surplus *per se* as it is an objection to attaching equal significance to a benefit (or cost) dollar without regard to who the recipient is. This is the distribution issue raised earlier, and we will return to it shortly.

MEASURING COSTS

Provided we can assume the availability of competitive prices on the inputs to a public project, and provided those prices do not change significantly as a result of the project, the methodology of evaluating costs is a straightforward application of principles developed in the preceding section. Resource prices under these circumstances reflect their opportunity cost, that cost being *both* their marginal value in alternative use *and* their marginal cost of production. Hence, we simply evaluate cost as the total dollar value of resources used, basing our evaluation on existing market prices at the time of use.

Changing Prices and Economic Rent

The assumption that input prices do not change significantly is of decisive importance and if it does not hold true, further adjustments are indicated. Normally, the assumption can be justified if the project plays a relatively minor role in the total demand for each of its inputs. In addition, many inputs are produced under conditions of relatively constant costs, and even massive increases in their demand will not bring about long-term increases in the supply price. Short-term increases during the time required to expand productive capacity are referred to as "quasi-rents," and do not count even though they do involve transfers of income, or redistribution. The appropriate perspective for cost benefit is the long-term view.

By the same token, an increase in cost due to "intramarginal rent" constitutes an income transfer but does not involve a real opportunity cost, and hence should be deducted from the cost calculation. Economic rent may be defined as that portion of payment to a given productive factor greater than its earning in the next best alternative use. To illustrate, suppose a project results in increased demand for coal, raising its price and causing marginal mines to be opened. The higher price will be paid on all coal mined, and owners of intramarginal mines will enjoy an appreciation in the revenue earned by their production. All of this apparently higher cost of coal, however, does not constitute a true opportunity cost. The situation is depicted in Figure 11.6, which shows supply and demand for coal, with an initial price P_o and production level X_o.

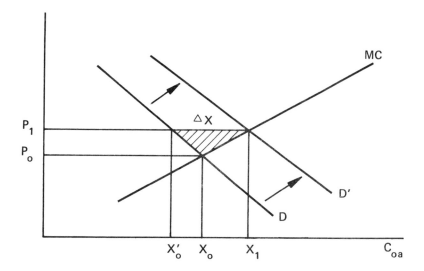

Figure 11.6 Opportunity Cost When Prices Change

Suppose that the project being analyzed will require ΔX units of coal, raising the demand from D to D$'$, the price from P_0 to P_1, and output from X_0 to X_1. What is the opportunity cost to society of these ΔX units of coal? Note that two costs have been imposed. First, consumption by other users has been reduced from X_0 to X'_0 (using the argument of the preceding section). Second, there is the cost of expanding production from X_0 to X_1. This cost is correctly measured as the area beneath the marginal cost curve between X_0 to X_1 (the demonstration that this is true directly parallels the analysis presented in equations 11.2 through 11.4).

The total cost to society of the ΔX units of coal, therefore, is *not* the monetary cost of the coal, given by $P_1 \cdot \Delta X$. This would overstate both the cost of reducing consumption from X_0 to X'_0 and the cost of increasing production from X_0 to X_1. The correct opportunity cost of the coal is the actual monetary cost, $P_1 \cdot \Delta X$, *less* the shaded triangle. If both demand and marginal cost curves are straight lines, the opportunity cost is given by $\frac{1}{2}(P_1 + P_2)\Delta X$, regardless of what share of ΔX comes from increased production and what share comes from reduced demand in other uses. The shaded area represents a change in "intramarginal rent" distributed between gains by coal mine owners and losses by alternative use consumers, but it does not represent a real opportunity cost to society as a whole.

Changes in Other Prices

It is, of course, conceivable that the prices of goods other than the direct inputs or outputs of the project may change. If this occurs, further adjustments are indicated. For example, a project that provides gas to a rural region may result in a decrease in demand for electricity. If electricity were produced under conditions of decreasing costs, the reduced demand would result in a lower price. Consumer surplus would increase by some amount, approximated by the change in the price of electricity times the quantity of electricity consumed. In principle, this amount should be added as a benefit.

It should be noted, however, that the essence of Cost Benefit is *partial analysis*. It examines the impact of a change in allocation in one sector of the economy, using supply and demand curves that assume that other prices remain cosntant. If prices change significantly, the result is a chain reaction in which supply and demand curves shift, leading to changes in consumer's surplus and in costs elsewhere in the system. The task of tracking down and estimating each change on a step-by-step basis is not feasible. Hence, if widespread changes in prices occur, the methods of Cost Benefit analysis fail. In practice, about the only circumstance in which it is ever feasible to make adjustments for other price changes is in the case of very close substitutes or complements to the output of the project.

DISCOUNTING AND CAPITAL BUDGETING

Cost Benefit analyses typically involve projects with long economic lives, as much as fifty years or more in some cases. The analysis must take the time dimension into account, and this is normally done by evaluating all benefits and costs in terms of present value (PV), discounting future values according to the formula

$$PV = V_t \left(\frac{1}{1 + r}\right)^t \tag{11.7}$$

where r is the appropriate annual rate of interest, t is the time in years from the present, V_t is value at time t, and PV represents present value.

Net Discounted Present Value of a Project

A projected stream of costs and benefits is depicted in Figure 11.7. In this case the cost stream consists of an initial investment that takes place during the first three years, annual operating costs that remain constant for ten years, and a final outlay due to expenses involved in closing-out the project, e.g., repairing environmental damage due to a mining operation. Benefits build gradually over three years to a maximum that continues for the duration of the project. Some salvage value is obtained at the end of the project's useful life.

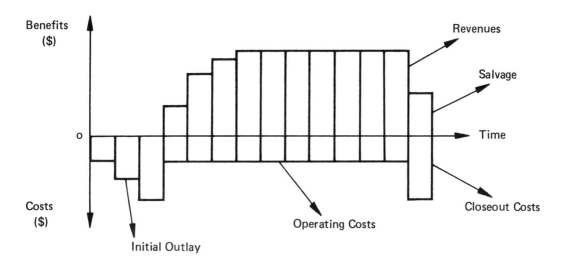

Figure 11.7 Cost and Benefit Stream

The fact that the project's cost, C, and benefits, B, are spread out in time does not change our approach to their estimation. The only difference is that all costs and benefits must be evaluated at some specific time. Applying the standard discounting formula, we have the Net Discounted Present Value (NDPV) of this stream as

$$NDPV = \sum_{t=1}^{n} (R_t - C_t) \left(\frac{1}{1+r}\right)^t, \tag{11.8}$$

If NDPV⟩O, benefits exceed costs, and the project passes in terms of our efficiency criterion.

Uncertainty and the Time Horizon

Application of the above formulation raises a host of conceptual and practical difficulties. Probably the most serious problem is that benefits or costs projected years into the future depend on, and may be highly sensitive to, a host of dubious assumptions. Such assumptions embrace the state of the world, the weather, the economy, technology, the behavior of other nations—the list goes on *ad infinitum*. Hence our benefit and cost estimates are, at best, subject to considerable uncertainty, and the further into the future we attempt to project them, the shakier they become. We will presently discuss the problems due to uncertainty. For the moment, we are assuming that projections of future costs and benefits are certain. The principles involved are not affected by this assumption, but you should recognize that in practice such projections are always beset by some degree of uncertainty.

A related issue concerns how far into the future we seek to project the analysis in estimating costs and benefits. This depends partly on the expected useful life of the project, and partly on the degree of our confidence in available projections. Obviously we cannot project into the future indefinitely; one must draw a line at some point, beyond which possible outcomes are ignored. In the case of extremely long-lived projects, such as dams, this *time horizon* may be as much as fifty years. In other cases the period may be as short as five years. Since in most cases the major costs of an investment occur at the outset—or in the early years of its life—setting too short a time horizon will understate its net value. On the other hand, estimates of outcomes in the very distant future are of doubtful validity. One technique for resolving this dilemma through compromise involves the inclusion of an estimate of salvage value at the end of the planning horizon. The results of the analysis may not be highly sensitive to the choice of time horizon since the importance of outcomes in the distant future are attenuated by discounting. In addition, if the analysis involves a ranking of similar projects, their relative performance may remain the same, whatever time horizon is chosen.

The Discount Rate

The next problem we will consider is that of the choice of an appropriate rate of discount. A public use of funds, such as that depicted in Figure 11.7, employs current resources in return for future benefits. In a simple extension of the arguments previously developed, the price we set on current resources diverted to future use should reflect their social opportunity cost. That opportunity cost, however, may take several forms, depending, for example, on whether the resources involved are diverted from current consumption, from private investment, or from other public investment. If the alternative use is current consumption, the cost of the project is deferring consumption to the future, and the appropriate measure of opportunity cost is the return on private savings, which represents the rate at which consumers are willing to defer current consumption in return for greater future consumption. If the alternative use is private investment, then the ultimate opportunity cost is a reduction in future consumption by an amount determined by the rate of return on investment in the private sector, and that rate would be the appropriate one for discounting purposes. If, however, the resources are drawn from other public investments—for example, the public authority is operating under a fixed capital constraint—then the opportunity cost might better be defined in terms of the marginal return on investment in the public sector.

In a Pareto Optimal world, all of these rates should be equal, and hence the appropriate discount rate would be unambiguously defined. In the real world, however, there are reasons to anticipate significant disparities in these rates.

First of all, in a dynamic economy in which positive net investment is taking place, it may be inferred that the opportunity cost of providing capital is less than its productivity. This means a continuing disequilibrium, in which the "social rate of time preference" is less than the rate of return on society's capital stock, with the market rate of interest fixed somewhere in between. Even if capital markets functioned perfectly, this would create some ambiguity as to the appropriate discount rate, at least in circumstances in which it might be argued that public investment comes out of current consumption, as society's rate of time preference is presumably less than the market rate of interest.

On a more practical level, capital markets do not, of course, function perfectly, tax schemes that create systematic divergences between the return to savings and investment are prevalent, and public investment takes place subject to a host of political constraints. With respect to the taxation problem, for example, consider a case in which earnings from investment are taxed at a rate of 50 percent. If an individual's rate of time preference is 5 percent, given the tax situation, he will refuse opportunities affording less than a 10 percent rate of return. Stated another way, if earnings on savings are taxed at 50 percent and the market rate of interest on savings is 10 percent, this implies a social rate of time preference of only 5 percent, since that will be the actual after-tax return individuals receive on their savings. Under these circumstances, in evaluating a public project that is financed out of current consumption, the appropriate discount rate would be 5 percent. If, however, the public investment supplants investment in the private sector, the appropriate rule is to discount at the higher rate of 10 percent. If the impact is divided between consumption and investment, it has been argued that an appropriately weighted sum of the two rates is proper. Given the practical difficulties of making such a determination, however, this approach does little to resolve the basic dilemma.

Even in the absence of discrepancies between the rate of return on private investment and the social rate of time preference, it may be appropriate to discount public investments at some other rate if such investment is subject to *capital rationing*. Suppose, for example, that a particular public authority has identified a number of projects that pass the Cost Benefit criterion. By this we mean that each is estimated to have a positive discounted net present value, based on the market rate. Further, suppose, however, that the public authority is politically constrained as to the amount of capital investment which will be permitted, forcing a choice among the available projects. In this circumstance it may be argued that the true opportunity cost of capital is the rate of return on the last or "marginal" project selected. That being the case, in establishing a priority among the available projects, it would be appropriate to use a higher discount rate, one just adequate to limit the number of acceptable projects so as to fall within the budget constraint.

In addition to the above problems, capital market imperfections, varying degrees of risk and creditworthiness, uncertainty as to future market conditions, inflation, and many other complicating factors all combine to further confuse the situation, creating a broad and shifting spectrum of interest rates on different types of investments. In the face of these complexities, discounting practices in Cost Benefit analysis have been less than perfectly consistent. Historically, the tendency has probably been to use too low a rate. Much of the early Cost Benefit analysis done by the U.S. Army Corps of Engineers, for example, was based on long-term, "risk free" bond rates of 2–3 percent or less. In the 1960s, in the early days of the Office of Systems Analysis in the Department of Defense, no consistent discounting policy was enforced, and in effect a zero rate was frequently employed. As interest in the analytical techniques has progressed, the trend has been to adopt more stringent discounting procedures, reflecting the view that public investments compete most directly with private investment. Rates on the order of 10 percent seem to be generally consistent with this view, and are widely employed in current practice.

INVESTMENT CRITERIA AND CAPITAL RATIONING

In the absence of capital constraints, once the appropriate discount rate is determined, the question of a "pass-fail" criterion for Cost Benefit projects is easily settled. The criterion is that the net present discounted value be positive, measuring all costs and benefits in terms of opportunity cost prices and discounting future values at the appropriate rate. This is the conceptually correct criterion, and nothing in the following discussion should be construed as contradicting this point. In actual practice, however, Cost Benefit analysis is frequently confronted with a requirement for establishing a priority or ranking for investment projects. This may be due to the fact that two or more projects are mutually exclusive, forcing a choice among them. It may also result from a budgetary constraint that limits the projects that can be approved to a subgroup of those that pass the present value criterion. This latter situation is referred to as the problem of capital rationing or capital budgeting. In both of these situations—mutual exclusivity and capital rationing—the present value rule continues to suffice. The criterion is to select that feasible project, or projects, that maximize net discounted present value. We will refer to this as the "NDVP criterion." Despite the general superiority of NDVP, past practice has been based on alternative criteria to such a large extent that it becomes necessary to understand how these criteria are employed and how they differ from NDVP. The ones we will examine are *pay-off period, internal rate of return* (IRR), *rate of return over cost* (RROC), and *benefit cost ratio*.

The Payoff Period

The most widely used naive criterion is the *payoff period*, which is nothing more than the time in years required to earn back the initial investment, applying a zero rate of discount to future earnings. The problems inherent in this approach are easily seen by reference to a simple example depicted in Table 11.1. Applying the payoff period criterion, Project A easily wins over B because it recoups the initial investment during the second year, whereas B only does so during the fourth year. The difficulty is in the discounting. We are, in effect, applying a zero rate of discount to any earnings during the first two years, and an infinite rate to anything thereafter. It turns out that B is preferred, i.e., gives a higher NDPV for any discount rate below 23 percent, but we could just as easily have imagined larger benefits for B in years 3 and 4. In fact, these benefits could be made large enough to make B preferred at *any* discount rate (short of infinity). Yet the payoff period, strictly applied, would still point to A. Not much else needs to be said in criticism of the payoff period. It might be noted that Soviet planners use a variant of the payoff period. For example, they sometimes require that investments return their (undiscounted) costs within a maximum period of five years.

Table 11.1

Comparing Two Projects Based on the Payoff Period

Project	Year				
	0	1	2	3	4
A	−100	60	50	0	0
B	−100	0	50	50	50

The Internal Rate of Return

The remaining criteria deserve more serious treatment, since there are contexts in which each can shed light on the characteristics of a given project choice. For this purpose, consider three hypothetical projects—A, B, and C—each of two years' duration with initial cost and benefits as depicted in Table 11.2. The table also gives the net discounted present value for each project over a range of discount rates. For example, the NDPV of project A at a discount rate of 10 percent is 8.68.

$$8.68 = (-50 + \frac{10}{1.10} + \frac{60}{1.10^2})$$

Table 11.2

Net Benefits and Discounted Present Value of Three Projects at Various Discount Rates

Project	Net Annual Cost (−) / Benefits (+) Year			NDVP Discount Rate						
	(0)	(1)	(2)	(0)	(.05)	(.10)	(.12)	(.20)	(.25)	(.33)
A	−50	10	60	20	13.95	8.68	6.64	0	−3.6	−8.56
B	−40	30	25	15	11.25	7.93	6.64	2.36	0	−3.31
C	−30	10	40	20	15.80	12.15	10.73	6.11	3.6	0

The internal rate of return (IRR) is widely employed as a criterion for ranking projects. IRR is defined as the rate of discount that creates a discounted present value of a given payments stream of zero. It may be thought of as the average annual yield or percentage earned on the initial investment. In other words, looking at Project A, if you borrowed $50 and paid back $10 and $60 one and two years later respectively, what effective annual rate of interest would you be paying on the initial loan? The answer in this case is 20 percent, obtained from Equation 11.8 by setting PV = 0, inserting the appropriate values for $(B_t - C_t)$ and solving for r. Although the computation of IRR is tedious when a longer project life is involved, modern business calculators routinely include such a capability.

It is possible that IRR may not be uniquely defined. The difficulty arises in cases involving close-out costs at the end of the project. The main difficulty, however, is again in the treatment of discounting. In the case of IRR, the Cost Benefit stream of each project is discounted according to what is essentially an arbitrary rate, different for each project, and bearing no necessary relation to the social opportunity cost of capital. For the projects under discussion, IRR_A = 20 percent, IRR_B = 25 percent, and IRR_C = 33⅓ percent are those discount rates at which NDPV is equal to zero. The IRR criterion is to select the project with the highest internal rate of return. Hence, by this criterion, C is preferred to B, and B is preferred to A. Yet if we calculate the NDPV of A and B, using a different discount rate—say 10 percent—we find $NDPV_A$ = 8.68 and $NDPV_B$ = 7.93. In other words by the NDPV criterion, A is preferred to B, at least at a discount rate of 10 percent. This contradiction in the project ranking clearly stems from the discount rate used.

We can best understand the nature of the problem by reference to Figure 11.8, which portrays discounted present value as a function of the discount rate.

Note, first of all, that present value is a decreasing function of the discount rate, the reason being that for these projects benefits occur in the future, and their present value diminishes as we discount them at higher rates. Secondly, note that there is a crossover or reversal in the present value ranking of A and B that occurs at a discount rate of 12 percent. For any rate lower than 12 percent, A is preferred; for any higher rate, B comes out ahead. The reason for this is that B's benefit stream is skewed more to the future than is that of A. Hence, the relative attractiveness of the two projects is affected by the rate at which those future benefits are discounted. The IRR is shown on the diagram at the intersection of each present value curve with the horizontal axis. At high discount rates, B clearly comes out ahead, and since the IRR of B is high, the IRR criterion supports B over A. At interest rates below 12 percent, however, the IRR criterion conflicts with the correct NDPV criterion. Of course, such a reversal in ranking does not always occur, in which case the choice of the discount rate plays a less significant role.

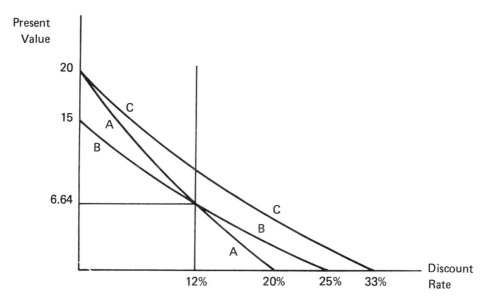

Figure 11.8 Present Value vs. Discount Rate

Rate of Return Over Cost

The reversal in ranking of A and B also illustrates the third criterion we wish to consider, namely the *rate of return over cost* (RROC). RROC is a criterion for comparing two projects, and is typically used in evaluating a choice between a given project and some alternative *larger* project involving a greater capital investment.

Imagine, for example, that B is a water resource improvement project and A is an alternative, larger, more ambitious scheme. If we consider choosing A over B, increasing the initial outlay by 10, a question naturally arises regarding the rate of return on the additional investment. RROC, which provides the answer to that question, involves nothing more than the calculation of the internal rate of return on the difference between the two streams. In this case, the stream A–B is –10, –20, 35 in years 0, 1, 2, respectively, and the internal rate of return of that stream can be calculated as 12 percent. This is the point at which the present value lines for each individual project cross. What this means is that the larger investment is justified at any discount rate lower than the RROC of 12 percent. If the appropriate discount rate is known, then RROC provides nothing new in terms of ranking A and B. It may be extremely useful in cases of this type, however, in determining the highest discount rate that would still justify the move to the more expensive project.

The problem of ranking projects may be complicated by the presence of a capital constraint, such as a specified maximum outlay during each year within the planning horizon. Net discounted present value remains the appropriate criterion. In such a situation, however, the task becomes one of selecting the feasible set of projects that maximizes NDPV. If a large number of projects is involved, the search procedure can become tedious. The only time the NDPV rule may require modification is when the capital constraint results in rejection of projects with a positive present value. In that case, the relevant opportunity cost of capital would be the rate of return on the marginal project, which would be greater than the opportunity cost in the unconstrained case. The NDPV criterion is always the appropriate technique. The only question concerns the appropriate discount rate.

Benefit Cost Ratio

The last project ranking criterion we will consider is that of the *Benefit Cost ratio*. In the absence of capital rationing or mutual exclusivity, use of the Benefit Cost ratio may be equivalent to maximizing NDPV. It may be used, for example, if the decision rule is to accept projects for which the ratio is greater than one and reject those for which the ratio is less than one. It is occasionally suggested, however, that the Benefit Cost ratio is an appropriate criterion to rank order projects in a capital rationing situation. Use of ratios can lead to erroneous results, and it is for that reason only that the idea is mentioned here. Suppose, for example, that a choice must be made between Project D (with a PV cost of $8 and PV benefit of $10) and Project B (with a PV cost of $3 and PV benefit of $4). The Benefit Cost ratio places B in first place ($4/3$ vs. $10/8$), yet the NDPV of A is twice that of B ($2 vs $1). The rule is that maximization of net discounted present value is the appropriate course of action under all circumstances. Benefit Cost ratios are not only superfluous, but are liable to lead to misallocation in many circumstances.

RISK AND UNCERTAINTY

As mentioned previously, to conduct analysis as if the Cost Benefit stream resulting from a given project is known with certainty is tantamount to conducting a play with the leading character absent. This is particularly true if the project life extends to a number of years. Dollar estimates of costs and benefits are in general highly uncertain, and at best they normally represent nothing more than the midpoint of a range of possible values. This factor needs to be taken into account.

In approaching this problem, it is useful to make a basic distinction between decision making, or problems of choice, in which we have some estimate of the probability distribution of various outcomes, and those in which we have none. The first, to which we shall refer as decision making under *risk*, is more amenable to analyis than the latter, to which we shall refer as decision making under *uncertainty*.[4]

With respect to decision making under risk, a further distinction is sometimes made between *objective* and *subjective* risk. *Objective* risk involves a situation in which the relevant probabilities can be estimated on the basis of a formal scientific model. For example, the outcome of a certain decision may be dependent on a sample drawn randomly from a population with known characteristics. Meteorological estimates of probable amount of rainfall or incidence of floods of various magnitudes also afford examples of (occasionally) objective ways of assigning a probability distribution, in this case to the benefits of flood control projects. A *subjective* estimate, by contrast, might be based on the opinion of the analyst, "experts," or economic forecasters. The distinguishing feature is that because individual opinions vary, the probability estimate is less reliable in a subjective risk situation than it is in an objective risk situation.

Table 11.3
Expected Value vs. Risk

Present Value (under different "States of Nature")			Mean Expected Value	Standard Deviation
Project	"a" (.5)*	"b" (.4)*	"c" (.1)*	
A	40	20	20	30	10
B	−20	80	80	30	50
C	0	0	300	30	90

*Probability of occurrence.

None of the projects presented is inherently better than the other two. How they will be ranked is a matter of personal preference regarding risk. If the decision maker is a "risk-averter," A will be preferred. On the other hand, he may be inclined to favor riskier choices and quite rationally rank C ahead of the other two. Examples of both types of behavior occur widely, perhaps most conspicuously in the form of gambling and the purchase of insurance. Indeed, individuals commonly indulge in both activities simultaneously. The most intellectually satisfying approach to rationalizing such apparently contradictory behavior is based on the idea that decision makers act on the basis of maximizing expected *utility* or satisfaction, rather than maximizing expected *monetary value*. The significance of this distinction is dependent on variations in the utility of money income at different income levels. If, for example, an individual decision maker's utility function is shaped as portrayed in Figure 11.9 so that the marginal utility of additional money income *declines* over the range depicted, the implication is that the individual is a risk-averter. If we use this function to evaluate projects that are equivalent in terms of expected monetary value, those with lower risk will be preferred.

For example, the utility function shown in Figure 11.9 translates monetary values into utility terms for an individual decision maker. The function, $U = f(V)$, shows that as the monetary value of a project increases, the utility attached to the project also increases. The concave shape of the function, however, suggests that the utility associated with higher monetary values increases at a diminishing rate. The marginal utility, or slope of the utility function, is declining.

Suppose that a risky project has two possible outcomes, with monetary values of V_1 and V_2. The probabilities associated with each outcome are p_1 and p_2, respectively, where $p_1 + p_2 = 1.0$. The expected monetary value of the project, V_e, is therefore computed as

$$V_e = p_1 V_1 + p_2 V_2.$$

If there were an alternative *risk free* project with an expected value of V_e, its utility would be read on the utility function as point B in Figure 11.9. In this case, however, both outcomes, V_1 and V_2, have their own expected utilities, and the expected utility of the risky project is given by

$$U_e = p_1 U(V_1) + p_2 U(V_2).$$

The expected utility of the risky project is shown at point A in Figure 11.9. Point A lies below point B because of declining marginal utility. *Despite both projects having the same expected monetary value, the expected utility of the risky choice is less than that of the project without risk.* If, conversely, the utility function were concave upward over a given range, indicating increasing marginal utility, riskier projects would be preferred.[7]

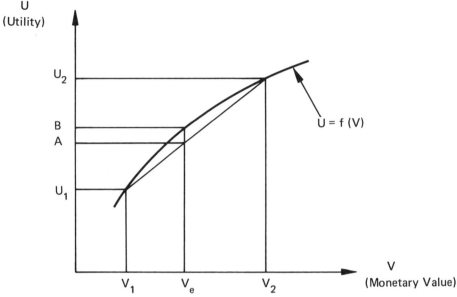

Figure 11.9 Expected Value vs. Expected Utility*

Note:

Point A represents the expected utility of a project with two possible outcomes, with monetary values V_1 and V_2 and an expected value of V_e. Point B represents the utility of a riskless project with a certain outcome V_e.

Unfortunately, expected utility analysis is not very helpful for Cost Benefit purposes, as it depends on the idea of differing individual utility weights for dollars at different individual income levels.

In Cost Benefit analysis we are dealing with aggregate data, and we are forced to treat all dollars as equally weighted. Even if we knew that *all* individuals were risk averters over the Cost Benefit range of the three projects, which we do not know, we still could not infer that A was *socially* preferable without further stipulations regarding the distributional impact. In other words, who bears the risk? In B, for example, the —20 outcome might be borne out of general revenues, i.e, by society as a whole, and the + 80 concentrated on low-income earners for whom additional income is considered, on distributional grounds, to be highly desirable. Conversely the apparently low risk indicated by the aggregate estimates for A may conceal not only an adverse distribution of costs and benefits, but an adverse distribution of risk as well. For example, suppose the aggregate benefit of 40 under State of Nature "a" goes, in its entirety, to one social group; the 20 of State "b" to some other social group; and the 20 of State "c" to a third group. From the viewpoint of the groups or of their individual members, A would be risky indeed.

These examples should suffice to illustrate that there is an aggregation problem in dealing with risk. The degree of risk conveyed by aggregate data bears no necessary relationship to risk from the point of view of individuals. Furthermore, this problem is inextricably bound with the distribution or equity problem, which we have already set aside as requiring separate treatment. Our means of doing this is to treat all cost and benefit dollars as having equal social significance for purposes of the efficiency analysis, deferring final judgment until a separate analysis of distributional considerations has been made. Clearly, however, assigning equal weight to each dollar implies a neutral attitude towards risk: projects of the same mean expected value are equally attractive, no matter how they vary regarding the dispersion of the possible outcomes. In terms of Figure 11.8, the implied utility function is a straight line, and any two projects having equal expected dollar value will also have equal expected utility.

The above discussion suggests that it is very difficult to improve upon mean expected value as the criterion for comparing public projects with risky outcomes. It may be that public decision makers are inclined to be "risk-averse," but this is for reasons that have more to do with political or bureaucratic considerations than with economic ones. In any event, the most that the economic analyst can do is seek to portray the full spectrum of possible outcomes. In cases where the probability distributions are known or can be estimated, the format of Table 11.3 is the most straightforward way of doing this.

In cases in which outcomes are *uncertain*, however, the problem is exacerbated since not even the mean expected value is unambiguously defined. To continue with our previous example, this might mean that the three contingency columns in Figure 11.8 were identified, but that there was no basis for assigning a probability to the three contingencies. Hence, there are no means of calculating the expected value or standard deviation, and the decision maker has only the payoff matrix itself on which to base his choice. Under the title Decision Theory a number of criteria have been suggested for coping with this type of situation. None of them, however, are generally satisfactory. Even for an individual decision maker, the ultimate choice is clearly subjective, and there really is nothing further that can be done to rank these projects in a Cost Benefit context. The crucial point is that the areas of uncertainty and range of outcomes must be identified as comprehensively as possible. Beyond that, economic rationality has little to offer.

PRACTICAL PROBLEMS IN ESTIMATING COSTS AND BENEFITS

The conceptual basis for estimating costs and benefits is the cumulative monetary value of whatever resource reallocation a project involves. This value is measured in terms of what the recipients would be willing to pay for the change in the case of gainers, and in terms of what they would be willing to accept in compensation for the change in the case of losers. The market pricing system is the key source of this information. As previously mentioned, such prices are normally either not available or seriously flawed, and a major portion of the analytical effort is expended in generating usable data. The methods are eclectic, and they often involve very crude approximations. It would not be appropriate here to seek to catalogue in detail either the types of problems that arise or the various techniques of resolving them. We will, however, briefly mention some of the major categories of problems, simply to illustrate how inexact Cost Benefit analysis can be.

Most of the problems involved in cost and benefit estimation can be explained in terms of the absence of true opportunity cost prices. First, there may be no price at all, because there is no market for the good in question. Recreational benefits of park areas and reservoirs, for example, may be provided without charge. In such cases, unless resources are provided to permit collection of survey data, the analyst is forced to very rough approximations, extrapolating data from the closest parallel he can find in which market values are available, or devising a proxy measure of some type. One approach to the benefits of recreational areas has been to use transportation costs expended in getting there as a lower bound of the estimate. If the benefits involve a public good, as national defense or police protection do, the estimation problems are further compounded. There is no way to establish a market in such goods, and the beneficiaries may be inclined to systematically bias their answers if survey methods are employed in estimating benefits.

Even when prices are available, there are a host of reasons why they may be seriously flawed. The presence of monopoly power, upward or downward skews due to government intervention (subsidies and controls), and externalities offer three major examples. When such distortions are present they should be corrected, but it is not always clear how this should be done. Consider the situation in which part of the alleged benefits of a public project is the increase of production of some agricultural commodity, the price of which is currently supported by government subsidy. Obviously, the presence of a price subsidy has already introduced a disparity between the marginal social cost and marginal social value of the commodity in question. Which level is appropriate to the Cost Benefit analysis is not always clear. If the purpose of the subsidy is to increase production, we might prefer the high estimate. On the other hand, if the purpose of the subsidy is to support the income of those already involved in producing the commodity, additional production begins to sound more like a cost than a benefit!

Externalities play an increasingly important role, particularly in the analysis of public projects that have some type of environmental impact. These projects pose particularly difficult problems, since the absence of property rights in air and water systems means there is no available market price for evaluating the impact. The most important externality is, of course, pollution. Pollution, and policies that affect pollution control, have been possibly the most popular subject for Cost Benefit analysis in recent times. Suffice it to say that problems of estimating both the cost and the benefit, at the margin, of more or less pollution are formidable, and estimates may vary widely. Furthermore, in many areas a significant gap exists *between* the marginal benefit and the marginal cost of pollution. Confronted with such ambiguity, which measure is the analyst to use? The problem is analogous to that of subsidies and price controls, and it can result in the well-known affliction of "what you think depends on where you sit."

These problems are particularly acute when the allocation of a given good or resource is controlled on a *de facto* basis by existing law, regulation, or government policy. This can occur as the result of intervention in the pricing system in the form of controls and subsidies, or it can occur because there is no market, and the issue is handled by regulation instead. Pollution control laws provide a good example. Such laws put an *implicit* (or shadow) price on pollution, that implicit price being the marginal cost of meeting the specified standards. To put the issue in more general terms, we are talking about cases in which the opportunity costs of resource use are defined by political constraints, rather than by market forces. As long as the constraints are such that the resulting shadow prices do not violate economic rationality—that is, as long as they tend toward Pareto Optimal resource allocation as discussed in Chapter 10—the analyst can in principle move right along, just as he would with market prices. If, however, the government law, regulation, or policy sets implicit or explicit prices that violate our rules of efficient allocation, such as those created for the purpose of achieving better income distribution or as the result of special interest groups, the analyst begins to lose his way. His frame of reference is economic rationality, and he has to save the distribution issues for last, for a separate evaluation. Yet, such political constraints (perhaps realities is a better word) inject distribution and politics into the heart of the analysis. Different analysts approach these issues in different ways. Perhaps the best rule is to be as explicit as possible in dealing with such problems.

Many other examples of inadequacies and ambiguities in the available measures of opportunity costs could be cited. One especially troublesome question concerns the treatment of the value of human life. Efforts to translate this particular commodity into a monetary value run into obvious difficulties, yet policy actions analyzed with Cost Benefit methods typically involve some need to deal with this issue. The amount of monetary compensation an individual would accept in lieu of saving his life is presumably very large, perhaps so large that very few policies that pose any hazard to human life would pass the Cost Benefit test. Yet people do voluntarily expose themselves to fatal risks. (They are more cautious under conditions of certainty.)

Another major difficulty concerns the problem of the proper measure of opportunity cost when the resources involved would otherwise be unemployed. The conventional approach to Cost benefit assumes full employment—taking the long-term view since the projects are long-term in nature—and in the long term we should be able to employ fully all resources. Experience has shown, however, that unemployment can persist on a long-term basis, particularly in declining regions. Hence it is sometimes argued that it is appropriate to use a low—even zero—opportunity cost when dealing with resources subject to persistent unemployment. The converse argument may be applied when a project is expected to *create* unemployment, at least on a temporary basis, until resources made redundant can be reallocated. Reallocation costs are real costs and deserve inclusion. The issue concerns how high those costs may appropriately be set. In dealing with *regional* impacts, the analyst is likely to encounter sharp controversy on this subject. Regional spokesmen tend to set the reallocation costs somewhat higher than those that are consistent with a national point of view.

The examples cited, while by no means all inclusive, should be adequate to convey some sense of the range and degree of difficulty confronting Cost Benefit estimates in specific situations. In meeting these problems in practical terms, analysts in the past have developed an astonishingly—sometimes distressingly—imaginative array of techniques. Consequently, the results of Cost Benefit are almost inevitably open to a great deal of discretion on the part of the analyst. If the discretion is exercised in an objective and explicit fashion, the public interest is well served. If, on the other hand, the technique is allowed to become a vehicle for the advocacy of special interests, rather different results will follow.[8]

CONCLUSION

The bottom line of Cost Benefit analysis is that the benefits, comprehensively defined and appropriately discounted, are either found to exceed the costs or fail to do so. In the former case, this means that we have identified a Potential Pareto Improvement. That is to say, with appropriate compensation among gainers and losers, this project could be converted to a Pareto Improvement, a change in which everyone gains. If such compensation is feasible, and will in fact be paid, a green light is obviously appropriate.

If, however, as is usually the case, such compensation is not practical or politically feasible, the situation is much more complex. If we were willing to treat all dollars of benefit and cost as having equal social weight, we could argue for the green light even in the absence of compensation. Clearly, however, it makes a great deal of difference on whom the benefits and costs fall, and in any event the judgment on the distributional impact is inevitably subjective. Some leverage may be gained on the issue by considering the extent to which the *redistribution* inherent in the project is consistent with, or at odds with, existing public laws and policy affecting that issue. For example, if the society is on record, given existing tax law, in support of redistribution toward a more egalitarian distribution of income, a public project that had such a distriubtional impact might be assessed favorably, if it also passed the efficiency criterion. It might, of course, be assessed favorably on distributional grounds alone, even if it failed the efficiency test. The question should be asked, however, as to whether some less costly and more precise means of accomplishing the desired redistribution could not be found. Perhaps the major contribution of Cost Benefit analysis is to expose proposed uses of resources that are inefficient, and thereby help society towards more efficacious means of achieving its distributional objectives.

Finally, it is, of course, possible that the project fails on *both* counts, representing *neither* an efficient use of resources nor a socially desirable redistribution of income. If the reader is becoming skeptical as to the utility of Cost Benefit analysis, he should keep in mind that a great deal of scarce resources have been used in this manner. A systematic Cost Benefit analysis provides really our only defense against such misuse of public funds. That alone is ample justification for the use of the technique.

NOTES

1 The ordinary demand curve depicts the amount that would be purchased at each price, assuming the buyers treat the price as fixed, pay the fixed price for all units purchased, and that other factors affecting demand remain constant. Such factors include consumer preferences, incomes, and prices of other goods.

2 It should be emphasized that the area under the demand curve is only an approximation, for reasons to be discussed shortly; however, it is the approximation that is used in practice.

3 Note that for a price *increase*, the relationship is reversed, and the compensated demand curve would lie *above* the ordinary demand curve.

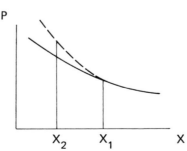

4 For a survey of efforts to develop criteria for decision making under uncertainty see W. J. Baumol, *Economic Theory and Operations Analysis,* 4th ed. (Englewood Cliffs, N.J.: Prentice-Hall, Inc., 1977).

5 The mean expected value is given by

$$V_e = \overset{i}{\Sigma}\ P_i V_i$$

where P_i and V_i respectively represent the probability of occurrence and expected value of each possible outcome.

6 The standard deviation is given by

$$\partial = (\ \overset{i}{\Sigma}\ P_i(V_i - V_e)^2)^{1/2}.$$

7 There is extensive literature on the utility analysis of choices involving risk, originally inspired by the development of game theory. For further reading and references, see Baumol, *op. cit.*

8 For further discussion of the principles and techniques of Cost Benefit, see Mishan, *Cost Benefit Analysis, op.cit.*

SELECTED REFERENCES

I. M. D. Little, *A Critique of Welfare Economics* (London: Oxford University Press, 1960).

E. J. Mishan, *Welfare Economics* (New York: Random House, 1964).

E. J. Mishan, *Cost-Benefit Analysis*, 2nd ed. (New York: Praeger Publishers, 1976).

Chapter 12
Cost Effectiveness Analysis

INTRODUCTION

Cost Effectiveness analysis is analogous in many ways to Cost Benefit as described in the previous chapter, since it also involves techniques for applying basic economic principles to policy choices, with the ultimate objective being efficient use of scarce resources. The principal distinction is that Cost Effectiveness methods are used in cases in which the output from a given resource use cannot be measured in dollar terms. Particularly in defense allocation problems, it frequently is not feasible to measure the output—or effectivess—of a given policy action in dollar terms. In evaluating a weapons system, for example, various dimensions of performance characteristics may be specified, such as speed, range, and firepower. Generally, however, there is no agreed way of combining these characteristics into a single measure of overall effectiveness, and even if this is possible to some extent, the effectiveness cannot be measured in dollar terms.

Despite this difficulty, however, decisions have to be made regarding (1) how much of the nation's resources should be devoted to defense purposes and (2) how those resources should be utilized. Although the absence of a dollar measurement of effectiveness complicates matters, the difficulty in no way changes the basic economic nature of the problem. Scarce resources are involved, and they need to be used efficiently.

The reason for our concern with the efficient use of defense resources should be fairly obvious. Defense uses the same scarce resources that go to satisfy general economic needs, and it uses a large quantity of those resources, ranging roughly between 25 and 50 percent of the federal budget over the past two decades. Those billions constitute an enormous opportunity cost—reduced consumption, and reduced availability of resources for other government programs with high social value. Furthermore, *specific* defense expenditures also entail an opportunity cost in terms of reduced availability of resources for *other defense needs*. In other words, the hard reality of scarcity pervades each sector of the economy, including defense; in a very real sense there is never "enough." Hence, we must ensure not only that resources are not wasted in any area, but also that they are being allocated efficiently. The essence of Cost Effectiveness analysis is the recognition of the economic nature of this problem. This means that costs are just as relevant as effectiveness or desirability in analyzing any program. To attempt to allocate resources on the basis of weapon effectiveness *without* systematic treatment of costs literally makes no sense at all in terms of making efficient use of resources.

These ideas are hardly controversial. Nevertheless, efforts to implement them have caused great controversy. After surveying the basic principles and methods of Cost Effectiveness analysis, we will return to this question of why what appears to be nothing than economic common sense has been able to generate such passionate opposition.

THE ELEMENTS OF COST EFFECTIVENESS ANALYSIS

As in the case of Cost Benefit, the methods of Cost Effectiveness analysis are eclectic, and there is no standard prescription for the best methodology to be employed. There are, however, certain essential elements that are always present. The conventional list contains five elements: (1) The objective(s) to which the system, doctrine, or policy being evaluated are dedicated, (2) two or more alternative ways of achieving the objective, (3) a model of some type that provides the basis for comparing effectiveness of the alternatives, (4) costs, and (5) a decision criterion. We add to this a sixth element, sensitivity analysis.

The need for an objective is quite apparent. Unless there is an explicit purpose for the systems being evaluated, we obviously are going to have trouble measuring their effectiveness. Some systems are much more amenable to a clear statement of purpose than others, and not surprisingly, Cost Effectiveness has been most useful in such cases. All cases are fraught with uncertainty, but the easiest cases tend to be those involving expensive hardware that is to be used in a narrowly defined way in a particular context in order to accomplish a specific purpose. An example might be a case deciding the type of armament to be used on planes employed in a ground support role, e.g., conventional bombs versus expensive "smart" bombs. A somewhat more difficult case might involve the mix of medium, heavy, and light planes in the air transport fleet, or the mix of conventional versus nuclear power in naval ships. Strategic weapons systems afford examples of narrowly definable objectives, and they have been fruitful subjects of analysis. General purpose forces, by contrast, are acquired for possible use for a wide variety of purposes and in a wide variety of circumstances. They have been more resistant to analysis.

The need for alternatives stems directly from our inability to measure effectiveness in dollar terms. Because effectiveness is not commensurable with dollar cost, we must specify alternatives to provide a basis for comparison. Although the alternatives evaluated need to have a common purpose, they may, of course, achieve that purpose in very different ways. If the purpose of a strategic weapons system is to add to our capability for assured destruction of enemy targets in a second strike situation, for example, this might be accomplished by adding additional delivery systems, it might be accomplished by improved accuracy or penetration capability of existing delivery systems, or it might be accomplished by improved active or passive defense of existing systems. If the purpose is to provide combat ready units in various contingent locations overseas within specified time limits, this might be accomplished by increased transport capability or by increases in forward based troops and prepositioned equipment stockpiles. Although the specification of various alternatives is an essential element in getting the analysis started, the list is open ended and one improtant goal of analysis is to develop new approaches.

The determination of an objective, and of the various ways of achieving that objective, constitutes the definition of the problem. The heart of the analysis consists of the next three elements: the measurement of effectivess, the measurement of costs, and the establishment of a criterion for choice, based on costs and effectiveness. In the following sections we will consider these three elements, beginning with the criterion problem and two important and closely related issues: the role of marginal analysis and the problem of suboptimization.

THE CRITERION PROBLEM:
THE MEANING OF COST EFFECTIVENESS ANALYSIS

Cost Effectiveness analysis is, in principle, applicable to any policy question that involves the use of scarce resources. Although procurement, or capital investment, decisions have been the most common subject of study, the methods are equally applicable to the evaluation of issues such as strategic policy, tactical doctrine, and the allocation of research and development funds. For the purpose of discussing the criterion problem, however, consider the following hypothetical procurement issue. Suppose a new fighter plane, the FX, has been proposed. The FX is still on the drawing boards, and no prototype has yet been built. Suppose, however, that the FX promises certain advantages—measurable in terms of performance parameters such as speed, endurance, and firepower—in comparison to similar planes either currently in use or proposed. To put the problem in the ususal format, let us assume that the FX appears to be the better plane, but that it is significantly more expensive.

Various questions may be posed: Is the FX really a better plane? If so, how much better and under what circumstances? Is it needed? Should the FX be adopted? If so, when, and how many units should be purchased? Should competing designs be carried to a further stage of development before any decision on FX is made? A host of problems in answering these and similar questions comes quickly to mind. It is the purpose of Cost Effectiveness analysis to assist us in organizing our thinking about such issues. The hope is that systematic analysis will lead to better decisions.

As the first step in reviewing the basic principles involved, we must confront the problem of the incommensurability of the costs of this plane and the benefits to be gained from having it. If it were possible to put a dollar value on the plane's usefulness, we could simply add up the costs and subtract them from the benefits, asking whether the net discounted present value is positive. If the plane were to be sold to the private sector, a dollar amount indicative of the value of various performance characteristics could be obtained from the market place, based on the willingness of consumers to pay. Since the ultimate purpose of goods sold in the private sector is the satisfaction of consumer wants, we are willing to accept this measure, and private goods are produced if the willingess to pay exceeds costs, i.e., if there is a profit. In the case of the FX, however, as is generally true for defense procurement items, there is no marketplace in which the value of the good for defense purposes can be ascertained.[2] The implication of this difficulty is that we cannot evaluate the desirability of purchasing the FX by comparing its costs to its benefits. Accordingly, we are going to drop the word benefits and instead will speak of "effectiveness," denoting that it represents something other than a dollar measure of the usefulness of the plane for defense purposes.

The way Cost Effectiveness analysis circumvents this difficulty, or attempts to do so, is to break the problem down into smaller pieces, enabling us to ask some easier questions. This is the technique of "suboptimization," and it really involves nothing more than narrowing the frame of reference. Rather than comparing the usefulness of the FX with the *unrestricted* next best alternative use of the resources involved, we compare the usefulness of the FX with a *restricted* definition of the alternative use of the resources involved. Basically, we restrict the alternative use to other means of achieving the same objectives as that of the project in question. For example, in evaluating the desirability of purchasing the FX, the comparison would be with alternative fighter planes with similar roles. If the FX is conceived primarily in a ground support role, other ground support fighters would be analyzed. If however, the plane has other purposes, such as air superiority and interdiction, the context of the analysis would have to be broadened to include these possibilities. In this case we would be seeking to evaluate the effectiveness of various tactical air fleet mixes, some of which include the FX.

Obviously, weapons systems vary widely in terms of how specific or how general their uses are. An ICBM has a fairly specific role; an infantry division, on the other hand, has a much more general purpose. In the latter case it is inherently far more difficult to define the purpose in measurable terms, and it is also far more difficult to define alternative systems for achieving the purpose. What this means is that some issues are more amenable to Cost Effectiveness than others.

In any case, however, the normal point of departure is the specification of a fixed level of resources, a fixed budgetary outlay. We then proceed to identify alternative ways of employing that fixed amount of resources to achieve some specified purpose or purposes. In the case of the FX, the assumed budget could be the total outlay on ground support planes (in the narrow conception of the role of FX), or it could be the total outlay on a tactical air fleet (taking the broader conception). The purpose in these two cases, respectively, would be effectiveness in ground support or effectiveness of the tactical air fleet in all its roles.

This specification of the budgetary outlay is the key to the exercise. It insures that the opportunity cost of adding various numbers of FX in the alternatives considered is taken into account, in the form of an equivalent reduction, in budgetary terms, of other planes in the fleet. If the FX is a very expensive plane, the opportunity cost is high. The purpose of the analysis is to determine whether its enhanced performance is sufficient to justify the higher cost.

Assuming for the moment that some means of estimating the "effectiveness" of various tactical airplanes or fleets is available, and that we have adequate cost data enabling alternative packages with equivalent resource costs to be defined, the criterion for selecting the optimum package is straightforward. We simply search for *that alternative which gives the greatest effectiveness, subject to the specified budgetary constraint.* This is the criterion most widely used in Cost Effectiveness studies, and for most purposes it is the most convenient approach. In certain applications, the analysis may begin by specifying some minimum effectiveness level and then proceed by searching for *that alternative which involves least cost, subject to the specified effectiveness constraint.* These two criteria are logically equivalent. The least cost way of achieving a given level of effectiveness is identical to the maximum effectiveness way of using a specified budget—provided of course that we are operating at the same scale of endeavor in both cases. The form in which the criterion is stated depends partly on whether our advance information gives a better idea regarding the ultimate level of cost or of effectivenss, and partly on whether it is more convenient to define the alternatives to be analyzed in terms of a fixed level of cost or a fixed level of effectiveness. Done properly, the ultimate outcome of the analysis should be the same.

THE MARGINAL PRINCIPLE IN COST EFFECTIVENESS: USES AND LIMITATIONS

In conceptual terms, the approach outlined above is analogous to the so-called "factor mix problem" discussed in Chapters 9 and 10. In this problem our objective is to maximize the level of output of some production process, using two or more factors of production, subject to a budgetary constraint on the total amount of factors employed. If we assume that unlimited amounts of each factor may be purchased at a constant market price, and that the underlying production process is characterized by a diminishing marginal rate of factor substitution (MRFS), the problem may be portrayed graphically for the two-factor case as shown in Figure 12.1. In the case shown, feasible fighter fleets consisting of varying numbers of each of two fighters, FX and FN, are given by points on the budget constraint. Three specific options have been singled out for scrutiny. Each production contour (E_1, E_2, and E_3) represents a given level of effectiveness, and any point on a given contour is equally desirable. (We set aside for the moment the question of how the effectiveness levels depicted by the contours are derived, although the ability to come up with a reasonably sound set of estimates is crucial to our ability to pass judgment on the correct choice of options.)

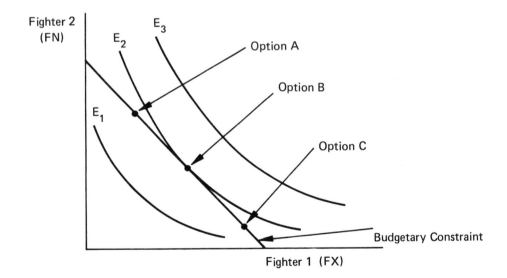

Figure 12.1 Choosing the Optimal Factor Mix

The optimal choice, that is to say the most "Cost Effective" composition of the fighter fleet, is Option B. The familiar rule is that the optimal solution occurs at a point of tangency of the budget line to a production contour. What this means is that the rate at which we can substitute (at the margin) one fighter for the other, holding the effectiveness of the fleet at a given level, must be equal to the price ratio of the two planes. Algebraically,

$$ \text{MRFS} = \frac{P_1}{P_2} $$

The reader should recognize that this rule is identical to the condition for Pareto Optimality in factor allocation developed in Chapter 10, where it was shown that competitive markets lead to the optimal allocation pattern. Hence, what we have is a rule that in effect seeks to replicate the market solution to the allocation problem. There are a number of important caveats to using this rule for Cost Effectiveness studies, and we will discuss them presently. The rule is, nevertheless, an extremely powerful tool for cutting complex allocation problems down to manageable size, and its importance would be hard to overstate.

We state the rule in the following alternative but equivalent form, which we will refer to as the "marginal rule": *In allocating resources to various factors used to produce some common goal, the optimal allocation pattern requires that the marginal contribution to achievement of the goal (i.e., to raising the effectiveness level) must be the same for incremental expenditure on each and every factor used.* Stated in this fashion, the marginal rule amounts to nothing more than economic common sense. In the illustrative case, the last dollar spent on Fighter 1 must make the same contribution to effectiveness as the last dollar spent on Fighter 2. If this condition is not satisfied, greater effectiveness can be achieved from the same total amount of resources employed by reallocating dollars *from* the activity with the *lesser* marginal return *to* the activity with the *greater* marginal return. The marginal rule is independent of the units in which effectiveness is measured. Hence, it permits us to "trade-off" resources among alternative means of achieving any of the numerous objectives of defense policy, wherever such objectives may be defined in commensurable terms.

In permitting us to dip into the defense allocation process and conduct a test of allocative efficiency in any area where alternative means may be used in achieving an objective, the marginal rule constitutes a powerful tool for identifying and correcting inefficiency. It is easily the single most powerful tool that the analyst has. Under fairly general conditions, the rule provides a valid test of allocative efficiency, and thoroughgoing adherence to the rule throughout the defense sector leads to the most effective use of the defense budget.

Partial Analysis

The marginal rule plays a strategic role in Cost Effectiveness analysis. There are, however, a number of important qualifications to its use; we turn now to those qualifications. The first qualification to bear in mind is that marginal analysis is what economists refer to as *partial analysis*. In isolating a particular defense output or objective to be analyzed, we in effect have to assume that all the rest of the world stays put. If other conditions change, and especially if they change in response to the policy being analyzed, there is a possibility that these shifts will invalidate the assumptions and, consequently, the results of our own study. There is also a possibility of spillover effects on the costs or effectiveness of systems outside the purview of the analysis. The vulnerability of marginal analysis to these dangers tends to be greatest when large shifts in defense posture are involved.

A particularly important example of this problem results from the basic assumption of our marginal rule, which states that the budget is fixed at a given level. Figure 12.2 illustrates that this may or may not be a problem, depending on the nature of the production function. In each case, the dashed line represents the combinations of fighters that provide the highest level of effectiveness at each budget level. The dashed line represents the path to be followed as the budget expands and is therefore termed the "expansion path." In Case A, on the lefthand side we have what is known as a "homothetic function," which is such that any straight line through the origin intersects production contours at some common slope. In other words the expansion path of a

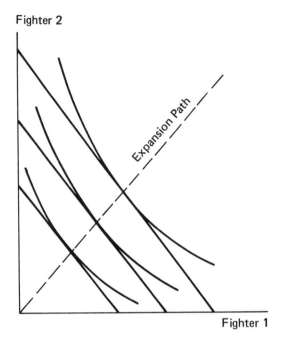

Case a. Homothetic Function

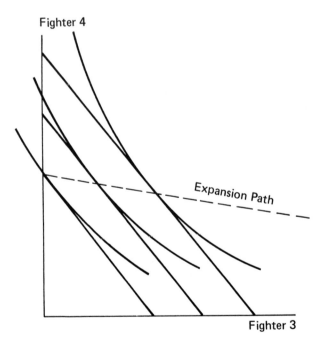

Case b. Non-Homothetic Function

Figure 12.2 Optimal Mix With Changing Budget

homothetic function is linear and passes through the origin. This means, given our marginal rule, that the optimal mix of Fighter 1 and Fighter 2 is independent of the budget level—only the price ratio matters. In Case B on the right hand, by contrast, the budget level matters a great deal. At the lowest level depicted, the optimal mix contains zero units of Fighter 3. As the budget is increased, however, the mix changes, with 3 introduced in increasingly larger quantities, and 4 diminishing in absolute terms.

There is no *a priori* basis for predicting which of these two situations will hold in a given analysis. The point is that Case B is always a possibility, and must be guarded against. The technique for doing this is straightforward: simply vary the budget and test whether the optimum mix is sensitive to such variations. This technique, known as *sensitivity analysis*, is of crucial importance to Cost Effectiveness. It applies generally to any assumption of dubious validity, and we will refer to it repeatedly in the following pages. Nothing more complicated is involved in sensitivity testing than repetition of the analysis over a range of assumptions regarding the value of the dubious variable (in this case, the budget). Of course, such explorations may be costly, depending on the techniques employed in particular analysis, and if the number of dubious assumptions is large, the number of permutations rapidly approaches astronomical size. Nevertheless, prudent use of sensitivity tests is the *sine qua non* of good analysis. Properly executed, it handles not only the budget assumption problem, but also most of the other difficulties we will raise.

Discontinuities

A second fundamental limitation on the marginal rule applies when the alternatives under consideration involve nonincremental changes or "discontinuities." In the previous discussion, we made the implicit assumption that the weapons mix can be varied continuously. This, however, is frequently not the case, the most notable exception occurring when the analysis involves a *new* system, introduction of which would occasion a substantial one-time outlay for research and development. Under such circumstances marginal analysis breaks down. A lump sum outlay, such as the payment for R&D required to bring FX into production, involves a discontinuity in the alternatives. In order to properly evaluate such nonincremental changes, our only alternative is to abandon marginal analysis and compare alternatives in terms of their *total* effectiveness. The nature of the problem is illustrated in Figure 12.3. FN is a plane already in the inventory and available at a given price. FX,

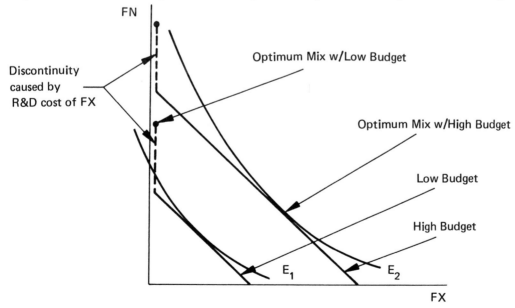

Figure 12.3 Failure of Marginal Rule Due to Discontinuities

however, would require a large initial outlay represented by the vertical dashed line. At the low budget level, FX is not cost effective, and the optimum mix contains only FN. In the case shown, FX does come into the optimal mix at the higher budgetary level, where the R&D costs are relatively less important. In either case, however, marginal analysis alone is incapable of identifying the optimal solution.

Decreasing Costs

A third limitation of marginal analysis applies in cases where the costs of one or more systems under consideration decrease with increasing scale. Economies of scale can occur in weapons system production for the same reasons as in the private sector, and indeed are probably more likely to occur in defense production, as the scale of production is liable to vary over wide extremes as the result of procurement decisions. The problem this may cause for marginal analysis is illustrated in Figure 12.4. The impact of decreasing costs is the change in the budget constraint from the straight line previously assumed, to the shape shown in the figure. Whether or not this creates a problem for marginal analysis depends on the relative curvature of the budget line and the production contours. In Figure 12.4a, the marginal rate of substitution between the two planes diminishes at a rapid rate and overcomes the influence of decreasing costs. The marginal rule correctly identifies Point A as the optimum mix. In Figure 12.4b, however, the situation is reversed, with the influence of decreasing costs overwhelming the diminishing marginal rate of substitution. The optimum mix is at Point B, with complete specialization on System Y. Applciation of the marginal rule in this case would result in selection of the mix represented by Point C—the worst possible choice since it is the one which *minimizes* effectiveness.

It should be noted that a similar problem would arise if the effectiveness contours did not exhibit the characteristic diminishing marginal rate of factor substitution shown in Figure 12.4 and indeed throughout the text. A function with this characteristic is said to be *quasi-concave*. Although this characteristic is conventionally assumed, in some instances it quite conceivably would not be present, in which case the contours would have the opposite curvature from that depicted. Use of marginal analysis in such cases is not permissible, and in fact will lead to the worst choice, even if the budget constraint is a straight line. *Second order conditions*, based on the mathematical properties of the production function and constraint, may be specified to test whether these

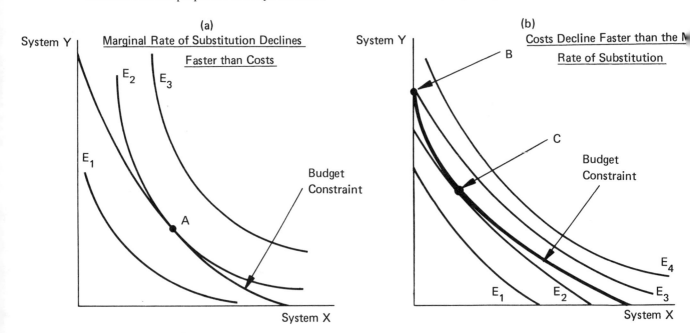

Figure 12.4 Failure of Marginal Rule Due to Decreasing Costs

problems are present and insure that a point identified as optimal is in fact a maximum—and not a minimum. However, provided that the production contours have the conventional shape, *and* that the budget constraint is linear, such procedures are not required.[3]

In practical terms the latter condition is the one most likely to fail. The moral here is that extraordinary care must be taken in applying marginal analysis, particularly in any case in which decreasing costs are present.

THE PROBLEM OF SUBOPTIMIZATION

Cost Effectiveness analysis is based on *suboptimization,* and as such is vulnerable to the problems that beset any suboptimizing approach. The meaning of suboptimizing, and the related problems, may be illustrated by reference to Figure 12.5, which depicts two levels of optimization. At the lower level we have our previous problem, choosing between two tactical air fleets, System A1 (the current mix) and System A2 (a proposed new mix which incorporates the new ground support plane FX). The ground forces are also subject to continuing analysis, and here two alternatives are also depicted: System G1 (the current ground force) and G2 (a proposed new ground force mix, incorporating a new tactical missile system known as TX).

The air and ground forces are used in conjunction, their joint objective being a combined force with maximum combat effectiveness, given the size of the general purpose forces budget. This represents the second level of optimization, namely the allocation of the (given) general purpose forces budget between air and ground, resulting in the maximization of the combat effectiveness of the general purpose forces. We could, of course, go on to higher levels of optimization, such as the trade-off between general purpose and strategic forces. We could also formulate alternatives at even lower levels of optimization, by considering alternative mixes of light infantry and armor units in G1, or go to lower levels still by considering alternative configurations of the light infantry units themselves, and so on. What we have is a multilevel hierarchy of allocation problems. Only two levels are required, however, to illustrate the dangers of suboptimization, and for that purpose we need not complicate the situation beyond that which is depicted in the diagram.

Suppose our immediate problem is a determination of whether A2 should be adopted in lieu of A1, i.e., whether we should purchase FX. The customary suboptimizing procedure would be to take as given the current ground force structure, represented by G1. Meanwhile, another group of analysts may be hard at work studying the issue of whether or not TX should be adopted, making a parallel set of assumptions, i.e., that the air force structure retains its current configuration. The basic issue is the following: Will this suboptimizing procedure always lead to optimal air and ground force structures? If not, under what circumstances, and how may the resulting problem be remedied?

The answer to these questions, as suggested by the broken line in the diagram, depends on the extent to which the Cost Effectiveness of FX and TX may be mutually interdependent. Suppose, for example, that they

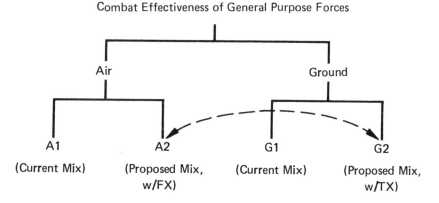

Figure 12.5 Mutual Interdependence of Weapon Systems

are strongly complementary systems. Perhaps TX is a tactical missile, the utility of which will be greatly enhanced by target acquisition equipment carried by FX, but not by other planes currently in the tactical fleet. Under these circumstances, suboptimization in choosing the mix of air and ground forces is obviously an unreliable technique. Introduction of both FX and TX may be highly Cost Effective, even though neither passes the Cost Effectiveness criterion when considered separately.

In such situations, in which the effectiveness of a given system is sensitive to the weapons mix in a separate category outside the purview of the analysis in question, something more is required. In general, two types of remedies are available, both of which have serious shortcomings. The first remedy is to conduct sensitivity analysis in which Cost Effectiveness is tested under alternative assumptions regarding such factors as the weapons mix, tactical doctrine, and policy to be employed in related systems. In the case under consideration, the air force analysis would examine the impact of TX on the Cost Effectiveness of FX, and army analysts would do the same, taking into account the impact of FX on the Cost Effectiveness of TX. Such sensitivity analysis is of crucial importance; it is, however, subject to several handicaps. First, FX analysts may be unaware of TX and its capabilities. They may be unable to obtain necessary data, and even if they do obtain information on TX, they may lack the expertise to make proper use of it. Secondly, bureaucratic factors may intrude in the form of interdepartmental rivalry, particularly if the weapons mix *within* air and ground systems affects the budgetary allocation *between* air and ground systems. Finally, at some point we have to question the sense of conducting the analyses of air and ground mixes separately, given the increasing redundancy of the efforts as the mutual interdependence increases.

The alternative solution is to shift the analysis to a higher level so that the interdependence may be taken into account. At the next higher level the problem, as presented in Figure 12.5, is the allocation of the general purpose forces budget between air and ground forces. In the absence of interdependence between the effectiveness of ground and air force mixes, the higher level problem may be stated simply in terms of trading off airpower versus ground power, so as to get maximum effectiveness for a given general purpose force budget. Of course, the problem is in fact not simple, because it is no easy matter to evaluate the combat effectiveness of general purpose forces. In general, the difficulty of estimating force effectiveness increases as the diversity and complexity of the force increases. Trading off air versus ground tactical forces is a tougher job than trading off one airplane against another airplane or one tank against another tank.

If in making this trade-off we also have to vary the air force mix and the ground force mix, the difficulties of making objective estimates are compounded even further. This difficulty was, of course, what motivated the suboptimization approach in the first place. Hence, in seeking to resolve suboptimization problems by moving to higher levels of analysis, we pay a price in terms of increasing complexity. A somewhat more subtle but nonetheless important issue is that moving the small allocation decisions to higher levels, i.e, centralizing the allocation decisions, moves the allocation process further and further away from the experts—individuals with detailed knowledge and field experience in use of the systems involved. At some point, the gain in comprehensiveness of the analysis may be more than offset by loss of reliability in the estimates of effectiveness.

COSTS

From a practical point of view, perhaps the most important aspect of applying Cost Effectiveness to defense allocation decisions has been the institution of procedures to collect total systems costs. A typical weapons system cost stream may look something like the pattern depicted in Figure 12.6. The pattern of this typical cost stream has several implications. The first is that a significant time period is involved, from the moment of inception until retirement. This means that efficient defense resource allocation requires a much longer perspective than the normal budgetary cycle. Decisions made in any given budget year carry implications extending at least five years into the future, and normally beyond. In deciding whether to proceed with any given system, the total systems cost must be taken into account, over the entire life of the system. A second implication is that the constraints imposed by annual congressional budget limitations bear little relation to trade-offs among various types of defense capabilities and various means of achieving such capability. In addition to the year to year nature of budget limitations, there is also the problem that expenditures for R&D, pro-

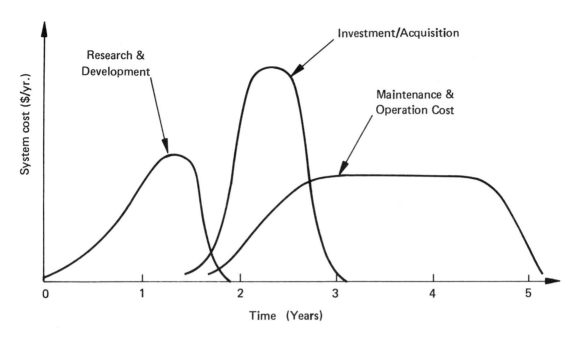

Figure 12.6 Lifecycle Costs of a Weapons System

curement, maintenance, training, and manning associated with a given system show up in different portions of the budgetary authorization. Hence, from the defense planner's and user's points of view, the budgetary trade-offs tend to occur within functional categories (R&D, manpower, procurement) rather than across "final" defense products. Thus the costs of a large weapons system are dispersed across many budget categories and across many separate budget cycles. In the face of this confusion, it is extraordinarily difficult to cast defense choices in economic terms. Organization of the data to permit identification of opportunity costs is the key function of Cost Effectiveness analysis.

For most purposes, the concept of cost employed in Cost Effectiveness studies is conceptually identical to that used in Cost Benefit analysis. Those ideas presented with respect to treatment of costs in Chapter 11 are equally applicable to Cost Effectiveness studies, and they need not be repeated here. The basic principle is that of opportunity cost, and our objective is to compare the effectiveness of resources used in a particular system with the effectiveness of the same amount of resources directed to the given objective via some alternative system. As noted, this means we are restricting the opportunity cost to the next best alternative use for the objective at hand. When we specify the "same amount of resources" by fixing the budget at a given dollar level, however, we mean exactly the same thing as is meant in a Cost Benefit analysis: a resource package whose opportunity cost to the economy as a whole is given by that dollar amount. As in Cost Benefit, this means that costs should be comprehensively defined, ideally taking into account any divergence between the actual budgetary figures and the true opportunity cost resulting from externalities, price distortions, etc.

Where future costs are involved, they should be converted into present value using an appropriate discount rate reflecting the social opportunity cost of capital. The issues concerning selection of the discount rate do not differ fundamentally from those discussed in Chapter 11.[4] There is, however, one important difference on the benefits side. Because effectiveness cannot be evaluated in dollar terms, the question arises as to whether any attempt should be made to discount future benefits. In principle, the same discount rate would apply. In fact, however, it frequently is not feasible to specify effectiveness, by year, in terms of a cardinal scale. Normally we are comparing the effectiveness of two systems, however, and all that is required is a choice between them. If their benefits are distributed differently over time, the choice necessarily involves some implicit discounting. That is usually as far as we can take the discounting process.

MEASURING EFFECTIVENESS:
MODELS, GAMES, AND EXPERIENCE

The most difficult aspect of Cost Effectiveness is the devising of a reliable, objective method for evaluating system effectiveness. The ideal technique—a full scale test under field conditions—is obviously not available in most cases. Failing that, the analyst has to make do with any of a variety of less reliable alternatives, based on some combination of experience and conjecture. The methods available vary widely, and some give greater assurance than others; the results, however, are rarely if ever fully satisfactory. Frustration over the difficulty of the problems leads some critics to conclude that systematic analysis is not worthwhile, but complexity does not constitute a case against analysis. A more reasonable interpretation is that the complexity of the issues demands systematic analysis.

Denied the oportunity to conduct full scale field tests, the analyst must devise some alternative means of predicting how a system will perform under actual field conditions. When the system being analyzed is relatively simple, it may be possible to describe the essential features of system performance using an abstract mathematical model. The effectiveness of a strategic weapons system, for example, may be fairly adequately characterized with a simple model incorporating probabilities of successful launch, penetration of enemy defenses, guidance system accuracy, and so on. Sometimes very large models are helpful. One of the most fruitful examples of Cost Effectiveness analysis was a large linear programming model of alternative transportation systems for providing rapid overseas deployment of forces.

As we move from single purpose to multipurpose systems, however, the feasibility of describing system performance in a single mathematical model dwindles rapidly. Whereas the principal objective of a new tank may be to destroy opposing armor, the probability of getting the first round on target may be sensitive to hundreds of factors in ways that defy quantification and explicit inclusion in a mathematical model. The analyst may resort to *proximate criteria*, or partial measures of effectiveness, such as speed, operating range, weapons range and accuracy, armor protection, maintenance, and training requirements. How to weight these partial measures in arriving at a final judgment can be highly problematical. There is a role for expert opinion, and there may be a role for some form of gaming or simulation technique. Whichever method of predicting performance is employed, a host of assumptions is usually involved as to the context in which the system will be used—terrain, climate, nature and strength of opposing forces, logistical factors, enemy reaction, and so on.

It would not be feasible to attempt here to catalog the whole array of effectiveness measurement techniques, identifying the strengths and pitfalls of each in each type of application. The list would be too long, and in any event Cost Effectiveness is not a "cookbook" type of activity. Its object is to develop new dishes, not to apply old recipes. The vital ingredient is an active, questioning inquiry into allocation issues, based on the few fundamental principles we have elucidated. Routine application of a standard technique is liable to be not only useless—precisely right on an issue of trivial importance, but also dangerous—grossly wrong on an issue of major importance.[5]

SENSITIVITY ANALYSIS

This thought brings us to the last, but probably most crucial, of our six elements of Cost Effectiveness, namely sensitivity analysis, which is the practitioner's insurance against being "grossly wrong." Given the complexity of the problems, obviously Cost Effectiveness studies have been and are subject to error. That is not an argument against analysis, but rather an argument against poor analysis. Serious mistakes have been made, but equally serious mistakes have also been made in weapons design, budgetary allocations, and policy formulation. Despite such occurrences, these activities must go on. The challenge is to raise the performance level. Cost Effectiveness can make a contribution in this regard, provided it is performed carefully and the results interpreted carefully.

The most important aspect of guarding against gross error—and avoiding spurious precision—is sensitivity analysis, which is nothing more than a continual questioning of methods and assumptions by the asking of "what if?" type questions. The purpose of sensitivity analysts is to identify those areas of uncertainty that have significance for the outcome of the analysis, and to estimate and make explicit the nature of the impact. In a sense, this problem is analogous to the uncertainty problem in Cost Benefit. The required treatment, however, is quite different.

As in the case of Cost Benefit, we may usefully distinguish between statistical risk, in which a probability distribution of possible outcomes is available, and uncertainty, in which a probability estimate is not available. Certain types of statistical risk can be handled in a straightforward manner by incorporating explicit confidence levels that in effect eliminate the risk, or reduce it to a tolerable level. For example, if the circular probable error (CEP) of a missile is known, we can calculate the number of rounds per target to insure a hit with any specified level of assurance, e.g., 99 percent. Weapons of varying accuracy can be traded off in this fashion.

If it is not feasible to eliminate the risk in this manner, the problem is much less tractable. Unlike Cost Benefit, we cannot retreat to expected value, because our measures of effectiveness are generally much more qualitative in nature. The kind of problem involved is depicted in Figure 12.7, which shows the estimated impact of a particular assumption on the performance of three systems. The first point to note is the FX and FY outperform FN across the entire range. Those systems are said to be *dominant*.[6] This is a useful piece of information, and with respect to the choice of either FX or FY over FN nothing more need be said. With respect to the choice between FX and FY, however, the situation is less clear. We can see that FX is better under certain conditions, but that its performance is far more sensitive to Assumption α, and in some instances the results may be "disastrous." Now, if performance were measurable in dollar terms, and if we could assign probabilities to various values of α, we might propose calculation of the expected value as a criterion of choice. But our scale of effectiveness is not measurable in dollar terms, and in general it will not do to treat equal distances on various portions of the performance scale as having equal importance. Getting from "disastrous" to "indifferent," for example, might be far more important than getting from "indifferent" to "superb." Because of this problem, it is

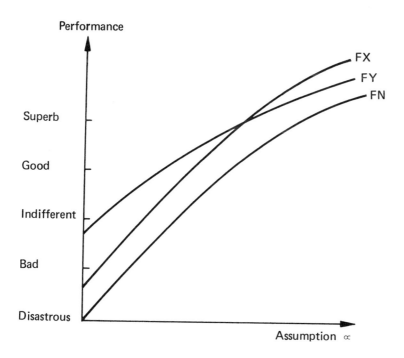

Figure 12.7 Sensitivity Analysis

not permissible for the analyst to hide risk by converting to some expected value. The same argument applies with even greater force in cases of uncertainty regarding factors involving the state of the world in the future, examples being technology, the strategic context, and the enemy and his reactions. Even with an acceptable performance scale, expected value is not a feasible solution in these cases, because there is no generally acceptable estimate of the probabilities.

Accordingly, the Cost Effectiveness analyst should endeavor to make explicit the sensitivity of his results to varying assumptions. A standard technique for doing this is to carry through the calculations for several versions of the assumptions, e.g., Best, Optimistic, and Pessimistic, the so-called "BOP" method.

When one considers that hundreds of crucial assumptions like α are involved in a typical analysis, and that assumptions gone awry can have a cumulative effect, the importance of sensitivity testing becomes even more evident. In cases such as the choice between FX and FY, the result is to reduce the persuasiveness of the analysis in identifying preferred chocies. The final outcome may be to demonstrate the essential ambiguity of the situation, and consequently may not get the policymaker much further along in making those choices that, sooner or later, have to be made. On the other hand, if the choice is in fact ambiguous, the policymaker is hardly well served if the analyst pretends otherwise.

The distinction between analyst and policymaker raises an underlying philosophical issue regarding the proper role of Cost Effectiveness studies. It may be argued, for example, that the analyst should scrupulously abstain from smuggling any policy biases or values of his own into what purports to be objective, scientific analysis. Adhering to this principle tends, for reasons elucidated above, to attenuate somewhat the force of any recommendations contained in the analysis. The analyst in this mold bends over backward to avoid inserting value judgments, many of which, in the final analysis, boil down to decisions as to how uncertainties should be treated.

The disadvantage of such a "purist" approach is, of course, that it inhibits the analyst from incorporating his own best judgment and the best judgment of experts and other sources he employs in his detailed study. The final product is the proverbial waffle, and clear policy choices do not emerge. A more realistic approaeh is to recognize that such a clear-cut distinction between normative and positive methodology in conducting analysis is not really possible and that the analyst inevitably imposes his value judgments on his work. Rather than avoid value judgments altogether, the good analyst will make some of his own, but he will be careful to identify the "crucial" issues. How do we define the crucial issues? Perhaps the best we can do is define them as those issues the policymaker himself would identify as crucial, if he had as much time and resources as the analyst to devote to the problem under study. In other words, identification of the crucial issues is itself a value judgment, and in practice it is a judgment that the analyst makes. The good analyst discharges the responsibility well, using sensitivity analysis to evaluate uncertain aspects, and explicitly reporting any crucial issues identified by the sensitivity analysis.

CONCLUSION

In the introduction to this chapter it was noted that, although Cost Effectiveness represents nothing more than the application of some very conventional and uncontroversial economic principles to defense policy, its use has occasioned considerable controversy. A number of explanations may be offered to explain this paradox. Part of the problem, especially during the initial intense period of its application under Secretary of Defense McNamara, was due to the fairly widespread belief that defense spending should not be subjected to the Cost Effectiveness test. The ideas were not new to economists, but they were new to some policymakers, and the vigor with which they were applied in the Department of Defense in the 1960s was definitely new. The feeling persists in some quarters, but in general the services have accepted the concepts, developed their own analytical capabilities, and today perform first-rate Cost Effectiveness analysis within their own staffs.

A second explanation of the controversy, which also has some validity, is that policy was being made by whiz-kids with no military experience and inadequate appreciation of its role in developing sound military policy. A third and more telling explanation is to be found in the nature of the budgetary process. There is inherent in all budgetary processes a strong adversarial element in which constituent groups with loyalties to and vested interests in particular programs constantly struggle to increase their share of the limited budget pie. The thoroughgoing institution of Cost Effectiveness methods in DOD in the 1960s constituted, first and foremost, a centralization of budgetary power, and consequently a threat to both the size of the individual services' share of the budget and their control of how that share would be used. Because of the threat to service autonomy in budget matters, a certain degree of hostile reaction was inevitable and would have occurred no matter how circumspect the DOD analysts might have been in preparing and using their findings.[7]

There is an additional consideration to be kept in mind in assessing the strengths and weaknesses of Cost Effectiveness, and this consideration may also help explain some of the controversy. As noted in the above discussion of sensitivity analysis, the complexity of the problems create enormous latitude for the individual analyst in designing his evaluation model, and in dealing with the manifold uncertainties involved. This open-ended nature of the problem places an extremely high premium on objectivity, and also indicates the need for caution in accepting particular recommendations that flow from the analysis. These are normal hazards in coping with complex issues, and there is little point in complaining about them—they are here to stay. If we inject into this environment a strong adversarial relationship, as in fact is frequently the case, several types of mischief may result. One is that the analyst may be tempted to claim a somewhat greater degree of factual underpinning for his conclusions than the situation actually warrants. Another is that disgruntled victims of program disapprovals or budgetary reallocations may be tempted to suspect lack of objectivity on the part of analysts. Both of these phenomena have accompanied the use of Cost Effectiveness in DOD, and on occasion the relationship between policymaker and analyst has been one of outright animosity. With the passage of time the situation has improved, but the price of effective use of the Cost Effectiveness approach is continuing vigilance to insure scrupulous objectivity, comprehensive sensitivity testing, and moderation with regard to findings.

NOTES

1 An excellent collection of essays on defense applications of Cost Effectiveness analysis is contained in E. S. Quade and W. I. Boucher, eds., *Systems Analysis and Policy Planning: Applications in Defense* (Santa Monica: The RAND Corporation, 1968).

2 From the perspective of the private producer, there is, of course, a marketplace in the form of the U.S. government and, increasingly in recent years, foreign governments who serve as prospective buyers. But our interest here is in how *governments* should decide, and from that perspective a market does not exist.

3 See the appendix by Alain Enthoven in Charles J. Hitch and Roland N. McKean, *The Economics of Defense in the Nuclear Age*, (Santa Monica: The RAND Corporation, 1960).

4 For a more detailed discussion, see Robert Shisko, *Choosing the Discount Rate for Defense Decisionmaking* (Santa Monica: The RAND Corporation, 1976).

5 For two recent, unclassified examples of Cost Effectiveness, see *The U.S. Sea-Based Strategic Force: Costs of the Trident Submarine and Missile Programs and Alternatives*, Congressional Budget Office, U.S. Congress (Washington, D.C.: Government Printing Office, February, 1980) and *Shaping the General Purpose Navy of the Eighties: Issues for Fiscal Years 1981–1985*, Congressional Budget Office, U.S. Congress (Washington, D.C.: Government Printing Office, January, 1980).

6 Note that the comparison assumes a common, fixed outlay for all three systems. In other words, the criterion in this case is maximum effectiveness for a given level of costs.

7 For more detailed discussions of the introduction in DOD of Cost Effectiveness on a broad scale, see Alain Enthoven and K. Wayne Smith, *How Much Is Enough? Shaping the Defense Program, 1961–69* (New York: Harper and Row, 1964). For a more critical perspective, see Bernard Brodie, "The McNamara Phenomenon," *World Politics* (July, 1965).

SELECTED REFERENCES

William J. Baumol, *Economic Theory and Operations Analysis,* 4th ed. (Englewood Cliffs, N.J.: Prentice Hall, Inc., 1977).

Gene H. Fisher, *Cost Considerations in Systems Analysis* (New York: American Elsevier Publishing Co., Inc., 1971).

Charles J. Hitch and Roland N. McKean, *The Economics of Defense in the Nuclear Age* (Santa Monica: The RAND Corporation, 1960).

E. S. Quade and W. I. Boucher, eds., *Systems Analysis and Policy Planning: Applications in Defense* (New York: American Elsevier Publishing Co., Inc., 1968).

James R. Schlesinger, *Uses and Abuses of Analysis,* Memorandum prepared for the Subcommittee on National Security and International Operations of the U.S. Senate Committee on Government Operations, 90th Congress, 2nd Session (Washington, D.C.: U.S. Government Printing Office, 1968).

"U.S. Army Force Design: Alternatives for Fiscal Years 1977–1981," Staff Working Paper (Washington, D.C.: Congressional Budget Office, 1976).

"U.S. Naval Force Alternatives," Staff Working Paper (Washington, D.C.: Congressional Budget Office, 1976).

"U.S. Tactical Air Forces: Overview and Alternative Forces, Fiscal Years 1976–81," Staff Working Paper (Washington, D.C.: Congressional Budget Office, 1976).

Part IV

Microeconomic Issues

Production is not the application of tools to materials, but logic to work.

Peter Drucker

High heaven rejects the lore
Of nicely calculated less or more.

William Wordsworth

Chapter 13
Markets:
The Laws of Supply and Demand

INTRODUCTION

In Chapters 10 to 12 the basic concepts of efficiency in resource allocation were discussed and related to the problem of choice in the defense sector. In this section, Chapters 13 to 17, we look behind the supply and demand curves, which were briefly discussed in those preceding chapters, to make a detailed examination of the various aspects of choice in defense economics.

The managers of defense policy are required not only to budget, but also to spend substantial amounts of money in a variety of different markets. In terms of goods, defense expenditures run the gamut from those goods produced in very competitive markets, to those produced in very noncompetitive markets. Our purpose in these chapters is to examine the variety of markets in which the defense sector participates, and the characteristics of these markets. Because in most cases the defense sector buys factors of production to support its activities, we will be emphasizing factor markets, although a general discussion of market activities follows below.

The primary purpose of this chapter is to discuss the basic laws of markets, and the common forms of alternative market structures. Chapters 14 and 15 discuss the specifics of the labor and capital markets in which defense planners frequently deal. Chapters 16 and 17 apply these market concepts to an analysis of defense mobilization and the impact of technological change.

The demand for a particular commodity can originate from one of three primary sources. Demand can emerge from the desire for consumers to satisfy primary wants; we call this the demand for final *consumer goods*.[1] Demand can originate from the need to produce materials to use in the production process; this is the *derived demand for intermediate goods*. Or lastly, the demand for goods can arise from producers' desires to buy primary factors of production such as capital or labor; this is the *derived demand for primary factors*.

Consumer Demand

The demand for consumer goods originates from an analysis of consumer tastes or preferences for the spectrum of commodities available in the economic system. Such preferences can be rank ordered by a utility function, which assigns an ordinal value to any specified combination of commodities. The value of the ordinal ranking determines the priority the consumer places on a specified collection of commodities.

Such a utility function is shown in Figure 13.1 for two commodities, X and Y. The function is shown in terms of utility contours, or "indifference curves," which represent combinations of goods X and Y that leave the individual indifferent between the various combinations in terms of satisfaction. A movement to the northeast on the XY plane represents an increase in the value of the utility function and consequently a movement to a higher level of satisfaction. Hence, U_3 represents a higher level of satisfaction than U_0.

The individual consumer is assumed to maximize utility, subject to a given level of income and prices of the commodities. The constraints under which the consumer operates can be represented by a budget line, shown in Figure 13.1 as the line X_0Y_0. The budget line, as discussed in Chapter 10, represents the possible combination of commodities that a single consumer can buy, given the consumer's level of income and the prices of each of the commodities. If all income were spent on X, then X_0 could be purchased with the income implicit in line X_0Y_0. If all income were spent on good Y, then Y_0 could be purchased. Any combination along X_0Y_0 is possible, with the slope of the budget line being the negative of the price ratio of good X to good Y. [2]

The consumer will maximize satisfaction by selecting that combination of goods X and Y at which the marginal rate of substitution (the slope of the indifference curve) is equal to the ratio of price X to price Y (the slope of the budget line). This is illustrated by point Z in Figure 13.1. Given the budget line, X_0Y_0, the consumer reaches the highest level of satisfaction by purchasing $\bar{Y}$ units of good Y and $\bar{X}$ units of good X. At this combination, the consumer reaches the U_1 indifference curve. Given the budget constraint, no higher level of satisfaction can be reached. Note that this solution depends on the consumer's utility function, a fixed income constraint, and fixed prices for X and Y. If any of these factors should change, the quantities of X and Y "demanded" or preferred by the consumer would change.

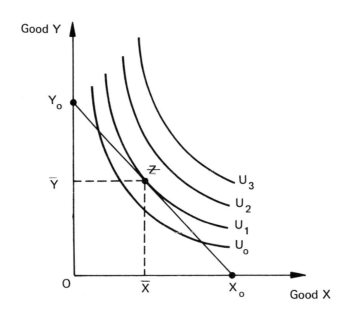

Figure 13.1 An Individual Function Represented by Indifference Curves

The demand curve for good X is derived by noting the amount of X that would be preferred at various prices. Graphically, the derivation of the demand curve is shown in Figure 13.2, which shows the optimum amounts of goods X and Y preferred when the price of good X is changed. Note that in this case a decrease in the price of good X is shown by a shift in the budget line from X_0 to X_2. As the price of X declines, the quantity of good X that can be purchased with a given level of income increases and, as the figure shows, more of good X is purchased. If the amount of good X demanded is plotted as a function of the price of good X, the result is the standard downward sloping demand curve shown in Figure 13.3. Note that points 1, 2, and 3 in Figure 13.3 correspond to the same points indicated in Figure 13.2.

The industry demand curve, representing the total demand for good X, is found by horizontally adding the individual demand curves at each price for good X. The resulting demand curve, shown in Figure 13.4, gives the amount that all individuals in the particular market are willing to buy at each price for good X. Thus at price $\bar{p}_X$, the total amount demanded by all consumers would be $\bar{Q}_X$.[3]

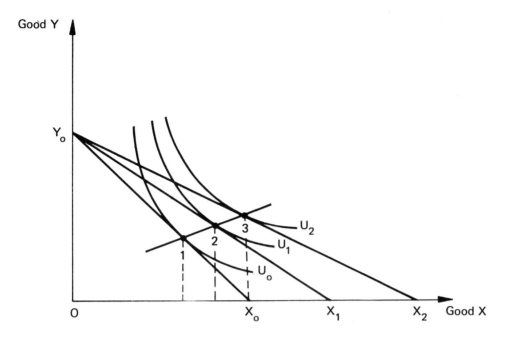

Figure 13.2 Derivation of the Demand Curve

Figure 13.3 The Demand Curve of the Individual

Note:
Points 1-3 correspond to points 1-3 on Figure 13.2.

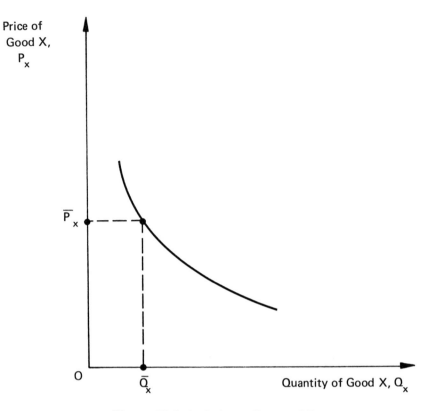

Figure 13.4 An Industry Demand Curve

Derived Demand

The analysis above gives the derivation of the demand curve for products utilized by consumers. In analyzing the defense sector, however, many of the markets that we shall be concerned with are those in which intermediate goods or primary factors of production are purchased. The demand for these products does not derive from the level of satisfaction resulting from consumption of the intermediate goods or primary factors, but rather from the goods or services that the primary factor or intermediate product produces. Such a demand is entitled *derived demand*.

The derivation of the derived demand curve for both intermediate goods and primary factors follows the same principles. To illustrate the process, we will focus on the derived demand for a factor using the production function approach developed in Chapter 9. We assume that output, Q, is a function of capital, K, and labor, L. In order to develop the derived demand for labor, we must determine how the quantity of labor demanded will vary as we change the price of labor, or wage, *assuming that the technology, input of capital, price of capital, and price of the output all remain constant*. In other words our analysis will be based on partial, or marginal, analysis.

As we increase the input of labor we will observe an increase in output, but because of the diminishing returns in most production processes, we will note that the additonal output from equal increments of labor will begin to decline. This diminishing marginal product of labor is reflected in the shape of the revenue curve shown in Figure 13.5. As more labor is used, revenue increases, but at a declining rate (total revenue is increasing, but marginal revenue is declining). Because we assume a constant wage, w, in the figure, costs continue to expand at a constant rate as we expand the input of labor.

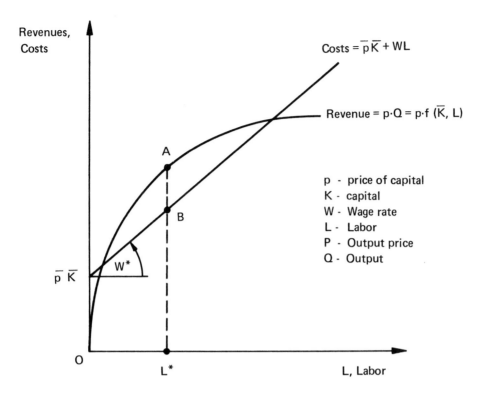

Figure 13.5 Revenue and Cost Based on Variations in Labor Input
(Holding the Output Price, Price of Capital, and Capital Input Constant)

Note that the revenue curve is a function of the fixed price of the output, $\bar{p}$, and the physical product, $Q = f(\bar{K},L)$, where $\bar{K}$ is the fixed stock of capital, and L is the amount of labor employed. Given a wage rate, w^*, the profit maximizing entrepreneur will choose that value of labor, L^*, which maximizes profit or the distance between the revenue and the cost functions. In Figure 13.5 this amount of labor is given as L^*, at which point revenues are given at point A and costs at point B. We know that L^* is the profit maximizing amount of labor, because at this point the slope of the revenue curve, the "marginal value product," is equal to the slope of the cost curve. To the left of L^*, the slope of the revenue curve is greater than the slope of the cost curve, and the two curves must be diverging; hence, profit is increasing. This merely indicates that at all points to the left of L^* the value to the entrepreneur of adding another unit of labor is greater than the cost; hence, the labor input should be increased. For all points to the right of L^* the slope of the revenue function is less than the slope of the cost function; hence, profits are decreasing. Only at the point where the marginal value product of labor is equal to the marginal cost, or wage rate, are profits maximized.

If the wage rate is increased, the cost curve rotates upward around point $\bar{p}\bar{K}$. If nothing else changes, the profit maximizing labor input will decline as the point at which the marginal value product of labor is equal to the new wage rate shifts to the left. If each optimum labor input is plotted horizontally as a function of the associated wage rate, the derived demand curve for labor services results. A typical curve is given in Figure 13.6. A similar type of derivation can develop the derived demand for capital as well as the derived demand for all intermediate goods.

Our discussion thus far has examined the demand side of the market for goods and services. The following section looks at the supply side of market forces and the theory of production.

Figure 13.6 The Derived Demand for Labor

THE THEORY OF FIRM AND SUPPLY

The amount of a particular product that entrepreneurs are willing to produce depends on the demand for the product, the cost structure of the industry, and the optimizing behavior of firms. The typical firm experiences costs associated with various output levels similar to those shown in Figure 13.7. Costs are distinguished as *fixed costs*, or those that in the short run do not vary with output, and *variable costs*, or those that vary in the short run with output. Fixed costs are represented by the distance OA in Figure 13.7, while variable costs are those lying above point A.

Total costs are shown to increase rapidly at first as output rises, then to slow down, and then to increase sharply again as output increases further. The initial rapid rise in costs is due to the operation of the firm at a less than efficient plant size. As output approaches the most efficient scale, costs increase less rapidly. As output continues to increase, diminishing returns set in and costs begin again to rise sharply.

In a competitive market, each firm is assumed to be too small to affect the market price. Thus total revenues are given simply by the product of a constant price, times quantity sold. Total revenues versus total costs in a competitive market are plotted in Figure 13.8. The total revenue curve OBCE gives total revenues for each quantity. The profit for the competitive firm is given by the vertical distance between the total cost curve and the total revenue curve. Note, for example, that the break even points for this firm are given at points B and E.

If it is assumed that the objective of the firm is to maximize profits, the output level that the firm selects is output level Q* where profits, CD, are a maximum. We know that the output level Q* is the profit maximizing level, because Q* is the point where the slope of the total revenue curve, or marginal revenue, is equal to the

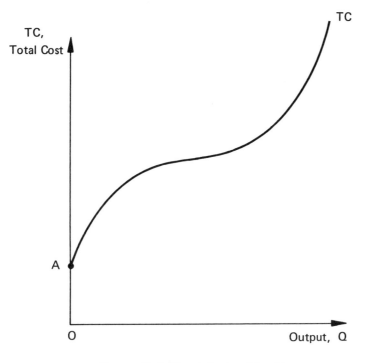

Figure 13.7 Total Costs of the Firm

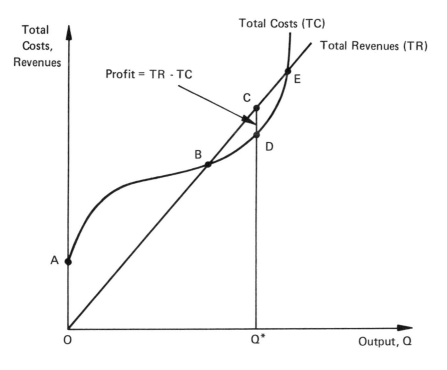

Figure 13.8 Total Revenues and Total Costs

slope of the total cost curve, or marginal cost. At the point to the left of Q*, revenues are rising faster than costs, and therefore, profits are increasing as the two curves are diverging. At Q* the slopes become equal, after which the slope of the cost curve exceeds the slope of the revenue curve, and profits begin to decline. The equality of the slopes of the two curves gives the marginal condition necessary for a profit maximum: the marginal revenues must equal marginal costs.[5]

The cost and revenue curves are replotted in average and marginal terms in Figure 13.9. The average total cost curve plots the cost per unit of output at each output level. This can be derived from the total cost curve by dividing the value given on the total cost curve by the level of output. The marginal cost curve plots the slope of the total cost curve, or the cost of producing the marginal unit of output.

Average total costs are first very high as output is low and fixed costs are spread over very few units of output. As output increases, average costs fall until diminishing returns set in, whereupon average total costs begin to rise. Marginal costs, similarly, first fall then rise, cutting through the average total cost curve at the minimum point on the average total cost curve.

The average and marginal revenue curves are identical for a competitive firm; each is a constant value equal to the price of output. This follows from the assumption that each firm in a competitive industry is so small relative to the output of the industry that shifts in the firm's output have no impact on the market price.

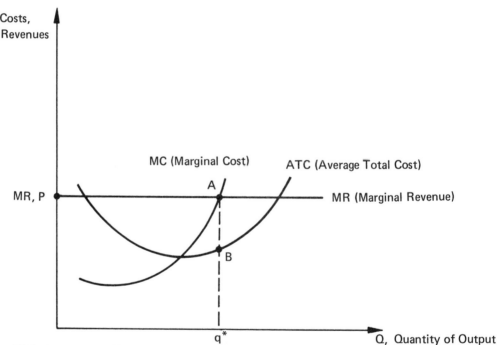

Figure 13.9 Average and Marginal Cost and Revenue Curves for the Competitive Firm

Note:
MC must intersect ATC at the minimum point on the ATC curve. To the left of this point the MC is lower than the average and producing one more unit pulls the average down. To the right of this point the MC is higher than the average and producing one more unit pulls the average up.

The profit maximizing output level, q* in Figure 13.9, is found at the point where marginal revenue and marginal cost are equal. The excess profit of the competitive firm in this case is given by the profit per unit, AB, times q*, the number of units produced. Note that if the price that the firm can get for its output is increased, the profit maximizing level of output will increase. The amount of output the competitive firm will produce at any price, therefore, is found by selecting the output at which price equals marginal cost. Thus the marginal cost curve for the competitive firm is equal to its supply curve.[6] If the marginal cost curves for each firm in an industry are summed horizontally, the result is the supply curve of the industry. This curve is illustrated in Figure 13.10. The industry supply curve shows how much all firms in the industry would be willing to supply at any specified price. Thus, at price P_o in Figure 13.10, the industry would be willing to supply Q_o units of output.

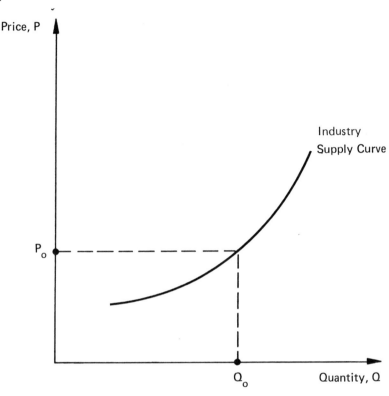

Figure 13.10 The Supply Curve for a Competitive Industry

EQUILIBRIUM

The price and quantity exchanged in a market are determined by the interactions of buyers and sellers. The demand and supply curves for a particular commodity are shown in Figure 13.11. These curves, together with a description of the disequilibrium bidding process, determine the price and quantity that result in the market.

The bidding process used here is assumed to be a simple "Walrasian" bidding process, where prices rise when demand exceeds supply.[7] Thus if the demand and supply curves are those shown in Figure 13.11 and the prevailing price in the market is p*, there would be an excess demand for the commodity and the bids of buyers would drive the price up. As the price rises, fewer consumers would buy the product and firms would be willing to supply more output to the market. The price would continue to rise until it reached the equilibrium level (P_e), where $Q_s = Q_D$. At that point supply and demand are equal, and the market would be in equilibrium at price p_e, and quantity, Q_e.

If the market equilibrium were "stable" there would be no tendency for price or quantity to change. Thus the market price and quantity would tend to remain at p_e and Q_e unless something occurred to cause either the supply or demand curves to shift. Recalling our demand curve discussion, we can now discuss several factors that would result in a shift in the demand curve. These factors include consumer income, the price of complements and substitutes, and consumer tastes for a particular commodity.

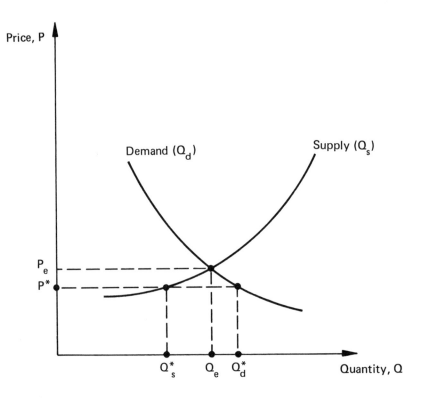

Figure 13.11 Market Equilibrium

Shifts in Demand and Supply

An increase in the level of consumer income is assumed, under most circumstances, to result in an increase in the demand for a particular commodity, assuming all other factors are constant. This can be seen by noting in Figure 13.1 that the effect of an increase in income is a shift in the budget line to the northeast, thus increasing the utility maximizing level of the consumption of both commodities. Thus the effect of an increase in income is to increase the demand for a particular commodity at every given price, or to shift the demand curve to the right.

Using a similar line of reasoning, the effect of changes in the other variables noted above can also be analyzed. Increases in the prices of *complementary goods*—goods used *with* the good in question—will result in a decrease in the demand for a particular commodity, or a leftward shift in the demand curve. An increase in the price of *substitutes*—goods used in lieu of the good in question—will increase demand. Demand will also increase with an increase in consumer tastes, reflecting greater preference for the good in question. Thus, increases in either the price of substitutes or consumer tastes will result in a rightward shift in the demand curve.

These points can be summarized by expressing the demand curve in the following manner:[8]

$$Q_D = f\ (\overset{-}{p},\ \overset{+}{p_s}\ \overset{-}{p_c},\ \overset{+}{y},\ \overset{+}{CT}) \tag{13.1}$$

where

Q_D	= quantity demanded	p_c	= price of complements
p	= price	Y	= income
p_s	= price of substitutes	CT	= consumer tastes

The signs on top of each independent variable indicate the effect on the quantity demanded of a positive change in that independent variable. When we draw a demand curve, we assume that all of the variables but price are held constant. The minus sign above price indicates that as price increases, the quantity will fall. When any variable other than price changes, the demand curve will shift. Increases in those variables with a positive sign over them result in a rightward shift of the demand curve. Increases in those variables with a negative sign over them result in a leftward shift in the demand curve.

Similar analysis on the supply side leads to the development of a similar functional relationship:

$$Q_s = g \; (\overset{+}{p}, \; \overset{-}{p_i} \; \overset{+}{K}, \; \overset{+}{T}, \; \overset{-}{BL}) \tag{13.2}$$

where

Q_s	= quantity supplied	K	= capital stock
p	= price	T	= technology
p_i	= price of inputs	BL	= bad luck

Bad luck is included to emphasize the risk associated with any production decision. The quantity we expect to see supplied will, in fact, be a function of a wide range of factors beyond the control of the producer.

Once again, increases in those variables with a positive sign over them result in a rightward shift in the supply curve, while increases in those with a negative sign result in a leftward shift in the supply curve.

Short Run Equilibrium

Let us now examine the effect of a shift in one of the curves on the equilibrium price and quantity. We will assume that we are concerned with the market for bullets, and that the initial equilibrium is that depicted in Figure 13.11, with the quantity of bullets on the horizontal axis and the price of bullets on the vertical axis. In equilibrium, the price of bullets is given by p_e and the quantity of bullets is given by Q_e. Assume now that an increase in the price of metal used in shell casings leads to a leftward shift in the supply curve. The new initial situation for the industry is shown in Figure 13.12. At the old equilibrium price, p_e, there is an excess demand

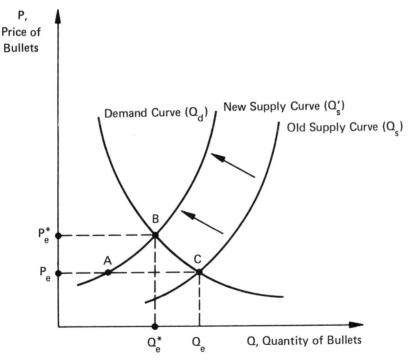

Figure 13.12 A Shift in Supply

for bullets as a result of the shift in the supply curve, i.e, $Q_D\rangle Q_s$. According to our hypothesis on the bidding behavior which occurs in markets, however, the price is is up when $Q_D\rangle Q_s$. Thus in this case the price begins to rise. As the price rises, less bullets are demanded or some consumers are squeezed out of the market by higher prices, and firms also begin to respond to the higher prices by moving along the new supply curve.

The effect of the higher market price on consumers is indicated by the movement along the demand curve from point C to point B in Figure 13.12. The effect of the higher market price on producers is indicated by a movement along the supply curve from point A to point B. Both of these adjustments occur simultaneously and the bidding process in the market continues until the quantities supplied and demanded are equal at point B. At price p_e and quantity Q_e, the market is again in "short-run" equilibrium. In the short run, we assume that the capital stock is fixed and that firms can neither enter nor leave the industry.

Long Run Equilibrium

The fact that the quantities demanded and supplied are equal at the new price, $p_e{}^*$, and quantity, Q_e, does not necessarily imply that the situation will remain unchanged. Figure 13.13 shows the typical firm in the bullet industry at the new equilibrium price, $p_e{}^*$. At this price the typical firm produces $q_e{}^*$. The excess profit for the firm—profit above and beyond the normal profit for the bullet industry already included in total cost—is given by area ABCD. Because the typical firm in the bullet industry is now earning a rate of profit greater than that which can be earned in investments of comparable risk, in the long run, resources will be moving into the bullet industry, and more bullet firms will begin to be established. With more bullet firms, however, the number of marginal cost curves increases, and the industry-wide supply curve consequently shifts to the right.[9]

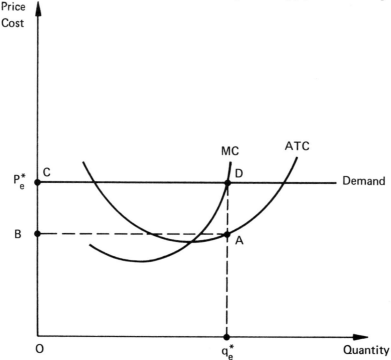

Figure 13.13 Short-Run Equilibrium of the Firm in the Bullet Industry

Note:
In the short run, we assume that the capital stock is fixed and that firms can neither enter nor leave the industry.

As the supply curve shifts to the right, the market price will begin to fall because excess supply will develop at the new equilibrium price as new firms enter the market. The price will continue to fall until it reaches a minimum point on the average total cost curve for the typical firm in the industry. This is depicted in Figure 13.14, where the industry supply and demand curves are shown on the left, and the cost curves of the typical firm are shown on the right. As the supply curve for the industry continues to shift to the right, the bidding process results in a decrease in price until pe** is reached. At this point, the price is equal to the lowest average total cost attainable by the firm. If the price were to drop any lower than this, the rate of return being earned in the bullet industry would be less than that earned on alternative investments of comparable risk, and firms would leave the industry. The industry supply curve, therefore, tends to stabilize when the price drops to the lowest point on the average total cost curve for the typical firm in the industry.

The above example showed the effect of an increase in the price of an input on short-run equilibrium in a competitive market. Similar analyses yield similar results for changes in any of the other variables that affect either the supply or demand curves.

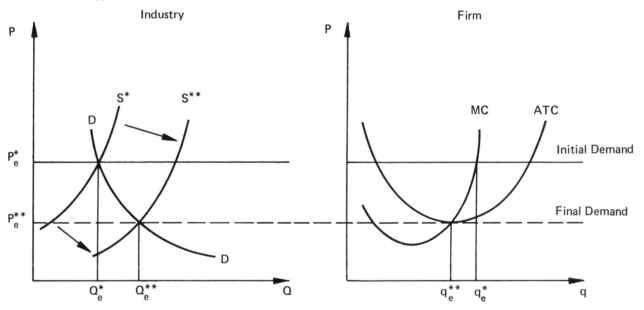

Figure 13.14 Long-Run Equilibrium of the Firm in the Bullet Industry

Note:
Entry of New Firms Shifts Industry Supply to the Right.

Note: When the Industry Price Drops to P_e^{**}, the Firm no longer makes Excess Profits and there is no Further Impetus for the Entry of New Firms.

ALTERNATIVE MARKET STRUCTURES

Monopoly

The analysis developed above assumes that the output decisions of individual firms do not affect the price received by the firm. This assumption implies that the capacity of the average firm in the industry is small in terms of the output of the entire industry. Thus, the actions of a single producer do not appreciably affect the industry supply curve and, therefore, do not greatly affect the price determined in the market. The opposite is true when a single firm is the entire industry, as in the case of a monopoly. Here the firm faces the industry demand curve, and changes in output result in changes in the price received by the firm. In the case of a monopoly, the analysis developed in the preceding section to determine the optimum output level of the individual firm must be modified to take into account the fact that total revenues are not a simple linear function of price.

In Chapter 10 we noted that the price set by a monopolist will, in general, be greater than the opportunity cost, or marginal cost, to society. Here we demonstrate that, whereas the perfect competitor sets price equal to marginal cost, the monopolist sets price above marginal cost. To develop this argument we assume a simple linear demand curve for the industry

$$P = a - bQ \qquad (13.3)$$

where a and b are constants. The total revenues for the industry are therefore given by

$$TR = PQ = aQ - bQ^2 \qquad (13.4)$$

In Figure 13.15, the total revenue expression above is graphed as a function of Q along with the cost curves of the firm developed in the preceding section. Note that the total revenue curve in this instance is not linear, but rises at a falling rate, peaks at a value of $Q = a/2b$, and then falls.[10] The level of output that maximizes profits in this case is Q^*, where the slope of the total revenue curve is greater than the slope of the total cost curve, the two curves are diverging and profits are rising. At points to the right of Q^*, where the slope of the total revenue cost is greater than the slope of the total revenue curve, the curves are converging and profits are declining. Only at Q^*, where the slopes are equal, are profits a maximum. This is the point once again where marginal revenues (the slope of the total revenue curve) equal marginal costs (the slope of the total cost curve).

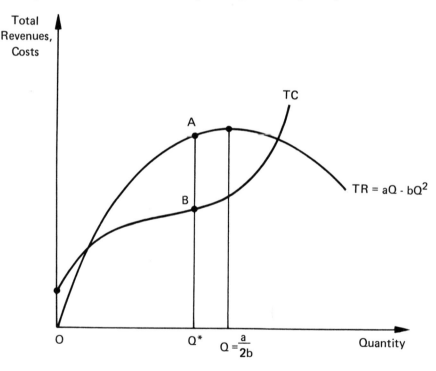

Figure 13.15 Total Revenues and Costs for a Monopoly

The above situation can also be shown in terms of the more conventional average and marginal revenue and cost curves. Figure 13.16 shows the average and marginal curves associated with the monopolistic firm. Note that in this situation, which differs greatly from that of the competitive firm, the demand curve for the firm is downward sloping, indicating the effect of increasing quantities of output on the price that the firm receives for its output. Also graphed is the slope of the total revenue curve, or the marginal revenue curve. Marginal revenues are below the demand curve, reflecting the fact that increased levels of output result in a falling price, hence lower revenues at the margin for the firm than those indicated by the price at the preceding level of output.

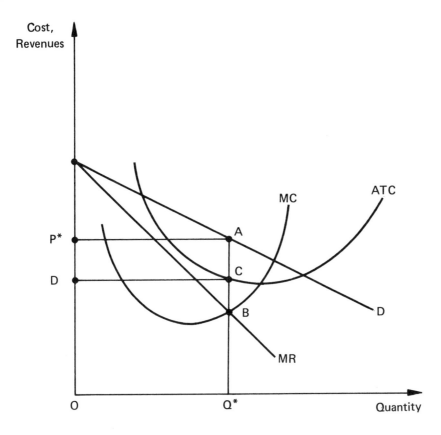

Figure 13.16   Cost and Revenue Curves for the Monopolist

The profit maximizing level of output is again given by Q*, where marginal revenues and marginal costs are equal. Notice that, in this case, the profits of the firm are given by rectangle ACDP.* The price charged at the profit maximizing point is given on the demand curve at point A, while costs per unit are given on the average total cost curve at point C. The difference between these two is profit per unit AC, which, when multiplied by the number of units OQ*, gives total profit.

An essential difference between the monopolistic and competitive market structures is that the monopolist will remain at the position described above in the long run, while the competitive industry will shift to eliminate excess profits. The monopolistic industry will not change, because a single firm supplies the entire market; competitors are eliminated by either legal or economic barriers to entry. Legal barriers include exclusive charters to do business granted by the state, or the granting of a patent. Economic barriers might include either large start-up costs and imperfect capital markets, or industries where the most efficient scale of plant would preclude more than one plant supplying the entire industry (decreasing cost industries).

For whatever the reason, the existence of a monopoly implies the existence of excess profit, and output being supplied at a price that is in excess of the opportunity cost. As noted in Chapter 10, this means that less output is supplied than is socially optimal. If the demand curve in some sense reflects the marginal benefit to the consumer that results from the consumption of the commodity in question, the monopolist produces at a point where marginal benefit, or price (point A in Figure 13.16), is greater than marginal cost (point B).[11] Thus marginal analysis would imply that for society, the optimal level of output should be greater, and the price of that output lower, than is indicated in the monopoly case. The private profit maximizing behavior of the monopolist, however, leads to the monopoly result, with too few resources in the monopolized industry, and no economic forces to change things.

Monopsony

A form of imperfect competition that is of particular interest to the defense sector is *monopsony*. As opposed to a monopoly market where there is a single *seller*, in the monopsonistic market there is a single *buyer*. In some markets the Department of Defense is the only buyer, and hence exercises monopsony power. In the case where the demand curve reflects a demand by a single buyer for a factor service, and the industry supplying the factor service is competitive, the solution of the monopsony problem is similar to that of the monopoly. Each point on the derived demand curve of the monopsonist in this case reflects the marginal product of the factor being purchased. The buyer, in order to maximize profits, will only purchase the factor until its marginal cost is equal to the price reflected on the demand curve. If the competitive industry has an upward sloping supply curve, the marginal cost curve for the monopsonist will be above the industry supply curve.[12] This situation is shown in Figure 13.17, where the profit maximizing monopsonist ends up at point A, purchasing Q* units of output at a price P.* Note in this case, as in the case of the monopoly, that the point at which output is produced is the point at which the marginal benefit of the good, i.e., the marginal product of the good in the using industry, is greater than marginal cost to producers. As a result of the monopsonistic situation, less than a socially optimum amount of good A will be produced.

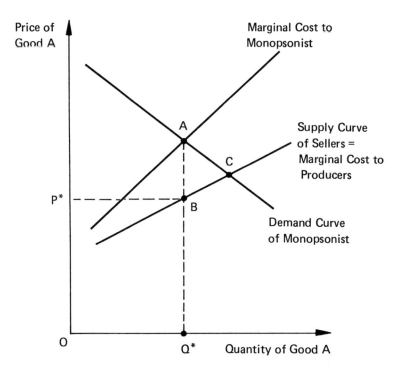

Figure 13.17 Monopsony Pricing and Output

Bilateral Monopoly

Another market structure that is of particular interest to the defense sector is *bilateral monopoly*. Here the market structure consists of a monopolist and a monopsonist. Such a situation is shown in Figure 13.18. In this case, the seller attempts to reach a contract along the buyer's demand curve, in which case the maximum profit is obtained with output Q_0 (where the seller's marginal cost is equal to his marginal revenue), to be sold at price P_0. The buyer, on the other hand, seeks a contract along the seller's marginal cost curve. From the buyer's perspective, the optimum output is Q_1 (where the buyer's marginal cost is equal to his marginal benefit), to be purchased at price P_1. Thus the seller wishes to sell output Q_0 at price P_0. The buyer wishes to purchase output Q_1 at price P_1. These objectives conflict and cannot be achieved simultaneously; hence, the ultimate outcome is indeterminate without some additional specification as to the relative bargaining power or negotiating skill of buyer and seller.

The optimal solution, from the standpoint of allocative efficiency, is to produce output Q_2, for which the seller's marginal cost is equal to the buyer's marginal benefit. One interesting aspect of bilateral monopoly from the defense sector perspective has been noted by Stigler.[13] If both buyer and seller attempt to maximize joint profits, the optimal solution will be achieved. In this case production will occur at Point D, with Q_2 being produced at price P_2. This opportunity to maximize joint profits provides an incentive for both firms to set jointly production and pricing decisions. The indeterminacy of the bilateral monopoly model is of particular interest to the defense sector in that it raises the issue of whether a large defense firm, which deals primarily with the government, should privately set price and output, or should in fact merge with the government and become publicly controlled.

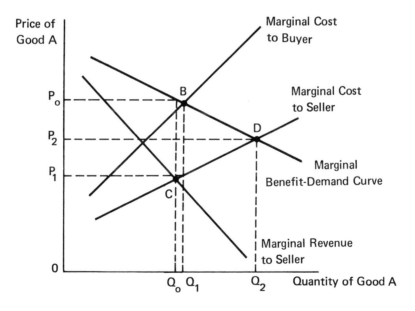

Figure 13.18 Bilateral Monopoloy

Oligopoly

Another interesting form of market structure, from the perspective of the defense sector, is oligopoly. Oligopoly is of interest not only from the perspective of buying and selling defense goods, but also for the parallels that the oligopoly model allows us to draw in terms of arms race models (see Chapter 26).

Oligopoly is a form of market structure in which there are few sellers and many buyers. The best studied example of an oligopoly is a *duopoly*, where there are two sellers and many buyers. The essential problem of an oligopoly is that the decisons of firms in an oligopolistic industry are dependent upon the actions taken by other firms in the industry. There are a number of solutions to the oligopoly problem. We shall briefly discuss three of the more interesting possibilities: the Cournot Solution, the Stackelberg Solution, and the Collusion Solution.

The Cournot Solution

One of the first solutions to the duopoly problem was that proposed by Cournot. To examine the Cournot solution we shall use a simple numerical example with two firms, each of which acts independently of the other in setting output of a given product. The results, however, can be generalized and extended to any number of firms.

Assume that two firms produce good A. The demand curve for the good is given by:

$$P = 200 - (Q_1 + Q_2)$$

where P is price, Q is quantity, and the subscripts refer to each firm. Cost curves for each firm are given by:

$$TC_1 = 50 + .5 Q_1^2$$
$$TC_2 = 100 + 0.25 Q_2^2$$

where TC is total cost. Cournot assumed that each firm would set output so as to maximize its profit, taking the other firm's output as fixed. Defining profit (π) as total revenue minus total cost, Firm 1 seeks to maximize the following expression:

$$\pi_1 = [200 - (Q_1 + Q_2)] Q_1 - 50 - .5Q_1^2 \tag{13.5}$$
$$= 200Q_1 - Q_1^2 - Q_1Q_2 - 50 - .5Q_1^2$$

Taking Q_2 as fixed, differentiating π, with respect to Q_1, and setting the result equal to zero gives:

$$\frac{d\pi_1}{dQ_1} = 200 - 2Q_1 - Q_2 - Q_1 = 0 \tag{13.6}$$

or

$$Q_1 = 66.7 - .33Q_2 \tag{13.7}$$

Equation 13.7, which is referred to as Firm 1's *reaction curve*, gives Firm 1's output as a function of Firm 2's output.

Following the same procedure, the condition for maximum profit for Firm 2 is given by:

$$\frac{d\pi_2}{dQ_2} = 200 - Q_1 - 2Q_2 - .5Q_2 = 0 \tag{13.8}$$

or

$$Q_2 = 80 - .4Q_1 \tag{13.9}$$

These reaction curves are plotted in Figure 13.19. As the figure shows, an equilibrium solution of the duopoly problem results when the output of both firms simultaneously satisfies the reaction functions, or when $Q_1 = 46.43$ and $Q_2 = 61.43$.

Thus the Cournot approach leads to a solution providing that each seller takes the output solution of his competitor as a given.

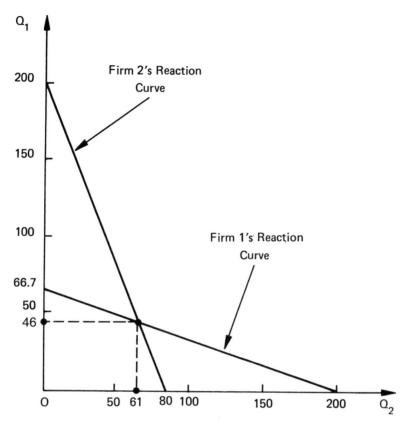

Figure 13.19 Duopoly Reaction Curves

The Stackelberg Solution

The assumption that each seller takes the output of his competitor as given implies imperfect information, in the sense that each seller does not know the reaction function of his competitor. The German economist Stackelberg noted that if information on the reaction function of each seller is available, and if each assumes the other will follow output leadership, then the solution of the duopoly problem will generally be indeterminate. To illustrate this, we assume that both sellers in our example above assume output leadership, and maximize profits using the other seller's reaction function as a datum. In this case, Firm 1's profits are given by substituting Firm 2's reaction function for Q_2 in Equation 13.5 or:

$$\pi_1 = (200 - Q_1 - 80 + .4Q_1) Q_1 - 50 - .5Q_1^2 \tag{13.10}$$
$$= 200 Q_1 - Q_1^2 - 80Q_1 + .4Q_1^2 - 50 - .5Q_1^2$$

Maximizing this expression with respect to Q_1 gives:

$$\frac{d\pi_1}{dQ_1} = 200 - 80 - 2.2Q_1 = 0 \tag{13.11}$$

or $Q_1 = 54.6$ with a profit of $\pi_1 = 3222.7$. The same analysis of Firm 2's profit maximizing position yields a profit function of:

$$\pi_2 = (200 - (66.7 - .33Q_2)) Q_2 - 100 - 100 - .25Q_2^2 \tag{13.12}$$
$$= 133.3Q_2 - .92Q_2^2 + 100$$

Maximizing Firm 2's profits with respect to Q_2 gives:

$$\frac{d\pi_2}{dQ_2} = 133.3 - 1.84 Q_2 = 0 \qquad (13.13)$$

or $Q_2 = 72.5$, with a profit of $\pi_2 = 4928.5$. Note that although this solution happens to have optimum outputs that are close to each other, they are not the same, and in general can be quite divergent. Thus, in the Stackelberg case, the oligopoly solution to the output problem is indeterminate.

The Collusion Solution

A relatively simple solution of the oligopoly problem is the Collusion Solution. Here both (or in the case of oligopoly, the several) firms in the industry collude and act as a monopolist. In this case, the profits of the industry are maximized, as in the case of a monopoly, but the division of the profits is left indeterminate. The profit question can only resolved by negotiations between the firms in the cartel. This problem is sometimes resolved by reverting to a market share solution, where the profits are divided based on past market shares. The question of profit division, however, may lead to discord within the cartel and create an unstable organization. Thus the Collusion solution, although determinate, may not often be observed due to either anti-trust laws or instability surrounding the division of profits.

Imperfect Competition

The last form of market structure to be considered here is imperfect, or "monopolistic," competition. This form of market organization exists when firms within an industry possess some market power due to "product differentiation." Product differentiation implies that a firm is able—through advertising or slight variations in product design—to make consumers buy its product, rather than a close substitute, even when the price may be higher. In this type of market structure the demand curve is downward sloping, but due to the availability of close substitutes, the slope of the curve is much less negative in general than a monopolist's demand curve, reflecting the availability of close substitutes.

The typical firm in an imperfectly competitive market would, therefore, have cost and revenue curves very similar to those in a monopolistic industry. The key difference between the two, however, is that in an imperfectly competitive industry the share of the market held by one firm may rise or fall due to the existence of excess profits.

A typical imperfectly competitive firm is shown in Figure 13.20. The original market position of this firm is reflected in the demand curve and marginal revenue curve, respectively labeled D_1 and MR_1. Given these curves, the profit maximizing level of output for the imperfect competitor would be at Q_1, where $MR = MC$ with a profit per unit of AC. These profits, however, create competition for the imperfect competitor that tends to reduce the demand for its product. Firms would continue to enter this market until the market share of the typical firm is reduced so that the demand curve and the marginal revenue curve are given by curves D_2 and MR_2. The profit maximizing level of output given by these new curves occurs at Q_2 where $MC = MR_2$, and where excess profit per unit are zero. The industry at this point is in long-run equilibrium, in that no more firms tend to enter or exit the market, and normal profits are being returned.

The difference between imperfect competition and pure or perfect competition is that, due to the downward sloping demand curve of the imperfect competitor, the long-run equilibrium in this market occurs at a point other than the lowest point on the average total cost curve, and at a point where price or marginal social benefit is greater than marginal cost. Thus the imperfect competitor produces inefficiently in the sense of producing a product at other than lowest average total cost, and also produces less than the socially optimal amount as indicated above in the case of a monopoly. The imperfect competitor, unlike the monopolist, is also placed in the unenviable position of having his excess profits eaten away by competition.

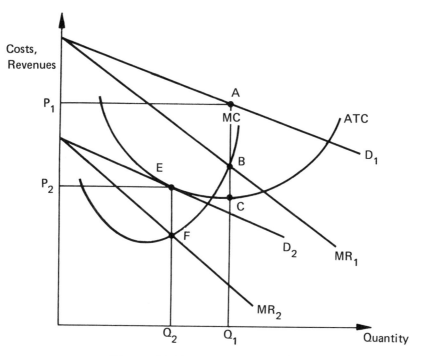

Figure 13.20 Imperfect Competition

Note:

At the initial output, Q_1, excess profits are earned. The entry of new firms shifts the demand for this firm's product from D_1 to D_2. At the new output, Q_2, there are no excess profits and hence no incentives for new firms to enter.

THE DEFENSE SECTOR AND MARKET STRUCTURE

The above discussion has indicated the various types of market structures commonly observed in most markets. In this section we will briefly review some of the major items that are purchased in the defense sector, and the nature of the markets in which the items are purchased.

Table 13.1 lists the fiscal year 1980 defense budget in terms of major purchases of defense inputs. The purchases are subdivided into components used in the yearly budget submission to Congress and indicate a breakdown of the defense budget viewed from the input side. As the table indicates, in terms of inputs, a large share of the budget is devoted to manpower. These expenditures are generally made in competitive labor markets, although DOD's size gives it some market power. The number of buyers and sellers of labor is large, and the product can generally be considered undifferentiated. The Defense Department is such a large buyer, however, that increases or decreases in the amount of labor purchased by the defense sector will result in some effect on wage rates. The features of this market are discussed in detail in Chapter 14.

Procurement purchases are made in a variety of different markets. The procurement of small items, such as small tools also used in civilian markets, are accomplished in competitive markets. The purchases of large end items, however, such as tanks or aircraft, primarily occur in markets where there are few buyers and few sellers. In this case the price of the commodity is initially determined by a supply side bidding process. The long lead times and changes in prices that occur during production delays, however, generally result in a determination of the final price by a "cost plus fee" arrangement between buyer and seller. The capital or hardware markets are discussed in detail in Chapter 15.

Operations and maintenance funds are used to buy consumable end items, which are purchased on a recurring basis. This category of goods includes such items as gasoline, lubricants, and spare parts for vehicles and aircraft. The number of different items that are included under this category is very large and includes items purchased in almost evry conceivable type of market. Many of these specific items are also stockpiled, and are further described in Chapter 16, which includes a discussion of mobilization.

Table 13.1

The Defense Budget: FY 1980

(Billions of Dollars)

Item	Budget
Military Personnel	$ 30.8
Retired Personnel	$ 12.0
Procurement	$ 35.8
Operations and Maintenance	$ 43.4
Other	$ 17.3
	$139.3

Source: Annual Report of the Secretary of Defense FY 1981, p. A–18.

CONCLUSION

Defense purchases are made in a variety of different market structures. Many of these markets are similar to those commonly described in most economics texts. This chapter has reviewed those common forms of market structures to give the reader a basic understanding of the determinants of pricing and output decisions in those cases where markets are competitive, monopolistic, and imperfectly competitive. The following two chapters describe the specific details of the markets for labor and hardware, the largest categories of defense purchases.

NOTES

1 This includes both public and private consumption goods.
2 The budget line is given by $p_aA + p_bB = I$ where p_a and p_b are the prices of A and B respectively, A and B represent the quantity of goods A and B consumed, and I is the level of money income. Solving the budget line equation for B we have:

$$B = \frac{I}{P_b} - \frac{P_a}{P_b} A$$

where I/P_b is the intercept on the B axis (the distance OX in Figure 13.1) and $-P_a/P_b$ is the slope.
3 The horizontal summation of individual demand curves to obtain the aggregate or market demand curve is valid only for private goods. In the case of public goods, where consumption of a given amount by one individual does not reduce consumption by others, the aggregate demand curve is obtained by vertical summation of the individual demand curves.
4 The isocost curve is given by $P_KK + p_LL = \bar{C}$ where $\bar{C}$ is the given cost, p_K is the price of capital, p_L the price of labor, K and L the quantities of K and L purchased.
5 Note that this condition also occurs at a point between points A and B on the total cost curve. A necessary and sufficient condition for a profit maximum is not only that marginal revenue equal marginal cost, but that the marginal cost curve be rising at a faster rate than the marginal revenue curve at the optimum point.
6 Strictly speaking, this is only true above the "shut-down" point for the firm. If the price is less than the average variable cost of production, the firm will maximize profits—or in this case minimize losses—by shutting down and producing no output.
7 Mathematically, the Walrasian bidding process is described by:

$$\Delta p = \alpha(Q_D - Q_S)$$

where Δp = the change in the market price
  α = positive constant adjustment parameter
  Q_D = quantity demanded
  Q_S = quantity supplied

8 The methodology used below is taken from James R. Golden and Robert H. Baldwin, *Economics and Public Policy: Principles, Problems and Applications* (Wayne, N.J.: Avery Publishing Co., 1979).

9 Remember that the industry supply curve is the sum of the marginal cost curves of all firms in the industry. If more firms enter the market, the number of individual marginal cost curves increases and the industry supply curve shifts to the right. This can be viewed as an increase in capital, K, in the industry in terms of the supply curves discussed in the text.

10 The total revenue curve in this case is actually an inverted parabola. The curve reaches a maximum where:

$$\frac{dTR}{dq} = O = a - 2bQ, \quad \text{or at} \quad Q = \frac{a}{2b}$$

The curve falls to zero where $Q = \dfrac{a}{b}$.

11 The demand curve reflects the amount that the marginal consumer is willing to pay for a particular commodity. As such it reflects, at the margin, what the consumer feels the benefit of the product is in terms of a *numeraire*, usually money. In this sense the demand can be said to reflect a marginal benefit curve for the market in question. At each point on the curve, the price reflects the benefit in terms of the *numeraire* of consuming an additional unit of output.

12 The reason that the marginal cost to the monopsonist lies above the industry supply curve is that the supply curve is upward sloping. Thus the cost to the user of an additional unit is always greater than the previous unit. For a straight line supply curve, this can be easily demonstrated. Assume the supply curve is given by:

$$P = a + bQ$$

Then total cost to the buyer is:

$$TC = PQ = aQ + bQ^2$$

Marginal cost is:

$$MC = \frac{dTC}{dQ} = a + 2bQ$$

Note that in this case the marginal cost curve to the monopsonist has the same intercept, a, and twice the slope of the industry supply curve.

13 George Stigler, *Theory of Price*, 3d ed. (Toronto: Macmillan, 1966).

SELECTED REFERENCES

James R. Golden and Robert H. Baldwin, Economics and Public Policy: Principles, Problems and Applications (Wayne, N.J.: Avery Publishing, 1979).

Edwin Mansfield, Microeconomics: Theory and Applications (New York: W. W. Norton & Co., Inc., 1970).

Paul A. Samuelson, *Economics*, 11th ed. (New York: McGraw-Hill Book Co., 1980).

Chapter 14
The Defense Labor Market

INTRODUCTION

Military manpower expeditures make up a significant share of the defense budget. In fiscal year 1980, the Department of Defense (DOD) budgeted $30.8 billion for manpower expenditures, out of a total of $139.3 billion for all defense items.

This chapter examines the defense labor market and the issues involved in defense manpower management. The emphasis in this chapter is on the active forces, with the issue of the reserves being primarily addressed in Chapter 16. We begin by examining the demand for military manpower and then look at the supply side. The chapter concludes with an examination of some major issues in defense manpower management, including an analysis of the issue of the draft versus volunteerism as systems of manpower procurement.

THE DEMAND FOR MILITARY MANPOWER

The demand for military manpower is a derived demand, dependent on the amount of defense services required as well as on the availability of alternative factors of production in the defense sector.

Following the approach introduced in Chapter 9, if we assume defense output is a function of capital and labor, then the production function for defense output can be represented by the following relationship:

$$Q = f(K,L) \tag{14.1}$$

where Q is defense output, K is capital employed in the defense sector, and L is the amount of labor employed in the defense sector. The production function can be graphically portrayed by means of isoquants, which are shown in Figure 14.1. Each isoquant represents alternative combinations of capital and labor that yield a given level of defense output. In Figure 14.1, for example, combinations of capital and labor represented by points A and B both result in output level Q_0.

The defense budget can be represented by the budget constraint line K_0L_0 shown in Figure 14.1. The budget constraint is algebraically given by the following relationship:

$$B = wL + rK \tag{14.2}$$

where B is the value of the defense budget, w is the wage rate, L is the amount of labor employed, r is the rental rate for capital, and K is the amount of capital employed in the defense sector.

The budget line in Figure 14.1 reflects the amounts of capital and labor that can be purchased with defense budget B_0. If all of the budget is spent on labor, the amount of labor that can be purchased is equal to

$$L_0 = B_0/W .$$

If all of the budget were to be spent on capital, the amount of capital that could be purchased would be

$$K_o = B_o/r .$$

The straight line connecting K_0 and L_0 represents all alternative combinations of commodities that can be purchased for B_0.

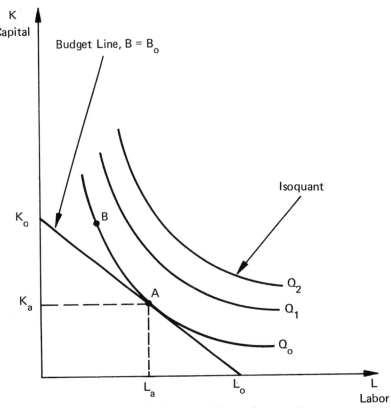

Figure 14.1 Defense Output Isoquants

Derived Demand for Military Manpower

The demand for military manpower can be developed from Figure 14.1 using the approach outlined in Chapter 13. If the demand for defense output is Q_0 and the prices of capital and labor are those implied by the budget line, then the combination of capital and labor represented by point A would minimize the cost of producing output level Q_0. Alternatively, if the defense budget were B_0, point A indicates the maximum level of output that could be produced, fully utilizing the budget, B_0.

The demand for labor at alternative wage rates can be developed by letting the wage rate vary and noting either the amount of capital and labor that minimize the cost of producing a given level of output, or the combinations of capital and labor that maximize output with a given budget. Figure 14.2 shows the result of such an analysis using the latter approach to deriving a demand curve for labor. The three budget lines shown reflect changes in the wage rate with wages falling, and the labor intercept shifting from L_0 to L_z. Plotting the amount of labor demanded as a function of the wage gives the demand curve for labor shown in Figure 14.3. The numbered points in the demand curve correspond to the numbered points shown in Figure 14.2.

The Factor Substitution Hypothesis

There is empirical evidence that defense planners actually do react to changing relative factor prices by varying the proportions of resources employed to produce defense output. The theory developed above implies that, as the relative price of labor increases, defense planners should reduce the proportion of labor uti-

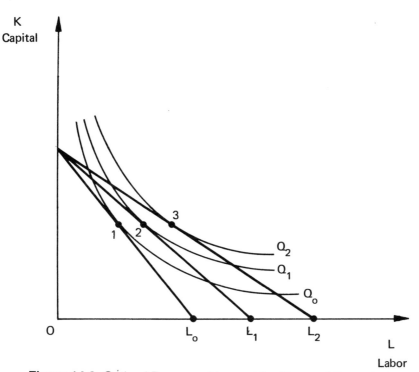

Figure 14.2 Optimal Resource Use and the Demand Curve for Labor

Note:
As the wage falls from W_0 to W_2, the intercept of the budget line on the labor axis increases from $L_0 = B/W_o$ to $L_2 = B/W_2$.

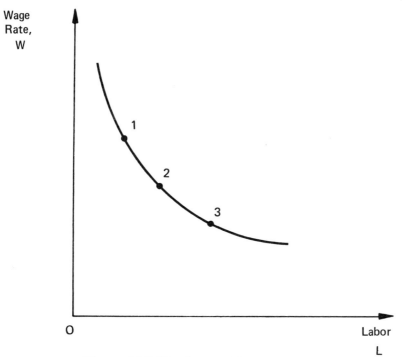

Figure 14.3 The Demand for Defense Labor

Note:
Points 1-3 correspond to points 1-3 on Figure 14.2.

lized to produce defense output. In Chapter 9 we cited Richard Cooper's conclusion that the relative defense use of labor and capital in the U.S. has not adjusted to changes in relative prices. However, data from a recent study of NATO countries appear to confirm the factor substitution hypothesis.[2]

Table 14.1
Capital Intensity and Wage Rates
(Armies of NATO Countries: 1973)*

Country	Troop Strength (L) (1000s of Men	Number of Medium Tanks (K)	$\frac{K}{L}$	Wage Rate ($/Hour)
Belgium (BE)	65.0	482	7.4	2.42
Britain (BR)	177.0	900	5.1	1.08
Canada (C)	33.0	330	10.0	3.85
Denmark (D)	24.0	250	10.4	3.85
France (FR)	332.4	820	2.5	1.50
Germany (GER)	334.0	3250	9.7	3.22
Greece (GR)	120.0	650	5.4	1.18
Italy (IT)	306.5	1200	3.9	1.59
Netherlands (NE)	70.0	885	12.6	2.83
Norway (NO)	18.0	158	8.8	3.25
Turkey (TUR)	365.0	1400	3.8	.51
United States (US)	801.5	8500	10.6	4.07

Sources: *Military Data: The Military Balance 1973–1974.*
Wage Rates: United Nations Statistical Yearbook, 1975.

* *Portugal and Luxembourg were excluded due to lack of tank data.*

Table 14.1 gives data from the study that shows the ratio of tanks to the troop strength of NATO armies, as well as the wage rate in each country. If it is assumed that capital is relatively mobile between countries, then the cost of capital among the various NATO countries should be relatively the same, and the wage rate variations should reflect variations in the relative price of labor. If the factor substitution hypothesis is correct, then those countries with a higher wage rate should utilize relatively less labor, and thus have a relatively more capital intensive force structure. Figure 14.4 plots the ratio of capital to labor as a function of the wage rate. The scatter diagram appears to confirm the hypothesis and indicates that in the long run, as labor costs increase, less labor tends to be utilized in the defense sector.

Defense Manpower Levels in the United States

The actual levels of active duty defense manpower in the United States for selected periods between 1960 and 1980 are shown in Table 14.2. As the data indicate, defense manpower levels in the United States rose substantially between 1960 and the 1965–1970 period, as a result of the Vietnam War. With the end of the war, manpower levels were reduced substantially in the face of reduced missions and, possibly, rising manpower costs. In any case, the current force structure of the United States is set so as to require about 2.1 million men.

From the perspective of the defense manpower planner, the flow or yearly demand for labor by the military does not relate directly to the desired military "end-strength," or strength at the end of each fiscal year. Most personnel on active duty have a multiyear enlistment contract, and the level of new accessions each year is a small fraction of the total manpower stock.

The relationship between the yearly demand for labor by the military services and the total stock of military manpower can be summarized in the following relationship:

$$A = t \cdot L \qquad (14.3)$$

where A is the yearly accession requirement, t is the turnover rate, and L is the desired military end-strength. The turnover rate for enlisted personnel is, in turn, a function of the career mix (i.e., the ratio of first-term enlistees to total reenlistees), the average length of the first-term contract, and the average first-term retention rate. Values for A, t, and L for enlisted personnel in the United States military force are shown in Table 14.3.[3]

Assuming the officer-enlisted ratio remains relatively constant, the military will require roughly 1.8 million enlisted personnel in the force in the near future. Given an average turnover rate of 22 percent, the requirement for nonprior service accessions will remain at roughly 400,000 personnel per year. This is the "baseline," or preliminary planning, figure that is used in analyzing manpower requirements and represents a figure often referred to in the literature on the volunteer force accession requirements. Note that this baseline projection assumes no factor substitution adjustments based on changes in input prices.

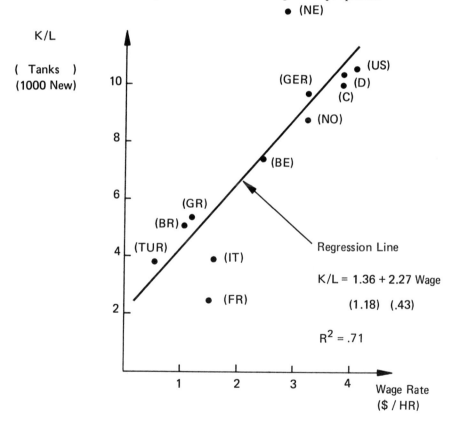

Figure 14.4 Wage Rates and Capital Intensity in NATO Armies—1973

Note:
The R^2 is one measure of how closely the data points cluster around the regression line, or the line that minimizes the sum of the squared deviations of the sample points from the estimated line. In this case, the R^2 of .71 means that the wage "explains" 71% of the variation in the capital labor ratios sample.

Table 14.2

**Defense Manpower Levels
1960–1980 (Millions)**

Year	Active Military Strength
1960	2.476
1965	2.655
1970	3.066
1975	2.127
1980	2.045*

Source: Annual Report of the Secretary of Defense FY 1981.

* *Projected.*

THE SUPPLY OF MANPOWER

The Quality Issue

Attracting 400,000 accessions into the military each year will not necessarily be a particularly difficult problem. Attracting 400,000 accessions of desired quality will, however, be a problem. Table 14.4 shows nonprior service accessions for the Department of Defense grouped by sex, mental category, and educational status for fiscal year 1974–1976.

Mental category and high school graduation status are the two most commonly used measures of accession quality, and the services encourage accessions of upper mental category high school graduates in their recruiting efforts. The reason for this bias on the part of manpower planners is understandable, given the data shown in Tables 14.5 and 14.6.

The retention data in Table 14.5 represent the average percentage of those enlisted personnel entering military service who remained on active duty at the end of each year in the first term of service, and at the end of the first term of service (which in fiscal year 1976 averaged 3.7 years). As the data show, those enlistees with high school diplomas had substantially better retention rates than those who did not finish high school. Higher retention rates imply not only lower turnover rates, and therefore lower accession requirements for the services, but also a greater return on the investment in basic and advanced training.

The data in Table 14.6 shows supervisor ratings of individuals of varying educational status and mental category. The ratings indicate the degree to which the supervisor felt the ratee compared to the average enlisted person with four years of experience. Once again, the data show that high school graduates and those individuals with higher mental categories do better than those without high school degrees, and those enlistees with lower mental categories. As a result of these factors, the emphasis in recruiting is on individuals of higher mental category and with high school diplomas.

Table 14.3
The Demand for Nonprior Service Enlisted Accessions
FY 1974–1976

Year	A (Accessions)	L_E (Enlisted Force Size)	t Turnover Rate Per Year
1974	.390	1.849	.21
1975	.403	1.824	.22
1976	.391	1.790	.22

Sources: A — Selected Manpower Statistics, OASD (Comptroller), May 1977, p. 26.
L_E — Unpublished data from Manpower Research and Data Analysis Center.
$t — A/L_E$

Table 14.4
Nonprior Service Accessions
by Quality Measures and Sexual Composition
FY 1974–1976
Thousands of Accessions (Percent of Total)

MALE

Year	Grouped by Mental Category		Grouped by High School Status		Total
	I–III	IV	Grad	Nongrad	
1974	320.1 (89.2%)	38.9 (10.8%)	207.5 (57.8%)	151.5 (42.2%)	359.0 (100%)
1975	341.9 (93.1%)	25.4 (6.9%)	229.2 (62.4%)	138.1 (37.6%)	367.3 (100%)
1976	340.5 (94.6%)	19.3 (5.4%)	234.9 (65.3%)	124.9 (34.7%)	359.8 (100%)

FEMALE

Year	Grouped by Mental Category		Grouped by High School Status		Total
	I–III	IV	Grad	Nongrad	
1974	30.9 (100%)	0.0 (0%)	28.3 (91.9%)	2.6 (8.1%)	30.9
1975	35.6 (100%)	0.0 (0%)	32.3 (90.7%)	3.3 (9.3%)	35.6
1976	30.8 (100%)	0.0 (0%)	27.9 (90.6%)	2.9 (9.4%)	30.8

Note:
Mental Category is determined from scores on the standardized ASVAB (Armed Services Vocational Aptitude Battery) Test. Mental categories range from I (highest) to IV (lowest). Category III is frequently subdivided into IIIA (higher) and IIIB (lower).

Source: Unpublished data provided by the Manpower Research and Data Analysis Center (MARDAC) of the Human Resources Research Organization. MARDAC Report—0816, as of June 30, 1976.

Table 14.5
Retention Percentages
by Year of Service and Mental Category
(Period Averages)

Year	High School Graduates		Non-High School Graduates	
	I–III	IV	I–III	IV
1	.91	.87	.81	.79
2	.83	.78	.67	.64
3	.77	.73	.56	.51
3.7	.72	.68	.47	.42

Source: *"First-Term Enlisted Attrition," unpublished Office of Management and Budget Study, August 9, 1978, p. 3. Attrition rates for mental category I–III were computed as .75 I–IIIA and .25 IVB. This reflects the proportions of mental categories I–IIIA and IIIB in the enlisted accessions of CY 1975. Data also reflect the average for the period shown, i.e., for the first year of service the retention rate at the midpoint of the year for high school graduates in mental categories I–III was .91.*

Table 14.6
Productivity Indices
by Mental Category

High School Graduates		Non-High School Graduates	
I–III	IV	I–III	IV
102	95	85	75

Source: *The estimated productivity figures are based on unpublished data compiled by Robert M. Gay from RAND cited in Cooper, op. cit., p. 139.*

A Supply Model

A number of analyses have been done on the supply of manpower to the armed forces. Most of these studies have found that enlistments of high quality nonprior service males can be explained by the following simple model:[4]

$$E = f(\overset{+}{WM}/WC, \overset{+}{u}, \overset{+}{I/S}, \overset{+}{R/S}, S)$$

where E   = enlistments
       WM/WC   = ratio of the military to the civilian wage rate for enlistees
       U   = unemployment rate
       I/S   = the ratio of those drafted to the population qualified and eligible for military service
       R/S   = the ratio of recruiters to the population qualified and eligible for military service
       S   = the population qualified and eligible for military service

The signs above each variable indicate the direction in which enlistments are expected to change with respect to an increase in each of the variables. The equation treats all enlistments equally. No quality adjustments are made.

The effect of the relative wage on enlistments is straighforward. As military wages rise relative to civilian wages, individuals in the labor market searching for a job will tend to find the military more attractive in terms of compensation than civilian jobs, and all other things being equal, this would tend to increase enlistments. Given this assumption, the supply curve for military labor would be similar to the supply curve for a competitive firm or industry, in that the amount of labor offered would rise with price.

Unemployment generally lowers the expected income to a civilian job seeker of attempting to find a civilian occupation as opposed to enlisting. As such, unemployment lowers the expected income derived from seeking civilian employment, and thus increases the expected ratio of military to civilian income. In this way, rising unemployment leads to increases in military enlistments.

The United States has procured military manpower in a volunteer environment since 1973. Prior to that time, however, the military also relied upon the draft to provide manpower when the number of volunteers fell short of desired enlistment objectives. During the periods when a draft is in effect, more individuals are induced to join the services, other things being equal, than would join in a volunteer environment. The probability that someone may be drafted lowers the expected income to selecting a civilian job if military wages are less than civilian wages (which usually turns out to be the case in a draft environment) and hence, in an economic sense, a draft makes the military more attractive as an occupation. A volunteer during a draft environment is also usually able to select the branch of service and possibly his military job specialty, which further increases the propensity to volunteer.

Recruiters make a great deal of information available to those in the youth labor market and attempt to affect attitudes regarding military service. The greater the number of recruiters and the greater the level of advertising expenditures on military service, the greater should be the number of enlistments.

The last variable specified in the recruiting model is the population base of those qualified and eligible for military service. As the population pool increases, other things being equal, so should enlistments.

To test the reasonableness of the above theory on enlistments, data on each variable in the model were gathered for the period from 1959 to 1976, as shown in Table 14.7. The enlistment variable refers to all DOD enlistments from mental categories I–III for each year shown. These mental categories were assumed to be appropriate in examining the supply aspects of armed forces enlistments, in that all enlistments from mental category IV were most likely demand- rather than supply-determined, while the enlistments of those individuals from the upper mental categories were most likely supply-determined. In other words, when the number of volunteers from the upper mental categories decreased, the manpower planners could offset this decline, to some extent, by increasing the intake of mental category IV individuals to meet specified recruiting objectives. Thus, when considering a supply model, it is appropriate to use, as a dependent variable, an enlistment group that is supply constrained. This should be the case for mental category I–III enlistments in this analysis.

The draft variable shown is for inductions of all individuals in the year shown. It is interesting to note that during the period of the Vietnam conflict, the number of mental category I-III enlistments was substantially greater than the number of draftees. Thus an analysis of supply considerations is important in a draft period, as well as in an all-volunteer period, in order to manage the quality composition of the force.

The civilian compensation variable, W_c, refers to real average annual full-time earnings for males ages 18–24 for the period shown. This age group was selected as being most representative of the population from which DOD enlistees are drawn. The military compensation variable, W_m, shown is for an E-2 under two years of service. This income level is that which an enlistee would expect to earn in his first few years of service.

The unemployment rate, u, shown is that for males aged 16–19. Increases in this rate are assumed to positively affect enlistments by increasing the relative attractiveness of military employment. The population base figure, S, is for males in the age cohorts between 18–20. Most enlistments are drawn from these age groups. Lastly, the recruiter variable, R, refers to the number of recruiters in the field during the year shown.

Table 14.7
Department of Defense Enlisted Supply Data Base:
CY 1959–1976

Year	E (Millions)	I (Millions)	W_c (CY 1967$)	W_m CY 1967$)	U (%)	S (Millions)	R Thousands
1959	.258	.096	4041	2959	15.3	5.928	6.909
1960	.299	.086	4185	2912	15.3	6.294	7.011
1961	.303	.146	4280	2883	15.2	6.591	7.114
1962	.301	.081	4358	2851	17.3	6.846	7.219
1963	.282	.119	4372	2868	17.2	7.016	7.070
1964	.284	.112	4427	2831	15.8	7.633	6.903
1965	.347	.232	4721	2783	14.1	7.941	7.056
1966	.480	.382	4717	2850	11.7	8.330	7.240
1967	.344	.229	4875	2858	12.3	8.735	7.370
1968	.408	.296	5077	2814	11.6	9.204	7.176
1969	.357	.285	5342	2750	11.4	9.203	6.987
1970	.286	.163	5446	2853	15.0	9.392	8.023
1971	.311	.095	5211	3287	16.6	9.599	9.058
1972	.344	.049	5517	4825	15.9	9.850	10.090
1973	.293	.001	5449	4738	13.9	10.054	13.728
1974	.331	.000	4987	4486	15.5	10.294	15.120
1975	.341	.000	5263	4300	20.1	10.490	14.860
1976	.349	.000	5681	4271	19.2	10.633	15.110

Sources:

E —   Mental category I–III male enlisted accessions. Data for 1959–1973 are from B. Karpinos, Male Chargeable Accessions: Evaluation by Mental Categories (1953–1973), Defense Manpower Data Center Report No. M–77–1. Data for 1974–1976 were constructed by the authors from unpublished Defense Manpower Data Center FY data from 1974–1976.

I —   Total draftees data are from the same sources as used for E.

W_c —   Year-round full-time male worker's mean earnings for ages 18–24, from Current Population Reports, Series P–60. Data for 1959–1966 show the median 20–24-year-old earnings multiplied by the ratio of mean 18-24-year-old earnings to median 20–24-year-old earnings for overlapping years of 1967 and 1969. Data for 1967–1975 came directly from the source. The data for 1976 were obtained by applying the increase in total private nonagricultural earnings between 1975 and 1976 obtained from the Economic Report of the President, 1977, page 227, to the 1975 value from the source.

W_m —   Base pay, BAQ with dependents, and subsistence for an E-2 under two years of service as of June 30 of the indicated year. Data are from Military Compensation Background Papers: Compensation Elements and Related Manpower Cost Items, August 1976, Department of Defense, Third Quadrennial Review of Military Compensation, OSD.

U —   the unemployment rate for male teenagers 16–19, from the Economic Report of the President, 1977, pages 220–221.

S —   the 17–21-year-old male population, from Current Population Reports, Series P–25.

R —   The number of enlisted production recruiters. Values for 1961 to 1969 are from S. Kemp, "The Production of U.S. Military Recruiting Systems," Gates Commission Background Papers, Volume II, p. IV–4-19. Figures for 1972 to 1976 are from Military Compensation Background Papers, Third Quadrennial Review, August 1976, p. 335. Figures for 1959 and 1960 were obtained by extrapolation of the 1961–1962 trend to 1960 and 1959. Figures for 1970 and 1971 were obtained by linear interpolation.

To test the model, linear regression analysis was used to assess empirically the effect of each variable on recruiting.[5] The results of the analysis are shown in Table 14.8 for two specifications of the enlistment model. The first includes the recruiting variable, while the second excludes the variable.

The model appears to explain 85 percent of the total variation of enlistments around the mean value for the sample as indicated by R^2 value for each relationship.[6] The sign of each variable appears to confirm the *a priori* expectation as to how each independent variable affects enlistments.

Of all the variables included in the model, only recruiting resources appeared to have a statistically insignificant effect on enlistments. This does not necessarily mean that recruiting resources do not have a significant affect on enlistments, but only that, in this analysis, the data do not confirm that effect. It should be noted that for most of the sample shown in Table 14.7, very little variation occurred in recruiting resources. Also, increases in recruiting resources occurred at the same time military compensation began to increase, and some of the effect of increasing recruiting resources may be picked up in the relative income variable. Omitting the recruiting variable had little effect on the model. The R^2 dropped negligibly, and the coefficient of the relative pay and unemployment variables increased slightly, while the induction coefficient dropped slightly. The population coefficient remained relatively constant.

Table 14.8

Regression Results for Enlisted Supply Models
(18 Observations 1959–1976)

COEFFICIENTS*

Regression Number	Dependent Variable	$\ln(W_c/W_m)$	$\ln(I{-}U)$	$\ln(I/S)$	R/S	S	Constant	R^2	Durbin-Watson
R.1	E	−.1816 (.0745) ((−2.438))	−.6031 (.3299) ((−1.828))	−6.6866 (1.0130) ((−6.601))	.0382*** (.0557) ((.686))	.0224 (.0041) ((5.463))	−.0366	.8597	1.936
R.2	E	−.2156 (.0544) ((−3.963))	−.6711 (.3081) ((−2.178))	−6.6426 (.9902) ((6.708))	**	.0228 (.0040) ((5.700))	−.0031	.8542	1.835

Note: See footnote 6 for a brief description of the Durbin-Watson statistics.

 * *Standard errors in single parentheses, t statistics in double parentheses.*
 ** *Variable not included in relationship.*
*** *Coefficient not statistically significant at the 95 percent level of confidence.*

The Supply Curve

The supply model can be used to indicate the nature of the supply curve for enlistments by holding all independent variables constant, with the exception of military income, and noting the effect on enlistments of varying the military income level. Figure 14.5 shows results of such an exercise in which the values of all explanatory variables other than income are set at their 1976 levels. The 1976 supply curve is then seen as an upward sloping function of income. As in the case of the general supply curve developed in Chapter 13, the supply curve shown in this chapter will shift if there are changes in any of the other variables noted in the general model other than military income.

As the supply curve indicates, the number of accessions increases with increases in the military wage rate, or in the price of labor. According to the graph shown in Figure 14.5, in 1976, with a military income of $2800 dollars—the income level prevalent during much of the draft era—the armed forces would have been able to recruit only 235,000 troops, or roughly two-thirds of those necessary to meet recruiting goals for mental category I–III accessions in 1976. The rapid increases in military compensation plus the high teenage unemployment rates that were prevalent in the mid-1970s enabled the volunteer force to meet almost 100 percent of its manpower requirements in the first few years.

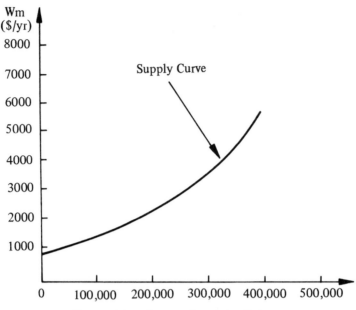

Figure 14.5 Supply Curve for Enlistments

Note:
The Supply Curve is estimated by substituting 1976 values into equation R.2 in Table 14.8.

ALTERNATIVE SYSTEMS OF MANPOWER MANAGEMENT

The Problem

The supply and demand curve analysis developed above can now be utilized to examine several major issues surrounding the military labor market. These issues generally center on the ability of the volunteer force to remain a viable concept, given recruiting difficulties foreseen in the 1980s and 1990s.

As the All-Volunteer Force (AVF) heads into the 1980s, serious questions have been raised about the ability of voluntary systems of labor procurement to meet adequately the demand for military labor. If the size of the enlisted force continues to remain at 1.8 million active military personnel, and turnover rates remain relatively constant at 20 percent to 22 percent, the active force will need to obtain roughly 400,000 new personnel each year. From the supply side of the issue, acquiring 400,000 new accessions each year in the next few decades will be a formidable problem. Apart from the cyclical problems associated with changes in the rate of unemployment, there are two significant problems that appear to signal trouble on the horizon: relative wage trends and demographic trends.

As noted in the discussion concerning the supply model, one of the significant variables that affect the supply of volunteers to the AVF is the ratio of military income to civilian income. An analysis of the trend in relative pay over the period from 1973 to 1978, shown in Figure 14.6, indicates a downward trend in relative compensation. If this trend were to continue, all else remaining constant, the services could expect to experience a failure to meet their recruiting objectives in the 1980s.

Another trend that will increase the difficulty of recruiting in the 1980s and 1990s is the decrease in the population of young males. Table 14.9 gives the estimates of the population of the 17-year-old and 17–21-year-old male groups. As the table indicates, the population of these age groups will decline until the early to mid-1990s, and then begin to rise again. During this period, as indicated in the supply model, downward pressure on the supply of enlistees can be expected to occur as a result of population pressures. In terms of the model, the decline in the population base, S, should shift the supply curve to the left.

Table 14.9

Projected Population Estimates: 1976–2000
(Millions)

Year	Males (age 17)	Males (ages 17–21)
1976	2.138	10.663
1980	2.093	10.740
1985	1.780	9.593
1990	1.640	9.005
1995	1.849	8.656
2000	2.115	10.253

Source: Current Population Reports, U.S. Department of Commerce, Bureau of the Census, Series P–25, No. 601, October 1975. Series II projections.

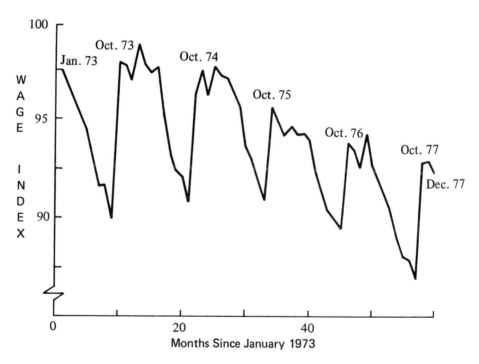

Figure 14.6 Relative Military–Civilian Wage Levels (January 1973 = 100.0)

Source: Department of Defense, America's Volunteers, 1978, p. 386.

Note:
Peaks in the index occur in the fall when annual military wage changes are appropriated in the budget cycle.

The problems associated with these trends can be summarized by the supply and demand curves shown in Figure 14.7. The figure shows a hypothetical supply curve for enlisted manpower similar to the actual empirical curve shown in Figure 14.6. The demand curve in this instance is shown to be vertical, representing a short-run demand for manpower, insensitive to the current military wage rate. The equilibrium wage rate in this market is shown as W_m^e. The relative wage and demographic problems discussed above generally imply that the market for military labor in the 1980s and 1990s will look something like the situation shown in Figure 14.7,, with the actual wage rate given by W_m^1. At this wage rate the military would experience a recruiting shortfall of B C personnel. The following section discusses the alternatives available to manpower planners to alleviate these shortfalls.

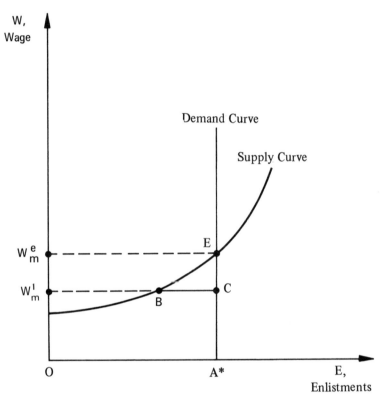

Figure 14.7 The Military Labor Market

The Alternatives

There are four general sets of policies that the military could undertake to offset the hypothetical shortfall BC shown in Figure 14.7. These sets of policies can be described in general terms as (1) compensation-increasing, (2) demand-reducing, (3) supply-increasing and (4) conscription. *Compensation-increasing* policies could rectify the shortfall by increasing the wage rate from W_m^1 to W_m^e. At the equilibrium wage rate, W_m^e, enough volunteers would be induced to enter the military through market processes to eliminate the shortfall. The problem with this option is that it may require Congress to pass increases in military compensation, which may run counter to other priorities, such as fighting inflation.

Demand-reducing policies imply taking some measures to reduce the demand for military manpower specified in the labor market model. Some of these measures were discussed above in the section on the demand for labor, but a list of some specific alternatives includes: (1) substitution of capital for labor, (2) substitution of career for noncareer military personnel, (3) substitution of lower mental category and non-high school diploma graduates for upper mental category and high-school diploma graduates, (4) substitution of women for men, and (5) relaxation of weight and medical standards.[7] All of the above measures reduce the demand for mental category I–III, male, nonprior service accessions needed to meet service requirements, or shift the demand curve shown in Figure 14.7 to the left. If it is assumed that the above list of measures can be accomplished at the military income level specified by W_m^1, then the services would be able to meet accession requirements given current trends in military compensation. In fact, many of these measures are currently being undertaken. What impact such changes on the demand side might have on the ability of the force to accomplish its mission or to hold down long-run personnel costs remains to be studied.

Supply-increasing measures that could be undertaken to solve the problem include actions to shift the supply curve of upper mental category or high school graduate, male, nonprior service enlistees to the right without the use of a draft. These include (1) restraint on private sector wages, (2) increasing rates of unemployment, (3) increasing the population of 17–21 year old males through such measures as increases in immigration or domestic birth rates, and (4) increasing recruiting resources. Some of these alternatives are currently being employed either directly (recruiting resources) or indirectly (voluntary restraint on wages) to increase the supply of enlistees. Alternatives 2 and 3 are controversial in the sense that they run against current economic priorities in other areas. Changes in domestic birth rates would obviously not help in the short run.

The last alternative to be considered is conscription. The draft has two effects on the shortage, as shown in Figure 14.8. Because of the draft effect on the supply curve, the supply of volunteers would shift to the right from S to S^1, thus reducing the shortage at W_m^1 from BC to GC. The second affect of the draft would be simply to fill the remaining shortfall of entlistees by conscription.

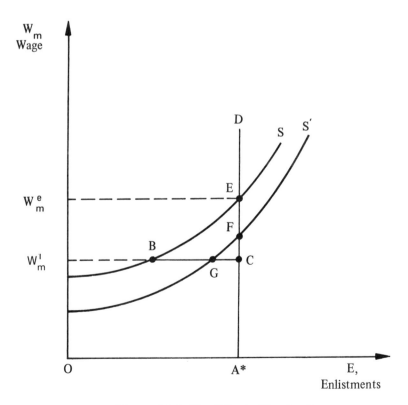

Figure 14.8 The Effect of the Draft

The Economics of the Draft vs. Volunteerism

The draft amounts to an implicit "conscription tax" on those who are drafted. In the case of a "perfect draft," i.e., where the individuals who are drafted are those that lie along the supply curve between points B and C, the draft amounts to a reduction in income of those who serve in the military by an amount equal to the area $W_m^1 W_m^e CE$ in Figure 14.8. This amount constitutes one definition of the "conscription tax" under the assumption of a "perfect draft." In the case of an imperfect draft, the conscription tax would have to be increased, dependent upon where those who were drafted lie along the supply curve.[8] In the best case, however, with a perfect draft, conscription can be viewed as a shift in the form of taxation that is used to finance the defense effort. In the case where the force is run in a voluntary fashion, the manpower portion of the defense effort is paid out of general revenues, while in a conscription system the manpower budget is financed by a combination of the general revenue system and the conscription tax. In one sense, therefore, the issue of conscription is an issue concerned with alternative forms of taxation, and the distribution of society's burden to finance public expenditure.

The draft, by effectively putting a ceiling on the price paid by the military for defense manpower, distorts the effect of prices as market signals of resource cost. Manpower planners perceive the cost of labor to be less than it would be if the costs were fully internalized (as they are under a volunteer system) and therefore tend to use more of it than they would or should from an efficiency perspective. If the defense establishment is led astray by the distortion in prices, then the result is a lower level of total real output than would occur under a volunteer system.

CONCLUSION

The issue of military manpower is of considerable importance. Labor is a vital input to the defense production process, and the method by which military labor is obtained raises serious economic and political issues.

There is no doubt, given the current trends in relative wages and population, that manpower planners in DOD will be faced with an increasingly difficult task over the 1980s and 1990s. This chapter has suggested a number of alternative solutions to the problems of insuring that the adequate supplies of labor are available to meet mission requirements. One of the most important issues here is whether the nation will return to a draft or continue with a volunteer system. There are a substantial number of alternatives to a draft, as indicated above. Many of these alternatives have not been fully studied in terms of their effect on cost or readiness. The sheer number of the alternatives, however, leads to the conclusion that given the distributional and efficiency questions surrounding the use of the draft, the reinstitution of conscription should be studied carefully in light of these alternatives before such a decision is made.

NOTES

1 *Annual Report of the Secretary of Defense*, FY 1981, p. A–18.
2. Robert Kelly, "Military Manpower Costs and Manpower Policy: An Economic Assessment," in William J. Taylor and Roger P. Arango, *Military Unions: and Trends* (Los Angeles: Sage, 1978), pp. 292–305.
3 The discussion in this chapter focuses primarily on enlisted strength requirements. There does not appear to be a significant problem in achieving officer accession targets in the active force. See Department of Defense, *America's Volunteers*, 1978, pp. 14–17.
4 Two of the most often cited studies in this regard are: Anthony C. Fisher, "The Cost of the Draft and the Cost of Ending the Draft," *American Economic Review*, June 1969, pp. 239-254; and Richard V. L. Cooper, *Military Manpower and the All Volunteer Force* (Santa Monica: The RAND Corporation, 1977).

5 Linear regression assumes a simple additive relationship between the dependent variable being explained and the independent or explanatory variables. In this case, a strong argument may be made that the relationships are multiplicative rather than additive. The linear-logarithmic function form of the equation, in which some of the variables are expressed in logarithms, assumes that some of the variables have a multiplicative impact on enlistments, while others are additive. See Fisher, *op. cit.*, for a rationale for a linear-logarithmic functional form.

6 Our test for the statistical significance of each variable's coefficient is the "t" statistic, or the ratio of the estimated coefficient to its standard error (shown in parentheses under the estimated coefficient in Table 14.8). If the coefficient is more than twice as large as the standard error—that is, if the t statistic is greater than roughly 2.0—we reject the null hypothesis that the true value of the coefficient is zero. This test assumes that the errors, or residuals between the estimated and actual number of enlistments in each year, are randomly distributed. The Durbin-Watson statistic tests for a pattern of serial correlation in the residuals. In both cases shown, the Durbin-Watson statistic indicates that there is no serial autocorrelation. In other words, we have confidence that our estimated coefficients are statistically significant if their t statistics are greater than 2.0.

7 See Cooper, *op. cit.*, for a detailed discussion of most of these alternatives.

8 See Cooper, *op. cit.*, Chapter 5.

SELECTED REFERENCES

Richard V. L. Cooper, *Military Manpower and the All-Volunteer Force* (Santa Monica, California: The RAND Corporation, 1977).

Department of Defense, *America's Volunteers* (Washington, D.C.: Department of Defense, 1978).

Anthony C. Fisher, "The Cost of the Draft and the Cost of Ending the Draft," *American Economic Review* (June, 1969), pp. 239-254.

Robert Kelly, "Military Manpower Costs and Manpower Policy: An Economic Assessment," in William J. Taylor and Roger P. Arango, eds., *Military Unions* (Los Angeles: Sage Publications, 1978).

Chapter 15
The Defense Capital Market

INTRODUCTION

To carry out their required missions, the services within the Department of Defense utilize a substantial amount of capital equipment. The annual flow of procurement purchases adds to the capital stock and represents a substantial portion of the defense budget. In fiscal year 1980, the Defense Department budgeted a total of $35 billion for procurement expenditures out of a total of $136 billion spent by the Defense Department for all types of expenditures.[1]

The acquisition of weapons systems is a controversial process and presents a number of difficult problems for defense managers. The process is controversial because of numerous reports of high defense industry profits, cost overruns, and conflicts of interest. The process poses a number of difficult problems because of the nature of the market for defense capital.

The Department of Defense procures defense capital from a variety of different sources and deals in a number of different types of markets. One indication of the nature of the defense capital markets is the relative size of the contracts that are awarded to Defense Department suppliers. In his study of the weapons acquisition process, *Arming America,* J. R. Fox notes the following:

> Ninety percent of the procurement actions, however, account for only 40% of the funds, and 90% of these actions involve less than $10,000 each. . . . Major contracts amount to less than 1% of all procurement actions, but they represent more than 50% of defense procurement dollars.[2]

Thus, DOD lets a large number of small contracts, and a few large dollar value contracts for major weapons systems. The small contracts of less than $10,000 are made for a variety of different commodities, and many of the purchases are made in markets for goods that have alternative civilian uses and that are let at generally competitive prices.

The large contracts, however, are usually made for weapons that have no alternative civilian uses, and are sold by a single supplier. Examples of such systems are shown in Table 15.1, which gives the major procurement programs of DOD and the amounts requested for fiscal year 1980. The major systems listed in Table 15.1 constitute about 35 percent of the total procurement budget for fiscal year 1980, yet only represent 14 major contractors. In each case shown, the weapons systems are specifically designed for military uses and are produced according to military specifications. The costs of such systems are determined by bargaining between the DOD and the contractor.

Thus, defense contracts range from those purchased in competitive markets to those procured in markets with one buyer, monopsony, and one seller, monopoly. This chapter examines the nature of these defense capital markets. The following sections examine both the theory and the institutional factors that affect defense capital purchases.

Table 15.1
Department of Defense Major Procurement Programs

Program	Number	Unit Cost ($Millions)	Total Cost ($Billions)	FY 1980 Request ($Billions)
Trident	14	1,714	24.0	2.3
DD6 - 47	16	881	14.1	.8
FF6 - 7	52	194	10.1	1.3
F-16	1,388	11	15.0	1.7
F-15	750	18	13.2	.9
F-18	1,366	17	23.8	1.0
F-14A	509	24	12.1	.7
SSN-688	36	267	9.6	.5
Patriot	15,000	.4	6.2	.6
XM-1	7,123	1.5	10.4	.7
A-10	733	6.3	4.7	.9
YAH-64	800	8.0	4.1	.2
Black Hawk	1,200	3.0	3.6	.4
ALCM	3,442	1.2	4.2	.5
TOTALS			155.1	12.5

Source: Lawrence J. Korb, *The FY 1980-1984 Defense Program: Issues and Trends* (Washington, D.C.: American Enterprise Institute, 1979), p. 14.

ECONOMIC THEORY AND CAPITAL PURCHASES

The amount of required defense capital can be determined with techniques similar to those used in analyzing the defense labor market. Figure 15.1 shows a set of defense production isoquants and alternative budget lines reflecting changes in the price of capital. The numbered points indicate the output combinations of capital and labor that maximize defense output, given the prices of capital and labor and the total budget. The price of capital is assumed to decrease as the K intercept changes from K_0 to K_z. The resulting demand curve for capital is shown in Figure 15.2. The curve shown represents the derived demand for capital as a function of the price of capital.

It should be noted at this point that one major difference between the purchase of capital and the purchase of labor services is that capital purchases typically involve a piece of equipment that will be used by the services over a long number of years, whereas labor is purchased for the current period. This spreading out of the benefits over a number of years requires that the concept of the time value of money be utilized to analyze the benefits and costs associated with the purchase of capital equipment. The specific methods of analyzing the inter-temporal costs and benefits associated with capital purchase decisions have already been discussed in Chapters 10 to 12.

The isoquant analysis developed above and in Chapter 14 indicates that as the relative price of capital falls, a greater amount of capital should be employed in the defense sector. As the NATO example in Chapter 14 indicated, in the long run, most countries with relatively expensive labor tend to substitute capital for labor in their defense sectors. The study by Cooper discussed in Chapter 9, however, indicates that in the past several decades, this may not have been the case in the United States.[3] Using a set of reasonable data for capital, labor, and prices, Cooper shows that from 1955 to 1977 the wage-rental ratio (based on an index with a value of 100 in 1964) increased from approximately 90 to 130, an increase of over 40 percent, while the ratio of capital to labor remained virtually constant. Thus, while some efficiency apparently could have been gained by switching to amore capital intensive force structure, it appears that the Defense Department did not choose to move in this direction over the 1956 to 1977 time period.

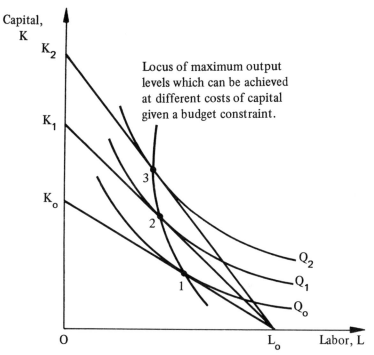

Locus of maximum output levels which can be achieved at different costs of capital given a budget constraint.

Figure 15.1 Defense Output and the Demand for Capital

Note:
The equation for the budget line is B = rK + wL, where r is the price of capital and w is the wage. As the price of capital, r, declines, the intercept of the budget line on the capital axis increases from $K_0 = B/r_0$ to $K_2 = B/r_2$.

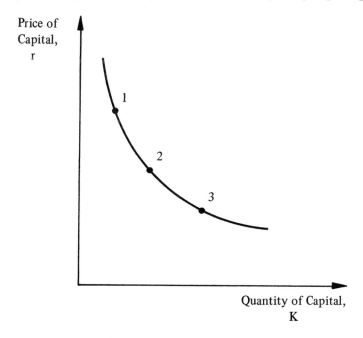

Figure 15.2 The Demand for Capital

Note:
Points 1-3 correspond to points 1-3 on Figure 15.1.

Cooper offers five reasons why such substitutions may not have been made:[4]

1. The pressure to reduce the current defense budget by foregoing costly hardware expenditures, which must be budgeted up front, as opposed to labor expenditures, which are paid as the services are delivered.
2. Cost increases in associated maintenance of high technology capital which offset the presumed efficiencies.
3. A misconception on the part of the military concerning the possibilities for substitutions.
4. Political constraints requiring the maintenance of manpower levels inconsistent with efficiency considerations.
5. Short-run preferences of the military leadership and Congress. Many long-run benefits of capital-labor substitution are ignored.

The above comments suggest that future capital labor substitutions in DOD may be of particular importance in holding down costs in the defense sector or improving efficiency in those areas where such substitutions can be adopted.

THE CAPITAL ACQUISITION PROCESS

The method by which defense capital is acquired was the object of an intense 1979 study by the Defense Organization Committee.[5] The results of the study, which was directed by Donald B. Rice, summarize the weapons acquisition process from two perspectives.

The first perspective is shown in Figure 15.3, which gives the *ideal acquisition process* as it should operate in accordance with the Defense Organization Committee's views of weapons acquisition. In this procedure an operational requirement is defined, the requirement is validated, full-scale development of the prototype of the weapons systems is begun, a performance test is conducted, operational tests are performed, and the system is put into operation and scheduled for full production.

Throughout this entire process the program is reviewed a number of times by the Defense System Acquisition Review Council (DSARC). The purpose of the DSARC is to discipline the acquisition process and to make the leadership within DOD aware of the progress of each program. Theoretically the DSARC is supposed to review each program at three critical times: (1) initiation of the contract definition, (2) the beginning of full-scale development, and (3) the beginning of production.

In reality, the Rice Study noted that the actual procurement cycle is often compressed, with systems being tested as they are put into operation. Any problems that turn up during the testing phase are then corrected during the modifications that are made on systems already on line or being produced. This process is shown in Figure 15.4.

Between the time that the services define the operational requirement and the full-scale development, the requirement must be validated. This includes the passing of authorizing legislation to begin the commitment of funds and the awarding of a contract. The method by which operational requirements become budget authori-

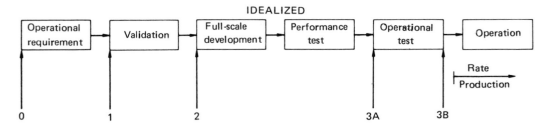

Figure 15.3 The Ideal Weapons Acquisition Process

Source: Figure II–1, Defense Resource Management Study, p. 29.

AS IT IS TOO OFTEN TODAY

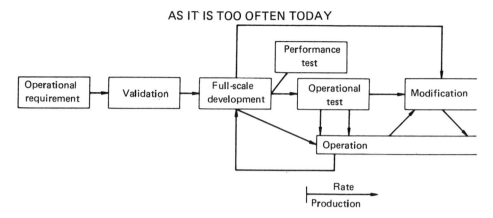

Figure 15.4 The "Actual" Weapons Acquisition Process

Source: Figure II–2, Defense Resource Management Study, p. 30.

zations is discussed in Chapter 8. The awarding of the contract for a major weapons system is reviewed in the following sections.

Bidding

The government generally obtains a contractor to perform a service or to provide a weapons system through one of two types of systems: (1) formal advertising or (2) negotiated procurement.[6]

The *formal advertising* approach assumes that a number of suppliers are available who have the expertise to provide the product in question. In this case, the requirement is advertised, and bids are accepted from a variety of sources. The bid offering the service at the lowest price is generally the one that is accepted. Thus, the formal advertising approach attempts to use the forces of competition to provide the product to the government in the least cost method.

In the *negotiation method of procurement*, the government does not advertise and then select the contractor by the lowest bid, but deals with specific contractors prior to accepting a bid. In this case, the specific contractors to be contacted in the procurement process are singled out in advance of bids. Negotiated contracts are used in lieu of advertised contracts when either (1) there is some question concerning the specification of the weapons system that only contractors can answer, or (2) there is a reason to hold down the number of bidders for technological or secrecy considerations.[7]

While there would appear to be obvious advantages to the competitive or advertising method of procurement, for a variety of reasons most contracts are let using the negotiation method. As Fox notes in *Arming America*:

> In 1971 less than 12% of defense procurements were awarded through formally advertised competitive procurement; the remaining 88% were awarded through negotiated procurement. No more than 25% of the negotiated procurements were conducted in situations where more than one contractor was a contender for the award. Thus, no more than 37% of defense procurement was awarded through competition of any form.[8]

There may be valid reasons for the use of negotiated contracts as opposed to competition. According to the Armed Services Procurement Regulations, Section III, there are seventeen different categories of contracts that enable the government to use negotiations as opposed to competitive bidding.[9] In most of these cases the use of formal advertising is too costly (the contracts have a value of less than $2500) or it is simply impractical to use advertising as a method of letting the contract (there are classified bids or bids where technology involved for specification purposes may reside with a specific corporation).

In general, however, when competitive contracts are available, the use of negotiated contracts leads to weapons systems that are more costly than those obtainable through competitive means. As noted by Fox:

> In a comparison of sole source negotiated vs. competitive procurement costs of components in six weapons systems, we observed that competition in specific contract awards effected savings of from 17% to 49% with an average of slightly less than 25%.

Contracts

Another feature of the weapons acquisition process that is important to understand is the nature of the contracts that are awarded after bidding. There are, in general, two major types of contracts that the Defense Department awards: fixed cost contracts, and cost-plus-fee contracts.

In *fixed cost contracts*, the government and contractor set a fixed price for the item in question at the time of the contract. The profitability of the contract is then dependent on the ability of the contractor to hold down costs, because the price of the item is not changed after the contract is let. In this case, therefore, the contractor assumes most of the risk in developing the system. The contractor also receives most of the benefits in the event of a technological breakthrough that leads to reduced costs.

Cost-plus-fee contracts fix the price of the weapons system at the cost of materials used in the production process, plus a fee to allow the contractor to earn a "normal" rate of profit on the capital invested in the project. The Department of Defense sets limits on the fees depending upon the nature of the work to be performed. In cases where the work is to provide a weapons system that requires experimentation, research, or development, the maximum fee under current regulation is 15% of the cost, while for supply or service contracts, the fee is set at a maximum of 10% of the costs.[11] In the case of the cost-plus-fee contract, therefore, the government accepts most of the risk involved in developing a weapons system, while the contractor is guaranteed a fee to insure some positive rate of return on investment.

Obviously, under the fixed cost contracts, the contractor assumes a greater degree of risk in developing the weapons system than does a contractor under the cost-plus-fee system. As a result, one might expect that the average planned rate of return on fixed cost contracts would be greater than the planned rate of return on cost-plus-fee contracts. In fact, this was the case in 1970 when straight fixed-price contracts averaged a negotiated profit rate of 11.1%, while cost-plus-fee contracts averaged a profit of 5.9 percent.[12]

Although from a cost standpoint it would seem that the Defense Department would move toward fixed price contracts, just the opposite has occurred. In 1952 the percentage of fixed cost contracts was 82%; in 1970 the percentage had fallen to 74%.[13] This trend may reflect the increasing risk in estimating costs of high-technology weapons systems.

Issues in Bidding and Contracting

As the above analysis indicates, the trend in defense bids and contracts appears to be toward negotiated bids and cost-plus-fee contracts. The trend towards negotiated bids is most likely caused by the increasing levels of sophistication in weapons systems. The trend towards cost-plus-fee contracts appears to be a move by defense contractors to reduce the risk associated with the ups and downs of the defense industry. As *Business Week* noted in February of 1980:

> Many companies once bid eagerly on defense contracts. . . . business suffered in the Aerospace slump of the 1970 [however], and they [subcontractors] have disappeared, and others steadfastly refuse to expand. They are concerned, explains Patrick S. Pinket, Chairman of Parker Hannifer, "about having to go out and make capital expenditures to take care of peaking government demand and then having the government say thanks and walk away."[14]

Thus the uncertainty associated with surges in defense spending has led many contractors to bid only on weapons systems for which there is some guarantee of a reasonable profit rate, or on a cost-plus-fee contract.

The problem with the above trend in bids and contracts is that it generally means higher prices on items procured. This may, however, be the optimal way of procuring weapons systems during periods of peak load demand for defense goods, as opposed to the alternatives of either government ownership of production facilities or subsidization of open production lines.

AREAS OF CONCERN IN THE ACQUISITION PROCESS

High Costs and Cost Overruns

The cost of weapons systems is of increasing concern to those who deal with procurement. High cost weapons systems have high opportunity costs not only within the Defense Department, but also to society. This section will determine whether weapons systems costs are rising substantially and, if so, will examine the causes for such increases.

In relative terms, the cost of capital goods used in the production of defense output has increased less rapidly than the cost of alternative inputs. As noted above, the wage-rental ratio from *1956* to *1976* increased by over 40 percent, indicating that capital costs have actually gone down, relative to the cost of labor, and based on efficiency considerations, it would make sense to substitute capital for labor in the defense production process.

There is no doubt, however, that the prices of weapons systems have increased dramatically over the past several decades. In an exhaustive study of armor development in the United States and the Soviet Union, Arthur Alexander traced the history of the cost of tanks in the United States from 1918 to 1980.[15] Alexander's data on tank costs are shown in Figures 15.5 and 15.6. Using 1972 dollars, Figure 15.5 shows the cost of the entire set of American tanks developed from 1918 to 1980. Excluding the now defunct MBT 70 and XM 803, the real cost of tanks appears to have increased rather significantly after 1955, although some increases occurred between 1918 and 1955. The price of going from the M-41 to the XM-1 increased in real terms at a compound average annual rate of roughly 5.2 percent per year. Increases in prices of tanks prior to 1955 were very slow, with price increases over the entire 1918–1980 period averaging only 1.2 percent.[16]

The explanation for the increase in prices is partially explained in Figure 15.6, which shows the cost per ton of tanks between 1918 and 1980. As the data show, much of the increase in tank prices prior to 1955 was due to increasing tonnage. Since 1955, however, the costs appear to be due to factors other than the increases in actual weight of the tank. Vehicles such as the M-551 Sheridan, a light, highly sophisticated reconnaissance vehicle, and the XM-1, employ the latest technological developments, including missile launching system and laser range-finders. These systems have dramatically improved the tank, thereby raising the cost.

Thus the increasing cost of weapons systems, if the tank is used as an example, can be attributed to both increases in quantity, or scale, and increases in quality. The issue of whether a weapons system's costs are excessive, therefore, must take these considerations into account.

The cost issue is particularly significant in terms of whether or not a weapons system that is selected, based on one set of projected costs, should be continued if the costs grow over the projected development of the project. The most controversial incident in this area is the size of the cost overruns encountered in the development of the C-5A long-range cargo aircraft. In 1965, the Air Force awarded Lockheed a fixed price contract to develop and produce the C-5A. The original cost estimates for research, development, design, testing, evaluation (RDT&E) plus production for 120 aircraft were roughly $3.1 billion, according to the Air Force. By 1968, a variety of factors pushed the Air Force cost estimates to $4.3 billion, or roughly a 40 percent increase over three years.[17]

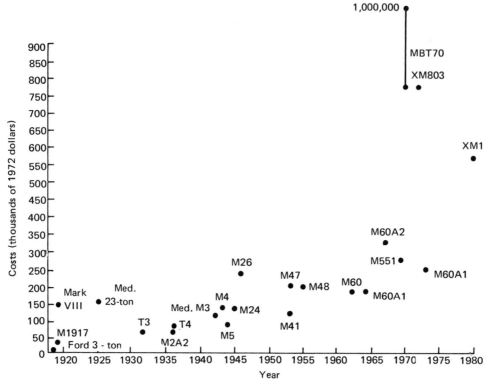

Figure 15.5 Tank Cost: 1918–1980 (Constant 1972 Dollars)

Source: Figure 1 from Arthur Alexander, Armor Development in the Soviet Union and the United States, p. 118.

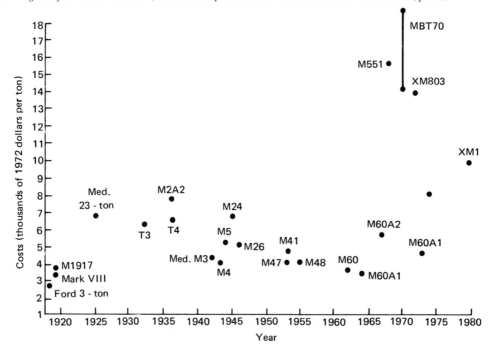

Figure 15.6 Tank Cost Per Ton: 1918–1980 (Constant 1972 Dollars)

Source: Figure 2 from Arthur Alexander, Armor Development in the Soviet Union and the United States, p. 118.

The C-5A case drew a great deal of attention because of pressure applied by A.E. Fitzgerald, a civilian DOD employee responsible for management controls in the C-5A program. Fitzgerald was particularly concerned with a shift in the contract from the original fixed price to a cost-plus-fee arrangement.[18] Because the cost-plus-fee contract gives little incentive to hold down costs, especially if the contract is renegotiated in the middle of the development phase of the project, there was apparently little incentive for Lockheed to hold down costs in problem areas.

Fitzgerald also disagreed with the official Air Force cost estimates. The Air Force excluded the cost of spare parts used in the design and testing phase of the procurement process. Fitzgerald's cost estimates, including spare parts, showed the cost of the contract rising from $3.4 billion in 1965 to $5.3 billion in 1968—an increase of about 56 percent over the three-year period.[19]

The central issue here is whether there are incentives or deterrents within the Department of Defense to hold down costs or to prevent the procurement of systems that become cost-ineffective during procurement because of cost overruns. The amount of pressure that can be placed on defense contractors to provide accurate cost estimates and to adhere to initial contracts is limited by a number of factors, to which we now turn.

Defense Profits

Underestimated costs do not necessarily mean that the new and higher procurement costs are not justified. What they do imply is that if the higher costs had been known during the period in which the costs and effectiveness of alternative ways of achieving the initial objectives of the system in question were analyzed, then the system being developed might not have been selected over alternative systems.

Another major issue is whether costs, either as originally estimated or ultimately obtained, are excessive. Without a competitive market to guide defense planners, there is no *a priori* method of devising a fair price for a weapons system other than to have the contractor specify his direct costs, and to give the contractor a reasonable fee for putting capital into the industry and undertaking the risk of production.

The key to whether a defense contractor's price is reasonable is therefore dependent upon whether the best technology is being used, whether costs are being accurately reported, and whether the contract gives the contractor a normal rate of return on the capital that the firm has invested in the industry.

The issue of the profit of defense contractors is a controversial one. In May, 1969, the *Report of the Subcommittee on Economy in Government of the Joint Economic Committee of Congress* noted:

> Although our present knowledge is incomplete, there is evidence that profits on defense contracts are higher than in related nondefense activities, and higher for the defense industry as a whole. There is also evidence that this differential has been increasing.[20]

One of the problems cited by the Joint Economic Committee and reiterated by other critics of defense contracting policy is that DOD contracts are negotiated or based on a fee or profit as a percentage of cost, rather than as a percentage of capital. For example, Lowell H. Goodhoe, in a *Harvard Business Review* study on profits in the defense industry in fiscal year 1970 noted:

> In preparation for each contract negotiation, DOD establishes a "prenegotiation profit objective" (the amount of profit it will try to negotiate with the contractor). By long-established policy these profit objectives are a percentage of the costs expected on the contract—a practice that lies at the heart of the cost-profit dilemma.[21]

Using cost rather than capital as a base for computing profits results in at least two significant problems in DOD contracting. The first problem is that using a cost base hides the rate of return on capital that a contractor can accrue by winning a defense contract. Without explicit knowing the rate of return on capital associated with a defense contract, it is difficult for a procurement officer to know whether the price of the contract is excessive. If the profit rate is too low, the contractor will most likely not accept the contract. If the profit rate is equal to or greater than the normal rate of return on capital invested in the industry, the contractor will accept the contract. To attain the contract at least cost, therefore, the contracting officers should strive to get the rate of return as close as possible to the normal rate of profit associated with firms producing similar items in the private sector (e.g., private aircraft for aircraft contracts, etc.). Assuming that costs have been accurately reported and that best known technologies are employed, using a rate of return on capital equal to the normal profit rate in the industry concerned should yield a defense contract at lowest cost.

A second major problem associated with using cost as a basis for profit calculations is that it leads to a perversion of the defense contractors' incentive to hold down costs. As noted by Goodhue:

> When profit is based on costs, any capital investment tends to reduce the profit-on-capital rate. And an investment that reduces costs can have a double effect. For example, the purchase of new machinery increases capital employed; and, at the same time, it tends to lower costs, thus reducing DOD's profit objective. Ironically, the more a capital investment reduces costs, the greater the probable reduction in profit.[22]

Thus the most efficient method of letting contracts would be to allow the contractor to attain a normal rate of return on capital employed in the industry. The problem with this criterion, however, is obtaining the data to make such computations. Critical questions such as (1) what is a normal rate of profit, (2) what is the value of the firm's capital, and (3) what portion of the capital stock is allocated towards defense output, need to be answered. Moreover, the answers must be provided to contracting officers in such a way that they can be applied effectively in the contracting process. Although there have ben proposals to employ such methods in defense contracting, many problems remain in working out the most efficient means of employing a rate of return criterion.

Given the above discussion, it will be helpful to examine the historical record of defense contracts to see what the rate of return figures look like. A 1971 study by the Industry Advisory Council noted the profit rates of 35 defense firms and 208 private commercial firms as shown in Table 15.2. As the table indicates, the average rates of return on capital in the defense sector appear to be comparable with those in the private sector. But as Fox notes:

> . . . it is misleading to average the profit data for all defense contractors. The defense industry may well consist of a few large contractors who are able to manage capital turnover effectively and thereby obtain a relatively high return on TCI (total capital invested) and equity, while the majority of defense contractors earn rates of profit substantially below the commercial average.[23]

To support his hypothesis, Fox goes on to note a separate DOD study, which showed that two of the five largest defense contractors had rates of return on total capital invested of over 50 percent.[24]

While the evidence does not support the hypothesis that defense contractors in general overcharge, the ability to price on a rate of return on capital basis should keep weapons systems costs down to lowest possible levels.

Table 15.2
Profit Rates of Defense Contractors and
Comparable Civilian Firms: 1965–1967
(Rate of Profit on Capital)

Quarter	35 Defense Firms	208 Commercial Durable Goods Firms
Top	31.4	37.1
Second	21.8	24.8
Third	14.5	19.0
Bottom	6.1	10.4
Average	15.5	22.9

Source: J. Ronald Fox, Arming America, p. 314.

ECONOMICS AND POLITICS OF DEFENSE CONTRACTS:
THE "FOLLOW-ON IMPERATIVE"

The above analysis assumes that short-run cost and efficiency considerations play a large role in the determination of which contractors get defense contracts. The procurement process discussed in the preceding sections also implies that defense contracts are based on a rational process involving national security considerations.

In reality, however, many other factors may enter into decisions concerning the procurement of weapons systems, and the awarding of defense contracts. As noted in the opening chapters of this book, there are a number of different elements that shape the defense budget. These include not only foreign policy considerations, but also domestic policy and institutional considerations.

In a classic study on weapons procurement policy, Ronald Kurth puts forth a view generally consistent with the defense spending model developed in the beginning of the book, by arguing that weapons procurement is a function not only of strategic considerations, but also of: (1) bureaucratic considerations—competition between bureaucracies in DOD; (2) democratic considerations—the outcome of political bargaining by the executive branch and Congress; and finally, (3) economic considerations—economic needs of certain sectors or geographical regions.[25]

Kurth goes on to argue that in the aerospace industry, both when procuring an aerospace system and awarding contracts, the key objective is to keep production lines in operation. The essential argument as noted by Kurth is as follows:

> A large and established aerospace production line is a national resource—or so it seems to many high officers in the armed services. . . . The Defense Department would find it risky and even reckless to allow a large production line to wither and die for lack of a large production contract.[26]

Thus, if one wished to predict which aerospace systems DOD would build and which contractors DOD would employ in the aerospace field, one would only have to see which production line was next available and what type of system that contractor was most suited to build. Kurth goes on to examine the data on aerospace procurement between 1960 and 1974 and finds empirical support for his hypothesis, at least in the aerospace field.

Is there a rational economic basis for such a policy? The answer is not clear. In the case of a mobilization, where single capability becomes important, the lack of working production lines may have substantial costs in terms of the inability to respond to external threats. In 1980, for example, the renewed emphasis on defense contracts after the Russian invasion of Afghanistan led to a study by *Business Week* on the "surge," or expansion, capability of the defense aircraft industry. As noted by Business Week:

> While many of the prime contractors stand ready to mobilize their own facilities, the underlying industrial base has been allowed to deteriorate since the end of the Vietnam War. Thus most of the industry's subcontractors who furnish materials, components and subsystems for weapons already have all the work they can handle.[27]

Thus while production lines are available, the cost of not keeping the production lines active is apparent in the subcontracting area.

Kurth defines the pressure on DOD to maintain production lines as the "follow-on imperative," suggesting that when existing contracts expire, DOD will select a new system to follow in its place. On the surface, the follow-on imperative would appear to be an inefficient rationale for deciding which weapons systems best meet current defense requirements. When mobilization requiremenmts are considered, however, the follow-on imperative makes more sense. Our evaluation of this policy as either a rational procedure for determining defense contracts or a reflection of political pressure, depends on our estimation of mobilization requirements; this subject will be examined in Chapter 16.

CONCLUSION

As noted at the beginning of this chapter, the procurement of weapons systems is a complex and controversial process. The application of economic principles to the weapons procurement system is perhaps easy to do in an abstract sense but, in all fairness to those involved in contracting, it is difficult to do in practice.

From an economic viewpoint, the key objective in the area of weapons procurement is the fulfillment of national security requirements at least cost. The methods to achieve this objective superficially appear to be related to the issues of competitiveness in defense contracting. As the discussion of the follow-on imperative indicates, however, short-run efficiencies garnered at the expense of longer-run surge capability may prove to be disastrous. The next chapter elaborates on this issue by examining mobilization capabilities from both the manpower and capital viewpoints.

NOTES

1 Department of Defense, *Annual Report of the Secretary of Defense FY 1980, p. C–10.*
2 J. Ronald Fox, *Arming America* (Cambridge, Mass.: Harvard University Press, 1974), p. 14.
3 Richard V.L. Cooper, *op. cit.*, pp. 277–290.
4 *Ibid.*, pp. 288–289.
5 Donald B. Rice, *Defense Resource Management Study* (Washington, D.C.: U.S. Government Printing Office, 1979).
6 Fox, *op. cit.*, pp. 250–251.
7 *Ibid.*, p. 252.
8 *Ibid.*, p. 256.
9 Ibid., p. 253.
10 *Ibid.*, p. 256.
11 *Ibid.*, pp. 230–231.
12 *Ibid.*, p. 236.
13 Ibid.
14 *Business Week* (February 4, 1980), p. 84.
15 Arthur Alexander, *Armor Development in the Soviet Union and the United States* (Santa Monica, Cal.: The Rand Corporation, 1976).
16 *Ibid.*, pp. 116–117.
17 *Report of the Subcommittee on Economy in Government of the Joint Economic Committee,* Congress of the United States (May, 1969) cited in Seymour Melman, ed., *The War Economy of the United States* (New York: St. Martins Press, 1971), p. 99.
18 *Ibid.*
19 *Ibid.*
20 Melman, *op. cit.*, p. 96.
21 Lowell H. Goodhue, "Fair Profits from Defence Business," *Harvard Business Review* (March-April 1977), p. 98.
22 *Ibid.*
23 Fox, *op. cit.*, p. 315.
24 *Ibid.*, pp. 315–316.
25 Ronald Kurth, "Why We Buy the Weapons We Do," *Foreign Policy* (Summer 1973), p. 34.
26 *Ibid.*, p. 40.
27 *Business Week, op. cit.*, p. 80.

SELECTED REFERENCES

J. Ronald Fox, *Arming America* (Cambridge, Mass.: Harvard University Press, 1974).
General Accounting Office, *Recent Changes in Department of Defense Profit Policy* (Washington, D.C.: Government Printing Office, 1979).
Seymour Melman, ed., *The War Economy of the United States* (New York: St. Martin's Press, 1971).
Donald B. Rice, *Defense Resource Management Study* (Washington, D.C.: Government Printing Office, 1979).

Chapter 16
Mobilization

INTRODUCTION

The preceding chapters have dealt with the allocation of defense resources, working on the assumption that the demand for defense output was relatively constant during the planning period. The demand for defense services, however, rises during an international incident or during a war. In such situations there is a surge in the purchases of defense-related items and a need to bring substantial amounts of capital and labor, as well as raw materials, into the defense sector.

Table 16.1 shows two indicators of the substantial change in the demand for resources that can occur as a result of an international incident or war. The data show the percentage of gross national product spent on defense and the amount of manpower in the armed forces in the year prior to and the peak year of the last three major conflicts that resulted in some form of mobilization: World War II, the Korean War, and the Vietnam War. As the data indicate, in each case substantial shifts in resources were accomplished in a relatively short time.

The data in Table 16.1 also show another interesting phenomenon: the steady increase throughout the middle of the twentieth century in the percentage of GNP spent on defense in the year prior to the start of a major conflict. This trend reflects the fact that the role of military power is changing, and that modern technology has reduced the time between the initiation of hostilities and the time when a nation must be prepared to respond militarily to a threat. This reduced response time results in the necessity to maintain a larger force in being, particularly theater and strategic nuclear forces, rather than some form of mobilization capabilty. This, in turn, necessitates a larger share of resources being spent to provide readily available military power.

This chapter looks at the problem of mobilization. We examine the issues surrounding the ability of the United States to rapidly increase its capability to deploy a large force in response to an international crisis or war. The following section examines the simple economics of mobilization. Subsequent sections examine the specific issues surrounding the mobilization of labor, capital, and raw materials.

THE ECONOMICS OF MOBILIZATION

The concept of mobilization generally refers to a buildup of conventional strength that occurs either in response to an external threat, or in furtherance of a nation's national security objectives. While a nation might retain some capability to mobilize strategic nuclear or theater nuclear capability, the warning times associated with the use of nuclear weapons and the uses to which they are put generally imply that the entire strategic and theater nuclear capability be "on-line," or readily available, in the event of an international crisis.

Advances in technology, such as the ability to conduct real time satellite reconnaissance (i.e., photographs are seen as soon as they are taken), have made it possible to be warned some time in advance of substantial buildups in conventional strength. This response time, therefore, enables nations to keep active conventional forces at levels below those necessary for a full-scale mobilization and only build up such forces in times of necessity.

Table 16.1

Percent of GNP Spent on Defense and
Number of Persons in the Armed Forces
(Selected Periods)

Period	Defense ÷ GNP (Percent)	Persons in Armed Forces (Millions)
World War II Period		
1940 (Pre-War)	2.2	.540
1944 (Peak)	41.6	11.410
Korean War		
1949 (Pre-War)	5.1	1.617
1952 (Peak)	13.2	3.592
Vietnam War		
1964 (Pre-War)	7.7	2.739
1968 (Peak)	8.9	3.535

Source: Economic Report of the President, 1978, Tables B–1 and B–27.

As shown in Table 16.2, over the past 100 years the United States has been involved in five major wars, or a major conflict every 20 years. Despite the continuing changes in the nature of conventional conflict, these figures suggest that it would be prudent to maintain some mobilization capability above and beyond that inherent in the productive capacity of the peacetime economy. This capability, provided by such measures as reserve forces, stocks of prepositioned capital equipment, or stockpiles of raw materials, allow a nation to mobilize more rapidly, achieving a higher rate of military capability within a shorter period of time.

Such measures pose an economic problem, since substantial costs are incurred over the period of time when the mobilization capability is unused. On the other hand, the existence of the mobilization capability may reduce the actual costs incurred during the period of mobilization. The economic issue thus becomes one of determining the level of mobilization capability that permits achievement of a specified increase in the level of active forces, within a given minimum warning time period, at least cost. This issue is shown in Figures 16.1 and 16.2.

Table 16.2
Major Wars with U.S. Involvement: 1880–1980

War	Period	Interval Since Last War
Spanish-American War	1898	33*
World War I	1914–1918	16
World War II	1939–1945	21
Korean War	1950–1952	5
Vietnam War	1965–1973	13

Average Interval = 17.6 years

* Previous Major War—Civil War 1861–1865.

Source: "Major War" is defined by Standard College Dictionary (New York: Harcourt Brace, 1963), p. 1511, except for Vietnam conflict.

Figure 16.1 presents the mobilization time paths for two force options—a *small reserve option* and a *large reserve option*—over the average nonconflict interval. The small reserve option is represented by the mobilization path $Q_A AC$, where Q_A is the initial level of active forces, and t_0 is the time after the minimum warning time that mobilization must begin with a small reserve in order to achieve the desired force size, Q_m, at the desired time T. The large reserve option is depicted at points $Q_A BC$. With a larger reserve, less time is needed to reach full mobilization.

Figure 16.2 shows the costs associated with the two options. Note that the small reserve option has lower costs associated with the pre-mobilization period, but takes a longer time to increase its force strength up to the desired mobilization level, and thus incurs higher costs over the mobilization period. The large reserve option allows the country to mobilize at a later period, involving lower costs during the mobilization period then those involved in the alternative. From an economic viewpoint, both options achieve the same result, a force of a given size, X_m at time period T, but follow different time, and hence cost, profiles.

Assuming that our only concern is with the active force required at time T, the option that is superior from an efficiency viewpoint is the one that generates the smallest stream of costs through time T. This approach further assumes that the stream of costs for both options after time T is the same. The costs for the large reserve option follow the path C_L-C-D on Figure 16.2, while the costs for the small reserve option follow the path C_S-A-B-D. The total cost from time 0 to time T is the area under each of these paths. Note that both paths include the shaded area shown on the figure. The cost of the small reserve option also includes Area Z, while the cost of the large reserve option also includes Area Y. In comparing the two cost streams we therefore need only be concerned with the difference between the two areas, Y and Z.

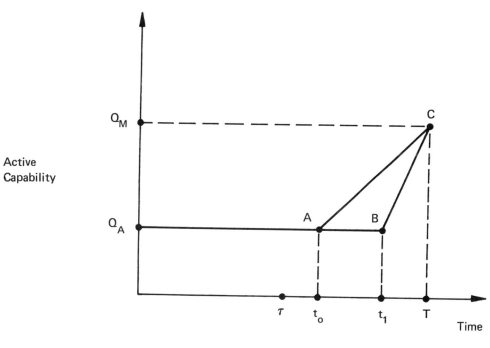

τ = minimum warning time t_1 = mobilization-high reserve option
t_0 = mobilization-low reserve option   T = average non-conflict interval

Figure 16.1   The Economics of Mobilization

Note:
The profile of active force capability under the small reserve option follows the path Q_A – A – C. The path under the large reserve option is Q_A – B – C.

Because these costs occur at different times, however, we must discount them back to some present value based on the appropriate rate of time preference for society. The appropriate efficiency criterion on which to judge the two options is the discounted present value of the difference in costs associated with each method. Referring to Figure 16.2, the efficiency criterion suggests that we should select the large reserve option if the present value of Area Y is greater than the present value of Area Z. Conversely, we should select the small reserve option if the present value of Area Z is greater than the present value of Area Y. Any force structure that minimized the total present value of the cost of attaining capability X_m at time T would be efficient.

Given the results of this highly simplified analysis we can now examine the factors that should affect optimum reserve capability. Recall that we have assumed that the time from mobilization to reaching full capability in both options was less than the minimum warning time. If this were not true, then options that had a buildup time greater than the minimum warning time could be ruled out as not being in the feasible set of force options.

Another consideration is the relative cost of reserve and active forces. If the cost of reserves increases relative to the cost of active forces, then the excess cost area indicated as Y in Figure 16.2 will increase, while area Z will decrease. Thus, given the optimum reserve force criteria stated above, the optimum sized reserve force will decrease.

Another major factor will be the average period between conflicts. If T is great, the carrying costs of a large reserve force (area Y in Figure 16.2) will be substantial. Thus in a period of prolonged peace and stability it may be more efficient to reduce the size of the reserves.

The rate at which a large reserve force allows the active force to grow in size towards the mobilization target is another critical parameter. If the larger reserve force substantially decreases the time to attain the mobilization capability, then the excess cost area Z in Figure 16.2 will increase, and given the optimum criteria developed above, the optimal sized reserve force will increase.

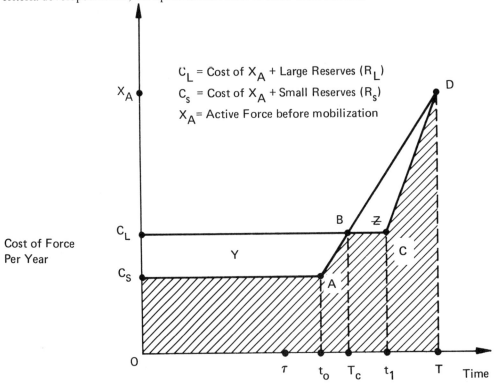

Figure 16.2 Costs of the Small Reserve and Large Reserve Force Options

In computing the present value of each cost stream we must apply an appropriate discount factor representing society's rate of time preference. If high discount factors are applied, reflecting a strong preference for current returns, our analysis will be tipped in the direction of a somewhat smaller reserve force.

Recall that that our only objective was to obtain an appropriate force at time T, and we were not concerned with the readiness profile prior to time T. However, both active and reserve forces have alternative purposes short of complete mobilization. In addition, the entire force acts as a deterrent to the use of force by our potential adversaries, and different combinations of active and reserve forces may have different deterrence implications.

Finally, our analysis assumes that we have acceptable estimates of all the time parameters and force structure requirements involved. In fact we have only rough estimates of the expected values of these parameters, and a vague idea about the distribution of possible outcomes. Thus our discussion in Chapter 11 of decision making under conditions of risk must certainly be applied here. Indeed, our analysis may simply underscore the importance of these estimates, and reinforce the need to commit resources to obtain better estimates in general and to improve the minimum warning time in particular.

THE MOBILIZATION OF LABOR

The United States Armed Forces operate under a "total force" concept. This concept implies that a combination of both active and reserve forces provide manpower to meet the nation's national security objectives. The preceding section has indicated some of the academic considerations involved in the rationale for, and the optimum size of, the reserve capability. In this section we examine the composition of the total force, the supply of labor to the reserves, and the requirements for mobilization resources.

The composition of the total force for the end of fiscal year 1977 is shown in Table 16.3. As the table indicates, the major readily available manpower assets include the active force and two reserve components: the selected reserve and the individual ready reserve.

The *active forces* represent those individuals currently on active duty with the U.S. armed forces. These forces are currently deployed in both Europe and Asia, and represent combat power available for use with little or no warning time.

The *Selected Reserve* consists of *units* pre-trained and available to deploy under a mobilization scenario. The selected reserve consists of the reserve components of the Army, Navy, Air Force, and Marine Corps as well as the Army and Air Force National Guards and the Coast Guard Reserve.[1]

The *Individual Ready Reserve* (IRR) consists of pre-trained *individuals* who generally have time remaining on their six-year total service obligation, and who elect not to serve in the Selected Reserve.[2] Members of the IRR are available to replace individuals in units who become casualties.

Table 16.3
The Total Force: FY 1977
(Readily Available Manpower)

Component	Total (Millions)
Active Forces	2.093
Selected Reserve	.808
Individual Ready Reserve	.375
Total Force Readily Available	3.276

Source: DOD, America's Volunteers, Appendix A.

The demand for mobilization manpower in the case of a major land war in Europe is summarized in Table 16.4, which indicates the Army's requirements for both combat units and individual replacements. The table also shows the availabilities of each category of troops in 1977,

The data shown in Table 16.4 illustrates the current problems existing with the mobilization capability in the manpower area, The current force structure is too small to meet projected manpower requirements in the event of a major land war in Europe. Virtually all of the shortfall lies in the selected reserve and the IRR.

It should be noted that the figures presented in Table 16.4 are probably a bit optimistic regarding supply. The supply figures assume that reserve units now on the books would be able to report within 120 days of mobilization and would be equally capable of joining in combat with active force units. Yet as Kenneth Coffey notes in *Manpower for Military Mobilization:*

> Many of the units are undermanned, however, and not all members are expected to report upon mobilization.[3]

Another point to note is that the above data assume that the only forces used during a mobilization would be the active forces, the selected reserve, and the IRR. Other alternatives might include the draft, volunteer increases, and the calling up of retired or discharged military personnel to active duty.

As far as the draft is concerned, the current state of the Selective Service System supports the assumption that no inductees would be available on M + 120. As noted in a recent DOD Study:

> In FY 1977, the Selective Service System reported that 110 days would be needed in FY 1978 before the first inductee could be called to active duty and 150 days would elapse before the first 100,000 could be put into the training process. Almost seven months would be needed before the first draftee would reach the theater.[4]

The draft might indirectly solve the mobilization problem, however, by increasing the number of volunteers. As noted in Chapter 14, the imposition of a draft increases the propensity of 18–20-year-old individuals to enlist. If this effect were significant, it might somewhat alleviate the M + 120 shortfall, although current law requires that an enlistee or draftee receive 12 weeks (84 days) of mandatory training before going into a combat zone.[5] Furthermore, if the conflict aroused strong public support for a military response, true volunteers might even make up a substantial pool of manpower, which could offset the shortfall.

The last assumption was that no retired or discharged military personnel would be called to active duty. In the case of a national emergency, however, retirees can be recalled to active duty by the president without legislation. In fiscal year 1978, DOD estimated that there were 244 thousand enlisted retirees available to be recalled to active duty who had less than 30 years time service, including retirement time.[6] The average age of this group was 44, and their average active time in service was 21 years.

Table 16.4
The Demand For and Supply of
Army Mobilization Assets
(M + 120 Days)

Category	Demand	Supply	Shortfall
Units	1,580,000	1,326,000	254,000
Casualty	200,000	160,000	40,000
Total	1,780,000	1,486,000	294,000

Source:

Demand—DOD Data cited in Kenneth J. Coffey, Manpower for Military Mobilization (Washington: American Enterprise Institute, 1978), p. 11.

Supply—DOD Data from Department of Defense, America's Volunteers (Washington, D.C.: Office of the Assistant Secretary of Defense for Manpower and Reserve Affairs, 1978), pp. 191, 216, 221. The Unit figures include the active duty Army, the Army Reserve, and Army National Guard. The casualty figures include the Army IRR.

Another potential group that could be used in a mobilization are those enlisted veterans who have been discharged and have no service obligation. In fiscal year 1977 a DOD study estimated that there were 1.184 million such persons who had left the service between fiscal year 1971 and fiscal year 1976.[7] The average age of this group was 27. This group could not be recalled in the case of a conflict, however, without some form of legislation.

The above alternatives to the supply problem noted in Table 16.4 represent rather Draconian measures that would require a national emergency and swift presidential and Congressional action. Other alternatives exist which could be implemented in the absence of such an emergency. One measure would be to increase the size of the reserve forces by increased accessions and better retention. The key to this program would be to increase the amounts currently allocated for compensation and recruit selected and individual ready reservists. Compensation increases, however, could prove expensive. In a 1979 study by Robert Kelly, the pay elasticity of selective reservists of the upper three mental categories from nonprior service personnel was estimated to be about .2.[8] Thus a 10 percent increase in pay could be expected to increase accessions by only 2 percent. The marginal dollar might be spent more productively on increasing enlistments through increased advertising, although little empirical evidence exists to support this hypothesis.

A second or potentially simpler solution to the shortfall in at least the IRR is to change the current requirement that those enlisting in the service have a total obligation of six years. The armed forces could increase the size of IRR by approximately .2 million individuals for every year by which the total commitment is extended.[9] Thus an increase in the service obligation to eight years would expand the IRR pool by .4 million persons. This would be more than enough to cover the total army mobilization shortfall if some of the IRR were used to augment shortages in the selected reserve.

CAPITAL MOBILIZATION

During wartime, the stock of capital equipment must be sufficient to complement manpower brought on line during a conflict, plus replace equipment lost during the initial stages of combat.

The matching up of men and equipment requires the availability of equipment for active and reserve units, the ability to move such equipment to the location of the conflict, and the ability to replace lost equipment during the initial stages of the conflict.

There are four general sources of capital (equipment) that can be used in the event of a crisis. These include:

1. TOE (Table of organization and equipment) stocks.
2. POMCUS (Pre-positioned overseas material configured to unit sets) stocks.
3. War Reserve Stocks.
4. Current Production.

TOE Stocks include the equipment currently allocated to existing active and reserve forces. This is the equipment that these units train with; it would be in varying stages of readiness in the event of an actual conflict.

POMCUS equipment includes pre-positioned stocks of capital, primarily in Europe, that would enable U.S. military units involved in an overseas conflict to leave the United States without equipment, and reduce the mobility assets necessary to move a large force overseas. Kenneth Coffey noted that this equipment is vital if the United States is to achieve national security objectives in Western Europe:

> The effectiveness of the Seventh Army reinforcement immediately after mobilization would depend on the equipment stockpiles in Germany, for it would be impossible to transport heavy equipment quickly from the United States to Western Europe. [10]

The Iranian and Afghanistan crises in 1979 indicated the limitations of the United States on projecting power in the Indian Ocean area. As a result, floating POMCUS Stocks are now being considered so that the U.S. forces will have heavy equipment readily available in distant areas in the event of a conflict.

The demand for *War Reserve Stocks* is based on ". . . schedules that establish the numbers and types of U.S. units in-theater and an assumed intensity of combat that drives attrition and consumption rates."[11] The status of War Reserve Stocks is affected by the fact that TOE and POMCUS equipment have received higher priority than the buildup of War Reserve Stocks. The buildup of War Reserve Stocks has been hindered by the impact of the Yom Kippur War on the U.S. military capital mobilization capability.[12] As Kenneth Coffey observed:

> Furthermore during the 1973 'Yom Kippur War' between Israel and the Arab States, the largest part of the Army's tanks and heavy weapons stockpiled in Germany was shipped to Israel to replace armaments lost in combat. Three years later, the tanks and other heavy equipment had not been fully replaced in the stockpiles.[13]

The last source of mobilization capital would be from increased *current U.S. production*. There are problems here, however, as noted in the 1980 report of the Secretary of Defense:

> The U.S. industrial base would be hard pressed to respond with the volume of war material necessary to assure uninterrupted support in a NATO conventional conflict after the inventories of war reserve material have been exhausted. This results primarily from the time required to accelerate production from existing sources and to open new production lines.[14]

In the last chapter we introduced the difficulties involved in providing the "surge" capability to rapidly expand the production of complex weapon systems. In many cases these systems have close counterparts in civilian production, and the mobilization problem would be limited to one of assigning priorities and accepting shortages of civilian goods. For example, in the wake of the increased emphasis on defense spending after the Soviet Union's invasion of Afghanistan in late 1979, *Business Week* reported a substantial backlog of civilian aircraft orders and severe limitations in the ability of subcontractors to respond to new orders by prime defense contractors. Table 16.5 shows the backlog for key aircraft components in early 1980.

In the event of a national emergency requiring full mobilization, such capacity constraints could be partially remedied by placing priority on defense contracts. However, when the objective is to expand capital prior to full mobilization, defense contracts must wait in the queue established by the market. In cases of shortages, contractors are more likely to meet the demands of regular customers than to absorb the costs of the retooling needed to meet requirements for a temporary expansion in defense contracts.

Table 16.5
Delays for Aircraft Components: 1980

Component	Maximum Production and Delivery Delay (Months)
Batteries	24
Landing Gear	38
Engines	29
Fuselages	34
Tails	24
Wings	27

Source: Business Week, February 4, 1980, p. 82.

Moreover, it often takes an extensive amount of time to acquire the machinery and expertise necessary for the production of sophisticated defense equipment. In the mobilization for World War II, the transition from civilian automobile and truck production to the production of tanks required relatively modest retooling, and U.S. industry handled the task brilliantly. The transition, however, still took considerable time. Today the transition from manufacturing automobiles and trucks to the modern main battle tank would be far more difficult. Given the higher rates of destruction expected on today's technological battlefield, the time for a transition to civilian production would also be more limited.

The central issue in capital mobilization centers on the economic trade-off between maintaining large stocks in peacetime and insuring a surge capability in the case of mobilization. Competing nondefense priorities, the trade-off between manpower and equipment in the total force, technological change, and maintenance problems would argue for emphasis on a surge capability. However, the time required for a transition from civilian production and the problems of strategic transport would argue for larger capital stocks in being.

The economic analysis involved directly parallels our discussion of labor mobilization. In this case the choice is between large prepositioned stock and smaller stocks with some surge capability. The surge capability could be provided by maintaining open production lines to insure the availability of defense contractors with the required technology. There may be a conflict between the objectives of obtaining military equipment at least cost and the desire to maintain an adequate surge capability. The "follow-on imperative" discussed in the last chapter may well be a sensible economic solution to the requirement for a surge capability, if defense planners anticipate sufficient time before and during a major conflict to use that capability. On the other hand, if planners anticipate limited warning and a short war with very high rates of attrition, the economic analysis would tilt toward greater emphasis on current stocks of equipment.

Table 16.6
The U.S. Strategic Stockpiles: Selected Commodities
March 31, 1978
(Market Value–Millions of Dollars)

Commodity	Unit	Goal	Total Inventory	Market Value
1. Alumina	ST*	11,532,000	0	$ 0
2. Aluminum	ST	0	1,684	$ 1.8
3. Aluminum Oxide, Abrasive Grain	ST	75,000	50,905	$ 36.6
4. Aluminum Oxide, Fused, Crude	ST	147,615	249,403	$ 45.0
5. Antimony	ST	20,130	40,730	$146.4
6. Asbestos, Amosite	ST	26,291	42,533	$ 14.5
7. Asbestos, Chrysotile	ST	0	10,956	$ 5.0
8. Bauxite, Metal Grade, Jamaica	LDT**	523,000	8,858,881	$213.9
9. Bauxite, Metal Grade, Surinam	LDT	0	5,299,597	$153.2

* ST—Short Tons   ** Long Dry Tons

Source: Stockpile Report to the Congress, October 1977–March 1978, pp. 6, 10.

RAW MATERIALS

One of the major constraints on the U.S. economy's ability to respond to a full-scale mobilization is the availability of raw materials. The Strategic and Critical Materials Stock-Piling Act of 1939 gives the president the authority to determine which materials are of critical importance to the United States and to make provisions to acquire such stockpiles. The major agencies responsible for administering the stockpile program within the General Services Administration include the Federal Preparedness Agency (FPA) and the Federal Supply Service (FSS). The FPA is responsible for stockpile policy, while the FSS is responsible for the actual administration of the program.

As noted in the Stockpile Report to the Congress, "Stockpile planning will be based on U.S. requirements during the first three years of a major war."[14] Examples of the materials authorized to be stockpiled and balances are shown in Table 16.6.

CONCLUSION

The optimum reserve capability of the United States is dependent upon a number of factors, which have been indicated in the above analysis. In reality, the stocks of manpower, capital, and raw materials available to support a major mobilization do not currently meet actual mobilization requirements. In most cases the deficiencies can be remedied with rather minor changes in the legislation or funding. In other cases current policy seems to rely upon the availability of the U.S. economy to respond to the increased demand on its resources as it has in the past.

If conventional conflicts continue to be as protracted as they have been in the past several decades, then this policy will probably enable the United States to adequately meet national security requirements. If the conventional war is conducted at a much more rapid pace, as the 1973 Yom Kippur war suggests, then the inability to respond with rapid reinforcements of men and equipment may increase the probability of the United States resorting to either theater or strategic nuclear weapons, or capitulating conventionally.

NOTES

1 The Coast Guard Reserve is controlled by the Department of Transportation in peacetime, but reverts to DOD in wartime.

2 All individuals enlisting to serve on active duty incur a six-year total service obligation. This may be served by any combination of active and reserve service.

3 Kenneth J. Coffey, *Manpower for Military Mobilization* (Washington, D.C.: American Enterprise Institute, 1978) p. 12.

4 Department of Defense, *America's Volunteers—A Report on the All Volunteer Force* (Washington, D.C.: Office of the Assistant Secretary of Defense for Manpower and Reserve Affairs, 1978), p. 129.

5 *Ibid.*

6 *Ibid.*, p. 127.

7 *Ibid.*, p. 128.

8 Robert Kelly, "The Supply of Selected Reservists: An Economic Analysis," unpublished paper presented at the Air Force Academy—Rand Conference on the Economics of National Security, August 1979.

9 The six-year total of veterans who had no service obligation between fiscal year 1971 and 1976 noted above was 1.2 million or a yearly average of .2 million.

10 Coffey, *op. cit.*, p. 5.

11 Department of Defense, *Annual Report of the Secretary of Defense 1980* (Washington, D.C.: Government Printing Office, 1979), p. 267.

12 *Ibid.*

13 Coffey, *op. cit.*, p. 5.

14 *Annual Report FY 1978*, p. 268.

15 General Services Administration, *Stockpile Report to the Congress, October 1977–March 1978*, p. 1.

SELECTED REFERENCES

Kenneth J. Coffey, *Manpower for Military Mobilization* (Washington, D.C.: American Enterprise Institute, 1978).

Department of Defense, "Mobilization Manpower Reserves," in *America's Volunteers—A Report on the All Volunteer Force* (Washington, D.C.: Office of the Assistant Secretary of Defense for Manpower and Reserve Affairs, 1978), pp. 101–140.

Department of Defense, *Reserve Compensation System Study* (Washington, D.C.: Office of the Deputy Assistant Secretary of Defense for Reserve Affairs, 1978).

Chapter 17
Technological Change

INTRODUCTION

In the preceding chapters of this book we looked at the production of national defense as if output were a simple function of the capital and labor inputs into the production process. It is clear, however, that both the civilian and military sectors of the economy are using more technologically advanced methods and equipment than were being used 10, 15, or 20 years ago, and that as an economic system develops and grows, technological changes increase the productivity of conventionally measured factors of production and result not only in new goods but also in old goods being produced at lower real resource costs.

Some technological change can be considered simply as manna dropped down upon the economic system. In reality, however, this type of technological change is usually the result of systematic study and experimentation by private entrepreneurs in search of ways to improve the efficiency of various economic processes. More often than not, technological change results from an explicit effort on the part of firms or agencies within the federal government to advance technology by means of research and development expenditures.

The purpose of this chapter is to review briefly the economics of technological change. We begin by discussing the classical analyses of technological change in the United States by Robert Solow and Edward Denison and then discuss the current state of research and development within the private sector and within the defense sector.

TECHNOLOGICAL CHANGE AND AGGREGATE OUTPUT

In his 1957 article, "Technical Progress and Productivity Change," Robert Solow pioneered the study of technological change in the United States essentially by developing the theory of what is called "growth accounting."[1]

Solow's analysis began by assuming an aggregate production function for output that differs in one key respect from the production functions used previously in this analysis:

$$Q = A(t) \cdot f(K,L) \tag{17.1}$$

where Q = real output

$A(t)$ = Shifts in output due to other factors than capital and labor (i.e., technological change)

K = Capital input

L = Labor input

It can be shown that proportional differentiation of the above relationship leads to the following expression for the rate of growth of real output.[2]

$$\frac{\dot{Q}}{Q} = \frac{\dot{A}}{A} + \left(\frac{K}{Q}\frac{\partial Q}{\partial K}\right)\frac{\dot{K}}{K} + \left(\frac{L}{Q}\frac{\partial Q}{\partial L}\right)\frac{\dot{L}}{L}$$

where a dot over a variable represents a time derivative, i.e.,

$$\dot{Q} = \frac{dQ}{dt}$$

By further assuming that the factors of production, capital, and labor, all paid their marginal products and that such payments exhaust total output, Solow shows the above expression can be rewritten:[3]

$$\frac{\dot{Q}}{Q} = \frac{\dot{A}}{A} + S_K \frac{\dot{K}}{K} + S_L \frac{\dot{L}}{L}$$

where S_K refers to the share of payments to capital in total output, and S_L refers to the share of payments to labor in total output.[4]

Using the above expression, Solow notes that the rate of growth in total output can be attributed to changes in capital,

$$S_K \frac{\dot{K}}{K}$$

changes in labor,

$$S_L \frac{\dot{L}}{L}$$

and technological change,

$$\frac{\dot{A}}{A}$$

Solow then goes on to estimate the effects of technological change on the United States economy between 1909 and 1949. Table 17.1 shows Solow's data for 1909 and 1940, while Table 17.2 shows Solow's method applied to estimate the average logarithmic rates of growth experienced between 1909 and 1940.

As the results indicate, Solow's method *attributes the largest share of increases by far in the growth of real output in the United States to technological change*. While there are a number of assumptions in Solow's analysis that can and have been challenged, the key point to note is that major gains in output appear to have been generated not only by increases in the conventionally measured inputs of capital and labor, but also by changes in technology.

Table 17.1
Output, Capital, Labor, and Technological Change in the United States: 1909–1940

Year	Q ($ x 10^9)	L (Man-Hrs x 10^9)	S_L	K ($ x 10^9)	S_K	A
1909	40.3	64.6	.665	133.1	.335	1.000
1940	107.8	99.7	.643	208.0	.357	1.590

Source: R. M. Solow, "Technical Progress and Productivity Change," in Artya Sen, ed., Growth Economics (Middlesex, England: Penguin Books, 1970), pp. 406–407.

Table 17.2

Solow's Growth Rate Estimates:
Average Compound Rate 1909–1940
(Percent Per Year)

Total Growth Rate of Output	3.28%
Growth Due to Capital	.53%
Growth Due to Labor	.96%
Growth Due to Technological Change	1.55%
Error	.24%

Source: See Text and Table 17.1.

In a more recent study, Edward F. Denison uses Solow's theory of growth accounting, but goes into much greater detail regarding the quality of capital and labor inputs, and causes of changes in technology. Table 17.3 shows Denison's analysis of the growth rate in the United States between 1929 and 1976 and the factors that contributed to the overall growth rate. Denison's analysis shows changes in specific aspects of each type of factor input and technological advancement that caused the growth in the aggregate factors shown at the top of each major heading.

Table 17.3

Denison's Analysis of U.S. Growth:
1929–1976
(Percent Per Year)

Total Growth Rate of Output	2.98%
Growth Due to Capital	.46%
of which:	
(Inventories	.09)
(Structures and Equipment	.18)
(Dwellings	.17)
(International Assets	.02)
Growth Due to Labor	1.36%
of which:	
(Employment of Persons	.09)
(Hours	−.24)
(Education	.41)
(Other	.10)
Growth Due to Technological Change	1.16%
of which:	
(Advances in Knowledge	.73)
(Improved Resource Allocation	.26)
(Economies of Scale	.27)
(Other	−.10)

Source: Edward F. Denison, Accounting for Slower Economic Growth (Washington, D.C.: Brookings, 1979), p. 104.

It is interesting to note that the percentages of the aggregate growth rate explained by Solow's earlier study and by Denison's more recent study show essentially the same result. *Most of the increases in the growth of output in the United States are the result of technological change and increases in the employment of labor*, with the impact of capital increases coming in significantly behind, in third place. Once again the important concept to take note of is that significant gains in output and efficiency result from technological change.

SOURCES OF TECHNOLOGICAL CHANGE IN THE UNITED STATES

As indicated by the data in Table 17.3, Denison attributes technological changes in the United States to three major factors: (1) advances in knowledge; (2) improved resource allocation; and (3) economies of scale. Each of these factors is related to improved efficiency resulting from either increased knowledge of various production technologies or increased specialization that results from changes in the scale of operations.

One major factor that significantly affects the trend in technological change is research and development expenditure. As noted by Denison:

> Secretary of Commerce Juanita Kreps, formerly professor of economics at Duke University, has stated that a 'probable source of the slowdown in productivity is the dramatic reduction in expenditures for research and development.' John W. Kendrick of George Washington University, an expert in productivity analysis, has repeatedly called attention to the decline in R&D. The conclusions of a two-day meeting held by the American Assn. for the Advancement of Science were summarized in the *Washington Post* as follows: "The United States is losing its competitive edge in technology because American industry is spending less on research and because the Federal Government withdrew much of its support for industrial research at the ends of the Apollo Space Program and the Vietnam War."[5]

As these sources indicate, much of the technological advantage of the United States was assumed to have been generated by American research and development. As cited by Denison:

> If expressed as a percentage of gross national product, total R&D expenditures rose from .95 percent in 1955 to a peak of 2.97 percent in 1964, then slipped gradually to 2.27 percent in 1976 and 1977.[6]

This decline in R&D expenditure probably contributed to the decrease in American productivity experienced in the 1970s. Some of the drop in R&D was due to declining military and space research programs. We turn now to the relationship between military and private sector R&D outlays.

MILITARY RESEARCH AND DEVELOPMENT

As noted in the preceding section, the drop in R&D in the United States is partially the result of a decrease in expenditures in research and development in the defense sector. Table 17.4 lists R&D in the defense sector as a share of GNP for various years from 1964 to 1980. The data clearly show the declining trend in the percentage of military R&D as a fraction of GNP. This decline appears to be even more pronounced than the shift in aggregate defense expenditures, which at least rose significantly during the Vietnam War, and then declined.

There are two important aspects of this decline in R&D expenditures. The first point is that the reduction in military R&D may have some impact on technological change in general in the economy. The central question is whether military R&D outlays "crowd-out" private research and development efforts by bidding away the most productive researchers and laboratories, or act as a stimulant to civilian efforts by providing transferrable basic and applied research. A thorough analysis of this issue would require a detailed industry-by-industry study, but in many high technology areas the costs of large-scale research compared with the uncertain returns are probably too great for the private sector. It cannot be denied that a number of civilian sector products and

Table 17.4
Research and Development (R&D) Military and GNP
in the United States: 1964–1979

Year	Military R&D (Billion Dollars)	GNP (Billion Dollars)	Military R&D/GNP (Percent)
1964	7.1	635.7	1.1
1968	7.3	868.5	.8
1972	7.6	1171.1	.6
1976	9.5	1702.2	.6
1979	12.8	2368.5	.5

Sources:
Military R&D—Annual Report of the Secretary of Defense FY 1980, p. A–1.
GNP—Economic Report of the President, 1980, p. 203.

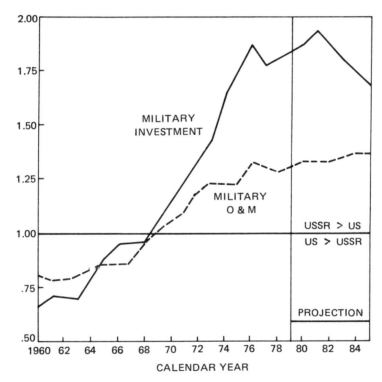

Notes:
1. Military Investment includes Research, Development, Testing, Evaluation, Procurement and Military Construction.
2. Military O & M (Operations and Maintenance) includes Personnel.
3. Retirement and Southeast Asia incremental costs excluded.
4. Includes non-DOD funded defense programs (Department of Energy and Coast Guard).

Figure 17.1 Ratio of Estimated Dollar Cost of
Soviet Investment Outlays to U.S. Investment Outlays

Source: Department of Defense, Annual Report of the Secretary of Defense FY 1981, Chart 4–2, p. 35.

services have benefited from military R&D. Clear examples include such innovations as radar, nuclear power, and rocket and satellite communications resulting from military-assisted expenditures in space research. Thus the decline in R&D by the military may have some effect on the growth of the civilian economy.

The second major point is that the decline in military R&D does affect the efficiency and productivity of the American defense effort. This becomes particularly clear when comparing U.S. and Soviet defense expenditures. Figure 17.1 shows the relative trend in U.S. and Soviet expenditures on R&D. As the data show, the Soviets have made substantial efforts to achieve technological breakthroughs in the area of weapons systems. One such breakthrough was noted by the *Annual Report* of the Secretary of Defense in Fiscal Year 1980:

> . . . the (Soviets) were the first to demonstrate modern anti-satellite (ASAT) systems. Though we have not yet responded with an ASAT of our own, the Soviets continue to work on and test new versions.[7]

Thus the decline in R&D may leave the United States vulnerable to Soviet advances in technology. Given these developments and the limited availability of U.S. R&D funds, it is clear that expenditures must be made in those areas where they will be most productive. In Fiscal Year 1980 the specific areas in which the Defense Advanced Research Projects Agency and the Defense Science and Technology program were concentrating their efforts included:

1. Very High Speed Integrated Circuits
2. Precision Guided Munitions
3. Laser Technology
4. Space Defense
5. Space Surveillance

These areas appear to be those which American defense planners feel will yield the greatest benefits in improving U.S. capabilities in the long run, and also are those in which some emphasis is placed by the Soviets.

CONCLUSION

Technological change is productive and can foster substantial increases in both efficiency and the rate at which new products are introduced in the civilian and military sectors. The rate at which new systems will be introduced depends to a large extent upon the level of research and development activities conducted in the future.

The amount of research and development that should be conducted.is essentially a simple resource allocation problem. Expenditures of limited funds available for defense output can be made on capital, labor, or research and development. The optimal amount of research and development conducted will be that which equates, at the margin, the net return from each of the three methods of increasing output. Thus the marginal dollar spent on research and development should yield the same amount of marginal output as a dollar's worth of capital or labor. If the marginal return to research and development is greater than those expenditures on either capital or labor, then expenditures on research and development should increase.

In the defense sector, a technological lead by an adversary may well result in a serious threat to the security of the country in question, and perhaps a loss of political independence. Any key breakthrough in a weapons system resulting from research and development by an adversary would result in serious consequences for all military rivals. Thus, the substantial decline in American R&D in the 1970s has led some observers to question the ability of the United States to remain ahead of the Soviets in the technology race. As the *Wall Street Journal* noted in 1980:

> The U.S. retains a lead in defense technology, but the Soviet Union is coming on fast and is ahead in some ways . . . . "The Soviets spent about $100 billion more than the U.S. on military research and development in the decade just ended," according to William Perry, Under Secretary of Defense for R&D. "We've been losing our (technological) advantage year by year," he believes.[9]

Given the major contribution that technological change makes to growth in the civilian sector, it is hard to justify the relatively low proportion of the defense budget that is allocated to research and development. In the short run, the emphasis on maintaining an adequate level of labor for the force and on procuring sufficient stocks of material may seem reasonable. But in the long run, limited attention to research and development can actually increase our requirements for both labor and capital.

NOTES

1 Robert Solow, "Technical Progress and Productivity Change," in Amartya Sen, ed., *Growth Economics* (Middlesex, England: Penguin Books, 1970), pp. 401–419.

2 (a)

$$\dot{Q} = A \times \dot{f} + f \times \dot{A}$$

(b)

$$\dot{f} = \frac{\partial f}{\partial L} \dot{L} + \frac{\partial f}{\partial K} \dot{K}$$

(c)

$$\dot{Q} = \left(A \times \frac{\partial f}{\partial L} \times \dot{L} \right) + \left(A \times \frac{\partial f}{\partial K} \times \dot{K} \right) + \left(f \times \dot{A} \right)$$

(d)

$$\text{But} \quad A \times \frac{\partial f}{\partial L} = \frac{\partial Q}{\partial L}$$

$$\text{and} \quad A \times \frac{\partial f}{\partial K} = \frac{\partial Q}{\partial K}$$

(e)

$$\dot{Q} = \frac{\partial Q}{\partial L} \dot{L} + \frac{\partial Q}{\partial K} \dot{K} + f \dot{A}$$

(f) Dividing both sides by Q gives:

$$\frac{\dot{Q}}{Q} = \frac{\partial Q}{\partial L} \cdot \frac{L}{Q} \frac{\dot{L}}{L} + \frac{\partial Q}{\partial K} \frac{K}{Q} \frac{\dot{K}}{K} + \frac{f}{f} \frac{\dot{A}}{A}$$

which is the expression shown.

3 Note that if each factor is paid its marginal product then:

$$w = \text{Wage} = \frac{\partial Q}{\partial L}$$

$$r = \text{Profit Rate} = \frac{\partial Q}{\partial K}$$

$$\left(\frac{\partial Q}{\partial L} \frac{L}{Q} \right) = \frac{wL}{Q} = S_L = \text{wages/income}$$

$$\left(\frac{\partial Q}{\partial K} \frac{K}{Q} \right) = \frac{rK}{Q} = S_K = \text{profits/income}$$

4 This assumption implies factor markets are competitive.

5 Edward Denison, *Accounting for Slower Economic Growth* (Washington, D.C.: Brookings Institution, 1979), pp. 122–123.

6 *Ibid.*, p. 123.

7 Department of Defense, *Annual Report of the Secretary of Defense FY 1980* (Washington, D.C.: Government Printing Office, 1979), p. 35.

8 *Ibid.*, pp. 255–259.

9 "Soviets Strive to Catch the U.S. in Technology and Make Some Gains," *The Wall Street Journal* (March 21, 1980), pp. 1, 39.

SELECTED REFERENCES

Edward Denison, *Accounting for Slower Economic Growth* (Washington, D.C.: Brookings Institution, 1979).

Amartya Sen, ed., *Growth Economics* (Middlesex, England: Penguin Books, 1970).

Robert Solow, "Technical Change and the Aggregate Production Function," *The Review of Economics and Statistics*, vol. 39 (August, 1957), pp. 312–320.

Part V

Interindustry Relations and the Defense Sector

I have yet to see any problem, however complicated, which, when looked at in just the right way, did not become still more complicated.

Paul Anderson

There is no limit to how complicated things can get, on account of one thing always leading to another.

E. B. White

Chapter 18
Input–Output Analysis

INTRODUCTION

Thus far in our examination of the economics of national security, we have looked at economic questions as they relate to the defense sector in either microeconomic or macroeconomic terms. One of the major problems with this type of approach is that microeconomics examines only a single market and ignores important interdependence, while macroeconomics treats issues with a great degree of aggregation and therefore skims over much of the detail that is important in examining defense economic issues.

The middle ground between microeconomics and macroeconomics is commonly referred to as "general equilibrium" theory. General equilibrium theory treats all markets in the economic system and develops the set of relationships and equilibrium conditions that show the effect of a change in one sector upon another. In the usual formulation of the general equilibrium problem, individual utility functions are specified for each consumer, and production functions are specified for each commodity.[1] Complex mathematical techniques are then used to show whether an equilibrium exists and, if so, whether it is stable, and the efficiency properties that result from the attempt of consumers to maximize utility and producers to maximize profits in a set of competitive product and factor markets. While general equilibrium theory is a useful theoretical tool for describing properties of an economic system, it has not resulted in much practical use because of the obvious data and computational problems.

A quasi-general equilibrium model is available, however, which is very useful in dealing with interdependencies on the supply side of the economy. The model, commonly referred to as an "input-output" model, was originally developed in sixteenth-century France by a group of economic-philosophers called the Physiocrats.[2] The physiocratic school of thought recognized the interdependencies of one sector of the economy with another, and actually constructed a hypothetical model of an interdependent economy called an "economique."

The ideas of the physiocrats were modernized in the early 1930s by Wassily Leontief at Harvard, who developed the theoretical analysis and some of the first empirical analysis using input-output economics. Leontief's model traced the requirements for producing a unit of output in one sector in the economy (e.g., aircraft) from all other inputs (e.g., steel, rubber, glass, etc.). Leontief's model allowed analysts to look at the effect of a changing set of macroeconomic final demands (consumption, government spending, investment, exports, and imports) on each sector of the economy.[3]

The purpose of this chapter is to develop the economic relationships involved in a simple input-output system. The model used as an example in this chapter contains only two sectors, but the results can be extended to a model with any number of sectors. The succeeding section describes input-output tables and the solution of the simple Leontief system. The third section discusses the variety of uses to which input-output tables can be put. Chapter 19 discusses the applications of input-output analysis to the defense sector.

INPUT-OUTPUT ECONOMICS:
AN ILLUSTRATION FOR A TWO-GOOD ECONOMY

Final Demands

The basic economic relationships that illustrate the input-output system can best be described by a simple input-output problem. In this problem we shall examine an economy that produces two goods—corn and steel—using two primary factors of production—capital and labor. The two goods that are produced can be purchased by final users for either private consumption, public consumption, or investment. The amounts of each commodity required for use as a final demand can be represented by the following relationship, which expresses the final demand for each commodity as a vector product of macroeconomic final demands and coefficients that indicate the fraction of final demand that is composed of purchases of each commodity:

$$F_c = b_1^c C + b_2^c G + b_3^c I \qquad (18.1)$$

and

$$F_s = b_1^s C + b_2^s G + b_3^s I \qquad (18.2)$$

where F_c is the final demand for corn, and F_s is the final demand for steel. The b_i^j refers to the fraction of the final macroeconomic demand i (i = 1,2,3) which is composed of demand for commodity j (j – C,S).

Suppose, for example, that 30 percent of all final consumption, 20 percent of all government purchases, and 10 percent of all investment is in purchases of corn. Equation 18.1 would then be written as:

$$F_c - .3C + .2G + .1I \qquad (18.3)$$

In matrix notation equations 18.1 and 18.2 can be compactly written as:

$$\begin{bmatrix} F_c \\ F_s \end{bmatrix} = [B]\ [D] \qquad (18.4)$$

where

$$[D] = \begin{bmatrix} C \\ G \\ I \end{bmatrix},$$

and [B] is the coefficient matrix—

$$[B] = \begin{bmatrix} b_1^c & b_2^c & b_3^c \\ b_1^s & b_2^s & b_3^s \end{bmatrix}$$

Table 18.1 provides some hypothetical values for our final demands and coefficients. Applying equation 18.4 to the data in Table 18.1 we may solve for F_c, the final demand for corn, as:

$$70\,(.3) + 20\,(.2) + 10\,(.1) = 26\ .$$

Note that this is the same as the result we would obtain from equation 18.3.[4]

Table 18.1

Data for Input–Output Problem

Final Demands	$[D] = \begin{bmatrix} C \\ G \\ I \end{bmatrix} = \begin{bmatrix} 70 \\ 20 \\ 10 \end{bmatrix}$	
Output Requirements Per Unit of Final Demand	$[B] = \begin{bmatrix} b_1^c & b_2^c & b_3^c \\ b_1^s & b_2^s & b_3^s \end{bmatrix} = \begin{bmatrix} .3 & .2 & .1 \\ .1 & .1 & .3 \end{bmatrix}$	
Interindustry Requirements	$[A] = \begin{bmatrix} a_c^c & a_s^c \\ a_c^s & a_s^s \end{bmatrix} \begin{bmatrix} .2 & .1 \\ .3 & .4 \end{bmatrix}$	
Labor Requirement	$L_D = [l_1\ l_2\ l_3]' = [20\ 30\ 10]$ $L_I[l_c\ l_s] = [40\ 10]$	
Capital Requirements	$K_D = [k_1\ k_2\ k_3] = [3\ 2\ 5]$ $K_I = [k_c\ k_s] = [2\ 6]$	

Intermediate Demands

The key to input-output analysis is the recognition of the fact that the production of outputs in one sector usually requires intermediate products from other sectors. Corn that is sold in cans, for example, will require steel as an intermediate input to the production process. The production of steel might also require corn oil as a lubricant and fuel for steel-making machinery. Thus the key point is that steel and corn output are required not only for final use, but also for intermediate or interindustry use.

The total amount of output in each sector for final *and* intermediate use can be represented by the following relationships for each sector:

and

$$X_c = F_c + a_c^c X_c + a_s^c X_s \qquad (18.5)$$

$$X_s = F_s + a_c^s X_c + a_s^s X_s \qquad (18.6)$$

where X_c and X_s represent the total output of the corn and steel sectors respectively; and the a_j^i represents the amount of output required from the jth sector (j = C,S) to produce a unit of output in the ith sector (i = C,S). Thus the coefficient a_c^c represents the amount of corn required in the corn sector (i.e., for seed, etc.) to produce ¨ unit of output in the corn sector.

For example, suppose that each unit of corn production required an input of .2 units of corn (seed) and each unit of steel production required an input of .1 units of corn (fuel). Equation 18.5 would then be written as:

$$X_c = F_c + .2X_c + .1X_s \qquad (18.7)$$

Equations 18.5 and 18.6 can be written in matrix notation as:

$$\begin{bmatrix} X_c \\ X_s \end{bmatrix} = \begin{bmatrix} F_c \\ F_s \end{bmatrix} + [A] \begin{bmatrix} X_c \\ X_s \end{bmatrix}$$

where [A] is the coefficient matrix,

$$[A] = \begin{bmatrix} a_c^c & a_s^c \\ a_c^s & a_s^s \end{bmatrix}$$

If we let [X] represent the vector of total outputs,

$$\begin{bmatrix} X_c \\ X_s \end{bmatrix}$$

and [F] represent the vector of final demands,

$$\begin{bmatrix} F_c \\ F_s \end{bmatrix}$$

equation 18.6 may be rewritten as:

$$[X] = [F] + [A][X] \tag{18.9}$$

Total Output

Using the hypothetical values in Table 18.1 and a final demand for corn of 26, and applying equation 18.9, we may solve for the total output of corn as:

$$X_c = 26 + .2X_c + .1X_s,$$

which, of course, is the same as equation 18.7. Note that this equation has two unknowns, X_c and X_s. By solving both of our total output equations simultaneously, we may obtain the values for X_c and X_s. In other words, if we know the set of final demands and the set of interindustry input coefficients, we may solve for the total output of each sector that will keep the interindustry flows in balance and just meet the required levels of final demand.

The general form of a solution may be obtained using our matrix notation. If we subtract [A][X] from both sides of equation 18.9 and then factor out the [X] matrix from the resulting expression, we have:

$$[I - A][X] = [F], \tag{18.10}$$

where [I] is the identity matrix.[5]

Equation 18.10 may be solved for the [X] matrix of outputs by premultiplying each side by the inverse of [I–A] to give:

$$[X] = [I–A]^{-1}[F] \tag{18.11}$$

where $[I–A]^{-1}$ is the inverse of [I–A].

Solving for Outputs: A Numerical Example

Equation 18.11 provides an expression for the vector of total production requirements for corn and steel based on a matrix of final demands and the matrix of technical coefficients (the technical coefficient matrix is frequently called the "Leontief Matrix"). In this section we will illustrate the solution for total production requirements using the data in Table 18.1.

The only major manipulation of the data to be performed prior to applying the relationships of the preceding section is to compute the inverse of the [I–A] matrix. In this case, the inverse can easily be computed manually. In large input-output models the computation of the inverse requires a significant number of calculations, and has to be done by computer.

The inverse of [I–A] for the [A] matrix, shown in Table 18.1, is given by:[6]

$$[I-A]^{-1} = \begin{bmatrix} 1.33 & .22 \\ .67 & 1.78 \end{bmatrix}$$

In this case the final demand production levels required to meet the specified final demand targets are given, using equation 18.4, as:

$$[F] = [B][D] = \begin{bmatrix} .3 & .2 & .1 \\ .1 & .1 & .3 \end{bmatrix} \begin{bmatrix} 70 \\ 20 \\ 10 \end{bmatrix} = \begin{bmatrix} 26 \\ 12 \end{bmatrix}$$

The total production in each sector required to meet the specified final demands is given by:

$$[X] = \begin{bmatrix} X_c \\ X_s \end{bmatrix} = [I-A]^{-1}[F] = \begin{bmatrix} 1.33 & .22 \\ .67 & 1.78 \end{bmatrix} \begin{bmatrix} 26 \\ 12 \end{bmatrix} = \begin{bmatrix} 37.22 \\ 38.78 \end{bmatrix}$$

These results are illustrated in Table 18.2. It may be noted that the total output of corn, 37.22, is divided among 26 units of final demand (21 for consumption, 4 for government pruchases, and 1 for investment) and 11.22 units of intermediate demand (7.35 to corn production and 3.87 to steel). The total output of steel, 38.78, is divided among 12 units of final demand (7 to consumption, 2 to government, and 3 to investment) and 26.78 units of intermediate demand (11.21 units to corn and 15.57 units to steel).

An interesting point to note is the significant difference between the two sectors in the interindustry production levels required to meet final demands. Interindustry production in the corn sector is only 30 percent of total corn production, while interindustry production in the steel sector is 74 percent of the final demand in the steel sector. The difference reflects the heavy interindustry use of steel in both the steel and corn sectors.

Note that our results satisfy equations 18.5 and 18.6 in that total output is equal to the sum of final and intermediate output requirements. Using the equations developed in the preceding sections, we may solve for the intermediate and total output requirements associated with any set of final demands.

Table 18.2
Final and Interindustry Demands for Corn and Steel

Output of Sector	Going to Sector		Going to Final Demand			Total Output
	Corn	Steel	C	G	I	
Corn	7.35	3.87	21.0	4.0	1.0	37.22
Steel	11.21	15.57	7.0	2.0	3.0	38.78

Factor Input Requirements

Observe that in Table 18.2 the total output of the corn sector is 37.22 units, but the inputs to corn production are only 7.35 units of corn and 11.21 units of steel. The difference between total output and interindustry inputs, in this case 18.66 units, is the "value added" to total output. This value added must be attributed to the factors used in the production process.

Factors are needed in both the process of producing final goods from intermediate goods and in producing the intermediate goods themselves. Direct labor requirements for final demands are given by the following relationship:

$$L_F = l_1C + l_2G + l_3I , \qquad (18.12)$$

where l_1, l_2, and l_3 are the direct labor inputs required per unit of output to satisfy final demands for C, G, and I respectively. Labor requirements for production in the corn and steel sectors are given by:

$$L_X = l_C X_C + l_S X_S , \qquad (18.13)$$

where l_C and l_S are the inputs required per unit of output of corn and steel respectively.

The corresponding relationships for the use of capital are given by:

$$K_F = k_1C + k_2G + k_3I, \qquad (18.14)$$

and

$$K_X = k_c X_c + k_S X_S . \qquad (18.15)$$

These relationships may be rewritten in matrix notation as:

$$[L_F] = [L_D][D] \qquad (18.16a)$$
$$[K_F] = [K_D][D] \qquad (18.16b)$$
$$[L_X] = [L_I][X] \qquad (18.17a)$$
$$[K_X] = [K_I][X]$$

where

$$[L_D] = [l_1\ l_2\ l_3] ,$$
$$[L_I] = [l_c\ l_S] ,$$
$$[K_D] = [k_1\ k_2\ k_3] ,$$
$$\text{and } [K_I] = [k_C\ k_S] .$$

The labor requirements for the specified final demands are given by substituting the output results from equation 18.1 into equations 18.16 and 18.17. Thus total labor requirements are given by:

$$L = L_F + L_X = [L_D][D] + [L_I][I-A]^{-1}[F] \qquad (18.18)$$

while total capital requirements are given by:

$$K - K_F + K_X = [K_D][D] + [K_I][I-A]^{-1}[F] \qquad (18.19)$$

Thus, once the level of desired final demands is given, total production targets, labor requirements, and capital requirements can be determined.

Solving for Inputs: A Numerical Example

Equations 18.18 and 18.19 provide expressions for factor input requirements given a vector of final demands, the Leontief matrix, the matrix of input coefficients for direct contributions to final demand, and the matrix of input coefficients for intermediate good production. In this section we illustrate the solution for input factor requirements using the data in Table 18.1.

Recall that in our example the final demand production levels required to meet the specified final demand targets were given by:

$$[F] = [B][D] = \begin{bmatrix} .3 & .2 & .1 \\ .1 & .1 & .3 \end{bmatrix} \begin{bmatrix} 70 \\ 20 \\ 10 \end{bmatrix} = \begin{bmatrix} 26 \\ 12 \end{bmatrix}$$

The total production in each sector required to meet the specified final demands was given by:

$$[X] = \begin{bmatrix} X_c \\ X_s \end{bmatrix} = [I-A]^{-1}[F] = \begin{bmatrix} 1.33 & .22 \\ 67 & 1.78 \end{bmatrix} \begin{bmatrix} 26 \\ 12 \end{bmatrix} = \begin{bmatrix} 37.22 \\ 38.78 \end{bmatrix}$$

Applying Equation 18.18, the labor requirements to produce the final demand levels and all intermediate output levels are given by:

$$[L] = [L_D][D] + [L_I][X] = [20\ 30\ 10] \begin{bmatrix} 70 \\ 20 \\ 10 \end{bmatrix} + [40\ 10] \begin{bmatrix} 37.22 \\ 38.78 \end{bmatrix} = 2100 + 1876.6 = 3976.6$$

The capital requirements are similarly given by:

$$[K] = [K_D][D] + [K_I][X] = [3\ 2\ 5] \begin{bmatrix} 70 \\ 20 \\ 10 \end{bmatrix} + [2\ 6] \begin{bmatrix} 37.22 \\ 38.78 \end{bmatrix} = 300 + 307.12 = 607.12$$

THE USES OF INPUT-OUTPUT ANALYSIS

Many types of economic problems, including a number of particular interest to defense economics, can be analyzed using the basic input-output model. In addition, there are many extensions of the basic model that further enhance the uses of the technique.

In its basic form as described above, the model normally begins with a given set of final demands, e.g., the result of a projection using a different type of macroeconomic model, a mobilization or demobilization plan, an economic growth goal, and so on. The usefulness of the model is its ability to further elaborate the implications of the given final demand vector by spelling out the implied levels of output by sector, as well as the input requirements in terms of primary factors, especially labor. One use of this analysis is to determine the *feasibility* of the projected set of final demands, that is, whether there are sufficient primary factors and sufficient productive capacity in each sector to satisfy the resulting derived demand. Another use might be to examine whether there is likely to be *unemployment* or *excess capacity*, and if so, the sectoral pattern of such unemployment.

Such information can be valuable in many ways to public policymakers. It also can be used by decision makers in the private sector, seeking to project the future of a particular industry.

The basic input-output model is also relevant to problems faced by planners in a nonmarket economy. In this case, central planners must specify an output target for each sector, some of which goes to final demand but much of which goes to satisfy input needs of other sectors. Clearly each sector's inputs and outputs are vitally dependent on what other sectors will be doing. In the absence of a coordinating mechanism, large shortages or surpluses are likely to develop. Input-output provides a basis for insuring *consistency*, so that the total demand for each sector's products—including intermediate demand—is consistent with the planned output level.

The above uses may be extended to include provision for analysis on a regional basis, to distinguish the domestic and foreign trade sectors, and to include a dynamic aspect to permit analysis of economic patterns over a period of time by examining the impact on capital formation.

It is important to recognize that input-output in its basic form is not an optimizing model in the usual sense, because it contains no element of choice within the model. The key economic choices must be specified in advance, and are assumed to be independent of the outcome of the analysis. These choices include those of technology, the sources of supply to each sector, and the pattern of final demand. However, it is possible to extend the basic model to permit choice and to incorporate a criterion for making optimal choices. Such extensions are referred to as *programming*.

The kinds of choices that may be incorporated include alternative technologies (i.e., different modes of production in various sectors), alternative sources of supply (i.e., different patterns of foreign trade, different regions, current production versus inventory depletion), and alternative patterns of final demand. Obviously once such choices are incorporated, there will be many possible solutions and some criterion must be specified for preferring one solution over another. Conceptually such criteria may involve maximization of output value, minimization of cost, or other functions of the choice variables.

Programming is conceptually a much richer technique, since it provides a basis not merely to predict the impact of a given policy but to evaluate the choice between alternative policies. Potentially it appears to offer great promise, especially in nonmarket and in developing economies with large-scale government involvement. However, programming is also much more demanding in terms of data and computational requirements and its uses to date in economy-wide applications have been limited for these reasons.[7]

The uses of the basic model can be illustrated with the numerical example of the preceding section. The first example is one where the model is used to test for the feasibility of an economic plan. In this case a typical problem might be to investigate whether the economic plan given by the following final demand vector

$$[D] = \begin{bmatrix} C \\ G \\ I \end{bmatrix} = \begin{bmatrix} 70 \\ 20 \\ 10 \end{bmatrix}$$

could be produced with a labor force and capital stock given by:

$$L = 4000$$
$$K = 700 \ .$$

From the preceding numerical example, it is obvious that the above economic program is feasible. The actual capital and labor requirements to produce the specified final demand vector are less than those shown above.

A second type of problem might be to determine whether the economic plan specified above implies full employment of labor and full utilization of capital capacity. The answer to both questions in this case is no. The final demands in the plan can be produced with less than the available capital stock and supply of labor. Obviously the excess capital and labor could be used to increase at least one final demand component and therefore increase total output.

The basic input-output model also works for *changes* in the final demand vector. For example we might be interested in examining the impact of a change in government spending, e.g., an increase of 25 percent, from 20 to 25. In this case the change in the final demand vector is given by:

$$\Delta D = [\Delta C \ \Delta G \ \Delta I] = [0 \ 5 \ 0] \ .$$

Equation 18-4 can be used to calculate the changes in final demand production levels required to produce the change in final demand.

$$[\Delta F] = [\Delta D] \ [B] = [0 \ 5 \ 0] \begin{bmatrix} .3 & .1 \\ .2 & .1 \\ .1 & .3 \end{bmatrix} = \begin{bmatrix} 1 \\ .5 \end{bmatrix}$$

The change in total output in each industry is found by using equation 18.11 as:

$$[\Delta X] = [I-A]^{-1} \ [\Delta F] = \begin{bmatrix} 1.33 & .22 \\ .67 & 1.78 \end{bmatrix} \begin{bmatrix} 1 \\ .5 \end{bmatrix} = \begin{bmatrix} 1.44 \\ 1.56 \end{bmatrix}$$

Finally, the labor and capital changes are given by equations 18.18 and 18.19 as:

$$[\Delta L] = [L_D] \ [\Delta D] \quad + \quad [L_I] \ [\Delta X] \ = [20 \ 30 \ 10] \begin{bmatrix} 0 \\ 5 \\ 0 \end{bmatrix} + [40 \ 10] \begin{bmatrix} 1.44 \\ 1.56 \end{bmatrix} = 223.2$$

$$[\Delta K] = [K_D] \ [\Delta D] \quad + \quad [K_I] \ [\Delta X] \ = [3 \ 2 \ 5] \begin{bmatrix} 0 \\ 5 \\ 0 \end{bmatrix} + [2 \ 6] \begin{bmatrix} 1.44 \\ 1.56 \end{bmatrix} = 22.2$$

These simple examples obviously are not exhaustive and they are limited by the lack of sectoral detail in the example model. A better appreciation of the power of the technique may be obtained by reference to an actual input-output model of the type used today in the United States.

Actual input-output tables of the United States economy are much larger than the ones used in the examples cited above. The first input-output table in the United States was constructed by Wassily Leontief at Harvard in 1949. The table, based on 1939 data, contained 42 sectors and the gathering of the data and the construction of the table took five years.[8]

Since that time input-output tables have become much larger and much more detailed. In 1979, the Department of Commerce had constructed a table with 496 sectors, as well as more aggregated tables of 365 and 85 sectors. The data for the tables were gathered from 1972 sources and therefore represent the state of the economy that existed in 1972.

In the Department of Commerce's 85-sector input-output table there is an 85 × 85 array of data that shows how much output of each sector was consumed by other sectors. This information provides the data for computing the [A] matrix discussed above. For example, 26.01 billion dollars worth of livestock (sector 1) went to inputs in producing food products (sector 14). After these interindustry flows come the columns that show how much output of each sector went to satisfy final demands—personal consumption expenditures, capital formation, exports, government purchases, and so forth. For example, 1.454 billion dollars of the output of livestock (sector 1) went to satisfy the final demand for personal consumption expenditures. Adding all of the final demands we find that the gross national product in 1972, the sum of all final demands for products produced in the United States in that year, was 1,132.766 billion dollars.

Assumptions and Limitations

The input-output model just described is a useful tool in economic planning and forecasting. However, those planning on using an input-output model to conduct such exercises should be aware of the assumptions and limitations implicit in the input output approach.

One of the key assumptions of the model is that the technical coefficients used in the input-output table are constant. Thus the model does not generally allow for *substitutions* in production when economic conditions warrant such changes. A good example of this limitation would be an instance where high oil prices induce industries to switch from oil to coal energy inputs in their production processes. In this case, an input-output model constructed using input coefficients when oil prices were low would overestimate the intermediate production and import requirements for oil inputs, while underestimating the production and import requirements for coal. This error would, of course, be compounded, because the intermediate inputs required in the oil and coal industries would also be in error.

A second key assumption of the input-output model is *static technology*. If the technology for producing a particular product changes, then the technical coefficients associated with the production process will also change. Again this will lead to errors in the estimation of intermediate inputs and imports required to produce the product in question, as well as the errors that result when these input requirements are multiplied throughout the system.

A third assumption of the model is that the number and types of products produced remain the same. This assumption of a *constant product mix* could lead to major errors in the analysis if new products are introduced. One example of this type of problem is the rise in the hand calculator industry that followed the improvements in micro-circuitry and liquid crystal technology. The mass production of hand calculators led to the demise of the slide-rule industry. Thus, over a a brief period of time, a new product with entirely different input characteristics replaced the slide-rule.

A final problem of the input-output model concerns the accuracy of *forecasts of final demands*. For example, the forecast of government spending may vary widely from the actual amount spent. This problem is not unique to forecasting with input-output analysis, but inaccuracies in the forecast of final demands can lead to significant shortages or overages of complementary inputs if production targets are based on the inaccurate forecast.

The above examples illustrate one major limitation of input-output analysis. This limitation results from the need to collect and process accurate and current data in order to construct an input-output table. To construct an 80 × 80 input-output table, for example, will require a minimum of 1600 pieces of data. Thus, in many cases, by the time the data for an input-output table are collected, processed, and the model is put in usable form, the model may be obsolete.

The 1972 model, for example, employs data gathered before the large oil shocks associated with the 1974 and 1979 oil markets. Are the technical coefficients used to compute interindustry requirements the same today as in 1972, or has the interindustrial structure shifted so as to make a significant difference in the results? If the input-output structure has remained the same, the technical coefficients are still appropriate; if it has changed, the employment of the tables could lead to significant errors in projecting variables of interest.

CONCLUSION

Input-output analysis is based on a highly simplified model of economic activity. It assumes that the technology is fixed and that inputs must be used in fixed proportions. Much of economic theory, however, emphasizes the adjustments in technology and the substitutions among inputs which will occur as relative prices change. Input-output analysis does not provide for such adjustments.

In the short run, however, it may well be true that technology is relatively fixed and that the input mix cannot be varied widely. In such cases input-output analysis provides a powerful tool to analyze the structural impact of a number of changes in the composition of inputs or outputs of an economic system. For example, if we are interested in the short run impacts of an oil embargo on the rest of the economy, input-output analysis may provide useful insights. Similarly, if a sector of the economy faces a natural disaster, a terrorist action, or a wartime attack, input-output techniques can provide important information on the expected extent of disruption throughout the economy.

Unfortunately the larger the disruption and the longer the period of analysis, the less appropriate the linear approach will be. In the short run the alternatives to a crude oil embargo may be quite limited, but, as we have discovered, in the longer run the possibility for substitutions through conservation or other energy sources is significant.

Input-output techniques are very useful in testing for feasibility and consistency, but they are less useful in determining an optimal solution. For example, the input-output approach can tell us whether or not a given set of final demands can be produced given available resources. It can also tell us the required pattern of interindustry flows to provide that output. However, input-output techniques by themselves cannot indicate the optimal allocation of resources because the key choices which affect optimality, the pattern of supply to each sector and the appropriate technology, have been assumed at the outset. If input-output solutions are iterated, however, using programming techniques, they may provide insights on optimal resource allocation.

Input-output techniques have had limited applications in the United States at the macroeconomic policy level. The significant data requirements, the long lag between gathering data and the employment of the model, and the problems in inverting the inverse of a large Leontief matrix, have all posed technical constraints. In general our reliance on the free market to allocate resources and to find appropriate substitutions has limited the role of aggregate input-output analysis. In the Soviet Union, however, with its greater emphasis on centralized planning, input-output techniques have been used to check the consistency of national plans.

NOTES

1 See James Quick and Ruben Saposnik, *Introduction to General Equilibrium Theory and Welfare Economics* (New York: McGraw-Hill, 1968) for an introductory treatment of general equilibrium theory.
2 Richard T. Gill, *Evolution of Modern Economics* (Englewood Cliffs, N.J.: Prentice Hall, 1967) has a brief review of the physiocratic school on p. 6.
3 Wassily Leontief, *Input-Output Economics* (New York: Oxford University Press, 1966).
4 Recall from matrix algebra that

$$\begin{bmatrix} b_1 & b_2 & b_3 \\ c_1 & c_2 & c_3 \end{bmatrix} \begin{bmatrix} a_1 \\ a_2 \\ a_3 \end{bmatrix} = \begin{bmatrix} a_1b_1 & + & a_2b_2 & + & a_3b_3 \\ a_1c_1 & + & a_2c_2 & + & a_3c_3 \end{bmatrix}$$

5 The identity matrix in this case is:

$$\begin{bmatrix} 1 & 0 \\ 0 & 1 \end{bmatrix}$$

6 The adjoint matrix of transposed cofactors, $[I-A]^T$, is:

$$[I-A] = \begin{bmatrix} .8 & -.1 \\ -.3 & .6 \end{bmatrix} \cdot \begin{bmatrix} .6 & .1 \\ .3 & .8 \end{bmatrix};$$

and

$$[I-A]^{-1} = \frac{[I-A]^T}{|I-A|}$$

or

$$[I-A]^{-1} = \frac{\begin{bmatrix} .6 & .1 \\ .4 & .8 \end{bmatrix}}{.45} = \begin{bmatrix} 1.33 & .22 \\ .67 & 1.78 \end{bmatrix}.$$

7 For an introduction to the uses of both input/output and programming methods, see Hollis B. Chenery and Paul G. Clark, *Interindustry Economics* (New York: John Wiley & Sons, 1965).

8 Wassily Leontief, *op. cit.*, pp. 25–26.

9 U.S. Department of Commerce, Bureau of Economic Analysis, *Survey of Current Business* (USPGO), April 1979, pp. 62-72.

SELECTED REFERENCES

Wassily Leontief, *Input-Output Economics* (New York: Oxford University Press, 1966).

William H. Miernyk, *The Elements of Input-Output Analysis* (New York: Random House, 1965).

James Quick and Ruben Saposnik, *Introduction to General Equilibrium Theory and Welfare Economics* (New York: McGraw-Hill, 1968).

Hollis B. Chenery and Paul G. Clark, *Interindustry Economics* (New York: John Wiley and Sons, 1965).

Chapter 19
National Security Applications of Interindustry Analysis

INTRODUCTION

In Chapter 18 the concept of interindustry analysis was introduced, and the general applicability of input-output techniques to economic decision making was discussed. In this chapter, the techniques of input-output analysis are applied to the economic problems of the defense sector.

Input-output analysis is useful in analyzing the interindustrial relationships among defense-related sectors in both the United States economy and in the economies of our adversaries. In the United States economy, the questions with which we will be concerned include the impact of changes in defense spending on the various sectors that supply the defense sector, the regional impact of defense spending changes, and the vulnerability of our resource base to disruptions caused by a conventional or nuclear conflict. The last consideration noted would be of most interest to those targeting either nuclear or conventional weapons against our adversaries or planning an economic blockade or embargo.

The following section of this chapter examines the specific relationship of the defense sector to the rest of the U.S. economy, using the 1972 input-output model of the Department of Commerce. The succeeding sections examine the analysis of Leontief on the impact of a reduction in defense spending on specific sectors in the United States economy; the geographical impact of changes in defense spending; and the usefulness of input-output analysis in targeting or planning economic warfare against our adversaries.

THE DEFENSE SECTOR AND THE UNITED STATES ECONOMY: AN INPUT-OUTPUT VIEW

The relationship of the defense sector to the other major sectors of the United States economy is shown in Table 19.1. The data in Table 19.1 show the composition of final demand that originated in each of the 81 sectors of the economy used in the 1972 Department of Commerce input-output study. This equates with the [B] matrix in Chapter 18, which indicated the impact of changes in the final demand on the change in demand for the output of specific sectors.

Five sectors in Table 19.1 accounted for over a billion dollars of defense outlays in 1972. These sectors included ordnance (sector 13 in the table), communications equipment (56), aircraft (60), transportation equipment (61), and imported goods (80). Final demands in each of these sectors are defined in more detail in Table 19.2, which shows the percentage of defense resources that was allocated to each sector in 1972.

Each of these "final demands" of defense spending creates further "intermediate" or "interindustry" demands on a wide variety of other sectors of the economy. For example, aircraft production requires inputs from the aircraft sector itself, primary iron and steel manufacturing, the nonferrous metal industry, miscellaneous machinery, communications equipment, and electronic components and accessories. The extent of these interindustry requirements is summarized in Table 19.3, which shows the percentage of aircraft inputs contributed by the major supplying industries.

Thus an increase in final demand for aircraft by the Department of Defense would trigger a corresponding intermediate demand in a number of other sectors, many of which might have little direct relationship to the defense sector. Moreover, each of these intermediate demands would trigger further interindustry requirements in an even wider array of sectors.

Table 19.1
The Sectoral Breakdown of National Defense Purchases: 1972
(Millions of $)

No.	Commodity	Federal Government purchases, national defense			
		Producers' prices	Transportation costs	Wholesale and retail trade margins	Purchasers' prices
1	Livestock and livestock products	(*)	0	−1	−1
2	Other agricultural products	(*)	0	−6	−5
3	Forestry and fishery products	−1	0	−1	−1
4	Agricultural, forestry, and fishery services				
5	Iron and ferroalloy ores mining	−25	−1	0	−25
6	Nonferrous metal ores mining	−8	−1	−1	−9
7	Coal mining	36	34	2	71
8	Crude petroleum and natural gas	0	0	0	0
9	Stone and clay mining and quarrying	−2	−3	0	−5
10	Chemical and fertilizer mineral mining	−2	−1	0	−3
11	New construction				
12	Maintenance and repair construction				
13	Ordnance and accessories	4,404	58	49	4,511
14	Food and kindred products	5	−1	−57	−52
15	Tobacco manufactures	0	0	−3	−3
16	Broad and narrow fabrics, yarn and thread mills	24	(*)	2	26
17	Miscellaneous textile goods and floor coverings	4	0	(*)	4
18	Apparel	82	1	5	87
19	Miscellaneous fabricated textile products	125	5	13	144
20	Lumber and wood products, except containers	17	(*)	1	19
21	Wood containers	9	(*)	1	9
22	Household furniture	15	(*)	1	16
23	Other furniture and fixtures	40	1	5	45
24	Paper and allied products, except containers	30	1	3	35
25	Paperboard containers and boxes	10	(*)	1	11
26	Printing and publishing	165	2	10	177
27	Chemicals and selected chemical products	795	52	25	873
28	Plastics and synthetic materials	35	(*)	(*)	36
29	Drugs, cleaning and toilet preparations	106	2	15	123
30	Paints and allied products	1	0	(*)	2
31	Petroleum refining and related industries	682	69	144	895
32	Rubber and miscellaneous plastics products	187	6	23	216
33	Leather tanning and finishing	(*)	0	0	(*)
34	Footwear and other leather products	6	(*)	1	6

35	Glass and glass products	16	(*)	2	18
36	Stone and clay products	10	0	1	11
37	Primary iron and steel manufacturing	168	4	13	184
38	Primary nonferrous metals manufacturing	−17	−2	1	−17
39	Metal containers	8	(*)	1	9
40	Heating, plumbing, and structural metal products	142	4	7	152
41	Screw machine products and stampings	44	(*)	3	47
42	Other fabricated metal products	130	3	18	151
43	Engines and turbines	191	3	11	205
44	Farm and garden machinery	9	(*)	1	10
45	Construction and mining machinery	112	1	18	1 30
46	Materials handling machinery and equipment	37	1	2	40
47	Metalworking machinery and equipment	66	0	4	70
48	Special industry machinery and equipment	44	(*)	2	46
49	General industrial machinery and equipment	152	2	16	170
50	Miscellaneous machinery, except electrical	46	8	5	58
51	Office, computing, and accounting machines	269	2	28	299
52	Service industry machines	45	(*)	8	54
53	Electrical industrial equipment and apparatus	405	1	13	419
54	Household appliances	7	0	1	8
55	Electric lighting and wiring equipment	24	(*)	3	27
56	Radio, TV, and communication equipment	4,633	14	80	4,727
57	Electronic components and accessories	456	3	17	476
58	Miscellaneous electrical machinery and supplies	91	4	10	105
59	Motor vehicles and equipment	455	13	18	485
60	Aircraft and parts	7,422	17	135	7,573
61	Other transportation equipment	1,410	(*)	9	1,419
62	Scientific and controlling instruments	431	2	48	480
63	Optical, ophthalmic, and photographic equipment	2 35	1	47	283
64	Miscellaneous manufacturing	45	3	9	56
65	Transportation and warehousing				
66	Communications, except radio and TV				
67	Radio and TV broadcasting				
68	Electric, gas, water, and sanitary services				
69	Wholesale and retail trade				
70	Finance and insurance				
71	Real estate and rental				
72	Hotels; personal and repair services exc. auto.				
73	Business services				
74	Eating and drinking places				
75	Automobile repair and services				
76	Amusements				
77	Medical, educational services, nonprofit org.				
78	Federal Government enterprises				
79	State and local government enterprises				
80	Noncomparable imports	2,919	0	(*)	2,927
81	Scrap, used, and secondhand goods	19	0	8	27

Source: Department of Commerce, *Survey of Current Business,* April, 1979, p. 52.

Table 19.2
Key Defense Sectors' Percent of Defense Output: 1972

Sector		Percent of Defense Output
13	Ordnance and accessories	6.1%
	Complete guided missiles	
	Ammunition, except for small arms	
	Tanks and tank components	
	Small arms	
	Small arms ammunition	
	Other ordnance and accessories	
56	Radio, TV, and communication equipment	6.3%
	Radio and TV receiving sets	
	Phonograph records and tape	
	Telephone and telegraph apparatus	
	Radio and TV communication equipment	
60	Aircraft and parts	10.3%
	Aircraft	
	Aircraft and missile engines and engine parts	
	Aircraft and missile equipment	
61	Other transportation equipment	1.9%
	Ship building and repairing	
	Boat building and repairing	
	Railroad equipment	
	Motorcycles, bicycles, and parts	
	Travel trailers and campers	
	Mobile homes	
	Transportation equipment	
80	Noncomparable imports	3.9%

Source: Department of Commerce, Survey of Current Business, April 1979, pp. 51–72.

Table 19.3
Major Suppliers to the Aircraft Industry: 1972

Number	Supply Industry	Percent of Aircraft Total Input Value
37	Primary Iron and Steel	2.4%
38	Non-ferrous Metals	3.3%
56	Communications Equipment	4.4%
57	Electronic Components	2.5%
73	Business Services	3.4%
74	Eating and Drinking Places	2.8%

Source: Department of Commerce, Survey of Current Business, April 1979, p. 65.

The purpose of tracing this chain of effects is to show how interdependent the defense sector is with all major industries in the economy. An earlier study by Wassily Leontief, using a 1958 input-output table, also indicates the interdependent nature of the United States economy.[1] Leontief's study, discussed briefly in Chapter 8, was constructed to show the effect of a significant reduction in the output of the defense sector, and a reallocation of this output to other final demand sectors, on output and employment in civilian industries. Although Leontief's data base is over 20 years old, the results of the Leontief study can be used as a rough guide to the impact of changes in defense spending.

Table 19.4 shows the top and bottom five industries affected by a 20 percent reduction in the defense budget, in terms of the percentage change in employment resulting in that industry. To generate these numbers, Leontief transferred the 20 percent reduction in military spending in pro rata fashion across all final demand categories other than defense purchases. The results, based on our preceding discussions, are somewhat predictable. The biggest losers in case of a defense spending cut would be those industries that have the largest sales to the defense industry: ordnance, aircraft and parts, ships and boats, and communications equipment. The biggest gainers are many of the industries that flourish with a rise in consumer spending, such as rail transportation, restaurants and amusements, and tobacco and alcoholic beverages. The shift in employment, taking into consideration the labor-intensive nature of the defense sector, would result in a net reduction of 120 thousand man-years, or the loss of employment of .2 of 1 percent of the entire 1958 labor force.[2]

The above conclusions can be reversed in the case of a mobilization. If the defense sector were suddenly required to increase by 20 percent, the percentage changes shown in the preceding paragraphs indicate which sectors would pick up a substantial increase in demand, under the assumption that the increases were financed by proportional decreases in the other sectors in the economy. This is an important point to note, because it indicates the significant pressure that an increase in military spending puts on the civilian labor market. Equal boosts in military and civilian spending do not result in similar increases in the demand for labor. Rather, increases in military spending generate a larger labor requirement.

Table 19.4
Industries Affected by a 20 Percent Reduction in Defense Spending and a 20 Percent Increase in Civilian Spending
(Percent Change in Employment)

Five Most Adversely Affected

Industry	Percent Change in Employment (1958 Man-Years)
1. Ordnance	−19.2
2. Aircraft and Parts	−17.9
3. Ships and Boats	−11.0
4. Radio	− 6.1
5. Aluminium	− 2.8

Five Most Favorably Affected

Industry	Percent Change in Employment (1958 Man-Years)
1. Railway Equipment	+ 2.0
2. Restaurants, Hotels, Amusements	+ 1.8
3. Tobacco, Alcoholic Beverages	+ 1.7
4. Banking, Finance	+ 1.7
5. Apparel	+ 1.6

Source: Wassily Leontief, Input-Output Economics (New York: Oxford, 1966), pp. 180–181.

Many observers have argued that this net increase in the demand for skilled and unskilled labor implies that military spending is, in some sense, more inflationary than comparable increases in civilian spending. This argument rests upon the specious assumption, however, that the complementary capital requirements for the civilian-related final demand and military-related final demand are unrelated to the rate of inflation. If the defense sector generates a greater increase in the demand for labor than does a comparable increase in the demand for civilian goods, it may be true that military spending results in greater pressure in the labor market than does civilian spending. This greater pressure will be translated into pressure on wages for those labor categories that are short in supply, and these cost increases will be inflationary.

It is equally true, however, that an increase in defense output also requires net increases in the direct and indirect demand for capital inputs. If the military spending increase also generates higher net capital requirements than does the nondefense increase, the argument could be made that, based on cost-pressure considerations, military spending is more inflationary than comparable increases in civilian spending. Unfortunately, however, the Leontief study did not compute the net capital requirements for the shift in expenditures, and therefore it is not clear that increases in the military budget are any more or less inflationary than changes in the civilian sector.

A related use of input-output analysis that has received considerable attention has been in connection with the size and composition of the strategic stockpile of raw materials mentioned briefly in Chapter 16. Given a set of assumptions regarding the impact of mobilization on final demand, an input-output model provides an estimate of the resulting increase in output levels across all sectors of the economy. Based on usage coefficients for various raw materials, the implied increase in total demand for those materials may easily be calculated using the I-O model. Most particularly in the case of materials provided by foreign suppliers and hence not a reliable source in wartime, these estimates may be used to identify potential problem areas and gauge stockpile requirements.

REGIONAL CONSIDERATIONS IN DEFENSE SPENDING

In a follow-up study to his analysis of the industrial impact of changes in the defense budget, Leontief constructed a regional input-output model to analyze the geographical impact of changes in defense spending. A regional input-output table disaggregates outputs and inputs on a regional basis and defines the regional impact of various changes in final demand.

Leontief used the same methodology as described in the preceding section to analyze the effect of changes in defense expenditures on various regions in the United States. A summary of Leontief's results is shown in Table 19.5. The data in the table show the percentage change in employment by regional grouping associated with a 20 percent decrease in final demand for defense purchases. The data shown give the five regions most positively and negatively affected by changes in military spending and the concomitant increase or decrease in labor for proportionate increases in all other components of aggregate demand.

Those most likely to suffer from a cut in defense spending would be the states in the western and southwestern United States. California heads the list of states most likely to benefit from increases in defense spending and, as a result of its aerospace industry, it would be most seriously affected in the case of a major defense reduction. The midwestern states, on the other hand, gain very little from defense spending in the aggregate, and would stand to gain substantially from a readjustment of final demand away from defense spending and towards civilian-related spending.

Such geographical insights are interesting for a variety of reasons. The most obvious is their impact on economic planning by states that are most affected by defense expenditure changes. A more subtle reason for interest is the political effect of geographical impact. The political representatives of those states that are most positively affected by increased defense spending will be legitimately biased to vote in favor of such increases, while those representatives from states that gain least from defense spending may be more inclined to oppose such outlays. Thus the geographical distribution of benefits may help explain defense spending voting behavior.

Table 19.5
Regions Affected by a 20 Percent Decrease in Defense Spending and a 20 Percent Increase in Nondefense Spending

Five Most Adversely Affected:

Region	Percent Change in Employment (1958 Man-Years)
1. California	−1.9
2. Colorado–New Mexico	−1.4
3. Arizona–Nevada–Utah	−1.4
4. Maryland, Virginia, Delaware, West Virgina, and District of Columbia	− 1.4
5. Texas	− 1.0

Five Most Favorably Affected

1. Minnesota, North Dakota, South Dakota	+ 1.5
2. Idaho, Montana, Wyoming	+ 1.3
3. Indiana, Illinois, Wisconsin	+ .9
4. Michigan, Ohio	+ .9
5. New York	+ .7

Source: Leontief, op. cit., 197.

TARGETING AND INPUT-OUTPUT ANALYSIS

The final area of interest in this brief review of the defense applications of input-output analysis is concerned with the economic consequences of profound disruptions, such as war or embargo. Our analysis of the structure of the American economy has shown us the relationship of the various sectors in the economic system to the defense sector. This information can be very useful to an enemy in either an era of increased tensions, in conventional conflicts, or in a strategic nuclear conflict. For example, in an era of increased tension it may become important to know the impact of trade restrictions on the production of defense services. If very little of a particular commodity is domestically produced, an input-output table would be very useful in determining the effect of a trade embargo on the defense sector or on key civilian sectors (i.e., food).

A second major use of an input-output model would be in the planning of strategic targeting. During World War II, the allied bombing effort was directed, in many cases, at industries which were key, in an intersectoral sense, to the German economic base. Two major examples of such strikes included the bombing of the oilfields at Ploesti and the ballbearing factory at Schweinfurt. In both of these cases the commodities were not of significant importance to the direct production of German defense output, but were critical in an interindustry sense to Germany's ability to wage war.

In the current environment, the use of an input-output analysis for planning conventional bombing missions as well as for counter-value strategic nuclear strikes would indicate those sectors that would economically cripple an opponent with the least number of strikes. Generating a set of tables similar to Tables 19.2 and 19.4 as well as the regional tables would enable targeters to set priorities regarding their use of sorties or warheads.

CONCLUSION

Defense expenditures have important impacts on a wide array of sectors of the United States economy. It is not surprising to discover that the final demands for defense purchases fall most heavily on the aircraft, ordnance, and communications sectors, but the ripple effects of such outlays on the rest of the economy are less intuitively obvious. Input-output analysis provides a powerful tool for estimating the impacts of changes in defense outlays on the entire economy, including those sectors which simply provide inputs to producers of defense-related outputs.

Leontief used the input-output technique to estimate the sectoral impact of a 20 percent reduction in defense expenditures which was offset by a corresponding increase in nondefense government purchases. This exercise has obvious relevance to situations of rapid mobilization or demobilization. His analysis indicated that the cuts in defense spending would hit most heavily on labor-intensive industries, and that the offsetting increases in other government programs would tend to stimulate activity in less labor-intensive sectors. As a result, a sharp cut in defense outlays could produce a significant increase in unemployment.

This example is only illustrative of the insights which input-output analysis can provide. The use of the technique in anticipating the impacts of economic disruptions on our defense capacity, or conversely in estimating the impact of such disruptions on adversaries, is extremely powerful.

An area of increasing concern is the ability of our industrial base to provide expanded defense production in the case of mobilization. Some industrial capacity can be quickly diverted to defense production. The reduction in the production of other non-defense goods, however, may have severe impacts on the rest of the economy. Input-output analysis permits planners to anticipate where critical shortages might occur, and to estimate the extent of stockpiling of critical items which should be completed before mobilization.

NOTES

1 Wassily Leontief, *Input-Output Economics* (New York: Oxford University Press, 1966), pp. 167–183.
2 The reduction in employment is given in Leontief, *op. cit.*, p. 181. The labor force data are from the *Economic Report of the President, 1978*, p. 288.
3 Leontief, *op. cit.*, pp. 184–222.

SELECTED REFERENCES

Economic Report of the President, 1976 (Washington, D.C.: Government Printing Office, 1976), pp. 39–47.
Wassily Leontief, *Input-Output Economics* (New York: Oxford University Press, 1966).

Part VI

The International Aspects of the Economics of National Security

There is no security on this earth; there is only opportunity.

Douglas MacArthur

Only one fellow in ten thousand understands the currency question, and we meet him every day.
Frank McKinney Hubbard

The future is like everything else—it isn't what it used to be.

Anonymous

Those who invented the law of supply and demand have no right to complain when this law works against their interest.

Anwar Sadat of Egypt on the price of oil

Chapter 20
Foreign Trade and Finance

INTRODUCTION

The study of economics in the United States has normally been preoccupied with the behavior of a "closed economy" with a small, relatively insignificant international sector. The decision-making process in the federal government has also tended to de-emphasize the importance of international economics and to treat the domestic economy as if it were essentially immune from international economic shocks. An acknowledgment of increasing economic interdependence was forced upon the United States by a variety of factors in the 1970s, particularly by the related declines in the value of the dollar relative to other currencies and a persistent excess of foreign imports over United States exports, exacerbated by the dramatic increase in the price of crude oil. The Organization of Petroleum Exporting Countries (OPEC) crude oil embargo in 1973 and the associated increases in oil prices for the rest of the decade underscored the vulnerability of the United States economy to international economic shocks.

Before we proceed to an analysis of the extent of economic interdependence in the last quarter of the twentieth century and the consequences of that interdependence for national security policy, we must review three important economic concepts: comparative advantage and the case for free trade, the balance of payments, and a supply and demand analysis of exchange rate determination. These are clearly related ideas. The benefits of specialization embodied in the idea of comparative advantage provide the impetus for international (as well as domestic) trade. The resultant flows of goods and services produce corresponding claims for transfers of currency to finance the transactions. The net accumulation of claims for different currencies in the hands of foreign citizens creates pressure for adjustments in the market values of those currencies. If currency markets are left free to balance these changes in the supply and demand for different currencies, exchange rates will be automatically adjusted to shifting trade patterns. If governments intervene to prevent fluctuations in exchange rates, they must also intervene in managing the supply and demand of different currencies, or even in adjusting the patterns of international trade.

We will begin by describing a "perfectly competitive" world in which there are no impediments to the free exchange of information, goods, and services. Producers analyze the costs of using foreign and domestic resources and consumers evaluate domestic and foreign products on the basis of quality and price alone: governments do not intervene to promote domestic products or impede foreign imports. Exchange rates are constantly adjusting relative currency values in line with changes in trade patterns, so that year after year the value of goods exported from each nation expressed in units of that nation's currency tends to equal the value of goods imported. This, of course, assumes that trade patterns adjust quickly to shifts in relative prices, and that exchange rates are also rapidly adjusted to reflect underlying shifts in comparative advantage.

Naturally, this perfectly competitive world is a far cry from the world we see around us with imperfect flows of information, tariff barriers, trade quotas, government subsidies, persisting imbalances in trade patterns, and government intervention in currency markets. But the competitive model does provide important insights into the underlying forces of international economics, and it is easier to understand the consequences of deviation from the competitive model once those underlying forces are understood. In the final sections of the chapter we will address the pressures resulting in deviation from the competitive model, and the implications of dynamic factors for our basic conclusions.

COMPARATIVE ADVANTAGE AND THE ARGUMENT FOR FREE TRADE

Comparative Advantage and Specialization

Trade occurs because individuals quickly discover that by specializing in the production of some goods and services, they can produce more than their own needs, sell the surplus to others, and then use their earnings to purchase the other goods and services that they want. Everyone benefits from this process as long as each individual produces those goods or services which he or she is *relatively* most efficient in producing. The market automatically creates this result by offering wage differentials based on the laws of supply and demand to attract individuals to the jobs in which they will receive the highest return. For example, the lawyer may be an excellent typist, but the market indicates a higher return from counseling clients, and the lawyer will find that a higher income may be earned by hiring a secretary to do the typing. The secretary does not have the qualifications to be a successful attorney, and will earn a higher income by typing.

Note that the market produced this pattern of specialization without any government decree to exploit the *comparative advantage* of each individual. In addition, specialization helped everyone. The lawyer was able to free more time for legal counseling by spending less time typing, and because the wage for counseling is higher than the wage for typing, this specialization increased the lawyer's net income. The typist, who may have been wrestling ineffectively with legal problems at home, can now concentrate on typing and earn enough income to hire legal assistance. The typist may never earn enough income to match that of the lawyer, but they will both be better off than they were before.

This principle, of course, applies in international as well as domestic trade. If, for some reason, all the individuals with a comparative advantage in typing lived in one nation, and those with a comparative advantage in law lived in another, the advantages of specialization would still exist. The only change would be that the wage payments would constitute claims for foreign rather than domestic currency. Moreover, the pattern of specialization would develop without any government program to exploit comparative advantage, and without any elaborate economic studies at the local universities.

The key to trade is a difference in "*opportunity costs*" among nations. Opportunitiy costs are simply the alternatives to any decision. In our simple example, the lawyer's opportunity cost in doing more typing is a reduced amount of legal counseling. Opportunity costs are the result of scarcity, in this case the limited amount of time available to the lawyer. The lawyer can shift outputs between counseling and typing by changing the amount of time allocated to each. We may think of this mix of outputs that the lawyer may produce from different allocations of time as a production possibility frontier, shown in Figure 20.1. The opportunity cost of more typing (a shift from A to B) is less legal counseling (a corresponding shift from C to D). The secretary, on the other hand, has a different set of opportunity costs, as reflected by the more gradual slope of the secretary's production possibility frontier. The secretary's opportunity cost of increasing typing from A to B is a reduction in legal counseling from E to F—a much smaller reduction than the lawyer's drop from C to D. Thus the secretary's opportunity costs from doing more typing are much lower than the lawyer's.

This difference in opportunity costs is the stimulus for trade. As an illustration, the lawyer can hire the secretary to complete an amount of typing corresponding to B-A, expand legal counseling by C-D, provide the secretary with an amount of legal counseling corresponding to E-F, and still have a surplus of legal counseling. Of course, common sense told us that the would be the case, but the illustration emphasizes the idea that trade occurs because of differences in opportunity costs.

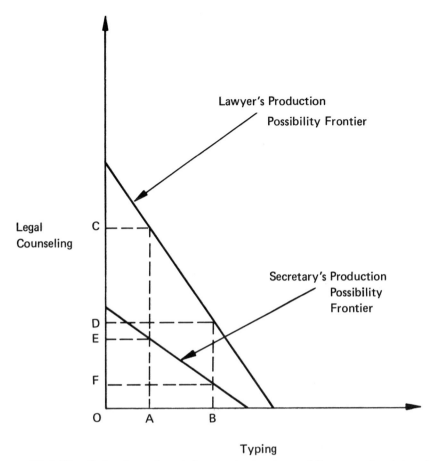

Figure 20.1 The Gains from Specialization in the Area of Comparative Advantage

Note:

In this case the lawyer has an *absolute* advantage in both counseling and typing, but the lawyer's greatest advantage—or *comparative advantage*—is in counseling.

Comparative Advantage and International Trade

Now let's shift our attention from individuals to nations. Differences in opportunity costs among individuals result from differences in intelligence, skills, education, and so forth. Differences in opportunity costs among nations result from different distributions of land, labor, capital, and entrepreneurial skill. The greater the differences in relative opportunity costs, the stronger the impetus for specialization and trade will be.

Consider Figure 20.2, which sketches hypothetical production possibility frontiers for the United States and Japan for wheat and cameras. The curves show the maximum amount of wheat and cameras that can be produced by allocating different portions of the nations' resources to the two products. Study the curves and determine which country has a comparative advantage in each product. Note that the United States has an absolute advantage in the production of each product, because if each country were to allocate all of its resources to the production of wheat, the United States can produce more wheat, and if each country allocated all resources to producing cameras, the United States could produce more cameras. But the principle of comparative advantage suggests that each nation will be better off by specializing in the product in which its opportunity costs are relatively lower, and then trading for the product in which its opportunity costs are relatively higher. The opportunity costs are reflected in the slopes of the production possibility frontiers. In this case, the

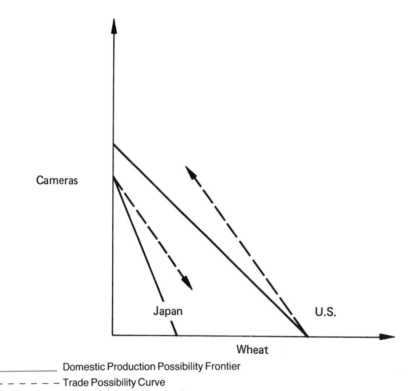

Cameras

Japan   U.S.

Wheat

———————————— Domestic Production Possibility Frontier

– – – – – – – – – Trade Possibility Curve

Figure 20.2 Hypothetical Production Possibility Frontiers and
Trade Possibility Curves for the United States and Japan

Note:

The slope of the trade possibility curve is $-\dfrac{\text{Price of Wheat}}{\text{Price of Cameras}}$

Japan moves along its trade possibility curve by producing cameras, selling some of them, and then buying wheat from the United States.

United States must give up more units of wheat than Japan in order to produce additional cameras, but the United States can produce more additional wheat with a smaller sacrifice in camera production. The United States, therefore, has a comparative advantage in producing wheat, and Japan has a comparative advantage in producing cameras.

The theory of comparative advantage simply explains a pattern of specialization that will automatically emerge as the result of market forces. United States wheat exporters will take advantage of the high cost of wheat in Japan by buying United States wheat and selling it in Japan. The increased demand for United States wheat will drive up wheat prices in the United States, increase farm profits, and lead to an expansion in resources allocated to the production of wheat. At the same time, Japanese exporters will be selling Japanese cameras in the United States, taking markets away from the higher cost United States producers and increasing the profits of Japanese camera producers. Resources in Japan will shift from wheat to cameras, while resources in the United States shift from cameras to wheat. The ratio at which cameras are exchanged for wheat in international trading will be determined by the overall supply and demand for the two products in both countries, but we know that the trade ratio must lie somewhere between the domestic production opportunity costs of the two countries in order for trade to occur.

Consider Figure 20.2 again. If Japan produces only cameras and then trades for wheat, it will only be better off if it gets more wheat per camera in trade than it could obtain by shifting resources in domestic production. The dotted line shows one trade ratio that would make Japan better off through trade. Japan could move along its trade possibility curve by selling cameras and buying back wheat from the United States, improving on its domestic possibilities. Similarly, the United States could produce wheat and then move along its trade possibility curve by selling wheat and buying cameras from Japan. The trade ratios for the two countries must be the same, because they are determined by relative prices on international markets. Thus the trade possibility curves on Figure 20.2 are parallel. Japan will benefit from a trade ratio that converts cameras to wheat at a higher rate than its domestic opportunity costs, and the United States will benefit from a trade ratio that converts wheat into cameras at a higher rate than its domestic opportunity costs. The domestic opportunity costs of the two nations therefore form the limit of trade ratios that would make each country benefit from trade. Any trade ratio between these limits would make each nation profit from specializing in its comparative advantage.

The advantages of trade, unfortunately, are not clearly reflected in the national income accounts. The difference between the value of exports and the value of imports (net exports) is entered as a component of the gross national product for each nation. But what is not obvious is that even if the level of imports and exports is equal, trade has increased the gross national product by permitting a more efficient allocation of resources in each nation. Suppose that the United States were exploiting its comparative advantage in wheat production, but United States camera producers were able to convince Congress to impose an import tariff on Japanese cameras. The Japanese would retaliate with a tariff on wheat, and in each case the tariff would be sufficient to completely eliminate trade. Resources in each country would now be reallocated to produce outputs that can be produced less efficiently at home than abroad. The result will be lower GNPs in each nation. Thus the case against imposing tariff barriers is that such restrictions hurt each nation through the resultant misallocation of resources.

Arguments Against Free Trade

Of course there are valid arguments against permitting the nation's economy to adjust freely to the pattern of production suggested by relative international prices. If a nation controls enough of the market for some product to affect the world price of the product, it may be to that nation's advantage to restrict foreign sales in order to raise the world price. Unfortunately, such a policy may lead to retaliation in other markets in which the nation has less market power. The "infant industry" argument is also frequently raised in defense of intervening in free trade patterns. According to this argument, a tariff would be applied to some import in order to provide a protected local market for domestic producers. As the scale of production of the domestic producers expanded they would become more efficient, and ultimately the protective barriers could be removed and the domestic industry could compete for world markets. Arguments against the infant industry's justification of protective tariffs are that the goals of stimulating domestic production can be accomplished more effectively through subsidies, and that the protective tariff laws are rarely repealed as the industry matures. Perhaps the distribution of income resulting from trade patterns may be undesirable on political grounds. Once again, other remedies might be found to redress income differentials, and adjusting trade patterns may be an inefficient way of achieving such objectives. Finally, the national defense argument is often raised suggesting that a nation should not become dependent on foreign sources of critical war materials. This argument is addressed in more detail in Chapter 22.

THE BALANCE OF PAYMENTS

International exchanges of goods and services produce claims for payment in the currency in which the sale is denominated. Claims for international payments also arise as the result of financial transactions such as the purchase or sale of plant and equipment, land, stocks, or bonds in a foreign country. The nation's balance of payments "deficit" is the amount by which foreign claims for payment exceed domestic claims for foreign payments each year. Such deficits must be offset by an exchange of reserves (currency, gold) to correct imbalances. As we will see, actions by individuals and central banks will always keep the total flow of transactions in balance, although particular types of payments may not be equal.

The balance of payments accounts include three types of transactions. The current account includes the debits and credits for the flow of goods, services, gifts, and other transfers. An export of a good creates a claim for foreign payment and enters the account as a credit, while an import of a good creates a claim for domestic payment and enters the account as a debit. That portion of the current account which deals only with the exchange of goods and services is termed the *balance of trade*. The second portion of the balance of payments is the *capital account*, which includes credits and debits for short- and long-term capital transfers. Short-term capital flows, such as international purchases of short-term debt instruments, are highly volatile and shift from country to country, chasing the highest rate of return based on relative interest rates, inflation rates, and exchange rate fluctuations. Long-term capital flows, such as direct investment in plant and equipment, foreign stocks, or long-term debt instruments, tend to be more stable year after year. Once again, any transaction that creates a claim for foreign payment enters the balance of payments accounts as a credit, and the United States capital accounts would therefore get credits for foreign purchases of United States bonds, and debits for the purchases of foreign bonds by United States citizens.

A surplus on current account means that a nation is accumulating claims for foreign payments based on the exchange of goods and services, and may use those claims to finance the purchase of foreign debt or assets. This was the case for the United States in the decades of the fifties and sixties, as current account surpluses were used to finance the acquisition of foreign assets. In the seventies, the United States balance on current account was often in deficit, and the claims accumulated by foreign citizens were used to purchase United States assets.

If the exchanges of currency brought about by transactions in the current account and the capital account are not in balance, the exchange value of the currency must shift, or the reserve position of a central bank must change. Consider the case of a Japanese exporter who has accumulated $100 million as the result of sales in the United States. If he simply holds the dollars, we will credit the United States with a short-term capital flow, and the payments will automatically balance. If he attempts to sell the dollars for yen, the value of the dollar in terms of yen (the exchange rate) will fall in international money markets. If the Japanese or United States central banks wish to prevent this change in the value of the yen and the dollar, they would have to enter the international markets with their reserves. In this case the United States Federal Reserve can use its reserves of yen to buy dollars and bid the exchange rate back up to the former level. In the case of a pure market adjustment, the exchange rate will adjust to bring the flow of payments enumerated in dollars back into balance. In the case of intervention by the Federal Reserve, the balance will be restored by the change in the official reserve position of the central bank.

Let's put all of these transactions together as they would appear in the balance of payments accounts. First, the current account balance is the sum of the balance on goods and services ($X - M$, Exports minus Imports) and net unilateral transfers ($T_{in} - T_{out}$) such as gifts, pensions to those retired overseas, etc:

$$\text{Current Account Balance} = (X - M) + (T_{in} - T_{out}). \tag{20.1}$$

Second, the capital account balance is the sum of net short-term capital flows ($S_{in} - S_{out}$) and net long-term capital flows ($L_{in} - L_{out}$).

$$\text{Capital Account Balance} = (S_{in} - S_{out}) + (L_{in} - L_{out}). \tag{20.2}$$

The sum of the current account and capital account balances is termed the Official Reserves Transactions Balance, since this amount must be settled by official transactions of central banks. The official reserve transactions are the sum of the change in liquid assets denominated in dollars held by central banks (CLA) and the change in foreign exchange reserves (CR), such as foreign currencies, gold, and special drawing rights that are held by central banks:[1]

$$\text{Official Reserve Transactions} = CLA + CR. \tag{20.3}$$

The net payments are always in balance, because there will either be a net balance between the current and capital accounts, or there will be an exchange rate adjustment, or there will be a change in official reserve transactions.

Balance of Payments $= 0 =$
Current Account Balance $+$ Capital Account Balance $+$ Official Reserve Transactions.   (20.4)

Transactions in each portion of the account occur continuously, and there is no great day of reckoning at the end of the year.

But to observe that the payments must always balance is not to argue that there can never be a balance of payments problem. Indeed, we are very concerned with what is happening in each area of the balance of payments accounts. If the current account is persistently in debit, we will observe either the foreign purchase of United States assets, a persistent decline in the reserve position of the Federal Reserve Bank, or continuing pressure on the exchange value of the dollar.

If we were willing to let the value of the dollar rise and fall on international markets, to allow our economy to adjust to shifting patterns of international comparative advantage, and to accept the redistribution of international assets resulting from free flows of capital, we would not be very concerned with the balance of payments. This is, of course, the judgment we have made about the flows of trade between New York and New Jersey. But to the extent that we wish to control the exchange rate, to shield the domestic economy against shifts in trade patterns, and to regulate the transfer of international assets, we attempt to influence the structure of our international payments.

Intervening in the economy to modify our balance of payments position can include tariff barriers, subsidies to exporters, import and export quotas, monetary and fiscal policies with broader effects on the national economy, or direct intervention in foreign exchange markets. Tariffs, subsidies, and quotas have a direct impact on current account transactions, but in addition to risking retaliatory acts by other nations, such actions reduce economic efficiency by misallocating our resources and blocking access to the gains from trade. Monetary policy can be used to adjust interest rates and attract foreign capital, but high interest rates also depress domestic investment and reduce aggregate demand. Restrictive monetary and fiscal policies may be used to reduce domestic inflation and make United States products more competitive overseas, and such restrictive policies may also lower national income and reduce the demand for imports. Depressing the national economy, however, is a high price to pay for stability in international payments. Direct intervention in currency markets may help, but such intervention is limited by available reserves and depends on the cooperation of other central banks. The real costs of problems with the balance of payments must therefore be measured in terms of the negative consequences of the policy alternatives available to redress persistent imbalances.

EXCHANGE RATES: FLOATING OR FIXED

Floating Rates and The Balance of Payments

In the wonderful world of the freely floating (perfectly competitive) exchange rates, we would encounter few problems with the balance of payments, or at least that was the conventional economic wisdom until the 1970s. As Paul Volcker, Chairman of the Federal Reserve Board, noted, "Mainly schooled in and preoccupied with the economics of a closed (or nearly closed) economy, the economists tended to see floating primarily as a way of freeing macro policy from the awkward external constraints of the balance of payments."[2]

Let us examine how floating exchange rates might free macroeconomic policy from the problems of adjusting the balance of payments. The "exchange rate" is the price of one currency in terms of another, or simply the rate at which one currency can be exchanged for another. In the early 1980s, the dollar could be exchanged for about 2 West German marks or 225 Japanese yen. The exchange rate may be used to convert the prices of an exporting nation's products into the currency units of the importing nation. Thus, a shift in exchange rates means a shift in the prices of imports and exports.

For example, assume that an American consumer is considering the purchase of a Japanese stereo system. The price of the stereo in dollars is the price in yen times the exchange rate expressed in dollars per yen. If the stereo sells for 22,500 yen, and the exchange rate is 1 dollar per 225 yen, the price in dollars is $100. The higher the exchange value of the dollar, the lower the price of the stereo is in the United States. If the exchange rate were 1 dollar per 450 yen, the price of the stereo in dollars would be $50. Thus a higher exchange value of the dollar should be associated with a larger volume of imports into the United States.

On the other hand, a high exchange value of the dollar would make United States exports expensive in terms of foreign currency. At an exchange rate of 225 yen per dollar, a bushel of soybeans selling for $8 in the United States would cost 1800 yen in Japan. At an exchange rate of 450 yen per dollar, the same bushel would cost 3600 yen in Japan. Thus a higher exchange value of the dollar should be associated with a lower volume of United States exports. Figure 20.3 shows how a shifting exchange rate can change the relative prices of imports and exports in two countries, alter trade patterns, and affect the supply and demand for a currency.

The demand for dollars by foreign citizens is a function of their desire to purchase United States goods, services, capital, or financial instruments. Any such transaction that created an obligation to make a payment to a United States citizen would be treated as a credit in the United States balance of payments. The demand for dollars by foreign citizens, as we have seen, will be a function of the exchange value of the dollar. At higher exchange rates, United States goods will be expensive when prices are expressed in the foreign currency, and thus the demand for United States exports will be low. At lower exchange rates, United States goods will be less expensive when prices are expressed in the foreign currency, the demand for United States exports will be higher, and the demand for dollars to finance the export sales will be higher.

Exactly the reverse pattern will apply to imports and the supply of dollars available to foreign citizens. At high exchange rates, the dollar will buy more foreign currency, and thus the prices of foreign products expressed in dollars will be low. The supply of dollar claims (debits in the balance of payments accounts) will be greater, the higher the exchange rate. At lower exchange rates, foreign goods will be more expensive in terms of dollars, imports will drop, and the supply of dollars will fall.

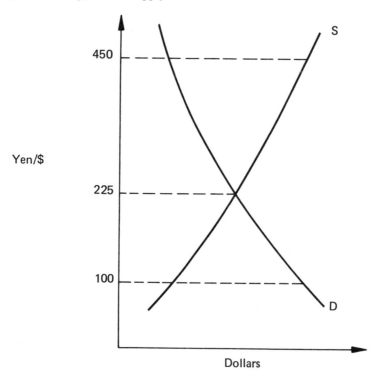

Figure 20.3 The Supply and Demand for Dollars as a Function of the Exchange Rate

Using the hypothetical curves shown in Figure 20.3, if the exchange rate were 450 yen per dollar, there would be a low demand for United States products (and hence for dollars) and a large supply of dollar claims as the result of large exports of foreign goods to the United States. At an exchange rate of 450 yen per dollar the supply of dollar claims would exceed the demand for dollars. Japanese banks would be accumulating dollar claims as Japanese firms exchanged them for yen. The Japanese banks would either sell the dollar claims in international money markets or sell them to the central bank. If the dollars were sold on international markets, the value of the dollar would have to fall in order to attract sufficient buyers to purchase the excess supply. If the central bank decided to hold the dollars and expand its dollar reserve position, the pressure on the dollar would be reduced. If the central bank decided not to support the dollar, the value of the dollar would fall.

Suppose the value of the dollar were bid all the way down to 100 yen. The devaluation of the dollar from 450 to 100 yen would increase the demand for the dollar (United States goods would now have a much lower price in yen) and decrease the supply of dollar claims (Japanese goods would now be much more expensive in terms of dollars). But there would then be an excess demand for dollars. Japanese importers would be exchanging yen for dollars to finance transactions, and banks would be forced to obtain dollars in international money markets or convince the central bank to reduce its dollar reserves. If the central bank made its reserves of dollars available at the new exchange rate, the pressure for a higher exchange rate would be reduced. But if the central bank did not support the yen, the excess demand for dollars would lead to an increase in the exchange rate as purchasers bid against each other to obtain the required dollars.

The exchange rate would continue to shift until it reached an equilibrium position at which the supply and demand for dollars was in balance. On Figure 20.3 this would occur at an exchange rate of 225 yen per dollar. At this point, payments made by United States citizens to finance foreign transactions (debits in the balance of payments) would be equal to payments made to United States citizens to finance transactions in the United States (credit in the balance of payments). Thus the process of permitting the market to determine the equilibrium exchange rate simultaneously insures that the balance in payments will occur without intervention by central banks. In other words, all of the adjustments will occur automatically in the current and capital accounts without any required change in the reserve positions of the central banks, or intervention by government in the form of monetary, fiscal, or tariff policy.

Problems with Floating Exchange Rates

Unfortunately, there are many problems with a freely floating exchange rate system. As we have seen, adjustments in exchange rates produce adjustments in relative international prices which should have some impact on trade levels. However, the price elasticity, or sensitivity, of demand may be very low, and large price adjustments and hence large exchange rate shifts may be required to create substantial shifts in the current account. In addition, the timing of impacts of an exchange rate shift may be different for imports and exports. For example, a devaluation of the dollar might be expected to stimulate United States exports and to reduce foreign imports. In the short run, however, traditional import patterns may persist, and it may take time for the new price advantage of United States products to have an impact on foreign export markets. In other words, the short run consequences of devaluation may simply be to increase the price of imports, thus adding to domestic inflation without a corresponding stimulus to exports. Economists call this the "J-Curve" pattern, because the immediate impact may be a deterioration in the current account balance, followed by a subsequent improvement. Moreover, most studies suggest that import levels are far more sensitive to income levels than to relative prices, and hence, changes in relative income levels tend to dominate price effects in the short run.

Thus, the impacts of exchange rate fluctuations on national income and inflation may be profound, and a floating exchange rate system may not be sufficient to shield the national economy from international economic shocks. Indeed, such a system may serve to transmit shocks based on shifts in expectations that may have little to do with underlying adjustments in comparative advantage. As Paul Volcker notes,

Above all, we have seen again and again what some had forgotten—in these circumstances, exchange rates can be dominated by expectations. . . . And those expectations will be volatile when divergences in national policies seem pronounced, or when those policies are subject to great uncertainty. . . . When patterns of trade or capital become influenced by monetary fluctuations rather than lasting comparative advantage, the underlying rationale of a liberal trade and investment order is undercut. The point is not merely theoretical. The instinctive political reaction in the face of seemingly capricious impacts on one industry or another is to protect or subsidize domestic industry, or to impede the flow of capital.[3]

Fixed Exchange Rates

To the extent that fluctuations in exchange rates are interpreted by policymakers as being inconsistent with underlying market forces, we would expect to see governments intervening to stabilize those rates. Indeed, if governments wished to insulate their economies from the price and output adjustments which would be triggered by changes in exchange rates, they could agree to fix, or *peg*, the relative values of their currencies.

Let's see how such a pegged exchange rate system works. Referring to Figure 20.3, suppose that Japan agreed to peg the exchange rate at 450 yen per dollar. At that exchange rate, the supply of dollars would exceed the demand, and there would be pressure for the exchange rate to drop. The central bank in Japan could enter the market, purchase the excess dollars at the pegged exchange rate, and eliminate the excess supply. The central bank would be supporting the dollar by agreeing to add to its dollar reserves at the agreed exchange rate. Of course, if this situation persisted, the Japanese central bank would accumulate more and more dollar reserves, and the United States would continue to run deficits in its combined current and capital accounts.

Under such a system of fixed exchange rates we would expect that the country which was forced to accumulate more and more foreign currency would ultimately object and demand some remedial action. In our illustration the Japanese would want the United States to adjust domestic monetary and fiscal policies to eliminate the trade imbalances. Such adjustments, however, would have adverse domestic consequences for the United States. In the case of a continuing deficit, the fiscal remedy would be to increase taxes or cut government spending, and the monetary remedy would be to restrict the money supply and force up interest rates, all of which would depress the national income, reduce imports, and improve the balance of payments. Unfortunately, these actions would also depress the national economy, lower investment, and increase unemployment. One would anticipate that governments might be reluctant to impose such restrictions on their economies in order to support a pegged exchange rate.

The alternatives in managing exchange rates, then, fall between two extremes. On the one hand, governments could permit the exchange value of their currencies to rise and fall with market conditions. This would automatically keep international payments in balance without requiring any domestic economic policy adjustments. Floating rates would, however, expose the domestic economy to continuous price, output, and employment adjustments as the economy adapted to different exchange rates. On the other hand, the government could attempt to fix the exchange rate in cooperation with other governments. This would shield the economy from continuous adjustments based on shifting exchange rates, but it would require Central Banks to intervene in the market to buy and sell currency, and it would require periodic, painful adjustments in domestic monetary and fiscal policy to support the fixed rate. As we shall see, the fixed exchange rate system adopted at the end of World War II gave way in 1971 to greater emphasis on floating rates. Since then a system has evolved in which Central Banks periodically intervene to moderate swings in exchange rates. The new system is often called a dirty float, to indicate that while rates do adjust to market forces the system is not pure, or clean, because Central Banks do intervene to control the extent and speed of such adjustments.

The Bretton Woods System

The arguments supporting free international trade as a way of exploiting the efficiencies of comparative advantage, presented so eloquently by Adam Smith and David Ricardo two centuries ago, did not exactly take the world by storm. British policies in the nineteenth century did slowly swing in the direction of free trade, but elsewhere, including the United States, high protective tariffs to defend developing domestic industry were the rule of the day. The Great Depression of the 1930s graphically illustrated the dangers of independent national policies directed at maximizing national balances of trade in the face of reduced domestic demand.

During the Great Depression, nations faced with falling national output attempted to increase their share of international markets by raising tariff barriers and devaluing their currencies. These competitive efforts simply reduced the potential gains from trade by lowering trade volume, as export reductions added to the tragedy of depression. The allies emerging from the Second World War decided to create a new economic order that would emphasize the benefits of free trade and simultaneously limit the possibility of competitive devaluations and tariff wars.

The Liberal Economic Order

The undamaged United States economy was to be the engine of the new liberal order, with the benefits of trade going first to the recovering economies of Western Europe and through them to the raw materials markets and the developing nations. In order to prevent competitive devaluations, the allies established a system of fixed, but adjustable, exchange rates, pegging currency values to the dollar based on the dollar's free convertibility into gold at a fixed price. In theory, this system, codified in the Bretton Woods Agreement of 1944, meant that participants would adjust national policies to insure an orderly pattern of exchange rates, and that the rates themselves would only be adjusted as a last resort.

Under the Bretton Woods System the value of the dollar was pegged to gold ($35 per ounce), and the United States government agreed to buy and sell gold at that price (although this was limited to purchases and sales by foreign governments in 1968). Other governments agreed to peg their currencies to the dollar, and the International Monetary Fund (IMF) was organized to assist members in securing the foreign exchange needed to support their currencies at the desired exchange rate. Small adjustments in exchange rates could be made unilaterally if required, but shifts over 10 percent were to be implemented only if the Fund approved of them on the basis of fundamental adjustments in trade patterns.

This new, liberal economic order was based on mutual commitment to free trade and lowered tariff barriers, to a system of swapping reserves when needed to defend established exchange rates, and to development assistance designed to spread the benefits of economic growth to poorer nations. The General Agreement on Trade and Tariffs (GATT) obligated the signatories to continuing reductions in tariff barriers, the International Monetary Fund (IMF) provided the mechanism for combining reserves and stabilizing exchange rates, and the World Bank established a framework for the multilateral transfer of funds for development. This overall structure was reinforced by the reduction of trade barriers in Western Europe through the establishment of the European Economic Community.

The postwar structure emphasized the interdependence of the western economies in general, and the merits of free trade in industrial products in particular. The communist nations were clearly exceptions to this general framework, but aside from the disruption of traditional trade patterns with Eastern Europe, this exclusion was not seen as a major problem. Similarly, agricultural and raw materials trade was never effectively drawn into the GATT framework, but these commodities were consistently seen as special cases which did not seriously erode the commitment to free trade in the industrial area.

For the 1950s and most of the 1960s, this liberal economic order prospered as long as central banks were willing to accumulate dollars. The dollar was overvalued compared to the level it would have reached in a free, floating market. The United States accumulated annual surpluses in its current account, because of its dominant position in manufacturing based on an industrial base that had escaped the ravages of war in Europe. The large deficits accumulated in the capital account resulting from heavy investment in Europe, however, more than offset the current account surpluses. The result was a steady flow of dollars overseas. The recovering economies of Europe and Japan benefitted from this arrangement, because of their tremendous requirements for capital investment. The Marshall Plan aid program or European Recovery Plan as it was officially known, which provided funds for restoring the industrial base in Europe, made the system even more palatable. The economic foundation of the Bretton Woods System was also reinforced by the convergence of political and military objectives reflected in the NATO alliance during the Cold War.

By 1971, however, many of these factors had changed. The level of dollars accumulated overseas made the gold exchange standard impractical. United States gold reserves were simply not sufficient to meet the potential claims at the announced price of gold. Moreover, the economies of Europe and Japan were fully recovered, and with newer capital incorporating the latest technology, they were very competitive with the United States in many markets. The umbrella of the Marshall Plan was no longer required, and there was a perceptible thaw in the Cold War. In short, the shift in economic, political, and military realities combined to make the Bretton Woods structure of pegged exchange rates obsolete.

Speculators were also having a field day with the fixed exchange rate system. International funds shifted from currency to currency, probing for weaknesses, and the speculators were frequently successful in anticipating and even forcing, devaluations. Such speculation in a pegged exchange rate system was a one-sided bet. Suppose you observed that Britain had a balance of payments problem, and the central bank was intervening to buy pounds to prevent a devaluation. Speculators would run in and sell their pounds for other currencies, anticipating the devaluation of the pound. If the central bank was unable to purchase all the pounds with its reserves of other currencies, the pound would have to be devalued. In this case, the speculators would win, because the currencies they held would now be worth more in terms of pounds. If the Bank of England successfully defended the pound, the speculators could simply buy back their pounds at the old exchange rate without incurring a loss. In the late 1960s the pound and then the French franc were devalued, and in 1971 there was enormous pressure for the value of the dollar to drop and the value of the German mark to rise.

The trade deficit that was generated in the United States in 1971—the first such deficit since before World War II—was the crowning blow to the Bretton Woods system of fixed exchange rates, as the United States first abandoned the convertibility of the dollar to gold, then negotiated two devaluations of the dollar, and finally permitted the dollar to float on international exchanges. At the same time that the economic order was adjusting to a system of floating exchange rates it was faced with a new problem of persisting high inflation that was strangely immune to the traditional medicine of restricting aggregate demand. Various experiments in price controls, most notably the United States controls structure that was in place from 1971 to 1974, failed to limit the upward pressure on prices.

The Soviet purchase of 25 percent of the United States grain crop in 1972 further fueled inflation and raised new questions of dealing with state-operated monopolies. The OPEC crude oil price increases of 1973 and the simultaneous embargo by the Organization of Arab Petroleum Exporting Countries (OAPEC) in retaliation for the Arab-Israeli War created major new strains on the economic system.

These shocks provided a major blow to the underlying rationale of the liberal economic order. That rationale suggested that the benefits of economic efficiency resulting from free exchange were worth the costs of adjusting to external economic shocks. It assumed that the problems of adjustment could be offset by internal economic programs, that the size of such shocks would be limited by exchange rate stability, and that major structural shifts in commodity prices would occur gradually, permitting ample time for the industrial nations to adapt. In the United States, the rationale was reinforced by the view that even abrupt shifts in international transactions could have little impact on a large national economy that had a relatively small foreign trade sector compared to the total level of annual output.

THE 1970s, A DECADE OF INTERNATIONAL ECONOMIC TURBULENCE

The decade of the 1970s began with the echoes of the collapsing Bretton Woods System ringing in the background. Refuge was ultimately sought in a system of floating exchange rates. As we noted earlier, such a system has clear advantages in immediately restoring any imbalances in international trade and capital flows. A deficit in the balance of payments would produce a surplus of claims for a nation's currency, the exchange rate would fall, and the prices of the nation's products would decline in terms of foreign currencies, stimulating exports and reducing imports. A surplus in the balance of payments would similarly produce an upward adjustment of the exchange rate, stimulating imports and reducing exports. If the required adjustments were moderate, such a system would have great merit. On the other hand, if exchange rates shifted rapidly the adjustments would be much more painful.

Unfortunately, the required adjustments in the 1970s were large and painful. The self-equilibrating mechanism of floating exchange rates worked slowly and clearly added to inflationary pressures in the United States. The devaluation of the dollar over the course of the decade added to the cost of imports immediately, but stimulated exports only with a long lag and exacerbated problems with the balance of payments rather than alleviating them. By the end of the decade the status of the dollar as the leading reserve currency was being eroded as central banks diversified into the German mark and the Japanese yen as protection against further devaluation of the dollar.

Current Account Dilemmas

The major economic shift in the 1970s was the dramatic increase in the price of crude oil (see Table 20.1), which came at a time when the United States, Western Europe, and Japan were already struggling against

Table 20.1
The Rising Price of Crude Oil: 1960–1982
(Average Price per Barrel)

Year	Current Dollars	Constant 1972 Dollars
1960	1.72	2.50
1970	1.78	1.95
1971	1.97	2.05
1972	2.10	2.10
1973	3.17	3.00
1974	11.37	9.80
1975	11.44	9.00
1976	12.17	9.10
1977	12.40	8.75
1978	12.16	8.00
1979	16.50	10.00
1980	28.12	15.85*
1981	31.84	16.45*
1982	32.40	15.70*

* Authors' estimate

Source: "The Cartel's Deadly New Sting," *Business Week* (April 9, 1979), p 99; Central Intelligence Agency, *Economic and Energy Indicators* (Washington, D.C.: August 6, 1982), p. 10.

Note: Estimating the "average" price of crude oil in a given year is a very tricky business because of significant differences in quality from different sources and because of a very complicated pricing system. These figures should therefore be taken as indicators of general trends in prices rather than precise levels in a given year.

growing inflation, when the dollar was already under attack as the international reserve currency, and when the rate of growth of productivity in the United States was declining. These trends all combined to place tremendous economic pressures on our major allies, and they threatened to undermine the economic pillar of our alliance structure. The dramatic upward surge in the price of gold as the decade ended was the crowning testimony to the widespread uncertainty over the stability of the international economic order.

Figure 20.4 portrays the imbalance of United States merchandise trade during the 1970s. The recession in 1974 and 1975 reduced income and hence the demand for imports, but from 1976 to 1979 imports exceeded exports by a significant amount. For example, in 1978 the United States ran a trade deficit of about $34 billion. In that year there was the usual trade surplus in agricultural products, but the traditional surplus in manufacturing goods (which constitute about 60 percent of United States trade) almost evaporated, and there was a large deficit of nearly $40 billion in fuel trade. The volume of oil imports peaked in the first quarter of 1977, but continuing OPEC price increases continued to drive up the dollar value of oil imports much faster than the overall rate of inflation.

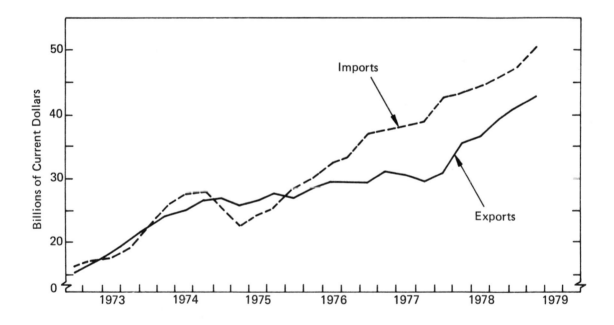

Figure 20.4 U.S. Merchandise Imports and Exports: 1973–1979
(Billions of Current Dollars)

Source: Congressional Budget Office, The U.S. Balance of International Payments and the U.S. Economy (Washington, D.C.: Government Printing Office, 1979), p. 9.

These deficits in merchandise trade were partially offset by the income on foreign assets owned by United States citizens, but as indicated in Table 20.2, the net impact was a persisting imbalance in the United States current account. This pattern of current account deficits, caused in large part by high energy prices, was not unique to the United States. Indeed, as shown in Figure 20.5, most of the developed and non-OPEC developing nations experienced dramatic current account deficits during this period.

Table 20.2
U.S. Current Account Balance: 1975–1979
(Billions of Dollars)

	1975	1976	1977	1978	1979*
Merchandise Trade					
Exports	107.1	114.7	120.8	141.9	168.3
Imports	98.0	124.1	151.7	176.1	195.9
Trade Balance	9.0	− 9.2	−30.9	−34.2	−27.7
Services					
Net Income on Foreign Assets	27.1	31.9	35.2	43.3	57.0
Net Military Transactions	− .7	.7	− 1.7	.5	− .1
Other	−12.5	−13.7	−15.5	−18.4	−24.5
Services Balance	13.9	18.9	21.4	25.4	32.0
Net Unilateral Transfers	− 4.6	− 5.0	− 4.7	− 5.1	− 5.4
Current Account Balance	18.3	4.6	−14.1	−13.9	− 1.1

* Figures for the first half of 1979 at annual rates.

Source: Congressional Budget Office, The U.S. Balance of International Payments and the U.S. Economy: Developments in 1978 and Early 1979 (Washington, D.C.: Government Printing Office, 1979), p. 4.

Note: Detail may not add to totals because of rounding.

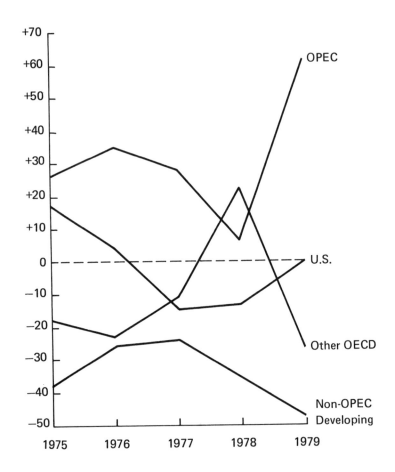

Figure 20.5 Current Account Balances in Selected Nations: 1975–1979
(Billions of Dollars)

*Source: Council of Economic Advisers, Economic Report of the President, 1980, Washington, D.C.: Government Printing Office, 1980,
p. 169.*

Note:
Figures for 1979 are preliminary.

Recycling

Some of the funds that flowed into the OPEC nations were "recycled" by capital investment flows into the United States, Europe, and Japan. A significant portion of these dollars wound up in the "Eurodollar Market" of dollars deposited in banks outside the United States. This "overhang" of dollars accumulating outside the United States, which has persisted for three decades, has a significant impact on the exchange value of the dollar. Many of these eurodollars were used in turn to finance expanded loans to the developing nations, loans which partially offset their current account problems.

Thus the international banking system faced the task of recycling billions of petrodollars into assets in other nations. The net result was a sharp expansion in the eurodollar market, an expansion of OPEC ,real wealth and investments in the developed countries, and an expanding level of debt in the developing nations financed by the international banking system. This pattern of "recycling" depended quite heavily on the dollar as the major reserve currency. However, as we shall see, the declining exchange value of the dollar placed this pattern in jeopardy by the end of the decade.

Terms of Trade

The increased price of crude oil changed the terms of trade, or relative prices of imports and exports, for the developed and developing nations in favor of the OPEC nations. This shift is illustrated in Figure 20.6. The

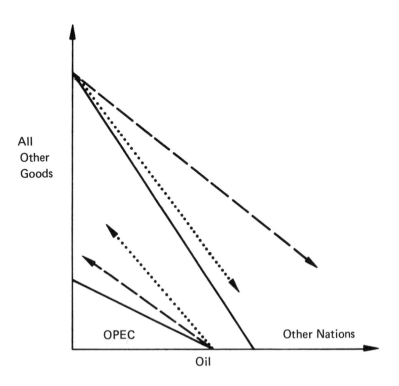

Figure 20.6 The Impact of a Shift in the Terms of Trade in Favor of OPEC

—————————— Domestic Production Possibilities Frontier
– – – – – – – – – Trade Possibilities Curve Based on a Low Relative Price of Crude Oil
· · · · · · · · · · · · · Trade Possibilities Curve Based on a High Relative Price of Crude Oil

Note:
The slope of the trade possibilities curve is

$$- \frac{\text{Price of Crude Oil}}{\text{Price of Other Goods}}$$

As the price of crude oil rises the slope of the trade possibilities curve becomes steeper.

dashed line shows the trade possibilities that were open to the OPEC nations and the rest of the world based on the low relative price of crude oil. Note that everyone gained from trade, but non-OPEC nations gained more than OPEC. The dotted lines show the terms of trade after the increase in the relative price of crude oil. Note that the gains from trade have improved dramatically for OPEC nations and declined sharply for everyone else. The shift in terms of trade meant a real loss in income for the non-OPEC nations. Attempts to redress this loss in income through inflation were unsuccessful in the 1970s because OPEC was able to impose continuing oil price increases above the rate of inflation for all other products.

Devaluation of the Dollar

Over the course of the decade, the value of the dollar fell relative to most other major currencies.[4] The growing dollar value of fuel imports contributed to this pattern, but it was definitely not the only factor. If the oil-producing nations had decided to simply hold on to the dollars, or to buy dollar-denominated assets, there would have been no downward pressure on the dollar. As shown in Table 20.3, the dollar fell most sharply after the oil deficit peak in early 1977. As we have seen, the oil deficit is only one part of the current account problem, and the decline of the dollar may be even more related to net changes in current account, which are dominated by manufacturing flows. Once again, however, the real question concerns what foreign citizens do with dollars when they begin to accumulate.

One major deterrent to holding dollars or assets denominated in dollars is the fear of devaluation, and with floating exchange rates, such devaluations are certainly possible. Even if there were no particular reason to expect a devaluation of the dollar, it might still be prudent to diversify holdings over several currencies to reduce the risk. We would, of course, expect most such diversification toward those currencies that had the best record of and prospects for future stability. Such diversification clearly occurred toward the German mark and the Japanese yen.

The decline in the dollar over the decade of the 1970s, then, is partially traceable to the current account problems in the United States and to the desire to diversify in the face of the floating exchange rate system. On the other hand, inflation and relative unit labor costs do not seem to explain the decline in the dollar very well.

Table 20.3
The Exchange Value of the Dollar: 1971–1981

December of	Cents/Unit of Currency			
	German Mark	Japanese Yen	United Kingdom Pound	Multilateral Trade Weighted Average, 1973 = 100.00
1971	30.6	.312	252.7	112.3
1972	31.3	.332	234.5	110.1
1973	37.6	.357	231.7	101.5
1974	40.8	.333	232.9	98.6
1975	38.1	.327	202.2	103.5
1976	42.0	.339	167.8	105.3
1977	46.5	.415	185.5	98.4
1978	53.2	.510	198.6	88.5
1979	57.7	.416	220.1	86.3
1980	55.1	.443	232.6	87.4
1981	44.4	.452	202.4	102.9

Source: Economic Report of the President, 1982.

Note:
Compared to the trade-weighted index of other currencies, the value of the dollar generally fell from 1971 to 1974, rose through 1975 and 1976, and then declined for the remainder of the decade. In 1979 the value of the dollar rose relative to the yen, and fell compared to the mark and the pound.

If the rate of inflation in the United States were consistently greater than the rate of inflation elsewhere, we would, of course, expect a decline in the dollar, because the purchasing power of the dollar would slowly erode over time in relation to other currencies. While the rate of inflation was higher in the United States in some periods, this was not true for most of the decade, as shown in Figure 20.7. In the figure, each index represents the price or cost in the United States compared to a weighted average of eleven industrialized countries. The graphs show that over the decade, export prices, industrial wholesale prices, and unit labor costs (the cost of labor per unit of output) all *declined* in the United States relative to other industrialized countries.

Reliance on observed inflation rates may, however, be misleading. The key variable in deciding whether to buy or sell dollars is not the actual rate of inflation, but the expected future rates of inflation in different countries. The major factor in the decline of the dollar may have been a subjective assessment of the United States' willingness to control future inflation with restrictive monetary and fiscal policies, to remain in the forefront of continuing innovation and adaptability, and to reduce its dependence on imported energy sources.

If the decline in the dollar reflected persisting relative price patterns, most economists would argue that the decline should simply be accepted. But the swings in exchange rates may be excessive in terms of redressing fundamental current account imbalances if capital flows are heavily speculative and if the lags of price effects are not fully appreciated. In the 1970s, indeed, exchange rates were managed so as to prevent wide fluctuations by the intervention of central banks. The philosophy behind such a "dirty float," manifested in the fall of 1978 and the fall of 1979 by significant intervention in defense of the dollar by the Federal Reserve Board, was to permit gradual adjustments based on underlying economic shifts, but to prevent speculative fluctuations. Of course, if the exchange rate is not permitted to restore balance of payments equilibrium, changes in central bank reserves must make up the imbalances.

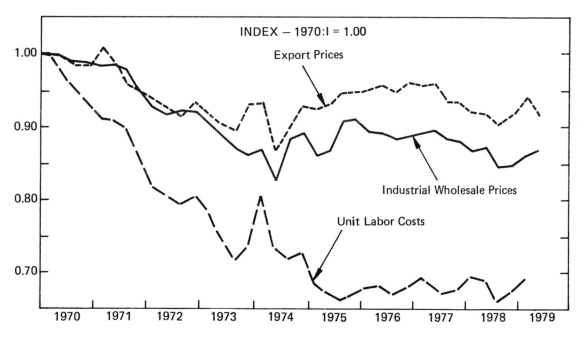

Figure 20.7 Some Measures of U.S. International Competitiveness: 1970–1979 (Seasonally Adjusted)

Source: Congressional Budget office, The U.S. Balance of International Payments and the U.S. Economy: Developments in 1978 and 1979 (Washington, D.C.: Government Printing Office, 1979), p. 22.

CONCLUSION

A strong case can be made for permitting national economies to follow patterns of specialization dictated by market forces which reflect different opportunity costs for different products in each nation. Unless governments intervene to block such market pressures, national economies will automatically adjust to exploit their comparative advantages.

Such specialization, however, may expose the economy to severe adjustment costs when international terms of trade, reflected in relative international prices, shift. If such shifts are gradual, the arguments for efficiency through shifting patterns of specialization may be overwhelming. On the other hand, if relative international prices swing sharply, the adjustment costs may outweigh the gains in efficiency. In the long run the failure to shift in the direction of comparative advantage would sharply reduce the national product available to a country, but in the short run there may be cogent reasons to attempt to moderate the rate of transition.

This argument also applies to adjustments in international exchange rates. Fixed rates which diverge from market equilibrium exchange rates can only be supported in the short run by a willingness to tie domestic economic policies to the exchange rate and to commit central banks to intervene in markets to buy and sell currency as required. In the long run, domestic economic pressures and accumulations of foreign currency in central banks will force some adjustment in the exchange rate. This can occur by simply agreeing to a new exchange rate, and absorbing all of the resultant economic shocks at once, or by slowly permitting the exchange rate to float to its equilibrium level.

As the international economic system nears the middle of the 1980s the arguments for free trade and floating rates have the upper hand, but the basic dilemmas of those positions have not yet been resolved. Despite relatively stable oil prices in the early 1980s, the oil shock of the 1970s lingers on, continuing to exert strong pressures on the balance of payments positions of the industrial economies and the non-oil-producing developing nations. Those balance of payments pressures threaten to heighten competition among the industrialized nations for expanded exports, and raise the possibility of greater constraints against free trade. Shifting exchange rates continue to force severe domestic adjustments. In 1980 and early 1981 the pressure shifted from the dollar to the European currencies, producing a decline in the mark against the dollar of over 25 percent. Such dramatic swings suggest that the international economy has not yet found the answer to its exchange rate dilemma.

Specialization along the lines of comparative advantage fosters a complex system of international economic interdependence. The challenge is to manage that interdependence to permit the participants to reap the harvest of improved efficiency while buffering the system from the blight of rapidly transmitted economic shocks. That is a challenge which will continue to hold center stage in the coming decade.

NOTES

1 Special Drawing Rights or SDR's are entitlements to draw on reserves in the International Monetary Fund.
2 Paul A. Volcker, "The Political Economy of the Dollar," The Fred Hirsch Lecture at Warwick University, Coventry, England, November 9, 1978.
3 *Ibid.*, pp. 29–30.
4 The following discussion of this decline draws on the major points posed by Herbert Stein in "The Mystery of the Declining Dollar," *The AEI Economist* (September, 1978).

SELECTED REFERENCES

Robert Z. Aliber, *The International Money Game*, 3rd ed. (New York: Basic Books, Inc., 1979).
Robert E. Baldwin and J. David Richardson, eds., *International Trade and Finance* (Boston: Little, Brown and Co., 1974).
Charles P. Kindleberger and Peter H. Lindert, *International Economics*, 6th ed. (Homewood, Ill.: Richard D. Irwin, Inc., 1978).

Chapter 21
Economic Interdependence and Alliances

INTRODUCTION

In 1972 Richard Cooper, writing on "Economic Interdependence and Foreign Policy in the Seventies," noted that the traditional assumptions of economic policy relied on the independence of national markets.[1] In his view, markets had already become very interdependent by the early 1970s, and the sharp distinction between internal and external policies of the Westphalian, or state-oriented, System were no longer appropriate. In particular, he pointed to the integration of multinational industrial markets, international migration patterns, huge international investment flows, and the expanding role of joint economic decisions through the IMF, the World Bank, and EEC commercial and agricultural policies. Cooper concluded that a major issue for the seventies was whether nations would respond to the growing interdependence passively, accepting the loss of domestic autonomy suggested by the principles of the liberal order; defensively, by establishing barriers to trade; aggressively, by seeking to control the actions of citizen firms outside the nation's boundaries; or constructively, by seeking joint remedies to the problems of interdependence. His article preceded the Soviet grain sale and the OAPEC embargo which brought home the major risks associated with a passive response to interdependence.

A decade later, Cooper's central question remains unanswered. Will the challenge of interdependence prove to be the end of the liberal economic order as nations seek to defend themselves from economic shocks, or will the commitment to the principles of open markets be a sufficient incentive for constructive coordination of policies despite extraordinary economy shocks? Most observers detect a shift over the last decade in the direction of limiting risks at the cost of sacrificing some of the potential benefits of free exchange. As W. Michael Blumenthal, former United States Secretary of the Treasury, wrote:

> In the field of international trade, as in the field of exchange rate policy, governments are found to be struggling between the same powerful countervailing forces. On the one hand, governments are obliged to respond to various demands from their electorates for economic security and economic equity; at the same time, governments are obliged to maintain strong economic ties with other countries in order to keep their economies growing. . . . As overall rates of growth began to slow up, the United States and other countries began to give greater weight to the objective of limiting the risks and redistributing the benefits that an open international society has helped to generate.[2]

As Klaus Knorr observed in *Economic Interdependence and National Security*, the reaction to the risks of economic interdependence is as much a function of national will as it is a result of specific economic impacts. He argues that the western nations have become less resilient as their governments have become more responsive to various constituencies.

> The more open the national economy, the greater the need to absorb and adapt to disruptive impacts received from the external environment. These impacts now become more readily politicized and elicit stonger public demands for government protection. Vulnera-

bility to disturbing impacts is thus not a function of their intensity and breadth but also of the receiving economy's and society's resilience and desire to adjust. The more unwilling and unable domestic groups are to undertake adjustments and submit to this burden, the more sensitive they become to economic disruption.[3]

Economic interdependence therefore poses a major challenge to the liberal economic order, and also raises important national security issues. At one level, economic interdependence may be seen as providing an expanded range of foreign policy instruments, which could serve as alternatives to the threat or use of force. On the other hand, economic interdependence provides other nations with potential leverage on the economies of the United States and its allies. Moreover, the shock of economic disruptions may be viewed by the United States as an attack on its vital national interests, and could conceivably become a justification for military action.

Interdependence also suggests that the complex web of military, political, and economic interests that interact in our alliance structure is becoming increasingly sensitive to the expanding pattern of economic interaction. Thus, concerns over secure sources of energy, the distribution of military expenditures and the balance of payments implications of those expenditures, and issues of standardization all become intertwined with negotiations over exchange rates and capital flows.

In the following sections we will concentrate on the aspects of interdependence affecting the relationships of the major industrial powers, particularly as they affect the NATO alliance structure. Chapter 22 will explore the issues of sanctions and leverage in general, and their application to East-West economic relations in particular. The impact of economic interdependence on the relationships between the industrial powers and the developing nations will be explored in Chapter 26.

Our discussion begins with a recapitulation of the major dimensions of economic interdependence, continues with an analysis of measures of changing interdependence over the past decade, presents a framework for considering the trade-off between economic growth and domestic vulnerability, and outlines the emerging patterns of economic consultation. A case study on the impact of the energy crisis is discussed as an example of the difficulties inherent in economic interdependence, and a final section then presents an overview of the impact of the shifting pattern of interdependence on the evolving alliance structure.

THE DIMENSIONS OF INTERDEPENDENCE

Levels of economic interdependence cannot be measured precisely on any one-dimensional scale. The extent of interdependence depends not only on the nature, volume, and frequency of interactions, but also on the *perceived* importance of those transactions to each participant. Perceived importance is a function of many factors, including the capability and willingness to adapt to changes in patterns of interaction and exchange. As we suggested earlier, this willingness to adapt may be related to the dispersion of political power in each state. Thus simple ratios of exports to total output, or numbers of messages exchanged, or flows of international investment do not indicate shifts in the perceived level of interdependence.

However, while acknowledging that perceptions are not necessarily directly related to shifts in the level of interaction among states, such interactions do provide a first order estimate of underlying economic trends that should ultimately influence perceptions. We may examine patterns of interaction either by focusing on real exchanges of final products and the factors, or inputs, of production, or by tracing the financial flows that mirror those transactions.

Perhaps the most obvious measure of economic interaction is the exchange of goods and services reflected in the *balance of trade*. The difference between exports and imports—net exports—is one of the elements of the gross national product because it reflects a contribution to the total demand for the nation's output. Net exports, however, are a very poor measure of interdependence, because they do not indicate the underlying volume of trade, and because they do not indicate the gains from trade that have been generated through specialization. The level of either imports or exports compared with the total level of national output is a superior measure, but this can also be deceiving. Changes in export levels, for example, can mean significant changes in the scale of operations in many industries and can therefore have important consequences for the efficiency of production. In many cases, export sales may mean the difference between annual profits or losses for a large number of firms. Thus, even if the ratio of exports to total output is low, the impact of exports on particular industries may be extremely important. The real issue is how integrated particular international markets have become, and how rapidly price and output adjustments affect production in each country.

Looking beyond the product markets, integrated markets also exist for the mobile factors of production: labor, capital, and technology. Because workers are often permitted to cross international boundaries, they are often able to exploit their own comparative advantages in seeking out employment. Permanent shifts in the labor force, then, are reflected in emigration statistics, although we also anticipate temporary migration of workers to follow shifting employment opportunities. Therefore, the extent of integration of the labor market is suggested by the level of annual *migration*, although a better measure is the sensitivity of changes in migration patterns to shifts in such economic factors as relative wage rates.

Similarly, we find that corporations build new plants in those areas with the highest anticipated rate of return, considering input costs, the availability and cost of financing, tax policies, and risks to include the risk of future nationalization of the industry. Multinational corporations, therefore, serve an important function from the point of view of economic efficiency by directing resources to their most productive use. Once again, measures of *international capital flows*, either in absolute terms or in relationship to total levels of output, are suggestive of the extent of integration in the capital market, but a superior measure is the sensitivity of the pattern of capital flow to differentials in expected rates of return.

Technology transfers among nations are certainly related to patterns of capital investment, but there is a major distinction between the transfer of capital goods and the "know-how" to convert that capital into production processes with desired quality standards. We might call that know-how "entrepreneurial skill." Thus the implications of building a "turn-key" plant that is completely prepared for operation may be much different than that of exporting the capital equipment needed in such a plant. To the extent that such entrepreneurial skill is reallocated among nations based on economic incentives, the international technology market is integrated, and a new technology breakthrough is transmitted to other nations. Obviously if entrepreneurial skill is less mobile, technology differentials persist. In this case, as in those previously mentioned, the extent of interdependence is a function of the level of integration of the market, which may or may not be reflected in the figures on total levels of interaction or exchange.

The central measure of interdependence is the ability of the international market to react to new economic signals. Integration clearly depends on the willingness of governments to permit the free transfer of products and input factors of production, and such willingness is limited to the extent that the benefits of increased economic efficiency are perceived to be small in relation to competing national objectives. Integration is also a function of the international infrastructure that facilitates interaction and exchange.

Economic interdependence is greatly affected by the infrastructure of international communications, transportation, information, and financial transactions. Economic differentials cannot affect the allocation of resources unless those differences are communicated to decision makers. Similarly, the greater the costs of exchange, the greater the economic differentials must be to stimulate a shift of resources.

While many important economic signals are transmitted through the marketplace, many others are not. These sources of cost and benefit that are not transmitted through the marketplace, or the "externalities," arise when no economic actor has clear property rights to a resource or product. Thus the industry that dumps effluent into the ocean imposes a cost on all users of the ocean, but the users do not have clearly defined property rights that permit them to sue the polluter. At the other extreme, there may be many "public goods" that are desired by the public but will not be produced by the marketplace because there is no way to force the users to pay for the benefit they receive. National or international defense, some types of health and safety information, or even a lighthouse would be examples of public goods that might not be provided by a private market.

Many externalities are an important dimension of economic interdependence. The extent to which nations are concerned about joint defense, the use of common resources, or the adoption of common standards of health and safety are also a measure of the extent of economic interdependence. In these cases, however, we find few market signals that measure the interdependence, and we must rely instead on the extent and nature of international discussions and agreements as a measure of these external elements of interdependence.

Interdependence can also be measured by evaluating the number and influence of the international actors or interest groups that affect agreements and transactions. This dimension of interdependence is very difficult to quantify, but it can be extremely important. To the extent that major actors have transnational economic interests, they can be expected to press for fewer national restraints, for more international standards of behavior, and for more complete integration of product and factor markets. Such actors may also have an important impact on the perception of economic interdependence.

SHIFTING PATTERNS OF INTERDEPENDENCE

Historic Overview

The evaluation of shifting levels of interdependence depends on the time frame of analysis and the specific measures of interdependence that are being examined, but virtually all of the measures suggested in the last section indicate a dramatic increase in the integration of international markets over the past three decades. For example, if we trace world trade flows back over two centuries, as shown in Table 21.1, the post-World War II expansion is quite dramatic and certainly comparable to the peak rates of growth achieved in earlier periods. This dramatic expansion in trade, however, must also be viewed against the backdrop of the unprecedented interruption of world commerce during the 1930s.

Table 21.1
Rates of Growth in World Trade Per Decade: 1750–1968 (Percent)

Period	Increase in World Trade Flow
1750–1825	10.1
1825–1835	30.1
1835–1845	61.5
1845–1855	59.8
1855–1865	52.7
1865–1875	53.7
1875–1884	43.4
1885–1890	42.0
1890–1913	63.5
1928–1938	−55.1
1954–1961	63.3
1961–1968	86.1

Table 21.2
Ratio of Foreign Trade (Imports plus Exports) to National Product in the United States: Selected Periods (Percent)

Period	Ratio
1834–43	12.9
1904–13	11.0
1919–28	10.8
1954–63	7.9
1965	7.0
1970	7.0
1971	12.2
1972	12.7
1973	15.0
1974	19.1
1975	17.9
1976	18.7
1977	19.0
1978	20.0
1979	21.9

Source (Table 21.1):
Peter J. Katzenstein, "International Interdependence: Some Long-Term Trends and Recent Changes," International Organization (Autumn, 1975), p. 1024.

Sources (Table 21.2):
Simon Kuznets, Modern Economic Growth: Rate, Structure and Spread (New Haven: Yale University Press, 1966), pp. 312–314, and Council of Economic Advisers, The Economic Report of the President, 1980 (Washington, D.C.: Government Printing Office, 1980), p. 203.

Of course, shifts in trade flows must be studied from the perspective of changes in the overall level of economic activity if we are to gain a more comprehensive view of their relative impact. Table 21.2 traces the ratio of foreign trade (imports plus exports) to national production in the United States over selected periods. The figures suggest that the long-term decline in the ratio of trade to national output in the United States has been reversed in the past decade. Moreover the data for the 1970s suggest that the ratio of trade to output is quite sensitive to the business cycle, as evidenced by the reduction in the ratio during the 1975 recession. In particular, the import share of output tends to drop in recession and rise sharply during expansions.

U.S. Trade Patterns

As shown in Figure 21.1, United States trade is highly concentrated in particular commodity and product groups. On the import side, it comes as no surprise to learn that fuel imports have risen rapidly over the last decade and now constitute about one-quarter of total imports. However, machinery, transport equipment, and other manufactures still constitute over half of our total imports. On the export side, machinery, transport equipment, and other manufactures also account for over half of total exports. Grains, soybeans, and other agricultural products contribute over one fifth of all exports, and chemical products add another 10 percent.

To summarize these observations, international trade affects an increasing proportion of total United States output, the ratio of imports to exports is particularly sensitive to the business cycle, and most trade involves the import and export of machinery and other manufactures. Based on these patterns it is not surprising to find that the regional distribution of United States trade, summarized in Figure 21.2, is concentrated on Western Europe, Japan, and Canada. In 1978 these regions accounted for 68 percent of United States exports and 55 percent of United States imports, and imports from Canada alone exceeded United States imports from all OPEC nations. These data suggest that the expanding levels of United States trade are at least partially related to an increasing integration of industrial markets in North America, Japan, and Western Europe.

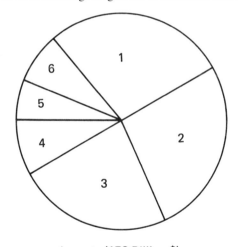
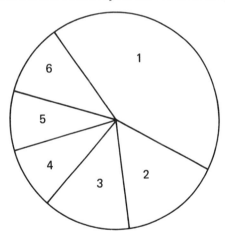

Imports (172 Billion $)   Exports (141 Billion $)

(1) Machinery and Transport Equipment (28%)   (1) Machinery and Transport Equipment (42%)
(2) Other Manufactures (27%)   (2) Other Manufactures (16%)
(3) Fuels (24%)   (3) Grains and Soybeans (12%)
(4) Agricultural Products (9%)   (4) Other Agricultural Products (9%)
(5) Non-fuel Crude Materials (5%)   (5) Chemical Products (9%)
(6) Miscellaneous (7%)   (1) Miscellaneous (12%)

Figure 21.1 Composition of U.S. Imports and Exports by Commodity Group in 1978

Source: U.S. Department of Commerce, Bureau of Economic Analysis, Survey of Current Business (July, 1979), pp. S22–24.

Imports   Exports

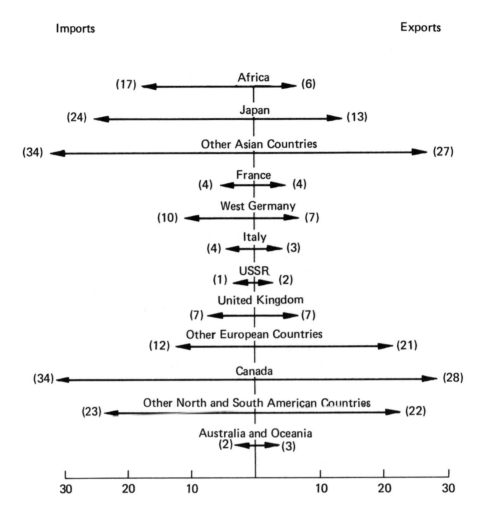

Figure 21.2 Composition of U.S. Exports and Imports by Destination in 1978 (Billion Dollars)

Source: U.S. Department of Commerce, Bureau of Economic Analysis, Survey of Current Business (July, 1979), pp. S22–24.

Market Integration

This pattern of integration becomes more striking when one considers the dramatic growth in Western Europe—particularly in West Germany—and Japan over the past two decades. In 1955 the United States gross national product of $399 billion represented over *one-third* of the entire world's output, and was 16 times the size of Japan's output and almost 10 times as great as the output of Western Germany. By 1975 the United States GNP of $1516 billion was less than *one-fifth* of the world's total, only 3 times larger than Japan's output and less than 4 times as great as West Germany's . In 1970 the output of the United States was more than one and a half times as great as the output of the European Community, but by 1979 their outputs were roughly equal. Similarly, in 1970 the exports of the United States ($43.2 billion) were roughly balanced by the exports of Japan and West Germany ($53.5 billion), but by 1979 the exports of Japan and West Germany had increased over 500 percent in current dollar terms to $276 billion compared to United States exports of $183 billion.[4] In summary, at the same time that the economic interdependence of the United States economy was expanding, its position as the world's dominant producer and trader was rapidly eroding.

The extent of integration of the markets of the major industrial powers is also reflected in the sensitivity of growth rates, unemployment rates, and inflation in each country to changes in those of the other major industrial countries. Relative growth rates in each of these nations are increasingly important, because they influence the rate of expansion of export markets. If the United States were to expand at a more rapid rate than West Germany and Japan, the United States market for German and Japanese exports would increase more rapidly than the market for United States exports, and as a result the United States would experience increasing balance of trade deficits. Indeed, in the late 1970s the United States put a great deal of pressure on its trading partners to pursue more expansionist monetary and fiscal policies in order to relieve its balance of payments problems. The extent of these international feedbacks was reflected in the coordination of the business cycle in the 1970s among these trading partners.[5] In the 1974 recession, the United States and Japan had negative real growth rates and West Germany expanded at only ½ percent in real terms. In 1975 Japan recovered to a real growth rate of 2½ percent per year, but the United States and West Germany continued to experience real declines. All three economies rebounded sharply in 1976 to real growth rates of 5½ to 6 percent in real terms. In this period inflation rates in each country were also highly correlated. The rate of inflation fell in each country in 1975, and fell again in 1976. By the end of the decade this correspondence of the business cycle declined somewhat as real growth in the United States declined as prices rose sharply. Japan and West Germany experienced higher growth rates and much less inflationary pressure.[6]

When such divergence in growth cycles does occur, it brings more intense pressure for coordination of other policies. For example, when the cycle was similar in each country in the mid-1970s, their trade balances were also in line. By the end of the decade, however, the trade balances were beginning to diverge sharply, increasing the risk of unilateral trade restrictions. These pressures for policy coordination, transmitted through balances of trade, have also been reflected in the growing integration of international capital markets.

Capital Flows

In the 1950s and 1960s, the United States dominated international capital markets, accounting for the vast majority of direct international investment. At the same time, very little international investment occurred in the United States. By the late 1960s the increased output growth in West Germany and Japan, and their associated increases in wealth, began to shift the pattern of international investment. By 1978 investment flows into the United States from other industrial nations were roughly equal to flows from the United States to those nations. These shifts in investment flows have reinforced the integration of international industrial markets. Foreign controlled firms account for over 20 percent of total sales or output in the United Kingdom, France, and Germany, and although the United States percentage was only 5 percent in 1974, that number has undoubtedly risen sharply since then.[7] Even Japan, the only large industrial country that significantly limited inflows of foreign capital in the postwar period, has begun to liberalize its policy in this area.

This pattern of direct international investment among the major industrial powers raises difficult issues regarding the national jurisdiction of multinational firms. It has also contributed to a tighter integration of short- and long-term capital markets, and expands the importance of international financial organizations. Perhaps the most obvious example of the expanding integration of capital markets is the growth of the so-called *Eurodollar Market* or, perhaps more precisely, the *Eurocurrency markets*.

Eurocurrency Markets

The Eurocurrency markets form a network of international banks that accept deposits and make loans in foreign currencies. The size of the Eurocurrency markets is normally estimated by adding the foreign currency deposits made in banks in Canada, Europe, and Japan and their branch banks elsewhere. In 1979 these deposits, net of interbank deposits, came to about $200 billion, after a growth rate of over 25 percent per year through the 1970s. The dollar accounts for roughly 75 percent of these Eurocurrency deposits.

The major depositors in the Eurocurrency markets have been the industrial countries, OPEC nations, and some developing nations that maintain their reserves in Eurocurrency markets. The largest share of Eurocurrency loans, about 40 percent, go to non-OPEC developing nations, although about 30 percent go to industrial countries. Most of the deposits are for short periods—90 percent have maturities less than 90 days—and the average loan is for 3 to 5 years, with a variable rate of interest depending on changes in financial markets. The larger loans are frequently arranged through international syndicates of banks in order to spread risks.

The Eurocurrency markets have led to an expansion in total international liquidity. For example, a Chase Manhattan deposit in a Eurocurrency bank does not reduce the total reserves held by Chase Manhattan, and therefore does not lead to a contraction in the United States money supply. There are no reserve requirements on the deposit in the Eurocurrency bank, and that deposit therefore permits an expansion of Eurocurrency deposits. This occurs because the deposit will lead to Eurocurrency loans, those loans will lead to further deposits, those deposits will lead to further loans, and so forth. This does not change the supply of money in the narrow sense, because the Eurocurrency deposits are time deposits. However, the existence of the Eurocurrency markets with relatively high interest rates for deposits may speed up the rate of circulation of domestic money supplies, and in practice many Eurocurrency deposits are converted into checking accounts overnight with little or no interest penalty. Thus for sophisticated multinational operators, Eurocurrency deposits are a direct substitute for domestic checking accounts. In this sense, the Eurocurrency markets permit a change in domestic money supplies outside the normal controls of central banks.

National Economic Policy Restrictions

This growing integration of product and capital markets among industrial nations places obvious limitations on conventional national economic policies. In his article, "Interdependence Has Its Limits," Gregory Schmid argues that these constraints on national economic policies are already leading to the end of the liberal trade epoch. Pointing to greater controls on capital flows designed to limit abrupt changes in exchange rates, to restrictions on movement of foreign workers into northern Europe, and to the end of the Bretton Woods "rules of the game," which limited "beggar-thy-neighbor" policies, Schmid concludes:

> Such controversies indicate that many countries are reaching an awareness that the risks inherent in the rapid growth of international transactions are now outweighing the expected gains. . . . The response of national political institutions to the dangers inherent in the free market system may well end 30 years of growing economic interdependence. . . . Already the results of this pressure are evident. The free market system will not be permitted to operate on the international level in agricultural trade because growing demand from a large number of prosperous countries will force prices to rise sharply in producer countries and could produce mass starvation in poor, drought-hit lands. The free market system will not

be permitted to operate in labor markets beyond the point already reached in Europe because large influxes of foreign workers or foreign immigrants threaten domestic employment in a slack labor market or cause massive problems for domestic social institutions in a tight labor market. The free market will not be permitted to operate in the goods market to the extent that it threatens jobs or imposes major adjustment costs on a single country. The free market system will not be permitted to operate in the financial market since it has been shown that it severely limits the ability of domestic monetary authorities to reach targets set by domestic political needs. . . . From some future perspective, the period of the 1980s and 1990s may even be seen as an era of a new mercantilism.[9]

As noted in the last chapter the system of floating exchange rates has not been able to achieve an adjustment of long-term imbalances in current account positions, and it therefore has not freed domestic economic policy from the impact of international economic shifts. Moreover, the floating exchange rate system transmits its signals of persisting imbalances in more subtle ways than the former system did, with its more fixed rates tied to convertibility. It has become increasingly clear that the international monetary system can no longer manage itself. In the 1950s and 1960s, the United States essentially served as the world's banker, earning "deposits" through surpluses in the balance of trade, making "loans" through direct international investment, and providing for international liquidity through the dollar exchange standard. In the 1970s a variety of institutional changes shifted the role of the United States, and a clear system of new international responsibilities has not yet emerged.

There is growing evidence in the monetary sector of greater emphasis on regional interdependence at the cost of some national autonomy. In March of 1979, eight European nations—West Germany, France, Belgium, Denmark, the Netherlands, Luxembourg, Italy, and Ireland—agreed to form a monetary union in order to assist in fighting inflation and restoring monetary discipline. This approach created a mini-Bretton Woods arrangement in which each nation pegged its currency to a regional standard, the mark, but the regional standard would float relative to other currencies. The exchange rates would be defended via a newly created European Monetary Fund to which reserve deposits would be made and from which credits could be received. The credits would be denominated in a new European Currency Unit, the ECU, based on an average of the currencies of all members and the British pound. Ultimately, the European Monetary Fund could become an international central bank, and the ECU would become a new international reserve currency. Commitment to such a monetary union represents the acceptance of further restrictions on national autonomy. National growth rates must now be coordinated to insure that currency values remain in line, and it is not yet known whether national governments will have the discipline and political strength required in such a system.

Whether a system of regional monetary spheres based on the ECU, the dollar, and the yen will emerge in the 1980s remains to be seen. The emerging pattern in the trade sector shows conflicting trends. Schmid's conclusion that despite all the evidence of increasing economic integration, the future holds a distinct danger of disintegration along nationalist lines warrants careful scrutiny. On the one hand, continuing GATT agreements hold out the prospect of greater cooperation; but on the other hand, there is sufficient evidence of a drift toward protectionism to cause some alarm.

The Tokyo Round: Conflicting Pressures

The "Tokyo Round" of negotiations under the General Agreement on Trade and Tariffs including representatives from nearly one hundred industrialized and developing nations, illustrates many of the conflicting pressures at work. The "Kennedy Round" of negotiations from 1962 to 1967 brought about agreements to reduce import duties in the industrial nations by about 35 percent for manufactured goods. While the Tokyo Round of negotiations from 1973 to 1979 cut tariff barriers by another 35 percent, it also undertook a major effort to reduce the complex maze of nontariff barriers to trade. The negotiations emphasized the development of behavioral codes to limit practices such as placing arbitrary values on imports to raise tariff duties, limiting large government contracts to domestic bidders, subsidizing export industries, and using health and safety standards to create unnecessary restraints on trade. However, while these codes would generally liberalize trade, the agreements also continue to permit domestic subsidies for virtually any reason and confirm continued restrictions in international agricultural trade. As Robert E. Baldwin points out in *The Multilateral Trade Negotiations*, the domestic costs of gaining agreement to the new codes may have been quite high in terms of protection for individual industries.[10] For example, during the Tokyo Round negotiations, the United States made trade concessions to the textile, sugar, and steel industries, and "orderly marketing agreements" or bilateral arrangements to limit exports of particular items to the United States were reached for such items as textiles, footwear, and television sets. The Congressional Budget Office viewed the failure of the Tokyo Round to deal with quantitative restrictions aimed at safeguarding a favorable balance of trade position as a major problem.

> The failure to achieve agreement on a safeguards code is in some respects only one aspect of a more general failure of the Tokyo Round participants to make any systematic progress on the general issue of quantitative restrictions. A number of specific quotas were removed or expanded, but no attempt was made to draw up guidelines for the use of quantitative restrictions or to negotiate their eventual elimination.[11]

The Congressional Budget Office also underscored the problem by granting industry concessions, which were apparently seen as a necessary cost of gaining agreement with the new trade codes.

> The Tokyo Round agreements represent an opportunity to reduce the distortions of trade flows created by government policies. But some critics complain that the concessions that governments have had to make to various domestic interest groups in order to assure acceptance of the agreements have introduced important new distortions. Supporters of the new government policies argue that in an imperfect trading system such concessions are necessary to protect the legitimate interests of domestic producers. In either view, however, these trade-limiting policies mark a failure of the Tokyo Round negotiations.[12]

Steel Trigger Pricing: An Illustration

The case of the steel industry provides an important illustration of the protectionist pressures in individual industries. In 1978 the United States became concerned with charges of "dumping," or sales in the United States at prices below average costs, by foreign steel exporters, particularly exporters from Western Europe. A trigger price system was established so that dumping investigations would be triggered only if the import steel price fell below the estimated costs of the most efficient producer (Japan) plus transport costs and an 8 percent profit margin. The impact of this trigger pricing system was to set a floor on import steel prices, a floor which, by some estimates, raised import steel prices in the first year of operation by about 8 to 10 percent, permitting domestic producers to raise their prices by 1 to 2 percent without losing their share of the market.[13] Such a system may be an effective deterrent against "dumping," but it also sets the price of steel in the United States above world market levels, increases the costs of domestic users of steel, and requires complex bureaucratic decisions on the appropriate trigger price—decisions that must be made under a great deal of domestic steel industry pressure. The Organization of Economic Cooperation and Development (OECD) has now established an International Steel Committee to review developments in the steel industry. Whether this committee will work to remove trade barriers or operate to block needed adjustments required to improve long term efficiency remains to be seen.

The Consequences of Interdependence

In summary, there is overwhelming evidence of a rapid shift toward greater economic interdependence—particularly among the industrialized nations—over the past thirty years, and considerable evidence that the pattern of interdependence accelerated in the 1970s. The reduction of domestic control over exchange rates, production patterns, investment flows, and even national money supplies, suggests a fundamental shift in international economic conditions in the direction of more fully integrated markets. What is not clear is the extent of defensive reaction such interdependence might bring in the coming decades. In the following sections we will examine the trade-off between growth and vulnerability in more detail, and suggest some of the implications of the choices that are ultimately made regarding the framework of international decision making in general, and the NATO alliance in particular.

INTERDEPENDENCE AND VULNERABILITY: AN APPLICATION OF GAME THEORY

We have seen that the classical argument in support of interdependence is that integrated markets permit expanded specialization, and therefore increase the potential gains from trade. On the other hand, expanded integration of markets also reduces the ability of nation states to control their economies and imposes adjustment costs when international conditions change. Nations, therefore, face difficult decisions requiring a trade-off between the objectives of efficiency and growth permitted by economic integration, and the vulnerability of their economic systems to external shocks.

The theory of games, discussed at the beginning of this chapter, provides one way of examining such a trade-off. Consider countries A and B, which have two trade options. Option 1 is free trade, and option 2 is a high protective tariff. In Table 21.3 the entries show the GNP for country A based on the options chosen by countries A and B. The GNP for country B is shown in parentheses.

Table 21.3
Tariff Options and Gross National Products:
The Case of Large Gains From Trade

		Country A 1	Country A 2
Country B	1	3000 (2000)	2500 (1000)
	2	2000 (1500)	1500 (500)

This is an illustration of a nonzero sum game, because the sum of the benefits (payoffs) available to both parties will vary depending on the options selected. Note that if each country selects the high tariff, option 2, the total GNP in both countries is only 2000; if they both select free trade, the total is 5000. The difference of 3000 represents the gains from trade made possible by specialization. Each country could impose a high loss on the other by imposing a protective tariff, illustrating the risk involved in a commitment to free trade. In this case, either country is better off selecting free trade even if the other country imposes a tariff, but not as well off as if both pursued free trade.

In this example, the potential gains from trade are so great that each nation would probably opt for free trade, although the distribution of the gains from trade and the political structure of each nation would clearly influence this decision. However, if the matrix in Table 21.3 were changed to the pattern in Table 21.4, the situation might be quite different.

Table 21.4
Tariff Options and Gross National Products:
The Case of Small Gains From Trade

		Country A 1	Country A 2
Country B	1	3000 (2000)	2980 (1710)
	2	2000 (1990)	2700 (1700)

In this case, the potential gains from trade are much smaller (5000-4400 = 600), and Country A can wipe out most of the gains from trade to the other nation by imposing a tariff without taking much of a domestic loss. Country B cannot impose much of a loss on Country A with a protective tariff, so it is quite vulnerable to a unilateral tariff imposed by Country A. In this situation it is certainly conceivable that industries in Country B that might be hurt by free trade could argue that the gains from trade were small compared to adjustment costs, and that free trade would make the economy too vulnerable to external shocks.

These examples suggest a broader range of possibilities. We can imagine cases in which the gains from trade and the losses imposed by a unilateral trade restriction are large for both countries, small for both countries, or large for one country and small for the other. Based on each option, we might deduce the type of equilibrium trade pattern that would develop. The case of large gains from trade and balanced vulnerability would probably produce a free trade equilibrium. The case of small gains from trade and unbalanced vulnerability would tend to produce a protectionist equilibrium. The intermediate cases could conceivably move in either direction.

Applying this framework to our previous discussion of the trends in interdependence, one might argue that although there have been major gains from the shifts toward integrated markets among the industrial countries since World War II, the incremental gains from further integration may be more limited. The adjustment costs and loss of national economic control accompanying interdependence may, therefore, come to have a great impact, restricting further integration. As former Secretary of the Treasury W. Michael Blumenthal has argued:

> The monetary, trade and investment issues discussed here are critical manifestations of a larger problem still. This is a world made up of separate nations, each with its own aspirations, its own history, and its own policies. It is also a world that is shrinking fast, creating new interdependencies and new opportunities. How best can these two unshakable facts be reconciled? How can we profit from the benefits of our growing interdependencies while pursuing our separate national needs? That is the basic challenge to which nations must respond. [14]

The challenge will be to manage further integration in a way that will prevent the industrial economies from slipping into a more protectionist equilibrium.

INTERDEPENDENCE AND VULNERABILITY: THE CASE OF ENERGY

The initial reaction to the flexing of monopoly muscle by the OPEC nations in 1973 was mixed. Many observers pointed to the disparate national objectives of the oil-producing nations and argued that the cartel would quickly collapse. Others saw the oil cartel as the wave of the future, and envisioned similar cartels growing up for a variety of raw materials. In retrospect, neither of these views proved to be correct. A decade later, OPEC is still able to set the floor price of crude oil, and the oil-importing nations have done very little to protect themselves against further price increases. On the other hand, the proliferation of resource cartels has not occurred, and there appears to be little prospect for such a trend.

If we apply our game theory model, the case of oil appears to be a situation in which the gains from trade are very great, and there is an imbalance in vulnerability. The size of the OPEC nations severely limits the prospect of retaliatory restrictions of the export of selected items—food is often mentioned as a possible example—to the oil-producing states. Aside from the ethical problems of restricting food exports, it is quite clear that the OPEC nations would be able to purchase sufficient imports to maintain acceptable dietary standards even if they were embargoed by the major food producers. This is also the case for other critical imports. On the other hand, the oil-consuming nations have not been able, or willing, to make the required substitutions of other energy sources, nor have they made the required cuts in consumption to limit their dependence on the OPEC nations.

The shift in the terms of trade of the OPEC nations constitutes a redistribution of world output, and imposes a real loss of output on the importing nations. This has placed great strains on the oil-importing nations as governments have attempted to shield their populations from the loss in real output, and have taken action to secure their own sources of crude oil in competition with other importers. In attempting to avert the loss in real income associated with higher oil prices, governments have the option of using expansionary monetary and fiscal policies. However, as discussed in Chapter 6, this has amounted to attempts to shift the aggregate demand curve to the right along an aggregate supply curve that is shifting to the left. The resulting inflation can be seen as a movement to alter the terms of trade back in favor of the oil-importing nations. If the rate of inflation exceeded the rate of increase in crude oil prices, the result would be a decline in oil prices in real, or constant dollar, terms. As shown in Table 20.1 in the last chapter, the *real* price of crude oil actually fell from 1974 to 1978, but the OPEC nations had sufficient market power to impose a new series of price increases at the end of the decade, once more shifting the terms of trade against the oil-importing nations.

The economist's answer to a shortage is to let the market price increase, thereby stimulating an expansion in supply. In the long run, this approach will probably make enough energy alternatives economically feasible to limit dependence on imported oil in many of the importing nations. The best prospects at the moment appear to be in the areas of conservation, solar energy, and coal—if the environmental and health consequences of expanded coal use can be reduced or accepted. Nuclear energy may prove to be a more efficient energy source in the long run, but for the moment, the problems of handling spent fuel and disputes over reactor safety prevent a major solution in this area. But how quickly could higher prices for energy bring these new sources of energy into play, and how high would the pri   have to go? Most current projections anticipate continued reliance on imported oil for 20 to 30 percent of the energy requirements of the United States, at least through the late 1980s.[15]

The picture is even bleaker for Western Europe and Japan where, aside from Britain's North Sea reserves, our allies lack the resources available to the United States. The prospects for significant increases in energy conservation in those nations is also less than in the United States, where the price of energy remains much lower than in other nations despite the increases of the past decade. An analysis of the 1975 ratio of energy use to output in selected nations, found in Figure 21.3, shows that nations with lower retail prices of gasoline use more gasoline. This, of course, is not surprising, but it does indicate the very low price of gasoline in the United States compared with that in other nations. Although prices have risen sharply in the United States since 1975, prices in the United States remain substantially below prices elsewhere.

Given the international shortages of energy and the continuing vulnerability to OPEC price increases, it is not difficult to understand the pressure being placed on the United States by its allies to lower energy consumption. Higher gasoline prices would place substantial adjustment costs on the United States with painful implications for the redistribution of income over different industries and regions. The reluctance to accept those adjustment costs has placed the United States in a difficult balance of payments position, has weakened confidence in the future purchasing power of the dollar, and has kept the economies of Western Europe, Japan, and the United States hostage to further OPEC price increases.

The redistribution of wealth associated with the increased price of oil has also raised the problem of efficiently recycling income flowing to OPEC. As noted earlier, the Eurodollar market has become a major means of channeling OPEC funds back into the industrial nations and through the banking system to the less developed nations. The limitations on the growth capacity of the OPEC nations, as well as the political consequences of rapid development illustrated by revolution in Iran, mean that direct OPEC purchases of goods, services, and capital will be constrained. Despite initial concerns, the OPEC nations have shown little interest in expanding direct investment in the industrial nations, and the developing countries already have large debt positions. Thus, there is very real concern with the banking system's ability to channel the expanding OPEC currency holdings back into real investment, particularly given the erosion in confidence in the dollar. The alternatives facing the United States in the 1980s may force a choice between a continuing defense of the dollar as a reserve currency, and the rate of growth of domestic output. In other words, expansionary policies added to a high underlying rate of inflation could conceivably put great pressure on the value of the dollar, and force a fundamental shift in the international monetary system.

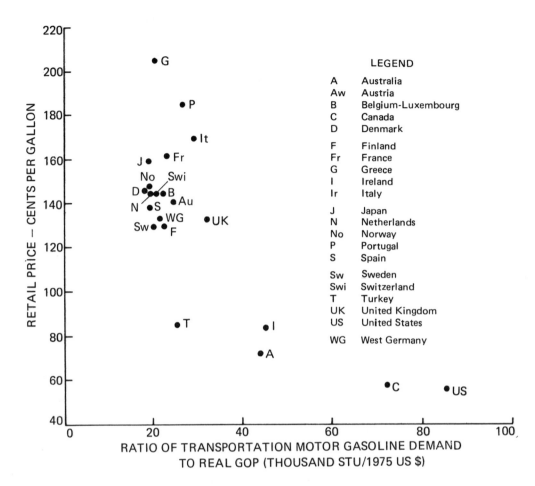

Figure 21.3 Cross-Country Comparison of Motor Gasoline Demand in 1975

Source: Council of Economic Advisers, Economic Report of the President, 1978, p. 189.

The strains on the United States alliance system imposed by the continuing energy dilemma have been obvious for some time. The crisis has forced an expanded range and frequency of international consultations, particularly through the OECD apparatus, but fundamental disagreements on energy policy persist. Competition for crude oil in the spot market was intense following the United States decision to end imports from Iran in 1979. For example, in December of 1979 the Carter administration attacked Japan for "unseemly haste" in purchasing Iranian oil. The oil importers were unable to agree to reductions in import levels, although there was an agreement to hold imports at least constant.[16] Recessions in the early 1980s reduced the demand for oil, produced a temporary excess supply, and alleviated the intense competition for oil supplies, but the long-term problem of energy supply remains.

It would be difficult to overstate the importance of the fundamental shift in world energy markets to the future of the industrial nations. President Carter declared in January of 1980 that the Persian Gulf area is of vital interest to the United States, and expanded defense budgets have been planned to provide a more rapid deployment capability in general, with specific emphasis on Middle East contingencies. Moreover, the dependence of the industrial nations on crude oil imports is tied up with the expanded interdependence of the economies of those nations and with common defense objectives.

INTERDEPENDENCE AND ALLIANCES: THE CASE OF NATO

National defense is a "public good" because all citizens in the nation benefit from defense, but a market system cannot develop an arrangement that forces each citizen to pay for the benefit being received. The benefits of defense accrue to those who are willing to pay for the defense they receive as well as to those who are not. Unless the government intervenes to tax citizens and provide defense expenditures, the level of defense provided will be below the social optimum. Similarly, in international defense, where the benefits of common defense are shared among several nations and where mutual capabilities affect the level of security available to all, we have the general problem of nations agreeing to an appropriate mix of expenditures in the common interest, despite the fact that they will receive increased security from the expenditures of others whether they contribute or not. Thus, as with other public goods, collective national security requires difficult negotiations and agreements on the appropriate sharing of the defense burden and the distribution of defense capabilities.

The nations of the NATO alliance have a great interest in what Lawrence Krause and Joseph Nye have called "collective economic security." This interest is based on the realization of the interdependence of their national economies. The extent to which governments accept the principle of collective economic security is reflected in their willingness to accept international surveillance of their economic policies, to respond to external criticism of the international impacts of those policies, and to permit international organizations to intervene in the operation of domestic and international markets.[17] Paralleling the NATO military alliance, which is aimed at common security, is a complex web of international economic organizations aimed at collective economic security. In practical terms it is impossible to isolate security interests and economic interests from each other, because the continuing negotiation processes involving security and economic considerations are conducted simultaneously, and frequently by the same individuals.

These security and economic interests merge most obviously in negotiations over sharing the burden of the NATO alliance. For example, the forward deployment of United States forces in West Germany imposes a balance of payments drain on the United States and makes United States defense expenditures subject to variations based on shifts in the exchange value of the dollar. In the late 1970s, the devaluation of the dollar compared to the mark meant not only an erosion of pay for United States forces stationed in Germany, but also an increase in outlays for procurement and operations. Such outlays can be "offset" by expenditures of NATO allies in the United States, particularly on weapon systems, or by a sharing of the operating expenses of United States forces overseas in the form of base construction or transportation. However, we could also contemplate a wider range of "offsets" which involve cooperation in regulating exchange rates, trade policies, capital flow restrictions, and so forth. Thus the sharing of the burden for common security cannot be evaluated separately from the burden for common economic security.

From World War II through the late 1960's, the convergence of economic and security interests provided a solid foundation for the NATO alliance. The reconstruction of Western Europe under the Marshall Plan meant a stronger economic base to deter Soviet expansion, and also meant larger, expanding markets for United States products and direct capital investment. The economic burden of the alliance for the United States was offset by a strong United States balance of trade position and by the stability of the dollar. The dramatic recovery of the economies of Western Europe and Japan, the balance of payments problems in the United States reflected in the devaluations of the early 1970s, the shift toward detente with the Soviet Union, and the failure of United States efforts in Vietnam, ended the tidy coincidence of economic and security objectives. The Nixon Doctrine, proclaimed in Guam in July, 1969, called on the United States to reduce its defense commitments and shift the burden of common defense to other nations. Real United States defense expenditures fell throughout most of the 1970s, even as the rapid increases in the price of oil imposed major resource drains on the United States and its allies, and the rate of growth in the United States slowed to less than 2 percent per year by the end of the decade. Accelerating inflation, an eroding dollar, and a shrinking defense commitment in the United States placed growing pressure on the foundations of the NATO alliance.

By the end of the 1970s, however, security objectives became more clearly defined by growing Soviet defense expenditures and expanding Soviet activity on the periphery of the vital Middle East oil fields. While negotiations continued on Mutual Balanced Force Reductions in Europe and on Strategic Arms Limitations, United States policy shifted toward managing competition with the Soviet Union from a position of greater military strength. It was also clear that the United States could no longer direct the NATO alliance from a position of overwhelming military and economic strength. Nuclear parity increased the relative importance of conventional forces, and the growing economic parity of the United States and its allies increased concern over the appropriate sharing of the economic burden for those forces. Moreover, the joint dependence of the United States and its allies on Middle East oil created not only a common concern for the defense of oil sources, but also strong national concerns for the protection of available energy sources. Thus, security and economic interests were increasingly intertwined, and not necessarily reinforcing.

The balancing of these security and economic interests has therefore become more complicated, and periodic consultations at the highest levels of government have become the rule of the day. In the late 1970s, annual economic "summits" were held to coordinate the economic policies of the major industrial powers, including Japan. These summits—at Ramboillet in 1975, in Puerto Rico in 1976, in London in 1977, in Bonn in 1978, in Tokyo in 1979, in Venice in 1980, in Ottawa in 1981, and in Versailles in 1982—provided a mechanism for coordinating policies that had in the past been fragmented over NATO, OECD, GATT, and other groups. While the summits themselves may not provide the best vehicle for reconciling fundamental differences, the international working groups established to provide the staff work for the summits have, in essence, become standing coordinating committees, facilitating negotiation at the highest levels.

At the London meeting in 1977, President Carter proposed a Long Term Defense Program (LTDP) for NATO. The LTDP, which was adopted in 1978, called for improvements in readiness, reinforcement, reserve mobilization, electronic warfare, air defense, logistics, theater nuclear modernization, maritime posture, communications, and rationalization of armaments production. Part of this program was an agreement with Europe to permit fair competition in international bidding in weapons procurement, to encourage specialization in the development of families of weapons systems, and to arrange for the dual production of some systems in several countries.

The sharing of the defense burden must be measured not only in terms of total outlays, the portion of national product allocated to defense or in active and reserve manpower levels, but also in terms of the effectiveness of resources allocated to the alliance. For example, if each nation produced its own tank system, relative expenditures would tend to exaggerate the contribution to total defense because of the high cost of domestic production and the limitations imposed on joint operations.

The issues of "interoperability" and "standardization" became central elements in NATO negotiations in the late 1970s. According to Dewey Bartlett, standardization may be defined as "the effort to adopt common doctrine, procedures, and equipment within NATO whenever major economic, military, or political benefits can be gained. Many approaches to standardization exist. Common equipment may be obtained through joint development (as in the case of the Multi-Role Combat Aircraft), coproduction of components (the F-16 fighter), licensing of production (Raytheon's Hawk missile), or direct purchase (the Lance missile)."[19] Interoperability, on the other hand, simply applies to the ability to use different weapons and systems together in the field. Interoperability is widely accepted as pure common sense, and the economic and political consequences of placing interoperability constraints on weapon system design are not severe. Standardization, however, is a continuing point of disagreement because it involves the selection of one weapon system for joint procurement, with major contract implications for different national producers.

The issue of standardization illustrates the growing interdependence of the allied economies, and the recovery of Western Europe relative to the United States. Until the late 1960s, standardization was a by-product of United States domination of arms production, but in the 1970s European arms production became a significant factor in the alliance structure. According to economist Herman L. Gilster, in 1978 NATO employed "4 different types of tanks, 31 different types of antitank weapons where 5 would suffice, and 11 different types of aircraft for 5 combat missions," resulting in wastes "estimated from $10-15 billion" annually.[20] According to economic theory, the answer to this dilemma is straightforward: comparative advantage. Unfortunately, the scale of production and the level of research and development in the United States gives the United States a comparative advantage for most weapons systems, and standardization through United States dominance is no longer politically acceptable in Europe. Thus arms production agreements are dominated by concerns for offsets, and the difficulty is to find a formula that preserves the economic efficiency available through standardization, while satisfying political concerns for the distribution of jobs and profits. Joint production and licensing agreements were reached for the F-16 and F-5 fighter aircraft in 1975, and negotiations in the late 1970s led to joint production of the Airborne Warning and Control System (AWACS). However, experience with such joint production agreements has been less than fully satisfactory. Gilster writes, "The fundamental problem with arrangements such as these is that there is no necessary correlation between the need to procure and the capacity to produce. Making procurement the basis for sharing production leads to inefficiency and increased cost."[21]

While quality and efficiency arguments are important, most analysts still use macroeconomic data on the share of GNP going to defense outlays as a measure of the contribution to the joint burdens of the alliance. Table 21.5 depicts the share of GNP committed to defense expenditure by NATO nations in 1980. There is a strong correlation between the size of the nation's GNP and the share of the GNP it allocates to defense. As an extreme illustration of this proposition note that Luxembourg, with the smallest GNP, devotes only 1.2 percent of its GNP to defense, while the United States, with the largest GNP, devotes 5.6 percent of it GNP to defense. There are, of course, important exceptions to this pattern—Turkey and Greece, for example—but the tendency of nations with larger GNPs to devote larger shares of their GNP to defense is clear. Mancur Olson and Richard Zeckhauser argue that this is the expected outcome when the larger country perceives a greater benefit from the public good provided by the international organization, in this case the defense provided by NATO.

Table 21.5
Share of GNP Devoted to Defense Expenditures
by NATO Nations in 1980
(Percentage)

Nation	Percent of GNP
Belgium	3.3
Britain	5.1
Canada	1.8
Denmark	2.4
France	4.1
Germany	3.3
Greece	5.6
Italy	2.4
Luxembourg	1.2
Netherlands	3.1
Norway	2.9
Portugal	3.6
Turkey	4.3
United States	5.6

Source: The International Institute for Strategic Studies, *The Military Balance, 1980–1981* (London: 1981).

As our model indicated, this is in part because each ally gets only a fraction of the benefits of any collective good that is provided, but each pays the full cost of any additional amounts of the collective good. This means that individual members of an alliance or international organization have an incentive to stop providing the collective good long before the Pareto-optimal output for the group has been provided. This is particularly true of the smaller members, who get smaller shares of the total benefits accruing from the good, and who find that they have little or no incentive to provide additional amounts of the collective good once the larger members have provided the amounts they want for themselves, with the result that the burdens are shared in a disproportionate way.[22]

However, while such a distribution of outlays might be anticipated, the perception of the distribution of the burdens of the alliance will become increasingly important as relative economic capabilities converge. Thus the commitment of NATO nations to an increase in real defense outlays of at least 3 percent per year beginning in 1978 was particularly important in demonstrating support for a balanced distribution of the defense burden.

Dollar measures of defense outlays may understate significant contributions to the alliance. The manpower balance, for example, is also extremely important to the alliance structure. As Secretary of Defense Harold Brown argued:

> The USSR maintains standing armed forces of roughly four million while we maintain two million. But our NATO allies contribute nearly three million throughout the alliance while non-USSR Warsaw Pact allies contribute only a million to their side. The two sides are therefore approximately equal in existing manpower, allowing the United States an all-volunteer force while at the same time giving us a counterweight to Soviet military strength in the world's most important theater of potential conflict. Through conscription a number of our allies obtain manpower at a lower budgetary cost than we can. . . Over 90 percent of the peacetime NATO forces deployed in Europe are European. European military aircraft comprise 75 percent of the total located in the NATO area in peacetime. The allies furnish to us, free of charge, a considerable amount of real estate and a number of facilities that might otherwise produce sizable revenues.[23]

In an even larger sense, however, the sharing of the military burden cannot be divorced from the sharing of the economic burden. In the fall of 1978 and 1979, the United States Federal Reserve Board announced a series of extraordinary actions designed to strengthen the exchange value of the dollar by restricting the supply of money and raising domestic interest rates. These actions were in direct response to pressures by our allies, particularly West Germany, to restrict our domestic economy in order to defend the reserve position of the dollar. Such a major concession to collective economic security is just as important to the NATO alliance as is a strengthening of United States forces in Europe. In an age of growing interdependence, economics and security are inseparable, and the future of the NATO alliance will depend as much on joint solutions to the problems of rising energy costs and international liquidity as it will on joint perceptions of common military interests and commitments.

CONCLUSION

The OPEC oil embargo of 1973 clearly illustrated the vital link between economic interdependence and national security. The markets of the industrialized nations have become increasingly interdependent on each other and heavily dependent on sources of critical raw materials. Such interdependence is not a new historical phenomenon, but the extent of interaction between the United States and other industrialized states has expanded dramatically over the past decade.

Several measures of interdependence have been suggested, including the integration of international labor, capital and technology markets, the ratio of trade to national output, the extent of the communications, transportation and information infrastructure, and concentrations of trade flows in different commodities and within different geographical patterns. The central measure of interdependence, however, is the speed and extent of reaction in a domestic economic market to shifts in market signals from abroad.

Increasing economic interdependence simply means that in accomplishing economic objectives, the responses of other nations to our own economic policies must be considered, because those responses will have a substantial impact on our ability to achieve domestic economic objectives. For example, the integration of international capital markets, illustrated by the emergence of the Eurocurrency markets, means that management of the domestic money supply must include an assessment of the impact on international monetary flows of interest rate differentials. As a further example, a judgment on whether or not to support Chrysler with further loan guarantees must be linked to import policies on automobiles from Japan and the European Community. To extend the illustration, if the European Community imposed tighter quotas on imports from Japan, the United States would face even greater pressure from diverted Japanese exports. The domestic economic objectives concerning Chrysler must clearly be viewed in the broader context of trade policy toward Japan and the European Community.

The traditional policy of the United States has been to support free trade, as reflected in a commitment to lowering tariff barriers through negotiations under the General Agreement on Trade and Tariffs. The Tokyo Round of negotiations continued the trend toward reduced tariff barriers. Agreements to reduce nontariff barriers to trade, however, have been more difficult to achieve. In the face of balance of payments problems throughout the industrialized nations caused by the rapid increases in crude oil prices, the pressure to expand nontariff barriers in the form of import quotas has increased.

Despite a decade of debate the Western industrialized nations remain highly vulnerable to disruptions in crude oil supplies. Higher energy prices have brought substantial conservation, particularly in the United States, and President Reagan's actions to decontrol the price of crude oil produced in the United States should accelerate that process. Production of coal in the United States has expanded and will continue to expand over the next decade, with an apparent willingness to accept the environmental impacts of stripmining and burning higher sulphur fuel. There are indications that greater reliance on solar energy will be more and more economically feasible. However, nuclear plant construction has come to a virtual standstill in the United States and no breakthrough in breeder reactor technology appears imminent.

Aside from Great Britain with its North Sea oil, the picture in Western Europe and Japan is more dismal. The possibilities for conservation in those nations are far more limited in the United States, because of much lower beginning gasoline consumption. Coal reserves are far less abundant, and coal transportation costs remain high. The outlook is for continuing dependence on oil from the Middle East, and there is even pressure to diversify energy sources through greater reliance on imports from the Soviet Union. West Germany has initiated an agreement for a natural gas pipeline with the Soviet Union. That agreement could make West Germany dependent on the Soviet Union for fully 30 percent of its natural gas.

Within this context of expanded interdependence among the industrialized nations and continuing dependence, at least for the next decade, on OPEC crude oil, the members of the NATO alliance must reconcile their economic and military objectives. The need to coordinate economic and military policies at the highest levels has produced increasing reliance on annual economic summits. The 1977 summit in London produced a long-term plan for upgrading NATO readiness, and subsequently an agreement was reached to expand defense outlays by 3 percent per year in real terms in each member nation. The Reagan administration has deemphasized the need to meet such precise spending targets, but it has emphasized the need for thorough consultation and a commitment to improved NATO readiness. The alliance faces continuing problems, however, in reconciling how the burdens of the alliance should be shared and in coming to grips with the security implications of continuing reliance on Middle East oil or new reliance on natural gas from the Soviet Union.

NOTES

1 Richard Cooper, "Economic Interdependence and Foreign Policy in the Seventies," *World Politics*, 24, No. 2 (January, 1972), pp. 159–181.
2 W. Michael Blumenthal, "Steering in Crowded Waters," *Foreign Affairs* (July, 1978), p. 82.
3 Klaus Knorr, "Economic Interdependence and National Security" in Klaus Knorr and Frank N. Trager, eds., *Economic Issues and National Security* (Lawrence, Kan.: Allen Press, Inc., 1977), p. 7.

4 *International Economic Report of the President, 1977* (Washington, D.C.: Government Printing Office, 1977), pp. 138 and 148, and *Economic Report of the President, 1980* (Washington, D.C.: Government Printing Office, 1980), pp. 323–325.

5 For a more detailed approach to growth cycle coordination, see Philip A. Klein, *Business Cycles in The Post-War World* (Washington, D.C.: American Enterprise Institute, 1976).

6 *Economic Report of the President, 1980, op. cit.*, pp. 325–327.

7 Federal Reserve Bank of New York, "National Policies Toward Direct Investment," *Quarterly Review*, Vol. 4, No. 4 (Winter 1979–80), p. 23.

8 This presentation of the Eurocurrency markets is based on the excellent summary by Edward J. Frydl, "The Debate Over Regulating the Eurocurrency Markets," *ibid.*, pp. 11–20.

9 Gregory Schmid, "Interdependence Has Its Limits," *Foreign Policy* (Winter 1975–76), pp. 192, 194.

10 Robert E. Baldwin, *The Multilateral Trade Negotiations: Toward Greater Liberalization* (Washington, D.C.: American Enterprise Institute, 1979).

11 Congressional Budget Office, *The Effects of the Tokyo Round of Multilateral Negotiations on the U.S. Economy: An Updated View* (Washington, D.C.: Government Printing Office, 1979), p. 47.

12 *Ibid.*, p. 48.

13 Estimates by Robert Crandall of the Brookings Institute as quoted in "Steel Fence," *Wall Street Journal* (February 11, 1980), p. 20.

14 W. Michael Blumenthal, *op. cit.*, p. 87.

15 See, for example, Robert Stobaugh and Daniel Yergin, eds., *Energy Future: Report of the Energy Project at the Harvard Business School* (New York: Random House, 1979), p. 232.

16 "Oil's New Power Structure," *Business Week* (December 24, 1979), p. 86.

17 Lawrence B. Krause and Joseph S. Nye, "Reflections on the Economics and Politics of International Economic Organization," in C. Fred Bergsten and Lawrence B. Krause, eds., *World Politics and International Economics* (Washington, D.C.: The Brookings Institution, 1975). See also, Ronald I. Meltzer, "Contemporary Security Dimensions of International Trade Relations," in Knorr and Trager, *op. cit.*, pp. 200–230.

18 Harold Brown, *Department of Defense Annual Report, Fiscal Year 1980*, pp. 45–49.

19 Dewey F. Bartlett, "Standardizing Military Excellence: The Key to NATO's Survival," *AEI Defense Review*, No. 6 (1977), p. 3.

20 Herman L. Gilster, *Economics and NATO Standardization*, Directorate for International Economic Affairs, Office of the Assistant Secretary for Defense for International Security Affairs (August, 1978), p. 1.

21 *Ibid.*, p. 7.

22 Mancur Olson, Jr. and Richard Zeckhauser, "An Economic Theory of Alliances," *The Review of Economics and Statistics* (August, 1966), p. 279. For a brief mathematical explication of this result, see Samuel Bowles and David Kendrick, *Notes and Problems in Microeconomic Theory* (Chicago: Markham Publishing Co., 1970), pp. 77–79.

23 Harold Brown, *op. cit.*, p. 221.

SELECTED REFERENCES

Ryan C. Amacher, Gottfried Haberler, and Thomas D. Willett, eds., *Challenges to a Liberal Economic Order* (Washington, D.C.: American Enterprise Institute, 1979).

C. Fred Bergsten and Lawrence B. Krause, eds., *World Politics and International Economics* (Washington, D.C.: The Brookings Institution, 1975).

James R. Golden, *NATO Burden Sharing: Risks and Opportunities* (New York: Praeger Press, 1983).

Klaus Knorr and Frank N. Trager, eds. *Economic Issues and National Security* (Lawrence, Kan.: Allen Press, Inc., 1977).

Robert Stobaugh and Daniel Yergin, eds., *Energy Future: Report of the Energy Project at the Harvard Business School* (New York: Random House, 1979).

Chapter 22
National Security Implications of East–West Trade

INTRODUCTION

As we saw in the last chapter, the period of the 1970s was marked by a growing level and awareness of economic interdependence, particularly among the nations in the Organization for Economic Cooperation and Development. Interrelationships among the advanced industrial nations are commonly referred to as "West-West" issues to distinguish them from interactions of the industrial democracies with communist states, "East-West" exchanges, and interactions with the developing nations, "North-South" relationships. This chapter will focus on the policy issues inherent in East-West economic interactions, and Chapter 26 will develop the importance of North-South economic relations for national security policy.[1]

The literature on economic interdependence in the 1970s included the traditional measures of trade statistics, population pressures, and resource availability, but there was also new emphasis on the threat to international liquidity, the transmission of balance of payments pressures through floating exchange rates, common environmental problems, communication linkages, and the future of space and the seas. The major thrust of these analyses of interdependence was that the postwar economic dominance of the United States would be constrained, at least to the point that international economic factors would have significant impacts not only on domestic economic policies, but also on policies in other areas affecting national security.[2] The post-World War II economic order, based on economic dominance of the United States and limited economic interaction with the communist states, had ended.

The most dramatic evidence of the impact of international markets on domestic economic policy came early in the decade of the 1970's in the form of the 1972 wheat sale to the Soviet Union, the so-called "Great Grain Robbery," and the OPEC oil embargo and associated increases in crude oil prices in 1973. In each case, substantial inflationary pressures were added to a domestic economy that was already suffering from a wage-price spiral whose origins could be traced to the failure of timely fiscal policy during the early phases of the Vietnam War. Domestic wage and price controls proved to be an insufficient response to those pressures and illustrated the dangers of partial, temporary tampering with a free market structure.

One response to the threat of increasing economic dependence was to emphasize programs that produced economic independence in vital areas. This was the avowed approach to growing energy dependence, although the actual steps taken in this direction were minimal. Stockpiling oil to limit vulnerability proved to be a popular but ineffective alternative to reducing domestic demand or subsidizing domestic supply. Although Presidents Ford and Carter proposed major energy conservation and development legislation to foster energy independence, their proposals met cool responses in Congress.

Another response was a search for economic levers that might be used to gain political influence or to deter aggressive economic policies against the United States. Many observers called for direct "linkage" between United States economic policy and a desired foreign political response. This argument was, and is, applied most strongly to economic relations with the Soviet Union. The underlying assumption in such analyses is that economic arrangements with the USSR are essentially asymmetrical; the Soviets rely on high technology and agricultural imports, but the United States has little need for Soviet exports. Thus, the argument continues, economic concessions to the Soviet Union should be made only when they are directly linked to specific political concessions.

The OPEC oil embargo raised the possibility of retaliating against similar actions with various types of economic sanctions. In such cases there would be less emphasis on political linkage, and more stress on deterring aggressive actions. Retaliatory economic policies might be announced in advance to increase their deterrent impact.

Against this background of concern for economic interdependence and the possibility of exerting economic leverage to achieve other policy objectives, United States economic policy toward communist nations has undergone a series of wrenching shifts. The 1970s began with a new euphoria over the prospects of easing military and political tensions through a pattern of expanded economic exchange. Trade restrictions were confined to items with clear military application, and the 1972 Trade Agreement with the Soviet Union was expected to usher in a new era of rapidly expanding trade. By the end of the decade, the euphoria had passed. Although trade did in fact expand, a series of Congressional actions in 1973 and 1974 and a gradual shift toward additional trade restrictions in the Carter administration sharply limited the level of United States trade with the Soviet Union.

At the same time, Western Europe welcomed the opportunity to restore traditional trading relationships with Eastern Europe and the Soviet Union. This growing divergence between the trade policy of the United States and its NATO allies presents a fundamental dilemma for United States foreign policy. If the United States does attempt to use economic leverage against communist nations, the cooperation of allies who are in a position to take up the economic slack is essential. There are only a few special cases in which unilateral sanctions imposed on high technology exports without the support of Western Europe and Japan have any promise of providing effective pressure on Soviet policy.

In the following sections we will provide an overview of the levels of East-West trade, and develop some of the issues involved in the transfer of Western technology. With this background we will then explore several cases that highlight the prospects and problems of applying leverage in these economic interactions. The Kama River Plant provides a classic example of trade-offs between the hope for a general relaxation of tension through economic interaction and the risk of diversion of technology for military purposes. United States wheat export policy reflects the importance of trade to the United States economy, the pressure of domestic economic interest groups, and the possibilities of imposing long-term constraints on Soviet growth. The case of the Occidental Petroleum ammonia deal further develops the domestic implications of East-West trade policy, and the prospects for sending foreign policy signals through trade restrictions. Finally, drawing on these illustrations of problems in integrating economic policy into the general process of formulating and implementing our overall foreign policy, we discuss some of the institutional adjustments that are needed to manage East-West economic exchanges.

AN OVERVIEW OF EAST-WEST TRADE AND TECHNOLOGY TRANSFER

Alexander Gerschenkron's seminal study of *Economic Backwardness in Historical Perspective* traced patterns of industrial development in nineteenth-century Europe and concluded, in part, that industrial spurts, if and when they occurred, were reinforced by technology transfers from leading economies to the more backward economy. The more backward the undeveloped nation was at the time of its industrial spurt, the greater was the transfer of technology. Applying this model to Russia, Gerchenkron attributed part of the rapid industrial spurt in the two decades preceding World War I to the emphasis of the Witte system on importing the latest Western technology.[3] Anthony Sutton extended the analysis of Soviet growth into the twentieth century and concluded that each major growth spurt followed an influx of Western capital and technology.[4]

Of course, Gerschenkron and Sutton would be the last to support a unicausal explanation of economic growth, but it is clear that technology imports have been an important factor in industrialization in general, and in Soviet expansion in particular. The argument for the control of high technology industrial exports follows directly from this conclusion. To the extent that such technology flows to potential adversaries can be restricted, the adversaries' overall economic growth can be reduced. More specifically, limitations on the export of technology and products required by an adversary's military establishment may reduce or eliminate some military capabilities, or at least increase the cost of obtaining them.

Views on the desirability of trade with the Soviet Union have varied sharply between those who agree with Lloyd George and those who believe Lenin.

> I believe we can save her (Russia) by trade. Commerce has a sobering influence. Trade, in my opinion, will bring an end to the ferocity . . . and the crudity of Bolshevism surer than any other method.
>
> Lloyd George, 1922

> The capitalist countries . . . will supply us with the materials and technology we lack and will restore our military industry, which we need for our future victorious attacks on our suppliers. In other words, they will work hard in order to prepare their own suicide.
>
> V. I. Lenin, 1921

Thus we are faced with two judgments. First, how dependent is the Soviet Union on transfers of Western technology in general, and United States technology in particular? Second, is the Soviet Union likely to alter other objectives in order to obtain Western technology? Until 1969, our policy judgment was that Western technology was important, but that Soviet objectives could not be influenced by trade. From 1969 to roughly 1976, the judgment was that slowing Soviet growth made Western technology even more important, and that trade could create an improved political climate. At some point between 1976 and 1980, the judgment shifted in degree to suggest that concessions in some areas of Soviet policy might be possible, but they could only be achieved by a more explicit linkage of trade to foreign policy and not by simply expanding the level of economic interaction.

As shown in Table 22.1, exports to the Soviet Union amounted to roughly .1 percent of total United States exports in 1960, .2 per cent in 1970, over 1.1 percent in 1973, and about .9 percent in 1977. The precise ratio obtained in any given year is very sensitive to the level of agricultural exports, which varied with domestic Soviet production, but these figures are illustrative of the rapid expansion in trade in the early 1970s, and the leveling off of trade at relatively low levels in the late 1970s. United States exports to Eastern Europe and the People's Republic of China reflect this same general pattern. Exports to the Soviet Union and Eastern Europe have far outpaced imports from those countries, reflecting trade surpluses for the United States and deficits for the communist states.

Table 22.1

United States Trade with Selected Communist Nations: 1960–1977

(Millions of Dollars)

	1960	1965	1970	1971	1972	1973	1974	1975	1976	1977
U.S. Exports to:										
Eastern Europe	154.9	94.8	234.9	222.2	276.9	606.5	823.4	951.0	1197.5	911.9
U.S.S.R.	39.6	45.2	118.7	162.0	542.2	1194.7	609.2	1836.0	2353.9	1623.5
P.R.C.	——	——	——	——	63.5	689.6	807.4	303.8	160.2	171.3
U.S. Imports from:										
Eastern Europe	58.3	94.8	153.5	165.8	225.0	306.1	539.4	472.9	648.7	683.7
U.S.S.R.	22.6	42.6	72.3	57.2	95.5	220.1	350.4	255.3	220.2	234.2
P.R.C.	.3	.5	.1	4.9	32.4	64.9	114.7	157.4	192.7	202.7

Source: *International Economic Report of the President (Washington, D.C.: Government Printing Office, 1977); U.S. Department of Commerce, "U.S. Trade Statistics with Communist Countries" (February 15, 1978).*

The euphoria over expanded trade associated with detente faded rapidly after the Congress imposed limitations on trade credits and denied most favored nation tariff status to the Soviet Union in 1974. The accumulating debt of the communist states also placed sharp limitations on the potential for expanding trade, as shown in Table 22.2. Without the prospect for trade credits, these debt restrictions posed a serious constraint. The sharp increase in Polish debt is particularly striking.

Table 22.2

Net Hard Currency Debt of Selected Communist Countries: 1970–1980

(Billion Dollars)

Country	1970	1974	1975	1976	1977	1979	1980
Bulgaria	.7	1.2	1.8	2.3	2.7	3.9	4.3
Czechoslovakia	.3	1.1	1.5	2.1	2.7	4.2	5.0
East Germany	1.0	2.8	3.8	5.2	6.0	10.5	12.0
Hungary	.6	1.5	2.1	2.8	3.4	8.1	7.6
Poland	.8	3.9	6.9	10.2	13.0	21.0	24.0
Romania	1.2	2.6	3.0	3.3	4.0	6.8	9.0
Total East Europe	4.6	13.1	19.1	25.9	31.8	54.5	61.9
U.S.S.R.	1.9	5.0	10.0	14.0	16.0	16.5	15.2

Sources:
1970–1977: Office of Economic Research, CIA.
1979–1980: Business Week (February 16, 1981), p. 86.

Western Europe, however, was under no self-imposed restriction on trade credits, and its trade with the Soviet Union and Eastern Europe continued to expand throughout the decade of the 1970s. For example, in 1978 East Germany did $9.6 billion worth of foreign trade with the West, or roughly 29 percent of its total exports. West Germany accounted for $4.4 billion of this trade, generating by some estimates about 500,000 jobs in some 4,500 West German firms. West Germany pursued this trade by charging East Germany no customs duties and providing interest-free "swing credit" to finance trade deficits. All other nations grant East Germany at least trade rights equal to those available to other states, but the United States prohibits trade credits and denies East Germany most favored nation tariff status. As a result, the United States generated only $.2 billion of trade with East Germany in 1978.[5]

Arnaud de Borchgrave emphasizes the critical importance of trade with the Soviet Union to West Germany.

> The Soviets are constantly proselytizing about the growing relevance of Soviet miltiary power to Europe's future—and, by implication, about the growing irrelevance of American power. And trade with the Soviet bloc—a two-way flow that amounted to nearly $80 billion last year (1979)—is much more important to the economies of Western Europe than it is to U.S. business. Soviet exports to West Germany, Russia's biggest Western trade partner, soared to $4.5 billion in 1979, up 28 per cent. West Germany gets 17 per cent of its natural gas from the U.S.S.R., along with 38 per cent of its enriched uranium for nuclear power. Negotiations are under way between the Russians and a German consortium for a $12 billion natural-gas pipeline deal.[6]

These illustrations suggest an important divergence in the trade policies of the United States and its European allies. Trade with the East is far more important for Western Europe than for the United States in both absolute and relative terms. In addition, Western Europe has stronger traditional political and economic ties with the East. As we will see later in this chapter, these differences pose major problems in orchestrating any form of economic leverage with the communist states.

The importance of the role of Western imports and Western technology in the Soviet Union is unclear. The low levels of trade compared with total Soviet output—exports were about 4 percent of total production in the late 1970s—suggest limited potential for trade leverage. Indeed, in Soviet planning trade is treated as a residual that makes up for shortfalls in domestic inputs. Total trade levels, however, can be deceiving, and there is substantial evidence that Western imports and technology are extremely important in some sectors. The agricultural sector is one obvious example, but there are also important weaknesses in the Soviet production of motor vehicles, natural gas, oil, timber, chemicals, and fertilizer, as well as in their ability to extract metals and to employ computer-assisted systems. These weaknesses were in areas emphasized in the 9th and 10th five-year plans.[7]

Donald Green and Herbert Levine have argued that Western machinery has made only a marginal contribution to Soviet growth in recent years. Their estimates suggest that from 1968 to 1973, Western machinery accounted for about 5 percent of total Soviet investment, and added only about 2½ percent to total industrial growth.[8] Philip Hanson supports the general finding that Western technology made a limited contribution to overall Soviet growth in this period, but he adds that the relative dependence was greater in the areas of computers, chemicals, light machinery, timber, paper, and shipbuilding.[9] Of course, the sample period for these studies was the early years of detente, and these results probably understate the potential impact of Western technology if restrictions were reduced and credits were available to finance expanded trade.

Hanson observed this potential for a larger future impact of Western technology, but noted that "the limits imposed by difference of economic system on the scale of negotiable technology transfer from the West may still prove to be severe," and that the central question concerns, "the capacity of the Soviet economic system to absorb foreign technology more rapidly and to procure indigenous innovation on a scale commensurate with the size of the economy." The Soviet Union faces numerous problems in the absorption of Western technology. Although a concerted effort is clearly being made to adapt the latest technology to local production processes, and particularly to screen such technology for possible military applications, the difficulties of reverse-engineering—that is, deducing manufacturing design from an end product—are severe in many high technology areas.[11] Moreover, in many instances an entire network of supply, servicing, and distribution must be established to support the new technology problems that have been particularly acute in the computer software area.[12]

Mark Miller summarizes these findings:

> To recapitulate, the Soviet investment in Western technology is rather small, and the total impact on the Soviet economy is modest. At the same time, the effect of Western technology on certain sectors has been substantial, raising both productivity and the quality of output. From this, it can be concluded that in the Soviet schema, Western technology serves as a "quick fix" for those industries that are most critical to the technical progress and basic strength of the Soviet economy. In lower priority areas, such as consumer goods, Moscow apparently believes that these requirements can be met by the country's indigenous capabilities and imports from Eastern Europe. In other words, hard currency is too precious to expend on technologies that do not augment the economic muscle of the state.[13]

Thus we are left with a mixed view of the importance of Western trade and technology to the Soviet Union. Overall levels of trade remain small compared to the total level of Soviet output, but in several sectors the contribution of Western technology has been important if not critical to Soviet planners. Even in those areas in which Western technology could potentially have a significant impact on the Soviet economy, important constraints on the capacity to absorb that technology remain. Finally, the trade patterns of the 1970s reflect a divergence in the trade policies of the United States and her West European allies, and this divergence has important implications for the structure of the alliance and the possibilities for the use of economic leverage to obtain political concessions.

HIGH TECHNOLOGY EXPORT CONTROLS

Although free international trade raises the prospects of greater economic efficiency through specialization, the potential gains in efficiency must frequently be weighed against other competing objectives. Trade with a potential adversary raises questions about the direct contributions of trade to military capacity, about the effect of enabling adversaries to divert their resources to the defense sector, and about the reliability of international sources of supply in a crisis. All of these arguments were used to justify industrial export controls following World War II.

Evolution of Export Control Policy

The Export Control Act of 1949 established trade restrictions that limited the economic and military potential of possible adversaries, and the leverage of Marshall Plan aid was used to gain broad support from Western Europe and Japan in enforcing an embargo of industrial exports to Eastern Europe, the Soviet Union, and the People's Republic of China. An informal Coordinating Committee (COCOM) was established to provide a forum to create itemized embargo lists and to review applications for exceptions to the embargo restrictions. Excepting Iceland, the members of NATO, as well as Japan, have joined COCOM, although there are no formal treaty agreements.

Until the late 1960s, export restrictions were directed against the broad economic potential of an embargoed nation. Distinctions between military and civilian products were rarely drawn, since the presumption was that even civilian imports would enable the embargoed nation to shift domestic production into military outputs. Then, in 1969, there was a fundamental shift in United States and COCOM industrial export controls policy.

The Export Administration Act of 1969 removed the criterion of contribution to economic potential as the test of a product or technology export, and limited restrictions of the "export of goods and technology which would make a signficiant contribution to the *military* potential of any other nation or nations which would prove detrimental to the national security of the United States." The act also added a new requirement to use "economic resources and trade potential to further the sound growth and stability of its [the United States] economy as well as to further its national security and foreign policy objectives."[14] Of course, the change in language did not simplify the process of administering export controls. Indeed, the act required far more subtle distinctions to be applied based on potential and intended use of the export. As the act has been applied, some exports with possible military applications have been permitted as long as adequate "safeguards" against diversion to military use are applied. Thus, during a period of rapid technological advances in products such as computers with dual military and civilian applications, the criteria for evaluating applications for export licenses became far more complex. Despite sharp reductions in the lists of restricted items, the shift in the overall attitude toward trade with communist states has led to an avalanche of requests for licenses in areas requiring sensitive, complex assessments.

Backlogs in the time required to process export applications and the strong markets for high technology exports have prompted a fundamental review of export control policy. In February, 1976, the *Defense Science Board Task Force on Export of U.S. Technology* submitted its report (widely known as the Bucy Report), which concluded that the control of design and manufacturing knowhow was "vital" and that restrictions should be limited to "critical items with direct military significance."[15] The report specifically challenged the value of safeguards that had been used to prevent the diversion of technology from approved uses in recipient countries, and questioned the effectiveness of COCOM in restricting end-product sales.[16] Although the study focused only on airframes, aircraft jet engines, and instrumentation and solid state devices, the conclusions were felt to be applicable in other high technology areas as well.

The implications of this report for United States high technology export controls were significant because it recommended sharp reductions in the list of restricted end-products and increased emphasis on controlling design and manufacturing technology flows even to COCOM countries. The decisions regarding the export of end-products rested on the difficulty of reverse engineering in the technology areas examined, on the problems of enforcing the current COCOM restrictions, and on the excessive time required to obtain decisions on many export applications.

The Export Control Process

The excessive amount of time required to process export applications led President Ford to establish a Presidential Task Force in 1976 to examine the administration of export controls. The Task Force found that of the 52,107 applications received in 1975 to export items in restricted categories, 4,856 were for communist destinations. In other words, most of the exports were to approved countries, and licenses could be issued as long as the appropriate safeguards on re-shipment to unauthorized deestinations were provided. The vast bulk of applications were then processed under the authority of the Office of Export Administration, within the Department of Commerce, without coordination with other agencies. Some licenses were issued after bilateral clearance with the Departments of Defense or State, or the Energy Research and Development Administration. The remaining 445 cases required formal approval by an Operating Committee with representatives from concerned agencies.[17] The Task Force found that an average Operating Committee Case required over six months of processing from initial application to a final decision, and a typical computer case lasted almost eight months. Some unusual cases remained in the review process for up to sixteen months.[16]

The detailed problems of interagency coordination are not of concern here, except to note that major precedent cases typically require the unanimous approval of Operating Committee representatives. Each concerned agency conducts its own technical and policy review in such cases, accounting for long delays in some instances. Where the Operating Committee cannot reach a decision, cases may be reviewed by the Export Administration Review Board at the cabinet level, or ultimately by the president. This process can, of course, be used to adjust application decisions to current foreign policy considerations, either by changing the list of embargoed items and destinations or by providing ad hoc exceptions to policy.

Such adjustments are constrained in part by the need for interagency concurrence. The "Jackson Amendment" to the Department of Defense Appropriations Act of 1975, for example, required that each application to export goods or technology to communist countries be referred to DOD for consultation. The amendment also required that in any case in which the president overruled the Secretary of Defense in an export decision, the president had to inform the Congress of the nature of the DOD concerns.[19] Thus, concessions in export restrictions to obtain other policy objectives would be closely scrutinized.

Export policy is restricted not only by the need for interagency agreement, but also by the requirement for COCOM approval of exceptions to policy. In order for export control policy to be effective, alternative sources of the export must also be restricted. Thus lists of embargoed items must be approved by all members. There have been some notable exceptions to this procedure, such as the unauthorized sale of 150 jet engines and the technology to build them to the People's Republic of China by Great Britain in 1973. In the bulk of cases, however, members have abided by the unanimous consent rule. Critics of the COCOM controls, however, argue that many exports are simply never submitted for COCOM review, since several members believe that the lists of embargoed items are too restrictive. Indeed, a 1976 study of East-West trade problems, conducted by the General Accounting Office, concluded that overseas export control verification and enforcment were insufficient to monitor United States exports, and that the United States had failed to press for acceptable, uniform international compliance standards.[20] Moreover, some restricted items may be purchased by embargoed nations from non-COCOM members, such as Sweden, Austria, or Switzerland. The Bucy Report responded to these criticisms in its call for a reduced embargo list and greater emphasis on enforcement of the reduced embargo, particularly in the area of technology transfer.

Export Controls and Leverage

Any leverage available to the United States through the manipulation of export policy must be coordinated through the COCOM structure. In some areas, United States unilateral export controls are more restrictive than is the overall COCOM embargo, and the United States could, of course, adjust these unilateral restraints. However, the areas in which United States technology significantly leads other COCOM members are limited, and therefore the range for unilateral action is also constrained.

There is, of course, significant pressure from United States firms to expand the range of approved exports and destinations. One major argument they present is that the inadequacy of COCOM controls permits exporters in other nations to exploit United States restrictions. Morevoer, the communist states provide a prime market for technology that is one or two generations removed from the latest Western innovations, and thus they form a profitable outlet for products and equipment with limited Western markets. Aggregate trade statistics that show the small impact of East-West trade on the total United States economy can be a very misleading indicator of the importance of such trade to the companies involved. For example, in 1975 the Herman Corporation, a small foundry in Zelienpole, Pennsylvania, was awarded a $34.5 million contract for a heavy tractor plant in the Soviet Union. Prior to that sale, Herman's best year had been $8 million in total sales.[21] In short, there are strong interest groups in the United States with deep concern over the level of East-West trade and the precise nature of export restrictions. Attempts to expand the controls program to provide increased leverage for some other objective meet with strong domestic opposition.

On the other hand, there are few parallel interest groups supporting expanded trade in communist states through which corresponding pressures could be placed on decision makers. In a perceptive critique of the group approach to Soviet politics, William Odom argued that a careful analysis throws "grave doubt on the emergence of even a limited pluralism in the Soviet system in the coming decades."[22] He concluded that the totalitarian model, despite the current disdain for an excessively monolithic view of Soviet power dispersion, "emphasizes what is truly important in Soviet politics: a high degree of centralized power, with policy initiative wholly reserved for the center."[23]

Central decision makers in the Soviet Union have thus far given little indication of a willingness to accept any direct linkage of economic and political concessions. Despite a widely acknowledged need for high technology imports, particularly in the areas of resource extractions and computers, the Soviet Union refused to accommodate its emigration policies to United States economic pressures in the early 1970s. The 1972 Trade Agreement called for a sharp expansion of U.S.-U.S.S.R. trade, credits for the U.S.S.R., and phased repayment of U.S.S.R. World War II Lend Lease debts totaling $700 million. Opposition to such trade expansion quickly emerged under the leadership of Senator Henry Jackson, and Congress subsequently restricted credits to about one-third of Soviet expectations and passed a Trade Reform Act in 1974 denying the Soviet Union Most Favored Nation tariff status. Under the act Most Favored Nation status could be granted only if the Soviet Union eliminated restrictions on the emigration of Jews.

In apparent response to the emigration provisions of the Trade Reform Act, the Soviet Union renounced the 1972 Trade Accord in January of 1975. Michael Kaser argues that the Soviet Union quickly modified its overall trade strategy, shifting emphasis from the United States to Eastern and Western Europe.[24] The rapid expansion of U.S.-U.S.S.R. trade that characterized the period of 1971 to mid-1974 slowed dramatically until the collapse of the Soviet wheat crop in 1975.

This scenario of events must be interpreted carefully. Most Favored Nation status undoubtedly had symbolic appeal to the Soviet Union, but most of her exports to the United States are duty-free raw materials such as chromium ore, platinum, and diamonds, and only 25 percent of Soviet exports are manufactured goods. Thus most Soviet exports would not be affected by tariff changes, because they are already exempt from tariffs. However, Export-Import credits were not symbolic; they were essential to finance the desired level of Soviet imports. Without them, significant changes in Soviet domestic and international economic planning would be required, and there was a major threat of reduced aggregate growth. Although the prospect of increased credits was not tied directly to emigration policy in United States legislation, the Soviet Union essentially closed the door to further credit negotiations with its rejection of the 1972 Trade Accord.

The important point is simply that the Soviet Union refused to accept any linkage of economic negotiations with its internal political affairs. This rejection was made in spite of the crucial importance of credit to further high technology purchases, and in spite of earlier concessions on Jewish emigration. The availability of some alternative credit sources in Western Europe, the possibility of modified arrangements with Eastern Europe, and the prospect of high technology purchases from sources other than the United States eased the pressure on the Soviet Union somewhat. But in the final analysis, the leadership of the Soviet Union was willing to accept slower growth in order to avoid direct political linkage.

The importance of the availability of non-United States high technology exports must be stressed. The high technology export control program operates at best to retard the rate of development of a military capability, or to increase the opportunity cost of obtaining it. Thus the alternatives to the target nation are to import less desirable substitutes for the embargoed item or to divert domestic resources, and any leverage from controls is limited to the cost of delay rather than the penalty of never achieving a capability.

This brief excursion into the complex arena of United States industrial export controls illustrates the major problems of gaining political leverage through export policy. The requirement for interagency coordination of export policy imposes lengthy delays in the decision process, and provides an arena for agencies that oppose any changes that endanger their positions. Moreover, since most high technology exports are also produced in Western Europe or Japan, policy adjustments must be coordinated with COCOM members. In addition, leverage can work in both directions. Restricting exports hurts U.S. firms as well as the Soviet Union. It is not at all obvious that an export restriction would impose greater pressure on Soviet planners than on United States exporters, and United States exporters are well organized to present their views to various elements of the government.

THE KAMA RIVER PLANT: AN EXERCISE IN DETENTE

The policy judgment from 1969 to roughly 1978 was that high technology export concessions were appropriate in cases that would reinforce the overall political climate of detente. In 1976, for example, the sale of two Control Data Cyber 172 computers to the People's Republic of China was approved as a gesture to the new Chinese leadership. Sale of a similar computer to the Soviet Union had been denied in 1975 on the grounds of inadequate safeguards against diversion to military use. According to the *New York Times*, the sale to China was opposed by the Energy Research and Development Administration on the grounds that the computer could be used to target nuclear missiles. The Department of Defense initially objected that the computers, which were supposed to be used for oil and seismic exploration, could also be used in submarine detection, but the Pentagon withdrew its objection based on the prescribed safeguards. Apparently, Secretary of State Henry Kissinger had recommended that the sale be completed on the "ground of overriding foreign-policy interests." The export license was actually granted to the Compagnie General Geophysique, a French affiliate of Control Data.[25]

The Kama River truck plant was perhaps the centerpiece of export concessions designed to foster a climate of relaxed political tension. The Soviet motor vehicle industry was organized by the Ford Motor Corporation in the 1930s, but by the 1960s Soviet truck design was some two decades behind the United States. The GAZ-51 truck was in continuous production for over 20 years without major modification. In 1966, Fiat built a plant on the Volga, and Fiat plants now contribute roughly one-half of all Soviet passenger car production. Construction of a modern truck production facility at Naberezhnye Chelmy on the Kama River began in 1969. The plant was constructed with 130 United States export licenses and has a design capacity of some 150,000 trucks and 280,000 spare engines per year. In 1979 production was estimated at 75,000 trucks per year with an annual rate of expansion of about 25,000 trucks.[26]

The entire project cost an estimated $3 billion, and roughly one-third of all equipment for the plant came from the United States. The Swindell Division of Pullman Incorporated did much of the design work, although most of the engineering was done by Renault. The impact of this single plant on Soviet truck production, in both volume and quality, was dramatic. In 1970, the Soviet Union was producing 15 vehicles in every four-minute period, and by 1975 that rate had more than doubled. Even TASS noted the contribution of Western technology to this effort: "It would be hard to create such a large modern enterprise with high performance indicators within such a short time without technical cooperation which draws on the best available in the country and abroad. . . ."[27]

Heavy trucks have a fairly obvious military capability, and granting licenses for such an enterprise meant major concessions in export policy. The appearance of Kama River Plant trucks in the Soviet military inventory graphically illustrated the extent of the concessions. In 1980 it was estimated that each Soviet division had between 55 and 60 of the Kama River trucks, and that some 4,000 of the heavy, three-axle vehicles were in East Germany.[28]

The United States commitment to assist in the construction of the Kama River plant came to a head in December of 1972, when IBM made an initial inquiry on the prospect of a major computer sale to the plant, and ultimately submitted a formal application in March of 1974. The case was quickly passed through the Office of Export Administration in the Department of Commerce to the Operating Committee and on to the cabinet level Export Administration Review Board (EARB). The EARB commissioned a special interagency study under DOD leadership to explore possible safeguards that might be employed to prevent military diversion of the computer. IBM initially rejected the proposed safeguards but finally accepted them after EARB insistence, and a license was issued in March 1975, after approval by COCOM.

The use of Kama River trucks in the Soviet Union's late 1979 invasion of Afghanistan triggered a fundamental review of the export of high technology by the Carter administration. The reassessment of high technology export policy had been underway since 1977, but the administration had been torn between the positions that such trade fostered a general climate of cooperation and the view that trade should be seen as an important element in continuing international competition with the Soviet Union. The Soviet invasion of Afghanistan tipped the balance.

OIL, AFGHANISTAN, AND THE NEW ORIENTATION IN EXPORT CONTROL POLICY

In August of 1976, candidate Jimmy Carter was asked, "In the case of the Soviet Union doing things like intervening in Angola, would you favor using our economic leverage and urging our allies to use their economic leverage to get the Russians to cease and desist?" He answered, "Yes, I would," and went on to explain that he would put the Russians on advance notice of the possibility of a "total withholding of trade."[29]

This view of the potential use of export restrictions suggested a larger role for foreign policy considerations in reviewing license requests. The Export Control Act of 1969 as amended grants the president the authority to impose export controls to the extent necessary:

1. to exercise necessary vigilance over exports from the standpoint of their significance to national security;
2. to significantly further United States foreign policies and aid in fulfilling international responsibilities, and
3. to protect the domestic economy from excessive drain of scarce materials and reduce the serious inflationary impact of abnormal foreign demand.[30]

The third provision requires a finding of short domestic supplies, and such controls have been rarely applied (an exception was the limitation of soybean exports to Japan in 1973). The second provision has been used to impose virtually complete embargoes on trade with Cuba, North Korea, and Vietnam, and to control exports to South Africa of items that might be used for military purposes. In the hypothetical case posed to candidate Carter in 1976, the rationale for controls would presumably be aimed at foreign policy objectives, because significance to national security has normally been defined as a direct contribution to military potential under the 1969 act.

Early in the Carter administration, the Soviet Union's anticipated problems with domestic energy sources in the 1980s raised the question of the appropriate policy regarding the export of oil and gas technology. The Soviet Union's need for Western technology in this area had long been understood.[31] Several projects to develop Soviet energy sources had been sidetracked by the denial of export credits under the amendments of the Export-Import Bank act of 1974 and the Trade Act of 1974, but the general United States policy was that the energy sector could be developed to the mutual advantage of the Soviet Union and the United States. A March, 1977, interview with outgoing Executive Secretary of the East-West Foreign Trade Board, Gerald Parsky, illustrates this position.

> **Question:** Do you foresee a possibility for American firms to participate in the development of Soviet oil and natural gas?

> **Answer:** I see this as a very real possibility. Not only does Soviet oil and gas represent a very high potential, but much of their reserves are located in areas of the country which are very difficult to reach. It will require advanced technology and expertise to develop those resources, which United States companies have. Given the size of the reserves involved the potential for cooperation is truly great . . . such cooperation could open up an avenue for our private sector to participate extensively in the development of a resource which we all need.[32]

However, the prospect of Soviet dependence on United States technology also raised questions about the potential for leverage created by restricting or threatening to restrict that technology. In August of 1977 President Carter signed Presidential Directive Number 18, which emphasized the dual cooperative and competitive nature of the relationship with the Soviet Union, and argued that the United States should take advantage of its economic and technological superiority to encourage Soviet cooperation in numerous areas of tension and potential conflict. In a June, 1978 speech, Samuel Huntington, then on the staff of the National Security Council, expanded on this position and argued that the alternatives in technology transfer of either complete denial or *laissez faire* were both unacceptable. Huntington noted that:

> At present, for instance, apart from purely military technology, the door on technological transfers to the Soviet Union is in many respects, wide open. The door on official credits, however, is nailed closed with a double lock—the Stevenson lock and the Jackson-Vanik lock. Consequently, in the economic field, we are in a position where we have little we can do to harm them. . . . We have denied ourselves both the carrot and the stick. If, however, we are to have [a] successful policy of conditioned flexibility, we need to be able to adjust the economic doors, to open or close them as our long-term security interests and the basic state of our political relations with the Soviet Union dictate.[33]

In the summer of 1978, this tilt toward "conditioned flexibility" was applied after the trials of Soviet dissidents Alexsandr Ginsburg and Anatoly Shcharansky. The sale of a Sperry Univac computer to TASS was denied, and the Dresser sale of drill bit technology was suspended. The drill bit technology sale was ultimately approved, but a broad review of energy technology exports was conducted in the fall of 1978. Although no new energy related sales were denied, several items were added to the control lists, and the National Security Council became more active in the interagency process of reviewing applications for high technology export licenses.

On balance, the technology export policy remained largely unchanged until the Soviet Union's invasion of Afghanistan in later 1979. Helmut C. Sonnenfeldt, former adviser to Henry Kissinger on policy toward the Soviet Union, summed up the shift in attitude when he observed that, "We now see that the dichotomy between cooperation and competition is false. The relationship is exclusively competitive, requiring a permanent strategy and an indefinite effort.[34] After suspending new high technology and feedgrain sales to the Soviet Union, the administration announced a new high technology export policy under which few exemptions from COCOM controls (600 United States exemptions were allowed in 1979) would be permitted, the export of oil and gas technology would be drastically restricted, and the policy on computer sales would revert to the stricter pre-1976 guidelines. Under this policy, oil equipment could be exported, but the technology to produce such equipment would be embargoed.[35]

This policy adjustment has significant implications for the 1980s. The Soviet Union is expected to encounter serious production constraints over the next decade, constraints which will limit energy exports to Eastern and Western Europe, restrict world energy supplies, and perhaps increase the risk of confrontation in the Middle East. On the other hand, the policy is designed to force the Soviet Union to bear a price for regional aggression. Of course, the extent of the pressure that can be placed on the Soviet Union is vitally dependent on the support of the new policy by other COCOM members, and support for the policy will undoubtedly be interpreted as a test for the alliance structure.

The alliance controversy came to a head over the planned Yamal natural gas pipeline deal which would be financed in part with European credits and lead to expanded natural gas exports from the Soviet Union to Western Europe. The Reagan administration argued vigorously that the deal would dangerously increase European dependency on the Soviet Union, alleviate Soviet hard-currency shortages, and provide direct support for the Soviet economy by offering credits at highly preferential terms. When Europeans persisted with the deal despite the declaration of martial law in Poland, the U.S. government first denied export licenses for the required pipeline technology to its own firms, and then extended the restriction to overseas firms who controlled such technology under U.S. licenses. Europeans ignored the new restrictions and continued the original pipeline arrangements.

Disagreements over industrial export policy extended to the area of agricultural exports as well, and Europeans were quick to point out the inconsistencies in the U.S. 1981 decision to lift the agricultural embargo against the Soviet Union which had been imposed in the wake of the invasion of Afghanistan while simultaneously pressing for a broader industrial embargo. In order to understand the U.S. decision on the agricultural embargo, it is first necessary to understand the dramatic shift in agricultural export policy over the decade of the 1970s, a shift to which we now turn.

THE CASE OF WHEAT: THE GREAT GRAIN ROBBERY

The traditional "farm problem" is that the supply and demand for most food products are relatively insensitive to price, or "price inelastic." As a result, shifts in supply resulting from weather variations produce sharp shifts in farm prices and farm income. Various schemes to stabilize farm prices have produced complex arrangements for government loans, export subsidies, and "set-aside" agreements in which farmers are induced to permit some of their land to lie fallow. In the early 1970s the Nixon administration decided to reduce the role of such farm programs by encouraging producton and export. By promoting export markets to absorb farm surpluses in high production years, farm income could be sustained, and the United States balance of trade would be improved. At the same time, the government would be able to sell the stocks of grain it had accumulated in the effort to stabilize prices, and the budgetary costs of storage would be reduced.

Meanwhile the Soviet Union was attempting to expand its own grain production in order to support larger livestock herds and a dietary shift toward meat. In the 1960s, shortfalls in production were absorbed in liquidated herds, which resulted in lower consumption. This pattern is shown in Figure 22.1. Note that in 1963 the level of grain consumption dropped with production, and the level of net imports rose only slightly. Again, in 1965, the sharp drop in production was offset with net imports equal to only about one-third of the shortfall. By the early 1970s, however, this policy of absorbing shortfalls with reduced consumption was reversed, probably because of increased emphasis on meeting expanded consumer expectations. As a result, net imports rose rapidly to offset the reduced production of 1971 and 1972.

The Soviet Union entered the international grain markets on a large scale at the same time that the United States was seeking to expand grain exports. In the spring of 1972 the United States granted the Soviet Union short-term credits in order to finance grain purchases. At the same time the United States was promoting exports by subsidizing an export price of $1.65 per bushel of wheat. The scale of Soviet wheat purchases was

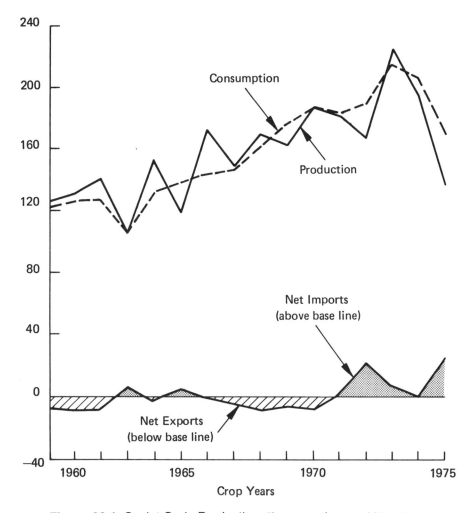

Figure 22.1 Soviet Grain Production, Consumption, and Net Trade: Crop Years 1960–1975 (Million Metric Tons)

Source: Congressional Budget Office, "U.S. Food and Agricultural Policy in the World Economy," (April 26, 1976), p. 27.

completely unanticipated, and because United States exporters carefully guarded the secrecy of their export agreements from each other and from the government, the size of the sale only became clear as the price of wheat skyrocketed. By September of 1972, the price of wheat in the United States had soared from $1.49 per bushel in July to a level of $2.26 per bushel. But that was only the beginning. The prices of all grain substitutes soared, meat prices rose to record levels as feed grain prices increased, and the prices of other protein substitutes such as soybeans also reached new heights.

The sale of roughly one-quarter of the United States wheat crop to the Soviet Union contributed to an increase in food prices of about 14% over the following two years and helped to defeat the wage-price controls that were then in effect. The sale did contribute to the United States balance of trade, but the secrecy of the transactions had serious repercussions. Farmers in the southern portions on the grain belt sold their crops early and missed out on the price increases. Moreover, the government continued to subsidize an export price of $1.65 per bushel until the end of August, and the Soviet Union was therefore able to complete the bulk of its purchases far below the current market prices.

The United States' response to the result of Soviet purchases was to suspend export subsidies, remove remaining constraints on domestic grain production, require grain exporters to report sales to the government on a systematic basis, seek improved information on Soviet crop projections, and negotiate upper and lower limits on future grain exports to the Soviet Union. The U.S.-U.S.S.R. Agreement on Cooperation in the Field of Agriculture, signed in 1973, provided for expanded exchanges of agricultural specialists, statistics, and forecasts. In the face of disastrous crops in 1974 and 1975, the Soviet Union agreed to a five-year commitment in October 20, 1975, to purchase a minimum of six million tons of grain each year in return for a United States minimum annual supply assurance of eight million tons of wheat and corn. Critics of these agreements point to the limited information being supplied by the Soviet Union and to the loopholes in the 1975 export agreement.

> Four years of persistent efforts by the U.S. side, however, have failed to elicit any Soviet forward estimates of agricultural production and utilization other than the well-publicized plan targets . . . the (1975) agreement will contribute little to stabilizing (the grain) market. In a situation of shortage it leaves the Soviet Union free to buy unlimited quantities in foreign markets, thus putting indirect pressure on United States supplies. In a period of glut there is nothing in the agreement that would keep the Soviets from offsetting their contractual imports by exports of their own grain to Eastern Europe or any other destination.[36]

The availability of alternative sources of grain, the difficulty of limiting grain re-shipments through third countries, and the relatively low ratio of grain imports to total grain production limit the ability to enforce grain embargoes and to create economic leverage. In contrast to the current heavy dependence of the United States, Western Europe, and Japan on imported crude oil, few developed countries import sufficient grain to be vulnerable to an embargo. Casting aside the serious moral implications of restricting food sales, the pressure that can be applied through such restrictions is limited. For example, in the 1979 crop year, the Soviet Union domestic output of wheat and coarse grains was roughly 173 million metric tons, compared with imports of only about 16 million metric tons. Of the major powers, only Japan, which imports about 50 percent of its agricultural needs, would appear to have a substantial vulnerability to a food embargo.

Of course, leverage is a relative term, and grain export restrictions could have some severe short-run impacts, particularly in years of low domestic production. On January 4, 1980, in retaliation for the invasion of Afghanistan, President Carter announced the suspension of all agricultural sales to the Soviet Union, except for the eight million tons of grain that were committed by the 1975 export agreement. This ban was subsequently relaxed for agricultural products not related to the feed-grain complex. This restriction coincided with projections of still another disastrous Soviet grain crop. The five-year plan for 1976 to 1980 called for Soviet production of some 220 million metric tons per year. In 1977–78, actual production was only 187 million tons, in 1978–79 output rose to 228 million tons, and projections for 1979–80 indicated production of only 173 million tons. The Carter embargo threatened to cut feed grain exports from some 11 million tons in 1978–79 to less than half that level in 1979–80.[37]

While the embargo held some promise of placing pressure on Soviet livestock herds, in practice the decision to abide by the 1975 agreement on minimum export levels and the availability of additional purchases on grain from Canada, Australia and Argentina limited the actual impact of the embargo. Moreover the real short-term constraints were in the availability of ships and harbor facilities rather than grain supplies, and extensions of the embargo would slowly have eliminated even those short-term constraints.

The embargo produced the anticipated outcry from U.S. farmers who objected that they were the only real victims of the trade restrictions. The original announcement of the embargo by President Carter had anticipated such a response, and had been accompanied with assurances that the government would take action to protect grain prices through expanded subsidies and government purchases. Nevertheless the embargo became a major campaign issue and candidate Reagan committed himself to a prompt termination of the embargo. The ultimate decision by President Reagan in 1981 to end the embargo was thus driven both by an assessment that the Soviet Union was escaping most of the economic pressure envisioned in the initial embargo decision and by concession to domestic political pressures.

THE CASE OF AMMONIA: AN ILLUSTRATION OF DOMESTIC INTERESTS

The subtle balancing of comestic interests and international economic objectives was reflected in the decision to limit the sale of phosphates to the Soviet Union in early 1980. The story begins in the early 1970s. In the midst of the rapid increase in food prices in 1973 and the effort to expand farm production, the price of anhydrous ammonia, used in the manufacture of fertilizer, soared from $90 to $400 per short ton. Occidental Petroleum Corporation reached a 20-year agreement to purchase anhydrous ammonia from the Soviet Union and in return, to sell the U.S.S.R. superphosphoric acid. This substance, also used in fertilizer production, was produced in Occidental's Florida plant. As part of the agreement, which was to take effect in 1978, Occidental agreed to assist the Soviet Union with the construction of the anhydrous ammonia plants and to provide technical services. The plants were financed with $180 million borrowed from the Export-Import Bank.

In 1978, the Soviet Union shipped 300,000 short tons of anhydrous ammonia to the United States, representing about 2 percent of United States domestic consumption. During 1979, Occidental purchased some 950,000 tons of ammonia worth roughly $100 million from the Soviet Union, and sold the U.S.S.R. some 480,000 tons of superphosphoric acid worth an equivalent amount. The 1979 purchases from the Soviet Union, however, amounted to over 5 percent of a weakening United States market, and in July of 1979 a group of domestic producers petitioned for relief under the Trade Act of 1974, arguing that they were being damaged by a rapid expansion of imports. The petitioners cited the reduction in employment in the industry from 4,700 in 1977 to 4,100 in 1979 as evidence of the domestic impact of the imports.

The International Trade Commission, which hears cases under the 1974 Trade Act, voted three to two that Soviet imports had caused material damage, and it recommended import quotas to be set at one million short tons in 1980. This quota compared with expected Occidental imports of some 1.2 to 1.4 million short tons in 1980. On December 12, 1979, President Carter rejected the finding of the International Trade Commission on the grounds that the real problem was an overexpansion of the domestic industry and the rising price brought on by the decontrol of natural gas, the main ingredient in ammonia. In addition, President Carter argued that the quota would only shift the imports to other countries and would not help domestic producers.

Following the Soviet Union's invasion of Afghanistan, President Carter reversed his decision and established an emergency restriction of imports to one million tons of ammonia in 1980, pending a more complete study by the International Trade Commission. In addition, in February 1980, Secretary of Commerce Philip Klutznick announced that phosphates would require validated export licenses, and that none would be granted pending an interagency task force study. Meanwhile the International Longshoremen's Association imposed their own boycott of the Soviet Union, refusing to unload Soviet ships at East Coast ports.

In this case, the export and import restrictions were widely supported in the farm belt. Soviet imports were limited slightly but not seriously curtailed, while United States exports were temporarily suspended. Both actions worked to lower the price of fertilizer to farmers. The Soviet Union faced some restrictions on sales, but the reductions were modest and preserved crucial foreign exchange earnings. In addition, Morocco provided an alternative, if higher cost, source of superphosphoric acid. Occidental, which had made the initial long-term agreement in the height of detente, faced a reduction in ammonia sales.[38]

CONCLUSION

It is clear that export controls work to limit the economic benefits of specialization and trade. In the case of the 1980 embargo of grain to the Soviet Union, the foregone sales may have totalled some $3.5 billion. Moreover, such controls have an uneven impact across various domestic industries and individual firms. On the other hand, trade with the Soviet Union accounts for a very modest proportion of total United States trade, and our national security objectives certainly transcend the modest restrictions such controls place on our quality of life.

But this distinction may present a false dichotomy. The more fundamental question is whether export controls can be applied in a way that enhances our national security, or whether an environment of freer economic interaction will serve as a vehicle for relaxing international tensions. This has been the basic issue in the debate over the past decade. A clear, strong concensus persists that the sale of military equipment to potential adversaries is not in the national interest. But when we shift to a discussion of items with civilian applications and less direct potential for military use, the waters become muddied, and when we generalize to any item that may help the economy of a potential adversary, the waters are murky indeed. In 1969 the pendulum swung sharply in the direction of restricting only items with direct military application, but by 1980 the Afghanistan invasion sent the pendulum sharply in the other direction.

The cursory analysis of industrial and agricultural export controls presented above merely scratches the surface of the issues involved. However, the arguments presented do suggest that the use of export controls to provide leverage on the actions of other nations is quite restricted, and far more complex than most popular discussions indicate. The problems of intragovernmental coordination, coordinated action with other suppliers, domestic interest group pressures, and adjusting long-term United States policy and current legislation are formidable. Moreover, there is little evidence that export restrictions, even if properly coordinated and efficiently administered, could force specific policy concessions in nations where decision makers are isolated from interest group pressures.

To observe that the prospect for leverage through export controls is limited is not to argue that controls are an unimportant element of our national security policy. Short-term adjustments in controls should not be expected to produce dramatic shifts in the fundamental policies of our potential adversaries, but the general framework of our economic policies does provide an important context for continuing negotiations on a wide variety of issues. Just as the easing of controls in the early 1970s was designed to reinforce the general shift toward detente, so the tightening of controls at the end of the decade was designed to protest the continuing expansion of Soviet military capabilities and repeated intervention in "wars of national liberation."

On balance, the interests of the United States will be better served by establishing a framework of export controls that is consistent with long-term policy rather than attempting to manipulate controls for short-term objectives. In the area of high technology exports, this suggests a simplified program that is coordinated with other COCOM members to obtain broad support and tougher enforcement. The Bucy Report suggestion that greater emphasis must be placed on all forms of technology transfer and somewhat less on specific products warrants careful scrutiny. Recent energy export decisions seem to follow this emphasis on technology, rather than end-products.

Export controls for agricultural products should similarly be tailored to avoid introducing uncertainties in trade relationships with our allies. To the extent that controls are required for the stability of domestic markets, they should be triggered by clearly defined market conditions to provide adequate early warning. Even in these cases, the foreign policy consequences must be carefully reviewed. On balance, the restrictions of soybean sales to Japan in 1973 probably produced more international damage than domestic advantage. As a major agricultural exporter, the long-term interests of the United States lie in stimulating free agricultural trade, and those interests can be seriously damaged by short-term tampering with established markets.

Long-term agreements with the Soviet Union that stabilize agricultural markets are in the interest of the United States. The 1975 export agreement lacked some of the enforcement provisions required to make such arrangements effective, but the principle that the United States economy should be protected against large swings in export demand is sound. It is certainly true that such long-term agreements limit the amount of pressure that can be exerted through export embargoes. In the case of the 1980 restrictions, the long-term agreement guaranteed the Soviet Union eight million metric tons of grain, and the Carter administraiton decided to honor that agreement despite the other retaliatory economic actions that were taken. This decision not only protected domestic farm markets, but also recognized the limited ability of agricultural sales restrictions to create economic pressure on the target nation.

Mechanisms to integrate export controls with other foreign policy considerations do exist. The Operating Committee, which considers high technology exports, has appropriate interagency representation, and a representative of the National Security Council is typically included in the most sensitive deliberations. Yet the greatest hope for the successful integration of economic and national security policy lies not in formal organization structures, but rather in the awareness of each participant in the policy process. Economic factors have become an increasingly important element in national security considerations, and there is a clear need for more individuals with backgrounds in both areas.

Such awareness is particularly important to forestall emotional responses to complex policy issues. Clarion calls for economic retaliation must be tempered with an accurate assessment of the short-term problems involved and the long-term consequences. Economic leverage clearly works in two directions, and in many cases the short-term pressure on the United States economy may be more effective than the influence on foreign decision makers.

The concept of leverage assumes a clear agreement on United States objectives and consensus on how pressure is to be applied. But in many policy areas objectives are defined by the interagency negotiation process where divergent interests are reconciled. Moreover, the short- and long-term consequences of such pressure are not at all clear, and predicting the political response of the target nation is a hazardous business. Unless the United States policy structure becomes far more centralized than it has been to date, and unless broader consensus emerges on the expected consequences of various forms of pressure, specific economic and political linkage will remain elusive. Nevertheless, United States export controls have an important impact on the broad framework of our national security policy, and they should be carefully coordinated for consistency with our longer-term policy objectives.

NOTES

1 An early version of this chapter was presented at the Fourth Annual Tripartite Conference at the Pennsylvania State University, University Park, Pennsylvania, October 2–5, 1977. This version is substantially revised and updated.

2 For example: Richard N. Cooper, *The Economics of Interdependence: Economic Policy in the Atlantic Community* (New York: McGraw Hill, 1968); Robert O. Keohane and Joseph S. Nye, Jr., eds., *Transnational Relations and World Politics* (Cambridge, Mass.: Harvard University Press, 1972); Richard N. Cooper, "Economic Interdependence and Foreign Policy in the Seventies," *World Politics*, Vol. 24, No. 2 (January, 1972), pp. 159–81; C. Fred Bergsten, ed., *The Future of the International Economic Order: An Agenda for Research* (Lexington, Mass.: D. C. Heath, 1973); Marina V. N. Whitman, "Leadership Without Hegemony: Our Role in the World Economy," *Foreign Policy*, Vol. 20 (Fall, 1975), pp. 138–164; Zbigniew Brzezinski, "The Deceptive Structure of Peace," *Foreign Policy*, Vol. 14 (Spring, 1974), pp.35–56.

3 Alexander Gerschenkron, *Economic Backwardness in Historical Perspective* (New York: Frederick A. Praeger, 1965).

4 Anthony C. Sutton, *Western Technology and Soviet Development, 1917–1930, 1930–1945, 1945–1965*, 3 Vols. (Stanford, Cal.: Hoover Institution, 1968, 1971, 1973).

5 James Hart, "Yeast Germany," *The New York Times* (March 13, 1980), p. A23.

6 Armand deBorchgrave, "The Embargo is Failing," *Newsweek* (March 10, 1980), p. 60.

7 Mark E. Miller, "The Role of Western Technology in Soviet Strategy," *ORBIS*, Vol. 22, No. 3 (Fall, 1978), p. 548.

8 Donald W. Green and Herbert S. Levine, "Macroeconomic Evidence of the Value of Machinery Imports to the Soviet Union," in John R. Thomas and Ursula M. Kurse-Vaucienne, eds., *Soviet Science and Technology: Domestic and Foreign Perspectives* (Washington, D.C.: George Washington University, 1977), p. 402.

9 Philip Hanson, "The Import of Western Technology," in Archie Brown and Michael Kaser, eds., *The Soviet Union Since the Fall of Khrushchev* (New York: The Free Press, 1975), pp. 38–39.

10 *Ibid.*, p. 43.

11 See, for example, the Defense Science Board Task Force on Export of U.S. Technology, "An Analysis of Export Control of U.S. Technology–a DOD Perspective" (Washington, D.C.: Office of the Director of Defense Research and Engineering, February 4, 1976).

12 See, for example, John Hardt, "Military Economic Implications of Soviet Regional Policy," in *Regional Development in the U.S.S.R.* (Newtonville, Mass.: NATO Information Directorate, 1979); Holland Hunter, "Soviet Economic Problems and Alternative Policy Responses," in *The Soviet Economy in a Time of Change* (Washington, D.C.: U.S. Congress, Joint Economic Committee, 1979); and S. E. Goodman, "The Transfer of Software Technology to the Soviet Union," in William Robinson and Ralph Crosby, eds., *Integrating National Security and Trade Policy: The United States and the Soviet Union* (West Point, N.Y.: United States Military Academy, 1978).

13 Mark E. Miller, *op. cit.*, p. 549.

14 Export Administration Act of 1969; Public Law 91-184, December 30, 1969; 83 Stat. 841; 50 U.S.C. App. 2401-2413. Emphasis added.

15 Defense Science Board Task Force on Export of U.S. Technology, *op. cit.*, p. iii.

16 *Ibid.*, p. 22.

17 *Report of the President's Task Force to Improve Export Administration Licensing Decisions* (January, 1977), p. 9.

18 *Ibid.*, pp. 30, 32.

19 Department of Defense Appropriation Authorization Act of 1975, Public Law 94-412, August 29, 1972, 86 Stat. 644, 50 U.S.C. App. 2401, Section 709.

20 Comptroller General of the United States, *The Government's Role in East-West Trade: Problems and Issues* (Washington, D.C.: General Accounting Office, 1976), p. 47.

21 Theodore Shabad, "U.S.–Soviet Trade Has Been Soaring Despite Absence of a Ratified Accord," *The New York Times* (January 15, 1975), p. 43.

22 William E. Odom, "A Dissenting View on the Group Approach to Soviet Politics," *World Politics*, Vol. XXVIII, No. 4 (July, 1976), p. 565.

23 *Ibid.*, p. 567.

24 Michael Kaser, "Soviet Trade Turns to Europe," *Foreign Policy,* No. 19 (Summer, 1975), pp. 123–134.

25 *The New York Times* (October 29, 1976), pp. A1, A7.

26 Armand de Borchgrave, *op. cit.*, p. 63, and *Business Week* (February 11, 1980), p. 37.

27 Mark E. Miller, *op. cit.*, p. 549.

28 *Business Week* (February 11, 1980), p. 37.

29 Arthur M. Cox, "Trade as a Weapon," *Washington Post* (August 8, 1976), p. C1.

30 Office of Export Administration, *Overview of the Export Control Program* (Washington, D.C.: Department of Commerce, 1975), p. 1.

31 See, for example, Philip Hanson, *op. cit.*, pp. 38–39; Mark Miller, *op. cit.,* p. 548; Robert W. Campbell, "Technology in the Soviet Energy Sector," *1976 NATO Colloquium*, p. 254; Arthur J. Klinghoffer, *The Soviet Union and International Oil Politics* (New York: Columbia University Press, 1977), pp. 280–288.

32 "A Conversation with Gerald Parsky," *Trialogue,* No. 4 (Summer, 1977), p. 20.

33 Samuel P. Huntington, "Banquet Address," in *Integrating National Security and Trade Policy, op. cit.*, p. 24. For a further elaboration of these views, see Samuel P. Huntington, "Trade, Technology and Leverage: Economic Diplomacy," *Foreign Policy*, No. 32 (Fall, 1978), pp. 63–80. For a counter view, see Jonathan Bingham and Victor Johnson, "A Rational Approach to Export Controls," *Foreign Affairs* (Spring, 1979), pp. 894–920.

34 Helmut C. Sonnenfeldt as quoted in *Business Week* (February 11, 1980), p. 37.

35 Richard Burt, "U.S. Curbs Technology for Soviet: Tightening Ends Exports Debate," *The New York Times* (March 19, 1980), pp. D1, D13.

36 Fred H. Sanderson, "U.S.–Soviet Agricultural Cooperation," *Trialogue,* No. 14 (Summer, 1977), pp. 5–6.

37 U.S. Department of Agriculture, *Agricultural Supply and Demand Estimates* (February 12, 1980), pp. 1, 4, and *Business Week* (February 11, 1980), p. 54.

38 This discussion of ammonia sales is based on *Business Week* (February 11, 1980), p. 46, and (March 10, 1980), pp. 43–4, and "Soviet Ammonia and Afghanistan," *Regulation: AEI Journal on Government and Society* (January/February, 1980), pp. 8–9, 55.

SELECTED REFERENCES

Jonathan Bingham and Victor Johnson, "A Rational Approach to Export Controls," *Foreign Affairs* (Spring, 1979), pp. 894–920.

Samuel P. Huntington, "Trade, Technology and Leverage: Economic Diplomacy," *Foreign Policy*, No. 32 (Fall, 1978), pp. 63–80.

Anthony C. Sutton, *Western Technology and Soviet Development, 1917–1930; 1930–1945; 1945–1965*, 3 Vols. (Stanford, Cal.: Hoover Institution, 1968, 1971, 1973).

John R. Thomas and Ursula M. Kruse-Vaucienne, eds., *Soviet Science and Technology: Domestic and Foreign Perspectives* (Washington, D.C.: George Washington University, 1977).

Part VII

Comparative Economic Issues

It is a socialist idea that making profits is a vice; I consider the real vice is making losses.

Winston Churchill

You show me a capitalist, I'll show you a blood sucker.

Malcolm X

In capitalism man exploits man. In communism it's vice versa.

Anonymous Roumanian official

.

Chapter 23
Comparative Economic Systems

INTRODUCTION

Our analysis of the economics of security issues has thus far been conducted on the premise that security issues are defined and security policy formulated and implemented within a particular institutional context—namely, that of a market economy. However our security needs, as well as the efficacy of steps taken to meet those needs, are very much a function of actions on the part of adversaries and allies, and some of those adversaries and allies conduct security policy in institutional contexts that are significantly different from those of the United States. The Soviet Union, for instance, operates on the basis of a command economy, in which resource allocation is accomplished primarily by central direction. There is no system of scarcity prices comparable to that found in the Western market economies. Hence many of those fundamental economic concepts on which we have relied in analyzing United States defense issues have little or no applicability to Soviet issues. This, of course, does not mean that the Soviets can avoid the economic burden of their defense outlays, but it does mean that they ignore the efficiency aspects of resource allocation, at least in the terms in which Western economists have defined efficiency.

These differences are major factors in any attempt to analyze Soviet economic capacity. As a result of these differences the Soviet system is subject to certain weaknesses, but on the other hand, it enjoys certain strengths. Clearly we cannot extrapolate United States experience as a basis for assessing either Soviet capability in a given situation or the impact of various United States policy actions on that capability. Accordingly, in this and the following chapter we will briefly examine the main variations in national economic systems, paying particular attention to the way in which the type of economic system affects security policy and capacity.

FUNCTIONS OF AN ECONOMIC SYSTEM

All modern economic systems must perform certain basic functions. These basic functions boil down to *allocation, coordination,* and *motivation.* Allocation functions, which have occupied the bulk of the attention of Western economists, take many forms, ranging across the traditional "What?" "How?" and "For Whom?" allocation problems discussed in Chapter 10. To that list, we should add a fourth function of providing for economic growth, which is really the question of allocation over time. The growth function is of particular importance in the comparative context, since one of the major claims of the nonmarket, command economy has been superior growth performance.

The *coordination* function concerns the interdependence of different sectors of the economy. In the crudest sense it simply means the avoidance of shortages and surpluses. For example, the optimal number of automobile tires to be produced in a given year depends on, among other things, the number of new cars to be produced; otherwise at the end of the year the economy will have either a surfeit of tires, or cars for which no tires are available. In most economies, this coordination of supply and demand of various goods and services is carried out by a market system. In the words of Adam Smith, who gave the first comprehensive account of how this function is performed in a modern specialized market economy, the market serves as "an invisible hand." As Smith's choice of words suggests, the market system is capable of performing this extraordinarily complex task with deceptive ease, and it is easy to overlook the importance of this particular aspect of allocation. In a command economy, which relies on central direction in setting output levels, coordination of this type becomes extremely important. Hence, we set it aside as a separate function.

In addition to working out how resources are to be allocated, and insuring coordination of allocation decisions, provision must also be made for incentives that motivate individual decision makers or managers to perform their various roles in an expeditious and efficient manner. Here, again, the importance of incentives is less apparent in a market system than in a command economy. In the former case there is no central plan, and allocation is the result of independent activities of millions of individual decision makers acting in their various capacities as consumer, producer, supplier of labor services and so on. Each is left, by and large, to pursue his or her own individual economic welfare on a decentralized basis. The market system has the remarkable feature of providing a congruence between the actions taken by individuals to satisfy selfish, personal objectives, and those actions that are necessary to satisfy the collective objectives of society as a whole. Self-interest is a powerful incentive, and although it obviously needs to be constrained in certain ways, there is no separate requirement for a system of incentives in a market economy. On the other hand, in the command economy, in which there is a central plan to be implemented, ways must be established to motivate individual behavior so that it will be in accordance with the plan. As will become apparent, this is by no means an easy task.

There is wide variety in the organization, goals, and methods adopted by individual nations to accomplish these basic economic functions of allocation, coordination, and motivation. Each case is the result of complex factors—history, ideology, political culture, state of economic development, current circumstances, and so on—and each case is unique. There are as many ways of going about the tasks as there are nations, and no simple model can hope to explain even a single system, much less capture the behavior of several. There are, however, two opposing organizational concepts that have fundamental significance and provide a basis for comparing economic systems. These two *organizational* concepts are, of course, that of the *market economy* and that of the *command economy*.

Before discussing these two organizational concepts, we hasten to point out that "pure" market economies and "pure" command economies do not exist in practice. Any economic system is a "mixed system," containing elements of both concepts. Nevertheless, as a basis for comparing the ways in which economies function and for assessing their individual strengths and vulnerabilities, there can be little doubt that this distinction between market allocation and command allocation is the dominant consideration. Furthermore, it clearly constitutes the crucial difference between the economies of the United States and the Soviet Union, representing respectively the current leading examples of the market and command economy.

THE MARKET ECONOMY

The crucial feature of the market economy, or as it is sometimes referred to the "exchange economy," is that it operates on the basis of *voluntary* and, hence, mutually beneficial transactions among economic agents. Individuals engage in economic activity because they choose to do so. The type of activity, the manner in which they perform it, and the amount of effort they exert are chosen voluntarily. The range of available choices is, of course, limited. Nevertheless, the individual choices are based on the reward of the activity itself, without outside direction or coercion.

In a primitive, barter economy, in which the extent of specialization is limited, it is easy to understand how such a decentralized, unplanned approach is feasible. As long as we assume that the typical primitive laborer provides a substantial proportion of his own basic needs, and that his barter is limited to items that he will consume or use directly in his own productive activities, the information requirements are minimal and the primitive economy can proceed without a coordinating mechanism. As the extent of specialization increases, however, the coordination problem rapidly becomes more complex. In a modern industrial economy such as that of the United States, a preponderant proportion of economic production is used to provide inputs to other industries, which in turn are providing inputs to other industries, and so on, with a relatively small fraction of the total gross output going to sastisfy final demand. An incredible variety of intermediate and final products is involved, flowing back and forth through the production process in an intricate, constantly evolving pattern. The task of coordinating these flows is one of extraordinary complexity. Merely balancing supply and demand at each stage is itself a monumental task. This level of allocation, which entails avoiding shortages and surpluses, is the function we have referred to as coordination. On a more sophisticated level, but one that's equally important to efficient resource use, are the problems of choosing both the pattern of output and the production techniques to be employed in each production process. Production techniques must be chosen so as to employ each factor of production in the best possible way. As discussed in Chapter 10, optimal production patterns are difficult to formulate. Western economists, however, have worked out a conceptual framework for tackling these issues, based on the central concept of Pareto Optimality. As was also outlined in Chapter 10, a market pricing system can be shown to lead to optimal allocation in this sense, subject to the various qualifications that were given.

The key to this allocation process is the pricing system, which not only acts to coordinate for each good the quantity supplied and demanded, but does so in a manner such that for each good or service the marginal cost and marginal value are equal. In fulfilling this role, the system of market prices functions as a vast information network that is accessible to decision makers throughout the economy and thus provides a basis for economic choices on a decentralized basis. The pricing system avoids the need for a centralized coordination scheme or plan. As shifts occur in supply or demand conditions, the system responds automatically with price changes, initially in those markets directly affected, but spreading eventually throughout the economy.[2]

Finally, the system of relative prices not only provides information regarding the relative values and best uses of different items, but also serves as the incentive for economic decision makers to put factors to those best uses.

There are, of course, many qualifications to this parable of an idyllic Pareto Optimal world in which each economic transaction is voluntary and mutually beneficial to both parties. Real world markets perform less effectively than the story implies, and governmental intervention is necessary in many areas to supplement or modify the market process. This command element of the market economy—the portion of resource allocation done by government direction—takes many forms, involving both direct provision of goods or services (e.g., national defense) by governmental agency and indirect provision of goods or services through subsidization or regulation means short of government ownership.

The diversion of resources from private uses to satisfy public goals may be accomplished through government ownership of assets, taxation of income on privately owned assets, or expansion of government debt. While there is no single "correct" method of specifying the relative proportion of total economic activity done under market aegis as opposed to that done under government direction, perhaps the most popular measure of the extent of the government's role is the share of national income that goes to taxes. Figure 23.1 graphs this particular index for the United States economy over the past fifty years.

The trend in the government share of GNP is up, with all the earmarks of irreversibility. An examination of similar data for other high income, industrialized market economies shows, in most cases, an even more extensive government role. Because of the ever-increasing extent of government intervention, it is sometimes argued that predominantly market economies like that of the United States and predominantly command economies like that of the Soviet Union are growing increasing similar, and eventually will converge in a form of mixed economy. There may be some merit in this idea as a description of very long-term trends. Despite the broad scope of government activity in market economies, however, the market system continues to play a crucial role in resource allocation. In establishing opportunity cost prices, it serves as a guide to resource allocation in both the private and public sectors of the economy.

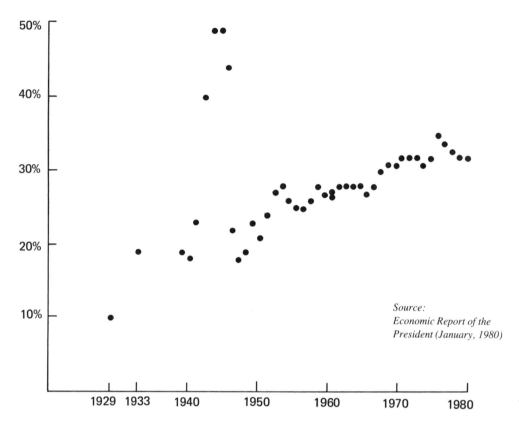

Figure 23.1 Total Government Expenditure in the United States as Percent of GNP: 1929–1980

THE COMMAND ECONOMY

At the opposite extreme to the unplanned, market economy we find the command economy, in which the pattern of resource allocation is based on central direction. The pattern of national output is specified in a national economic plan, which sets output goals for both final and key intermediate products. The plan reflects national economic priorities as they are determined by the political mechanism. Economic forces and the market mechanism play a very small role in setting output goals, except, of course, for their constraint of what is possible.

The Aggregation Problem

Whereas the hallmark of the market economy is the individual firm that chooses its own output and input patterns in response to opportunities defined by market prices, the hallmark of the command economy is the state owned firm that produces in response to specified quotas. In the most extreme cases these quotas are specified in physical units. We can, of course, conceive of the pricing system being dispensed with altogether, although this would mean that the national economic plan would have to be totally disaggregated. Without prices and a numeraire for converting disparate commodities into a common measure, no aggregation would be possible. We would also have to dispense with the conventional macroeconomic concepts such as national income and the rate of economic growth. As a practical matter, national economic planning without aggregation across different types of commodities is not feasible. The level of detail involved would be staggering.

Some appreciation for the problems involved may be obtained by contemplating the difficulties of planning a disaggregated annual budget for a single United States household. Note that none of the conventional aggregate concepts such as food and clothing could be utilized. Instead, detailed lists specifying hundreds of individual items would have to be prepared. Inevitably there would be some aggregation in physical units, such as kilos of fruit or sets of winter clothing. Obviously, however, such aggregation quickly runs into danger of concealing massive variations in quality. For instance, a kilo of fresh, out-of-season strawberries may be equivalent in "value" terms to tens of times the comparable physical quantity of low quality apples.

The problems are even more serious with respect to items of capital such as housing. A house or apartment is, by its very nature, a collection of disparate items. Except in the crudest sense, we cannot even make sense of measuring "how much" housing a family consumes without making use of some form of pricing system that allows aggregation across disparate items. In practice, of course, the command economy does retain at least a rudimentary pricing system, which permits a degree of aggregation in specifying planning goals and evaluating performance. However, how well the rudimentary system performs these tasks is open to serious question.

Coordination

In order to explore the many questions concerning the ways in which the command economy accomplishes the basic functions of resource allocation, we must begin with the concept of coordination discussed above. Consider an economy in which the basic determinant of the production pattern is a national economic plan that specifies exactly what the level of output will be, on a firm by firm, product by product basis. Suppose further that, to the extent feasible, these specifications are made in physical units. Obviously, the ability of a given firm to meet its specified output quotas will be determined by the availability of the necessary inputs. Yet the inputs to one firm are, in turn, the outputs of other firms. The initial and primary problem confronting the planners is recognition of this basic interrelationship and formulation of the plan so that inputs and outputs "balance." Soviet planners refer to this as the problem of *material balances*.

If we assume that there is a fixed relationship between outputs and input requirements, this sounds like a fairly mechanical problem. Beginning with the vector of final product goals, the planners would simply work their way backwards through the interim production stages, calculating the cumulative requirements for primary and intermediate goods implied by the final product goals. These cumulative requirements could then be checked against the availability of primary factors and capacity constraints on individual sectors. Where shortages were indicated, provision would be made for either greater output or lesser requirements of the scarce commodity.

Analytically this is equivalent to inverting the matrix of input-output coefficients for the entire economy. Given the necessary data and the willingness on the part of the planning hierarchy to employ the technique, input-output is at least theoretically capable of translating any final product vector into the associated production levels for each economic sector as well as the labor requirements. However, these are both very large "if's," and to date command economies such as that of the Soviet Union have not yet progressed to the level of computerized, "push button" planning and coordination that the input-output model suggests.[3] The technique employed in practice is a crude, iterative procedure within the planning hierarchy. It relies heavily on projections of the existing pattern, and falls far short of achieving the theoretical ideal of a perfectly coordinated plan. As will become clear when we discuss the motivation function and the associated problems of bureaucracy in economic planning, it is quite unlikely that any planned national economy will ever approach the extreme degree of centralization suggested by use of an economy-wide input-output matrix to coordinate planning.

Efficient Resource Allocation

Before discussing the problems of bureaucracy, the point needs to be stressed that perfect coordination—even if it were a practicable goal of economic planning—is not a criterion of efficient resource allocation in other than a very limited sense. What this means may be understood by considering how central planners are forced to resolve the traditional economic problems of "What?" and "How?" given the absence of a functional market pricing system.

The "what" problem essentially concerns the determination of the vector of final products. In a market system this determination is left primarily to consumer preferences as expressed by expenditure patterns, with the pricing system providing an interface between the preferences for individual goods and services and the resource costs involved in providing them. Subject to the constraint that preference for an item must be expressed by payment of a price indicative of the marginal resource cost, consumers exercise sovereignty over the pattern of output, except insofar as that pattern is modified by various forms of government intervention in the process.

In the command economy, by contrast, planners' preferences take over, and the basic pattern of production is determined by the national economic plan, which specifies those planners' preferences in terms of production levels in the various economic sectors. Consumer sovereignty in the Western sense does not exist in the command economy. The division of national output between consumption and investment is set by the plan, and even within the consumer goods sector, the pattern of output may be set by the plan. Once the output is made available for sale, it is distributed on the basis of willingness of consumers to pay a set price. The prices may be market clearing prices, so that inventories maintain a steady level and embarrassing shortages and surpluses are avoided. If, on the other hand, the planning priority is high rates of investment, prices may be set at a relatively low level, so that shortages of consumer goods are widespread and queueing becomes the basis for allocating items in particularly short supply.

While this use of a market is an improvement over a system of rationing, it is important to realize that it is in no way comparable to the consumer sovereignty concept. Under that concept, prices are adjusted (by the market) to reflect opportunity costs, and any shortages or surpluses which develop lead to changes in the pattern of production. Adjusting prices to clear the market, or allowing shortages to occur generally, severs the link between the production pattern and consumer desires. Hence there is no basis for assuming that the output pattern is well designed to meet consumer needs and preferences. The command economy approach to the "what" question, therefore, misses the mark in terms of allocative efficiency—at least as that concept has been defined in Western market economies.

A similar difficulty afflicts the command economy's approach to the "how" problem. In this case the problem is that the planners' allocation mechanisms afford no basis for the rational selection of alternative technologies to be used for meeting output quotas. In the market economy, these choices are made on a decentralized basis, motivated by a drive to minimize resource costs as measured by their best alternative uses. In the command economy, however, these choices flow primarily from the plan for input allocation, which is based essentially on historical usage coefficients. Inputs are allocated in physical terms, based on the established production norms, and production managers are charged with achieving output quotas with the inputs provided. There is neither an incentive nor a basis for exploration of alternative techniques that might afford the requisite outputs at a lesser resource opportunity cost. There may, of course, be incentives for reducing overall input requirements. However, there can hardly be an incentive for seeking more economical approaches to resource use, because there is no measure of the relative value of resources such as the market pricing system provides. Hence, even if the planning hierarchy were inclined to seek efficient allocation in the Western sense, it would not be able to do so, since there is no available criterion for assessing economic performance in efficiency terms.

The nature of this problem may be clarified by a short digression to a famous debate in the 1920's between Ludwig von Mises and Oskar Lange as to whether it would be theoretically possible for a "planned" economy to achieve Western type efficiency in resource allocation.[4] On the affirmative side Lange held that, indeed, a planned economy could replicate the essential allocative characteristics of a market system. Although the practical significance of the scheme by which this was to be achieved is open to serious challenge, the method proposed nonetheless constitutes one of the clearest explanations of how a market pricing system functions.

The idea suggested by Lange was that the central planners initially set prices arbitrarily, and that they instruct plant managers and other decision makers in the production process to set output levels not on the basis of a production quota, but so as to equate marginal production costs with the prices given. The key idea was that at the end of a specified production period the initial price structure would be adjusted, with increases in the price of items in short supply and decreases for items in surplus. Managers would continue to follow this marginal cost "rule" in adjusting outputs, and at the end of each production period prices would be adjusted on the basis of supply and demand relationships.

There is considerable force in the argument that such an interative price-setting procedure, combined with production decisions in accordance with the marginal cost rule, would in fact replicate the market solution to resource allocation. The interesting aspect of the procedure, however, is that it is tantamount to a surrender of the planners' control over the direction in which the economy proceeds. In other words, in order to generate a system of scarcity prices, it proves necessary to base resource allocation decisions on those prices. However, if the planning hierarchy in command economies were willing to base output levels on prices, the obvious question is why not do the job properly and reintroduce the profit incentive as a means of motivating decision makers to follow the marginal cost rule. But this begins to sound suspiciously like a capitalistic system! Not too surprisingly, command economies have shown marked reluctance to introduce pricing reforms and to devise incentive systems based on prices. To some extent this reflects an ideological bias, but perhaps to a greater extent it reflects the unwillingness of planners to surrender control over allocation decisions.

In any event, the typical use of the pricing system in command economies is only that of a supplemental accounting and control system. Prices are not adjusted frequently, and production choices are not geared to relative prices in a significant way. The prices do not reflect opportunity costs, and hence they do not constitute a reliable basis for identifying the most economic production methods. The "How" question has to be resolved in an essentially arbitrary fashion.[5]

Motivation

The previous discussion of the absence of a scarcity pricing system in a command economy leads naturally to the problem of motivation: the provision of incentives to induce managers and decision makers at lower echelons to act in accordance with the priorities established in the national economic plan, and to pursue those goals in an energetic and effective fashion. This so-called problem of "success indicators" involves both the provision of rewards for correct behavior and some means of identifying and correcting inadequate performance. Here again, as we shall see, the problem is complicated by the absence of prices that reflect opportunity costs.

In order to understand why "success indicators" constitute a problem, two crucial factors must be kept in mind. The first is that there is inevitably a significant adversarial element in the relationship between higher and lower echelons of the command economy (i.e., planners and managers). In the command economy the traditional emphasis of planners has been on achieving ever higher levels of economic performance, with this drive to improve productivity reflected in continually increasing output quotas. To the extent that it succeeds, such pressure on the manager inevitably constitutes an implicit threat to his status, and the manager responds defensively. Managers and bureaucrats in a command economy are human and demonstrate the same tendencies toward self-preservation as do their counterparts elsewhere. Earlier Utopian ideas notwithstanding, the dismantling of capitalism has not succeeded in altering this basic aspect of human nature. This means that "success indicators," such as meeting output targets with specified inputs, are needed. It also means that the natural reaction to them is to find ways of beating the system, such as lowering output quality or hoarding inputs. Hence the success indicators, if they are to be effective, have to be safeguarded against various forms of evasion.

The second factor to be kept in mind is that no economic plan is ever comprehensive in spelling out all aspects of desired performance. The output quotas of a particular plant, for example, will normally involve some degree of aggregation across various types and sizes of the plant's products. More importantly—and this is the crux of the problem—output quotas expressed in terms of physical measurements tend to omit various aspects of product quality. Furthermore, to the extent that product quality is specified, the specification may bear little relationship to the needs of the users. In a market system, the enterprise manager is judged on the basis of the (net) value of the output his plant produces, and the value of that output is based on the willingness of users to buy it. It is the users who are capable of making detailed judgments on product design and quality, and they are able to express those judgments through their purchasing decisions which in turn influence the market price. In the command economy, by contrast, users are generally forced to accept whatever products they are allocated, and hence are denied this crucial role in controlling product quality. In addition, since the product prices bear no relation to opportunity cost or user satisfaction, there is no basis for measuring a plant's total output in value terms, aggregating across various types, designs, sizes, and qualities of products. Even if the manager were inclined to make a satisfied customer his most important product, he has no adequate basis for doing that. Customer satisfaction, however, does not normally rank high in the manager's scale of values, because his success as a manager is judged in terms of physical output quotas—not the number of satisfied customers.

Soviet experience is replete with frequently humorous examples of how physical output quotas may lead to obviously undesirable outcomes. One of the most publici zed examples was a cartoon illustrating a single, giant nail being hauled out of a nail factory at year end. The caption reported the plant's success in meeting its annual production quota, which had been specified in terms of weight without reference to the size and variety of nails to be produced. Specification of the output in terms of the number of nails would, of course, lead to the opposite extreme. This fictitious example is indicative of a very real problem that has arisen with respect to a wide variety of products. When roofing materials were measured in terms of area, they became too thin; when specified in terms of weight, they became too thick. Women unloading bricks from a truck smashed many of them since greater care would mean they would produce less and be paid less, the truck driver would be paid less, and his enterprise would clock up fewer ton-kilometers.[6]

The central dilemma for central planning that is highlighted by these examples is really the same as in the previous discussion of the "What" and "How" problems. The dilemma is that an inherent cost of establishing a centralized system of resource allocation seems to be the abandonment of a scarcity pricing system, and with that the loss of a rational basis for determining how resources can best be allocated. In setting forth this dilemma we have deliberately couched the argument in rather extreme terms. That is, we have given scant consideration to schemes that seek to combine the maintenance of a scarcity pricing system with some degree of central planning. Certainly such possibilities exist. For example, there is the French concept of "indicative planning." The economies of Eastern Europe display a variety of gradations along this spectrum. However our main interest here is in drawing some comparisons between United States and Soviet economic performance. For that purpose, the market versus the command economy is the appropriate conceptual starting point, since the Soviets have shown no serious inclination to revive their pricing system. The discussion so far has also been couched in terms that are less than flattering to the command economy approach, spelling out some of the allocation problems associated with the abandonment of the market pricing system and little reference to compensating advantages. It is time now to examine some of the compensations—real and alleged—and to evaluate their net impact on relative performance.

COMPARATIVE PERFORMANCE OF COMMAND VERSUS MARKET ECONOMIES

Any attempt to make generalizations concerning the relative effectiveness of alternative economic systems is best prefaced by a strong caveat that predictions of the behavior of complex national economies are hazardous when based on simple conceptual models. In the case of the command versus the market economy, however, the differences are sufficiently pronounced to enable us to characterize them with some confidence, and to include the identification of particular strengths and vulnerabilities.

The principal economic advantages of the market system follow directly from the characteristics enumerated above and in Chapter 10. Stated simply, the market provides far and away the most effective means of accomplishing the tasks of resource allocation, at least insofar as the ultimate purpose of resource allocation is seen to be the satisfaction of human wants. The quantity, quality, and composition of the goods and services provided under the market system approach simply cannot be achieved in the absence of a scarcity pricing system. Not only do relative prices provide the information necessary to achieve the desired allocation, but they also provide a robust system of incentives. These incentives permit the allocation decisions to be carried out in a highly decentralized manner, for the most part eliminating the need for a central plan and for centralized supervision of managerial behavior. This decentralization has the additional advantage of affording a high degree of resource mobility and a wide scope for the exercise of individual initiative and ingenuity. It is highly unlikely that any centrally planned economy can perform equally well in terms of the level of innovation that exists in the United States across the whole range of economic activity. A related advantage of the market system is its compatibility with a democratic political tradition, which sets some value on the degree of individual autonomy in economic affairs.

The ways in which the market system fails to satisfy individual or social, economic, and political objectives are well documented, and none of the above advantages preclude the need for or desirability of various forms of government intervention: redistribution of income/wealth, provision of public goods and services, prevention or regulation of excessive private accumulations of market power, correction for external economies and dis-economies, and so on. All these forms of governmental intervention, however, may be accomplished within the context of the market pricing system. Indeed, the criteria for designing and evaluating the regulatory activities are themselves based largely on the concept of competitive market prices as a measure of value.

In the face of these rather strong claims for the efficacy of the market process, what are the countervailing claims in support of the command economy? Perhaps the most widely made claim for the command economy approach is that it can afford the central government the opportunity to bring about a radical shift in a society's economic structure, by means of a large-scale industrialization program. There is an associated claim that the command economy approach permits a higher rate of GNP growth, partially as a result of more rapid industrialization, and partially as a result of the higher level of GNP that is devoted to investment. A third claim is that the command economy affords a more equitable, i.e., more egalitarian, distribution of the national income.

The extent to which these claims have merit is a controversial topic, and one on which views have shifted over time as more has become known about the performance of the principal test case to date: namely, the Soviet Union. No doubt, subsequent developments in that area will lead to continued revision of the judgment. However, it seems to us that certain generalizations can already be made with some confidence.

With respect to the claim that the command economy has the capacity to achieve a more rapid structural change than does an unplanned market economy, we say, "Yes, but . . ." The problem is that rapid structural change per se is not really a meaningful economic objective, at least not in the long run. Quite obviously, a command economy can achieve structural changes that would not take place in a market economy simply by directing uneconomic activities. Whole new industries may be created by fiat of the planners. The issue is how well these industries will perform in the long run. One can conceive of an array of new, planned industrial sectors—so-called "infant industries"—that never achieve a sufficient degree of productivity to justify their creation. They may continue to be operated "at a loss," but in that case the structural change they represent serves only as a monument to bad planning. Even if the structural change does survive the performance test of time, a question remains as to whether other means of industrialization would have been more effective. The obvious alternative is some form of planning within the context of a market pricing system.

Moving to the question of performance, or economic growth, the prognosis for the command economy, after several decades of optimism, seems to have taken a decided turn for the worse in recent years. The change in thinking is directly linked to the Soviet case, which, after a period of apparently quite rapid growth, seems now to have encountered serious obstacles to sustaining that level. We will examine that question in the subsequent chapter.

Before going on to consider the Soviet experience in more detail, the point should be made that a high level of overall economic performance is neither necessary nor sufficient for a high level of military capability. Comparisons of overall economic capacity using aggregate measures such as GNP can be virtually meaningless with respect to defense economics. In the short run—and the short run has assumed increasing importance—it is primarily the forces in being that count, and these are determined over time by not only the *size* of GNP, but also the *share* of GNP devoted to military purposes. Although the command economy may indeed prove inferior on the first count, with respect to the latter the conclusion is quite different. The same caveat applies to comparisons of overall capability in the area of technological progress. It may well be true that a Soviet type command economy proves vastly inferior in terms of total, across-the-board technological advances. However, if a much larger share of its research and development capablity is dedicated to military purposes, and particularly if military priority is placed on the very best talent in that smaller resource pool, the technological competition in the military sphere may also be won by the command economy.

CONCLUSION

In this chapter we have briefly reviewed the basic functions that all economic systems must perform, and we have highlighted the crucial differences between the market and command economy in discharging those functions. We have seen that, although there is a common underlying structure of functions to be performed in any economy, the methods employed differ in fundamental ways. The principal difference lies in the presence or absence of a system of relative prices for evaluating and allocating resources and products. The command economy, eschewing this device for decentralized allocation decisions, relies on a cumbersome centralized plan to determine the composition of output and to direct the pattern of resource use. There are reasons to believe this central planning approach to be inherently subject to limitations in its ability to generate efficient patterns of resource allocation, thereby imposing constraints on the overall level of economic performance. The magnitude of the problems involved is problematical and expert opinion has been divided as to its long-term significance. Indeed a major claim for the command economy has been higher rates of economic growth, and apparent success with growth rates in the Soviet Union in previous decades lent some credence to this view. As we shall examine in the following chapter, recent experience has caused the balance of opinion among Western analysts to shift toward a more negative assessment of the efficacy of the command approach.

No matter how the debate over the strengths and weaknesses of the various economic systems is ultimately resolved, it must be recognized that the command economy's ability to create military capability may be largely independent of aggregate measures of economic performance. The existence of a state-controlled, centralized planning authority confers government power over resource allocation unmatched in market economies. This caveat applies not only to the production of military manpower and hardware, but also to the advancement of military technology. Soviet performance with respect to these aspects of their economic system will be examined in Chapter 25.

NOTES

1 The reader should be careful to distinguish the gross output of an industry from its value added to GNP. Value added is obtained by subtracting from gross output all purchases from other businesses, so as to avoid double counting. GNP is the summation of value added for all producers. The summation of gross output is a meaningless figure from the viewpoint of Western economists because of the double counting involved, although Soviet aggregate output data is based on this concept.

2 For a classic statement of this function see Friedrich A. Hayek, "The Price System as a Mechanism for Using Knowledge," *American Economic Review*, Vol. XXXV, No. 4 (September, 1945), pp.519–530, reprinted in Morris Bornstein, ed., *Comparative Economic Systems: Models and Cases*, (Homewood, Ill.: Richard D. Irwin, Inc., 1965), pp. 30–50.

3 Conceputally, the problem involves nothing more than multiplying the final demand vector by the inverse matrix (I-A)$^{-1}$ as discussed in Chapter 18. The resulting sectoral outputs would be "consistent" in the sense described. In practice, there are severe limitations on the extent to which this technique can supplant the planning process. A key consideration is that much of the planning process involves negotiation as to what the I-O coefficients will be. See Alec Nove, *The Soviet Economic System* (London: George Allen and Irwin, Ltd., 1977), p. 37.

4 Oskar Lange and Fred M. Taylor, *On the Economic Theory of Socialism,* Benjamin E. Lippincott, ed. (Minneapolis: University of Minnesota Press, 1938), pp. 72–86. For the negative case, see Friedrich A. Hayek, "Socialist Calculation: The Competitive Solution," *Economics*, New Series, Vol. VII, No. 26 (May, 1940), pp. 125–149.

5 In the words of Sitnin, the Head of the Prices Committee, "Market prices are, in our view, alien to our economy and contradict the task of centralized planning. It is . . . incorrect to imagine that prices should balance supply and demand . . . [That] is the task of the planning organs." Quoted in *Nove, op. cit.,* p. 179.

6 *Ibid.*, p. 107.

SELECTED REFERENCES

Richard L. Carson, *Comparative Economic Systems* (New York: Macmillan, 1973).

Milton Friedman, *Capitalism and Freedom* (Chicago: University of Chicago Press, 1962).

Vaclav Holesovsky, *Economic Systems: Analysis and Comparison* (New York: McGraw-Hill, 1977).

Alec Nove, *The Soviet Economic System* (London: George Allen and Unwin, Ltd., 1977.)

Joseph A. Schumpeter, *Capitalism, Socialism and Democracy*, 3rd ed. (New York: Harper and Row, 1976).

Chapter 24
Soviet Economic Performance

INTRODUCTION

The Soviet economic system supports the continuing growth of a powerful military establishment, the existence of which constitutes the central threat to United States security and the principal motivation for our own considerable expenditure for defense. The Soviets have themselves proclaimed the importance of relative economic strength in the competition between the two superpowers, and have asserted their advantages in this area. Clearly, the prospects for Soviet economic growth are of crucial importance in assessing the ability of the Soviet Union to continue to boost its military potential and to uphold Soviet interests in other parts of the world.

In this chapter we will survey the results of efforts to evaluate Soviet performance, seeking to identify and project the major strengths and weaknesses of the Soviet system. The subsequent chapter will extend the analysis, comparing Soviet military spending with that of the United States, and assessing the economic burden of Soviet military outlays and the impact which the special characteristics of the Soviet economy have on those military outlays.

The previous chapter highlighted the principal conceptual reasons for the scepticism of Western economists concerning the ability of a command system to perform well in comparison with a market system. It will be recalled that the central deficiency of the command economy involved the absence of a system of scarcity prices, the essential basis for rational allocation decisions and for motivating and evaluating the decision makers. Apologists for the Soviet system, on the other hand, have consistently downplayed the significance of the Western concept of efficiency, stressing other aspects of economic performance, with particular emphasis on the rate of economic growth and the equity of income distribution. Growth is obviously a crucial performance standard, since presumably a higher rate of growth will in time generate sufficient productive capacity to compensate for losses due to inefficient allocation. In assessing Soviet performance, therefore, we are less interested in abstract notions of allocative efficiency than in the actual level of productive capacity and the capability of the system to expand that capacity by sustained economic growth.

SOVIET-UNITED STATES GNP COMPARISONS

Before presenting some results of recent efforts to measure Soviet output and growth performance, it is appropriate to note that such estimates are inherently subject to serious ambiguities and consequently have to be interpreted with great caution. There are several problems with efforts to compare the level of GNP in two different countries such as the Soviet Union and the United States. As mentioned in the previous chapter, measurement of an aggregate such as GNP must be carried out in terms of a numeraire, such as a ruble or dollar value, permitting disparate items to be lumped together in terms of a common unit of measure. If we wish to be able to compare the level of United States and Soviet GNP, however, it won't do to measure one in terms of dollars and the other in terms of rubles. For comparative purposes, we need either an estimate of Soviet GNP in dollar terms or an estimate of United States GNP in ruble terms.

Estimating Soviet GNP in Dollar Terms

Suppose that the approach of estimating Soviet GNP in dollar terms is adopted. Ideally the procedure is to convert the ruble value of the output of each item produced in the Soviet Union into a dollar amount by multiplying the output in rubles by the ratio of the United States dollar price of the item to the Soviet price in rubles. Provided that each item is produced in both economies, according to the same quality specifications, this procedure, although statistically tedious, yields a straightforward method for attaching a dollar figure to the Soviet GNP. This is known as the *purchasing power parity* approach, and it is the method normally employed, although some aggregation is necessary for practical purposes. Here, however, is where the caveats begin.[1]

In the first place, many items are not produced in both economies, and even when they are there may be significant disparities in quality. Soviet consumer goods, for example, are notoriously inferior to United States products. In such cases, the analyst is required to make an adjustment, which is inevitably arbitrary to some degree and in many instances woefully inadequate. For instance, with respect to residential housing there is no Soviet equivalent to the United States single-family dwelling, and the unit in which housing is measured is square meters of floor space.

Setting this computational difficulty aside, a second problem arises with respect to the interpretation of the results. Suppose, for example, that we measure Soviet output in dollars using the purchasing power parity method, and that the dollar value of Soviet GNP in a given year is estimated to be about one-half that of the United States GNP. What does this suggest? Is it a measure of relative productive capacity, or is it a measure of relative economic welfare? Unfortunately, we cannot give a strong affirmative answer to either interpretation.

Consider first the issue of relative productive capacity. Our example suggests that *if* the Soviet output were produced in the United States, its cost would amount to one-half the total value of United States output. However, this does not mean that the United States economy is capable of producing twice as much of every item that the Soviet Union produces. The GNP estimates are based on the aggregation of different production mixes, using a common set of relative prices. In order for the prices used to measure alternative production possibilities, they must reflect the opportunity costs for every item. Even if prices do reflect current opportunity costs, however, the opportunity costs will change as the production pattern shifts.

In addition to this dynamic problem of re-estimating opportunity costs as the level and composition of production shifts, we face the dilemma that current prices might not be an accurate measure of current opportunity costs in either economy. In the United States' case, which is subject to the distortions created by monopoly pricing and other market imperfections, the condition is reasonably well satisfied. In the Soviet case, however, the rigidity of the pricing system renders it completely unacceptable as a measure of opportunity cost. There is the additional problem that consumer goods prices include indirect tax—the so-called *turnover tax*—on which the Soviets rely for the bulk of their revenue.

Similarly, for the GNP measure to be valid as a measure of economic welfare it is necessary that the prices used in the computations reflect the marginal value to consumers of the items purchased, at least in terms of the amount consumers would be willing to pay, given free choice. Here again the pricing systems fall short of the ideal in both countries, and the problems are particularly acute in the Soviet case. Although market clearing prices for consumer goods have been widely used to avoid embarrassing surpluses in the Soviet marketplace, the economy has been characterized by chronic shortages of many consumer items. The result is long waits and queues, indicating that the Soviet consumer places a higher value on items in short supply than the price would indicate.

These problems are even more acute when we consider the public sector and the investment sector. It may be argued that in the case of the United States, the marginal value of both investment and public spending is *roughly* equivalent to the marginal value of consumption. There are, at least, mechanisms available whereby consumers may exercise some influence on the share of GNP going to these uses. In the Soviet case, however, a substantially larger share of GNP goes to public spending, which we may think of as including both public spending and investment in the United States sense. Clearly we cannot ascribe this allocation to the exercise of sovereignty by Soviet consumers, who are usually portrayed as being held by authoritarian planners to far lower levels of consumption than they would opt for, given the opportunity to choose. Hence an economic welfare interpretation of the significance of Soviet outlays for defense and investment is problematical, to say the least.

The Index Number Problem

The above discussion, while not all inclusive, is indicative of the caution with which we should interpret comparisons of the dollar value of Soviet and United States GNP, whether to signify either relative productive capacity or income levels. A further source of ambiguity aises from the differences in the pattern or composition of output in the two economies.

The procedure described for converting Soviet output into dollar terms is based on the Soviet pattern of production. Alternatively, following the reverse procedure we can estimate the value of United States GNP in terms of rubles. In this case the comparison would be used either to evaluate the relative ability of the two economies to produce output in terms of the United States economic pattern, or to evaluate the relative income levels in terms of the United States patterns.

The ambiguity arises from the fact that the two procedures give widely disparate results, due to the fact that those items that are in relatively plentiful supply in one economy generally have a relatively lower price in that economy. For example, in 1976 $.43 bought as much canned orange juice in the United States as one ruble would buy in the Soviet Union, whereas it took over $5.00 to buy the same amount of frozen cod in the United States as one ruble would buy in the Soviet Union.[2] It turns out that, in comparison to the United States, in the Soviet Union frozen cod is relatively more plentiful than is canned orange juice. Hence, if we compare the aggregate value of canned orange juice and frozen cod produced in each economy, obviously it makes a great deal of difference whether the comparison is made in dollars or rubles. The dollar comparison favors the Soviet Union, while the ruble comparison favors the United States. This pattern, in which the most plentiful commodities in an economy are relatively cheaper, accords with basic economic principles and tends to occur across all commodities produced, although, of course, there are many exceptions. The consequence is that if the GNP comparison is made in dollars, the Soviet GNP appears relatively larger because a heavier weight is assigned to items that are more expensive in dollar terms. Conversely, making the comparison in terms of rubles favors the United States, since the United States production pattern is heavily weighted with items that are relatively expensive in terms of rubles. Indeed, United States output contains large quantities of items that the Soviets lack the capacity to produce in any quantity. Neither approach is inherently superior to the other, and we are left without a clear basis for comparison. The dilemma that this situation creates is known as the *index number* problem. It applies not only to comparisons across two economies with different output patterns, but also to comparisons over time within a single economy in which the output pattern changes.

One resolution of this dilemma is to make the comparison in terms of the geometric mean of the dollar and ruble GNP ratios. In a very approximate sense the idea is to compare production and income levels on the basis of an output pattern that lies somewhere between the actual patterns of the two economies. The approach is controversial, because it is essentially an arbitrary procedure with no theoretical claim to superiority over the measurements in either dollars or rubles. About the most we can say is that the geometric mean will lie somewhere between the two ratios from which it is calculated. It does afford a useful summary statistic, however, provided caution is exercised in its interpretation.[3]

Comparative GNP Estimates

Table 24.1 presents the results of recent comparative estimates of United States and Soviet GNP as a percentage of United States GNP, both in aggregate and by major categories of final products, calculated in terms of rubles, dollars, and as the geometric mean of the two.

These estimates indicate that Soviet GNP falls somewhere in the range of 49.5 to 73.7 percent of the comparable United States figure, making it the second largest economy in the world although still a distant second behind the United States. The low estimate of 49.5 percent is, as expected, based on the value of United States output in terms of rubles.

The GNP comparison, however, conceals major variations in the pattern of output. Relatively speaking, the Soviet economy in 1976 was allocating far more resources to investment and to defense spending, so that even in *absolute* terms, the Soviet output level was greater than that of the United States in both categories, and by a substantial margin—23 and 36 percent greater in investment and defense respectively, using the geometric means as our measure.

The source of these massive outlays for investment and defense, given the relatively smaller overall size of the Soviet economy, was obviously consumption, the Soviet-United States ratio in this category falling somewhere between 35.2 and 54.3 percent. In other words, the Soviet economy, while significantly smaller in "size" than the United States economy, appears to be generating a larger amount of investment and defense spending than the United States, and it is able to do this by devoting a much lower share of its total output to consumption. Within the consumption category, the lowest values occur in consumer durables and housing—apparently the two areas in which the Soviet consumer fares the worst compared to his United States counterpart. In terms of welfare comparisons the situation is in fact even worse. There are more Soviet consumers than

Table 24.1
Soviet and U.S. GNP in 1976
(in billions)

	Rubles			Dollars			U.S.S.R. as percent of United States geometric mean
	U.S.S.R.	United States	U.S.S.R. as percent of United States	U.S.S.R.	United States	U.S.S.R. as percent of United States	
GNP	505	1,020	49.5	1,253	1,700	73.7	60.4
Consumption . . .	285	810	35.2	644	1,188	54.3	43.7
Food	137	230	59.6	175	242	72.3	65.4
Soft goods . . .	61	159	38.4	85	140	60.7	48.3
Consumer durables	26	159	38.4	85	140	60.7	48.3
Household services	31	127	24.4	143	420	34.0	28.8
Health	11	43	25.6	96	118	81.4	45.6
Education . . .	20	25	80.0	112	105	106.7	92.4
Investment	142	132	107.6	390	278	140.3	122.9
Machinery and equipment .	44	51	86.3	164	116	141.4	110.5
Construction . .	83	81	102.5	181	162	117.7	107.0
Capital repair .	15	—	—	45	—	—	—
Administration . .	12	21	57.1	77	128	60.2	58.6
Defense and space	62	48	129.2	131	91	144.0	1 36.4
Other	5	10	50.0	11	37	64.7	56.9

Source: Imogene Edwards, Margaret Hughes, and James Noren, "U.S. and U.S.S.R.: Comparisons of GNP," U.S. Congress, Joint Economic Committee, Economy in a Time of Change, Vol. I (Washington, D.C.: Government Printing Office, 1979), p. 378.

United States consumers and the per capita figures are even lower, reflecting on a per capita basis a range of 30 to 45 percent of the United States values for the total consumption category, and substantially lower values for the consumer durables and housing components.[4] Despite its enormous size, the Soviet economy provides a lower per capita level of income than any of the developed countries, excepting Ireland and South Africa.[5]

Soviet Growth Performance

Possibly the most extravagant claims made by Soviet spokesmen have been those concerning the system's growth performance. From the inception of the Soviet system, rapid growth—particularly in the industrial sector—has been the central theme of Soviet economic policy. As the data in Table 24.1 graphically portray, this theme continues to be supported by a massive commitment of resources to investment purposes. Although the methods employed to achieve this social commitment of resources have been unacceptable in terms of Western values, the results in terms of economic growth have won grudging support from many Western observers.

Between the beginning of the first Five Year Plan in 1928 and the onset of World War II, the Soviet economy was transformed from a predominantly rural, agricultural economy into an urban, industrial economy. The fact that the economy was undergoing such a radical transformation, combined with lack of data, renders the task of evaluating growth performance during this period exceedingly difficult, and studies on this subject reflect a wide range of estimates. The annual growth of industrial production over the 12-year period stretching from 1928 to 1940 has been estimated as low as 8 percent and as high as 16 percent.[6] The most authoritative study of overall GNP growth cites a range of 5.5 to 11.9 percent for the period from 1928 to 1937, depending on the price-weights used.[7]

The impact of the price-weights is analogous to the dollar-ruble problem discussed earlier. The high estimate is based on 1928 prices, at which time the industrial products that received high priority were relatively scarce, and hence relatively higher priced. It might be argued that even the 5.5 percent figure is an impressive one, especially given what was happening in the remainder of the industrialized world during that period, and the achievement was duly noted at that time. However, for the purpose of comparing United States and Soviet growth performance, the period beginning with the recovery from World War II affords a better basis for comparison.

As discussed previously, comparative analysis of the growth performance of two economies is hampered by the presence of the index number problem in two forms—the pattern of output differs between the two economies, and within each economy the pattern of output is changing over time. This means that our comparisons are inherently arbitrary, and various methods may be used, each giving somewhat different results and highlighting somewhat different aspects of the comparison. Obviously, a great deal of interest has been attached to trends in the relative size of the two economies and this is one method of comparison frequently employed, perhaps because of the dramatic flavor it gives to the issue of United States-Soviet performance. GNP comparisons based on purchasing power parity as described in the previous paragraph afford a means for doing this, and the results of such an analysis for the past 20 years are presented in Figure 24.1.

Ambiguities in the measurements notwithstanding, the obvious message of this figure is that, for the period in question, the Soviet economy has outperformed the United States economy in terms of growth, moving from 40 percent of GNP in 1955 to a high value of 62 percent in 1975.

To put this picture in a somewhat less dramatic perspective, we can compare the relative growth rates using the data contained in Table 24.2, which presents trends in Soviet and United States GNP components in selected years since 1955.

During this 22-year period, United States GNP increased in real terms from $880 billions to $1782 billions, approximately doubling, with an average annual growth rate of about 3.3 percent.[8] During the same period the Soviet GNP increased from 174 to 523 billion rubles, approximately tripling, with an annual aver-

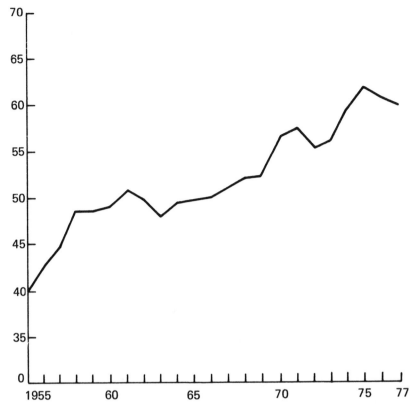

Figure 24.1 U.S. and U.S.S.R. Trends in Relative Size of GNP
(Soviet GNP as Percent of U.S. GNP Geometric Mean Comparison)

Source: Edwards, et. al., op. cit., p. 383.

age growth rate of 5.1 percent. Because of the larger size of the United States GNP, the difference between the two has continued to increase, with the United States pulling further ahead in absolute terms. The point has now been reached, however, where continuation of the growth differential will begin to narrow the absolute gap. Should these trends continue, the Soviet GNP will eventually exceed that of the United States.

The growth of individual components is also of considerable interest in our comparison, and particular interest is attached to the behavior of consumption, investment, and military expenditure categories. The relative shares in these categories are useful in strengthening our understanding of the priorities of Soviet planners and the future capabilities of the Soviet economy. They also have a bearing on our appraisal of the economy's performance.

The continuing Soviet emphasis on investment is apparent in the GNP trends. Taking 1955 as the base year, and again using the data in Table 24.2 for the period from 1955 to 1977, Soviet investment grew at an annual rate of about 7.2 percent in 1976 rubles, in contrast to the growth rate of consumption which was only 4.9 per cent per year. In other words, investment growth occurred at a rate substantially higher than GNP growth, whereas consumption growth, despite the relatively poor lot of the Soviet consumer, failed to keep pace with GNP. Therefore, although the Soviet consumer did enjoy modest progress, the share of GNP going to consumption in fact declined slightly due to the rapid growth in investment spending. Whereas in 1955 Soviet investment spending was only half of the United States figure, the rapid growth caused them to surpass United States spending by 1975. As Table 24.2 shows, this is true whether the comparison is made in terms of dollars or rubles. A similar pattern occurred in the defense sector, and will be discussed more fully in the following chapter.

Table 24.2
Trends in Soviet and U.S. GNP: 1955–1977

	1955 U.S.S.R.	1955 United States	1965 U.S.S.R.	1965 United States	1975 U.S.S.R.	1975 United States	1976 U.S.S.R.	1976 United States	1977 U.S.S.R.	1977 United States
BILLION 1976 RUBLES										
GNP	174	560	304	773	486	955	505	1,020	523	1,071
Consumption	104	415	171	569	277	759	285	810	295	849
Food	61	151	92	191	136	218	137	230	140	237
Soft goods	17	78	33	111	58	153	61	159	63	164
Consumer durables	4	102	9	139	24	201	26	225	28	248
Household services	9	62	16	88	29	122	31	327	32	131
Health	5	14	8	26	11	40	11	43	11	45
Education	9	8	34	15	19	24	20	25	20	26
Investment	32	78	77	118	135	123	142	132	147	145
Machinery and equipment	6	19	18	34	40	47	44	51	46	57
Construction	23	59	46	84	81	76	83	81	85	88
Capital repairs[1]	6	——	7	——	14	——	15	——	16	——
Administration	6	7	7	10	11	20	12	21	12	22
Defense and space	NA	48	38	60	59	47	62	48	64	45
Other	32	13	16	15	4	6	5	10	5	6
BILLION 1976 DOLLARS										
GNP	464	880	793	1,252	1,202	1,607	1,253	1,700	1,294	1,782
Consumption	257	561	410	807	623	1,123	644	1,186	664	1,238
Food	84	160	121	200	172	230	175	242	179	251
Soft goods	23	68	45	98	81	136	85	140	89	145
Consumer durables	5	67	12	93	30	143	33	160	36	175
Household services	47	194	81	283	136	402	143	420	148	437
Health	45	38	69	70	94	111	96	118	97	122
Education	53	33	82	61	110	101	112	105	115	108
Investment	86	167	202	249	367	262	390	278	406	305
Machinery and equipment	27	51	80	83	150	111	164	116	173	129
Construction	50	116	102	167	175	151	181	162	185	176
Capital repairs[1]	8	——	20	——	42	——	45	——	47	——
Administration	41	44	49	64	75	122	77	128	80	137
Defense and space	NA	87	90	108	127	90	131	91	133	92
Other	80	20	42	24	11	10	11	17	11	10

[1]Capital repair is not an accounting category in U.S. national accounts.

Source: Edwards, et. al., op. cit., p. 384.

Evaluating Soviet Growth Performance

Presented in these gross terms, the initial reaction may be to give the Soviet system high marks for its growth performance. The system has sustained over a long period a rather steady rate of increase, which, while by no means comparable to the top performances in the West, has exceeded that of the United States. In terms of capacity to sustain military expenditure, the data are clearly impressive, as we will see in the following chapter.

There are, however, a number of qualifications that set the comparative growth issue in better perspective, considerably dimming the luster of Soviet performance. Obviously the key question concerns their ability to continue their high growth rates in the future, and the preponderance of expert opinion seems to be that they will not. Two kinds of argumentation are involved. First, we can look at growth trends during recent decades, and the evidence there indicates a slowing down. Secondly, we can examine the nature of Soviet growth and attempt to project future prospects on that basis. Here again most observers conclude that prospects are not favorable and believe that the growth slowdown will persist.

Declining Soviet Growth Rates

Table 24.3 presents average annual growth rates of total Soviet GNP and the sectors of origin by five-year periods since 1955. An examination of these data reveals a general slowing of growth rates in the 1960s compared to the 1950s, and a further decline in the 1970s. Furthermore, the slowdown seems to have occurred across the board, excepting services (which includes military services) and, possibly, communications.

Table 24.3
Average Annual Rates of Growth in U.S.S.R. GNP
by Sector of Origin (Percent)

	1951–55	1956–60	1961–65	1966–70	1971–75	1976–78
Industry	10.6	9.8	6.6	6.3	5.9	3.8
Ferrous metals	10.7	7.5	6.9	4.9	3.8	2.2
Nonferrous metals	12.8	6.9	7.7	8.1	5.9	2.1
Fuel	9.4	8.9	6.1	5.0	5.0	3.6
Electric power	13.1	11.4	11.5	7.9	7.0	5.0
Machinery	11.9	12.2	7.8	7.0	8.1	5.9
Chemicals	11.2	10.7	11.5	8.6	8.6	4.7
Forest products	7.5	5.9	2.6	2.7	2.5	.1
Construction materials	15.5	14.5	5.1	5.6	5.1	1.5
Light industry	8.6	8.0	3.0	7.1	2.6	2.7
Food industry	10.0	8.8	5.8	5.9	4.2	.8
Construction	11.6	10.7	5.2	5.5	5.3	2.6
Agriculture	4.1	4.1	2.4	4.2	–2.1	4.4
Transportation	11.0	10.7	8.1	7.5	6.6	4.3
Communications	8.1	7.1	7.1	8.9	7.2	6.1
Trade	10.4	8.5	4.7	6.4	4.8	3.7
Services[1]	2.3	2.2	4.5	4.2	3.4	3.0
Gross National Product	5.8	6.0	4.9	5.3	3.7	3.7

[1]Including military personnel costs.

Source: Office of Economic Research, CIA, published in H. Block, "Soviet Economic Performance in a Global Context," U.S. Congress, Joint Economic Committee, Soviet Economy in a Time of Change (Washington, D.C.: Government Printing Office, 1979), p. 136.

Patterns of Factor Productivity

Quite a variety of explanations have been offered to account for the slowdown phenomenon, most of which suggest that it will be exceedingly difficult to reverse. While it is extraordinarily difficult to assess the relative importance of the various explanations, their cumulative impact is a bleak picture for Soviet growth in the coming decade. All the sources of growth—labor, capital, raw materials, and improvements in factor productivity—present problems.

One major source of Soviet growth for the past 25 years has been additions to the labor force. Between 1950 and 1975, total employment rose by an average rate of 2.2 percent annually, exceeding both the 1.4 percent rate for the total population and the 1.3 percent rate for the able-bodied population.[9] The more rapid rate of growth of the labor force was largely due to the recruitment of women to the labor force. Obviously there is a limit to this source. Furthermore the underlying population growth rates are down. The Soviet Union faces an unprecedented decrease in the annual increments to the population of able-bodied during the 1980s.[10] Hence a decline in labor force growth appears inevitable.

This decline in labor force growth could be compensated either by an increase in the rate of additions to the capital stock or by better performance in terms of enhancing factor productivity. For a number of reasons, higher rates of investment do not appear to have much promise as the solution. The opportunity cost of higher investment rates would, of course, be a reduction in the growth of either consumption or military expenditure or both. To a considerable extent this phenomenon has already been taking place. Table 24.4 illustrates the trend of a rsing share of GNP going to investment, and a falling share to consumption. Although data are not available to separate out the military expenditure shares in this table, the military expenditure trends reflected in other estimates do not suggest any curtailment in that area to permit greater investment. The future may of course be different, and we will return to this subject in the following chapter.

The immediate question, then, is whether the Soviet consumer can be squeezed further to provide more investment resources. Given his already disadvantaged state relative to the rest of the industrialized world, the answer might be "possibly—but it would not be a very pleasant alternative for consumers or for planners." To accept this possibility one almost has to assume that the attitudes of Soviet consumers are inconsequential to the leadership. Such an assumption is not supported by the rhetoric of the Brezhnev regime. According to the draft directives for the 1971–1975 plan, the "chief task" was the "increase in the people's material and cultural standard of living."[11] The actual allocations, however, seem to reflect somewhat different priorities.

Table 24.4
U.S.S.R.: Shares of GNP by End Use (Factor Cost): 1950–1978

	1950	1955	1960	1965	1970	1975	1978
Consumption	62.1	61.0	59.8	57.3	57.3	56.8	56.2
Consumer goods	35.5	36.0	36.1	33.4	34.6	34.3	34.1
Consumer services	26.6	25.0	23.7	23.8	22.8	22.5	22.1
Fixed investment	14.8	19.5	23.7	26.0	27.2	29.5	31.4
New fixed investment	11.9	16.5	20.1	21.7	22.8	23.8	25.3
Capital repair	2.8	3.0	3.6	4.3	4.4	5.7	6.1
Research and development . . .	1.8	2.0	2.7	3.3	3.5	3.9	4.2
Administrative and other services .	7.3	4.4	3.0	2.6	2.6	2.6	2.5
Outlays not elsewhere classified[1] .	14.0	13.1	10.8	10.8	9.4	7.2	5.7
Gross national product	100.0	100.0	100.0	100.0	100.0	100.0	100.0

[1]Includes defense, net exports, change in inventories and reserves, unidentified outlays, and statistical discrepancy.

Source: H. Block, op. cit., p. 137.

Even if sources for an increase in investment rates were readily available, there are good reasons to question the viability of this approach. The pattern of Soviet growth has been one of high reliance on investment, and for more than a decade the growth of investment and the capital stock have exceeded the growth of both the labor force and output. The consequence is that capital productivity has been falling, creating apparently a classic case of diminishing returns. There may, of course, be other culprits, such as more costly raw materials or just plain bad management, and estimates of the productivity of investment are fraught with difficulty. Nevertheless the general conclusion seems inescapable that growth via more rapid investment will be an increasingly costly proposition, especially in the absence of progress in the remaining area—productivity.

As pointed out in Chapter 17, the key ingredient in long-term growth in the United States economy has been the increase in factor productivity. A man-hour of labor and a unit of capital have each, over time, become increasingly productive. To a large extent such improvements are associated with the progress of science and technology, as reflected in new forms of capital equipment and new techniques of production. In part it is also attributable to improvements in human capital through better health, education, and training. In general the accumulation of capital is accompanied by qualitative improvements that embody scientific advances. In the industrial world these improvements have been more than adequate to permit continuing increases in the capital-to-labor ratio over a long time period without a drop in the marginal productivity of capital. Overall factor productivity has steadily risen.

In the Soviet case, the productivity performance has been less successful. The main sources of growth have come from additions to the industrial labor force and additions to the capital stock, with the latter taking place at a higher rate. However, at least in recent years, industrial output seems to have been growing at a slower rate than the combined inputs.[12] It would appear either that the new capital is too much like the existing stock, permitting the law of diminishing returns to operate, or else that—from a management viewpoint—insufficient advantage is being taken of the productive capacity of the new capital.

Alternative Approaches to Productivity Problems

Alternative sources of relief to the productivity problem could conceivably come from access to new and cheaper raw materials, or from a step-up in Soviet capability to obtain and implement Western technology. The latter possibility has been addressed in Part VI and, barring a major change in East-West relations, does not seem likely. In the raw materials area, the expected outcome is also bleak. As the better resources are exhausted, raw materials are becoming more expensive to extract. Although the subject is controversial at this time, many foresee major problems for the Soviets in the energy area, and it is expected that they will shift from their current position as the world's second largest oil exporter to that of a net importer by 1990.[13] Since the oil exports have played a key role in Soviet foreign exchange earnings, this forecast also implies major repercussions with respect to Soviet ability to import the Western technology that they so badly need.

In the case of agriculture—the traditional Achilles heel of the Soviet economy—the prospects for major improvement in productivity performance appear equally remote. Given that the Soviets continue to employ almost a third of their work force in agriculture—a much larger fraction than Western industrial nations—agriculture would appear to be a promising candidate for enhanced factor productivity. The Soviets have in fact invested heavily in agriculture during the last 25 years, as well as having increased their sown acreage, and they have succeeded in achieving an average output growth of about 3½ percent per year.[14] This is not a disreputable rate of output growth, given the environmental limitations faced by Soviet agriculture.

When it comes to factor productivity, however, the picture is much less favorable, in terms of both the current level and the apparent trends. Whereas Soviet agricultural labor productivity has been increasing, compared to United States performance they have fallen steadily behind, despite massive investment on their part in the agricultural sector. The value of output per man-day in the U.S.S.R., expressed in dollars, dropped from about 7 percent of the United States figure in the mid-1960s to 5½ percent in the mid-1970s.[15] This is remarkable in that in the period from 1970 to 1977, total direct farm investment in the Soviet Union was 6.3 times the United States amount.[16] Furthermore the factor productivity performance displays the same downward trend as that in industry, reflecting a substantial drop in the 1960s from the level of the 1950s, and a further decrease in the 1970s. The measurement of total factor productivities is, to repeat, a hazardous undertaking, especially in the Soviet case. However, barring fundamental reforms in management and incentive systems, available data do not reflect any greater hope in agriculture than in industry for a sharp turnabout in productivity trends.

In the final analysis, the issue comes back to that of efficiency. As discussed in the previous chapter, the command economy encounters major impediments to efficiency, particularly in the area of incentives and motivation and in the area of innovation. The Soviets have responded to their productivity malaise with waves of "reforms" involving planning and management structures and incentive systems. The question naturally arises as to the prospects that recent or prospective reforms might be successful in effecting a productivity turnabout. To that subject we now turn.

THE ROLE OF REFORMS

The previous account of the Soviet growth slowdown seems to confirm the doubts presented in two other sources of insight into Soviet economic performance. One of these sources is the body of Western literature that addresses the efficiency problems inherent in a highly centralized economy.[17] The other is the steady stream of anecdotal evidence of specific Soviet problems, such as inconsistent plans, perverse incentives, and bad management resulting in inferior product quality and shortages. The endemic nature of these difficulties has been reflected in continuing efforts by the Soviet government to solve the problems by various reforms of the system. The last 15 years have seen particularly intensive activity in this area, inspired by the Kosygin reforms of 1965.

Chapter 23 briefly outlined the main problems faced by a centrally directed economy in organizing, planning, and motivating desired economic activity. In addressing these problems, the Soviet leadership can either:

1. Attempt to reform the mechanisms of central control in order to make them more effective, or
2. Surrender some degree of central control, granting greater autonomy to individual decision makers throughout the economy, hoping by the decentralization to remedy some of those bureaucratic excesses that may account for the productivity problem. Essential to the decentralization approach is a greater reliance on market mechanisms for coordinating and motivating economic behavior.

Thus, the Soviets must decide whether their goals will be pursued through more perfect centralization or through decentralization. When Western critics talk about "fundamental" reforms, it normally is the latter approach that they have in mind. In general, the Soviets have not been favorably inclined to this philosophy, although it is, of course, possible to mix the two approaches, and to some extent they have done so. Although certain reforms contain elements of decentralization, on balance it seems clear that the contrary philosophy is still dominant and is likely to remain so for quite some time.

The distinction between the two types of reform can be illustrated in respect to the role played by the plant manager in the Soviet system. Basically the manager works to satisfy an output quota that is specified in a production plan in terms of either physical units or monetary units based on state-administered prices. The inputs used to accomplish this goal—raw materials and producer goods—are also allocated by plan: they are rationed rather than obtained in a free market. Inputs are typically in short supply, and the output quotas are set so as to achieve "tautness" in the system and thereby encourage full utilization of capacity and continuing increases in factor productivity.

The plant manager plays some role in the planning phase, generally seeking to protect himself by holding the output quotas down and the input requirements up. In the implementation phase, the plant manager tends to behave conservatively—a flashy performance this year will mean tougher norms next year. If inputs are short, he will revert to black markets and extra-legal supply sources. In producing the output he will concentrate on satisfying the plan rather than the customers who will eventually use the product. Since he normally operates in a sellers' market, quality in his product is liable to go unnoted.

The fundamental reform of this situation would involve the following steps:

1. The output quotas would be abandoned as the manager's goal, in favor of net profit based on the willingness of customers to buy the product.
2. The producer's goods would be obtained in a market and would be allocated to the highest bidder rather than by government rationing.
3. The prices at which producer and consumer goods exchange would be determined on the basis of supply and demand, rather than by fiat. To whatever extent desired, these steps could be further supplemented by the direction of investment funds to those areas experiencing the largest return on invested capital.

The Soviet reforms have not yet involved any of these fundamental changes except in the most peripheral way. The output quota specified by the plan has been retained as the primary success indicator. However, the quota has been supplemented by a list of additional measures of worker and manager performance that seek to remedy the problems noted. For the most part, incentives take the form of bonus funds, to be awarded on the basis of improvements in factor productivity; independent measures of product quality; customer satisfaction as measured by contract fulfillment; and so on. Thus a given manager's scorecard contains a large number of items, most of which are mutually competitive—doing better in one area entails a cost in another. All, of course, is done within the context of the central planning framework.

No doubt some of the changes represent movements toward greater rationality in resource use. The incorporation of the rate of return on invested capital as a measure of plant efficiency, for example, would appear to be a step in the right direction. The talk of allocating some producer goods on a market basis would be even more significant, but this is not occurring in practice.[8] Finally, the institution of market prices reflecting demand as well as production costs and the determination of production levels to satisfy demand—rather than a plan—seem to remain anathema to the Soviet leadership. In short, the reforms to date have not been of the fundamental variety that Western critics believe are essential.

A related topic concerns the issue of whether more sophisticated planning mechanisms, such as the use of computers, can remedy the problems. The Soviets have in recent years placed increasing stress on the importance of enhancing the "scientific basis" of planning, and a number of possibilities exist for them to do so. The Input-Output analysis described in Chapter 18, for example, is an obvious candidate. Without denigrating the utility of this approach, however, it seems quite unlikely that computer models will be a panacea for the efficiency and productivity problems we have described. A number of considerations may be cited.

First of all computer models—even the largest ones contemplated—involve rather heroic simplifications of an economy's functioning. Furthermore, even if we limit the problem to optimizing in terms of existing technology, models are only as good as the input data. If the data do not reflect true opportunity costs, there is no basis for assuming that computer models can lead to optimal allocations. In a market economy this information is developed by the pricing system. In a command economy, however, the information does not exist.

Even greater than the problem of insufficient data is that which is created by the basic limitations of computer models. The parameters of economic models, e.g., the coefficients of an Input-Output model, basically represent average values collected from previous experience. Innovation and the growth of productivity, on the other hand, involve something quite different from the maintenance of past averages. They involve *changes* in parameter values, and this is something that models are inherently incapable of providing.

Thus, economic models would be of little use to the Soviets in terms of helping them improve factor productivity. The same problem occurs in the area of product quality, which is the locus of much of the dynamism in Western economies, but is extraordinarily difficult to specify as part of an economic plan. In our view, what is required is an incentive system tied to the ultimate test—the challenge of a satisfied customer. It is difficult to see how even the most elaborate computer models can alleviate these problems, within the context of the centralized approach. If the centralized control is relinquished to permit greater reliance on market forces, then, of course, computer models are not required. But the ideological barriers to such reform appear to be insuperable.

CONCLUSION

The Soviet economy has sustained a high rate of GNP growth in the last 25 years. The growth rate has, in fact, been better than that of the United States, although not nearly as good as those of many other countries. Given the growth differential, in combination with a high priority to investment and military expenditure, the Soviets have achieved at least comparability with United States levels, and perhaps more, in these sectors. This performance, however, is clouded by the lack of comparable improvement in the consumption sector, where income levels are very low by industrialized economy standards, and by unfavorable trends that suggest continuation of their recent, serious slowdown in GNP growth in the coming decade. The support for this view is especially compelling because each of the possible sources of a turnaround—labor, capital, raw materials, and level of factor productivity—present significant problems. Declining increments to the labor force, an already tightly squeezed Soviet consumer, and questions as to the adequacy of domestic sources are key elements in this pessimistic prognosis. General Secretary Andropov's initial reactions in this area have been to press for increased effort without fundamental reform. It is highly unlikely that mere exhortations can increase productivity in the long run. On the other hand, there is the possibility of fundamental reforms in the allocative mechanisms employed. If enacted, such reforms might enhance factor productivity sufficiently to compensate for the problems cited and restore higher growth rates.

From our perspective the most effective means of reform would be a revitalization of the pricing system with, *pari passu,* some decentralization of resource allocation decisions. Changes to date have lacked this essential ingredient. In our view, continuing emphasis on reforms that retain the highly centralized control of the economy will achieve only marginal success and are unlikely to reverse the growth slowdown.

NOTES

1 See Imogene Edwards, Margaret Huges, and James Noren, "U.S. and U.S.S.R.: Comparisons of GNP," office of Economic Research, Central Intelligence Agency, published in *Soviet Economy in a Time of Change*, Vol. 1, Joint Economic Committee, U.S. Congress (Washington, D.C.: Government Printing Office, 1979), pp. 369–401.

2 *Ibid.*, p. 374.

3 For a critique of this concept see Abraham Becker, "Comparisons of United States and U.S.S.R. National Output: Some Rules of the Game," *World Politics*, Vol. 13, No. 1 (October, 1960), pp. 99–111.

4 Edwards, *et al., op. cit.,* p. 379.

5 *World Development Report 1978,* The World Bank, Washington, D.C., August, 1978, p. 77. Such comparisons are, of course, subject to the qualifications made previously. In 1976, however, median GNP for Industrialized Countries was $6,200, vesus the Soviet figure of $2,760.

6 Howard J. Sherman, *The Soviet Economy* (Boston: Littl, Brown and Company, 1969), p. 96.

7 Abram Bergson, *The Real National Income of Soviet Russia Since 1928* (Cambridge, Mass.: Harvard University Press, 1961).

8 the percentage reflects the constant annual rate of compound growth which would produce the increase from $880 billions to $1782 billions in a 22-year period. Thus $880(i + r)^{22} = 1782$, and $r = .033$.

9 Stephen Rapawy, "Regional Employment Trends in the U.S.S.R.: 1950 to 1975," *Soviet Economy in a Time of Change*, p. 601. The Soviets define able-bodied as males 16–59 years of age and females 16–54 years of age, inclusive.

10 Not only are the aggregate increments to the population of able-bodied ages dropping, such increase as will occur is heavily concentrated in the republics of Central Asia and Kazakhstan. Projections indicate there will be no increase in the other ten republics in the first half of the 1980s and even a net decrease in the second half. See Frederick A. Leedy, "Demographic Trends in the U.S.S.R.," *Soviet Economic Prospects for the Seventies*, Joint Economic Committee, U.S. Congress (Washington, D.C.: Government Printing Office, June, 1973), pp. 492–493.

11 See M. Elizabeth Denton, "Soviet Consumer Policy: Trends and Prospects," *Soviet Economy in a Time of Change*, Vol. 1, pp. 759–789.

12 Empirical estimates of factor productivity are notoriously suspect. For an effort to estimate recent trends in Soviet factor productivity, see F. Douglas Whitehouse and Ray Converse, "Soviet Industry: Recent Performance and Future Prospects," *Soviet Economy in a Time of Change*, Vol. 1, pp. 402–422.

13 Tyrus W. Cobb, "The Soviet Energy Dilemma," *Orbis* (Summer, 1979), p. 353–385.

14 Douglas B. Diamond and W. Lee Davis, "Comparative Growth in Output and Productivity in U.S. and U.S.S.R. Agriculture," *Soviet Economy in a Time of Change*, Vol. 2, pp. 20–21.

15 *Ibid.*

16 *Ibid.*

17 Possibly the most persuasive account is to be found in Nove, *The Soviet Economic System, op. cit.*

18 *Ibid.*, pp. 310ff.

SELECTED REFERENCES

Abram Bergson and Simon Kuznets, eds., *Economic Trends in the Soviet Union* (Cambridge, Mass.: Harvard University Press, 1963).

Tyrus W. Cobb, "The Soviet Energy Dilemma," *Orbis* (Summer, 1979), pp. 353–385.

Paul R. Gregory and Robert C. Stuart, *Soviet Economic Structure and Performance* (New York: Harper and Row, 1974).

Alec Nove, *The Soviet Economic System* (London: George Allen and Unwin, Ltd., 1977).

Hedrick Smith, *The Russians* (New York: Ballantine Books, 1976).

Soviet Economy in a Time of Change: A Compendium of Papers, 2 Vols., Joint Economic Committee, U.S. Congress (Washington, D.C.: Government Printing Office, October, 1979).

Chapter 25
Comparative Military Expenditure

INTRODUCTION

Defense analysts have a continuing interest in comparative studies of the amount of resources devoted to defense by different societies, allies, and adversaries. A companion topic is the assessment of the "economic burden" of defense spending, normally approached in terms of the share of total GNP allocated to defense. Such examinations can serve a variety of useful purposes. In the case of a potential adversary, the general objective is to enhance our understanding of the state and trends of enemy capabilities and intentions, thereby better equipping our own strategy and programs for countering the explicit or implicit threats to United States security. In the case of allies, where both the level of capability and the proper sharing of the defense burden are at issue, useful purposes may also be served.

Despite the obvious utility of such comparisons, there are also severe limitations and ample opportunities for misuse of the results. In the following paragraphs we will set forth the principal caveats to be observed in conducting comparative analyses of defense spending as well as some of the principal findings in the case of greatest interest, namely that of the Soviet Union.

MILITARY EXPENDITURE AND MILITARY POWER

In measuring and comparing military expenditure, ideally we would like to obtain some insight into the comparative levels and trends of military power in the countries being examined. How do the size and effectiveness of opposing military establishments compare? Does either one possess a decided advantage? What are the trends?

One approach would be to conduct such comparisons in physical units, like item by like item. Of necessity, this would be done on a disaggregated basis, since a wide variety of weapons systems and types of military capability are involved. Such comparisons are made and indeed play important roles in defense analysis. The limitations of this approach are that trends for individual items move in various directions, that there are wide variations in the quality of most items, and that some aggregation is inevitable.

Clearly, it would be very useful if an index could be devised to measure the overall size and effectiveness of the defense output, just as GNP measures economic output. What is needed for this purpose is a price or weighting scheme in which the weights reflect military effectiveness, much in the same sense that market prices are said to reflect the utility of consumer goods. Unfortunately such effectiveness weights are not available. There is no market for defense output, and the methods of estimating military effectiveness are far too rudimentary to permit determination of effectiveness weights in an explicit way. In the face of our inability to measure the *output* from defense spending, the standard approach is to fall back upon estimates of the *input* as the next best alternative.

When we measure military expenditure, we are attempting to evaluate in aggregate monetary terms the volume of resources flowing into defense spending in a given time period, normally one year. The significance of the dollar amount, say in the case of the United States, is best understood in terms of the concept of opportunity cost. A given amount of dollars has significance only in terms of the foregone opportunities for the resources involved to be used in some alternative way, e.g., for private consumption or investment. If the prices used in evaluating defense spending are market prices of the resources employed, reflecting their value in alternative uses, the defense budget may then be given the opportunity cost interpretation.[1]

The first point to note about this concept is that it is a *cost* concept, based entirely on the value of the resources employed in terms of other than military uses. As such it has absolutely nothing to do with military power or effectiveness, which depend on the force mix for which the resources are used, the contingencies which must be faced, the nature of opposing forces, climate, geography, and a host of additional factors. It is easy to conceive of defense resources being wasted, devoted to the wrong uses, and so on. Thus the connection between military spending and military power is tenuous at best.

Such connection as there is between the two concepts—military spending and military power—derives from some assumption regarding the rationality of military planners and the budget formulation process. Economic theory teaches us that the optimal expenditure pattern for a given defense budget is one in which the cost ratio of alternative items is equal to their effectiveness ratio. If we assume that defense planners are capable of estimating the effectiveness of alternative expenditure patterns, that they are free to choose, and that they seek to maximize military effectiveness in terms of the given budget, then there is some basis for treating military expenditure as being related to military effectiveness. We would expect, for instance, that the relationship is positive, with an increase in military expenditure being associated with an increase in military effectiveness. A larger budget expands the decision maker's options and, given our assumptions, should lead to productive choices which enhance military power.

Although we can say that more is better, however, we cannot say how much better. An analogy with the ordinal utility function of consumer theory is appropriate. Military effectiveness (utility) increases with higher budgets (income), but we cannot even measure the effectiveness (utility) level in a cardinal sense, and most certainly not in money terms.

The above discussion presumes that other factors affecting military effectiveness do not change. However, other factors in general do change, most notably the size and configuration of the military forces of potential adversaries. This brings us to the next step, which is the *comparison* of military spending levels.

COMPARATIVE MILITARY EXPENDITURE

Using analyses of defense spending in two different economies (e.g., the United States and the Soviet Union) to indicate *relative* military power is a complex procedure. Comparisons are particularly suspect where the Soviet Union is involved, because of the lack of data and the deficiencies of the Soviet pricing system which have previously been noted. Soviet military expenditures are not revealed in official budget data, which contain a single line item entry—averaging about 17 billion rubles annually during the 1970s—which is generally agreed to be unrealistically low and virtually worthless as an indicator of trends.[2]

Although a few Western scholars have sought to deduce defense expenditure figures from Soviet budget data, by and large the field has been left to the intelligence community as the only entity with sufficient resources to be able to tackle the problem with any hope of success.[3] The method used, known as *dollar costing*, essentially involves counting the effort in physical terms and translating the implied flow of resources into a dollar value, based on estimated United States prices for the production of similar items. Recalling the discussion of GNP comparisons in the previous chapter, the conceptual approach is analogous to that used in estimating the Soviet GNP in dollar terms. It is also subject to the same criticisms.

The central problem is that the relative price structure and the force mix vary significantly between the two economies—the classic index number problem. For example, labor is the plentiful good in the Soviet Union, carrying a lower relative price and being used relatively more intensively in the Soviet military force. Such disparities create significant problems of interpretation. To continue the example, if the relative price of labor goes up in the United States, even with no quantitative changes in the composition of military procurement, the Soviet military expenditure in dollar terms will go up more than the United States expenditure. Thus with no change on either side in the actual quantities of items purchased, an apparent relative increase in Soviet military spending will have occurred.

As long as we stick with a strict interpretation of the data, namely an estimate of what it would cost *in dollars* to duplicate the Soviet effort, there is no problem. If, however, we go beyond that interpretation and seek to interpret the relative dollar costs of the two defense budgets as somehow measuring the relative increments to military power that each budget contributes to its respective side, the results are likely to be confusion and error. But that, of course, is precisely the interpretation that users of the data tend to make, because it permits addressing the question of greatest interest, namely what are the trends in relative military power.

As in the case of the GNP estimates, one helpful corrective is to make a second comparison, based on ruble prices. Whereas the dollar cost comparison tends to exaggerate the size of the Soviet outlay, the ruble cost comparison has the opposite effect, tending to make the United States outlay appear larger. The practical difficulties are far greater with this approach, since it is much harder to obtain the price in rubles of United States military equipment, a significant amount of which the Soviet economy is not even capable of producing. As a result, use of this method has been relatively limited.

It turns out that, according to CIA estimates, the level of Soviet military spending in recent years has exceeded that of the United States whether measured in terms of dollars or rubles, the U.S.S.R./U.S. expenditure ratio for 1979 being 1.5 and 1.3 respectively for the dollar and ruble comparisons. The consistency of these two measures relieves some of the ambiguity that the index number problem creates.[4] Presumably, defense planners on both sides, if they could agree with the CIA data, would also agree that the Soviet Union in 1979 allocated a larger amount of economic resources to defense activities than did the United States. Unless one quarrels with the data—and admittedly there are important questions to be raised—or unless one assigns to United States force planners a higher level of ingenuity in converting their resources into military output, it would appear that in 1979 Soviet military capability expanded relative to that of the United States.

RECENT TRENDS IN UNITED STATES-SOVIET MILITARY EXPENDITURE

In any event, it is important to remember that budgetary outlays in a given year represent only a small fraction of the existing military capability, which is primarily derived from the cumulative effect of many years of training and equipping the military force. Hence in comparing the levels of military outlay, greater interest has been attached to long-term trends than to the year-to-year fluctuations in spending.

The levels and trends of United States and Soviet aggregate defense costs for the past two decades, as estimated by the CIA's National Foreign Assessment Center, are presented in Figure 25.1. Bearing in mind that these are dollar cost comparisons and remembering the care that must be exercised in interpreting them, a number of salient features may be identified. With respect to the comparative level of expenditure, the Soviet Union moved ahead of the United States in dollar terms in 1971 and has steadily widened the gap since that time. By 1979, the annual outlay was 50 percent higher than that of the United States. The cumulative Soviet outlay for the last decade, 1970–79, was 30 percent higher.

Disaggregation of the spending totals reveals a number of sharp divergencies, both between and within the major mission categories. In strategic forces, as shown in Figure 25.2, Soviet expenditure was already well ahead at the start of the decade and continued to increase the gap, amounting to two-and-two-thirds that of the United States for the decade as a whole. Within this category, the Soviets devoted a much greater share of their resources to strategic *defense*—cumulatively about half—versus only 15 percent in the case of the United States. In the area of intercontinental attack activities, additional divergencies appear, with the Soviets devoting a much higher proportion to ICBM forces than the United States, one-half versus one-fifth, and a lower proportion to bombers, less than 5 percent versus one-third.[5] The Soviets have exceeded United States spend-

BILLIONS OF FY 1980 DOLLARS

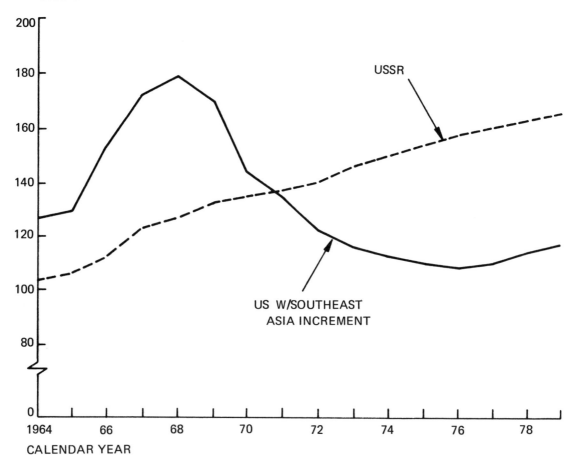

Figure 25.1 Comparison of U.S. Defense Outlays and Estimated Dollar Cost
of Soviet Defense Programs: 1964–1979

Source: Department of Defense Annual Report, 1980, and
CIA, Soviet and U.S. Defense Activities, 1970–79: A Dollar Cost Comparison.

ing for General Purpose Forces by a relatively constant gap since 1973. In the case of Support Forces, the Soviets have exhibited a continuing increase, whereas United States spending in real terms has declined for most of the period under discussion.

These differences in the levels and trends of spending in subcategories are important to keep in mind when comparisons of aggregate military expenditure are made. The differences are the result of many factors, including not only relative costs but also differences in geography, doctrine, the nature of the perceived security threats, and capabilities of allies—in short, all the factors that affect the security problem.

Despite these divergencies in the spending patterns, the picture that emerges from the estimates is one in which the Soviets have steadily outspent the United States in virtually all of the major categories that analysts might choose to distinguish. Whereas United States military expenditures in real terms declined in the first half of the 1970s, and held roughly constant thereafter, Soviet spending has grown steadily during the past decade, averaging about 1.8 percent annually by the 1979 dollar cost measure. The measurement in rubles, which is probably a more reliable indicator of trends in Soviet military expenditure, gives a much higher rate, an annual increase of 4 to 5 percent for the period from 1967 to 1977. This is approximately the same growth rate as that for the Soviet economy as a whole during the same period.[6]

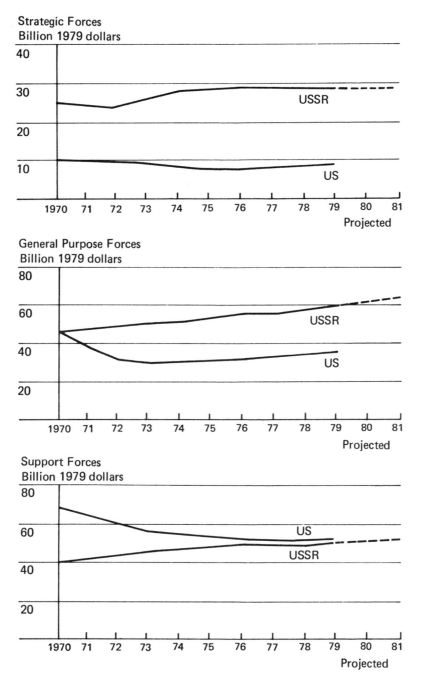

Figure 25.2 U.S. and Soviet Military Expenditure by Major Mission Category: 1970–1981

Source: CIA, Soviet and U.S. Defense Activities, 1970–79: A Dollar Cost Comparison.

By 1980 the cumulative impact of these disparate outlays on the relative military capability of the U.S. and U.S.S.R.—exacerbated by Soviet actions in Afghanistan and Poland and Soviet proxy actions in Ethiopia and Angola—had set the stage for a resurgence in U.S. military spending. Beginning with the fiscal year 1979 budget, the Carter administration announced its determination to reverse the adverse trend and begin the process of countering the long-term Soviet military buildup. A related action was a commitment to concerned NATO allies to increase United States military spending by 3 percent per annum in real terms. The Reagan administration, having made this a key issue in the 1980 Presidential campaign, set a priority goal of even more substantial increases in real defense spending. Administration projections in the Five-Year Defense Plan called for an average real growth rate of 7.4 percent in Total Obligational Authority through FY 1987, taking FY 1982 as the base year.[7] Such a buildup, which would be unprecedented for the U.S. during peacetime, represents a substantial diversion of resources from the private sector or other government programs. This leads us to the concept of the economic burden of military expenditure.

THE ECONOMIC BURDEN OF MILITARY EXPENDITURE

As we have noted throughout, the opportunity cost of military spending is best understood in terms of other goals to which the resources involved might be applied. These goals include the current levels of consumption and investment, the latter, of course, being a determinant of the rate of economic growth and hence of the future capacity to satisfy these goals. In comparing military spending patterns, it is common to measure the size of the defense effort relative to the total capacity of the economy to satisfy its goals. This is the normal sense in which the concept of the economic burden of military expenditure is employed, and the most common measure is the fraction of total GNP devoted to defense. The concept has some legitimate uses, but it is also easily subject to abuse.

When calculating the economic burden of military spending, we note first that, by conventional national income accounting procedures, each dollar spent on defense also counts as a dollar of GNP. We do not treat security costs as an operating expense, as would be done for an individual firm, in which case the outlays would not enter into final product or value added. Hence military expenditure does not constitute a burden in the sense that it detracts from the size of GNP. Clearly, however, a dollar spent on defense does impose an opportunity cost, and the share of total GNP going to defense is one means of putting that cost in perspective.

The main legitimate use of the "burden" concept is to provide a better feel for the significance of the opportunity cost of military spending. An annual military outlay of one billion dollars is difficult to comprehend. Therefore, in seeking to assess the significance of the amount, it helps to know whether the amount represents 5 or 50 percent of the GNP of the country involved. Allies sharing a common defense burden, for example, frequently employ the concept in negotiating "fair" share.

By the same token, the burden concept may be useful in efforts to interpret a country's defense spending behavior. For example, if Country A's annual defense budget is increasing at approximately 4 percent per year in real terms, the significance of that increase might be assessed differently if it were occurring in the context of a GNP growth rate of 8 percent as opposed to one of 2 percent. In the former case, the defense share of GNP is dropping at about 4 percent per annum in real terms; in the latter case it is increasing at about 2 percent. Other things being equal, a rising share of GNP or a sudden increase in the share may be a better indicator of a government's intentions or a society's level of commitment than are changes in the absolute amount or its rate.

If we agree that GNP constitutes a rough measure of military spending capacity, the burden concept can also be used as a measure of the extent to which that capacity is being utilized, and hence as a measure of the capability to expand. However, as noted in Chapter 6, the use of GNP as a measure of defense spending capacity is fraught with difficulty. The fact that a society is physically capable of a certain level of military production loses significance if the necessary political and social ingredients are lacking.

Because political and social factors vary widely among countries, cross-cultural comparisons of GNP are virtually useless as a measure of relative national ability to mount a defense effort. The economic burden, as we have defined it, is equally suspect as an indicator of the capacity to sustain or expand the military effort. United States-Soviet comparisons illustrate this point.

In addition to the conventional share of GNP measurement of the military burden, the impact on various economic sectors may also be of interest. For example, we may wish to know the share that goes to defense of various components of GNP, such as total investment, or total expenditures on research and development. How these components are utilized has significant implications for long-term economic performance in the defense and nondefense sectors, and the extent to which a government devotes these key resources to defense may shed additional light on both the magnitude of the defense burden and trends in military power. The hazards of cross-cultural comparisons discussed in the previous paragraph also apply to these categories.

With these caveats in mind, it may be noted that the burden of Soviet military expenditure, by the most recent C.I.A. estimates, amounts to some 11 to 12 percent of Soviet GNP, and the figure seems to have held roughly constant for the past decade.[8] The crucial question is, of course, what the longer term Soviet spending pattern will be. In light of the unfavorable prospects for Soviet growth and the relatively disadvantaged status of the Soviet consumer, clearly the large military spending share of GNP constitutes a substantial and growing burden for the Soviets. There is the possibility that these pressures may occasion a reassessment of Soviet policies, with some diversion of resources from the military sector to improve long-term economic prospects.[9]

In contrast, in the U.S. case the pattern has been one of a long-term decline in the defense burden, at least until quite recently. The peak post-World War II year was 1955, with a defense share of the GNP in excess of 9 percent. Thereafter the share gradually declined, excepting the late 1960s, when Vietnam spending occasioned an increase. By FY 1979 the defense share had dropped to 5 percent. As noted above, President Carter undertook a reversal of this trend and, subsequently, President Reagan set an even more ambitious goal, projecting an average real growth rate in defense spending in excess of 7 percent for his first term of office. Obviously such a rate would boost the share of GNP going to defense. According to administration estimates the defense share would amount to 7.4 percent by FY 1987.[10] A shift of this magnitude involves a substantial increase in the defense burden, and it is by no means clear at the time of this writing that the increase can be sustained at that rate. Yet by comparison to the entire post-World War II period, and by comparison to Soviet behavior, the goals might be judged relatively modest.

This reversal of the United States trend in military spending had an obvious connection with the disparate Soviet pattern, which raises the quesiton of interaction in military spending levels.

INTERACTION IN MILITARY SPENDING: THE ARMS RACE

The previous paragraphs have set forth some generalities regarding the way in which economic considerations enter into a society's capability and willingness to undertake military expenditure to secure national values and interests against external threat. The need to apply scarce national resources to such purposes is, of course, contingent on the nature of the threat. So far, the discussion has been couched in terms that imply the threat is exogenously determined. This would mean, for example, that the magnitude and quality of the Soviet military threat to United States interests is fixed independently of the United States security policies that are designed to protect against that threat. Obviously, however, if United States military expewnditure is determined to some degree in response to Soviet military expenditure, the possibility exists that Soviet actions likewise may be affected by what the United States does. If so, it follows that our own military expenditure to counter the Soviet threat has some impact on the threat itself. Such a pattern of interaction might also be inferred by Soviet planners, namely, a pattern in which U.S. military capabilities are shaped in response to changes in Soviet military capabilities. Of course, there is no reason to suppose that the reaction patterns are similar.

This type of action-reaction behavior, commonly referred to as the arms race, is of obvious importance to national security strategy. Any progress in achieving a better understanding of interaction in the arms process is likely to be helpful in devising better strategies to achieve national security objectives or to reduce the required expenditure of national resources for that purpose. A central concern is the irrational aspect of an escalating situation that involves both sides expending substantial amounts of resources, arming against a growing threat, but creating no net gain in terms of improved security. Indeed, it seems to have created the possibility of increased risk of a nuclear conflict in which both sides will lose. Such a situation would appear to offer some basis for attenuating the growth of armaments. The possibilities include, but are not limited to, formal arrangements to limit certain weapons systems. It is also conceivable that unilateral policy actions might achieve similar benefits, provided of course that the expected reaction did in fact materialize. One variant of such policy would be to avoid certain actions that seem likely to provoke a neutralizing response on the other side, or to escalate the arms competition to a higher level or a more dangerous form. For example, in the design of the strategic nuclear deterrent, such considerations might support measures to reduce the vulnerability of the existing missile force rather than an increase in the size of that force. Both approaches are ways to increase the attack capability surviving a first round enemy strike. However, the latter approach also constitutes an additional threat to the opponent's own retaliatory force and hence is more likely to stimulate increases in the opponent's capability.

It would not be appropriate here to attempt a full-scale discussion of the many issues involved in the general area of arms control. However, the idea of an arms race clearly is relevant to the topic of comparative military spending. Furthermore, the problems involved are closely related to some conventional economic principles previously introduced in Chapter 13, under the heading of oligopoly. It seems that economic theory, while useful in explaining the fundamental nature of the arms race problem, has not been especially helpful in providing practical ways of coping with the problem. The following discussion elaborates briefly on the subject.

Actions and Reactions

As explained in Chapter 13, oligopoly theory deals with problems in which rival actors, who share some interests but are opposed in others, seek to formulate rational decision-making rules that take into account the reaction of the rival to one's own policies. In the classic case of duopoly, for example, two firms have a mutual interest in extracting as large a total amount of profit as possible from a given market, but also have a conflicting relationship as to what their relative market shares will be. It would be in the interest of both parties to agree to limit production, thereby maximizing the total profit pie. However, in seeking to enlarge their own share of the pie, or in preventing the rival from gaining a larger share, each side feels an incentive to expand production. In the process, the mutual interest may be sacrificed.

The arms race situation presents somewhat the same dilemma, in that each side shares an interest in constraining the total amount of "defense production," but each side has a competing interest in achieving a larger amount of defense production than the rival. The arms race problem is more severe than the oligopoly problem in that the concern not to fall behind one's rival in defense capability is far more intense than the competition for a share of the market in the conventional economic context. The penalty for being second best in the military arena may be very high, or may be so perceived.

A useful device for illustrating some of the possibilities and dilemmas of the action-reaction problem with respect to armaments is the *reaction function*. Consider a situation in which two competing sides, Red and Blue, confront a choice concerning the level of military capability.

We assume that each side has a preference for military superiority, conditioned by the opportunity cost of achieving it. Figure 25.3 uses indifference contours to depict the preferences of Red as a function of the level of military capability of each side. Red's utility increases with a move to the left, i.e., a reduction in Blue's capability. Thus U_2^R is preferred to U_1^R, U_3^R to U_2^R, and so on. The shape of the contours may be explained by considering the series of points a . . . d along Contour U_3^R. We begin with Point a, which represents a zero capability level for Blue and some positive level of capability of Red, and examine the changes in the marginal rate of substitution along this contour as we move to higher levels of Red capability. Note that initially (a to b) the trade-off is positive, with an increase in Red capability compensated by an increase in Blue, but that the trade-off worsens as Red capability increases (b to c). This reflects the increasing opportunity cost of Red capability. In fact, beyond c the cost is so high that to remain on the same utility contour requires that Blue capability *decline*. The point on each contour where the slope is vertical represents that point at which the benefit to Red of additional military capability vis-a-vis Blue is just balanced by the opportunity cost of that capability.[10]

The locus of these points of vertical slope is referred to as the *reaction function* of Red. For each level of Blue capability, the reaction function depicts the optimal response by Red, on the assumption that Red regards Blue's capability as fixed.

The location and shape of the reaction function are of particular interest, and it would be very helpful if we could impose any *a priori* restrictions regarding what the shape might be. Unfortunately that is not possible. The shape depicted, however, is a highly plausible one for the following reasons.

Note first that the reaction function shown in Figure 25.3 depicts Red as choosing a positive level of capability in response to zero Blue capability. This pattern might result from a Red desire for stability, the reasoning being that if both sides have a very low or zero capability, the military balance is subject to large short-run swings.

Secondly, note that the reaction function is shown with a positive slope. This is the pattern we would normally expect—as Blue increases capability, Red counters by an increase in Red's own capability. However, the slope of the reaction function is shown to be decreasing, approaching zero at some level of Red capability.

Whether, or at what level, the reaction function will "flatten out" in this manner is problematical. Such a pattern might occur if, at some high level of Red capability, further additions to the Blue threat become insignificant. For example, in an era in which strategic weapons are targeted primarily on the population or economic capacity of the opposing side, at some point diminishing returns to additional striking power will presumably occur, simply because the number of targets remains constant. If on the other hand, strategic weapons have a "counterforce" capability, the Red reaction function can retain its positive slope indefinitely because the targets, i.e., enemy missiles, continue to increase. It is interesting to note in this regard that the previously mentioned shift in United States policy to counter the continuing Soviet military buildup was accompanied by news of a shift in strategic doctrine. As reported, the revised policy requires American strategic forces to be able to undertake strikes against specific military targets, including enemy missiles. Previous thinking placed primary emphasis on threats to major cities as the means to achieving deterrence.[11]

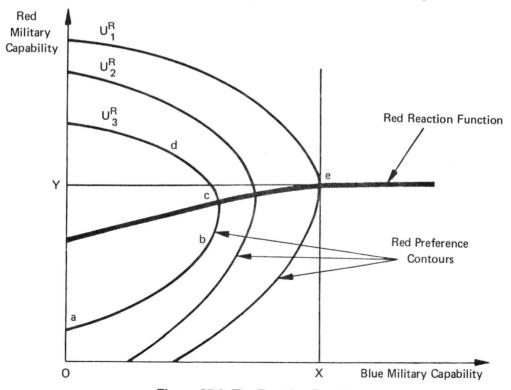

Figure 25.3 The Reaction Function

Figure 25.4 expands the illustration to include preference maps and reaction functions for Blue as well as Red. In the Blue case, for the purposes of the discussion, the reaction curve is shown with a relatively constant slope over the range depicted. It might be inferred either that Blue's economic capacity is somewhat greater than that of Red, or that Blue's preference for military "superiority" does not attenuate for doctrinal or other reasons, even at very high capability levels.

The reaction functions in Figure 25.4 represent, for the respective sides, the preferred levels of military capability as a function of the strength of the opposing side. Each point in the diagram symbolizes a particular combination of capabilities. Any point that does not lie on Blue's reaction function symbolizes a disequilibrium for Blue; the figure works the same way for Red. Point b, for example, indicates a situation in which both Red and Blue, given their respective preference functions, would be motivated to add to their existing capability by additional military expenditure. In general, any point below Red's reaction function leads Red to invest in additional capability, any point to the left of Blue's reaction function provokes a similar response by Blue, and vice versa. The pattern of Point g would lead to *disinvestment* by both sides. Point e represents the only equilibrium in which both parties are satisfied and, in the case shown, the equilibrium would be stable.[12]

The reader should keep in mind that the axes in the diagram reflect the cumulative level of military capability, resulting from previous flows of investment expenditures, less, of course, depreciation. The model does not stipulate the significance of annual expenditures relative to total capability. For example, the change in capability involved in the vertical movement by Red from Point f up to the Red reaction function might represent many annual increments to Red's military capital. Thus the actual pattern of relative military capabilities of two countries such as the United States and the Soviet Union, observed at a time when both countries are accumulating additional capability, would normally be taken to represent a point such as f, with both countries in a state of disequilibrium.[13]

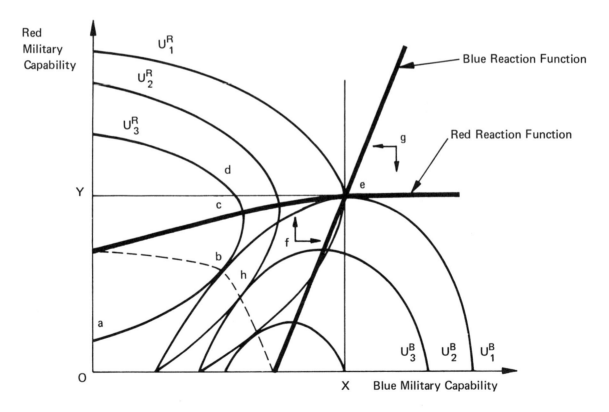

Figure 25.4 Interaction and Equilibrium in Military Capability

Applications of the Model

Not surprisingly, this highly abstract model does not afford much assistance in interpreting the nature of the interaction of armaments levels in particular instances. It does, however, provide a number of interesting insights into the general nature of the problem. The principal inference to be drawn from the model is the perversity of the underlying incentive structure. Point e does represent a stable equilibrium in the sense that, if the point were reached, neither side would have an incentive to modify its military capability. However, the equilibrium is not optimal. The implied levels of military spending are excessive—in the sense that lower outlays, if undertaken by both sides, would benefit both sides.

The optimal levels of military capability are shown by the dashed line through Points b and h; the line represents the locus of points of tangency between the Red and Blue preference contours, and is analogous to the contract curve of Chapter 10. Note that Point h, for example, represents an improvement for both Red and Blue over Point e. Once any point on the contract curve is attained, such as h, any readjustment would be disadvantageous for at least one of the two sides.

The reasons for the difficulty in achieving the mutual gains available by a move to the contract curve are closely analogous to problems faced by duopolists seeking to collude. For example, in seeking to negotiate a mutual reduction from Point e, Red will aspire to move along the Red reaction function, and Blue along the Blue reaction function. However, the opportunities for mutual gains are to be found by each side agreeing to move *off* its own reaction function, to the middle ground represented by points such as b, f, or h. Furthermore, even if such a point, say h, is achieved both parties will experience an incentive to cheat; either would benefit by a unilateral move up or to the right, for Red and Blue respectively. Thus, distrust of the other side is not only likely, but also well founded.

Many additional questions may be posed regarding the nature of the interaction process in a particular instance, such as that of the United States—Soviet arms competition. Is there an equilibrium point such as e, which would entail an eventual slowdown in either the strategic or conventional arms competition? Or, on the other hand, is there no equilibrium, with the possibility of an ever-escalating pace of arms spending? If some eventual equilibrium does exist, what magnitude of additional arms spending is implied before equilibrium is reached? Is it legitimate to suppose, as the simple model does, that either side's military expenditure patterns are heavily conditioned by the other side's capability, or do other factors such as internal bureaucratic pressures play the predominant role? The importance of this question lies in the fact that, if the former supposition is valid, a strong argument can be made in support of unilateral moderation in weapons spending as a means of curbing the arms race. If the latter is true, however, such policies are likely to be at best useless, and most probably perilous.

Clearly what is needed is some basis for sharpening our understanding of the determinants of military spending, particularly concerning the component attributable to interaction. The basic question to be addressed is how does a particular society or ruling elite trade off the costs of military expenditure against the advantages of the associated increase in relative military capability? About the only thing we can say from a deductive viewpoint is that, presumably, a trade-off does in fact exist, i.e., military expenditure—at some point—entails a positive opportunity cost. What the trade-off is, however, and how it varies over different points in the expenditure and relative capability spectrum, cannot be deduced from axioms of rational choice, and, unfortunately, efforts to elicit underlying behavioral patterns from the experience to date have not yielded results in which we can place great confidence.

The Richardson Equations

Perhaps the most influential work in modelling arms races was done by Lewis Richardson.[14] The basic postulate of Richardson's work was that the rate of change in rival military capability could be explained in terms of the relations

$$\frac{dB}{dt} = a - bB + cR \qquad\qquad (25.1)$$

$$\frac{dR}{dt} = d - eR + fB \qquad\qquad (25.2)$$

where B and R represent military capability of the Blue and Red sides and the parameters a . . . f represent positive constants. Thus, according to the basic Richardson model, the time rate of change of a nation's addition to military capability is positively related to the magnitude of the opposing force and negatively related to its own strength, with a constant term that may be variously interpreted. The reaction functions in this model are assumed to be straight lines and are given for Blue and Red respectively by the equations

$$a - bB + cR = o \qquad\qquad (25.3)$$

$$d - eR + fB = o .^{15} \qquad\qquad (25.4)$$

Countless variations in this basic model are possible, and in theory such models, and elaborated versions thereof, are susceptible to empirical estimation and testing on the basis of actual data.[16]

The practical problems, however, are profound. The difficulty is essentially to be found in the inherent complexity of the arms process. It is extraordinarily difficult to devise meaningful measures of military capability, both in the strategic weapons category and in the conventional category. For example, if the model is to be applied to the strategic weapons race, the candidates for measurement criteria might be the number of missiles, the number of warheads, or the megatonnage equivalent. The study cited above employed a measurement based on total megatonnage yield raised to the 2/3's power. A crucial issue concerns the ability of the deterrent force to survive a first strike. Obviously one's reaction to an adversary's buildup of capability can greatly vary, depending on the extent to which one's own capability is threatened in this manner. However, none of the criteria mentioned address this issue. By the same token, technological changes, such as improved accuracy, which can rewrite the strategic balance, tend to be omitted from aggregate data. It should also be noted that any single measure of military capability—such as the one used in this study—can be highly misleading.

A further problem is that of leads and lags, which separate policy formulation and implementation. Investment in a particular strategic system may involve decades, with continuing opportunities for adjustment of the scope and characteristics of the system. This makes it very difficult to impute the decisions to specific actions by the other side.

An additional problem is the obvious fact that many other factors impinge on military spending decisions. The best model for predicting Soviet military expenditure during the past decade, for example, would most likely be the level of Soviet GNP, of which military spending involved a remarkably constant share. By the same token, United States military spending after declining in real terms for almost a decade, has increased recently, no doubt in response to the Soviet pattern. However, this only occurred after a very long time lag and the additional stimulus of world events, which had no direct connections with the Soviet spending level.

The most significant problem, of course, is the weakness of the fundamental assumption that each side bases its policy on the adversary's level of capability, as opposed to some more complex set of factors. Although military planners emphasize the importance of enemy capabilities as opposed to that of intentions, each side is inevitably affected by its perceptions of the other side's intentions regarding the utilization of present or future capabilities. Perceptions may be affected by many factors outside the realm of the current capability level, ranging from sharp changes in the rate of military spending to hostile acts in other areas. In turn, such changes in perceptions may radically affect either side's assessment of the importance of its own military capability, in which case the preference function in effect shifts, and military spending patterns shift with it. The Berlin Wall, the Cuban missile crisis, and the Afghanistan invasion all provide examples of events that have had the potential to trigger such shifts.

CONCLUSION

To date, it has not been possible to "explain" with confidence either Soviet or United States variations in military expenditure patterns in terms of what the other was doing. However, simple oligopoly type models of military spending do shed some light on the possible patterns of interaction in the arms process. They reveal, for example, the perversity of the underlying incentive structure, which motivates both sides to continue to expend resources in a mutually disadvantageous process. This insight constitutes a powerful rationale for formal efforts to negotiate mutually advantageous limitations on arms spending. At the same time it illustrates not only the profound obstacles to the success of such efforts, but also the vital importance of verification to insure compliance with any agreement reached.[17]

NOTES

1 In general all the caveats of the previous chapter on interpreting and comparing GNP data apply equally to military spending aggregates. For a useful summary see Abraham Becker, "The Meaning and Measure of Soviet Military Expenditure," *Soviet Economy in a Time of Change*, Vol. 1, pp. 352–366.

2 *Ibid.*, p. 362.

3 The following discussion will follow CIA estimates as the most authoritative available. For a description of some of the alternative estimates, see Becker, *op. cit.*, p. 362.

4 Data from Central Intelligence Agency, *Soviet U.S. Defense Activities, 1970–79: A Dollar Cost Comparison* (Washington, D.C.: CIA, January, 1980), p. 3. It should be noted, however, that the ruble cost comparison is subject to question, given the inevitably convoluted nature of the estimating procedure. More detailed data may well reduce the U.S.S.R./U.S. ruble cost estimate.

5 *Ibid.*

6 For the ruble figures see Central Intelligence Agency, *Estimated Soviet Defense Spending: Trends and Prospects* (Washington, D.C.: CIA, June, 1978). The disparity in the dollar and ruble growth rates is a further illustration of the index number problem. An argument might be made that the dollar weights are more indicative of the "late period" prices and ruble weights of "early period" prices. Even in that event, however, both approaches have equivalent claims to legitimacy. See Becker, *op. cit.*, p. 356.

7 Department of Defense, *Annual Report, Fiscal Year 1983* (Washington, D.C.: Government Printing Office, January, 1983), p. I-4.

8 CIA, *Estimated Soviet Defense Spending, op. cit.*, p. 1. This is the "narrow" estimate, excluding such categories as internal security, certain civil defense activities, military stockpiling, foreign military assistance, and space programs, which would normally not be counted in the U.S. Inclusion of these items, which might reflect a more accurate measure in terms of Soviet perceptions, raises the estimate to 12 to 13 percent. It should be noted that in 1976 the CIA revised its estimate from 6–10 percent to the current 11–13%.

9 Andrew Marshall, "Sources of Soviet Power: The Military Potential in the 1980's," *Prospects of Soviet Power in the 1980's*, Part II, *Adelphi Papers*, No. 152, International Institute for Strategic Studies (London: The Eastern Press, Ltd., September, 1978).

10 Department of Defense, *Annual Report, op. cit.*, p. IV-10.

11 The rationale underlying the preference contours may be clarified as follows. Suppose Blue's utility to be given by $U = f[X, Y, Z]$, where the arguments X, Y, and Z respectively represent military capability of the adversary, Blue's own military capability, and capability to satisfy nonmilitary goals. We assume utility to be a decreasing function of X, and increasing functions of Y and Z. Assume further that the production frontier which defines Blue's ability to achieve various combinations of Y and Z is given by $Z = g(Y)$. As Blue increases Y, Z necessarily falls. We may think of Blue's objective as maximizing $U = f[X, Y, Z] = f[X, Y, g(Y)]$, which may be rewritten as $U = F[X, Y]$. This is the function depicted. Applying the usual 1° Order condition, for any given *fixed* level of X, maximum utility occurs where

$$\frac{\partial U}{\partial Y} = 0$$

12 Richart Burt, "Carter Said to Back Plan for Limiting Nuclear War," *New York Times* (August 6, 1980), p. 1.
13 The condition for stable equilibrium is that Blue's reaction function, as drawn, has a greater slope than Red's at the point of intersection. It is, of course, conceivable that the opposite is true, and there is no guarantee that the functions intersect.
14 Alternatively, only one of the countries may be on its reaction function.
15 Lewis Richardson, *Arms and Insecurity* (Pittsburgh: Boxwood Press, 1960) and *Statistics of Deadly Quarrels* (Chicago: Quadrangle Press, 1960).
16 By definition, each side's reaction function consists of those capability levels for which no change in capability is desired. Thus $dB/dt = 0$ defines Blue's reaction function.
17 See Martin C. McGuire, "A Quantitative Study of the Arms Race in the Missile Age," *Review of Economics and Statistics* (August, 1977), pp. 328–39.
18 For alternative approaches to the conceptual aspects of the interactive nature of arms spending, see Kenneth E. Boulding, *Conflict and Defense* (New York: Harper Torchbooks, 1962), and Thomas Schelling, *The Strategy of Conflict* (Cambridge, Mass.: Harvard University Press, 1960).

SELECTED REFERENCES

Kenneth E. Boulding, *Conflict and Defense* (New York: Harper and Row, 1960).
Central Intelligence Agency, *Estimated Soviet Defense Spending: Trends and Prospects* (Washington, D.C.: CIA, June, 1978).
Central Intelligence Agency, *A Dollar Cost Comparison of Soviet and U.S. Defense Activities, 1968–78* (Washington, D.C.: CIA, January, 1979).
Department of Defense, *Annual Report* (Washington, D.C.: Government Printing Office, Annual).
Albert Wohlstetter, "Is There a Strategic Arms Race?" *Foreign Policy, No. 15 (Summer, 1974), pp. 3–20* and "Rivals But No Race," *Foreign Policy*, No. 16 (Fall, 1974), pp. 48–81.
Soviet Economy in a Time of Change: A Compendium of Papers Submitted to the Joint Economic Committee, Congress of the United States (Washington, D.C.: Government Printing Office, October, 1979).

Chapter 26
National Security
and the Developing Nations

INTRODUCTION

It is appropriate to conclude this book on economics and national security with a brief examination of the economic situation in the developing countries. The benefits of industrialization have not been spread equally among the nations of the world, and the lack of economic progress in widespread areas, particularly the nations of the southern hemisphere, has been a matter of concern since World War II. The concern has in significant part been a humanitarian concern, and rightly so, especially with respect to the worst cases—the 800 million who continue to live in abject poverty. The concern has also been based on the recognition that security interests are at stake. Without doubt, the willingness on the part of the industrialized countries to provide foreign aid to stimulate economic development and ameliorate proverty has been vitally dependent on the notion that enhanced economic performance for the developing nations is conducive to peace and security.

The extent to which the motivation for foreign assistance is altruistic or based on self-interest varies from case to case, and the two forms of motivation are not mutually exclusive. The distinction is nevertheless important. The rationale for economic assistance determines the results expected and conditions not only the level of assistance provided, but also the terms of assistance, the selection of recipients, and in turn the attitudes of recipient governments and peoples. The discussion that follows will emphasize the pragmatic approach, recognizing however that the self-interest involved is very much a long-term proposition. Just as there are no short-term solutions to the problems of poverty and underdevelopment, there are unlikely to be short-term rewards for efforts to combat these problems. The connection with national security is nonetheless vital. In the following pages we will attempt to briefly set forth the nature of that connection, the dimensions of the problems confronting the developing countries, and the uses of various economic policy instruments by the United States and other industrialized nations in seeking to ameliorate those problems.

THE RATIONALE OF FOREIGN ASSISTANCE

In the two hundred years since the industrial revolution, the associated increases in productivity have led to dramatic improvements in income levels for those societies in which the industrialization process has taken place. However, the benefits of economic progress have not been evenly distributed. The grim reality is that more than one-third of the developing world's population continues to subsist in absolute poverty, and average income levels in a few rich industrial economies are several times the levels typical elsewhere in the world. On balance, the disparities are increasing.

Humanitarian considerations alone would suffice to justify efforts to narrow this gap. In a more pragmatic vein, however, the United States has a strong self-interest in the ability of the developing countries to achieve political stability, avoiding the excesses of totalitarianism and adhering to those basic principles of human rights contained in our Constitution and supported by the charter of the United Nations. A world characterized by political unrest is a dangerous world. Unstable governments provide opportunities and create demands for

380 THE ECONOMICS OF NATIONAL SECURITY

intervention. Trade relations may be interrupted, the rights and lives of foreign nationals may be threatened, and the mere existence of disorder may invite intervention, lest a competing power do so first. Wherever armed conflict occurs there is a possibility of wider involvement, into which the superpowers might be drawn.

The conventional wisdom holds that a satisfactory level of economic progress in the developing countries is conducive—even essential in the long run—to political development and enhanced prospects for political stability. The proposition seems to us to be a valid one; however, it is subject to significant qualifications. The interrelationships between economic and political development in the overall modernization process are not simple. Indeed, there is ample evidence that rapid economic development can be destabilizing. While Iran is the single most dramatic instance of economic development gone awry, throughout the developing world the achievement of economic progress has not generally been accompanied by comparable gains in the political sphere.

Various explanations can be cited. In the first place, the benefits of economic progress are usually not equitably distributed within a given society. Groups living in abject poverty are forced to coexist with the most lavish styles of conspicuous consumption. Secondly, the experience of some improvement in material well-being has a tendency to raise the level of what is expected. As the following section describes, in the past several decades there has been substantial progress in absolute terms with respect to the economic standard of living of people in the developing countries. Yet dissatisfaction with the status quo and the intensity of demand for more rapid progress and a greater aid commitment by the industrialized nations have never been higher. In the third place, the process of economic development disturbs cultural patterns in ways that may cause instability. For example, it may result in the dislocation of workers from the traditional family setting to urban areas. Finally, and most significantly, the challenge of developing effective political institutions within the mold of Western democratic values has proved to be a very difficult proposition. Adoption of the forms of constitutional government does not guarantee achievement of the substance. Time after time the fundamental ideas—that political power must be won by competition, exercised with restraint, and surrendered peacefully according to established rules—have fallen victim in the struggle for political and economic spoils. The upshot of these complexities is that the governments of developing nations may be unstable or undemocratic or both.

Such problems undermine the rationale for economic assistance to developing countries. However, if the granting of development assistance does not lead to satisfactory results, it clearly is not likely that withholding it will do better. The moral is not that better economic conditions in the developing countries are unimportant to their political development, but rather that the interrelationships are complex and that expectations must be tempered accordingly.

A related issue concerns the extent to which the granting of development assistance is linked by the donor to conditions that the recipient government respond in particular ways. Such conditions might involve a simple *quid pro quo* in the form of a return favor, such as the granting of a trade concession or military basing rights. On the other hand, the conditions might extend to more fundamental issues affecting the domestic or foreign policy of the recipient country. For example, the recipient government might be asked to refrain from human rights violations, or it might be pressed to move more rapidly toward an open society with wider participation in government.

The efficacy of linking foreign aid to requirements for political reform is highly limited. It is likely to be perceived as unwarranted, ill-advised meddling which constitutes an encroachment upon national sovereignty. Furthermore, the requested actions are likely to be perceived as a threat to the power of the existing regime, and governments clearly do not surrender power lightly, certainly not for a few dollars of economic assistance, the benefits of which are diffuse and conferred on the population as a whole. Hence, except in the rare case in which the assistance itself is deemed vital to the regime's continuation, major reforms are not to be expected in return. Finally, political reforms externally imposed in this manner are inherently simplistic and liable to compound rather than reduce the problem.

This discussion highlights one of the most painful dilemmas of United States foreign policy, namely the choice between dealing with a foreign government which violates the basic standards we cherish versus terminating the relationship, thereby losing valuable military or other support. The cost of such dealings is that the United States' image is tarnished, and we lose credibility elsewhere. On the other hand, for the reasons given, neither the threatened nor actual denial of aid is likely to be more than a hollow gesture in terms of achieving fundamental political reforms.

In summary, the basic rationale of foreign aid is to assist in accelerating the rate of economic progress in developing countries, and the criterion against which particular aid programs are evaluated is their efficacy in that regard. For this purpose, the concepts and methods of Cost-Benefit analysis as discussed in Chapter 11 are appropriate. The premise of this approach is that accelerated economic progress, in addition to enhancing the economic welfare of the peoples involved, is conducive to the achievement of broader objectives. These objectives include stable governments that respect the basic rights of their own people in their domestic affairs and of other nations in their foreign policy. Although the premise that economic progress is complementary to these broader objectives is accepted as having long-term validity, in the short run the connection is at best tenuous. From time to time, donor nations do seek to link economic assistance to other objectives, using the granting or withholding of aid as a foreign policy instrument. Although this may be effective in securing limited, short-term objectives, the willingness of recipient governments to subordinate their interests in return for economic assistance is severely limited. Before examining the economic policy instruments, we turn now to a brief survey of the nature and extent of the development gap.

THE DEVELOPMENT GAP

Economic development has many dimensions, and the rank ordering of the development level of the countries that comprise the world economy will vary somewhat, depending on the particular indices chosen and the weights assigned to them. While clearly the level of per capita income is the key dimension, the underlying structure of an economy and its capacity to sustain growth are also important. In some cases very high per capita income levels, such as that derived from massive oil resources in the case of Kuwait, are not accompanied by comparable performance along other dimensions of development. Allowing for such variations, certain characteristics typify poor or less developed economies. The World Bank groups countries into Low Income, Middle Income, and Industrialized categories based on average annual per capita Gross Domestic Product (GDP) of less than $250 (1976 dollars) for the Low Income group and a dividing line between the Middle Income and Industrialized groups of about $4000.[1]

Characteristics of the Low Income Group

The Low Income group, which consists primarily of African and South and Southeast Asian countries, is characterized by a heavy reliance on agriculture (about 50 percent of GDP), high population growth rates (in excess of 2 percent), and relatively low rates of savings (less than 10 percent of GDP). Exports are virtually all primary commodities. Health-related and education indicators present a dismal picture. Worst of all, such GDP growth as occurs is neutralized by population growth. The GDP growth per capita over the period from 1960 to 1976 has averaged less than 1 percent for this group. Four of these countries—Bangladesh, India, Indonesia, and Pakistan—account for three-fourths of the Low Income country population and, by the World Bank's estimate, for two-thirds of the world's absolute poor.

Characteristics of the Middle Income Group

The Middle Income Group consists of some 58 countries which include most of Latin America and the Middle East, some of the relatively better off African and Asian nations, and a few of the poorer European nations. Although there are enormous variations within this group, the average income levels are generally well above the subsistence level. As a group, these countries in the last two decades have been able to sustain GDP growth rates well above the growth of population, permitting absolute increases in levels of income and improvements in the quality of life for at least a substantial portion of the population. For most of these countries the initial tendency for population growth to increase with improvement in health-related factors has been more than compensated by higher investment levels and greater productivity, with the result that for the Middle Income countries, the median per capita GNP growth was some 2.8 percent for the period from 1960 to 1976. This growth represents substantial progress and, if sustained, will in time raise income to the high levels enjoyed by the industrailized countries today.

Associated with these higher rates of per capita growth is a generally much higher rate of aggregate investment, financed in part by international credit but primarily by domestic savings. For the Middle Income countries, the median savings rate in 1976 was 20 percent of GDP, which contrasts with the less than 10 percent rate in the Low Income group. The higher rates of saving and investment are, of course, a key factor in generating sustained GDP growth in excess of population increase.

In addition to higher rates of savings and investment, there are a number of other structural changes that commonly accompany the transition to higher levels of productivity and growth found in the Middle Income group. One of these is a shift in the relative importance of agriculture, industry, and services in the composition of GDP.[2] Whereas agriculture normally accounts for as much as 50 percent of GDP in the Low Income group, it occupies a less predominant position in the Middle Income group, typically on the order of about 25 percent and—especially among the better off countries—as little as 10 percent. On the demand side this shift is attributable to the low income elasticity of demand for food as we move beyond the basic subsistence level of income. However, the accompanying shift to industry and services, especially the former in the early stages, is a vital ingredient in the development process, so much so that frequently the tendency is to equate the process with "industrialization." Indeed, as we have noted, the World Bank categorization of countries is Low Income, Middle Income, and *industrialized*.

The presence of a substantial "modern," industrial sector can contribute to economic progress in various ways. It can provide employment for the surplus labor generated by agriculture, it can provide a focus for capital investment, it can save scarce foreign exchange by substituting domestic production for imports of manufactured goods as demand shifts to that sector, and finally—hopefully—it can earn foreign exchange through the development of an export trade in selected industrial products.

These structural shifts are reflected in trade patterns. Whereas the Low Income group relies on exports of primary commodities for virtually all their foreign exchange, higher income levels and the creation of a modern sector enhance the opportunities for diversifying export trade by increasing the proportion of manufactured items.

The Middle Income group exhibits—again with considerable variation within the group—generally higher levels of education. The median adult literacy rate jumps from 23 to 63 percent (1974) as we move from a Low Income group to a Middle Income group, and the median figure on primary school enrollment is well over 90 percent (versus less than half in the Low Income group), with the secondary school enrollment figure averaging over one-third of the eligible population (versus less than 10 percent in the Low Income group). Health-related indicators such as life expectancy, infant and child mortality rates, access to safe water, and population per physician also typically show major improvements as we move up the per capita GDP scale in the Middle Income group.

Despite the considerable dynamism and progress that some of the Middle Income group countries have exhibited during the past several decades, there are a number of disquieting aspects of their status and prospects, even among these relatively fortunate members of the community of less developed nations. When we consider the massive numbers of people in the relatively stagnant Low Income group, the overall picture is definitely not one to inspire complacency. There is an enormous gap between rich nations and poor, and the gap is continuing to increase.

Characteristics of the Industrialized Group

Looking at the high income, "Industrialized" group, consisting of the English-speaking nations, most of Western Europe, and Scandinavia, we find not only much higher per capita income levels (typically 40 times that of the Low Income group and perhaps 8 times that of the Middle Income group), but also generally higher rates of growth. The median growth of per capita GNP for the Industrialized group for the period from 1960 to 1976 is given by the World Bank to be some 3.4 percent, in contrast to median rates of .9 and 2.8 percent for the Low and Middle Income groups.

There are, of course, certain development success stories among the Middle Income group, where per capita growth rates have been quite high. For example, Korea, China, Romania, Yugoslavia, Portugal, Iran, Hong Kong, Greece, Singapore, and Spain all reported average annual per capita GNP growth rates in excess of 5 percent for the period from 1960 to 1976. Even where the per capita growth rate was less, frequently the overall growth rate was high—the benefits attenuated by extraordinarily high rates of population growth. In these cases the low per capita growth performance may conceal a high degree of dynamism and rapid diffusion of technology. As population growth eventually tapers off, such economies should be able to accelerate per capita GNP growth. Although projections call for fertility rates to eventually decline with increasing income, the initial impact on population growth has been an increase due to reductions in mortality rates. Real relief from this problem is only expected well into the next century.[3] On the whole, in terms of per capita income, the industrialized nations are continuing to pull away from most of the rest of the world.

A second disquieting aspect concerns the distribution of the benefits of economic development within those countries that have made impressive progress. Again there are exceptions, however rapid growth of per capita GNP clearly does not mean that the implied opportunity for enhanced levels of economic welfare is distributed equitably across all members of society. Indeed, a frequent pattern is for income distribution to tend toward greater inequality. One reason this occurs is that productivity and income growth tend to be concentrated within the modern, industrialized sector of the economy, in effect bypassing the traditional, low income sectors.[4] The benefits "trickle down," but the pace is slow and the pattern uneven.

Under the circumstances it is not surprising that expectations often run ahead of achievement, and that growth performance which is high by a country's historical standards, and even high in comparison to others, fails to induce either domestic political tranquility or friendly attitudes toward those rich nations contributing economic assistance.

MODELS OF ECONOMIC GROWTH

If we take acceleration of the rate of per capita economic growth as the central objective of policy regarding the developing countries, an appropriate preliminary step is to set forth some ideas concerning the determinants of growth. Economic growth is constrained by the quantity and quality of productive factors available, namely, at the highest level of aggregation, labor, capital, and raw materials. Technology, or the technical "know how" by which these factors are combined in the productive process, may be considered separately as a fourth factor. To a considerable extent, technology is embodied in the capital equipment employed in a given process. Additions to the capital stock, involving improvements in its quality, and training of the labor force that mans the new equipment, represent the principal methods of enhancing technology. Hence technology tends to be defined by the existing capital stock, and it advances primarily as a result of changes in the capital stock.

This is not to say that additions to capital automatically generate the labor and management skills necessary for its effective use. Obviously there are limits to the rate at which additional capital can be absorbed, determined by the availability of the necessary complementary factors. An "oil rich" developing country, for example, may have unlimited access to capital by virtue of its foreign exchange earnings. However, its ability to absorb additional capital could be sharply constrained by other factors, in particular the time required to train labor and management in modern industrial methods.

In general, however, if we set aside the case of oil rich developing countries, the rate of growth is constrained by the lack of capital. What is required for accelerated growth is additional resources with which higher rates of investment and additions to the capital stock may be financed. In principle, these additional resources may come from either domestic or foreign sources. The domestic source is reduced consumption, obtained on a voluntary basis by increased savings, or on a compulsory basis by higher rates of taxation. The foreign source can take several forms: direct investment, long- or short-term loans, or grants.

The distinction between domestic and foreign sources of additional capital is important. The importance stems from the fact that, for a variety of reasons, developing countries tend to be chronically short of foreign exchange. Hence an additional dollar of resources in terms of foreign currency may be more valuable than an equivalent amount generated domestically. Investment resources provided from foreign sources satisfy two needs, supplementing domestic saving as a source of additional investment, and at the same time providing additional foreign exchange with which vital imports of capital or materials may be purchased. These two distinct problems may be referred to respectively as the *savings gap* and the *foreign exchange gap*. Which problem is predominant will vary from country to country. Naturally the predominant problem determines the nature of the developing country's need. We will now consider the savings gap in more detail, returning later to the special problems of foreign exchange.

A central concept in models that emphasize capital accumulation is the incremental capital output ratio (ICOR), which expresses the idea that additions to a country's capital stock result in a given increment to output. Thus if the ICOR is represented by k, additions to the capital stock by I, and level of output by Y,

$$k = \frac{I}{\Delta Y} \tag{26.1}$$

If we make the additional assumption that the average savings rate, s, is constant, and impose the condition that savings equals investment, it follows that

$$sY = k\Delta Y \tag{26.2}$$

or,

$$\frac{\Delta Y}{Y} = \frac{s}{k} \tag{26.3}$$

Equation 26.3 expresses the rate of growth of output as a function of the savings rate and the ICOR. Thus if the ICOR is 3.5, a rate of growth of 5 percent requires a savings rate of 17.5 percent.

Quite obviously this simple relationship, devised originally to analyze stability problems in growing, developed economies, tends to conceal more than it reveals of the complexity of the modernization process, and it can hardly serve as the basis of a development strategy.[5] There are many ways of tackling the problem of enhancing economic productivity, and to focus on the rate of capital accumulation in aggregate terms entails serious risks—so much so that some writers decry even the use of the concept. It does, however, represent a useful starting point, and it does convey a crucial aspect of the long-term problem confronting those developing countries at the low end of the income spectrum, with savings rates below 10 percent.

For a country with a savings rate of only 10 percent, and for which the incremental capital output ratio is on the order of 3.5, the implied GNP growth rate from Equation 26.3 is under 3 percent. Given a high rate of population growth, figures of 2.5 percent or higher being common, most of the GNP growth is required to accommodate the additional population, leaving very little surplus for increase in per capita income. In order to accelerate the GNP growth rate, some means must be found of increasing the rate of investment. Essentially two alternatives are possible: (1) revise the domestic savings rate, or (2) rely on foreign borrowing to make up the difference.[6]

Increasing the domestic savings rate means reducing consumption, and for societies in the very low income range that option is not particularly attractive. Improvement in savings institutions may help to some extent, even in the worst cases, but it is difficult, at least on a voluntary basis, to extract higher rates of savings from individuals living close to the subsistence margin. Alternatively, savings may be increased on a compulsory basis in the form of increased taxation and use of the revenues for investment purposes. This is an important aspect of any development plan, and the extent to which a developing country engages this mechanism of *self help* is an important determinant of the willingness of others to provide development assistance. However, this source is also limited. Typically the administrative machinery for tax collection is ineffectual. More importantly, a large portion of productive activity takes place outside the money economy, as in the case of subsistence agriculture, and hence is inaccessible to taxation.

Confronted with urgent fiscal demands, governments of developing economies, frustrated in their inability to generate adequate tax revenue, frequently resort to deficit financing and, in effect, levy a tax through the resulting inflation. Although this method may succeed in transferring resources from the private to the public sector, it has a number of adverse consequences: the primary impact may be a reduction in private saving and investment, which tends to offset any gains from increased public investment; the development of financial institutions is retarded by an environment of chronic inflation; the inflation tax burden may be very inequitably distributed; and efforts to stimulate foreign trade and attract foreign investment may be adversely affected. Even in the absence of these administrative obstacles to generating adequate amounts of capital from within a developing country's resources, the hard fact remains that a large proportion of the population is subsisting right at the margin of survival and is literally incapable of saving—hence the need for an external supplement to investment resources.[7]

The gap between savings resources and investment needs may be reduced in a number of ways. One approach is to borrow abroad, building up an external debit in return for current resources to fuel higher rates of economic growth and development. This is a popular approach, and has been utilized extensively by the developing countries. The problem with accelerated growth based on foreign debt is that debts must be serviced. As with any debt-financed investment, the operative principle is that the return on the invested funds must be higher than the interest rate paid for the loan. In the case of private, domestic transactions this rule is enforced by the discipline of the marketplace, and investors who fail to satisfy the rule rapidly lose their access to funds. In the case of foreign borrowing for development purposes, the situation is considerably more complicated. In the first place, the need is for resources to finance investments with at least initially a low rate of return. If there were an abundance of attractive investment opportunities with high rates of return, the development problem could be addressed simply by facilitating the flow of foreign capital. Under those circumstances it presumably could and would come in suitable quantities. Unfortunately there is no such abundance; the challenge is to create an environment in which such opportunities exist.

In the past three decades, much has been written about alternative strategies for meeting this challenge. Some writers have envisioned "balanced growth" across all sectors of the economy.[8] The balanced growth concept emphasizes the dependence of each sector on demand from other sectors. An alternative view, the so-called "unbalanced growth" approach, stresses decision making as the strategically scarce capability, and advocates a more selective approach based on leading sectors.[9] According to this view, the dynamic sectors that receive planning priority can, by various linkages, pull the rest of the economy along.

Critics of the balanced versus unbalanced growth debate have noted that ". . . the crucial question is not whether to create unbalance, but what is the *optimum* degree of unbalance, where to unbalance and *how much*, in order to accelerate growth."[10] In any event, development planners normally are not confronted with a plethora of high return projects. Invariably there is a need for investments in infrastructure, to provide economical transportation, communications, and power, along with investments in health and education and training of the labor force. Such improvements in the economic infrastructure, while they may play a crucial development role, do not generally yield a high return in the short run.

Governments that run up a large foreign debt to finance such investments quickly find themselves confronting debt service problems. Increasing debt service ratios cause foreign sources to dry up and make it especially difficult to prevent a reduction in the average maturity of the debt, further increasing the magnitude of the debt service and making it more difficult to manage. The outflow of foreign exchange to service debt has exactly the reverse impact of borrowing—it means less resources available for domestic investment as well as a reduction in scarce foreign exchange reserves.

The practical consequence of these so-called problems of *return flow* is that foreign borrowing on commercial terms is of limited help. This is not to say that commercial capital flows are unimportant; indeed they play a vital and increasing role in the successful performance found in the Middle Income group. However, this source must be supplemented by assistance on *concessional* terms if development resources are to be expanded without creating insurmountable repayment problems, particularly in the Low Income and poorer Middle Income countries.

The importance of official grants and concessional loans is reflected by the fact that in 1975 they accounted for 67 and 26 percent of net medium and long-term capital flows to the Low Income and Middle Income countries, respectively.[11] The Low Income group figure is expected to rise to 92 percent by 1985, meaning that only 8 percent of the capital inflow to those countries will consist of loans at market terms. This Official Development Assistance comes primarily from the OECD countries, which have been donating on average about one-third of 1 percent of their GNP for this purpose.[12] The top performers in 1977 were the Netherlands and Sweden, allocating .76 and .81 percent, respecively; the United States figure in that year was .17 percent, well below the OECD average.

Even though the concessional assistance represented by Table 26.1 constitutes a significant portion of the total capital inflow to the developing countries, the amounts are not particularly large from the perspective of the donor countries. The informal normative lending standard advocated by the international lending agencies was originally set at 1 percent of GNP, and subsequently revised downward to 0.7 percent for purposes of realism. Clearly that target is not even close to achievement. Furthermore, the United States amount reflects a long-term decline, from 2.49 percent in 1949 at the beginning of the Marshall Plan, to .53 percent in 1960, .31 percent in 1970, and 0.17 percent in 1977.[13]

A continuing source of divisiveness between donor and recipient nations concerns the extent to which the specific uses of concessionary aid will be stipulated or influenced by the donor government. In part this involves the general issue of attempting to link the provision of aid to actions desired of the recipient government. A related issue concerns the degree to which the donor government is permitted to take part in shaping

Table 26.1
Foreign Aid as a Proportion of GNP, 1977 (%)

Australia	0.57
Austria	0.16
Belgium	0.59
Canada	0.59
Denmark	0.64
France	0.61
West Germany	0.31
Italy	0.13
Japan	0.21
Netherlands	0.76
New Zealand	0.47
Norway	0.69
Sweden	0.81
Switzerland	0.15
United Kingdom	0.30
United States	0.17
Average	0.30

Source: Roger D. Hansen, et al., The U.S. and World Development: Agenda for Action 1976 (New York: Praeger, 1976), p. 203.

development strategy and tactics. Normally the donor government feels entitled to somewhat more influence than the recipient is eager to permit.

This tension over the degree to which "strings" will be attached to foreign aid is at the root of the choice between bilateral aid, in which the donor country deals directly with the recipient government, and multilateral aid, in which the assistance is funnelled through an international lending agency. Developing countries strongly support the multilateral approach because it minimizes the influence of the donor country over who shall receive assistance and how the assistance will be used. For similar reasons, developing countries prefer program assistance, in which funds are provided in support of the overall development program or major portions thereof, versus project assistance, in which the aid is tied to specific development projects of which the donor approves. Donor preference for bilateral, project assistance reflects distrust on the part of donors of host government planning, combined with a lack of enthusiasm for multilateral agencies and for aid which does not provide an identifiable, tangible return.

One important point to keep in mind in assessing the merits of this debate is that the efficacy of "strings" in shaping the recipient country's development strategy is frequently illusory because of the "fungibility" problem. This is well illustrated by the traditional United States insistence that its bilateral assistance be used to "Buy American." Since the assistance normally constitutes only a fraction of the recipient's foreign exchange in a given year, and since the pattern of use of the remainder may as a result be diverted away from United States imports, the net impact of the "Buy American" provision is highly problematical. Over the past decade the share of Official Development Assistance channeled through multilateral agencies has increased, from less than 10 percent in the mid-sixties to more than 25 percent in 1974.[14]

Concessionary aid in the form of capital flows is only one of many policy instruments through which developing economies may be assisted in the pursuit of their development objectives. While it would not be feasible to attempt a full catalogue of the many other means through which their economic objectives may be helped—or hindered—two such policy instruments are of particular interest to security economics, namely trade policy and military assistance. We now turn to consider these topics.

TRADE AND ECONOMIC DEVELOPMENT

Trade with the industrialized countries occupies a position of strategic importance to the developing countries, with a long-term impact on their growth prospects easily comparable to that of capital flows. As discussed previously, developing countries are dependent on foreign exchange to purchase imports vital to growth and development, and they characteristically confront chronic balance of payments problems as their appetite for imports tends to exceed their foreign exchange earning power. In the short run, the problem may be partially alleviated by capital imports, whether on market or concessional terms. However, loans eventually must be repaid, and increases in the volume of external loans entail mounting debt service requirements which serve to compound the foreign exchange problem. Hence, in the long run, export growth is essential.

In a free trade environment, the developing countries could pursue their interest in expanding exports without benefit of foreign assistance for that purpose, and trade matters would not assume particular importance as a development policy issue. In practice, of course, international trade does not take place in a free environment. Both sides benefit from trade, but the benefits do not extend automatically to all members of society. Although consumers benefit from cheap imports, producers and workers in competing domestic industries have a different perspective. To them imports constitute a threat in the form of increased competition and reduced demand for their own products and consequently reduced employment opportunities in their own industry. The result is a trading world in which imports are restrained by tariffs, quotas, and other trade barriers.

The level of trade restrictions varies widely, by both country and product. At times progress has been made toward freer trade, while at other times protectionist tendencies are reasserted. By and large, the Post World War II period has been characterized by rapidly expanding world trade and by a commitment to international economic cooperation. Since the early 1970s, however, the picture has darkened considerably, and although there is no simple statistic for measuring the general degree of restrictions on international trade, there is general agreement that the recent tendency has been toward increasing protectionism.

Domestic economic performance is the crucial determinant of protectionist pressures in an industrialized country. In a fully employed, rapidly growing economy, imports can be absorbed with relative ease. As unemployment and excess capacity occur, however, pressures for protection rapidly increase. In 1974 the industrialized countries slid into what was to become the most widespread recession since World War II, exacerbated by chronic inflationary problems which have persisted since that time. At the same time, sharp increases in energy prices began to impose severe balance of payments pressures on oil importing countries. The result has been not only a sharp drop in world trade growth, but also widely felt pressures for a new wave of protectionism which, it is feared, will have a long-term adverse impact on trade.

At the same time that trade performance has been falling in objective terms, the subjective evaluation of matters—in particular attitudes among the developing countries—seems to reflect growing dissatisfaction. Perhaps the trend is best described by saying that the widening gap between the economic welfare levels of the rich and poor nations has been accompanied by a widening gap between the extent of economic assistance felt by the developing countries to be their rightful due, and the extent of assistance that the industrialized nations are prepared to provide. With respect to trade policy, for example, the issue is no longer simply that of the developing countries being allowed free and equal access to markets; it has become increasingly a matter of demands for preferential treatment of various kinds.

In the case of the Low Income countries that are heavily dependent on primary commodity exports, the issues concern the level and stability of commodity prices, access to markets, and the opportunity to diversify exports, e.g., by processing of the primary commodities prior to their export. The commodity price issue is an old one, going back to the Prebisch thesis that in the long run the terms of trade would tend to turn against raw materials, a thesis that has been influential in the high priority given to industrialization in the development aspirations of most countries.[17] The empirical record on this issue is mixed regarding both the stability and long-term trends of commodity prices. Western economists have tended to question not only the thesis but also the wisdom and practicability of stabilization schemes. This is one of those areas on which views diverge sharply. Nevertheless, the developing countries continue to seek arrangements to support and stabilize prices. Oil, of course, provided a dramatic and, depending on one's point of view, either inspiring or frightening example of sellers' ability to raise a primary product's price by acting in concert. However, oil appears to be uniquely well suited to cartel action. Other primary commodities—by virtue of lesser importance, more readily available substitutes, more diverse sources of supply, or greater ease of stockpiling—are much less amenable to this approach.

More important than price stability is the need for access to markets. Usually this issue does not arise in the case of nonagricultural primary products, since such products are permitted to enter freely without tariffs or other restrictions. However those *agricultural* commodities that are also produced in the industrialized countries are normally heavily protected. Agriculture in industrial economies typically suffers the problems of being a shrinking sector, and the pressures for protection against even further encroachment by foreign competition are severe.

Moving up the economic development spectrum, the issue becomes one of getting manufacturing started and gaining access to foreign markets for manufactured products. Naturally the most promising candidates for initiating a manufacturing export sector are low technology industries, for example, processing of primary commodities, in which cheap labor and raw materials are used intensively. Textiles and clothing products have played a strategic role in export growth for a large number of countries, and these industries offer perhaps the best example of the problem that protectionism poses for economic development.

Textile and clothing exports to the industrial nations are controlled by a system of bilateral, country-to-country quotas on each group of products. In the mid-seventies, established quotas not only limited the growth of textile exports but, in some cases, called for absolute reductions in the levels. The restrictions have been alleviated somewhat by the fact that actual growth has frequently exceeded the established quotas. If the pattern of growing restrictions continues, however, it seems likely the quotas will be enforced with increasing stringency.

Among the developing countries, the three leading exporters of textile products are China, Korea, and Hong Kong, which together account for over half of the developing countries' clothing exports to the industrialized nations. The large volume and dynamic behavior of these three countries' exports give them a special importance in the overall picture. However, the trade quotas also have an adverse impact on countries just emerging as significant exporters and on those seeking to get started. The problem is not simply that of trade relations between the industrialized and developing countries. It is also a function of the degree of success the industrialized nations have in maintaining open trade conditions among themselves. Increasing trade restrictions in one industry tends to set off retaliatory measures in others.

In their efforts to promote exports, the developing countries frequently resort to some form of export subsidy, which opens the way to charges by threatened industries in the target countries of *dumping*, or selling products in foreign markets at prices below production costs. From the perspective of the developing country, the subsidies are vital. It frequently can be argued—and with justification—that the subsidy is needed to compensate for the anti-export bias caused by import controls and overvalued exchange rates. However, from the perspective of threatened domestic producers in the importing countries, such practices are clearly discriminatory, and the origin of the offending items matters little. Existing laws that offer protection against such practices usually make no distinction regarding the level of economic development in the country of origin. Whether such practices are to be interpreted as legitimate development efforts or as unfair means of competition is a potentially divisive issue.

MILITARY SALES AND ASSISTANCE

The Pattern of Arms Transfers

In addition to general economic assistance, for more than three decades the United States has provided security assistance in various forms to help strengthen the defense posture of nations with which we share military and political interests. The principal forms of security assistance are grants and credits for foreign military sales. Grants to foreign governments of United States combat equipment, materials, and all services except training are provided under the Military Assistance Program (MAP). MAP comprised the bulk of the United States security assistance program at the time of its inception in 1950, and for many years thereafter. However, as Figure 26.1 shows, recent years have seen a dramatic rise in foreign military sales (FMS), both in absolute terms and in terms relative to MAP.

Foreign military sales are only partially subsidized in the form of official credit assistance or guarantees. However, since the act of providing sophisticated military equipment involves such important foreign policy considerations, the total amount of arms transfers is the measure of the program commonly employed. Of course, not all foreign military sales go to developing countries, but a substantial proportion does. In fact, during the 1968 to 1977 period, worldwide arms deliveries to the developing nations increased from 68 to 78 percent of the total arms trade.[18] The regional distribution of this flow is presented in Table 26.2.

While the United States transfers the largest "dollar" amount, the Soviet Union runs a substantial second and, in fact, is the leading supplier of certain items, including combat aircraft, tanks, self-propelled guns, and artillery. The nations of Western Europe are also a major source and, along with new entrants, such as Israel and Brazil, have been stepping up their efforts in recent years to reap the advantages of expanded sales.

Figure 26.2 indicates the volume of economic aid and arms exports to developing countries from the five leading arms suppliers during a recent five-year period. During this period, France, Germany, and the United Kingdom shared the greatest rates of increase in arms exports, although all three provided a substantially larger amount of economic aid than arms exports.[19] The Soviet Union occupied the opposite extreme, exporting over $16 billion in arms, but expending relatively little for economic aid. The United States generated the largest volume in both categories, with arms exports substantially in excess of the economic aid amount.

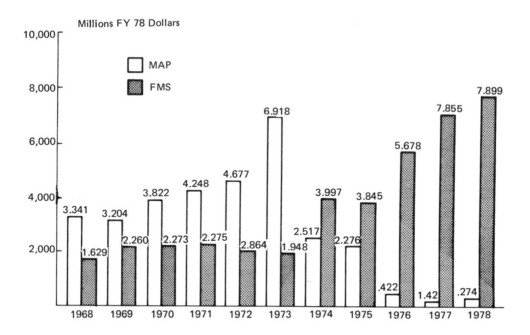

Figure 26.1 U.S. Military Assistance and Foreign Military Sales Deliveries: 1968–1978

Source: Department of Defense, Annual Report, FY 1980, p. 225.

Table 26.2
Worldwide Arms Deliveries by Recipient Region

	1958 ($ millions)	(% of total)	1977 ($ millions)	(% of total)
Africa	135	2.5	2,915	16.6
East Asia	2,070	38.5	1,120	6.4
Europe	1,790	33.3	4,455	25.3
Latin America	155	2.9	1,025	5.8
Middle East	635	11.8	6,940	39.4
North America	240	4.5	290	1.6
Oceania	70	1.3	120	0.7
South Asia	280	5.2	740	4.2
TOTAL	5,375	100.0	17,605	100.0

Source: ACDA, World Military Expenditures and Arms Transfers: 1968–1977.

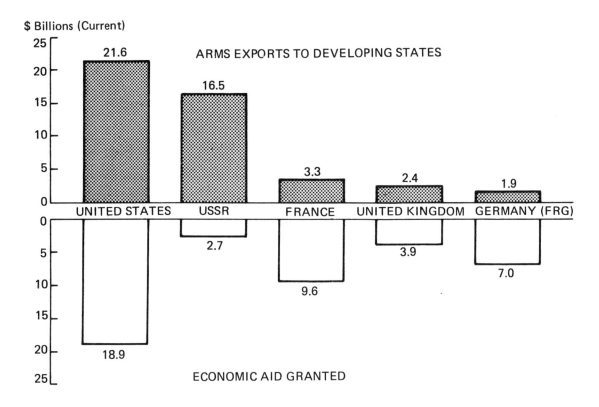

Figure 26.2 Arms Exports and Economic Aid to Developing States: 1973–1977

Source: ACDA, World Military Expenditures and Arms Transfers: 1968–1977.

The boom in arms transfers to the third world, the shift in the pattern from grants to sales, and the increasing diversity of suppliers have raised a number of questions about United States policy in this area. From the perspective of arms suppliers, the trends involve a curious reversal of the traditional relationship between economics and national security. As we have elaborated this relationship, economic considerations normally have served to *constrain* the use of resources for security purposes. In the military sales arena, however, economic considerations work to *stimulate* the magnitude of armaments production, even though the result may very well not be in the interest of peace and security.

The commercial incentives to export arms are, of course, substantial. In addition, military sales can also lead to budgetary savings. These savings occur in two principal forms: recovery of fixed costs associated with research and development, and economies of scale. Given the nature of the savings, they apply primarily to the latest and more sophisticated forms of equipment and hence are sensitive to the sales mix. According to some estimates, the recent pattern of United States arms exports may generate budgetary savings at a rate as high as ten cents per dollar of sales. In addition, the foreign exchange earnings are also welcomed. A third argument is occasionally made that such sales benefit mobilization planning by permitting production lines to remain open, although such benefits are speculative in nature and difficult to identify.[21] All of the above arguments apply also to other nations in the military sales business.

The Rationale of Arms Transfers

The rationale for military assistance in the form of grants of equipment and services is both conceptually awkward and fraught with practical hazards. The problem, of course, is that being the provider of military hardware involves no guarantee that the recipient government will conduct its affairs or use the equipment in a way that is acceptable to the supplying nation. Weapons provided may subsequently support or actually be used for internal repression or external aggression. They may lead to an armaments race among third world countries. There is the additional hazard that governments change, as the case of Iran has made so eloquently clear.

These considerations suggest that extreme care should be exercised in shaping the military assistance program, both in terms of the selection of recipients and the type of assistance to be provided. The booming business in military sales is in many ways even more troublesome than that of military assistance. A substantial amount of these arms transfers go to those developing countries for whom the opportunity costs, in terms of investment capital and foreign exchange, are most crucial. Although the military burden varies widely among the developing countries, their average level of military expenditure is slightly higher than for the industrialized nations. In many cases, of course, the arms satisfy legitimate security needs. Frequently, however, a far better use of the resources would be for purposes of economic development.

The United States' ability to constrain the pattern or consequences of arms sales is sharply limited. First of all, there is inherently less of a basis for controlling the future use of items sold than there is for controlling the use of those provided on concessionary terms. After paying hard-earned exchange, buyers are naturally more reluctant to agree to limitations. Secondly, there are the substantial economic advantages to be gained from the sale and these advantages generate internal pressures in support of sales and confuse the motives of the transactions. The benefits of arms sales are assuming increasing importance as the growing sophistication of armaments raises their costs, and as the impact of "oil shocks" continues to create foreign exchange problems for the industrial nations. Finally, because of the widespread desire to indulge in military sales, the United States' refusal to supply an item has much less of an impact than it does in the case of grants. The likely consequence of such a refusal is that the item will be purchased elsewhere, further reducing our limited ability to influence the process. It should also be noted that military sales involve very long lead times. As a consequence, the actual flow of goods in a given year is largely the result of contracts let previously. Efforts to control the flow apply only to new contracts, and hence have a delayed impact.

The incentive structure that underlies the arms transfer problem contains many perverse elements, similar to those outlined in the previous discussion of interaction in military spending, and compounded by commercial motives on the part of sellers. The net result of these mixed motivations and additional complications is that military sales represent an extraordinary challenge to policymakers. Clearly the United States cannot afford to conduct policy in this area on the basis of commercial considerations alone, and we are bound to encourage our allies and competitive suppliers to exercise similar restraint. In 1977 the United States announced a policy of unilateral restraint, including a dollar limit on United States arms transfers, and a call for multilateral cooperation to seek to bring this problem under control. Whether this initiative can be sustained and lead to a reversal of the military expenditure trends in the developing countries is not yet clear.

CONCLUSION

Economic conditions within the developing countries have been a matter of concern to national security in the last quarter century, during which time substantial efforts have been made to share the benefits of industrialization and economic development. Our survey of the results has revealed a mixed picture. There are, of course, a number of economic success stories. In general, however, the per capita income gap between the rich nations and the low and middle income groups continues to widen. The prospects are worst for those countries near the bottom of the income spectrum—those most dependent on concessional loans or trading opportunities for improving their economic condition. These disturbing aspects of the economic outlook for developing nations are accentuated by a worsening in the overall economic environment; the industrial nations are confronting reduced growth prospects, balance of payments problems of their own due to higher energy prices, and mounting pressures for protectionism. There has been some diminution in the support for both capital assistance and concessional trade arguments.

The link between United States security and economic progress in these countries is through political development and, as discussed above, the relationship is a tenuous one. Rapid economic development provides no guarantee of comparable progress in the political realm and in some contexts may even operate as a destabilizing factor, at least in the short run. At the same time, experience has revealed severe limitations on the use of economic aid as a bargaining tool to seek to induce healthy political change or even to achieve limited United States foreign policy objectives. Thus, although the humanitarian rationale for foreign assistance has never been higher, the national security rationale is in some disarray. Despite these kinds of qualifications, we believe the security rationale is a valid one. In the long run, the widening gap between the economic performance of the industrial and developing nations presents a dangerous risk of political turmoil and military conflict. It is unlikely that the United States could remain immune from the consequences of such unrest. Assistance to promote economic development may be a small price to pay to avoid future conflict.

NOTES

1 The classification and data following are drawn from The World Bank, *World Development Report, 1978* (Washington: The World Bank, August 1978).
2 See also Simon Kuznets, *Modern Economic Growth: Rate, Structure and Spread* (New Haven: Yale University Press, 1966).
3 World Bank, *op cit.*, p. 5.
4 *Ibid.*, p. 64
5 All economic growth models or strategies tend to highlight certain strategic variables in the development process, inevitably to the detriment of other important considerations. For an excellent discussion of the pitfalls, see Henry Burton, *Principles of Development Economics* (Englewood Cliffs, N.J.: Prentice-Hall, Inc., 1965), esp. Ch. 18.
6 A third possibility, of course, is to reduce the capital output ratio, e.g., by more effective dissemination of improved technologies. To reiterate the point of the previous note, it is essential that concentration on the strategic role of capital not lead to the neglect of alternative development tools.
7 It is also conceivable that lack of foreign exchange itself is the binding constraint on growth, in which case increased domestic saving may not help. See Hollis Chenery and Allen Strout, "Foreign Assistance and Economic Development," *American Economic Review*, vol. 56, no. 4, part 1 (September, 1966), pp. 679–733.
8 Ragnar Nurkse, *Problems of Capital Formation in Underdeveloped Countries* (New York: Oxford University Press, 1967).
9 See Albert Hirschman, *Strategy of Economic Development* (New Haven: Yale University Press, 1958).
10 Paul Streeten, "Balanced versus Unbalanced Growth," *The Economic Weekly* (April 20, 1963).
11 World Bank, *op. cit.*, p. 67
12 The usual criteria for distinguishing official development assistance from other capital flows are that it is provided to developing countries or multilateral institutions by official agencies for the purpose of promoting economic development or welfare and is concessional in character, with a grant element of at least 25 percent.
13 Charles P. Kindleberger and Bruce Herrick, *Economic Development*, 3rd ed. (New York: McGraw Hill, 1977), p. 306.
14 See Roger Hansen, *The U.S. and World Development,* (New York: Praeger Publishers, 1976).
15 Robert S. McNamara, "Countering the New Protectionism," *Finance and Development* (September, 1979).
16 See Roger Hansen, "North-South Policy—What's the Problem?" *Foreign Affairs* (Summer, 1980), pp. 1104–1128.
17 Raul Prebisch, "Commercial Policy in the Underdeveloped Countries," *American Economic Review,* Vol. 49, No. 2 (May, 1959), pp. 251–73.
18 U.S. Arms Control and Disarmament Agency, *World Military Expenditures and Arms Transactions 1968–77,* (Washington, D.C.: U.S.A.C.D.A., October, 1979), p. 16.

19 *Ibid.*

20 Congressional Budget Office, "Budgetary Cost Savings to the Department of Defense Resulting from Foreign Military Sales," Staff Working Paper (Washington, D.C.: Government Printing Office, May 24, 1976), p. 22.

21 *Ibid.*, p.5.

SELECTED REFERENCES

"America and the World, 1979," *Foreign Affairs,* Vol. 58, No. 3, 1980.

Willy Brandt and Anthony Sampson, *North-South: A Program for Survival [The Brandt Report] (Cambridge, Mass.: MIT Press, 1980).*

Charles P. Kindleberger and Bruce Herrick, Economic Development, 3rd ed. (New York: McGraw Hill, 1977).

Simon Kuznets, *Modern Economic Growth: Rate, Structure, and Spread* (New Haven: Yale University Press, 1966).

The World Bank, *World Development Report* (Annual) (Washington, D.C.: The World Bank).

INDEX

Standardization, 314. *See also* Interoperability
Steel trigger pricing, 308. *See also* European
   Economic Community; Tariffs; Quotas
Stein, Herbert, 53, 55, 75
Stigler, George, 197
Stockman, David, 76
Stockpiling, 243-244, 274, 319
Strategic arms limitations talks, 16, 314
Strategic forces, 18, 21, 84, 91-92, 114, 164,
   171. *See also* Defense budget; Triad
Strategy, 13, 15, 22, 48. *See also* Deterrence;
   Flexible response; Massive retaliation; Mutual
   assured destruction
Sub-optimization, 164-165
Subsidies, 159, 283-285, 308, 331-332
Substitute goods, 190
Substitution among factors, 206
Summits, economic, 314
Supply
   curve, 125, 189
   of labor, 9
   shift in, 191-193
   See also Elasticity; Aggregate supply
Supply-side economics, 29, 54, 70-71, 76, 97
Surge capability, 242-243
Sutton, Anthony, 320
Sweden, 325
Systems analysis, 84, 153. *See also* Cost-benefit
   analysis; Cost-effectiveness analysis; Program
   analysis and evaluation

Tangency condition, 134
Tanks, 314
Targeting, 275
Tariffs, 49, 283, 285, 289, 307, 309-310, 317. *See
   also* Imports; Quotas
Taxation, 28, 71, 73-74, 76, 78. *See also* Fiscal
   policy; Income tax
Technological change
   and aggregate output, 247-250, 383
   and military research and development,
   250-253
      See also Research and development
Technology transfer, 301, 319-330, 334. *See also*
   Export controls; Reverse engineering
Terms of trade, 388
Theater nuclear forces, 18, 314. *See also* Nuclear
   weapons; Strategy
Third world. *See* Developing nations
Three percent commitment, 316-317
Time horizon, 151-152. *See also* Investment

Tokyo Round. *See* General Agreement on Trade
   and Tariffs
Total force concept, 239. *See also* Reserves,
   military
Trade, 3, 49, 279-298, 302-304, 316, 319-335,
   382, 387. *See also* Balance of payments;
   Balance of trade; Current account; Exports;
   Imports; Quotas; Tariffs
Trade possibility curve, 282-283, 295
Trade Reform Act of 1974, 326, 329
Transfer payments, 56, 73, 97. *See also* Budget;
   Fiscal policy
Transportation, 269, 272-273, 316
Triad, 18. *See also* Nuclear weapons; Strategy
Trident submarine, 91. *See also* Triad
Troika, 76-78, 86. *See also* Economic policy
   board; Economic policy group
Truman administration, 32, 95
Turnover tax, 352

Uncertainty, 151, 156, 159, 175. *See also*
   Risk
Unemployment, 2, 27-29, 54-55, 60-61, 63,
   67-71, 77, 160, 263, 273-276, 305. *See also*
   Economic policy goals; Manpower; Phillips
   curve
Unified commands, 39
Union of Soviet Socialist Republics. *See* Soviet
   Union
United Kingdom, 304-305, 307, 311, 317, 325.
   See also North Sea crude oil reserves; Pound
   sterling
Utility
   and consumer theory, 158, 181
   maximization, 157
   See also Demand; Indifference curves; Marginal
   rate of substitution

Vietnam War, 15-16, 67, 93, 98, 100, 116, 208,
   313, 319, 371
Volcker, Paul, 285, 287-288
Volunteer force. *See* Manpower
Von Mises, Ludwig, 344

Wage-price controls, 70, 99, 104, 290, 319, 331
Walrasian bidding process, 189, 202
Ways and Means Committee, House of Represen-
   tatives, 79
Welfare economics, 128
West Germany. *See* Germany, Federal Republic of
Wheat, 319-320, 326, 330-332. *See also*
   Embargoes